NEW FRONTIERS IN GRAPH THEORY

Edited by **Yagang Zhang**

INTECHOPEN.COM

New Frontiers in Graph Theory
Edited by Yagang Zhang

CBS, Edition 2016

Published by InTech

Janeza Trdine 9, 51000 Rijeka, Croatia

Publishing Process Manager Oliver Kurelic

Technical Editor Teodora Smiljanic

Cover Designer InTech Design Team

Additional hard copies can be obtained from orders@intechopen.com

New Frontiers in Graph Theory, Edited by Yagang Zhang
p. cm.
ISBN 978-953-51-0115-4

INTECH

open science | open minds

Contents

Preface

The Königsberg bridge problem is well known, and is often said to have been the birth of graph theory. Nowadays, graph theory has been an important analysis tool in mathematics and computer science. Many real world situations can conveniently be described by means of a diagram consisting of a set of points, with lines joining certain pairs of these points. In mathematics and computer science, graph theory is the study of graphs: mathematical structures used to model conjugated relations between objects from a certain collection. A graph is an abstract notion of a set of nodes and connection relations between them, that is, a collection of vertices or nodes and a collection of edges that connect pairs of vertices. A graph may be undirected, meaning that there is no distinction between the two vertices associated with each edge, or its edges may be directed from one vertex to another.

Because of the inherent simplicity of graph theory, it can be used to model many different physical and abstract systems such as transportation and communication networks, models for business administration, political science, psychology and so on. Efficient storage and algorithm design techniques based on the graph representation make it particularly useful for utilization in computers. There are many algorithms that can be applied to resolve different kinds of problems, such as Depth-first search, Breadth-first search, Bellman-Ford algorithm, Dijkstra's algorithm, Ford-Fulkerson algorithm, Kruskal's algorithm, Nearest neighbor algorithm, Prim's algorithm, etc. Graph theory also has a very wide range of applications in physical science, biological science, social science, engineering, linguistics, and many other fields.

The purpose of this book is not only to present the latest state and development tendencies of graph theory, but to bring the reader far enough along the way to enable him to embark on the research problems of his own. It is a multi-author book. Taking into account the large amount of knowledge about graph theory and practice presented in the book, it has two major parts: theoretical researches and applications. The scientists have discussed in detail the properties of spectral null codes, graph invariants and large cycle structures, the fifth degree chordal rings, poly-dimension of antimatroids etc. The selected applications of various graph theory approaches are also wide, from power networks, genome, machine failure prognosis, computer recognition, communication networks, wireless sensor networks, chemical warehouses to law and policy, and so on.

It is our hope that this book will prove useful both to professional graph theorists interested in the applications of their subjects, and to engineers in the particular areas who may want to learn about the uses of graph theory in their own and other subjects. The book is also intended for both graduate and postgraduate students in fields such as mathematics, computer science, system sciences, biology, engineering, cybernetics, and social sciences, and as a reference for software professionals and practitioners. The wide scope of the book provides them with a good introduction to the latest approaches of graph theory, and it is also the source of useful bibliographical information.

Yagang Zhang
North China Electric Power University, Baoding,
China

1

A Graph Theoretic Approach for Certain Properties of Spectral Null Codes

Khmaies Ouahada and Hendrik C. Ferreira
Department of Electrical and Electronic Engineering Science,
University of Johannesburg, Auckland Park, 2006
South Africa

1. Introduction

In this chapter, we look at the spectral null codes from another angle, using graph theory, where we present a few properties that have been published. The graph theory will help us to understand the structure of spectral null codes and analyze their properties differently.

Graph theory [1]–[2] is becoming increasingly important as it plays a growing role in electrical engineering for example in communication networks and coding theory, and also in the design, analysis and testing of computer programs.

Spectral null codes [3] are codes with nulls in the power spectral density function and they have great importance in certain applications such as transmission systems employing pilot tones for synchronization and track-following servos in digital recording [4]–[5].

Yeh and Parhami [6] introduced the concept of the index-permutation graph model, which is an extension of the Cayley graph model and applied it to the systematic development of communication-efficient interconnection networks. Inspiring the concept of building a relationship between an index and a permutation symbol, we make use in this chapter of the spectral null equations variables in each grouping by representing only their corresponding indices in a permutation sequence form. In another way, these indices will be presented by a permutation sequence, where the symbols refer to the position of the corresponding variables in the spectral null equation.

Presenting a symmetric-permutation codebook graphically, Swart *et al.* [7] allocated states to all symbols of a permutation sequence and presented all possible transpositions between these symbols by links as depicted for a few examples in Fig. 1 [7].

The Chapter is organized as follows: Section II introduces definitions and notations to be used for spectral null codes. Section III presents few graph theory definitions. Section IV presents the index-graphic presentation of spectral null codes. Section V makes an approach between graph theory and spectral null codes where we focus on the relationship between the cardinalities of the spectral null codebooks and the concepts of distances in graph theory and also we elaborate the concept of subgraph and its corresponding to the structure of the spectral null codebooks. We conclude with some final remarks in Section VI.

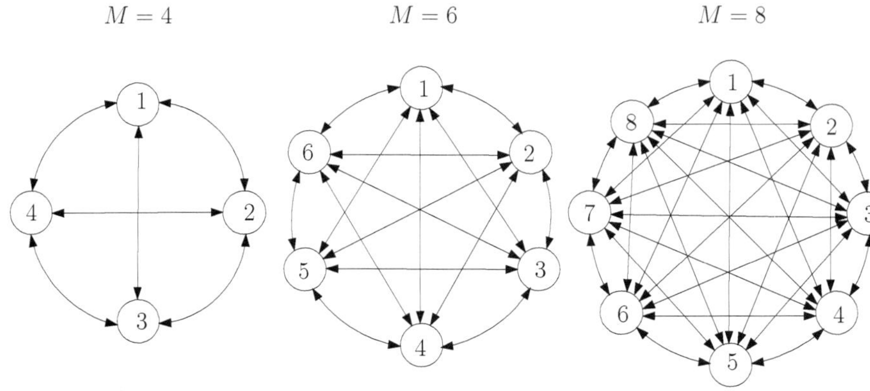

Fig. 1. Graph representation for permutation sequences

2. Spectral null codes

The technique of designing codes to have a spectrum with nulls occurring at certain frequencies, i.e. having the power spectral density (PSD) function equal to zero at these frequencies, started with Gorog [8], when he considered the vector $\mathbf{X} = (x_1, x_2, ..., x_M)$, $x_i \in \{-1,+1\}$ with $1 \leq i \leq M$, to be an element of a set S, which is called a codebook of codewords with elements in $\{-1,+1\}$. We investigate codewords of length, M, as an integer multiple of N, thus let

$$M = Nz,$$

where N represents the number of groupings in the spectral null equation and z represents the number of elements in each grouping. The values of $f = r/N$ are frequencies at spectral nulls (SN) at the rational submultiples r/N [9]. To ensure the presence of these nulls in the continuous component at the spectrum, it is sufficient to satisfy the following spectral null equation [10],

$$A_1 = A_2 = \cdots = A_N, \tag{1}$$

where

$$A_i = \sum_{\lambda=0}^{z-1} x_{i+\lambda N}, \quad i = 1, 2, \ldots, N, \tag{2}$$

which can also be presented differently as,

$$\begin{array}{l} \overbrace{\phantom{x_1 + x_{1+N} + x_{1+2N} + x_{1+3N} + \cdots + x_{1+(z-1)N}}}^{z} \\ A_1 = x_1 + x_{1+N} + x_{1+2N} + x_{1+3N} + \cdots + x_{1+(z-1)N} \\ A_2 = x_2 + x_{2+N} + x_{2+2N} + x_{2+3N} + \cdots + x_{2+(z-1)N} \\ A_3 = x_3 + x_{3+N} + x_{3+2N} + x_{3+3N} + \cdots + x_{3+(z-1)N} \\ \vdots \quad \vdots \quad \vdots \quad \vdots \quad \vdots \\ A_N = x_N + x_{2N} + x_{3N} + x_{4N} + \cdots + x_{zN}. \end{array} \tag{3}$$

If all the codewords in a codebook satisfy these equations, the codebook will exhibit nulls at the required frequencies. henceforth we present the channel symbol -1 with binary symbol 0.

Definition 2.1. *A spectral null binary block code of length M is a subset $C_b(M,N) \subseteq \{0,1\}^M$ of all binary M-tuples of length M which have spectral nulls at the rational submultiples of the symbol frequency $1/N$.*

Definition 2.2. *The spectral null binary codebook $C_b(M,N)$ is a subset of the M dimensional vector space $(\mathbb{F}_2)^M$ of all binary M-tuples, where $\mathbb{F}_2$ is the finite field with two elements, whose arithmetic rules are those of mod-2 arithmetic.*

For codewords of length M consisting of N interleaved subwords of length z, the cardinality of the codebook $C_b(M,N)$ for the case where N is a prime number is presented by the following formula [10],

$$|C_b(M,N)| = \sum_{i=0}^{M/N} \binom{M/N}{i}^N, \tag{4}$$

where $\binom{M/N}{i}$ denotes the combinatorial coefficient $\frac{(M/N)!}{i!(M/N-i)!}$.

Example 2.3. *If we consider the case of $M = 6$, we can predict two types of spectral with different nulls since N can take the value of $N = 2$ or $N = 3$. Their corresponding spectral null equations are presented respectively as follows:*

$$x_1 + x_3 + x_5 = x_2 + x_4 + x_6 \tag{5}$$

$$x_1 + x_4 = x_2 + x_5 = x_3 + x_6 \tag{6}$$

The corresponding codebooks for (5) and (6) are respectively as follows:

$$C_b(6,2) = \left\{ \begin{matrix} 0\,0\,0\,0\,0\,0 \\ 0\,0\,0\,0\,1\,1 \\ 0\,0\,0\,1\,1\,0 \\ 0\,0\,1\,0\,0\,1 \\ 0\,0\,1\,1\,0\,0 \\ 0\,0\,1\,1\,1\,1 \\ 0\,1\,0\,0\,1\,0 \\ 0\,1\,1\,0\,0\,0 \\ 0\,1\,1\,0\,1\,1 \\ 0\,1\,1\,1\,1\,0 \\ 1\,0\,0\,0\,0\,1 \\ 1\,0\,0\,1\,0\,0 \\ 1\,0\,0\,1\,1\,1 \\ 1\,0\,1\,1\,0\,1 \\ 1\,1\,0\,0\,0\,0 \\ 1\,1\,0\,0\,1\,1 \\ 1\,1\,0\,1\,1\,0 \\ 1\,1\,1\,0\,0\,1 \\ 1\,1\,1\,1\,0\,0 \\ 1\,1\,1\,1\,1\,1 \end{matrix} \right\},$$

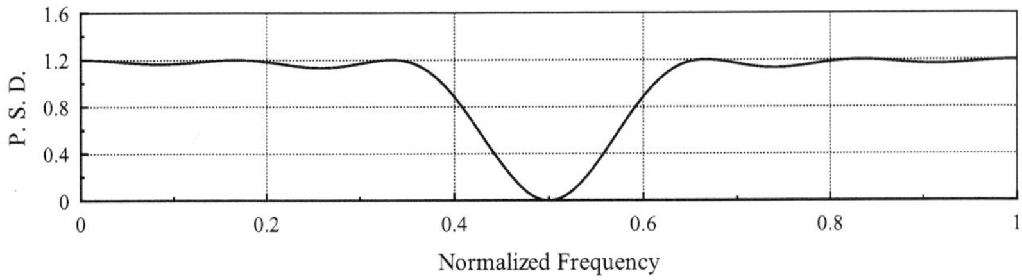

Fig. 2. Power spectral density of codebook $N = 2, M = 6$.

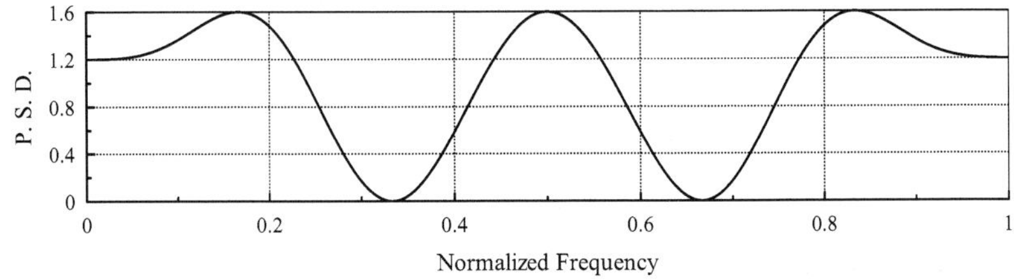

Fig. 3. Power spectral density of codebook $N = 3$, $M = 6$.

and

$$C_b(6,3) = \begin{Bmatrix} 0\,0\,0\,0\,0\,0 \\ 0\,0\,0\,1\,1\,1 \\ 0\,0\,1\,1\,1\,0 \\ 0\,1\,0\,1\,0\,1 \\ 0\,1\,1\,1\,0\,0 \\ 1\,0\,0\,0\,1\,1 \\ 1\,0\,1\,0\,1\,0 \\ 1\,1\,0\,0\,0\,1 \\ 1\,1\,1\,0\,0\,0 \\ 1\,1\,1\,1\,1\,1 \end{Bmatrix}.$$

The cardinalities of $C_b(6,2)$ and $C_b(6,3)$ are respectively equal to 20 *and* 10. *This also can be easily verified from* (4).

We can see clearly the power spectral density $C_b(6,2)$ and $C_b(6,3)$ respectively presented in Figures 2 and 3 where the nulls appear to be multiple of $1/N$ as presented in Definition 2.1.

3. Graph theory: Preliminary

We present a brief overview of related definitions for certain graph theory fundamentals which will be used in the following sections.

Definition 3.1. *[1]–[2]*

(a) *A graph G = (V, E) is a mathematical structure consisting of two finite sets V and E. The elements of V are called vertices, and the elements of E are called edges. Each edge has a set of one or two vertices associated with it.*

(b) *A graph $G' = (V', E')$ is a subgraph of another graph $G = (V, E)$ iff $V' \subseteq V$ and $E' \subseteq E$.*

Definition 3.2. *[1]–[2] The graph distance denoted by $\mathcal{G}_d(u,v)$ between two vertices u and v of a finite graph is the minimum length of the paths connecting them.*

Definition 3.3. *[1]–[2] The adjacency matrix of a graph is an $M \times M$ matrix $\mathcal{A}_d = [a_{i,j}]$ in which the entry $a_{i,j} = 1$ if there is an edge from vertex i to vertex j and is 0 if there is no edge from vertex i to vertex j.*

4. Index-graphic presentation of spectral null codes

The idea of the index-graphic presentation of the spectral null codes is actually based on the presentation of the indices of the variables in each grouping of the spectral null equation (1).

Definition 4.1. *We denote by $I_p(i,\lambda)$ the permutation symbol of the corresponding index of the variable $x_{i+\lambda N}$ in* (2).

$$I_p(i,\lambda) = i + \lambda N \quad where \quad \begin{cases} i = 1,2,\ldots,N, \\ \lambda = 0,1,\ldots,z-1. \end{cases} \tag{7}$$

Definition 4.2. *We denote by $\mathcal{P}_{I_p}(M,N)$ the index-permutation sequence from a spectral null equation for variables of length $M = Nz$ as presented.*

$$\mathcal{P}_{I_p}(M,N) = \prod_{i=1}^{N} \prod_{\lambda=0}^{z-1} I_p(i,\lambda). \tag{8}$$

The product sign in (8) is not used in its traditional way, but just to give an idea about the sequence and the order of the permutation symbols.

Example 4.3. *To explain the relationship between the spectral nulls equation, the index-permutation sequences and their graph presentation, we take the case of $M = 4$ where we have only two groupings since $N = 2$.*

$$A_1 = A_2 \rightarrow x_1 + x_3 = x_2 + x_4 \tag{9}$$

We can see from (9)*, that the indices of the variables x_i, using* (8)*, are represented by the symbols $I_p(1,0) = 1$, $I_p(1,1) = 3$, $I_p(2,0) = 2$ and $I_p(2,1) = 4$. The index-permutation sequence is then $\mathcal{P}_{I_p}(4,2) = (13)(24)$.*

An index-permutation symbol is presented graphically by just being lying on a circle, which it is called a state. The state design follow the order of appearance of the indices in (9)*. The symbols are connected in respect of the addition property of their corresponding variables in* (9) *as depicted in Fig. 4.*

Spectral null codebooks have the all-zeros and all-ones codewords [10], where all the variables y_i are equal. We call the corresponding spectral null equation, which is $x_1 = x_2 = x_3 = x_4$ as the all-zeros spectral null equation, which still satisfying (9) *since it is a special case of it. If we substitute the variables in* (9) *by using the all-zeros spectral null equation, we obtain the following relationships:*

$$\begin{cases} x_1 + x_3 = x_2 + x_4, \\ x_1 = x_2 = x_3 = x_4, \end{cases} \Rightarrow \begin{cases} x_2 + x_3 = x_1 + x_4, \\ x_1 + x_2 = x_3 + x_4. \end{cases} \tag{10}$$

Equation (10) *shows the resultant equations derived from* (9) *and the all-zeros spectral null equation. Fig. 5 shows that the same graph G_1 in Fig. 4 is actually a special case of the graph G_2 when we take into consideration the all-zeros spectral null equation.*

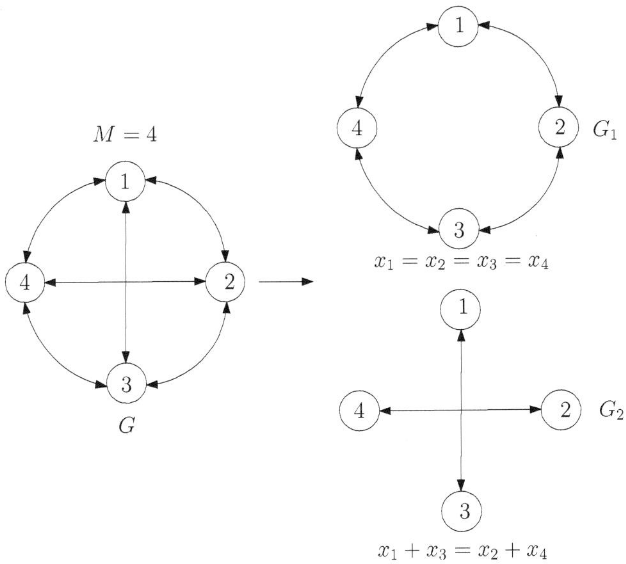

Fig. 4. Equation representation for Graph $M = 4$

Since the obtained relationship between the variables $x_1 = x_2 = x_3 = x_4$ is a special case of the equation representing the graph G_2 in Fig. 4, we limit our studies to (1) *and to its corresponding graph to study the cardinality and other properties of the code.*

Fig. 4 shows that the graph G, which is the general form of all possible permutations is the combinations or the union, $G = G_1 \cup G_2$, of other subgraphs related to the spectral null equation.

5. Graph theory and spectral null codes

In this section we will present certain concepts and properties for spectral null codes and try to confirm and very them from a graph theoretical approach.

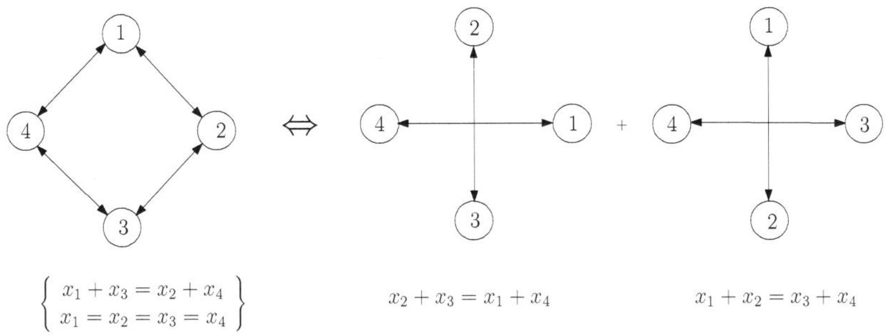

Fig. 5. All-zero equation representation for Graph $M = 4$

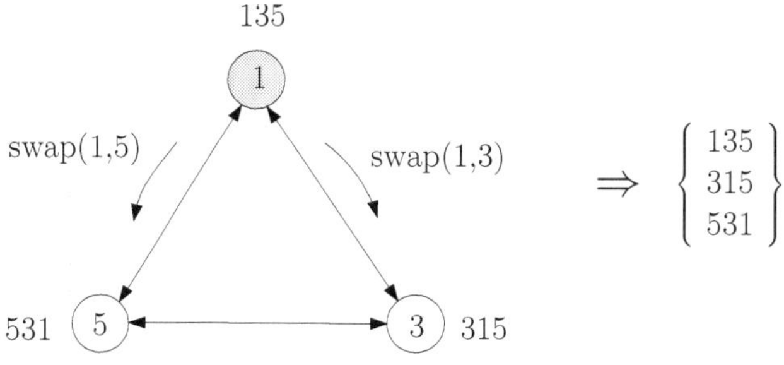

Fig. 6. Index-permutation sequences

5.1 Cardinalities approach

5.1.1 Hamming distance approach

The use of the Hamming distance [11] in this section is just to refer to the number of places that two permutation sequences representing the index-permutation symbols of each grouping A_i of the spectral null equation differ, and not in the study of the error correction properties of the spectral null codes.

To generate the permutation sequences, we start with any state representing an index-permutation symbol in each grouping as appearing in (1). A permutation sequence used as a starting point, contains the symbol from the start state followed by the rest of symbols from the other states taking into consideration the order of the symbols as appearing in (1). Fig. 6 shows the starting permutation sequence as 135. We swap the state-symbol with the following state-symbol in the permutation sequence based on the k-cube construction [12]. We end the swapping process at the last state in the graph. We do not swap symbols between the last state and the starting state for the reason to not disturb the obtained sequences at each state. As an example, for $M = 6$, Fig. 6 depicts the swaps and shows the resultant index-permutation codebooks for one grouping.

Definition 5.1. *The Hamming distance $d_H(\mathbf{Y}^i, \mathbf{Y}^j)$ is defined as the number of positions in which the two sequences $\mathbf{Y}^i$ and $\mathbf{Y}^j$ differ. We denote by $\mathcal{H}_d(M,N)$ the distance matrix, whose entries are the distances between index-permutation sequences from a spectral null code of length $M = Nz$ defined as follows:*

$$\mathcal{H}_d(M,N) = [h_{i,j}] \quad \text{with} \quad h_{i,j} = d_H(\mathbf{Y}^i, \mathbf{Y}^j). \tag{11}$$

Definition 5.2. *The Hamming distance between the same sequences or between sequences with non connected symbols is always equal to zero.*

Definition 5.3. *The sum on the Hamming distances in the $\mathcal{H}_d(M,N)$ distance matrix is*

$$|\mathcal{H}_d(M,N)| = \sum_{i=1}^{M} \sum_{j=1}^{M} h_{i,j}. \tag{12}$$

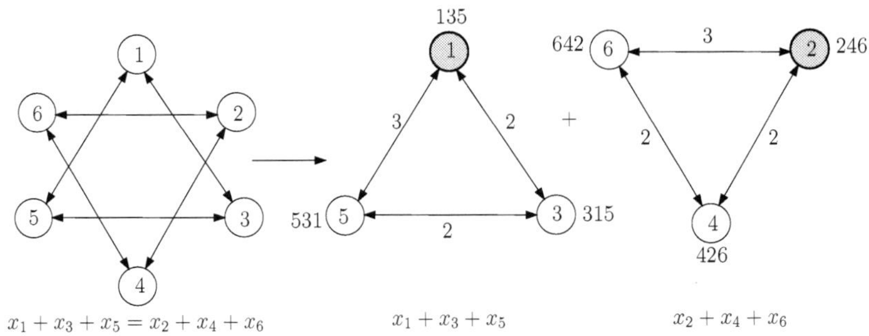

Fig. 7. Distances for Graph $M = 6$ with $N = 2$

In the following examples we consider different cases of number of groupings and number of elements in each grouping and we discuss their impact on the resultant Hamming distance and its relationship with the cardinalities of the spectral null codebooks.

Example 5.4. *We consider the case of $M = 6$ where the number of groupings is $N = 2$ and the number of variables in each grouping is $z = 3$. The corresponding spectral null equation is*

$$\overbrace{x_1 + x_3 + x_5}^{A_1} = \overbrace{x_2 + x_4 + x_6}^{A_2} \tag{13}$$

The equation (13) is presented by the graph in Fig. 7, where the index-permutation symbols are presented with their corresponding Hamming distances.

$$\mathcal{H}_d(6,2) = \begin{array}{c} \\ 135 \\ 315 \\ 513 \\ 246 \\ 426 \\ 624 \end{array} \begin{array}{c} \begin{array}{cccccc} 135 & 315 & 513 & 246 & 426 & 624 \end{array} \\ \begin{bmatrix} 0 & 2 & 3 & 0 & 0 & 0 \\ 2 & 0 & 2 & 0 & 0 & 0 \\ 3 & 2 & 0 & 0 & 0 & 0 \\ 0 & 0 & 0 & 0 & 2 & 3 \\ 0 & 0 & 0 & 2 & 0 & 2 \\ 0 & 0 & 0 & 3 & 2 & 0 \end{bmatrix} \end{array} \tag{14}$$

Each grouping in (13) is represented by a subgraph as depicted in Fig. 7. The Hamming distance matrix for all possible index-permutation sequences is presented in (14), where "0" represents the Hamming distance between same sequences or sequences with non connected symbols as defined in Definition 5.2. From Definition 5.3, we have,

$$|\mathcal{H}_d(6,2)| = 28.$$

Example 5.5. *For the case of $M = 6$ where $N = 3$ and $z = 2$, the corresponding spectral null equation is*

$$\overbrace{x_1 + x_4}^{A_1} = \overbrace{x_2 + x_5}^{A_2} = \overbrace{x_3 + x_6}^{A_3}. \tag{15}$$

The equation (15) is presented by the graph in Fig. 8. Using the concept of graph distance and the permutation sequences, we can have the distance values as depicted in Fig. 8.

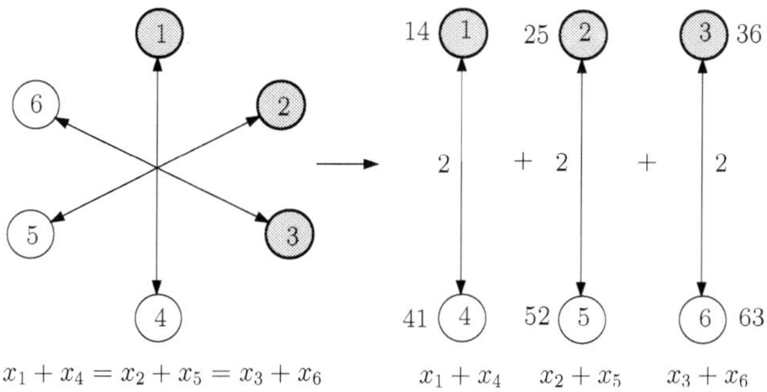

Fig. 8. Distances for Graph $M = 6$ for $N = 3$

The corresponding subgraphs for each grouping A_1, A_2 and A_3 are presented in Fig. 8.

$$\mathcal{H}_d(6,3) = \begin{array}{c} \\ 14 \\ 41 \\ 25 \\ 52 \\ 36 \\ 63 \end{array} \begin{array}{c} \begin{array}{cccccc} 14 & 41 & 25 & 52 & 36 & 63 \end{array} \\ \begin{bmatrix} 0 & 2 & 0 & 0 & 0 & 0 \\ 2 & 0 & 0 & 0 & 0 & 0 \\ 0 & 0 & 0 & 2 & 0 & 0 \\ 0 & 0 & 2 & 0 & 0 & 0 \\ 0 & 0 & 0 & 0 & 0 & 2 \\ 0 & 0 & 0 & 0 & 2 & 0 \end{bmatrix} \end{array} \tag{16}$$

The Hamming distance matrix for all possible index-permutation sequences is presented in (16). *From Definition 5.3, we have,*

$$|\mathcal{H}_d(6,3)| = 12.$$

Comparing the two results we have,

$$|\mathcal{H}_d(6,2)| > |\mathcal{H}_d(6,3)|.$$

Example 5.6. *In this example we take the case of N not a prime number, where we have to suppose that $N = cd$, where c and d are integer factors of N. The equation, which leads to nulls, is*

$$\begin{aligned} A_u &= A_{u+vc}, \\ u &= 0,1,2,\ldots,c-1, \\ v &= 1,2,\ldots,d-1, \\ N &= cd, \end{aligned} \tag{17}$$

We consider the case of $M = 8$, where N can be whether $N = 2$ or $N = 4$. The corresponding graph of each case is respectively depicted depicted in Fig. 9 as G_1 and G_2. From Definition 5.3, we have,

$$|\mathcal{H}_d(8,2)| = 40.$$

and

$$|\mathcal{H}_d(8,4)| = 16.$$

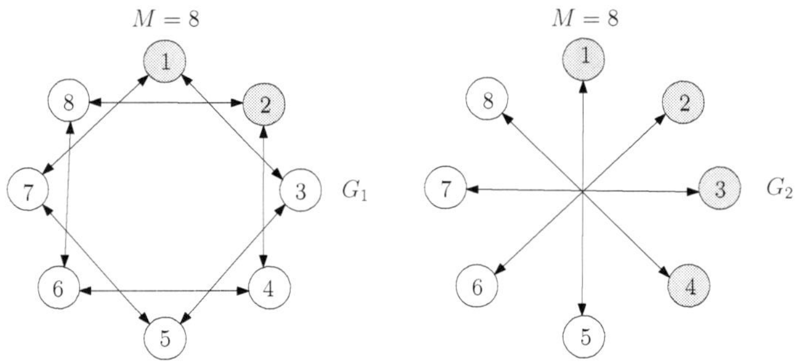

$x_1 + x_3 + x_5 + x_7 = x_2 + x_4 + x_6 + x_8$ $\quad$ $x_1 + x_5 = x_2 + x_6 = x_3 + x_7 = x_4 + x_8$

Fig. 9. Equation representation for Graph $M = 8$

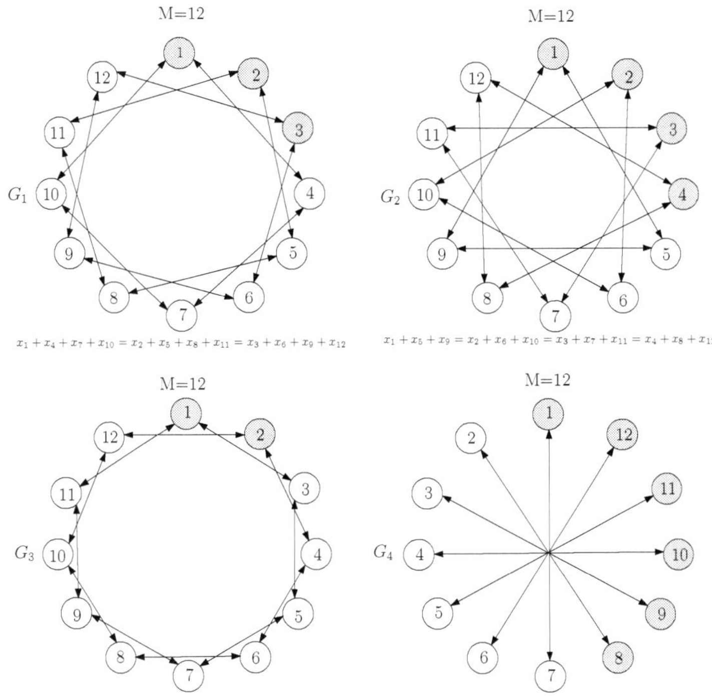

$x_1 + x_4 + x_7 + x_{10} = x_2 + x_5 + x_8 + x_{11} = x_3 + x_6 + x_9 + x_{12}$ $\quad$ $x_1 + x_5 + x_9 = x_2 + x_6 + x_{10} = x_3 + x_7 + x_{11} = x_4 + x_8 + x_{12}$

$x_1 + x_3 + x_5 + x_7 + x_9 + x_{11} = x_2 + x_4 + x_6 + x_8 + x_{10} + x_{12}$ $\quad$ $x_1 + x_7 = x_2 + 8 = x_3 + x_9 = x_4 + x_{10} = x_5 + x_{11} = x_6 + x_{12}$

Fig. 10. Equation representation for Graph $M = 12$

Comparing the two results we have,

$$|\mathcal{H}_d(8,2)| > |\mathcal{H}_d(8,4)|.$$

Example 5.7. *In the case of $M = 12$, we have four combinations where the value of N could be $N = 4$, $N = 3$, $N = 2$ or $N = 6$ as depicted in (17). In each case we have a graph representing the spectral null equation as depicted in Fig. 10.*

From Definition 5.3, we have,

$$|\mathcal{H}_d(12,2)| = 64,$$
$$|\mathcal{H}_d(12,6)| = 24,$$
$$|\mathcal{H}_d(12,3)| = 60,$$

and

$$|\mathcal{H}_d(12,4)| = 56.$$

Comparing all the results we have,

$$|\mathcal{H}_d(12,2)| > |\mathcal{H}_d(12,6)|,$$
$$\text{and } |\mathcal{H}_d(12,3)| > |\mathcal{H}_d(12,4)|.$$

Theorem 5.8. *The sum on the Hamming distances for all index-permutation sequences is*

$$|\mathcal{H}_d(M,N)| = \begin{cases} 4N, & \text{for } z = 2, \\ 2N(3z-2), & \text{for } z \geq 3. \end{cases}$$

Proof. Since the matrix $\mathcal{H}_d(M,N)$ is clearly symmetric, we can just prove half of the results of the theorem and then the final will be the double. For the case of $z = 2$ the proof is trivial since we swap only two symbols in each index-permutation sequence. Thus the sum on the distances is $4 \times N$. For the case of $z \geq 3$ we have a cycle graph [1]-[2], where the number of edges is equal to the number of vertices. Since we swap two symbols each time we move from one state to another, the distance at each edge is equal to two, except for the last edge connecting the first state to the last state where all symbols are swapped and the distance is equal to the length of the index-permutation sequences, which is z. The sum on the Hamming distances for a cycle graph for each grouping is $2 \times (z-1) + z = 3 \times z - 2$. Thus the result on the sum of the Hamming distances in the matrix is $2 \times N \times (3 \times z - 2)$. □

5.1.2 Graph-swap distance approach

The length of each grouping A_i, which is equal to the value of z plays an important role in cardinalities of the corresponding codebooks. We make use of the graph distance theory to see how z also plays an important role in the value of the graph distance.

Definition 5.9. *The graph-swap distance denoted by $\mathcal{G}_d$ between two index-permutation symbols represented by the vertices u and v of a finite graph is the minimum number of times of swaps that symbol u can take the position of symbol v in the graph.*

Definition 5.10. *The graph-swap distance between the same index-permutation symbol or between non connected symbols is always equal to zero.*

Definition 5.11. *We denote by $\mathcal{M}_{\mathcal{G}_d}(M,N)$ the graph-swap distance matrix, whose entries $m_{i,j}$ are the graph distances between two index-permutation symbols from a spectral null code of length $M = Nz$.*

Definition 5.12. *The sum on the graph-swap distances in the $\mathcal{M}_{\mathcal{G}_d}(M,N)$ distance matrix is*

$$|\mathcal{M}_{\mathcal{G}_d}(M,N)| = \sum_{i=1}^{M}\sum_{j=1}^{M} m_{i,j}. \tag{18}$$

Example 5.13. *We consider the case of $M = 8$ with $N = 2$ or $N = 4$, the corresponding graph-swap distance matrices are respectively as*

$$\mathcal{M}_{\mathcal{G}_d}(8,2) = \begin{array}{c|cccccccc} & 1 & 2 & 3 & 4 & 5 & 6 & 7 & 8 \\ \hline 1 & 0 & 0 & 1 & 0 & 2 & 0 & 1 & 0 \\ 2 & 0 & 0 & 0 & 1 & 0 & 2 & 0 & 1 \\ 3 & 1 & 0 & 0 & 0 & 1 & 0 & 2 & 0 \\ 4 & 0 & 1 & 0 & 0 & 0 & 1 & 0 & 2 \\ 5 & 2 & 0 & 1 & 0 & 0 & 0 & 1 & 0 \\ 6 & 0 & 2 & 0 & 1 & 0 & 0 & 0 & 1 \\ 7 & 1 & 0 & 2 & 0 & 1 & 0 & 0 & 0 \\ 8 & 0 & 1 & 0 & 2 & 0 & 1 & 0 & 0 \end{array}, \quad \text{and} \quad \mathcal{M}_{\mathcal{G}_d}(8,4) = \begin{array}{c|cccccccc} & 1 & 2 & 3 & 4 & 5 & 6 & 7 & 8 \\ \hline 1 & 0 & 0 & 0 & 0 & 1 & 0 & 0 & 0 \\ 2 & 0 & 0 & 0 & 0 & 0 & 1 & 0 & 0 \\ 3 & 0 & 0 & 0 & 0 & 0 & 0 & 1 & 0 \\ 4 & 0 & 0 & 0 & 0 & 0 & 0 & 0 & 1 \\ 5 & 1 & 0 & 0 & 0 & 0 & 0 & 0 & 0 \\ 6 & 0 & 1 & 0 & 0 & 0 & 0 & 0 & 0 \\ 7 & 0 & 0 & 1 & 0 & 0 & 0 & 0 & 0 \\ 8 & 0 & 0 & 0 & 1 & 0 & 0 & 0 & 0 \end{array}.$$

From Definition 5.12, we have $|\mathcal{M}_{\mathcal{G}_d}(8,2)| = 32$ and $|\mathcal{M}_{\mathcal{G}_d}(8,4)| = 8$. where we can see clearly that

$$|\mathcal{M}_{\mathcal{G}_d}(8,2)| > |\mathcal{M}_{\mathcal{G}_d}(8,4)|.$$

Theorem 5.14. *The sum on the graph distances for all index-permutation symbols is*

$$|\mathcal{M}_{\mathcal{G}_d}(M,N)| = \begin{cases} \left(\frac{z}{2}\right)^2 M, & \text{for } z \text{ even}, \\ \frac{z^2-1}{4} M, & \text{for } z \text{ odd}. \end{cases}$$

Proof. The graphs that we are using are cycle graphs. As long as we go through the edges of a graph the graph distance is incremented by one. When z is even, the first state has the farthest state to it located at $\frac{z}{2}$. So the graph distances from the first state to the $\frac{z}{2}$ state are in a numerical series of ratio one from one to $\frac{z}{2}$. From the state at the position $\frac{z}{2} - 1$ till the first state, the graph distances are in a numerical series of ratio one from one to $\frac{z}{2} - 1$. Adding the two series we get the final sum equal to $\left(\frac{z}{2}\right)^2 M$. Same analogy for the case of z as odd with a numerical series from one till $\frac{z-1}{2}$. □

5.1.3 Adjacency-swap matrix approach

We introduce the adjacency-swap matrix inspired by graph theory as follows.

Definition 5.15. *The adjacency-swap matrix of index-permutation symbols is an $M \times M$ matrix $\mathcal{N}_{\mathcal{A}_d}(M,N) = (n_{i,j})$ in which the entry $n_{i,j} = 1$ if there is a swap between an index symbol i and an index symbol j and is 0 if there is no swap between index symbol i and index symbol j as presented in each grouping of a spectral null equation.*

Example 5.16. *For the case of $M = 6$ with $N = 2$ or $N = 3$, the corresponding adjacency-swap matrices are*

$$\mathcal{N}_{A_d}(6,2) = \begin{array}{c} \\ 1 \\ 2 \\ 3 \\ 4 \\ 5 \\ 6 \end{array}\!\!\begin{array}{c} \begin{matrix} 1 & 2 & 3 & 4 & 5 & 6 \end{matrix} \\ \begin{bmatrix} 0&0&1&0&1&0 \\ 0&0&0&1&0&1 \\ 1&0&0&0&1&0 \\ 0&1&0&0&0&1 \\ 1&0&1&0&0&0 \\ 0&1&0&1&0&0 \end{bmatrix} \end{array}, \quad \text{and} \quad \mathcal{N}_{A_d}(6,3) = \begin{array}{c} \\ 1 \\ 2 \\ 3 \\ 4 \\ 5 \\ 6 \end{array}\!\!\begin{array}{c} \begin{matrix} 1 & 2 & 3 & 4 & 5 & 6 \end{matrix} \\ \begin{bmatrix} 0&0&0&1&0&0 \\ 0&0&0&0&1&0 \\ 0&0&0&0&0&1 \\ 1&0&0&0&0&0 \\ 0&1&0&0&0&0 \\ 0&0&1&0&0&0 \end{bmatrix} \end{array}.$$

We can see that $|\mathcal{N}_{A_d}(6,2)| = 12 > |\mathcal{N}_{A_d}(6,3)| = 6.$

M	N	z	$\|\mathcal{C}_b(M,N)\|$	$\|\mathcal{H}_d(M,N)\|$	$\|\mathcal{M}_{\mathcal{G}_d}(M,N)\|$	$\|\mathcal{N}_{A_d}(M,N)\|$
6	3	2	10	12	4	6
6	2	3	20	28	12	12
8	4	2	36	16	8	8
8	2	4	70	40	32	24
10	5	2	34	20	10	10
10	2	5	252	52	60	40
12	6	2	250	24	12	12
12	4	3	300	56	24	24
12	3	4	346	60	48	36
12	2	6	924	64	108	60
15	5	3	488	70	30	30
15	3	5	2252	78	90	60

Table 1. Graph Distances and Cardinalities of Different Codebooks

Theorem 5.17. *The total number of swaps in an adjacency-swap matrix is*

$$|\mathcal{N}_{A_d}(M,N)| = (z-1)M$$

Proof. The proof is trivial as per grouping we have z index-permutation symbols. Thus we have $z-1$ ones in each row of the matrix $\mathcal{N}_{A_d}(M,N)$ which refer to the possible swaps of each symbol with others in the same grouping. The total number of swaps is $(z-1) \times M$. □

Table 1 presents few examples of the relationship between the cardinalities of spectral null codes denoted by $\mathcal{C}_b(M,N)$ and their correspondences of graph distances. It is clear from Table 1 that the cardinalities of different codebooks with the same length of codewords, increase when the number of swaps increases. This results is also verified in Table 1 based on the concept of distances from graph theory perspective.

5.2 Subsets approach

5.2.1 Subgraph theory

In this section we make use of one of the properties in graph theory related to the design of subgraphs as presented in Definition 3.1.

The elimination of states from any graph corresponding to the index-permutation symbols is in fact the same as eliminating the corresponding variables from the spectral null equation (1). The elimination of the variables is performed in such a way that the spectral null equation is always satisfied. This leads to the basic idea of eliminating an equivalent number of variable equal to N as a total number from different groupings in the spectral null equation. This is true when we eliminate only one variable from each grouping. In the case when we eliminate t variables with $1 < t < z$ from each grouping, we have a total number of eliminated variables of tN.

$\frac{1}{2}C_b(8,2) =$ (19)

N bits		N bits			
0	0	0	0	0 0 0 0	$C_b(4,2)$ (rows 1–6); $C_b(6,2)$ (rows 1–20)
0	0	0	0	0 0 1 1	
0	0	0	0	0 1 1 0	
0	0	0	0	1 0 0 1	
0	0	0	0	1 1 0 0	
0	0	0	0	1 1 1 1	
0	0	0	1	0 0 1 0	
0	0	0	1	1 0 0 0	
0	0	0	1	1 0 1 1	
0	0	0	1	1 1 1 0	
0	0	1	0	0 0 0 1	
0	0	1	0	0 1 0 0	
0	0	1	0	0 1 1 1	
0	0	1	0	1 1 0 1	
0	0	1	1	0 0 0 0	$C_b(4,2)$ (rows 15–20)
0	0	1	1	0 0 1 1	
0	0	1	1	0 1 1 0	
0	0	1	1	1 0 0 1	
0	0	1	1	1 1 0 0	
0	0	1	1	1 1 1 1	
0	1	0	0	0 0 1 0	
0	1	0	0	1 0 0 0	
0	1	0	0	1 0 1 1	
0	1	0	0	1 1 1 0	
0	1	0	1	1 0 1 0	
0	1	1	0	0 0 0 0	
0	1	1	0	0 0 1 1	
0	1	1	0	0 1 1 0	
0	1	1	0	1 0 0 1	
0	1	1	0	1 1 0 0	
0	1	1	0	1 1 1 1	
0	1	1	1	0 0 1 0	
0	1	1	1	1 0 0 0	
0	1	1	1	1 0 1 1	
0	1	1	1	1 1 1 0	

Example 5.18. *We construct the code for the case of $M = 8$, with $N = 2$ and $z = 4$, which is represented by the codebook $C_b(8,2)$ in (19) (we present only the half of the codebook because of space*

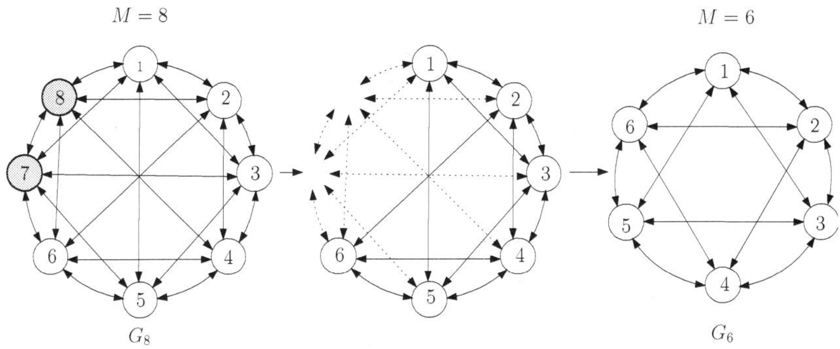

Fig. 11. Subgraph design from $M = 8$ to $M = 6$ with $N = 2$

limitation in the page) and which is designed from the spectral null equation presented as follows:

$$\overbrace{\underbrace{y_1 + y_3 + y_5 + y_7}_{}^{z=4} = \overbrace{y_2 + y_4 + y_6 + y_8}^{z=4}}^{N=2}. \tag{20}$$

The corresponding graph for $C_b(8,2)$ is G_8 as presented in Fig. 11.

From the spectral null equation (20) we eliminate the variables y_7 and y_8 using the addition property. Thus we get,

$$\overbrace{\overbrace{y_1 + y_3 + y_5}^{z=3} = \overbrace{y_2 + y_4 + y_6}^{z=3}}^{N=2}. \tag{21}$$

This resultant equation is the spectral null equation for the case of $M = 6$ with $N = 2$ and the corresponding codebook is denoted by $C_b(6,2)$. Fig. 11 depicts the elimination of the states from a graph theory perspective.

Based on the same approach, we eliminate the variables y_5 and y_6 from the equation (21). The resultant spectral equation for the case of $M = 4$, with $N = 2$ and $z = 2$ is presented as follows:

$$\overbrace{\overbrace{y_1 + y_3}^{z=2} = \overbrace{y_2 + y_4}^{z=2}}^{N=2}. \tag{22}$$

The code generated from the spectral null equation (22) is denoted by the codebook $C_b(4,2)$ as depicted in (19). The corresponding graph for $C_b(4,2)$ is G_4 as presented in Fig. 12.

It is clear that from the codebook presented in (19), we have $C_b(4,2) \subset C_b(6,2) \subset C_b(8,2)$ in terms of the existence of elements from the codebooks $C_b(4,2)$ and $C_b(6,2)$ in the codebook $C_b(8,2)$, which is the same as for the subgraps where we have $G_4 \subset G_6 \subset G_8$.

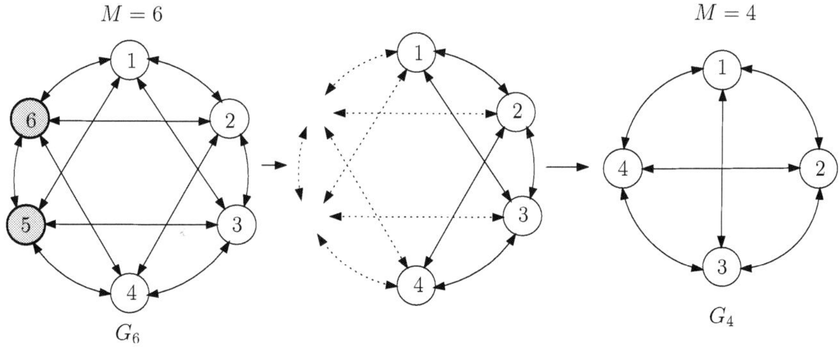

Fig. 12. Subgraph design from $M = 6$ to $M = 4$ with $N = 2$

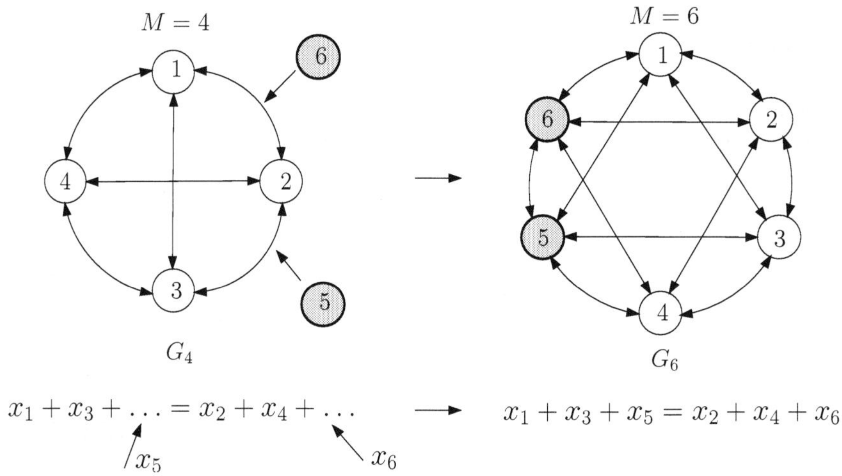

Fig. 13. Supergraph design: From $M = 4$ to $M = 6$ with $N = 2$

5.2.2 Supergraph theory

The concept of supergraphs is totally opposite to what was introduced with the subgraphs. Although this concept is not treated in graph theory because of its complexity and the conditions that we should have to add vertices to any graph. This problem is already solved in the design of spectral null codes since we are dealing with spectral null equations where it is easy to add variables in all groupings in such a way the spectral null equations are satisfied. Thus it results in the addition of the corresponding states of the symbols in the corresponding permutation equation.

Definition 5.19. *A spectral null preserving supergraph is an extension of a graph with a multiple of N states, which always keeps the spectral null equation satisfied.*

Fig. 13 presents the mechanism of the addition of states to an existing graph. The example of a graph of six states, which is related to the case of $M = 6$, is actually an extension of the graph of four states which corresponds to the case of $M = 4$. An addition of a state corresponds to the addition of its corresponding variable in a way to keep the equation (1) satisfied.

6. Conclusion

Spectral shaping technique that design codes with certain power spectral density properties is used to construct codes called spectral null codes that can generate nulls at rational submultiples of the symbol frequency. These codes have great importance in certain applications like in the case of transmission systems employing pilot tones for synchronization and that of track-following servos in digital recording. these codes are not confined to magnetic recorders but they ware taken further to their utilization in write-once recording systems.

In this investigation we have shown how the use of graphs can give a new insight into the analysis and understanding the structure of the spectral null codes, where with incisive observations to spectral null codebooks, we could derive important properties that can be useful in the field of digital communications.

The relationship between the spectral null equations for our designed codes and the permutation sequences corresponding to the indices of the variables in those equations have lead to a very important derivation of certain properties based on graph theory approach.

The properties that we have presented could potentially lead to the discovery of other interesting properties for specific applications like those that we have investigated in [13].

The use of certain graph theory properties helped in understanding certain properties of spectral null codes. The introduction of the index-permutation sequences and the use of the concept of distances gave us an idea about the structure and the design conditions of spectral null codes.

7. References

[1] R. J. Wilson, *Graph theory and Combinatorics*. England: Pitman Advanced Publishing Program., 1979.

[2] J. L. Gross and J. Yellen, *Graph theory and its Applications*. USA: Chapman and Hall/CRC., 2006.

[3] K. A. S. Immink, "Spectral null codes," *IEEE Transactions on Magnetics*, vol. 26, no. 2, pp. 1130–1135, Mar. 1990.

[4] N. Hansen, "A head-positioning system using buried servos,Ť *IEEE Transactions on Magnetics*, vol. 17, no. 6, pp. 2735–2738, Nov. 1981.

[5] M. Haynes, "Magnetic recording techniques for buried servos,Ť *IEEE Transactions on Magnetics*, vol. 17, no. 6, pp. 2730–2734, Nov. 1981.

[6] C. Yeh and B. Parhami, "Parallel algorithms for index-permutation graphs. An extension of Cayley graphs for multiple chip-multiprocessors (MCMP)"*International Conference on Parallel Processing*,pp. 3–12, Sept. 2001.

[7] T. G. Swart, "Distance-Preserving Mappings and Trellis Codes with Permutation Sequences", Ph.D. dissertation, University of Johannesburg, Johannesburg, South Africa, Apr. 2006.

[8] E. Gorog, "Alphabets with desirable frequency spectrum properties," *IBM J. Res. Develop.*, vol. 12, pp. 234–241, May 1968.

[9] B. H. Marcus and P. H. Siegel, "On codes with spectral nulls at rational submultiples of the symbol frequency," *IEEE Trans. Inf. Theory*, vol. 33, no. 4, pp. 557–568, Jul. 1987.

[10] K. A. S. Immink, *Codes for mass data storage systems*, Shannon Foundation Publishers, The Netherlands, 1999.

[11] A. Viterbi and J. Omura, *Principles of Digital Communication and Coding*. McGraw-Hill Kogakusha LTD, Tokyo Japan, 1979.

[12] K. Ouahada and H. C. Ferreira, "A *k*-Cube Construction mapping mapping binary vector to permutation," in *Proceedings of the International Symposium on Information Theory*, South Korea, pp. 630–634, June 28–July 3, 2009.

[13] K. Ouahada, T. G. Swart, H. C. Ferreira and L. Cheng, "Binary permutation sequences as subsets of Levenshtein codes, run-length limited codes and spectral shaping codes," *Designs, Codes and Cryptography Journal*, vol. 48, no. 2, pp. 141–154, Aug. 2008.

2

Pure Links Between Graph Invariants and Large Cycle Structures

Zh.G. Nikoghosyan*
Institute for Informatics and Automation Problems,
National Academy of Sciences,
Armenia

1. Introduction

Hamiltonian graph theory is one of the oldest and attractive fields in discrete mathematics, concerning various path and cycle existence problems in graphs. These problems mainly are known to be NP-complete that force the graph theorists to direct efforts toward understanding the global and general relationship between various invariants of a graph and its path and cycle structure.

This chapter is devoted to large cycle substructures, perhaps the most important cycle structures in graphs: Hamilton, longest and dominating cycles and some generalized cycles including Hamilton and dominating cycles as special cases.

Graph invariants provide a powerful and maybe the single analytical tool for investigation of abstract structures of graphs. They, combined in convenient algebraic relations, carry global and general information about a graph and its particular substructures such as cycle structures, factors, matchings, colorings, coverings, and so on. The discovery of these relations is the primary problem of graph theory.

In the literature, eight basic (initial) invariants of a graph G are known having significant impact on large cycle structures, namely order n, size q, minimum degree δ, connectivity κ, independence number α, toughness τ and the lengths of a longest path and a longest cycle in $G\setminus C$ for a given longest cycle C in G, denoted by $\overline{p}$ and $\overline{c}$, respectively.

In this chapter we have collected 37 pure algebraic relations between $n,q,\delta,\kappa,\alpha,\tau,\overline{p}$ and $\overline{c}$ ensuring the existence of a certain type of large cycles. The majority of these results are sharp in all respects.

Focusing only on basic graph invariants, as well as on pure algebraic relations between these parameters, in fact, we present the simplest kind of relations for large cycles having no forerunners in the area. Actually they form a source from which nearly all possible hamiltonian results (including well-known Ore's theorem, Pósa's theorem and many other

* G.G. Nicoghossian (up to 1997)

generalizations) can be developed further by various additional new ideas, generalizations, extensions, restrictions and structural limitations:

- **generalized and extended graph invariants** - degree sequences (Pósa type, Chvátal type), degree sums (Ore type, Fun type), neighborhood unions, generalized degrees, local connectivity, and so on,
- **extended list of path and cycle structures** - Hamilton, longest and dominating cycles, generalized cycles including Hamilton and dominating cycles as special cases, 2-factor, multiple Hamilton cycles, edge disjoint Hamilton cycles, powers of Hamilton cycles, k-ordered Hamilton cycles, arbitrary cycles, cycle systems, pancyclic-type cycle systems, cycles containing specified sets of vertices or edges, shortest cycles, analogous path structures, and so on,
- **structural (descriptive) limitations** - regular, planar, bipartite, chordal and interval graphs, graphs with forbidden subgraphs, Boolean graphs, hypercubes, and so on,
- **graph extensions** - hypergraphs, digraphs and orgraphs, labeled and weighted graphs, infinite graphs, random graphs, and so on.

We refer to (Bermond, 1978) and (Gould, 1991, 2003) for more background and general surveys.

The order n, size q and minimum degree δ clearly are easy computable graph invariants. In (Even & Tarjan, 1975), it was proved that connectivity κ can be determined in polynomial time, as well. Determining the independence number α and toughness τ are shown in (Garey & Johnson, 1983) and (Bauer et al., 1990a) to be CD_{λ}-hard problems. Moreover, it was proved (Bauer et al., 1990a) that for any positive rational number t, recognizing t-tough graphs (in particular 1-tough graphs) is an NP-hard problem.

The order n and size q are neutral with respect to cycle structures. Meanwhile, they become more effective combined together (Theorem 1). The minimum degree δ having high frequency of occurrence in different relations is, in a sense, a more essential invariant than the order and size, providing some dispersion of the edges in a graph. The combinations between order n and minimum degree δ become much more fruitful especially under some additional connectivity conditions. The impact of some relations on cycle structures can be strengthened under additional conditions of the type $\delta \geq \alpha \pm i$ for appropriate integer i. By many graph theorists, the connectivity κ is at the heart of all path and cycle questions providing comparatively more uniform dispersion of the edges. An alternate connectedness measure is toughness τ - the most powerful and less investigated graph invariant introduced by Chvátal (Chvátal, 1973) as a means of studying the cycle structure of graphs. Chvátal (Chvátal, 1973) conjectured that there exists a finite constant t_0 such that every t_0-tough graph is hamiltonian. This conjecture is still open. We have omitted a number of results involving toughness τ as a parameter since they are far from being best possible.

Large cycle structures are centered around well-known Hamilton (spanning) cycles. Other types of large cycles were introduced for different situations when the graph contains no Hamilton cycles or it is difficult to find it. Generally, a cycle C in a graph G is a large cycle if it dominates some certain subgraph structures in G in a sense that every such structure has a vertex in common with C. When C dominates all vertices in G then C is a Hamilton cycle. When C dominates all edges in G then C is called a dominating cycle introduced by Nash-Williams (Nash-Williams, 1971). Further, if C dominates all paths in G of length at least some fixed integer λ then C is a PD_λ (path dominating)-cycle introduced by Bondy (Bondy, 1981). Finally, if C dominates all cycles in G of length at least λ then C is a CD_λ (cycle dominating)-cycle, introduced in (Zh.G. Nikoghosyan, 2009a). The existence problems of generalized PD_λ and CD_λ-cycles are studied in (Zh.G. Nikoghosyan, 2009a) including Hamilton and dominating cycles as special cases.

Section 2 is devoted to necessary notation and terminology. In Section 3, we discuss pure relations between various basic invariants of a graph and Hamilton cycles. Next sections are devoted to analogous pure relations concerning dominating cycles (Section 4), CD_λ-cycles (Section 5), long cycles (Section 6), long cycles with Hamilton cycles (Section 7), long cycles with dominating cycles (Section 8) and long cycles with CD_λ-cycles (Section 9). In Section 10 we present the proofs of Theorems 6, 21 and 27. Concluding remarks are given in Section 11.

2. Terminology

We consider only finite undirected graphs without loops or multiple edges. A good reference for any undefined terms is (Bondy & Murty, 1976). The set of vertices of a graph G is denoted by $V(G)$ and the set of edges by $E(G)$. For S a subset of $V(G)$, we denote by $G\setminus S$ the maximum subgraph of G with vertex set $V(G)\setminus S$. For a subgraph H of G we use $G\setminus H$ short for $G\setminus V(H)$. Denote by $N(x)$ the neighborhood of a vertex x in G. Put $d(x)=|N(x)|$

A simple cycle (or just a cycle) C of length t is a sequence $v_1v_2...v_tv_1$ of distinct vertices $v_1,v_2,...,v_t$ with $v_iv_{i+1}\in E(G)$ for each $i\in\{1,...,t\}$, where $v_{t+1}=v_1$. When $t=2$, the cycle $C=v_1v_2v_1$ on two vertices v_1,v_2 coincides with the edge v_1v_2, and when $t=1$, the cycle $C=v_1$ coincides with the vertex v_1. So, all vertices and edges in a graph can be considered as cycles of lengths 1 and 2, respectively. A graph G is hamiltonian if G contains a Hamilton cycle, i.e. a cycle containing all vertices of G. Let λ be an integer. A cycle C' in G is a PD_λ-cycle if $|P|\le\lambda-1$ for each path P in $G\setminus C'$ and is a CD_λ-cycle if $|C''|\le\lambda-1$ for each cycle C'' in $G\setminus C'$. In particular, PD_0-cycles and CD_1-cycles are well-known Hamilton cycles and PD_1-cycles and CD_2-cycles are often called dominating cycles.

We reserve n,q,δ,κ and α to denote the number of vertices (order), number of edges (size), minimum degree, connectivity and independence number of a graph, respectively. Let c denote the circumference - the length of a longest cycle in a graph. In general, $c\ge 1$. For C a longest cycle in G, denote by $\overline{p}$ and $\overline{c}$ the lengths of a longest path and a longest cycle in $G\setminus C$, respectively. Let $s(G)$ denote the number of components of a graph G. A graph G is t-tough if $|S|\ge t\cdot s(G\setminus S)$ for every subset $S\subseteq V(G)$ with $s(G\setminus S)>1$. The toughness of G, denoted $\tau(G)$, is the maximum value of t for which G is t-tough (taking $\tau(K_n)=\infty$ for all $n\ge 1$).

An (x,y)-path is a path with end vertices x and y. Given an (x,y)-path L of G, we denote by $\overrightarrow{L}$ the path L with an orientation from x to y. If $u,v \in V(L)$ then $u\overrightarrow{L}v$ denotes the consecutive vertices on $\overrightarrow{L}$ from u to v in the direction specified by $\overrightarrow{L}$. The same vertices, in reverse order, are given by $v\overleftarrow{L}u$. For $\overrightarrow{L} = x\overrightarrow{L}y$ and $u \in V(L)$, let $u^+\left(\overrightarrow{L}\right)$ (or just u^+) denotes the successor of u $(u \neq y)$ on $\overrightarrow{L}$, and u^- denotes its predecessor $(u \neq x)$. If $A \subseteq V(L) \setminus \{y\}$ then we denote $A^+ = \left\{v^+ \mid v \in A\right\}$. Similar notation is used for cycles. If Q is a cycle and $u \in V(Q)$, then $u\overrightarrow{Q}u = u$.

Let a, b, t, k be integers with $k \le t$. We use $H(a,b,t,k)$ to denote the graph obtained from $tK_a + \overline{K}_t$ by taking any k vertices in subgraph $\overline{K}_t$ and joining each of them to all vertices of K_b. Denote by L_δ the graph obtained from $3K_\delta + K_1$ by taking one vertex in each of three copies of K_b and joining them each to other. For odd n, where $n \ge 15$, construct the graph G_n from $\overline{K}_{(n-1)/2} + K_\delta + K_{(n+1)/2-\delta}$, where $n/3 \le \delta \le (n-5)/2$, by joining every vertex in K_δ to all other vertices and by adding a matching between all vertices in $K_{(n+1)/2-\delta}$ and $(n+1)/2-\delta$ vertices in $\overline{K}_{(n-1)/2}$. It is easily seen that G_n is 1-tough but not hamiltonian. A variation of the graph G_n, with K_δ replaced by $\overline{K}_\delta$ and $\delta = (n-5)/2$, will be denoted by G_n^*.

3. Pure relations for Hamilton cycles

We begin with a pure algebraic relation between order n and size q insuring the existence of a Hamilton cycle based on the natural idea that if a sufficient number of edges are present in the graph then a Hamilton cycle will exist.

Theorem 1 (Erdös & Gallai, 1959). Let G be an arbitrary graph. If

$$q \ge \frac{n^2 - 3n + 5}{2}$$

then G is hamiltonian.

Example for sharpness. To see that the size bound $(n^2 - 3n + 5)/2$ in Theorem 1 is best possible, note that the graph formed by joining one vertex of K_{n-1} to K_1, contains $(n^2 - 3n + 4)/2$ edges and is not hamiltonian.

The next pure algebraic relation links the size q and minimum degree δ insuring the existence of a Hamilton cycle. In view of Theorem 1, it seems a little surprising, providing, in fact, a contrary statement.

Theorem 2 (Zh.G. Nikoghosyan, 2011). Let G be an arbitrary graph. If

$$q \leq \delta^2 + \delta - 1$$

then G is hamiltonian.

Example for sharpness. The bound $\delta^2 + \delta - 1$ in Theorem 2 can not be relaxed to $\delta^2 + \delta$ since the graph $K_1 + 2K_\delta$ consisting of two copies of $K_{\delta+1}$ and having exactly one vertex in common, has $\delta^2 + \delta$ edges but is not hamiltonian.

The earliest sufficient condition for a graph to be hamiltonian is based on the order n and minimum degree δ ensuring the existence of a Hamilton cycle with sufficient number of edges by keeping the minimum degree at a fairly high level.

Theorem 3 (Dirac, 1952). Let G be an arbitrary graph. If

$$\delta \geq \frac{n}{2}$$

then G is hamiltonian.

Example for sharpness: $2K_\delta + K_1$.

The graph $2K_\delta + K_1$ shows that the bound $n/2$ in Theorem 3 can not be replaced by $(n-1)/2$.

The minimum degree bound $n/2$ in Theorem 3 can be slightly relaxed for graphs under additional 1-tough condition.

Theorem 4 (Jung, 1978). Let G be a graph with $n \geq 11$ and $\tau \geq 1$. If

$$\delta \geq \frac{n-4}{2}$$

then G is hamiltonian.

Examples for sharpness: Petersen graph; $K_{\delta,\delta+1}$; G_n^*.

This bound $(n-4)/2$ itself was lowered further to $(n-7)/2$ under stronger conditions $n \geq 30$ and $\tau > 1$.

Theorem 5 (Bauer et al., 1991a). Let G be a graph with $n \geq 30$ and $\tau > 1$. If

$$\delta \geq \frac{n-7}{2}$$

then G is hamiltonian.

Furthermore, the bound $n/2$ was essentially lowered to $(n+\kappa)/3$ (when $k < n/2$) by incorporating connectivity κ into the minimum degree bound.

Theorem 6 (Zh.G. Nikoghosyan, 1981). Let G be a graph with $\kappa \geq 2$. If

$$\delta \geq \frac{n+\kappa}{3}$$

then G is hamiltonian.

Examples for sharpness: $2K_{\delta} + K_1; H(1, \delta - \kappa + 1, \delta, \kappa)\ (2 \leq \kappa < n/2)$.

A short proof of Theorem 6 was given by Häggkvist (Häggkvist & Nicoghossian, 1981).

The minimum degree bound $(n+\kappa)/3$ in Theorem 6 was slightly lowered to $(n+\kappa-2)/3$ for 1-tough graphs.

Theorem 7 (Bauer & Schmeichel, 1991b). Let G be a graph with $\tau \geq 1$. If

$$\delta \geq \frac{n+\kappa-2}{3}$$

then G is hamiltonian.

Examples for sharpness: $K_{\delta,\delta+1}; L_{\delta}$.

Another essential improvement of Dirac's bound $n/2$ was established for 2-connected graphs under additional strong condition $\delta \geq \alpha$.

Theorem 8 (Nash-Williams, 1971). Let G be a graph with $\kappa \geq 2$. If

$$\delta \geq \max\left\{\frac{n+2}{3}, \alpha\right\}$$

then G is hamiltonian.

Examples for sharpness:
$(\lambda+1)K_{\delta-\lambda+1} + K_{\lambda}\ (\delta \geq 2\lambda); (\lambda+2)K_{\delta-\lambda} + K_{\lambda+1}\ (\delta \geq 2\lambda+1); H(\lambda, \lambda+1, \lambda+3, \lambda+2)$.

Theorem 8 was slightly improved by replacing the condition $\kappa \geq 2$ with a stronger condition $\tau \geq 1$.

Theorem 9 (Bigalke & Jung, 1979). Let G be a graph with $\tau \geq 1$. If

$$\delta \geq \max\left\{\frac{n}{3}, \alpha - 1\right\}$$

then G is hamiltonian.

Examples for sharpness: $K_{\delta,\delta+1}\ (n \geq 3); L_{\delta}\ (n \geq 7); K_{\delta,\delta+1}\ (n \geq 3)$.

For λ a positive integer, the bound $(n+2)/3$ in Theorem 8 was essentially lowered under additional condition of the type $\delta \geq \alpha + \lambda$, including Theorem 8 as a special case.

Theorem 10 (Fraisse, 1986). Let G be a graph, λ a positive integer and

$$\delta \geq \max\left\{\frac{n+2}{\lambda+2} + \lambda - 1, \alpha + \lambda - 1\right\}.$$

If $\kappa \geq \lambda + 1$ then G is hamiltonian.

Examples for sharpness:
$(\lambda+1)K_{\delta-\lambda+1} + K_{\lambda}$ $(\delta \geq 2\lambda)$; $(\lambda+2)K_{\delta-\lambda} + K_{\lambda+1}$ $(\delta \geq 2\lambda+1)$; $H(\lambda,\lambda+1,\lambda+3,\lambda+2)$.

Later, Theorem 8 was essentially improved for 3-connected graphs by incorporating the connectivity κ into the minimum degree bound.

Theorem 11 (Zh.G. Nikoghosyan, 1985a). Let G be a graph with $\kappa \geq 3$. If

$$\delta \geq \max\left\{\frac{n+2\kappa}{4}, \alpha\right\}$$

then G is hamiltonian.

Examples for sharpness: $3K_2 + K_2; 4K_2 + K_3; H(1,2,\kappa+1,\kappa)$.

The graph $4K_2 + K_3$ shows that for $\kappa = 3$ the minimum degree bound $(n+2\kappa)/4$ in Theorem 11 can not be replaced by $(n+2\kappa-1)/4$.

Finally, the bound $(n+2\kappa)/4$ in Theorem 11 was reduced to $(n+\kappa+3)/4$ without any additional limitations providing a best possible result for each $\kappa \geq 3$.

Theorem 12 (Yamashita, 2008). Let G be a graph with $\kappa \geq 3$. If

$$\delta \geq \max\left\{\frac{n+\kappa+3}{4}, \alpha\right\}$$

then G is hamiltonian.

Examples for sharpness: $3K_{\delta-1} + K_2$; $H(2,n-3\delta+3,\delta-1,\kappa)$; $H(1,2,\kappa+1,\kappa)$.

The first pure relation between graph invariants involving connectivity κ as a parameter was developed in 1972.

Theorem 13 (Chvátal and Erdös, 1972). Let G be an arbitrary graph. If

$$\kappa \geq \alpha$$

then G is hamiltonian.

Example for sharpness: $K_{\delta,\delta+1}$.

4. Pure relations for dominating cycles

In view of Theorem 2, the following upper size bound is reasonable for dominating cycles.

Conjecture 1. Let G be a graph with $\kappa \geq 2$. If

$$q \leq \frac{3\left(\delta^2+\delta-2\right)-1}{2}$$

then each longest cycle in G is a dominating cycle.

In 1971, it was proved that the minimum degree bound $(n+2)/3$ insures the existence of dominating cycles.

Theorem 14 (Nash-Williams, 1971). Let G be a graph with

$$\delta \geq \frac{n+2}{3}.$$

If $\kappa \geq 2$ then each longest cycle in G is a dominating cycle.

Examples for sharpness: $2K_3+K_1$; $3K_{\delta-1}+K_2$; $H(1,2,4,3)$.

The graph $2K_3+K_1$ shows that the connectivity condition $\kappa \geq 2$ in Theorem 14 can not be replaced by $\kappa \geq 1$. The second graph shows that the minimum degree condition $\delta \geq (n+2)/3$ can not be replaced by $\delta \geq (n+1)/3$ and the third graph shows that the conclusion "is a dominating cycle" can not be strengthened by replacing it with "is a Hamilton cycle".

The condition $\delta \geq (n+2)/3$ in Theorem 14 can be slightly relaxed under stronger 1-tough condition instead of $\kappa \geq 2$.

Theorem 15 (Bigalke & Jung, 1979). Let G be a graph with $\tau \geq 1$. If

$$\delta \geq \frac{n}{3}$$

then each longest cycle in G is a dominating cycle.

Examples for sharpness: $2(\kappa+1)K_2+\kappa K_1$; L_3; G_n^*.

The bound $(n+2)/3$ in Theorem 14 can be lowered to $(n+2\kappa)/4$ by incorporating κ into the minimum degree bound.

Theorem 16 (Lu et al., 2005). Let G be graph with $\kappa \geq 3$. If

$$\delta \geq \frac{n+2\kappa}{4}$$

then each longest cycle in G is a dominating cycle.

Examples for sharpness: $3K_2+K_2$; $4K_2+K_3$; $H(1,2,\kappa+1,\kappa)$.

The graph $4K_2+K_3$ shows that for $\kappa=3$ the minimum degree bound $(n+2\kappa)/4$ in Theorem 16 can not be replaced by $(n+2\kappa-1)/4$.

In 2008, the bound $(n+2\kappa)/4$ itself was essentially reduced to $(n+\kappa+3)/4$ without any additional limitations, providing a best possible result for each $\kappa\geq 3$.

Theorem 17 (Yamashita, 2008). Let G be graph with $\kappa\geq 3$. If

$$\delta\geq\frac{n+\kappa+3}{4}$$

then each longest cycle in G is a dominating cycle.

Examples for sharpness: $3K_{\delta-1}+K_2$; $H(2,n-3\delta+3,\delta-1,\kappa)$; $H(1,2,\kappa+1,\kappa)$.

5. Pure relations for CD_λ-cycles

In 1990, the exact analog of Theorems 3 and 14 was established In terms of generalized CD_3-cycles.

Theorem 18 (Jung, 1990). Let G be a graph with

$$\delta\geq\frac{n+6}{4}.$$

If $\kappa\geq 3$ then each longest cycle in G is a CD_3-cycle.

Examples for sharpness:
$\lambda K_{\lambda+1}+K_{\lambda-1}$ $(\lambda\geq 2)$; $(\lambda+1)K_{\delta-\lambda+1}+K_\lambda$ $(\lambda\geq 1)$; $H(\lambda-1,\lambda,\lambda+2,\lambda+1)$ $(\lambda\geq 2)$.

In 2009, a common generalization of Theorems 3, 14 and 18 was proved by covering CD_λ-cycles for each integer $\lambda\geq 1$.

Theorem 19 (Zh.G. Nikoghosyan, 2009a). Let G be a graph, λ a positive integer and

$$\delta\geq\frac{n+2}{\lambda+1}+\lambda-2.$$

Then each longest cycle in G is a $CD_{\min\{\lambda,\delta-\lambda+1\}}$-cycle.

Examples for sharpness:
$\lambda K_{\lambda+1}K_{\lambda-1}$ $(\lambda\geq 2)$; $(\lambda+1)K_{\delta-\lambda+1}+K_\lambda$ $(\lambda\geq 1)$; $H(\lambda-1,\lambda,\lambda+2,\lambda+1)$ $(\lambda\geq 2)$.

In (Zh.G. Nikoghosyan, 2009a), an analogous generalization has been conjectured in terms of PD_λ-cycles.

Conjecture 1 (Zh.G. Nikoghosyan, 2009a). Let G be a graph, λ a positive integer and $\kappa\geq\lambda$. If

$$\delta \geq \frac{n+2}{\lambda+1} + \lambda - 2$$

then each longest cycle in G is a $PD_{\min\{\lambda-1,\delta-\lambda\}}$-cycle.

In view of Theorems 6 and 17, the next generalization seems reasonable.

Conjecture 2 (Yamashita, 2008). Let G be graph, λ an integer and $\kappa \geq \lambda \geq 2$. If

$$\delta \geq \frac{n+\kappa+\lambda(\lambda-2)}{\lambda+1}$$

then each longest cycle in G is a $PD_{\lambda-2}$ and $CD_{\lambda-1}$-cycle.

6. Pure relations for long cycles

The earliest and simplest hamiltonian result links the circumference c and minimum degree δ.

Theorem 20 (Dirac, 1952). In every graph,

$$c \geq \delta + 1.$$

Example for sharpness: Join two copies of $K_{\delta+1}$ by an edge.

For C a longest cycle in a graph G, a lower bound for $|C|$ was developed based on the minimum degree δ and $\overline{p}$ - the length of a longest path in $G \backslash C$.

Theorem 21 (Zh.G. Nikoghosyan, 1998). Let G be a graph and C a longest cycle in G. Then

$$|C| \geq (\overline{p}+2)(\delta-\overline{p}).$$

Example for sharpness: $(\kappa+1)K_{\delta-\kappa+1} + K_{\kappa}$.

The next similar bound is based On the minimum degree δ and $\overline{c}$ - the length of a longest cycle in $G \backslash C$.

Theorem 22 (Zh.G. Nikoghosyan, 2000a). Let G be a graph and C a longest cycle in G. Then

$$|C| \geq (\overline{c}+1)(\delta-\overline{c}+1).$$

Example for sharpness: $(\kappa+1)K_{\delta-\kappa+1} + K_{\kappa}$.

In 2000, Theorem 22 was improved involving connectivity κ as a parameter combined with $\overline{c}$ and δ.

Theorem 23 (Zh.G. Nikoghosyan, 2000b). Let G be a graph with $\kappa \geq 2$ and C a longest cycle in G. If $\overline{c} \geq \kappa$ then

$$|C| \geq \frac{(\overline{c}+1)\kappa}{\overline{c}+\kappa+1}(\delta+2).$$

Otherwise,

$$|C| \geq \frac{(\overline{c}+1)\overline{c}}{2\overline{c}+1}(\delta+2).$$

Example for sharpness: $(\kappa+1)K_{\delta-\kappa+1}+K_{\kappa}$.

In view of Theorem 23, the following seems reasonable for PD_{λ} -cycles.

Conjecture 3 (Zh.G. Nikoghosyan, 2009a). Let G be a graph with $\kappa \geq 2$ and C a longest cycle in G. If $\overline{p} \geq \kappa - 1$ then

$$|C| \geq \frac{(\overline{p}+2)\kappa}{\overline{p}+\kappa+2}(\delta+2).$$

Otherwise,

$$|C| \geq \frac{(\overline{p}+2)\overline{p}}{2\overline{p}+2}(\delta+2).$$

7. Pure relations for Hamilton cycles and long cycles

The following direct generalization includes Theorem 3 as a special case.

Theorem 24 (Alon, 1986). Let G be a graph and λ a positive integer. If $\delta \geq n/(\lambda+1)$ then

$$c \geq \frac{n}{\lambda}.$$

Examples for sharpness: $(\lambda+1)K_{\lambda}+K_1$; $\lambda K_{\lambda+1}$.

In 1952, a relationship was established linking the minimum degree δ, circumference c and Hamilton cycles for 2-connexted graphs.

Theorem 25 (Dirac, 1952). Let G be a graph with $\kappa \geq 2$. Then

$$c \geq \min\{n, 2\delta\}.$$

Examples for sharpness:
$(\lambda+1)K_{\lambda+1}+K_{\lambda}$ $(\lambda \geq 1)$; $(\lambda+3)K_{\lambda-1}+K_{\lambda+2}$ $(\lambda \geq 2)$; $(\lambda+2)K_{\lambda}+K_{\lambda+1}$ $(\lambda \geq 1)$.

For 1-tough graphs the bound 2δ in Theorem 25 was slightly enlarged.

Theorem 26 (Bauer and Schmeichel, 1986). Let G be a graph with $\tau \geq 1$. Then

$$c \geq \min\{n, 2\delta + 2\}.$$

Examples for sharpness: $K_{\delta,\delta+1}$; L_2.

The first essential improvement of Theorem 25 was achieved by incorporating connectivity κ into the relation without any essential limitation.

Theorem 27 (Zh.G. Nikoghosyan, 1981). Let G be a graph with $\kappa \geq 3$. Then

$$c \geq \min\{n, 3\delta - \kappa\}.$$

Examples for sharpness: $3K_{\delta-1} + K_2$; $H(1, \delta - \kappa + 1, \delta, \kappa)$.

In (Voss & Zuluaga, 1977), it was proved that the bound $\min\{n, 2\delta\}$ in Theorem 25 can be essentially enlarged under additional condition $\delta \geq \alpha$ combined with $\kappa \geq 3$.

Theorem 28 (Voss and Zuluaga, 1977). Let G be a graph with $\kappa \geq 3$. If $\delta \geq \alpha$ then

$$c \geq \min\{n, 3\delta - 3\}.$$

Examples for sharpness: $(\lambda + 2)K_{\lambda+2} + K_{\lambda+1}$; $(\lambda + 4)K_{\lambda} + K_{\lambda+3}$; $(\lambda + 3)K_{\lambda+1} + K_{\lambda+2}$.

In 2009, a direct generalization was established for each positive integer λ, including Theorem 28 as a special case $(\lambda = 1)$.

Theorem 29 (Zh.G. Nikoghosyan, 2009a). Let G be a graph and λ a positive integer. If $\kappa \geq \lambda + 2$ and $\delta \geq \alpha + \lambda - 1$ then

$$c \geq \min\{n, (\lambda + 2)(\delta - \lambda)\}.$$

Examples for sharpness: $(\lambda + 2)K_{\lambda+2} + K_{\lambda+1}$; $(\lambda + 4)K_{\lambda} + K_{\lambda+3}$; $(\lambda + 3)K_{\lambda+1} + K_{\lambda+2}$.

In 1985, the bound $3\delta - \kappa$ in Theorem 27 was enlarged to $4\delta - 2\kappa$ under additional condition $\delta \geq \alpha$ combined with $\kappa \geq 4$.

Theorem 30 (Zh.G. Nikoghosyan, 1985b). Let G be a graph with $\kappa \geq 4$ and $\delta \geq \alpha$. Then

$$c \geq \min\{n, 4\delta - 2\kappa\}.$$

Examples for sharpness: $4K_2 + K_3$; $H(1, n - 2\delta, \delta, \kappa)$; $5K_2 + K_4$.

The bound $4\delta - 2\kappa$ in Theorem 30 is sharp for $\kappa = 4$.

Furthermore, the bound $4\delta - 2\kappa$ in Theorem 30 was essentially improved to $4\delta - \kappa - 4$ without any additional limitations providing a best possible result for each $\kappa \geq 4$.

Theorem 31 (M.Zh. Nikoghosyan & Zh.G. Nikoghosyan, 2011). Let G be a graph with $\kappa \geq 4$ and $\delta \geq \alpha$. Then

$$c \geq \min\{n, 4\delta - \kappa - 4\}.$$

Examples for sharpness: $4K_{\delta-2} + K_3$; $H(1,2,\kappa+1,\kappa)$; $H(2, n-3\delta+3, \delta-1, \kappa)$.

The next theorem provides a lower bound for the circumference in terms of n, δ and α under the hypothesis of Theorem 14.

Theorem 32 (Bauer et al., 1990b). Let G be a graph with $\kappa \geq 2$. If $\delta \geq (n+2)/3$ then

$$c \geq \min\{n, n+\delta-\alpha\}.$$

Examples for sharpness: $2K_\delta + K_1$; $3K_{\delta-1} + K_2$; $K_{2\delta-2,\delta}$.

An analogous bound was established for 1-tough graphs.

Theorem 33 (Bauer et al., 1988). Let G be a graph with $\tau \geq 1$. If $\delta \geq n/3$ then

$$c \geq \min\{n, n+\delta-\alpha+1\}.$$

Examples for sharpness: $K_{\delta,\delta+1}$; L_δ; G_n^*.

8. Pure relations for dominating cycles and long cycles

The exact analog of Theorem 25 for dominating cycles can be formulated as follows.

Theorem 34 (Voss & Zuluaga, 1977). Let G be a graph with $\kappa \geq 3$. Then either

$$c \geq 3\delta - 3$$

or each longest cycle in G is a dominating cycle.

Examples for sharpness:
$(\lambda+1)K_{\lambda+1} + K_\lambda$ $(\lambda \geq 1)$; $(\lambda+3)K_{\lambda+1} + K_{\lambda+2}$ $(\lambda \geq 2)$; $(\lambda+2)K_\lambda + K_{\lambda+1}$ $(\lambda \geq 1)$.

The bound $3\delta - 3$ in Theorem 34 was enlarged to $4\delta - 2\kappa$ by incorporating connectivity κ into the bound.

Theorem 35 (Zh.G. Nikoghosyan, 2009b). Let G be a graph with $\kappa \geq 4$. Then either

$$c \geq 4\delta - 2\kappa$$

or G has a dominating cycle.

Examples for sharpness: $4K_2 + K_3$; $5K_2 + K_4$; $H(1, n-2\delta, \delta, \kappa)$.

Theorem 35 is sharp only for $\kappa = 4$ as can be seen from $5K_2 + K_4$. Further, the bound $4\delta - 2\kappa$ in Theorem 35 was essentially improved to $4\delta - \kappa - 4$ without any limitation providing a sharp bound for each $\kappa \geq 4$.

Theorem 36 (M.Zh. Nikoghosyan & Zh.G. Nikoghosyan, 2011). Let G be a graph with $\kappa \geq 4$. Then either

$$c \geq 4\delta - \kappa - 4$$

or each longest cycle in G is a dominating cycle.

Examples for sharpness: $4K_{\delta-2} + K_3$; $H(2,\delta-\kappa+1,\delta-1,\kappa)$; $H(1,2,\kappa+1,\kappa)$.

9. Pure relations for CD_λ -cycles and long cycles

TThe following theorem can be considered as a common generalization of Theorems 25 and 34 by covering CD_λ-cycles for all $\lambda \geq 1$ including Hamilton and dominating cycles as special cases.

Theorem 37 (Zh.G. Nikoghosyan, 2009a). Let G be a graph and λ a positive integer. If $\kappa \geq \lambda + 1$ then either

$$c \geq (\lambda+1)(\delta-\lambda+1)$$

or each longest cycle in G is a $CD_{\min\{\lambda,\delta-\lambda\}}$-cycle.

Examples for sharpness:
$(\lambda+1)K_{\lambda+1} + K_\lambda$ $(\lambda \geq 1)$; $(\lambda+3)K_{\lambda-1} + K_{\lambda+2}$ $(\lambda \geq 2)$; $(\lambda+2)K_\lambda + K_{\lambda+1}$ $(\lambda \geq 1)$.

In (Zh.G. Nikoghosyan, 2009a), another version of Theorem 37 was conjectured in terms of PD_λ-cycles, instead of CD_λ-cycles.

Conjecture 4 (Zh.G. Nikoghosyan, 2009a). Let G be a graph and λ a positive integer. If $\kappa \geq \lambda + 1$ then either

$$c \geq (\lambda+1)(\delta-\lambda+1)$$

or each longest cycle in G is a $PD_{\min\{\lambda-1,\delta-\lambda-1\}}$-cycle.

In view of Theorems 27 and 36, the following common generalization seems quite reasonable.

Conjecture 5. Let G be a graph and $\lambda \geq 2$ an integer. If $\kappa \geq \lambda + 1$ then either

$$c \geq (\lambda+1)\delta - \kappa - (\lambda+1)(\lambda-2)$$

or each longest cycle in G is a $PD_{\lambda-2}$ and $CD_{\lambda-1}$-cycle.

10. Proofs of theorems 6, 21 and 27

In proofs of theorems and lemmas, the end of the proof is marked by $\square$. In proofs of claims, the end of the proof is marked by Δ.

Proof of Theorem 27 (Mosesyan et al., 2009). Let G be a 3-connected graph and S a minimum cut-set in G. Choose a longest cycle C in G so as to maximize $|V(C)\cap S|$. The result holds immediately if $|C|\geq 3\delta-3$, since $3\delta-3\geq 3\delta-\kappa$. Otherwise, by Theorem 34, C is a dominating cycle. Assume first that $S\not\subseteq V(C)$ and let $v\in S\setminus V(C)$. Since $\overrightarrow{C}$ is dominating, $N(v)\subseteq V(C)$. Let $\xi_1,\ldots,\xi_t$ be the elements of $N(v)$, occurring on $\overrightarrow{C}$ in a consecutive order. Put

$$M_1=\left\{\xi_i \mid V\left(\xi_i^+\overrightarrow{C}\xi_{i+1}^-\right)\cap S\neq\varnothing\right\},\quad M_2=N(v)\setminus M_1.$$

Since $v\in S$, we have

$$|M_1|\leq\kappa-1,\qquad |M_2|=|N(v)|-|M_1|\geq\delta-\kappa+1.$$

Further, since C is extreme and $|V(C)\cap S|$ is maximum,

$$N(v)\cap N^+(v)\cap M_2^{++}=\varnothing.$$

Hence

$$\begin{aligned}|C|&\geq|N(v)|+|N^+(v)|+|M_2^{++}|\\&=2|N(v)|+|M_2|\geq 3\delta-\kappa+1.\end{aligned}$$

Now assume that $S\subseteq V(C)$. Let $H_1,\ldots,H_h$ be the connected components of $G\setminus S$. If $V(G\setminus C)=\varnothing$ then $|C|=n$ and we are done. Let $x\in V(G\setminus C)$. Assume without loss of generality that $x\in V(H_1)$. Since C is dominating, $N(x)\subseteq V(C)$. Put $Y_1=N(x)\cup N^+(x)$. Clearly $|Y_1|\geq 2\delta$ and to prove that $|C|\geq 3\delta-\kappa$, it remains to find a subset Y_2 in $V(C)$ such that $Y_1\cap Y_2=\varnothing$ and $|Y_2|\geq\delta-\kappa$. Abbreviate, $V_1=V(H_1)\cup S$. Suppose first that $Y_1\subseteq V_1$. If $V(H_2)\subseteq V(C)$ then $Y_2=V(H_2)$ since $|V(H_2)|\geq\delta-\kappa+1$. Otherwise, there exist $y\in V(H_2\setminus C)$. Since C is dominating, $N(y)\subseteq V(C)$ and we can take $Y_2=N(y)\setminus S$. Now let $Y_1\not\subseteq V_1$. Assume without loss of generality that $Y_1\cap V(H_2)\neq\varnothing$. Since $N(x)\subseteq V_1$, we have $N^+(x)\cap V(H_2)\neq\varnothing$. Let $z\in N^+(x)\cap V(H_2)$. If $N(z)\subseteq V(C)$ then take $Y_2=N(z)\setminus S$, since $N^+(x)$ is an independent set of vertices (by standard arguments) and therefore, $N(z)\cap N^+(x)=\varnothing$. Otherwise, choose $w\in N(z)\setminus V(C)$. Clearly

$$N(w)\subseteq V(C),\ w\in V(H_2),\ N(w)\cap N^+(x)=\{z\}.$$

Then by taking

$$Y_2=(N(w)\setminus\{z\})\setminus(S\setminus\{z^-\})$$

we complete the proof of Theorem 27. □

Proof of Theorem 6 (Mosesyan et al., 2009). Let G be a 2-connected graph with $\delta \geq (n+\kappa)/3$ and let S be a minimum cut-set in G. Since $\delta \geq (n+\kappa)/3 \geq (n+2)/3$, by Theorem 14, every longest cycle in G is a dominating cycle. As in proof of Theorem 27, we can show that either G is hamiltonian or $c \geq 3\delta - \kappa$. Since $n \leq 3\delta - \kappa$ (by the hypothesis), it follows from $c \geq 3\delta - \kappa$ that $c = 3\delta - \kappa = n$. So, in any case, G is hamiltonian. □

To prove Theorem 21, we need some special definitions. Let G be a graph, C a longest cycle in G and $\overrightarrow{M}$ a longest path (or a cycle) in $G \backslash C$. Further, let $u_1,...,u_m$ be the elements of $V(M)$ occurring on $\overrightarrow{M}$ in a consecutive order.

Definition 1 {M_C-spreading; $\overrightarrow{\Upsilon}(u)$; $\dot{u}$; $\ddot{u}$}. An M_C-spreading Υ is a family of pairwise disjoint paths $\overrightarrow{\Upsilon}(u_1),...,\overrightarrow{\Upsilon}(u_m)$ in $G \backslash C$ with $\overrightarrow{\Upsilon}(u_i) = u_i \overrightarrow{\Upsilon}(u_i) \ddot{u}_i$ $(i = 1,...,m)$. If $u \neq \ddot{u}$ for some $\overrightarrow{\Upsilon}(u)$, then we use $\dot{u}$ to denote the successor of u along $\overrightarrow{\Upsilon}(u)$.

Definition 2 $\{\Phi_u; \varphi_u; \Psi_u; \psi_u\}$. Let Υ be any M_C-spreading. For each $u \in V(M)$, put

$$\Phi_u = N(\ddot{u}) \cap V(\Upsilon), \quad \varphi_u = |\Phi_u|,$$

$$\Psi_u = N(\ddot{u}) \cap V(H), \quad \psi_u = |\Psi_u|.$$

Definition 3 $\{U_0; \bar{U}_0; U_1; U^*\}$. For Υ an M_C-spreading, put

$$U_0 = \{u \in V(M) \mid u = \ddot{u}\}, \quad \bar{U}_0 = V(M) \backslash U_0,$$
$$U^* = \{u \in \bar{U}_0 \mid \Phi_u \subseteq V(\Upsilon(u))\}, \quad U_1 = V(M) \backslash (U_0 \cup U^*).$$

Definition 4 {(U_0)-minimal M_C-spreading}. An M_C-spreading Υ is said to be (U_0)-minimal, if it is chosen such that $|U_0|$ is minimum.

Definition 5 $\{B_u; B_u^*; b_u; b_u^*\}$. For Υ an M_C-spreading and $u \in V(M)$, set

$$B_u = \{v \in U_0 \mid v\dot{u} \in E\}, \quad b_u = |B_u|.$$

Further, for each $u \in U_0$, set

$$B_u^* = \{v \in \bar{U}_0 \mid u\dot{v} \in E\}, \quad b_u^* = |B_u^*|.$$

Lemma 1. Let C be a longest cycle in a graph G and M a path in $G\backslash C$. Let $\overrightarrow{L}_1,...,\overrightarrow{L}_r$ be vertex disjoint paths in $G\backslash C$ with $\overrightarrow{L}_i = v_i \overrightarrow{L}_i w_i$ $(i=1,...,r)$ having only $v_1,...,v_r$ in common with M and let . $Z_i = N(w_i)\cap V(C)$ $(i=1,...,r)$ .. Then

$$|C| \geq \sum_{i=1}^{r}|Z_i| + \left|\bigcup_{i=1}^{r} Z_i\right|.$$

Proof. We can assume without loss of generality that $v_i = w_i$ $(i=1,...,r)$, since otherwise, we can use the same arguments. If $\bigcup_{i=1}^{r} Z_i = \varnothing$, then there is nothing to prove. Let $\bigcup_{i=1}^{r} Z_i \neq \varnothing$ and let $\xi_1,...,\xi_t$ be the elements of $\bigcup_{i=1}^{r} Z_i$ occurring on $\overrightarrow{C}$ in a consecutive order. Set

$$F_i = N(\xi_i)\cap\{w_1,...,w_r\} \quad (i=1,...,t).$$

Suppose first that $t=1$. If $|F_1|=1$ then $\sum_{i=1}^{r}|Z_i| = \left|\bigcup_{i=1}^{r} Z_i\right| = 1$ and the result follows from $|C|\geq 2$ immediately. If $|F_1|\geq 2$, then choosing a largest segment $u\overrightarrow{M}v$ on M with $u,v\in F_1$, we get a cycle $C' = \xi_1 u\overrightarrow{M}v\xi_1$ satisfying

$$|C| \geq |C'| \geq \sum_{i=1}^{r}|Z_1| + 1 = \sum_{i=1}^{r}|Z_1| + \left|\bigcup_{i=1}^{r} Z_i\right|.$$

Now assume $t\geq 2$. Put

$$f(\xi_i) = \left|\xi_i\overrightarrow{C}\xi_{i+1}\right| \quad (i=1,2,...,t),$$

where $\xi_{i+1} = \xi_1$. Then it is easy to see that

$$|C| = \sum_{i=1}^{t} f(\xi_i), \quad \sum_{i=1}^{t}|F_i| = \sum_{i=1}^{r}|Z_i|, \quad t = \left|\bigcup_{i=1}^{r} Z_i\right|. \tag{1}$$

For each $i\in\{1,...,t\}$, let $x_i\overrightarrow{M}y_i$ be the largest segment on $\overrightarrow{M}$ with $x_i, y_i \in F_i\cup F_{i+1}$ (indices mod t). Now we need to show that

$f(\xi_i) \geq (|F_i| + |F_{i+1}| + 2)/2$. Indeed, if $x_i\in F_i$ and $y_i\in F_{i+1}$, then $f(\xi_i) \geq \left|\xi_i x_i \overrightarrow{M} y_i \xi_{i+1}\right|$ since C is extreme. It means that

$$f(\xi_i) \geq \max\{|F_i|,|F_{i+1}|\}+1 \geq \frac{1}{2}(|F_i|+|F_{i+1}|+2).$$

The same inequality holds from $f(\xi_i) \geq \left|\xi_i y_i \overleftarrow{M} x_i \xi_{i+1}\right|$ if $x_i \in F_{i+1}$ and $y_i \in F_i$, by a similar argument. Now suppose that either $x_i, y_i \in F_i$ or $x_i, y_i \in F_{i+1}$. Assume without loss of generality that $x_i, y_i \in F_i$. In addition, we have $x_i, y_i \notin F_{i+1}$, since otherwise we are in the previous case. Let $x_i' \overrightarrow{M} y_i'$ be the largest segment on $\overrightarrow{M}$ with $x_i', y_i' \in F_{i+1}$. If $\left|x_i \overrightarrow{M} x_i'\right| \geq (|F_i|-|F_{i+1}|)/2$, then $f(\xi_i) \geq \left|\xi_i x_i \overrightarrow{M} y_i' \xi_{i+1}\right|$ and hence

$$f(\xi_i) \geq \frac{1}{2}(|F_i|-|F_{i+1}|)+|F_{i+1}|+1 = \frac{1}{2}(|F_i|+|F_{i+1}|+2).$$

Finally, if $\left|x_i \overrightarrow{M} x_i'\right| \leq (|F_i|-|F_{i+1}|-1)/2$, then

$$f(\xi_i) \geq \left|\xi_i y_i \overleftarrow{M} x_i' \xi_{i+1}\right| = \left|x_i' \overrightarrow{M} y_i\right|+2 = \left|x_i \overrightarrow{M} y_i\right| - \left|x_i \overrightarrow{M} x_i'\right|+2$$
$$\geq |F_i|-1-\frac{1}{2}(|F_i|-|F_{i+1}|-1)+2 > \frac{1}{2}(|F_i|+|F_{i+1}|+2).$$

So, $f(\xi_i) \geq (|F_i|+|F_{i+1}|+2)/2$ $(i=1,\ldots,t)$ in any case, implying that

$$\sum_{i=1}^{t} f(\xi_i) \geq \sum_{i=1}^{t}\frac{1}{2}(|F_i|+|F_{i+1}|+2) = \sum_{i=1}^{t}|F_i|+t$$

and the result follows from (1). □

Lemma 2. Let C be a longest cycle in a graph G and M a longest cycle in $G \setminus C$ with a U_0-minimal M_C-spreading Υ. Then for each $u \in U_1$, $|M| \geq \varphi_u + b_u + 1$.

Proof. Let $u \in U_1$. For each $x \in V(M)$, put

$A_u(x) = (\Phi_u \cup B_u) \cap V(\Upsilon(x))$. By the definition,

$$|\Phi_u \cup B_u| = \sum_{x \in V(M)} |A_u(x)|. \quad (2)$$

If $A_u(x) \neq \varnothing$ for some $x \in V(M)$, then we choose a vertex $\rho_u(x)$ in $A_u(x)$ such that $|x \overrightarrow{\Upsilon}(x) \rho_u(x)|$ is maximum. By the definition, $\rho_u(u) = (\ddot{u})^-$. Put $\overline{\rho}_u(x) = \ddot{u}$ if $\rho_u(x) \in \Phi_u$, and $\overline{\rho}_u(x) = \dot{u}$ if $\rho_u(x) \in B_u \setminus \Phi_u$. Clearly $\overline{\rho}_u(u) = \ddot{u}$.

Let $\Lambda_u = \{x \in V(M) \mid A_u(x) \neq \varnothing\}$. Further, for each distinct $x, y \in \Lambda_u$, put $\Lambda_u(x,y) = x\ddot{u}y$ if either $x = u$, $y \in U_0$ or $y = u$, $x \in U_0$. Otherwise,

$$\Lambda_u(x,y)=x\overrightarrow{\Upsilon}(x)\rho_u(x)\overline{\rho}_u(x)\Upsilon(u)\overline{\rho}_u(y)\rho_u(y)\overleftarrow{\Upsilon}(y)y.$$

Let $\xi_1,...,\xi_f$ be the elements of Λ_u, occurring on $\overrightarrow{M}$ in a consecutive order with $\xi_1=u$. For each integer i $(1\le i\le f)$, set

$$M_i=\xi_i\overrightarrow{M}\xi_{i+1},\quad \omega_i=|A_u(\xi_i)|+|A_u(\xi_{i+1})|\quad (indices \bmod f)$$

Claim 1. $\sum_{i=1}^{f}|M_i|\ge\sum_{i=1}^{f}\omega_i$.

Proof. Since M is extreme, for each $i\in\{2,...,f-1\}$,

$$|M_i|\ge|\Lambda_u(\xi_i,\xi_{i+1})|\ge|A_u(\xi_i)|+|A_u(\xi_{i+1})|=\omega_i.$$

If $\Phi_u\cap V(\Upsilon(\xi_2))\ne\varnothing$ and $\Phi_u\cap V(\Upsilon(\xi_f))\ne\varnothing$, then the inequality $|M_i|\ge\omega_i$ $(i=1,f)$ holds as in previous case and we are done. Now let $\Phi_u\cap V(\Upsilon(\xi_2))=\varnothing$ and $\Phi_u\cap V(\Upsilon(\xi_f))=\varnothing$. It means that $A_u(\xi_2)=\{\xi_2\}$ and therefore, $|M_1|\ge 2=|A_u(\xi_2)|+1=\omega_1-|A_u(u)|+1$. Analogously, $|M_f|\ge\omega_f-|A_u(u)|+1$. By the definition of Λ_u, $\dot{u}\xi_2\in E$ and $\dot{u}\xi_f\in E$. Since $u\in U_1$, we have $\Phi_u\cap V(\Upsilon(\xi_s))\ne\varnothing$ for some $3\le s\le f-1$. Then we can choose i,j such that $2\le i\le s-1$ and $s\le j\le f-1$ with $|M_i|\ge\omega_i+|A_u(u)|-1$ and $|M_j|\ge\omega_j+|A_u(u)|-1$, and the result follows. Finally, because of the symmetry, we can suppose that $\Phi_u\cap V(\Upsilon(\xi_2))=\varnothing$ and $\Phi_u\cap V(\Upsilon(\xi_f))\ne\varnothing$. Clearly $|M_1|\ge\omega_1-|A_u(u)|+1$. By the definition of Λ_u, $\dot{u}\xi_2\in E$. Then we can choose $i\in\{2,...,f-1\}$ such that $|M_i|\ge\omega_i+|A_u(u)|-1$ and again the result follows. Δ

Claim 2. If $|\Upsilon(u)|\ge 2$ then $\Phi_u\cap U_0=\varnothing$.

Proof. Suppose to the contrary and let $v\in\Phi_u\cap U_0$. Then replacing $\Upsilon(u)$ and $\Upsilon(v)$ by $u\overrightarrow{\Upsilon}(u)(\dot{u})^-$ and $v\dot{u}$, respectively, we can form a new M_H-spreading, contradicting the (U_0)-minimality of Υ. Δ

By (2) and Claim 1,

$$\begin{aligned}|M|&=\sum_{i=1}^{f}|M_i|\ge\sum_{i=1}^{f}\omega_i=\sum_{i=1}^{f}\left(|A_u(\xi_i)|+|A_u(\xi_{i+1})|\right)\\&=2\sum_{i=1}^{f}|A_u(\xi_i)|=2\sum_{x\in V(M)}|A_u(x)|=2|\Phi_u\cup B_u|.\end{aligned}\tag{3}$$

If $|\Upsilon(u)|\geq 2$ then by Claim 2, $|\Phi_u \cup B_u|= \varphi_u + b_u$, which by (3) gives $|M| \geq 2(\varphi_u + b_u) \geq \varphi_u + b_u + 1$.

Finally, if $|\Upsilon(u)|= 1$, i.e. $\ddot{u} = \dot{u}$, then $|\Phi_u \cup B_u|= |B_u|+|\{u\}|= b_u + 1 = \varphi_u$ and again by (3)

$|M| \geq 2|\Phi_u \cup B_u| \geq 2\varphi_u \geq \varphi_u + b_u + 1$. □

Lemma 3. Let C be a longest cycle in a graph G and L a longest path in $G\backslash C$ with a U_0-minimal L_C-spreading Υ. Then for each $u \in \bar{U}_0$, $|L| \geq \varphi_u + b_u$.

Proof. Put $L = u_1 ... u_m$. Let Λ_u, $\Lambda_u(x,y)$ and ω_i be as defined in proof of Lemma 2. Let $\xi_1,...,\xi_f$ be the elements of Λ_u occurring on $\vec{L}$ in a consecutive order. Set

$$\vec{M}' = u_1 \vec{L} \xi_1, \quad \vec{M}'' = \xi_f \vec{L} u_m, \quad \vec{M}_i = \xi_i \vec{L} \xi_{i+1} \quad (i = 1,..., f-1).$$

Let G' be the graph obtained from G by adding an extra edge $u_m u_1$. Set $\vec{M} = u_1 ... u_m u_1$ and $M_f = \xi_f \vec{M} \xi_1$. Let $\Lambda_u'(\xi_f,\xi_1)$ and $\Lambda_u''(\xi_f,\xi_1)$ be the paths obtained from $\Lambda_u(\xi_f,\xi_1)$ by deleting the first and the last edges, respectively. Since L is extreme, $|M_i| \geq |\Lambda_u(\xi_i,\xi_{i+1})|$ $(i = 1,..., f-1)$. As for M_f, observe that

$$|M'| \geq |\Lambda_u'(\xi_f,\xi_1)| = |\Lambda_u(\xi_f,\xi_1)| - 1,$$
$$|M''| \geq |\Lambda_u''(\xi_f,\xi_1)| = |\Lambda_u(\xi_f,\xi_1)| - 1,$$

Implying that

$$|M_f| = |M'| + |M''| + 1 \geq 2|\Lambda_u(\xi_f,\xi_1)| - 1 \geq |\Lambda_u(\xi_f,\xi_1)|.$$

So, $|M_i| \geq |\Lambda_u(\xi_i,\xi_{i+1})|$ for each $i \in \{1,..., f\}$. Further, for each $u \in U_1$, we can argue exactly as in proof of Lemma 2 to get $|L| = |M| - 1 \geq \varphi_u + b_u$. Now let $u \in U^*$. By the definition, $\Phi_u \subseteq V(\Upsilon(u))$ and therefore, $|\Upsilon(u)| \geq |\Phi_u| = \varphi_u$. Since L is extreme, $|L| \geq 2(|B_u| + |\{u\}|) - 2 = 2b_u$. Hence,

$$|L| \geq |\Upsilon(u)| + \frac{1}{2}|\vec{L}| \geq \varphi_u + b_u.$$

Proof of Theorem 21 (Zh.G. Nikoghosyan, 1998). Let M be a longest path in $G\backslash C$ of length $\bar{p}$ with a (U_0)-minimal M_C-spreading Υ. If $\bar{p} = -1$, i.e. M is a Hamilton cycle, then $|C|\geq \delta + 1 = (\bar{p} + 2)(\delta - \bar{p})$. Let $\bar{p} \geq 0$. We claim that

(a1) if $u \in U_0$ and $v \in \overline{U}_0$ then $\Phi_u \cap V(\Upsilon(v)) \subseteq \{v, \dot{v}\}$,

(a2) if $u \in U_0$ then $\varphi_u \le \overline{p} + b_u^*$,

(a3) if $v \in \overline{U}_0$ then $\varphi_u \le \overline{p} - b_u$.

Let $u \in U_0$. If $v \in \overline{U}_0$ then to prove (a1) we can argue exactly as in proof of Claim 2 (see the proof of Lemma 2). The next claim follows immediately from (a1). To prove (a3), let $v \in \overline{U}_0$. Since M is extreme, by Lemma 3, $\overline{p} \ge \varphi_u + b_u$ for each $u \in \overline{U}_0$, and (a3) follows.

Observing that

$$\sum\nolimits_{u \in U_0} b_u^* = \sum\nolimits_{u \in \overline{U}_0} b_u$$

and using (a2) and (a3), we get

$$\sum_{u \in V(M)} \varphi_u \le \overline{p}(\overline{p}+1) + \sum_{u \in U_0} b_u^* - \sum_{u \in \overline{U}_0} b_u = \overline{p}(\overline{p}+1).$$

Since Υ is extreme, we have

$$\psi_u = d(\ddot{u}) - \varphi_u \ge \delta - \varphi_u$$

for each $u \in V(M)$.

By summing, we get

$$\sum_{u \in V(M)} \psi_u = (\overline{p}+1)\delta - \sum_{u \in V(M)} \varphi_u \ge (\overline{p}+1)(\delta - \overline{p}).$$

In particular,

$$\max_u \psi_u \ge \delta - \overline{p}.$$

By Lemma 1,

$$|C| \ge \sum_{u \in V(M)} \psi_u + \max_u \psi_u$$
$$\ge (\overline{p}+1)(\delta - \overline{p}) + \delta - \overline{p} = (\overline{p}+2)(\delta - \overline{p}).$$

11. Conclusions

Graph invariants provide a powerful and maybe the single analytical tool for investigation of abstract structures of graphs. They, combined in convenient algebraic relations, carry global and general information about a graph and its particular substructures such as cycle structures, factors, matchings, colorings, coverings, and so on. The discovery of these relations is the primary problem of graph theory.

We focus on large cycle substructures, perhaps the most important cycle structures in graphs: Hamilton, longest and dominating cycles and some generalized cycles including Hamilton and dominating cycles as special cases.

In the literature, eight basic (initial) invariants of a graph G are known having significant impact on large cycle structures, namely order n, size q, minimum degree δ, connectivity κ, independence number α, toughness τ and the lengths of a longest path and a longest cycle in $G\setminus C$ for a given longest cycle C in G.

We have collected 37 pure algebraic relations between $n,q,\delta,\kappa,\alpha,\tau,\overline{p}$ and $\overline{c}$ ensuring the existence of a certain type of large cycles. The majority of these results are sharp in all respects.

Focusing only on basic graph invariants, as well as on pure algebraic relations between these parameters, in fact, we present the simplest kind of relations for large cycles having no forerunners in the area. Actually they form a source from which nearly all possible hamiltonian results (including well-known Ore's theorem, Pósa's theorem and many other generalizations) can be developed further by various additional new ideas, generalizations, extensions, restrictions and structural limitations.

12. References

Alon, N. (1986). The longest cycle of a graph with a large minimum degree, *Journal of Graph Theory*, Vol. 10, No. 1, pp. (123-127).

Bauer, D. & Schmeichel, E. (1986). Long cycles in tough graphs, *Technical Report 8612, Stevens Institute of Technology*, Hoboken.

Bauer, D., Schmeichel, E. & Veldman, H.J. (1988). A generalization of a Theorem of Bigalke and Jung, *Ars Combinatoria*, Vol. 26, pp. (53-58).

Bauer, D., Hakimi, S.L. & Schmeichel, E. (1990a). Recognizing tough graphs is NP-hard, *Discrete Applied Mathematics*, Vol. 28, No. 3, pp. (191-195).

Bauer, D., Morgana, A., Schmeichel, E. & Veldman, H.J. (1990b). Long cycles in graphs with large degree sums, *Discrete Mathematics*, Vol. 79, No. 1, pp. (59-70).

Bauer, D., Chen, G. & Lasser, L. (1991a). A degree condition for Hamilton cycles in t-tough graphs with $t>1$, In: *Advances in graph theory*, V.R. Kulli, (Ed.), pp. (20-33), Vishwa International publications, Gulbarga, India.

Bauer, D. & Schmeichel, E. (1991b). On a Theorem of Häggkvist and Nicoghossian, *Graph Theory, Combinatorics, Algorithms and Applications*, pp. (20-25).

Bermond, J.C. (1978). Hamiltonian graphs, *In: Selected topics in graph theory, L. Beineke and R.J. Wilson, (Eds.),* Academic press, London.

Bigalke, A. & Jung, H.A. (1979). Über Hamiltonsche Kreise und unabhängige Ecken in Graphen, *Monatshefte für Mathematik*, Vol. 88, No. 3, pp. (195-210).

Bondy, J.A. & Murty, U.S.R. (1976). *Graph Theory with Applications*, Macmillan, London, ISBN 0-444-19451-7.

Bondy, J.A. (1981). Integrity in graph theory, *In: The Theory and Application of Graphs, G. Chartrand, Y. Alavi, D.L. Goldsmith, L. Lesniak-Foster, D.R. Lick (Eds.),* Wiley, New York, pp. (117-125). MR83e:05070.

Chvátal, V. & Erdös, P. (1972). A note on hamiltonian circuits, *Discrete Mathematics*, Vol. 2, No. 2, pp. (111-113).

Chvátal, V. (1973). Tough graphs and Hamiltonian circuits, *Discrete Mathematics*, Vol. 5, No. 3, pp. (215-228).

Dirac, G.A. (1952). Some theorems on abstract graphs, *Proceedings of the London Mathematical Society*, Vol. 2, No. 1, pp. (69-81).

Even, S. & Tarjan, R.E. (1975). Network flow and testing graph connectivity, *SIAM journal on computing*, Vol. 4, No. 4, pp. (507-518).

Erdös, P. & Gallai, T. (1959). On maximal paths and circuits of graphs, *Acta Mathematica Hungarica*, Vol. 10, No. 3-4, pp. (337-356).

Fraisse, P. (1986). D_λ -cycles and their applications for Hamiltonian graphs, Universite de Paris-sud, preprint.

Garey, M.R. & Johnson, D.S. (1983). *Computers and Intractability: A Guide to the Theory of NP-Completenes,* Freeman, New York.

Gould, R.J. (1991). Updating the Hamiltonian Problem - A survey, *Journal of Graph Theory*, Vol. 15, No. 2, pp. (121-157).

Gould, R.J. (2003). Advances on the Hamiltonian Problem - A survey, *Graphs and Combinatorics*,Vol. 19, No. 1, pp. (7-52).

Häggkvist, R. & Nicoghossian, G.G. (1981). A remark on hamiltonian cycles, *Journal of Combinatorial Theory*, Ser. B, Vol. 30, No. 1, pp. (118-120).

Jung, H.A. (1978). On maximal circuits in finite graphs, *Annals of Discrete Mathematics*, Vol. 3, pp. (129-144).

Jung, H.A. (1990). Long Cycles in Graphs with Moderate Connectivity, In: *Topics in combinatorics and graph theory, R.Bodendieck and R.Henn (Eds),* Phisika Verlag, Heidelberg, pp. (765-778).

Lu, M., Liu, H. & Tian, F. (2005). Two sufficient conditions for dominating cycles, *Journal of Graph Theory*, Vol. 49, No. 2, pp. (135-150).

Mosesyan, C.M., Nikoghosyan, M.Zh. & Nikoghosyan, Zh.G. (2009). Simple proofs of two Dirac-type theorems involving connectivity, *In: arXiv:0906.3630v2 [math.CO]*, 27 Jul 2009, Available from: http://arxiv.org/abs/0906.3630.

Nash-Williams, C.St.J.A. (1971). Edge-disjoint hamiltonian cycles in graphs with vertices of large valency, In: *Studies in Pure Mathematics, L. Mirsky, (Ed.),* pp. (157-183), Academic Press, San Diego/London.

Nikoghosyan, M.Zh. & Nikoghosyan, Zh.G. (2011). Large cycles in 4-connected graphs, *Discrete Mathematics*, Vol. 311, No. 4, pp. (302-306).

Nikoghosyan, Zh.G. (1981). On maximal cycle of a graph, *DAN Arm. SSR*, Vol. LXXII, No. 2, pp. (82-87) (in Russian).

Nikoghosyan, Zh.G. (1985a). A sufficient condition for a graph to be Hamiltonian, *Matematicheskie voprosy kibernetiki i vichislitelnoy tekhniki*, Vol. 14, pp. (34-54) (in Russian).

Nikoghosyan, Zh.G. (1985b). On maximal cycles in graphs, *DAN Arm. SSR*, Vol. LXXXI, No. 4, pp. (166-170) (in Russian).

Nikoghosyan, Zh.G. (1998). Path-Extensions and Long Cycles in Graphs, *Mathematical Problems of Computer Science,* Transactions of the Institute for Informatics and Automation Problems of the NAS (Republic of Armenia) and Yerevan State University, Vol. 19, pp. (25-31).

Nikoghosyan, Zh.G. (2000a). Cycle-Extensions and Long Cycles in Graphs, *Mathematical Problems of Computer Science,* Transactions of the Institute for Informatics and Automation Problems of the NAS (Republic of Armenia) and Yerevan State University, Vol. 21, pp. (121-128).

Nikoghosyan, Zh.G. (2000b). Cycle-Extensions and Long Cycles in κ-connected Graphs, *Mathematical Problems of Computer Science,* Transactions of the Institute for Informatics and Automation Problems of the NAS (Republic of Armenia) and Yerevan State University, Vol. 21, pp. (129-155).

Nikoghosyan, Zh.G. (2009a). Dirac-type generalizations concerning large cycles in graphs, *Discrete Mathematics,* Vol. 309, No. 8, pp. (1925-1930).

Nikoghosyan, Zh.G. (2009b). On the circumference, connectivity and dominating cycles, *In: arXiv:0906.1857v1 [math.CO],* 10 Jun 2009, Available from: http://arxiv.org/abs/0906.1857.

Nikoghosyan, Zh.G. (2011). A Size Bound for Hamilton Cycles, *In: arXiv:1107.2201v1 [math.CO]* 12 Jul 2011, Available from: http://arxiv.org/abs/1107.2201.

Voss H.-J. & Zuluaga, C. (1977). Maximale gerade und ungerade Kreise in Graphen I, *Wiss. Z. Tech. Hochschule,* Ilmenau, Vol. 4, pp. (57-70).

Yamashita, T. (2009). A degree sum condition with connectivity for relative length of longest paths and cycles, *Discrete Mathematics,* Vol. 309, No. 23-24, pp. (6503-6507).

3

Analysis of Modified Fifth Degree Chordal Rings

Bozydar Dubalski, Slawomir Bujnowski, Damian Ledzinski, Antoni Zabludowski and Piotr Kiedrowski
University of Technology and Life Sciences, Bydgoszcz, Poland

1. Introduction

Implementation of new telecommunications services has always been associated with the need to ensure network efficiency required to implement these services. Network efficiency can be described by a number of parameters such as: network bandwidth, propagation time, quality, reliability and fault tolerance. More and better performance, and thus network efficiency is achieved mainly by using more and more advanced technical and technological solutions. There were milestones solutions such as the use of coaxial transmission cables, optical fibers, and various techniques of multiplication like TDM or WDM (Newton, 1996). Significant impact on the way to deliver services had wireless transmission, which has found widespread use in communication networks since the end of last century.

In addition to technical and technological solutions to improve network efficiency by using system solutions such as: protocols or topology (topology control) appropriate for the type of connection or service. Type of system solutions in the network is closely related to the technology involved in the network, so it can be said that technology determines the solutions. Examples may be the different topological approaches as a result or a consequence of the limiters for a specific technology; e. g.:

- Networks based on SONET/SDH have limitations as to the path length (number of nodes in the path) as result of synchronization signals distribution,
- In turn, networks based on WDM technology, where network nodes are OADM (ALU: Alcatel-Lucent, 2011) multiplexers there are restrictions as to the length of the path (in the literal sense) associated with the phenomenon of dispersion,
- Recent example is the WSN networks, which are increasingly common application in various areas of life, such as the implementation of communication solutions for Smart Grid (Al-Karaki, 2004), which dealt with the Authors of this chapter, in the case of WSN network must resolve a number of problems associated with reliable transmission over a large area using short-range devices.

From the above examples it follows that in order to provide high efficiency network technology solutions are not always sufficient and require additional system solutions, which should always go hand in hand with these technological ones. Therefore, proposed in this publication the solutions are always up to date.

2. Background

A critical issue in designing telecommunications systems is choosing the interconnection network topology as it has the biggest impact on efficiency, speed, and reliability of the entire system (Bhuyan, 1987). Nowadays, analysis of regular network structures is one of the most important issues in telecommunications and computer science.

These networks can be model by symmetric digraphs, i.e., a directed graph G with vertex set $V(G)$ and edge set $E(G)$, such that, if $[v_i, v_j]$ is in $E(G)$, then $[v_j, v_i]$ is also in $E(G)$. So any edge of digraph connecting vertices v_i and v_j can be replaced by two directed edges $[v_i, v_j]$ and $[v_j, v_i]$ (Narayanan et al., 2001).

It is obvious that the best service and reliability parameters one can obtain by forming complete networks (described by a complete graph), but only small networks can be built in this way. In (Kocis, 1992) a survey of known topologies has been presented. Among the analyzed topologies that would be used in designing the distributed structures, the authors of this publication have chosen rings as they are very simple and extensible. They are characterized by connectivity equal to 2 (damage of one edge or node ensures possibility of transmission), are not expensive (number of edges is equal to the number of nodes), are regular and symmetric, but possess poor transmission parameters.

Halfway between the complete graph and the ring is the chordal ring structure (Arden & Lee, 1981). The chordal ring is a ring with additional chords. It is defined by pair (p,Q), where p is the number of nodes of the ring and Q is the set of chords. Each chord connects every pair of nodes of the ring that are at distance q_i in the ring.

The application of this type of structure is useful due to its simplicity, clear topology, resistance to damages, simplicity of routings, and good extension (Kocis, 1992).

The application of chordal rings in computer systems (Mans, 1999), TDM networks (communication between distributed switching modules) (Bujnowski, 2003), core optical networks (Freire & da Silva, 1999, 2001a, 2001b; Liestman et al., 1998; Narayanan & Opatrny, 1999; Narayanan et al., 2001), and optical access networks (Pedersen, 2005; Pedersen et al., 2004a, 2004b, 2005; Bujnowski et al., 2003) has been analyzed. The authors of this publication, in their earlier works on modeling of telecommunication and computer networks, present an analysis of chordal rings (Bujnowski et al. 2004a, 2004b, 2005).

In the beginning the general definition of chordal ring will be giving.

Definition 1. A chordal ring is a ring with additional edges called chords. A chordal ring is defined by the pair (p, Q), where p denotes the number of nodes of the ring and Q denotes the set of chord lengths $Q \subseteq \{1, 2, ..., \lfloor p/2 \rfloor\}$. Since it is a ring, every node is connected to exactly two other nodes (i.e. assume a numbering of the nodes $1,2,\ldots, p$ - then node i is connected to node i-1 and i+1 $(mod\ p)$. Node 0 is connected to p and 1). Each chord of length $q \in Q$ connects every two nodes of the ring that are at distance q. The chordal ring will be further denoted as $G(p; 1, q_1, ..., q_i)$, $q_1 < ... < q_i$. In general, the degree of chordal rings is $2i$, unless there is a chord of length $p/2$. In this case p should be even and rings' degree is $2i - 1$ (Gavoille, n.d).

In the papers (Bujnowski et al., 2008a, 2009b, 2010; Dubalski et al., 2007, 2008; Pedersen et al., 2009) the authors have previously analysed the transmission properties of third, fourth and sixth degree chordal rings and modified graphs of these types. These topologies are the subject of many publications of the researchers from Putra University (Farah et al, 2008, 2010a, 2010b; Azura et al., 2008, 2010; Farah et al. 2010, 2011).

In this publication the survey of the chordal rings consisting of fifth degree nodes (Fig. 1) will be presented. Until now this type of the regular structures is not widely examined, so authors decided to focus on it (Dubalski, 2010).

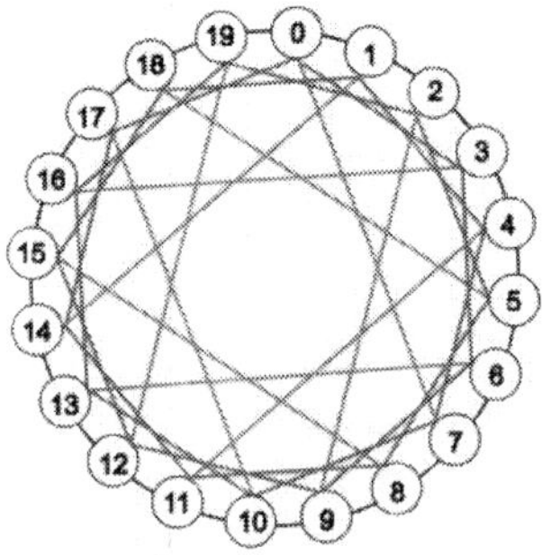

Fig. 1. An example of chordal ring fifth nodal degree

Average distance and diameter was chosen in order to provide a general and simple indication of transmission properties of the analyzed topologies. These follow standard definitions as summarized below. For more basic definitions of e.g. paths and path lengths, please refer to any basic graph theory book, such as (Distel, 2010).

Definition 2. The diameter *D(G)* is the largest path length among all of the shortest length of the paths between any pair of nodes. It is defined as follows:

$$D(G) = \max_{v_i v_j} \{d_{\min}(v_i, v_j)\} \tag{1}$$

where v_i means the number of the node, d_{min} minimal distance (number of edges) between *i-th* and *j-th* node.

Definition 3. The average path length d_{av} between all pairs of nodes is defined by the formula:

$$d_{av} = \frac{1}{p(p-1)} \sum_{i=0}^{p-1} \sum_{j=0}^{p-1} d_{\min}(v_i, v_j) \tag{2}$$

where d_{min} (v_i, v_j) is the minimal number of edges between a source node v_i and every other chosen node v_j,, and p denotes the number of nodes.

A Reference Graph (a virtual example is shown in Fig. 2) can be determined, which presents a reference for all regular graphs of degree 5. It represents lower bounds for average distance and diameter for all these graphs, but since it is a "virtual graph" these bounds may not always be achievable.

The Reference Graph possesses parameters as follows:

1. The number of nodes p_{dr} in d-th layer is determined by formula:

$$p_{1r} = 5$$
$$p_{dr} = 20 \cdot 2^{2(d-2)} \ when \quad d > 1 \tag{3}$$

2. Total number of nodes $p_{D(G)r}$ versus graph diameter is described by expression:

$$p_{D(G)r} = \frac{5 \cdot 4^{D(G)r} - 2}{3} \tag{4}$$

3. Value of diameter versus total number of nodes can be calculated following formula:

$$D(G) = \left\lceil \log_4 \left(\frac{3p_r + 2}{5} \right) \right\rceil \tag{5}$$

4. Average path length d_{avr} in function of diameter is equal to:

$$d_{avr} = \frac{1 + (3 \cdot D(G)_r - 1) \cdot 4^{D(G)_r}}{3 \cdot \left(4^{D(G)_r} - 1\right)} \tag{6}$$

5. This graph is symmetrical, its all parameters are equal regardless from which node they are calculated.

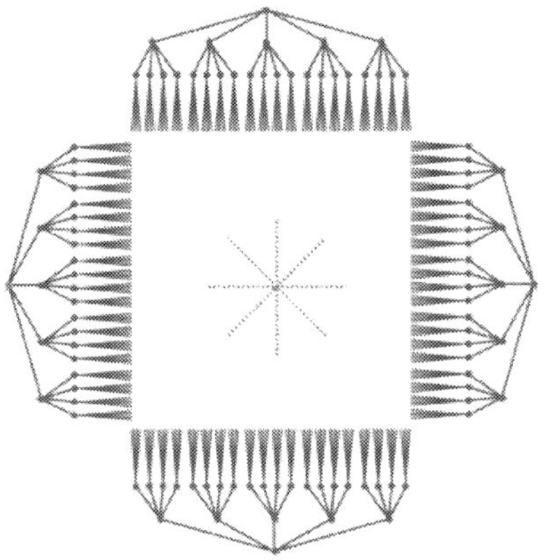

Fig. 2. General diagram of virtual infinite Reference Graph

Only one Reference Graph fifth nodal degree exists in reality, it is the complete graph consisting of 6 nodes.

Two other reference graphs, named as Ideal and Optimal graphs, are also useful for determining average distance and diameter of the chordal rings. They provide theoretical values, which in the following will be compared to values obtained in the real graphs. As for the reference graph mentioned above, the optimal and ideal graphs do not always exist.

In order to determine parameters of the theoretical calculated reference topologies of chordal rings two types of these structures were defined. The first one is called the ideal graph and the second one - optimal graph. In fact these graphs exist only in particular cases, but they are useful as reference models for evaluation expected parameters of tested graphs.

Definition 4. The ideal chordal ring with degree $D(G)$ is the regular graph with total number of nodes p_i given by the formula:

$$p_i = 1 + \sum_{d=1}^{D(G)-1} |p_d| + |p_{D(G)}| \tag{7}$$

where p_d means the number of nodes that belong to the *d-th* layer (the layer is the subset of nodes that are at a distance d from the source node), while $p_{D(G)}$ denotes the number of the remaining nodes which appear in the last layer. For ideal rings, for every n and $m < D(G)$ $p_n \cap p_m = \varnothing$. If for certain $D(G)$ the subset $p_{D(G)}$ of chordal ring reaches the maximal possible value, then such a ring is called the optimal ring (optimal graph).

For ideal chordal ring the average path length d_{avi} is expressed as:

$$d_{avi} = \frac{\sum_{d=1}^{d(G)-1} d|p_d| + D(G)|p_{d(G)}|}{p_i - 1} \tag{8}$$

whereas for the optimal graph the average path length d_{avo} is equal to:

$$d_{avo} = \frac{\sum_{d=1}^{d(G)} d\, p_d}{p_o - 1} \tag{9}$$

where d - layer number, p_d - number of nodes in *d-th* layer, p_o - number of nodes in optimal graph.

Optimal graphs were used to calculate the formulas describing parameters of each type of analyzed chordal ring, whereas ideal rings were served to compare calculated theoretically and obtained in reality parameters of analyzed structures.

The basic topology of fifth degree chordal rings in Fig. 3 is shown. The definition, short presentation and author's consideration concerned of this structure are given below.

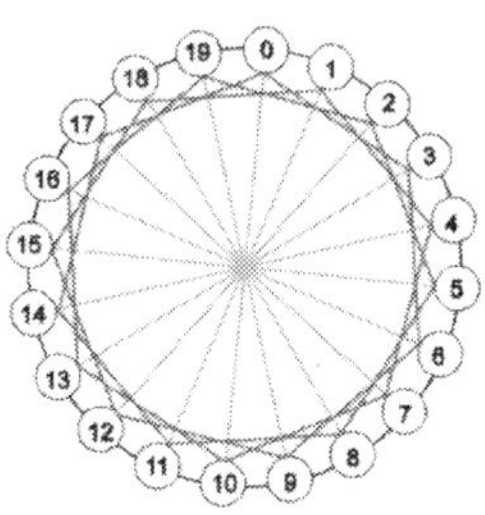

Fig. 3. Basic chordal ring fifth nodal degree CHR5(20; 3,10)

Definition 5. The basic chordal ring fifth nodal degree called CHR5 is an undirected graph, based on a cycle with additional connections (chords). It is denoted by CHR5(p; q_1,q_2) where p must be even and means number of nodes creating the ring, chord length $q_1 > p/2$ is odd, even too, chord length q_2 is equal to $p/2$. The values of p and q_1 must be prime each other (Bujnowski, 2011).

In order to calculate the diameters and average path lengths appearing in optimal graphs it is necessary to evaluate the maximal number of nodes appearing in each layer. In the table 1 the numbers of nodes in the first successive layers of virtual optimal ring are shown (d denotes the layer number, p_d - the number of nodes appearing in d-th layer).

d	1	2	3	4	5	6	7	8
p_{do}	5	12	20	28	36	44	52	60

Table 1. Maximal number of nodes in the layers

If $d > 1$ the power of these sets is described by formula:

$$p_{do} = 4(2d - 1) \tag{10}$$

Using the formula given above, the total number of nodes p_o in the optimal graph with diameter $D(G)$ can be calculated ($D(G) > 1$):

$$p_o = 4D(G)^2 + 2\,. \tag{11}$$

The total number of nodes in optimal graphs versus its diameter is shown in table 2.

$d(G)$	1	2	3	4	5	6	7	8
p_{do}	6	18	38	66	102	146	198	258

Table 2. Total numbers of nodes forming optimal graphs versus diameter

The average path length in optimal graphs is given by formula:

$$d_{avo} = \frac{8D(G)^3 + 6D(G)^2 - 2D(G) + 3}{3\left(4D(G)^2 + 1\right)} \tag{12}$$

Only one optimal graph exists in reality. It is the complete graph which possesses 6 nodes, but the ideal chordal rings can be found. Whereas it founded two groups of ideal graphs consisting of p nodes, which can be described by formulas given below.

The graphs belonging to the first group are defined as follows:

$$p_i = 4D(G)^2 \quad \left(D(G) > 1\right) \tag{13}$$

so

$$D(G) = \frac{\sqrt{p_i}}{2} \tag{14}$$

In this case a chord length q_1 of ideal graphs is equal to:

$$\begin{gathered} q_1 = 2D(G) - 1 \quad or \quad q_1 = 2D(G) + 1 \\ q_1 = \sqrt{p_i} - 1 \quad or \quad q_1 = \sqrt{p_i} + 1 \end{gathered} \tag{15}$$

these both graphs are isomorphic each other.

The average path length can be express by formula:

$$d_{avi} = \frac{8D(G)^3 + 3D(G)^2 - 8D(G) + 3}{3\left(4D(G)^2 - 1\right)} \tag{16}$$

The graphs belonging to the second group are described as follows:

If $D(G) > 2$ then:

$$p_i = 4D(G)^2 - 4D(G) = 4D(G)\left[D(G) - 1\right] \tag{17}$$

So when the number of nodes is equal to p_i then

$$D(G) = \frac{1 + \sqrt{1 + p_i}}{2} \tag{18}$$

The lengths of chords used to construct ideal graphs can be calculated using formulas:

$$q_1 = 2D(G) - 1 \quad or \quad q_1 = \sqrt{1 + p_i} \tag{19}$$

When the number of nodes creating chordal ring is given by equation:

$$\begin{aligned} & p_i = 4(9i^2 + 9i + 2) \quad or \quad p_i = 6(6i^2 + 10i + 4) \quad where \quad i \in (1, 2, \cdots, n) \\ & then \quad q_1 = 2D(G) + 1 \quad or \quad q_1 = \sqrt{p_i + 1} + 2 \\ & if \quad p_i = 4(9i^2 + 9i + 2) \quad then \quad q_1 = \frac{4D(G)^2 - 2D(G) - 3}{3} \\ & if \quad p_i = 6(6i^2 + 10i + 4) \quad then \quad q_1 = \frac{4D(G)^2 - 6D(G) + 3}{3} \end{aligned} \tag{20}$$

The average path length of all these graphs is described by formula:

$$d_{avi} = \frac{8D(G)^3 - 6D(G)^2 - 8D(G) + 3}{3\left(4D(G)^2 + 4D(G) - 1\right)} \tag{21}$$

Unfortunately the parameters of CHR5 graphs are considerably different of Reference Graph parameters, what is shown in fig. 4 and 5 given above.

It follows from the difference of number of nodes appearing in successive layers and thus the difference of total number of nodes appearing in dependence of its diameter as well.

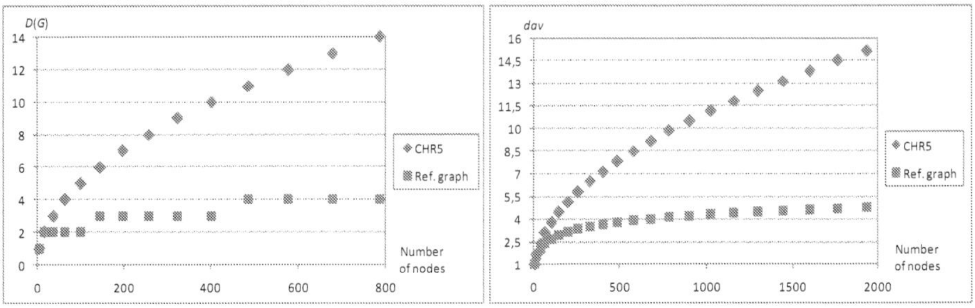

Fig. 4. Comparison of diameter and average path length of Reference Graphs and CHR5

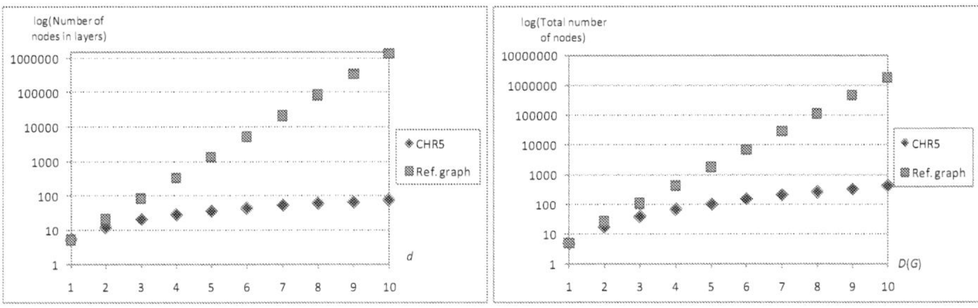

Fig. 5. Differences of number of nodes in successive layers and total number of nodes in Reference Graphs and CHR5

The aim of authors of this publication was to find structures possessing basic parameters which values would be closer to reference graph parameters.

3. Analysis of modified graphs fifth degree

The authors prepared two programs which were used to make it possible to examine the analysed graphs - "Program Graph Finder" and "Find the best distribution of nodes in the layers". The first one - "Program Graph Finder" was used in the first stage of analysis for quite simple topologies, the second one "Find the best distribution of nodes in the layers" - for more complicated structures, when the number of variables describing the way of connections is greater than 4.

The real values of parameters of modified chordal rings were calculated using these programs and compared to those obtained in a theoretical way.

In the following sections, an analysis of 15 different regular structures based on chordal rings is presented. Each of the type of graphs is defined, examples are given, the distribution of nodes in different layers is analyzed, and the ideal and optimal graphs are compared to real graphs. Also, basing on the analysis of nodes in different layers, the average distance and diameter can be calculated as a function of the number of nodes.

The graphs are divided into 3 groups, each consisting of 5 types of graphs. The first group of graphs needs to have a number of nodes divisible by two, and the second group of graphs a number of nodes divisible by 4. The third group of graphs also has a number of nodes divisible by 4, but for these no mathematical expressions of node distribution (and thus the average distance and diameter) were found.

3.1 First group of chordal rings

As previously mentioned, for each type of graph we present:

- Definitions
- Descriptions
- Distribution of nodes
- Expressions for key parameters
- Comparisons of parameters for real and theoretical graphs.

Graph CHR5_a.

Definition 6. The modified fifth degree chordal rings called CHR5_a (Fig. 6) is denoted by CHR5_a(p; q_1,q_2), where p is even and means number of nodes; q_1, q_2 are chords. Chords q_1 and q_2 are odd and $< p/2$. Chord q_1 generates a Hamiltonian cycle. whereas q_2 is odd too and $< p/2$. Each even node i_{2k} is connected to five other nodes: i_{2k-1}, i_{2k+1}, $i_{2k-q1(\text{mod } p)}$, $i_{2k+q1(\text{mod } p)}$, $i_{2k+q2(\text{mod } p)}$, while odd node i_{2k+1} is connected to i_{2k}, i_{2k+2}, $i_{2k+1-q1(\text{mod } p)}$, $i_{2k+1+q1(\text{mod } p)}$ and $i_{2k+1-q2(\text{mod } p)}$ ($0 \leq k < p/2$). The values of p and q_1 must be prime each other (this ensures that the Hamiltonian cycle is created). ☑

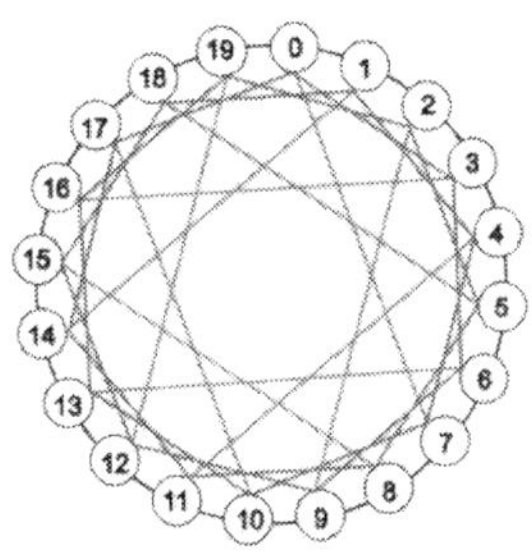

Fig. 6. Modified chordal ring CHR5_a(20; 3,7)

In table 3 the numbers of nodes in the layers of optimal rings as the function of node degree are shown.

d	1	2	3	4	5	6	7	8
p_{do}	5	16	33	58	89	128	173	226

Table 3. Maximal number of nodes in the successive layers

When d (layer number) is odd, then the power of these sets is described by the expression:

$$p_{do\ odd} = \frac{1}{2}(7d^2 + 3) \tag{22}$$

and when d is even:

$$p_{do\,even} = \frac{1}{2}(7d^2 + 4) \tag{23}$$

The general expression has the following form:

$$p_{do} = \frac{1}{2}(7d^2 + 4 - d(\mathrm{mod}\,2)) \tag{24}$$

The total number of nodes p_o forming an optimal graph which possesses diameter $D(G)$ is expressed as:

$$p_{o\,odd} = \frac{7}{12}\left(2D(G)^3 + 3D(G)^2 + 4D(G)\right) + \frac{3}{4}$$

$$p_{o\,even} = \frac{7}{12}\left(2D(G)^3 + 3D(G)^2 + 4D(G)\right) + 1$$

$$p_o = \frac{7}{12}\left(2D(G)^3 + 3D(G)^2 + 4D(G)\right) + 1 - \frac{D(G)(\mathrm{mod}\,2)}{4} \tag{25}$$

which confirms the results obtained by constructing the possible graphs, as shown in Table 4.

$D(G)$	1	2	3	4	5	6	7	8
p_o	6	22	55	113	202	330	503	729

Table 4. Diameters and total numbers of nodes in virtual, optimal graphs

The average path length in optimal graphs can be calculated as:

$$d_{avo} = \frac{3}{2}\,\frac{7d(G)^4 + 14d(G)^3 + 14d(G)^2 + 8d(G) - 2d(G)d(G)(\mathrm{mod}\,2) - d(G)\mathrm{mod}\,2}{14d(G)^3 + 21d(G)^2 + 28d(G) - 3d(G)\mathrm{mod}\,2} \tag{26}$$

Fig. 7 shows a comparison of diameters and average path lengths between theoretical and real graphs.

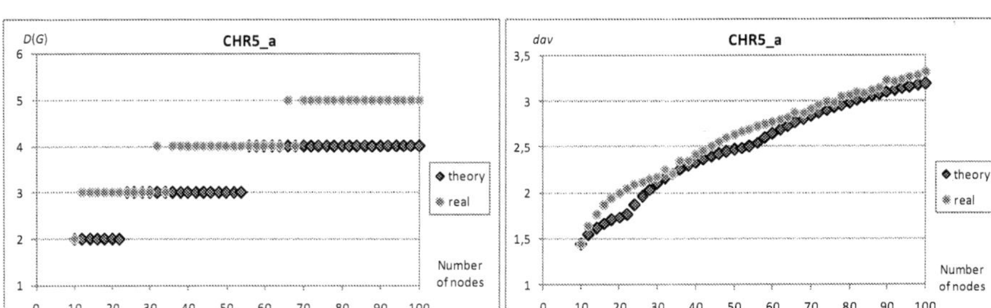

Fig. 7. Comparison of diameter and average path length of theoretical and real graphs CHR5_a

All graphs of this type are symmetrical, the values of their basic parameters do not depend on the number of source node.

Graph CHR5_b.

Definition 6. The modified fifth degree chordal ring called CHR5_b is denoted by CHR5_b(p; q_1,q_2,q_3) where p is even and means number of nodes; q_1, q_2, q_3 are chords, where chord q_1 and q_2 possess even lengths, whereas the length of q_3 is odd. The values of p and q_1, q_2, q_3 must be lower than $p/2$. Each even node i_{2k} is connected to five other nodes: i_{2k-1}, i_{2k+1}, $i_{2k-q1(\mathrm{mod}\ p)}$, $i_{2k+q1(\mathrm{mod}\ p)}$, $i_{2k+q3(\mathrm{mod}\ p)}$, while odd node i_{2k+1} is connected to i_{2k}, i_{2k+2}, $i_{2k+1-q2(\mathrm{mod}\ p)}$, $i_{2k+1+q2(\mathrm{mod}\ p)}$ and $i_{2k+1-q3(\mathrm{mod}\ p)}$ $(0 \le k < p/2)$.

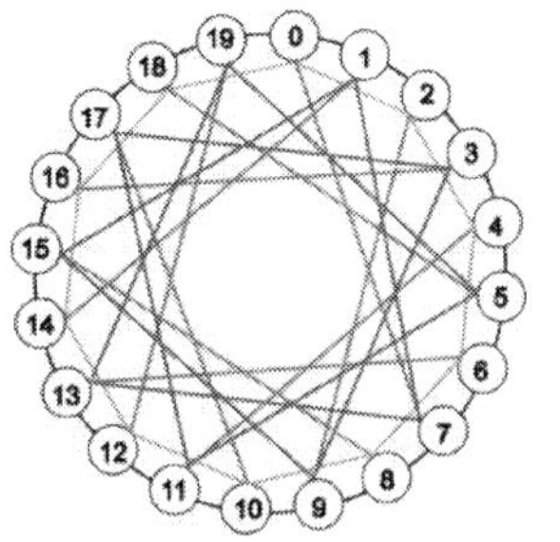

Fig. 8. Modified chordal ring CHR5_b(20; 2,6,7)

Fig. 8 shows an example of CHR5_b. In table 5, the numbers of nodes in the layers of an optimal graph is shown.

d	1	2	3	4	5	6	7	8
p_{do}	5	20	61	140	267	454	713	1056

Table 5. Maximal number of nodes in the layers

When d is bigger than 2, the maximal number of nodes which can appear in the successive layers is described by:

$$p_{do} = 2d^3 + 5d - 8 \tag{27}$$

The total number of nodes p_o in the optimal graph with diameter $D(G) > 1$ is given by:

$$p_o = \frac{1}{2}\left(D(G)^4 + 2D(G)^3 + 6D(G)^2 - 11D(G) + 18\right) \tag{28}$$

This was also confirmed by constructing the possible graphs. These results can be seen in Table 6.

$d(G)$	1	2	3	4	5	6	7	8
p_{do}	6	26	87	227	494	948	1661	2717

Table 6. Total numbers of nodes in optimal graphs versus diameter

The average path length in optimal graphs can be expressed as:

$$d_{avo} = \frac{12D(G)^5 + 30D(G)^4 + 70D(G)^3 - 45D(G)^2 - 97D(G) + 300}{15\left(D(G)^4 + 2D(G)^3 + 6D(G)^2 - 11D(G) + 16\right)} \tag{29}$$

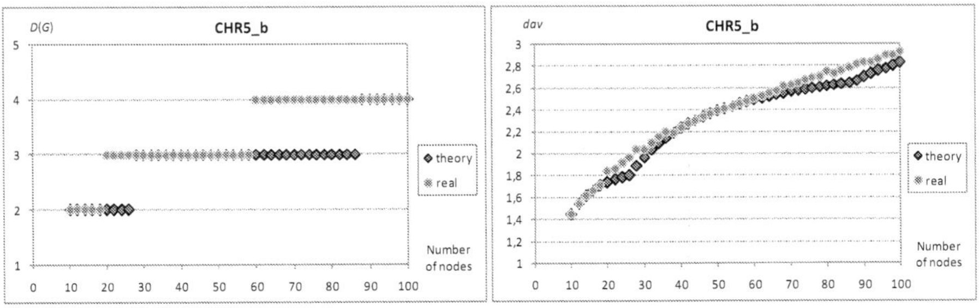

Fig. 9. Comparison of diameter and average path length of theoretical and real graphs CHR5_b

Fig. 9 shows a comparison of the diameter and average path length between theoretical and real graphs.

Not all these graphs are symmetric, but most of the graphs possessing parameters equal or close to ideal graphs are symmetric. In table 7 examples of the real and ideal chordal rings are presented.

Number of nodes	q_1	q_2	q_3	d_{av}
8	2	2	3	1.2857143
10	2	4	3	1.4444444
12	2	2	5	1.5454545
14	2	2	7	1.6153846
16	2	6	7	1.6666666
18	2	4	7	1.7058823
38	6	12	9	2.1891892
40	6	18	9	2.2307692
42	4	8	19	2.2682927
44	6	18	15	2.3023255
46	4	8	19	2.3333333
48	10	22	7	2.3617022
48	14	22	17	2.3617022
50	4	8	21	2.3877552
52	10	14	17	2.4117646
54	4	14	23	2.4339623
56	10	22	5	2.4545455
58	4	14	23	2.4736843

Table 7. Examples of ideal graphs CHR5_b

Graph CHR5_c

Definition 7. The modified fifth degree chordal ring called CHR5_c is denoted by CHR5_c(p; q_1,q_2,q_3), where p is even and means number of nodes; q_1, q_2, q_3 are chords, all chords possess odd lengths less then $p/2$. The values of p and q_1, q_2, q_3 must be prime each other. Each even node i_{2k} is connected to five other nodes: i_{2k-1}, i_{2k+1}, $i_{2k+q1(\text{mod } p)}$, $i_{2k+q2(\text{mod } p)}$, $i_{2k+q3(\text{mod } p)}$, while odd node i_{2k+1} is connected to i_{2k}, i_{2k+2}, $i_{2k+1-q1(\text{mod } p)}$, $i_{2k+1-q2(\text{mod } p)}$ and $i_{2k+1-q3(\text{mod } p)}$ where $(0 \le k < p/2)$. ☑

Fig. 10 shows an example of CHR5_c. In Table 8 the numbers of nodes in the layers of an optimal graph is shown.

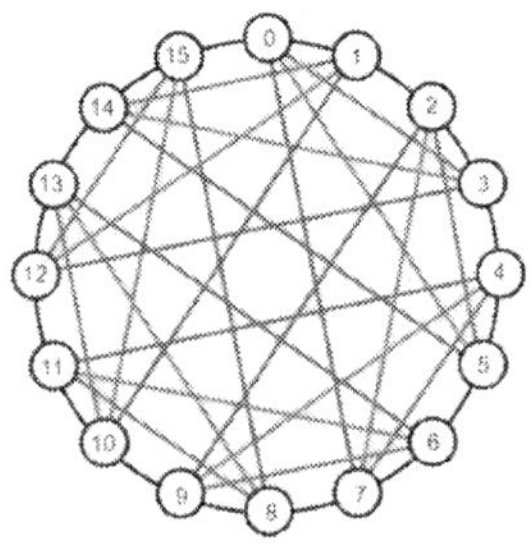

Fig. 10. Modified chordal ring CHR5_c(16; 3,5,,7)

d	1	2	3	4	5	6	7	8
p_{do}	5	20	50	110	200	340	550	850

Table 8. Number of nodes appearing in successive layers

In the case when d - number of layer is bigger than 2 the number of nodes in the layers can be described by the following expression:

$$p_{do} = 5\left(\frac{2}{3}d^3 - 5d^2 + \frac{67}{3}d - 30\right) \tag{30}$$

The total number of nodes p_o in the optimal graph with diameter $D(G) > 1$ is given by:

$$p_o = \frac{1}{6}\left(5D(G)^4 - 40D(G)^3 + 265D(G)^2 - 590D(G) + 516\right) \tag{31}$$

In table 9 the total number of nodes in virtual, optimal graphs, as described by the above expression, is shown.

$D(G)$	1	2	3	4	5	6	7	8
p_o	6	26	76	186	386	726	1276	2126

Table 9. Total numbers of nodes in optimal graphs

The average path length in optimal graphs can be calculated using the expression:

$$d_{avo} = \frac{8D(G)^5 - 55D(G)^4 + 310D(G)^3 - 305D(G)^2 - 678D(G) + 1260}{2\left(5D(G)^4 - 40D(G)^3 + 265D(G)^2 - 590D(G) + 510\right)} \tag{32}$$

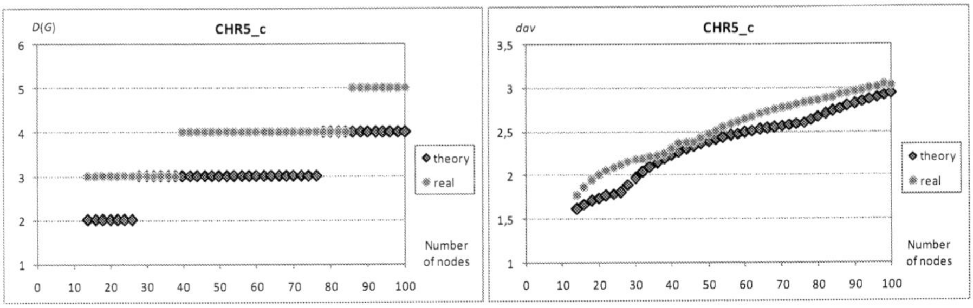

Fig. 11. Comparison of diameter and the average path length of theoretical and real CHR5_c graphs

Fig. 11 shows a comparison of diameter and the average path length between theoretical and real graphs. All graphs of this type are symmetrical, but they couldn't find any ideal graph.

Graph CHR5_d.

Definition 8. The modified fifth degree chordal ring called CHR5_d is denoted by CHR5_d(p; q_1,q_2,$p/2$), where p means the number of nodes and is positive and even; q_1, q_2 are chords which possess odd lengths less then $p/2$. The values of p and q_1, q_2 must be prime each other. Each even node i_{2k} is connected to five other nodes: i_{2k-1}, i_{2k+1}, $i_{2k+q1(\text{mod } p)}$, $i_{2k+q2(\text{mod } p)}$, $i_{2k+p/2(\text{mod } p)}$, while odd node i_{2k+1} is connected to i_{2k}, i_{2k+2}, $i_{2k+1-q1(\text{mod } p)}$, $i_{2k+1-q2(\text{mod } p)}$ and $i_{2k+1+p/2(\text{mod } p)}$ where $(0 \le k < p/2)$.

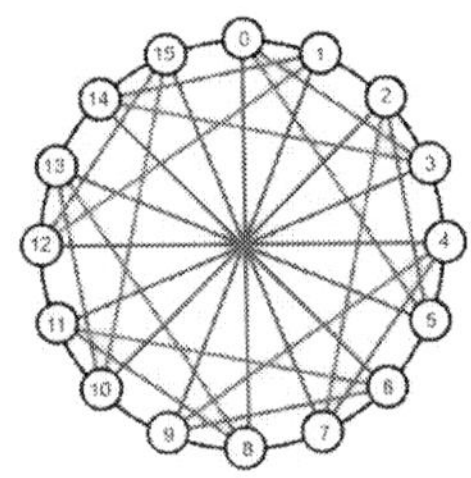

Fig. 12. Example of modified chordal ring CHR5_d(16; 3,5,,8)

Fig. 12 shows an example of CHR5_d. In table 10, the numbers of nodes in the layers of an optimal graph are shown. It should be noted that there are two different number of nodes in layers, depending on whether the total number of nodes is divisible by 4 or not.

d	1	2	3	4	5	6	7	8
$p_o = 0 \pmod 4$	5	16	36	66	106	156	216	286
$p_o \neq 0 \pmod 4$	5	18	39	72	113	166	227	300

Table 10. Maximal number of nodes in the successive layers

When the number of layer d is bigger than 1, the number of nodes in the layers can be described by the following expression:

$$\begin{aligned} &\text{If } p = 0 \pmod 4 \text{ then } \quad p_{do} = 5d^2 - 5d + 6 \\ &\text{if } p \neq 0 \pmod 4 \text{ and layer number is even then } \quad p_{do} = 5d^2 - 3d + 4 \\ &\text{if } p \neq 0 \pmod 4 \text{ and layer number is odd then } \quad p_{do} = 5d^2 - 3d + 3 \end{aligned} \tag{33}$$

The total number of nodes p_o in the optimal graph depending on the diameter is given by:

$$\begin{aligned} p_o &= \frac{D(G)\left(4D(G)^2 + 13\right)}{3} \quad \text{if } p_o = 0 \bmod 4 \\ p_o &= \frac{D(G)\left(10D(G)^2 + 6D(G) + 17\right)}{6} + 1 \quad \text{if } p \neq 0 \bmod 4 \text{ and } D(G) \text{ is even} \\ p_o &= \frac{D(G)\left(10D(G)^2 + 6D(G) + 17\right)}{6} + \frac{1}{2} \quad \text{if } p \neq 0 \bmod 4 \text{ and } D(G) \text{ is odd} \end{aligned} \tag{34}$$

In Table 11 the total number of nodes in virtual optimal graphs described by formula given above is shown.

$D(G)$	1	2	3	4	5	6	7	8
$p_o = 0 \pmod 4$	6	22	58	124	230	386	602	888
$p_o \neq 0 \pmod 4$	6	24	63	135	248	414	641	941

Table 11. Total numbers of nodes forming optimal graphs versus diameter

The average path length in optimal graphs can be calculated using the expressions:

$$\begin{aligned} &\text{If } p_o = 0 \bmod 4 \\ &d_{avo} = \frac{D(G)\left(2D(G)^4 + 5D(G)^3 + 12D(G)^2 + 10D(G) + 1\right)}{2\left(5D(G)^3 + 13D(G) - 3\right)} \\ &\text{if } p_o \neq 0 \bmod 4 \\ &d_{avo} = \frac{6D(G)\left(5D(G)^2 - 3D(G) + 3 + (D(G)+1) \bmod 2\right)}{D(G)\left(10D(G)^2 + 6D(G) + 17\right) + 3 + 3(D(G)+1) \bmod 2} \end{aligned} \tag{35}$$

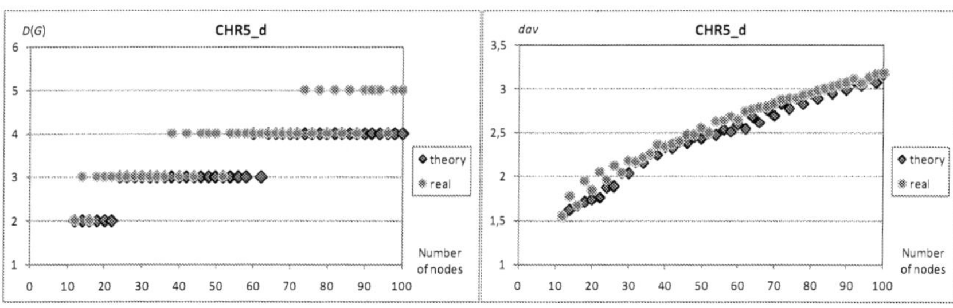

Fig. 13. Comparison of diameter and average path length of theoretical and real graphs CHR5_d

Fig. 13 shows a comparison of diameter and average path length between theoretical and real graphs.

All this type of chordal rings are symmetrical. Ideal graphs are only for the cases where the number of nodes is divisible by 4. Examples are given in Table 12.

Number of nodes	q_1	q_2	$p/2$	d_{av}
12	3	5	6	1,545455
16	3	5	8	1,666667
28	7	11	14	2,037037
32	5	13	16	2,16129
36	5	13	18	2,257143
40	7	17	20	2,333333
44	5	13	22	2,395349
52	5	17	26	2,490196
76	13	21	38	2,893333
80	7	25	40	2,949367
84	9	23	42	3,00000
88	7	27	44	3,045977
96	7	29	48	3,126316

Table 12. Examples of ideal graphs CHR5_d

Graph CHR5_e.

Definition 9. The modified fifth degree chordal ring called CHR5_e is denoted by CHR5_e(p; q_1,q_2,$p/2$), where p means the number of nodes and is positive and even; q_1, q_2 are chords which possess even lengths less then $p/2$. The values of $p/2$ and q_1, q_2 must be prime each other. Each even node i_{2k} is connected to five other nodes: i_{2k-1}, i_{2k+1}, $i_{2k+q1(\text{mod } p)}$, $i_{2k-q1(\text{mod } p)}$, $i_{2k+p/2(\text{mod } p)}$, while odd node i_{2k+1} is connected to i_{2k}, i_{2k+2}, $i_{2k+1+q2(\text{mod } p)}$, $i_{2k+1-q2(\text{mod } p)}$ and $i_{2k+1+p/2(\text{mod } p)}$ where $(0 \le k < p/2)$.

Fig. 14. Example modified chordal ring CHR5_e(18; 4,8,9)

Fig. 14 shows an example of CHR5_e. In Table 13 the number of nodes appearing in the successive layers of optimal graphs is shown. It should be observed that there are two different number of nodes in layers, depending on the total number of nodes are they divisible by 4 or not.

d	1	2	3	4	5	6	7	8
$p_o = 0 \pmod 4$	5	16	42	88	152	232	328	440
$p_o \neq 0 \pmod 4$	5	18	48	96	160	240	336	448

Table 13. Maximal number of nodes in the successive layers

When the number of layers d - is bigger than 1 the number of nodes in the layers can be described by the following expressions:

$$\begin{aligned} &if\ p = 0 \pmod 4\ and\ d \rangle 2\ then \quad p_{do} = 8d(d-1) \\ &if\ p \neq 0 \pmod 4\ and\ d \rangle 3\ then \quad p_{do} = 8d(d-1) - 8 \end{aligned} \tag{36}$$

The total number of nodes p_o in the optimal graph depending on the diameter is given by:

$$\begin{aligned} p_o &= \frac{8D(G)^3 - 32d(G) + 72}{3} = \frac{8D(G)\left(D(G)^2 - 4\right)}{3} + 24 \quad if\ p_o = 0 \bmod 4\ and\ D(G) \rangle 2 \\ p_o &= \frac{8D(G)^3 - 8d(G) + 24}{3} = \frac{8D(G)\left(D(G)^2 - 1\right)}{3} + 8 \quad if\ p_o \neq 0 \bmod 4\ and\ D(G) \rangle 1 \end{aligned} \tag{37}$$

In Table 14 the total number of nodes in virtual optimal graphs described by the above expressions is shown.

$D(G)$	1	2	3	4	5	6	7	8
$p_o = 0 \pmod 4$	6	22	64	152	304	536	864	1304
$p_o \neq 0 \pmod 4$	6	24	72	168	328	568	904	1352

Table 14. Total numbers of nodes forming optimal graphs versus diameter

The average path length in optimal graphs can be calculated using this expression:

$$\begin{aligned} &When\ p_o = 0 \bmod 4\ and\ D(G) \rangle 2 \\ &d_{avo} = \frac{6D(G)^4 + 4D(G)^3 - 18D(G)^2 - 16D(G) + 105}{8D(G)^3 - 32D(G) + 69} \\ &when\ p_o \neq 0 \bmod 4\ and\ D(G) \rangle 1 \\ &d_{avo} = \frac{6D(G)^4 + 4D(G)^3 - 6D(G)^2 - 4D(G) + 27}{8D(G)^3 - 8D(G) + 21} \end{aligned} \tag{38}$$

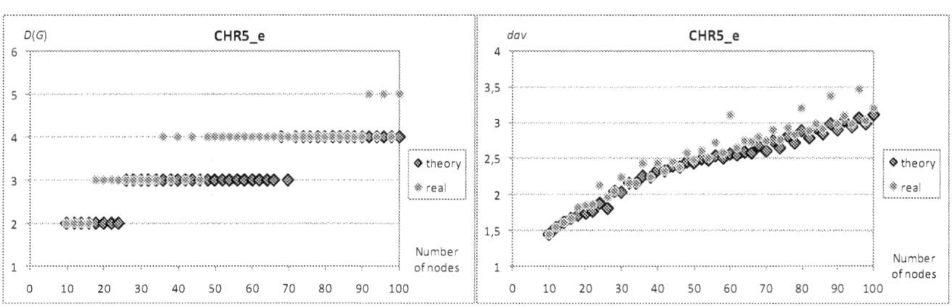

Fig. 15. Comparison of diameter and average path length of theoretical and real graphs CHR5_e

Fig. 15 shows diameter and average path lengths in theoretical and real graphs with up to 100 nodes.

Some but not all of these graphs are symmetric, and as illustrated in Fig. 15 the non symmetric graphs generally have parameters closer to those of ideal graphs. Only a few ideal graphs are found, of which some examples are shown in Table 15.

Number of nodes	q_1	q_2	$p/2$	d_{av}
10	2	4	5	1,444444
12	2	2	6	1,545455
14	2	4	7	1,615385
16	2	6	8	1,666667
28	6	10	14	2,037037
32	6	10	16	2,161290
34	4	10	17	2,151515
38	4	8	19	2,243243
42	4	8	21	2,317073

Table 15. Examples of ideal graphs CHR5_e

To sum up, in the first group of analyzed graphs the best parameters have CHR5_b graphs. They possess minimal diameter and average path length in comparison to the other analyzed chordal rings, and the parameters of the real graphs are close or equal to parameters of ideal graphs. Additionally, most of the best graphs are symmetric, what is also an advantage for the application in real networks.

Fig. 16 shows the comparisons of the real graphs in the first group.

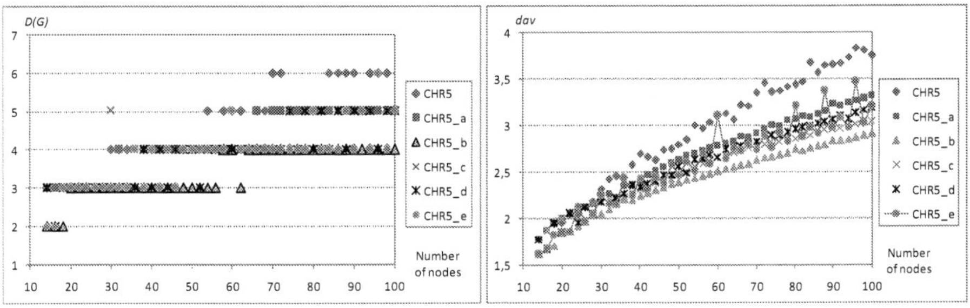

Fig. 16. Comparison of diameter and average path length of all real modified chordal rings belonging to the first group of analyzed graphs.

3.2 Second group of analyzed graphs

The chordal rings consisting of $4i$ nodes (i = 2, 3, 4, …,) belong to this group. These topologies are often more complicated, since they are less symmetric. Basing on patterns for ideal and optimal graphs it is possible to derive expressions for average distance and diameter for all of the different topologies in this group of graphs.

Graph CHR5_f.

Definition 10. The modified fifth degree chordal ring called CHR5_f is denoted by CHR5_f(p; q_1,q_2,q_3, $p/2$), where p means the number of nodes and is positive and divisible by 4; q_1, q_2, q_3, are chords which possess even lengths less then $p/2$. The values of $p/4$ and q_1, q_2, q_3 must be prime each other. Each even node i_{2k} is connected to five other nodes: i_{2k-1}, i_{2k+1}, $i_{2k+q1(\text{mod } p)}$, $i_{2k-q1(\text{mod } p)}$, $i_{2k+p/2(\text{mod } p)}$, while odd node i_{2k+1} is connected to i_{2k}, i_{2k+2}, $i_{2k+1+q2(\text{mod } p)}$, $i_{2k+1-q2(\text{mod } p)}$ and $i_{2k+1+p/2(\text{mod } p)}$ and node i_{2k-1} is connected to i_{2k}, i_{2k-2}, $i_{2k-1+q3(\text{mod } p)}$, $i_{2k-1-q3(\text{mod } p)}$ and $i_{2k-1+p/2(\text{mod } p)}$ where $(0 \le k < p/2)$.

An example is shown in Fig. 17.

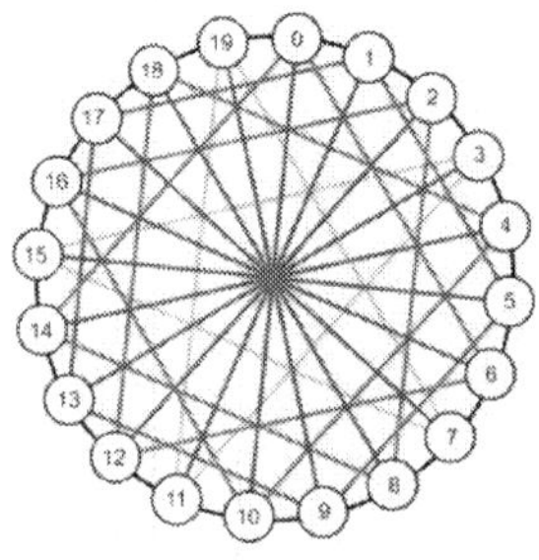

Fig. 17. Example of modified chordal ring CHR5_f(20; 4,6,,8,10)

This structure is more complicated since the number of nodes appearing in successive layers depends on whether the total number of nodes is divisible by 8 or not, and also on whether it seen from odd or even node number in the graph. This creates multiple cases, which also complicates deriving the basic parameters. Table 16 shows the experimentally obtained results, which are the basis for further analysis.

d	Number of nodes	1	2	3	4	5	6	7	8
$p_{do\ p=0\ (mod\ 8)}$	Even	5	16	44	112	248	488	888	1496
	Odd	5	16	46	116	262	536	984	1640
$p_{do\ p\neq 0\ (mod\ 8)}$	Even	5	16	48	136	312	616	1096	1784
	Odd	5	18	58	152	340	668	1172	1884

Table 16. Maximal number of nodes in the successive layers

The number of nodes in the layers can be described by the following formula:

$$\begin{aligned}
&\textit{When } p = 0\ (\text{mod}\,8)\ \textit{and } d \rangle\ 5\ \textit{then}\\
&p_{do\ even} = 5\frac{1}{3}d^3 - 8d^2 - 173\frac{1}{3} + 664 \quad p_{do\ odd} = 5\frac{1}{3}d^3 - 8d^2 - 125\frac{1}{3} + 424\\
&\textit{when } p \neq 0\ (\text{mod}\,8)\ \textit{and } d\ \rangle\ 4\ \textit{then}\\
&p_{do\ even} = 5\frac{1}{3}d^3 - 8d^2 - 93\frac{1}{3} + 312 \quad p_{do\ odd} = 5\frac{1}{3}d^3 - 8d^2 - 69\frac{1}{3} + 220
\end{aligned} \tag{39}$$

In Table 17 the total number of nodes in optimal graphs given by above expression is shown.

$d(G)$	Number of nodes	1	2	3	4	5	6	7	8
$p_{do\ p\ =\ 0\ (mod\ 8)}$	even	6	22	66	178	426	914	1802	3298
	odd	6	22	68	184	446	982	1966	3606
$p_{do\ p\ \neq 0\ (mod\ 8)}$	even	6	22	70	206	518	1134	2230	4014
	odd	6	24	82	234	574	1242	2414	4298

Table 17. Total numbers of nodes forming optimal graphs versus diameter

The total number of nodes p_o in the optimal graph as a function of the diameter is given by:

$$\begin{aligned}
&\text{When } p = 0\ (\text{mod} 8) \text{ and } d \rangle 4\\
&p_{o\,even} = 1\frac{1}{3}D(G)^4 - 89\frac{1}{3}D(G)^2 + 576D(G) - 1054\\
&p_{o\,odd} = 1\frac{1}{3}D(G)^4 - 65\frac{1}{3}D(G)^2 + 360D(G) - 554\\
&\text{when } p \neq 0\ (\text{mod} 8) \text{ and } d \rangle 3\\
&p_{o\,even} = 1\frac{1}{3}D(G)^4 - 49\frac{1}{3}D(G)^2 + 264D(G) - 402\\
&p_{o\,odd} = 1\frac{1}{3}D(G)^4 - 49\frac{1}{3}D(G)^2 + 264D(G) - 400
\end{aligned} \tag{40}$$

The average path length in optimal graphs can be calculated using expressions:

$$\begin{aligned}
&\text{When } p_o = 0 \bmod 8 \text{ and } D(G) \rangle 2\\
&d_{avo} = \frac{6D(G)^4 + 4D(G)^3 - 18D(G)^2 - 16D(G) + 105}{8D(G)^3 - 32D(G) + 69}\\
&\text{when } p_o \neq 0 \bmod 8 \text{ and } D(G) \rangle 1\\
&d_{avo} = \frac{6D(G)^4 + 4D(G)^3 - 6D(G)^2 - 4D(G) + 27}{8D(G)^3 - 8D(G) + 21}
\end{aligned} \tag{41}$$

Fig. 19 shows diameter and average path lengths in theoretical and real graphs with up to 100 nodes.

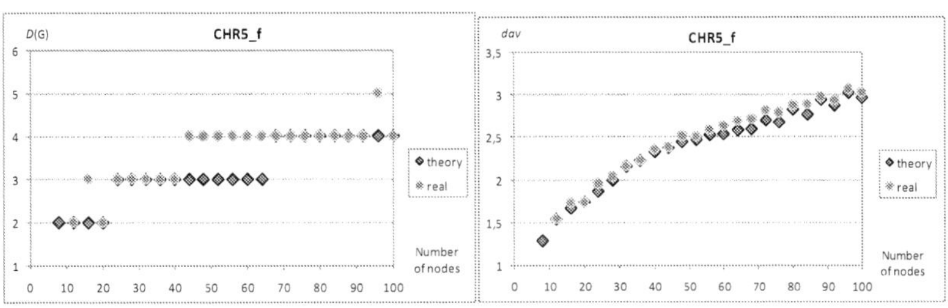

Fig. 18. Comparison of diameter and average path length of theoretical and real graphs CHR5_f

Only three ideal graphs found, which is presented in Table 18.

Number of nodes	q_1	q_2	q_3	$p/2$	d_{av}
12	2	4	4	6	1,545
20	6	4	4	10	1,737
32	6	12	12	16	2,161

Table 18. All founded ideal graphs CHR5_f with up to 100 nodes.

Graph CHR5_g.

Definition 11. The modified fifth degree chordal ring called CHR5_g is denoted by CHR5_g(p; q_1,q_2,q_3), where p means the number of nodes, is positive and divisible by 4; q_1 is chord has odd length; q_2, q_3 are chords which possess even lengths and less then $p/2$. The values of p and q_1 must be prime each other. Even node $i_{2k=0(\text{mod}4)}$ is connected to five other nodes: i_{2k-1}, i_{2k+1}, $i_{2k+q1(\text{mod } p)}$, $i_{2k-q1(\text{mod } p)}$ and $i_{2k+q2(\text{mod } p)}$, when $i_{2k=2(\text{mod}4)}$ than this node is connected to i_{2k-1}, i_{2k+1}, $i_{2k+q1(\text{mod}p)}$, $i_{2k-q1(\text{mod } p)}$ and $i_{2k-q2(\text{mod}p)}$; while odd node $i_{(2k+1)=1(\text{mod}4)}$ is connected to i_{2k}, i_{2k+2}, $i_{2k+1+q1(\text{mod}p)}$, $i_{2k+1-q1(\text{mod}p)}$, $i_{2k+1+q3(\text{mod}p)}$; and any node $i_{(2k+1)=3(\text{mod}4)}$ is connected to i_{2k}, i_{2k+2}, $i_{2k+1+q1(\text{mod}p)}$, $i_{2k+1-q1(\text{mod}p)}$, $i_{2k+1-q3(\text{mod}p)}$. ☑

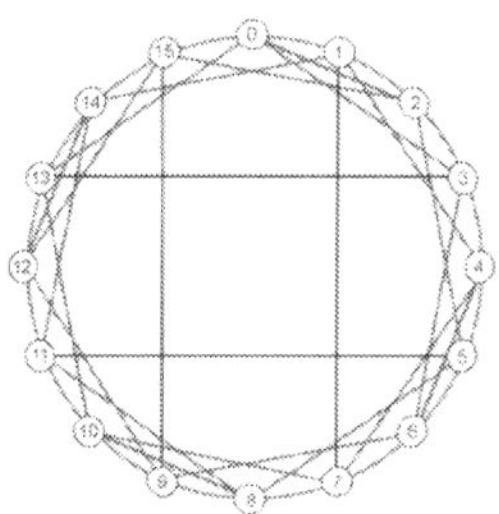

Fig. 19. Example of modified chordal ring CHR5_g(16; 3,2,6)

An example is shown in Fig. 20. The number of nodes in the layers of an optimal graph is given in table 19.

d	1	2	3	4	5	6	7	8
p_{do}	5	16	42	102	183	302	491	704

Table 19. Maximal number of nodes in the layers

In the case when the number of layer is bigger than 1, the number of nodes in the layers can be described by the following formula:

$$\begin{aligned}
&When \quad d = 0\,(\text{mod}\,3)\; then\; p_{do} = \frac{4}{3}d^3 + \frac{8}{3}d - 2 \\
&when \quad d = 1\,(\text{mod}\,3)\; and\; d \rangle 2\; then\; p_{do} = \frac{4}{3}d^3 + \frac{2}{9}d^2 + \frac{29}{9}d + \frac{2}{9} \\
&when \quad d = 2\,(\text{mod}\,3)\; and\; d \rangle 4\; then\; p_{do} = \frac{4}{3}d^3 - \frac{2}{9}d^2 + \frac{41}{9}d - \frac{8}{9}
\end{aligned} \tag{42}$$

The total number of nodes p_o in the optimal graph can be calculated using the expressions:

$$\begin{aligned}
&When\ \ d = 0\ (\text{mod}\,3)\ then\ \ p_o = \frac{1}{3}D(G)^4 + \frac{2}{3}D(G)^3 + 2D(G)^2 + \frac{2}{3}D(G) - 1\\
&when\ \ d = 1\ (\text{mod}\,3)\ and\ d \rangle\ 2\ then\ \ p_o = \frac{1}{3}D(G)^4 + \frac{2}{3}D(G)^3 + \frac{20}{9}D(G)^2 + \frac{5}{9}D(G) + \frac{2}{9}\\
&when\ \ d = 2\ (\text{mod}\,3)\ and\ d \rangle\ 2\ then\ \ p_o = \frac{1}{3}D(G)^4 + \frac{2}{3}D(G)^3 + 2D(G)^2 + \frac{4}{3}D(G) + \frac{2}{3}
\end{aligned} \tag{43}$$

In Table 20 the total number of nodes in optimal graphs described by formula given above is shown.

$D(G)$	1	2	3	4	5	6	7	8
p_o	6	22	64	166	349	651	1142	1846

Table 20. Diameters and total numbers of nodes in optimal graphs

The average path length in the optimal graphs as a function of its diameter can be calculated using equations (44).

$$When\ D(G) = 0\ (\text{mod}\ 3)$$

$$d_{avo} = \frac{64{,}8\left(\frac{D(G)}{3}\right)^5 + 54\left(\frac{D(G)}{3}\right)^4 + \frac{124}{3}\left(\frac{D(G)}{3}\right)^3 - 10\left(\frac{D(G)}{3}\right)^2 - \frac{47}{15}\frac{D(G)}{3} - 4}{\frac{1}{3}\left(\frac{D(G)}{3}\right)^4 + \frac{2}{3}\left(\frac{D(G)}{3}\right)^3 + 2\left(\frac{D(G)}{3}\right)^2 + \frac{2}{9}D(G) - 2}$$

$$when\ D(G) = 1\ (\text{mod}\ 3)$$

$$d_{avo} = \frac{64{,}8\left(\frac{D(G)-1}{3}\right)^5 - 54\left(\frac{D(G)-1}{3}\right)^4 + \frac{124}{3}\left(\frac{D(G)-1}{3}\right)^3 - 14\left(\frac{D(G)-1}{3}\right)^2}{\frac{1}{3}\left(\frac{D(G)-1}{3}\right)^4 + \frac{2}{3}\left(\frac{D(G)-1}{3}\right)^3 + \frac{20}{9}\left(\frac{D(G)-1}{3}\right)^2 + \frac{5}{27}(D(G)-1) - \frac{7}{9}} +$$

$$+ \frac{-\frac{43}{15}\frac{D(G)-1}{3} - 4}{\frac{1}{3}\left(\frac{D(G)-1}{3}\right)^4 + \frac{2}{3}\left(\frac{D(G)-1}{3}\right)^3 + \frac{20}{9}\left(\frac{D(G)-1}{3}\right)^2 + \frac{5}{27}(D(G)-1) - \frac{7}{9}}$$

$$when\ D(G) = 2\ (\text{mod}\ 3)$$

$$d_{avo} = \frac{64{,}8\left(\frac{D(G)-2}{3}\right)^5 + 162\left(\frac{D(G)-2}{3}\right)^4 + \frac{574}{3}\left(\frac{D(G)-2}{3}\right)^3 + 117\left(\frac{D(G)-2}{3}\right)^2}{\frac{1}{3}\left(\frac{D(G)-2}{3}\right)^4 + \frac{2}{3}\left(\frac{D(G)-2}{3}\right)^3 + 2\left(\frac{D(G)-2}{3}\right)^2 + \frac{4}{9}(D(G)-2) - \frac{1}{3}} +$$

$$+ \frac{-\frac{523}{15}\frac{D(G)-2}{3} + 1}{\frac{1}{3}\left(\frac{D(G)-2}{3}\right)^4 + \frac{2}{3}\left(\frac{D(G)-2}{3}\right)^3 + 2\left(\frac{D(G)-2}{3}\right)^2 + \frac{4}{9}(D(G)-2) - \frac{1}{3}} \tag{44}$$

Fig. 20 shows diameter and average path lengths in theoretical and real graphs with up to 100 nodes.

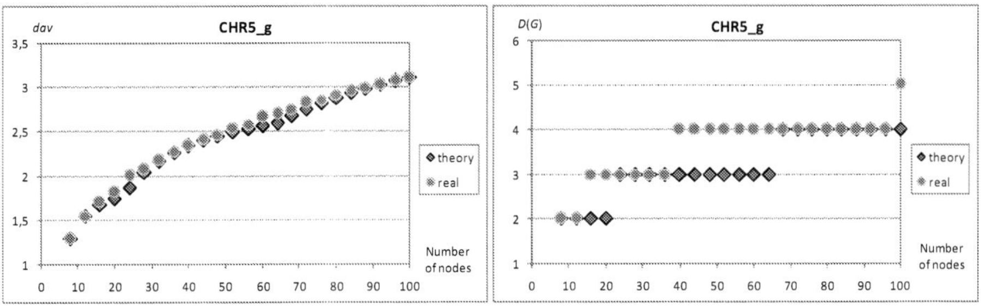

Fig. 20. Comparison of diameter and average path length of theoretical and real graphs CHR5_g

Graph CHR5_h.

Definition 12. The modified fifth degree chordal ring called CHR5_h is denoted by CHR5_h(p; q_1,q_2,q_3,q_4,q_5), where p means the number of nodes and is positive and divisible by 4; q_1, q_2, q_3, q_4 are chords which possess even lengths less then $p/2$, q_5=$p/2$. Even node i_{2k} is connected to five other nodes: i_{2k-1}, i_{2k+1}, $i_{2k+q5(\text{mod } p)}$ and to $i_{2k+q1(\text{mod } p)}$, $i_{2k-q1(\text{mod } p)}$ when number of node is equal to 0 mod 4 or to $i_{2k+q2(\text{mod } p)}$, $i_{2k-q2(\text{mod } p)}$ when number of node is equal to 2 mod 4, while odd node i_{2k+1} is connected to i_{2k}, i_{2k+2}, $i_{2k+1+q5(\text{mod } p)}$ and $i_{2k+1+q3(\text{mod } p)}$, $i_{2k+1-q3(\text{mod } p)}$ when number of node is equal to 1 mod 4 or to $i_{2k+1+q4\ (\text{mod } p)}$, $i_{2k+1-q4\ (\text{mod } p)}$ when number of node is equal to 3 mod 4.

An example is shown in Fig. 21, and the number of nodes in the layers of an optimal graph is shown in tables 21 and 22.

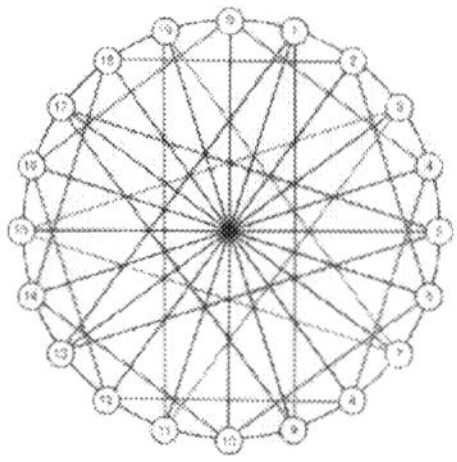

Fig. 21. Example of modified chordal ring CHR5_h(20; 4,4,8,8,10)

d	1	2	3	4	5	6	7	8
p_{do}	5	18	64	196	524	1244	2636	5068

Table 21. The number of nodes appearing in layers when p is not divided by 8

d	1	2	3	4	5	6	7	8
p_{do}	5	16	48	136	358	868	1908	3804

Table 22. The number of nodes appearing in layers when p is divided by 8

The number of nodes in the layers, as shown in Tables 21 and 22, can be described by the following expression:

$$\begin{aligned}
&\textit{When} \quad d > 5 \textit{ and } p \textit{ is not divisible by } 8 \textit{ then}\\
&p_{do} = \frac{8}{3}d^4 - \frac{16}{3}d^3 + 154\frac{2}{3}d^2 + 1133\frac{8}{3}d - 2292\\
&\textit{when} \quad d > 7 \textit{ and } p \textit{ is divisible by } 8 \textit{ then}\\
&p_{do} = \frac{8}{3}d^4 - \frac{16}{3}d^3 - 266\frac{2}{3}d^2 + 2285\frac{1}{3}d - 5604
\end{aligned} \tag{45}$$

In Table 23 the total number of nodes in optimal graphs described by expression given above is shown.

$D(G)$	1	2	3	4	5	6	7	8
p_o is not divisible by 8	6	24	88	284	808	2052	4688	9756
p_o is divisible by 8	6	22	70	206	564	1432	3340	7144

Table 23. Total numbers of nodes forming optimal graphs versus diameter

$$\begin{aligned}
&\textit{When} \quad D(G) > 4 \textit{ and } p \textit{ is not divisible by } 8 \textit{ then}\\
&p_o = \frac{8}{15}D(G)^5 - \frac{160}{3}D(G)^3 + 488d^2 + 1751\frac{1}{5}d + 2364\\
&\textit{when} \quad D(G) > 6 \textit{ and } p \textit{ is divisible by } 8 \textit{ then}\\
&p_o = \frac{8}{15}D(G)^5 - \frac{272}{3}D(G)^3 - 1008\frac{2}{3}D(G)^2 + 4505\frac{13}{15}D(G) + 7624
\end{aligned} \tag{46}$$

The average path length in optimal graphs:

$$\begin{aligned}
&\textit{When } D(G) > 4 \textit{ and } p \textit{ is not divisible by } 8\\
&d_{avo} = \frac{\frac{4}{9}D(G)^6 + \frac{4}{15}D(G)^5 - 40\frac{2}{9}D(G)^4 + 298\frac{2}{3}D(G)^3 - 618\frac{2}{9}D(G)^2 - 956\frac{14}{15}D(G)}{\frac{8}{15}D(G)^5 - \frac{160}{3}D(G)^3 + 488d^2 + 1751\frac{1}{5}d + 2363} +\\
&+\frac{3905}{\frac{8}{15}D(G)^5 - \frac{160}{3}D(G)^3 + 488d^2 + 1751\frac{1}{5}d + 2363}\\
&\textit{When } D(G) > 4 \textit{ and } p \textit{ is divisible by } 8\\
&d_{avo} = \frac{\frac{4}{9}D(G)^6 + \frac{4}{15}D(G)^5 - 68\frac{2}{3}D(G)^4 + 626\frac{2}{3}D(G)^3 + 1726\frac{2}{9}D(G)^2 - 2420\frac{14}{15}D(G)}{\frac{8}{15}D(G)^5 - \frac{272}{3}D(G)^3 - 1008\frac{2}{3}D(G)^2 + 4505\frac{13}{15}d + 7623} +\\
&+\frac{14695}{\frac{8}{15}D(G)^5 - \frac{272}{3}D(G)^3 - 1008\frac{2}{3}D(G)^2 + 4505\frac{13}{15}d + 7623}
\end{aligned} \tag{47}$$

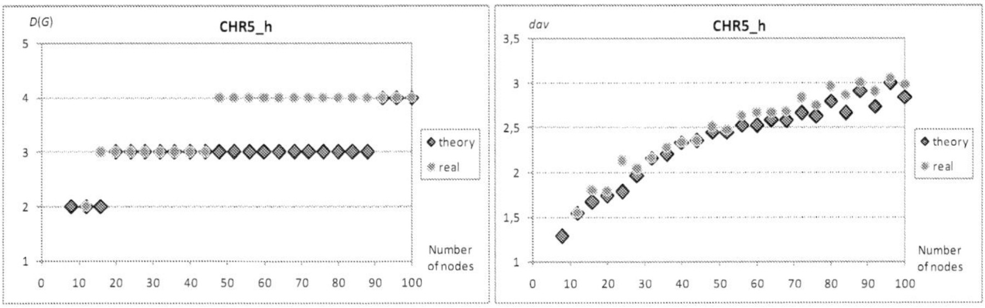

Fig. 22. Comparison of diameter and average path length of theoretical and real graphs CHR5_h

Fig. 22 shows diameter and average path lengths in theoretical and real graphs with up to 100 nodes.

There are only three chordal rings which possess basic parameters equal to parameters of theoretical graphs: These are: CHR5_h(12; 4,4,4,4,6), CHR5_h(40; 4,12,4,12,20) and CHR5_h(44; 4,8,12,16,22).

Graph CHR5_i.

Definition 13. The modified fifth degree chordal ring called CHR5_i is denoted by CHR5_i(p; q_1,q_2,q_3,q_4), where p means the number of nodes and is positive and divisible by 4; q_1, q_2, q_3, q_4 are chords which possess: q_1, odd length and q_2, q_3, q_4 - even lengths less then $p/2$. Each node is connected to five other nodes. Even node i_{2k} is connected to i_{2k-1}, i_{2k+1}, $i_{2k+q1(\text{mod } p)}$, $i_{2k-q1(\text{mod } p)}$ and $i_{2k+q2(\text{mod } p)}$, while odd node $i_{(2k+1)=1(\text{mod}4)}$ is connected to i_{2k}, i_{2k+2}, $i_{2k+1-q2(\text{mod } p)}$, $i_{2k+1+q3(\text{mod } p)}$, $i_{2k+1-q3(\text{mod } p)}$ and odd node $i_{(2k+1)=3(\text{mod}4)}$ is connected to i_{2k}, i_{2k+2}, $i_{2k+1-q2(\text{mod } p)}$, $i_{2k+1+q4(\text{mod } p)}$, $i_{2k+1-q4(\text{mod } p)}$.

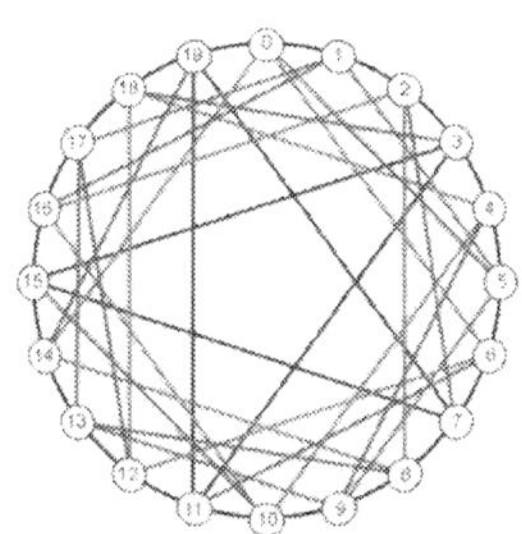

Fig. 23. Example of modified chordal ring CHR5_i(20; 5,6,4,8)

An example of a CHR5_i is shown in Fig. 23. The distribution of nodes in the layers depends on whether the graph is seen from odd or even node in Table 24 is given.

d	1	2	3	4	5	6	7	8	Node number
p_{do}	5	20	63	190	465	1010	2001	3594	even
	5	20	69	196	493	1094	2141	3790	odd

Table 24. Maximal number of nodes in the layers

The distribution of nodes in the layers can be described by the expression:

$$\begin{aligned} &\textit{When} \quad d > 4 \textit{ and node number is even} \\ &p_{do} = d^4 + 6d^2 - 192d + 650 \\ &\textit{when} \quad d > 4 \textit{ and node number is odd} \\ &p_{do} = d^4 + 6d^2 - 136d + 398 \end{aligned} \tag{48}$$

The total number of nodes in optimal graphs calculated depending on the source node number, given in Table 25, can be expressed as follows:

$$\begin{aligned} &\textit{When} \quad D(G) > 3 \textit{ and node number is even} \\ &p_{o\ even} = \frac{D(G)^5}{5} + \frac{D(G)^4}{2} + \frac{7}{3}D(G)^3 - 93D(G)^2 + 554\frac{29}{30}D(G) - 935 \\ &\textit{when} \quad D(G) > 3 \textit{ and node number is odd} \\ &p_{oodd} = \frac{D(G)^5}{5} + \frac{D(G)^4}{2} + \frac{7}{3}D(G)^3 - 65D(G)^2 + 330\frac{29}{30}D(G) - 475 \end{aligned} \tag{49}$$

$D(G)$	1	2	3	4	5	6	7	8	Node number
p_o	6	26	89	279	744	1754	3755	7349	even
	6	26	95	291	784	1878	4019	7809	odd

Table 25. Total numbers of nodes in the optimal graphs

The average path length in optimal graphs is equal to:

$$d_{avo} = \frac{d_{avoeven} + d_{avoodd}}{2} =$$

$$= \frac{\frac{D(G)^6}{6} + \frac{D(G)^5}{2} + 1\frac{11}{12}D(G)^4 - 42\frac{1}{3}D(G)^3 + 132\frac{5}{12}D(G)^2 + 176\frac{1}{3}D(G) - 764}{2\left(\frac{D(G)^5}{5} + \frac{D(G)^4}{2} + \frac{7}{3}D(G)^3 - 93D(G)^2 + 554\frac{29}{30}D(G) - 936\right)} + \tag{50}$$

$$+ \frac{\frac{D(G)^6}{6} + \frac{D(G)^5}{2} + 1\frac{11}{12}D(G)^4 - 61\frac{1}{3}D(G)^3 + 230\frac{5}{12}D(G)^2 + 293D(G) - 1646}{2\left(\frac{D(G)^5}{5} + \frac{D(G)^4}{2} + \frac{7}{3}D(G)^3 - 65D(G)^2 + 330\frac{29}{30}D(G) - 476\right)}$$

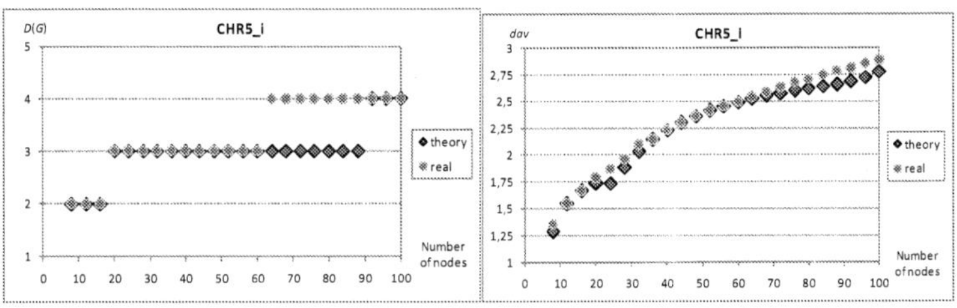

Fig. 24. Comparison of diameter and average path length of theoretical and real graphs CHR5_i

Fig. 24 shows diameter and average path lengths in theoretical and real graphs with up to 100 nodes.

For graphs with less than 72 nodes it is possible to find real graphs with parameters close to those of ideal graphs. However the difference becomes bigger for larger graphs. The differences seem to come from the different path lengths calculated from odd and even nodes. The ideal graphs found are shown in table 26.

Number of nodes	q_1	q_2	q_3	q_4	d_{av}
12	5	2	4	4	1,545
16	7	2	4	4	1,667
36	13	10	16	16	2,143
40	9	6	12	12	2,231
44	9	6	12	20	2,302
48	5	10	20	20	2,362
52	5	10	20	20	2,412

Table 26. Ideal graphs CHR5_i

Graph CHR5_j.

Definition 14. The modified fifth degree chordal ring called CHR5_j is denoted by CHR5_j(p; q_1,q_2,q_3,q_4), where p is the number of nodes. It must be positive and divisible by 4. Chords q_1 and q_2 have odd lengths; q_3 and q_4 possess even lengths, all chords lengths are less then $p/2$. Each node is connected to five other nodes. Even nodes i_{2k} are connected to i_{2k-1}, i_{2k+1} and to $i_{2k+q1(\text{mod } p)}$, $i_{2k+q2(\text{mod } p)}$ and $i_{2k+q3(\text{mod } p)}$ when $2k = 0$ (mod4) or to $i_{2k-q3(\text{mod } p)}$ when $2k = 2$ (mod4); while odd nodes $i_{(2k+1)}$ are connected to i_{2k}, i_{2k+2}, $i_{2k+1-q1(\text{mod } p)}$, $i_{2k+1-q2(\text{mod } p)}$ and to $i_{2k+1+q4(\text{mod } p)}$ when $2k+1=1$ (mod4) or to $i_{2k+1-q4(\text{mod } p)}$ when $2k+1 = 3$ (mod4).

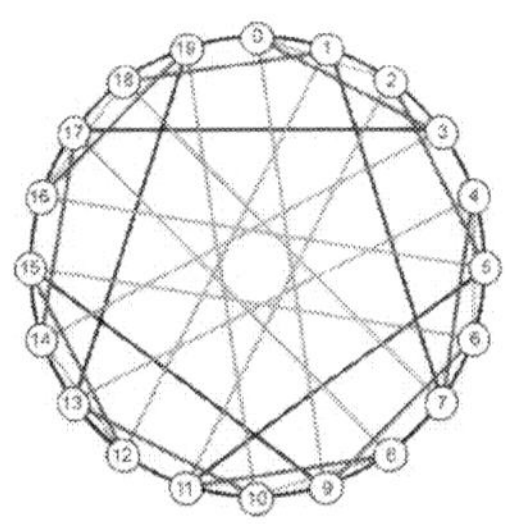

Fig. 25. Example of modified chordal ring CHR5_j(20; 3,9,2,6)

Based on going through all the real graphs, the distribution of nodes in the layers of CHR5_j is as follows (Table 27):

d	1	2	3	4	5	6	7	8
p_{do}	5	20	62	174	375	718	1303	2136

Table 27. Maximal number of nodes in the successive layers

The distribution of nodes in the layers of an optimal graph is described by expression:

$$\begin{aligned}
&When\ \ d \rangle 2 \ and\ d = 0\ (\mathrm{mod}\,3)\ then \\
&p_{do} = \frac{77}{162}\left(\frac{d}{3}\right)^4 + 27\frac{1}{2}\left(\frac{d}{3}\right)^2 - 4 \\
&when\ \ d \rangle 2 \ and\ d = 1\ (\mathrm{mod}\,3)\ then \\
&p_{do} = \frac{77}{162}\left(\frac{d-1}{3}\right)^4 + 52\frac{1}{3}\left(\frac{d-1}{3}\right)^3 + 53\frac{1}{2}\left(\frac{d-1}{3}\right)^2 + 24\frac{2}{3}\left(\frac{d-1}{3}\right) + 5 \\
&when\ \ d \rangle 2 \ and\ d = 2\ (\mathrm{mod}\,3)\ then \\
&p_{do} = \frac{77}{162}\left(\frac{d-2}{3}\right)^4 + 101\frac{2}{3}\left(\frac{d-2}{3}\right)^3 + 129\frac{1}{2}\left(\frac{d-2}{3}\right)^2 + 83\frac{1}{3}\left(\frac{d-2}{3}\right)^2 + 22
\end{aligned} \tag{51}$$

In Table 28 the total number of nodes in virtual, optimal graphs is shown as function of diameter.

$d(G)$	1	2	3	4	5	6	7	8
p_{do}	6	26	88	262	637	1355	2658	4794

Table 28. Total numbers of nodes in optimal graphs versus diameter

The total number of nodes in optimal graphs calculated as a function of its diameter can be expressed as follows:

$$\begin{aligned}
&When\ \ D(G) \rangle 2 \ and\ D(G) = 0\ (\mathrm{mod}\,3)\ then \\
&p_o = 23\frac{1}{10}\left(\frac{D(G)}{3}\right)^5 + 19\frac{1}{4}\left(\frac{D(G)}{3}\right)^4 + 31\frac{2}{3}\left(\frac{D(G)}{3}\right)^3 + \\
&+ 12\frac{3}{4}\left(\frac{D(G)}{3}\right)^2 + 2\frac{7}{30}\left(\frac{D(G)}{3}\right) - 1 \\
&when\ \ D(G) \rangle 2 \ and\ D(G) = 1\ (\mathrm{mod}\,3)\ then \\
&p_o = 23\frac{1}{10}\left(\frac{D(G)-1}{3}\right)^5 + 57\frac{3}{4}\left(\frac{D(G)-1}{3}\right)^4 + 84\left(\frac{D(G)-1}{3}\right)^3 + \\
&+ 66\frac{1}{4}\left(\frac{D(G)-1}{3}\right)^2 + 26\frac{8}{9}\left(\frac{D(G)-1}{3}\right) + 4 \\
&when\ \ D(G) \rangle 2 \ and\ D(G) = 2\ (\mathrm{mod}\,3)\ then \\
&p_o = 23\frac{1}{10}\left(\frac{D(G)-2}{3}\right)^5 + 96\frac{1}{4}\left(\frac{D(G)-2}{3}\right)^4 + 185\frac{2}{3}\left(\frac{D(G)-2}{3}\right)^3 + \\
&+ 195\frac{3}{4}\left(\frac{D(G)-2}{3}\right)^2 + 110\frac{7}{30}\left(\frac{D(G)-2}{3}\right) + 26
\end{aligned} \tag{52}$$

The average path length in optimal graphs is described by (53):

$$\text{When } D(G)\rangle 2 \text{ and } D(G)=0\,(\bmod 3) \text{ then}$$
$$d_{avo}=57\frac{3}{4}\left(\frac{D(G)}{3}\right)^6+57\frac{3}{4}\left(\frac{D(G)}{3}\right)^5+77\frac{5}{12}\left(\frac{D(G)}{3}\right)^4+$$
$$+39\frac{7}{12}\left(\frac{D(G)}{3}\right)^3+4\frac{251}{300}\left(\frac{D(G)}{3}\right)^2-2\frac{101}{300}\left(\frac{D(G)}{3}\right)-4$$
$$\text{when } D(G)\rangle 2 \text{ and } D(G)=1\,(\bmod 3) \text{ then}$$
$$d_{avo}=57\frac{3}{4}\left(\frac{D(G)-1}{3}\right)^6-173\frac{1}{4}\left(\frac{D(G)-1}{3}\right)^5+272\frac{11}{12}\left(\frac{D(G)-1}{3}\right)^4+ \tag{53}$$
$$-261\frac{3}{4}\left(\frac{D(G)-1}{3}\right)^3+146\frac{1}{3}\left(\frac{D(G)-1}{3}\right)^2-42\left(\frac{D(G)-1}{3}\right)+1$$
$$\text{when } D(G)\rangle 2 \text{ and } D(G)=2\,(\bmod 3) \text{ then}$$
$$d_{avo}=57\frac{3}{4}\left(\frac{D(G)}{3}\right)^6-57\frac{3}{4}\left(\frac{D(G)}{3}\right)^5+77\frac{5}{12}\left(\frac{D(G)}{3}\right)^4+$$
$$-42\frac{11}{12}\left(\frac{D(G)}{3}\right)^3+16\frac{5}{6}\left(\frac{D(G)}{3}\right)^2-2\frac{1}{3}\left(\frac{D(G)}{3}\right)-4$$

Fig. 27 shows diameter and average path lengths in theoretical and real graphs with up to 100 nodes.

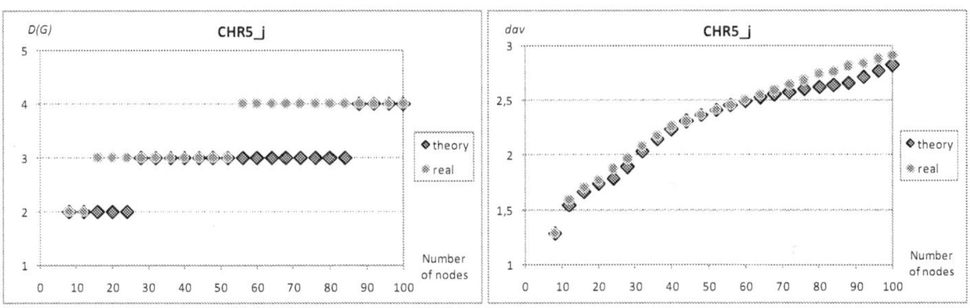

Fig. 26. Comparison of diameter and average path length of theoretical and real graphs CHR5_j

There are a few graphs having values of basic parameters equal to those of ideal graphs. For example: CHR5_j(44; 5,17,14,22), CHR5_j(48; 5,17,14,22), CHR5_j(52; 5,15,18,26), CHR5_j(56; 7,19,10,22).

Among all graphs belonging to the second group the best parameters (minimal diameter and minimal average path length given the number of nodes) were found in CHR5_i but other in minimal degree are slightly different it (especially from CHR5_j). In Fig. 27 the comparison of the second group of graphs is shown.

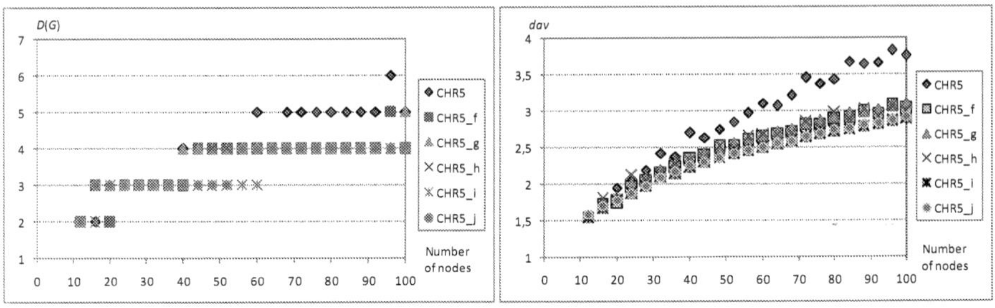

Fig. 27. Comparison of basic parameters of the chordal rings belonging to the second group of graphs

3.3 Analysed graphs – Third group

There are a number of other topologies, for which we have not found any nice expressions for the distribution of nodes in layers, and thus no expressions of the average distance and diameter could be derived. Due to the good basic parameters the topologies have been described, but further research is needed in order to provide more precise descriptions.

Graph CHR5_k.

Definition 15. The modified fifth degree chordal ring called CHR5_k is denoted by CHR5_k(p; q_1,q_2,q_3,q_4,q_5,q_6), where p is the number of nodes. It must be positive and divisible by 4. All chords have even lengths less than p/2. Each node is connected to five other nodes. Even nodes i_{2k} are connected to i_{2k-1}, i_{2k+1} and to $i_{2k+q1(mod\ p)}$, $i_{2k-q1(mod\ p)}$, $i_{2k+q5(mod\ p)}$ when 2k = 0 (mod4) or to $i_{2k+q2(mod\ p)}$, $i_{2k-q2(mod\ p)}$, $i_{2k-q5(mod\ p)}$ when 2k = 2 (mod4); while odd nodes $i_{(2k+1)}$ are connected to i_{2k}, i_{2k+2} and to $i_{2k+1+q3(mod\ p)}$, $i_{2k+1-q3(mod\ p)}$, $i_{2k+1+q6(mod\ p)}$ when 2k+1 = 1 (mod4) or to $i_{2k+1+q4(mod\ p)}$, $i_{2k+1-q4(mod\ p)}$, $i_{2k+1-q6(mod\ p)}$ when 2k+1 = 3 (mod4).

An example is shown in Fig. 28.

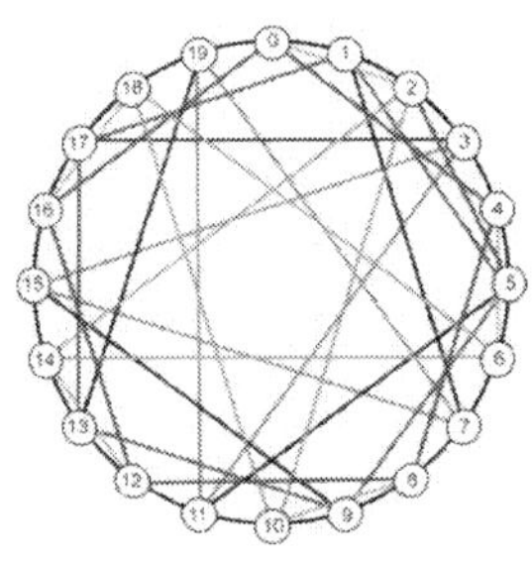

Fig. 28. Example of modified chordal ring CHR5_k(20; 4,8,4,8,2,6)

In Table 29 the distribution of nodes in layers is shown, based on observations of all graphs.

d	1	2	3	4	5	6	7	8
p_{do}	5	20	80	284	895	2520	6333	14334

Table 29. Maximal number of nodes in the successive layers

Using the results shown in Table 29, the counted total number of nodes in virtual optimal graphs is presented in table 30.

$D(G)$	1	2	3	4	5	6	7	8
p_0	6	26	106	390	1285	3805	10138	24472

Table 30. Total numbers of nodes forming optimal graphs versus diameter

In Fig. 29 comparison of diameter and average path length of theoretical and real graphs CHR5_k is shown.

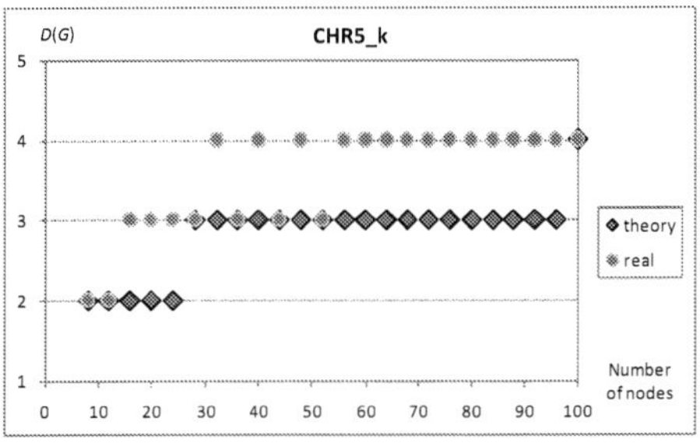

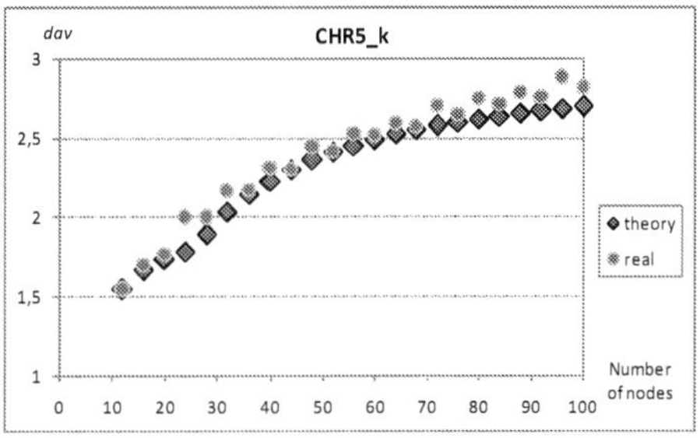

Fig. 29. Comparison of diameter and average path length of theoretical and real graphs CHR5_k

Only three graphs with average distance and diameter equal to those of ideal graphs can be found. These are CHR5_k(12; 4,4,4,4,2,6), CHR5_k(44; 4,8,12,16,18,22), CHR5_k(52; 4,8,12,16,22,26).

Graph CHR5_l.

Definition 16. The modified fifth degree chordal ring called CHR5_l is denoted by CHR5_l(p; q_1,q_2,q_3,q_4,q_5), where p means the number of nodes and is positive and divisible by 4. Chord q_1 has odd length, other chords have even length. The lengths of all chords are less than $p/2$. Each node is connected to five other nodes. Even nodes i_{2k} are connected to i_{2k-1}, i_{2k+1} and to $i_{2k+q1(\text{mod } p)}$ and to $i_{2k+q2(\text{mod } p)}$, $i_{2k+q3(\text{mod } p)}$ when $2k = 0$ (mod4) or to $i_{2k-q2(\text{mod } p)}$, $i_{2k-q3(\text{mod } p)}$ when $2k = 2$ (mod4); while odd nodes $i_{(2k+1)}$ are connected to i_{2k}, i_{2k+2}, $i_{2k+1-q1(\text{mod } p)}$, and to $i_{2k+1+q4(\text{mod } p)}$, $i_{2k+1+q5(\text{mod } p)}$ when $2k+1 = 1$ (mod4) or to $i_{2k+1-q4(\text{mod } p)}$, $i_{2k+1-q5(\text{mod } p)}$ when $2k+1 = 3$ (mod4).

An example is shown in Fig. 30.

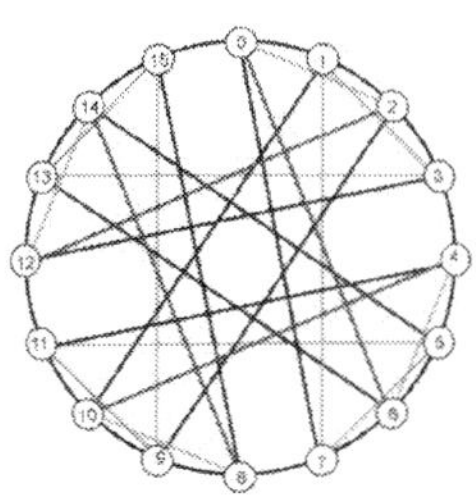

Fig. 30.Example of modified chordal ring CHR5_l(16; 7,6,2,2,6)

In Table 31 the distribution of nodes in the layers is shown.

d	1	2	3	4	5	6	7	8
p_{do}	5	20	71	228	555	1216	2442	4458

Table 31. Maximal number of nodes in the successive layers

Using the results shown in Table 31, the total number of nodes in virtual optimal graphs calculated in this way was presented in Table 32.

$D(G)$	1	2	3	4	5	6	7	8
p_o	6	26	97	325	880	2096	4538	8996

Table 32. Total numbers of nodes forming optimal graphs versus diameter

In Fig. 31 comparison of diameter and average path length of theoretical and real graphs CHR5_l is shown.

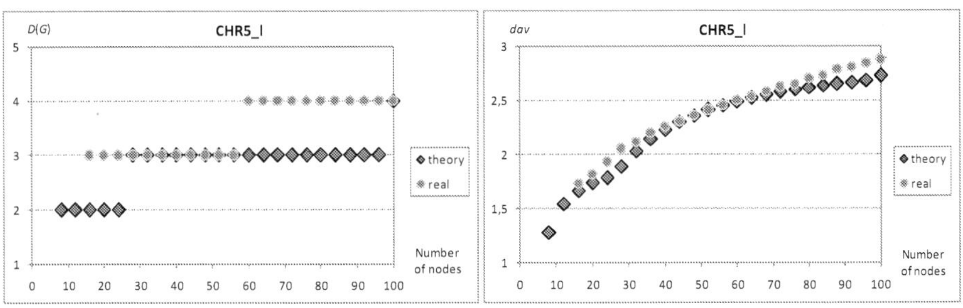

Fig. 31. Comparison of diameter and average path length of theoretical and real graphs CHR5_l

Examples of ideal graphs include: CHR5_l(16; 3,2,2,6,6), CHR5_l(44; 11,6,14,22,18), CHR5_l(48; 7,10,18,14,22), CHR5_l(52; 11,6,18,26,22), CHR5_l(56; 11,14,6,22,26).

Graph CHR5_m.

Definition 17. The modified fifth degree chordal ring called CHR5_m is denoted by CHR5_m(p; q_1,q_2,q_3,q_4), where p means the number of nodes and is positive and divisible by 4. All chords have even length less than $p/2$. Each node is connected to five other nodes. Even nodes i_{2k} are connected to i_{2k-1}, i_{2k+1}, $i_{2k+q1(\text{mod } p)}$, $i_{2k-q1(\text{mod } p)}$ and to $i_{2k+q2(\text{mod } p)}$ when $2k = 0$ (mod4) or to $i_{2k-q2(\text{mod } p)}$ when $2k = 2$ (mod4); while odd nodes $i_{(2k+1)}$ are connected to i_{2k}, i_{2k+2}, $i_{2k+1+q3(\text{mod } p)}$, $i_{2k+1-q3(\text{mod } p)}$, and to $i_{2k+1+q4(\text{mod } p)}$ when $2k+1 = 1$ (mod4) or to $i_{2k+1-q4(\text{mod } p)}$ when $2k+1 = 3$ (mod4).

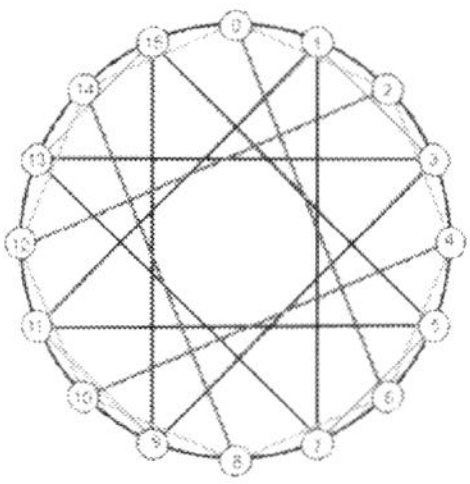

Fig. 32.Example of modified chordal ring CHR5_m(16; 2,6,6,2)

An example of CHR5_m is given in Fig. 32.

In Table 33 the distribution of nodes in layers is shown. The total number of nodes in optimal graphs, calculated based on these results, are shown in Table 34.

d	1	2	3	4	5	6	7	8
p_{do}	5	20	71	210	511	1064	1997	3440

Table 33. Maximal number of nodes in the layers

$D(G)$	1	2	3	4	5	6	7	8
p_o	6	26	97	307	818	1882	3879	7319

Table 34. Total numbers of nodes forming optimal graphs versus diameter

In Fig. 34 comparison of diameter and average path length of theoretical and real graphs CHR5_m is shown.

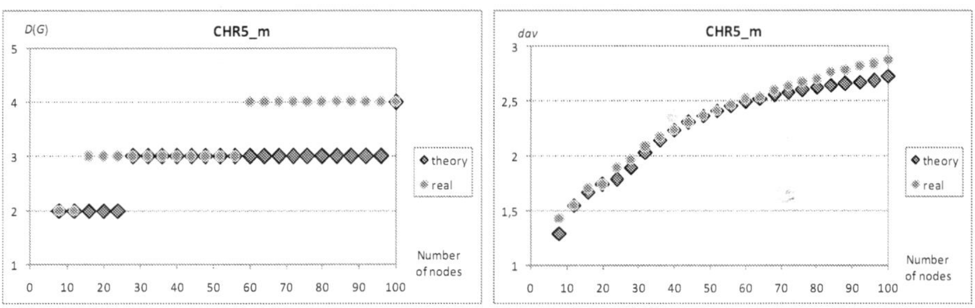

Fig. 33.Comparison of diameter and average path length of theoretical and real graphs CHR5_m

Examples of ideal chordal rings with up to 100 nodes include: CHR5_m(12; 2,2,6,6), CHR5_m(40; 6,14,10,18), CHR5_m(44; 6,14,10,18), CHR5_m(48; 10,22,6,14), CHR5_m(56; 18,26,14,6), CHR5_m(40; 6,14,10,18).

Graph CHR5_n.

Definition 18. The modified fifth degree chordal ring called CHR5_n is denoted by CHR5_n(p; q_1,q_2,q_3,q_4,q_5,q_6), where p means the number of nodes and is positive and divisible by 4. All chords have even length less than $p/2$. Each node is connected to five other nodes. Even nodes i_{2k} are connected to i_{2k-1}, i_{2k+1} and to $i_{2k+q1(\mathrm{mod}\ p)}$, $i_{2k+q2(\mathrm{mod}\ p)}$, $i_{2k+q3(\mathrm{mod}\ p)}$ when $2k = 0$ (mod4) or to $i_{2k-q1(\mathrm{mod}\ p)}$, $i_{2k-q2(\mathrm{mod}\ p)}$, $i_{2k-q3(\mathrm{mod}\ p)}$ when $2k = 2$ (mod4); while odd nodes $i_{(2k+1)}$ are connected to i_{2k}, i_{2k+2} and to $i_{2k+1+q4(\mathrm{mod}\ p)}$, $i_{2k+1+q5(\mathrm{mod}\ p)}$, $i_{2k+1+q6(\mathrm{mod}\ p)}$ when $2k+1 = 1$ (mod4) or to $i_{2k+1-q4(\mathrm{mod}\ p)}$, $i_{2k+1-q5(\mathrm{mod}\ p)}$, $i_{2k+1-q6(\mathrm{mod}\ p)}$ when $2k+1 = 3$ (mod4).

An example of a CHR5_n graph is shown in Fig. 34.

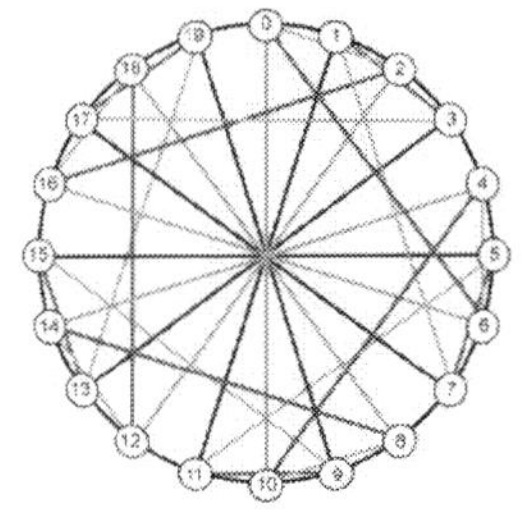

Fig. 34. Example of modified chordal ring CHR5_n(20; 2,6,10,2,6,10)

In Table 35 the distribution of nodes in layers is presented.

d	1	2	3	4	5	6	7	8
p_{do}	5	20	77	272	764	1916	4268	8696

Table 35. Maximal number of nodes in the layers

The total number of nodes in optimal graphs calculated based on the results given in Table 35 is shown in Table 36.

$D(G)$	1	2	3	4	5	6	7	8
p_o	6	26	103	375	1139	3055	7323	16019

Table 36. Total numbers of nodes in optimal graphs as a function of the diameter

In Fig. 36 shows the comparison of diameter and average path length of theoretical and real graphs CHR5_n.

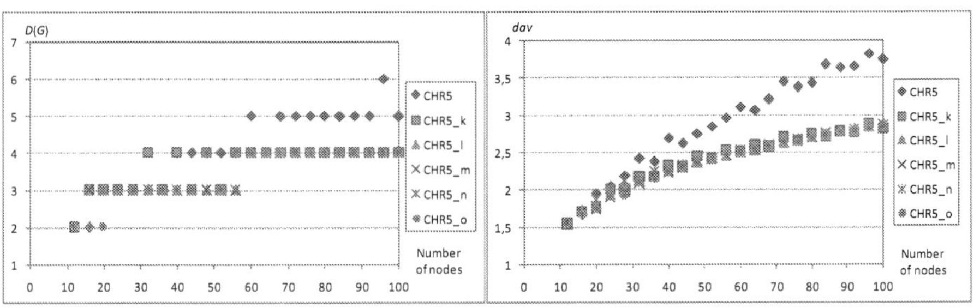

Fig. 35. Comparison of diameter and average path length of theoretical and real graphs CHR5_n

Going through all nodes with up to 100 nodes only one ideal graph was found, namely CHR5_n(52; 10,6,14,18,26,22) with 52 nodes.

Graph CHR5_o.

Definition 19. The modified fifth degree chordal ring called CHR5_o is denoted by CHR5_o(p; q_1,q_2,q_3,q_4,q_5) where p means the number of nodes and is positive and divisible by 4. All chords have even length less than (p/2+1). Each node is connected to five other nodes. Even nodes i_{2k} are connected to i_{2k-1}, i_{2k+1} and to $i_{2k+q1(\text{mod } p)}$, $i_{2k-q1(\text{mod } p)}$, $i_{2k+q2(\text{mod } p)}$ when $2k = 0$ (mod4) or to $i_{2k-q2(\text{mod } p)}$ when $2k = 2$ (mod4); while odd nodes $i_{(2k+1)}$ are connected to i_{2k}, i_{2k+2}, $i_{2k+1+q5(\text{mod } p)}$ and to $i_{2k+1+q3(\text{mod } p)}$, $i_{2k+1-q3(\text{mod } p)}$ when $2k+1 = 1$ (mod4) or to $i_{2k+1+q4(\text{mod } p)}$, $i_{2k+1-q4(\text{mod } p)}$ when $2k+1 = 3$ (mod4).

An example of a CHR5_o graph is shown in Fig. 36.

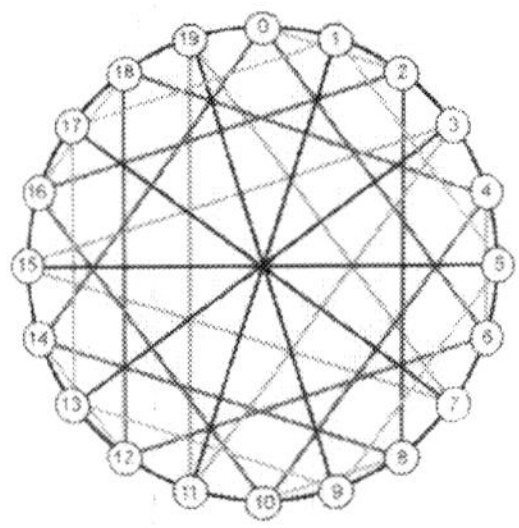

Fig. 36. Example of modified chordal ring CHR5_o(20; 6,2,4,8,10)

In Table 37 the distribution of nodes in layers is shown. Based on these numbers Table 38 is derived, showing the numbers of nodes in optimal graphs as a function of the diameter.

d	1	2	3	4	5	6	7	8	Node number
p_{do}	5	20	73	244	699	1726	3779	7498	even
	5	20	78	254	719	1778	3893	7696	odd

Table 37. Maximal number of nodes in the layers

$d(G)$	1	2	3	4	5	6	7	8	Node number
p_{do}	6	26	99	343	1042	2768	6547	14045	even
	6	26	104	358	1077	2855	6748	14444	odd

Table 38. Total numbers of nodes forming optimal graphs versus diameter

A number of ideal graphs can be found, such as CHR5_o(12; 6,2,2,4,4), CHR5_o(16; 2,6,6,4,4), CHR5_o(20; 10,10,6,4,4), CHR5_o(36; 10,18,14,4,8), CHR5_o(44; 6,14,10,20,4), CHR5_o(52; 6,10,14,20,24).

Fig. 37 shows the comparison of diameter and average path length of theoretical and real CHR5_o graphs.

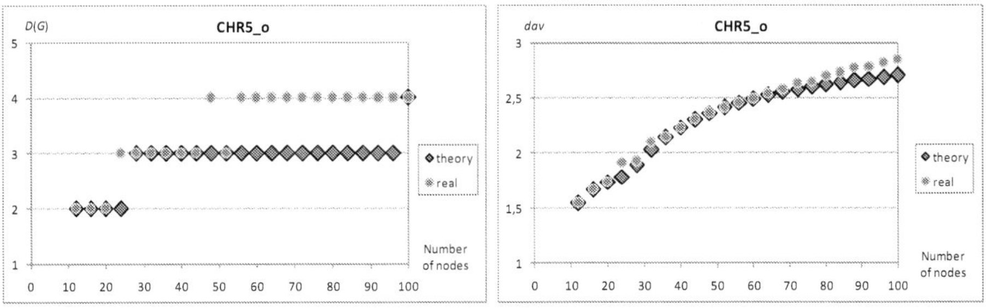

Fig. 37.Comparison of diameter and average path length of theoretical and real graphs CHR5_o

As for the previous group of graphs, the chordal rings of this group are compare with respect to the basic parameters. The comparison is given in Fig. 38.

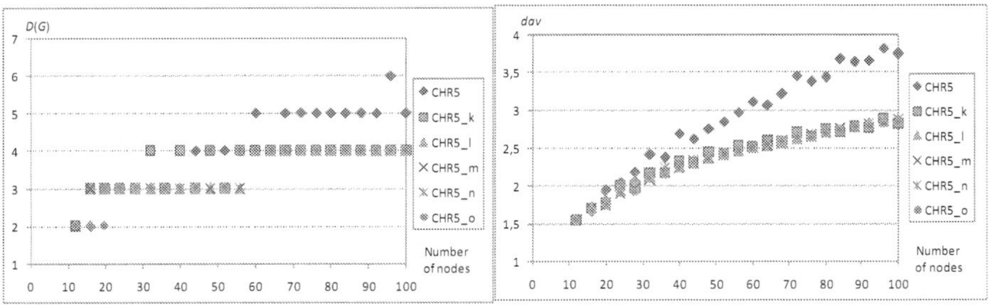

Fig. 38.Comparison of basic parameters of analyzing group chordal rings

From Fig. 38 it follows that all graphs belonging to third group of chordal rings have very similar properties when the number of nodes is smaller than 100.

4. Analysis of obtained results

Based on the obtained results for all 15 groups of graphs presented, the values of minimum diameter and average paths lengths can be compared. Despite the differences found between theoretical and real parameters the comparisons will be based on the theoretical values.

First, Fig. 39 presents the average path lengths as a function of the diameter in the graphs. This does not take into account the number of nodes in the graphs, which vary significantly between the different graphs as can be seen in Table 39 and Fig. 40. It can be seen that for a given number of nodes, CHR5_k has the smallest diameter.

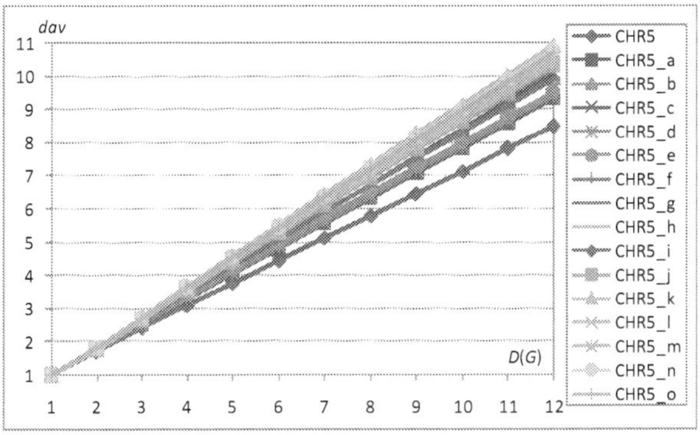

Fig. 39. Comparison of the calculated average paths length in the function of the diameter of graphs

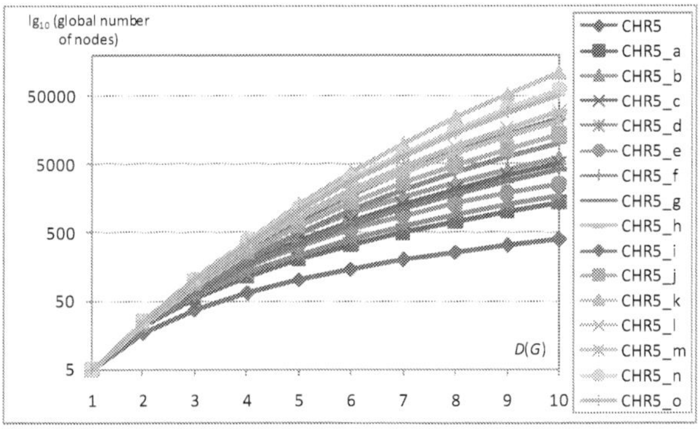

Fig. 40. Relationship between the total number of nodes and diameters

In the following section, a comparison of the average path length as a function of the number of nodes is presented. In order to compare graphs with different numbers of nodes, a "Normalized estimator of average path length" (E_{nav}) is introduced as follows:

$$E_{nav} = \frac{d_{avD(G)} \sum_{d=1}^{d(G)} p_{dr}}{d_{avrD(G)} \sum_{d=1}^{d(G)} p_d} \tag{54}$$

Where $d_{avD(G)}$ means the average path length of a particular graph when its diameter is equal to $D(G)$, and $d_{avrD(G)}$ means the average path length of the reference graph, $\sum_{d=1}^{d(G)} p_{dr}$ is the total number of nodes in relation graph, $\sum_{d=1}^{d(G)} p_d$ - total number of nodes in the particular graph.

	D(G)									
Graph	1	2	3	4	5	6	7	8	9	10
CHR5	6	18	38	66	102	146	198	258	326	402
CHR5_a	6	22	55	113	202	330	503	729	1014	1366
CHR5_b	6	26	87	227	494	948	1661	2717	4212	6254
CHR5_c	6	26	76	186	386	726	1276	2126	3386	5186
CHR5_d	6	23	61	130	239	400	622	915	1288	1753
CHR5_e	6	23	68	160	316	552	884	1328	1900	2616
CHR5_f	6	23	72	201	491	1068	2103	3804	6411	10196
CHR5_g	6	22	64	166	349	651	1142	1846	2840	4228
CHR5_h	6	23	79	245	686	1742	4014	8450	16430	29842
CHR5_i	6	26	92	285	764	1816	3887	7579	13674	23158
CHR5_j	6	26	88	262	637	1355	2658	4794	8148	13240
CHR5_k	6	26	106	390	1285	3805	10138	24472	54108	110878
CHR5_l	6	26	97	325	880	2096	4538	8996	16706	29420
CHR5_m	6	26	97	307	818	1882	3879	7319	12876	21406
CHR5_n	6	26	103	375	1139	3055	7323	16019	32520	62092
CHR5_o	6	26	102	351	1060	2812	6648	14245	28120	51864

Table 39.Total number of nodes versus diameters.

The results are shown in Table 40 and Fig. 41.

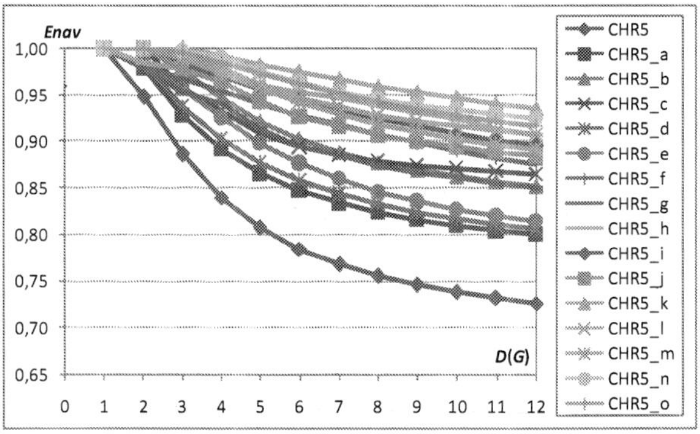

Fig. 41. Distribution of the normalized estimator of average path length versus graph diameter

From Fig. 41 it can be seen that he CHR5_k has the relatively shortest average path length.

Not surprisingly, the distributions of the number of nodes in the layers have a great impact on the two basic parameters. This can be seen also from expressions (7) and (9). The difference in the distribution for all graphs is shown in Fig. 42.

Graph	D(G)											
	1	2	3	4	5	6	7	8	9	10	11	12
CHR5	1,000	0,948	0,886	0,840	0,807	0,785	0,768	0,756	0,746	0,738	0,732	0,726
CHR5_a	1,000	0,979	0,928	0,892	0,866	0,848	0,834	0,824	0,816	0,810	0,804	0,800
CHR5_b	1,000	1,000	0,977	0,947	0,922	0,903	0,889	0,878	0,870	0,863	0,857	0,853
CHR5_c	1,000	1,000	0,958	0,932	0,909	0,894	0,885	0,879	0,875	0,871	0,868	0,865
CHR5_d	1,000	0,985	0,938	0,903	0,877	0,858	0,844	0,833	0,824	0,818	0,811	0,806
CHR5_e	1,000	0,985	0,957	0,926	0,898	0,877	0,860	0,847	0,836	0,828	0,820	0,814
CHR5_f	1,000	0,982	0,967	0,954	0,941	0,928	0,918	0,908	0,899	0,891	0,883	0,876
CHR5_g	1,000	0,979	0,953	0,940	0,914	0,895	0,885	0,874	0,866	0,861	0,855	0,851
CHR5_h	1,000	0,985	0,978	0,969	0,961	0,954	0,946	0,939	0,931	0,925	0,914	0,908
CHR5_i	1,000	1,000	0,984	0,971	0,957	0,945	0,935	0,925	0,916	0,909	0,901	0,896
CHR5_j	1,000	1,000	0,978	0,964	0,943	0,926	0,916	0,907	0,899	0,894	0,889	0,885
CHR5_k	1,000	1,000	1,000	0,992	0,983	0,975	0,967	0,959	0,953	0,946	0,941	0,936
CHR5_l	1,000	1,000	0,990	0,981	0,961	0,947	0,937	0,928	0,921	0,916	0,911	0,907
CHR5_m	1,000	1,000	0,990	0,974	0,957	0,941	0,929	0,919	0,910	0,903	0,897	0,892
CHR5_n	1,000	1,000	0,997	0,990	0,975	0,964	0,954	0,946	0,939	0,934	0,929	0,925
CHR5_o	1,000	1,000	0,995	0,985	0,973	0,962	0,952	0,943	0,935	0,928	0,922	0,917
	E_{nav}											

Table 40. Distribution of the normalized estimator of the average path length versus the graph diameter

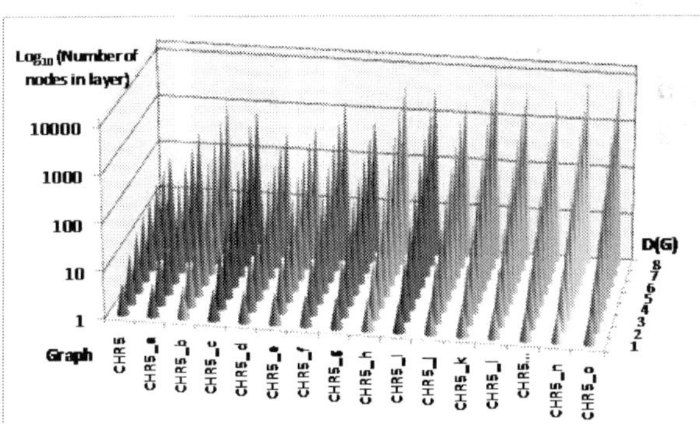

Fig. 42. Distribution of nodes numbers in the layers for all graphs

In the charts given below the comparison of the maximum number of nodes appearing in the layers of all analyzed graphs is presented.

On the basis of Fig. 42 and Fig. 43 it seems to be sufficient to analyze the distributions of numbers occurring in the first few layers to select a graph having the best basic parameters. This obviously reduces the time and effort for comparisons. The results again confirm that CHR5_k seems to be superior in terms of these basic parameters.

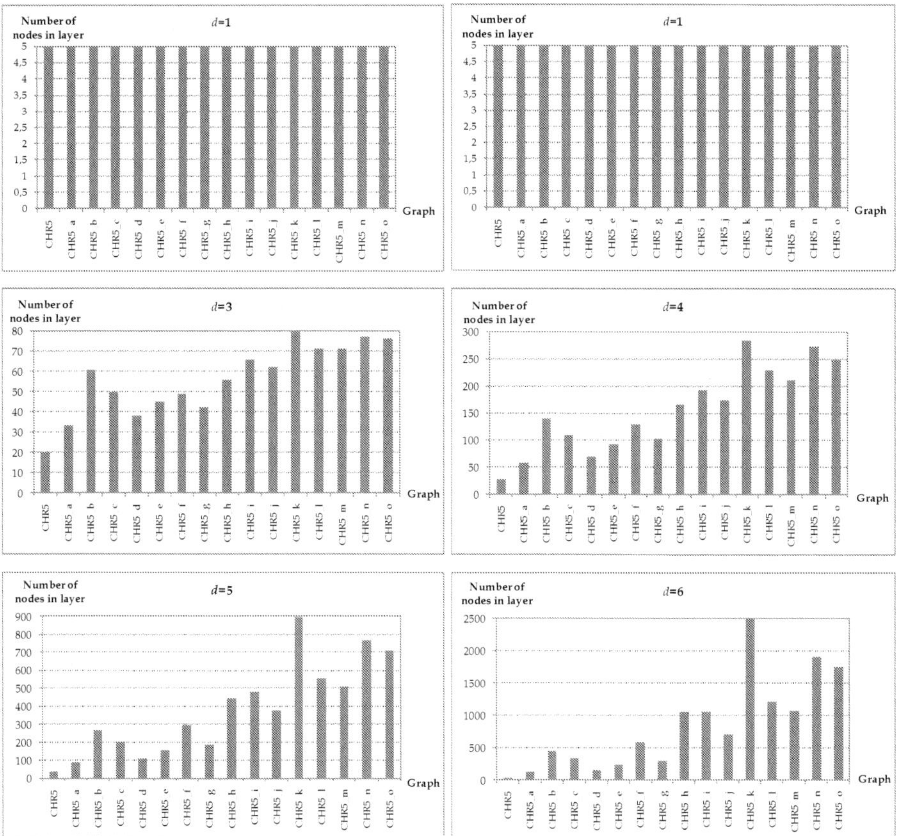

Fig. 43. Distribution of the number nodes in the first six layers

In order to make an objective assessment of the CHR5_k parameters, they were compared to the parameters of the Reference Graph as previously described. Table 41 and Fig. 44 show the distribution of nodes in different layers of these two graphs, as a function of their diameters.

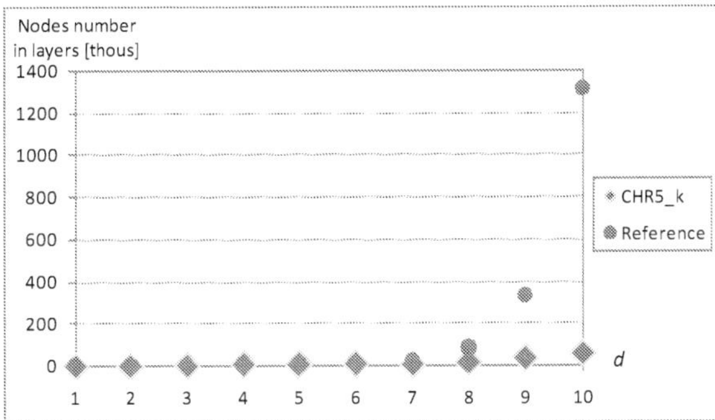

Fig. 44. Comparison of nodes number in successive layers

In Table 41 the total number of nodes in CHR5_k and reference graphs is compared for different diameters.

$D(G)$	1	2	3	4	5	6	7	8	9	10
CHR5_k	5	20	80	284	895	2520	6333	14334	29636	56770
Reference Graph	5	20	80	320	1280	5120	20480	81920	327680	1310720
	Total number of nodes									

Table 41. Total number of nodes in Reference Graph and CHR5_k

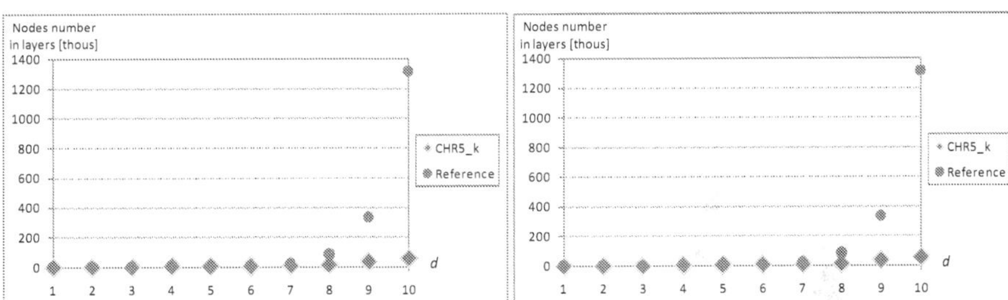

Fig. 45. Comparison the number of nodes in layers and total number of nodes versus layer number

In Fig. 45 a comparison of node numbers in successive layers and total number of nodes as a function of number layer in ideal CHR5_k and Reference Graph is shown.

Table 42 and Fig. 46 show a comparison of the average length as a function of the both graphs diameter, taking into account the total number of nodes corresponding to this diameter. As in the previous comparisons E_{nav} (54) is used.

$D(G)$	1	2	3	4	5	6	7	8	9	10
CHR5_k	1,0000	1,0000	1,0000	0,9920	0,9829	0,9747	0,9669	0,9595	0,9527	0,9465
	E_{nav}									

Table 42. The average path length as a function of the diameter

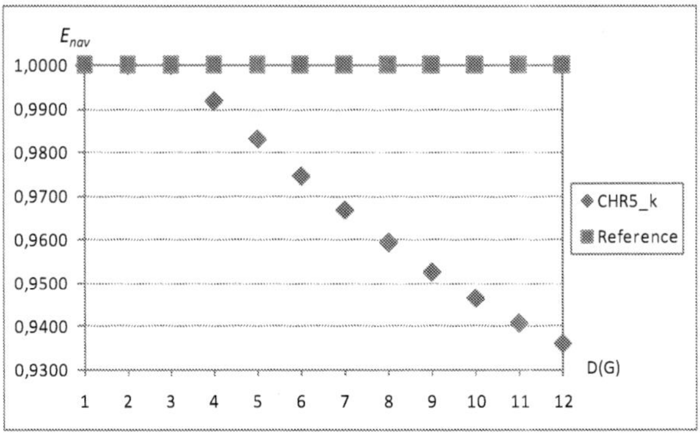

Fig. 46. Comparison of average path length as a function of the graphs diameter

5. Conclusions

In this publication the analysis of a different construction of 5th degree chordal rings was presented. The authors' main aim was to find structures which have the minimal diameter and minimal average of path in respect to number of nodes which create these graphs.

Presented considerations in the paper have rather theoretical nature, without a strict reference to practical applications. It is difficult to imagine a real regular WAN communication network that consists of thousands of nodes. However the interconnection structures connecting thousands of microprocessors, or sensors require the construction of such networks as the regular ones. The main objective function for regular interconnection structures is to minimize the network diameter or average path length. So, this is the main reason why such the structures were analyzed and studied in our paper.

In this regard the program was worked out which allows to calculate the analyzed parameters. It allowed describing virtual reference graphs namely optimal and ideal graphs. In this way we also found chordal rings which possess the smallest difference regards to average path length and diameter, which Reference Graphs have. They examined many types of structures and concluded that parameters of the real graphs are slightly different of the theoretically calculated graph parameter values. The obtained results became the basis for preparing the general formulas for determining these parameters without the need of simulation. As a side-result of the paper, we have shown that these reference graphs can be used for obtaining fairly good estimation of distance parameters in a simple manner. Additionally, they concluded that it is enough to inspect the maximal number of nodes which can appear in first few layers in aim to choose the best topology.

This publication presents the results of analysis of the modified chordal rings fifth degree. This analysis was carried out for 15 graphs divided into 3 groups. Each of the group included 5 types of graphs. Since the graphs were analyzed are regular graphs odd degree, hence all the graphs have to have an even number of nodes. The nodes number of all graphs belonging to the first group is divisible by two, the second and the third by four (it follows from used method of their construction).

For each group of graphs their analysis based on results obtained thanks to the application of testing programs constructed by authors. It made possible to carry out a distribution of maximal number of nodes in layers, to count total number of nodes in virtual, optimal graphs. Based on obtained results, for the first two groups of graphs they found strict mathematical expressions describing the distribution of nodes in layers, the total number of nodes, the average path length for optimal graphs, whilst for the third group such formulas were not found. Additionally the prepared programs allowed us to compare the basic parameters of real and theoretically constructed graphs.

Among the all analyzed graphs, the structures CHR5_f - CHR5_o have the most acceptable basic parameters. Those graphs however have a fundamental limitation: the network should consist of nodes with nodes number has to be divisible by 4. The parameters of these networks in more or less deviate from the parameters of the reference graph (graph ideal), and what's involved, they are usually asymmetrical (depending on the choice of the source node, obtained values differ). Also, computational process is rather complex, and takes long time.

From the point of view of application, according to the authors, the most appropriate structure of the regular network topology are graphs CHR5_b. These chordal rings are symmetrical, their parameters, if are not equal to the parameters of optimal graphs, they are very close to them; they are simple and easy to design and implement. The main limitation is the fact that the number of nodes, creating these networks, has to be even, but this follows from the assumption that the structure has to be regular, and the degree of nodes is five. Fig. 47 shows the comparison of the best two structures.

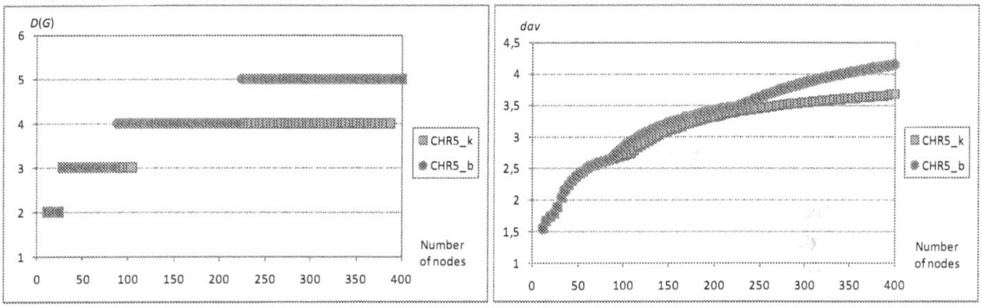

Fig. 47.Comparison of diameter and average length path both analyzing chordal rings versus the number of nodes

As the justification of this last conclusion the presented above diagrams can be used. In Fig. 47 we show the comparison of basic parameters of chordal rings CHR5_b and the best graph - CHR5_k. It can be observed that in up to 84 nodes, theoretically calculated parameters of both types of rings are identical, and up to 224 nodes - not much different from each another. Thus, taking into account the advantages of CHR5_b structure described before, it should be used to construct regular networks possessing not a huge number of nodes or in a large network consisting of a few identical regular structures.

Future work can focus on both theoretical and practical aspects. For the theoretical aspects, it would be a big help to find more precise and reachable bounds. This would make it possible to assess graph types, and to know how close to optimal they are. Moreover, a more thorough study of how precise distance estimates can be given using ideal and optimal graph would be interesting. Such a study could also cover other types of graphs. Another direction for further research would be to study new groups of graphs.

More practical aspects could deal with analyzing how well the good theoretical properties translate into good network properties. This could be done through simulation of different network configuration and traffic scenarios, and/or by studying how feasible the graphs are for assignment of physical, optical or logical links. In order to demonstrate that the topologies are useful in real-world settings, case studies would be a good place to start.

6. Acknowledgment

The authors would like to thank Associate Professor Jens Myrup Pedersen and Assistant Professor Tahir Riaz from Aalborg University, Department of Electronic Systems, and Professor Dr. Mohamed Othman from Universiti Putra Malaysia, Department of Communication Technology and Networks, for a fruitful collaboration with the work on analyzing chordal rings and other network topologies. Their inputs for this chapter have been particularly valuable.

7. References

A.N. Al-Karaki & A.E.Kamal. (2004). *Routing Techniques in Wireless Sensor Networks: a Survey,* IEEE Wireless Comm., pp. 6-28, Dec. 2004

ALU: Alcatel-Lucent 1830. (2011). *Photonic Service Switch 4 (Pss-4) Release 1.5.0/1.5.1 User Guide,* Issue 2, March 2011

W. Arden & H. Lee. (1981). *Analysis of Chordal Ring Network.* IEEE Transactions on Computers Vol. 30 No. 4 pp. 291-295, 1981

R. N. F. Azura; M. Othman; M.. H. Selamat & P. Y. Hock. 2008. *Modified Degree Six Chordal Rings Network Topology.* Proceedings of Simposium Kebangsaan Sains Matematik Ke-16, 3-5, pp. 515-522, Jun 2008

R. N. F. Azura; M. Othman; M.. H. Selamat & P. Y. Hock. (2010). *On properties of modified degree six chordal rings networks.* Malaysian Journal of Mathematical Sciences. 4(2), pp. 147-157.

L. N. Bhuyan. (1987). *Interconnection Networks for Parallel and Distributed Processing.* IEEE Computer Vol. 20 No. 6, pp. 9-12, 1987

S. Bujnowski. (2003). *Analysis & Synthesis Homogeneous Structure Networks Connecting Communications Modules.* PhD Thesis, UTP, Bydgoszcz, 2003.

S. Bujnowski; B. Dubalski & A. Zabłudowski. (2003). *Analysis of Chordal Rings.* Mathematical Techniques and Problems in Telecommunications. Centro International de Matematica, Tomar 2003, pp. 257-279

S. Bujnowski; B. Dubalski & A. Zabłudowski. (2004). *The Evaluation of Transmission Ability of 3rd Degree Chordal Rings with the Use of Adjacent Matrix.* The Seventh INFORMS Telecommunications Conference, pp. 219-221. Boca Raton 2004

S. Bujnowski; B. Dubalski & A. Zabłudowski. (2004). *Analysis of 4th Degree Chordal Rings.* Proceedings of International Conference on the Communications in Computing. Las Vegas, 2004, pp. 318 - 324

S. Bujnowski; B. Dubalski & A. Zabłudowski. (2005). *Analysis of Transmission Properties of 3rd Degree Chordal Rings.* Kwartalnik Elektroniki i Telekomunikacji. 2005, 51, z.4, pp. 521 - 539

S. Bujnowski; B. Dubalski; J. M. Pedersen & A. Zabłudowski. (2008). *Struktury topologiczne CR3m oraz NdRm.* Przegląd Telekomunikacyjny LXXXI, nr 8/9, 2008, pp. 1133 - 1141 (in Polish)

S. Bujnowski; B. Dubalski; J. M. Pedersen & A. Zabłudowski. (2009). *Analysis of Regular Structures Third Degree Based on Chordal Rings.* Image Processing and Communications. Vol. 14, nr 1, pp. 13-24, 2009 - 4

S. Bujnowski; B. Dubalski; A. Zabłudowski; D. Ledziński; T. Marciniak & J. M. Pedersen. (2010). *Comparison of Modified 6 Degree Chordal Rings.* Image Processing and Communications. Challenges 2. 2010, ISSN 1867-5662, pp. 435 - 446

S. Bujnowski; B. Dubalski; A. Zabłudowski; J. M. Pedersen & T. Riaz. (2011). *Analysis of Degree 5 Chordal Rings For Network Topologies.* Image Processing & Communications. Challenge 3, 2011, Springer. ISSN 1867-5662, pp. 445-459

R. Diestel, Graph Theory, 4th Edition. Springer-Verlag, Heidelberg. Graduate Texts in Mathematics, Volume 173. July 2001.

B. Dubalski; S. Bujnowski; A. Zabłudowski & J. M. Pedersen. (2007). *Introducing Modified Degree 4 Chordal Rings with Two Chord Lengths.* Proceedings of the Fourth IASTED Asian Conference "Communication Systems and Networks". Phuket 2007, ISBN CD: 978-0-88986-658-4, pp. 561-574 - 2

B. Dubalski; A. Zabludowski; S. Bujnowski & J. M. Pedersen. (2008). *Comparison of Modified Chordal Rings Fourth Degree to Chordal Rings Sixth Degree.* Proceedings of Electronics in Marine, ELMAR 2008, Zadar, Croatia. Volume 2, pp. 597-600

B. Dubalski; A. Zabłudowski; D. Ledziński; J. M. Pedersen & T. M. Riaz. (2010). *Evaluation Of Modified Degree 5 Chordal Rings for Network Topologies.* Proceedings of 2010 Australasian Telecommunication Networks and Applications Conference. Auckland - New Zealand, ISBN 978-1-4244-8171-2, pp. 66-71

R. N. Farah; M. Othman; H. Selemat & P.Y. Hock. (2008). *Analysis of Modified Degree Six Chordal Rings and Traditional Chordal Rings Degree Six Interconnection Network.* International Conference of Electronics Design, Penang, Malaysia, 2008

R. N. Farah & M. Othman. (2010). *In Modified Chordal Rings Degree Six Geometrical Representation Properties.* Proceedings of Fundamental Science Congress, Kuala Lumpur, Malaysia, May 18-19, 2010.

R. N. Farah; M. Othman & M. H. Selamat. (2010). *Combinatorial properties of modified chordal rings degree four networks.* Journal of Computer Science. 6(3), pp. 279-284.

R. N. Farah; M. Othman & M. H. Selamat (2010). *An optimum free-table routing algorithms of modified and traditional chordal rings networks of degree four.* Journal of Material Science and Engineering. 4(10), pp. 78-89.

R. N. Farah; M. Othman; M. H. Selamat & M. Rushdan. (2010). *In Layers Shortest Path of Modified Chordal Rings Degree Six Networks.* Proceedings of International Conference on Intelligent Network and Computing, Kuala Lumpur, Malaysia, November 26-28, 2010.

R. N. Farah; N. Irwan; M. Othman; M. H. Selamat & M. Rushdan. (2011). *In An Efficient Broadcasting Schemes for Modified Chordal Rings Degree Six Networks.* Proceedings of

International Conference on Information and Industrial Electronics, Chengdu, China, January 13-14, 2011

M. M. Freire & H.J.A. da Silva. (1999). *Assessment of Blocking Performance in Bidirectional WDM Ring Networks with Node-to-Node and Full-Mesh Connectivity*. European Conference on Networks and Optical Communications (NOC'99), Delft, 1999

M. M. Freire & H.J.A. da Silva. (2001). *Influence of Wavelength on Blocking Performance of Wavelength Routed Chordal Ring Networks*. Proceedings of 3rd Conference on Telecommunications, Figueira da Foz, 2001

M. M. Freire & H.J.A. da Silva. (2001). *Performance Comparison of Wavelength Routing Optical Networks with Chordal Ring and Mesh-Torus Topologies*. ICN (1), pp. 358-367, 2001

C. Gavoille. (n.d). *A Survey on Internal Routing*. http://deptinfo.labri.ubordeaux.fr/~gavoille/article/ survey /node28.html

G. Kotsis. (1992). *Interconnection Topologies and Routing for Parallel Processing Systems*. ACPC, Technical Report Series, ACPC/TR92-19, 1992

A.L. Liestman; J. Opatrny & M. Zaragoza. (1998). *Network Properties of Double and Triple Fixed Step Graphs*. International Journal of Foundations of Computer Science 9, pp. 57-76, 1998

B. Mans. (1999). *On the Interval Routing of Chordal Rings*. ISPAN '99 IEEE - International Symposium on Parallel Architectures, Algorithms and Networks, Fremantle, Australia, 1999, pp. 16-21

L. Narayanan & J. Opatrny. (1999). *Compact Routing on Chordal Rings of Degree Four*. Algorithmica, Vol. 23, pp. 72-96, 1999

L. Narayanan; J. Opatrny & D. Sotteau. (2001). *All-to-All Optical Routing in Chordal Rings of Degree 4*. Algorithmica Vol. 31, pp. 155-178, 2001

H. Newton. (1996). *Newton's Telecom Dictionary*. 11th Edition. A Flatiron/Publishing, Inc. Book, 1996,

J. M. Pedersen; A. Patel; T. P. Knudsen & O. B. Madsen. (2004). *Generalized Double Ring Network Structures*. Proc. of SCI 2004, The 8th World Multi-Conference On Systemics, Cybernetics and Informatics. Vol. 8, pp. 47-51. Orlando, USA, July 2004.

J. M. Pedersen; T. P. Knudsen & O. B. Madsen. (2004). *Comparing and Selecting Generalized Double Ring Network Structures*. Proc. of IASTED CCN 2004, The Second IASTED International Conference Communication and Computer Networks, pp. 375-380. Cambridge, USA, November 2004.

J. M. Pedersen. (2005). *Structural Quality of Service in Large-Scale Networks*. PhD. Thesis Aalborg University, April 2005

J. M. Pedersen; M. T. Riaz & O. Brun Madsen. (2005). *Distances in Generalized Double Rings and Degree Three Chordal Rings*. Proc. of IASTED PDCN 2005. IASTED International Conference on Parallel and Distributed Computing and Networks, pp. 153-158. Innsbruck, Austria, February 2005.

J. M. Pedersen; J. M. Gutierrez; T. Marciniak; B. Dubalski & A. Zabłudowski. (2009). *Describing N2R Properties Using Ideal Graphs*. Advances in Mesh Networks, MESH 2009. The Second International Conference on Advances in Mesh Networks. ISBN: 978-0-7695-3667-5, pp. 150-154

4

Poly-Dimension of Antimatroids

Yulia Kempner[1] and Vadim E. Levit[2]
[1]*Holon Institute of Technology*
[2]*Ariel University Center of Samaria*
Israel

1. Introduction

A partial cube is a graph that can be isometrically embedded into a hypercube. In other words, a partial cube is a subgraph of a hypercube that preserves distances - the distance between any two vertices in the subgraph is the same as the distance between those vertices in the hypercube. Partial cubes were first introduced by Graham and Pollak (Graham & Pollak, 1971) as a model for communication networks and were extensively studied afterwards.

Many important families of combinatorial structures can be represented as subgraphs of partial cubes, for instance, antimatroids. An antimatroid is an accessible set system closed under union. There are two equivalent definitions of antimatroids, one as set systems and the other as languages (Björner & Ziegler, 1992; Korte et al., 1991). An algorithmic characterization of antimatroids based on the language definition was introduced in (Boyd & Faigle, 1990). Later, another algorithmic characterization of antimatroids, which depicted them as set systems was developed in (Kempner & Levit, 2003). Dilworth (Dilworth, 1940) was the first to study antimatroids using another axiomatization based on lattice theory, and they have been frequently rediscovered in other contexts. An antimatroid can be viewed as a special case of either greedoids or semimodular lattices, and as a generalization of partial orders and distributive lattices. While classical examples of antimatroids connect them with posets, chordal graphs, convex geometries etc., a game theory gives a framework, in which antimatroids are considered as permission structures for coalitions (Algaba et al., 2004; 2010). There are also rich connections between antimatroids and cluster analysis (Kempner & Muchnik, 2003). Glasserman and Yao (Glasserman & Yao, 1994) used antimatroids to model the ordering of events in discrete event simulation systems. In mathematical psychology, antimatroids are used to describe feasible states of knowledge of a human learner (Cosyn & Uzun, 2009; Eppstein et al., 2008; Falmagne & Doignon, 2011).

The notion of "antimatroid with repetition" was conceived by Bjorner, Lovasz and Shor (Björner et al., 1991) as an extension of the notion of antimatroid in the framework of non-simple languages. Further they were investigated by the name of "poly-antimatroids" (Kempner & Levit, 2007; Nakamura, 2005), where the set system approach was used.

An antimatroid with the ground set of size n may be isometrically embedded into the **hypercube** $\{0,1\}^n$. A poly-antimatroid with the same ground set is isometrically embedded into n-dimensional integer **lattice** $\mathbb{Z}^n$. In this research we concentrate on interrelations between antimatroids and poly-antimatroids and prove that these two structures are isometrically isomorphic.

The *poly-dimension* of an antimatroid is the minimum dimension d such that the antimatroid is isometrically isomorphic to some d-dimensional poly-antimatroid. This definition is a direct analog of the lattice dimension of graphs (Eppstein, 2005). In this paper the exact characterization of antimatroids of poly-dimension 1 and 2 is given and a conjecture concerning antimatroids of any poly-dimension d is suggested.

This chapter is organized as follows.

Section 1 contains an extended introduction to the theory of antimatroids.

Section 2 gives basic information about distances on graphs and isometric isomorphisms. We concentrate on interrelations between antimatroids and poly-antimatroids. In particular, we construct an isometric isomorphism between these structures.

In Section 3 we introduce the *poly-dimension* of an antimatroid and prove our main theorem characterizing antimatroids of poly-dimension 2. In addition we present a linear labeling algorithm that isometrically embeds such an antimatroid into the integer lattice $\mathbb{Z}^2$.

Section 4 discusses an open problem.

2. Preliminaries

Let E be a finite set. A *set system* over E is a pair $(E, \mathcal{S})$, where $\mathcal{S}$ is a family of sets over E, called *feasible* sets. We will use $X \cup x$ for $X \cup \{x\}$, and $X - x$ for $X - \{x\}$.

Definition 2.1. *(Korte et al., 1991) A finite non-empty set system $(E, \mathcal{S})$ is an antimatroid if*

$(A1)$ for each non-empty $X \in \mathcal{S}$, there exists $x \in X$ such that $X - x \in \mathcal{S}$

$(A2)$ for all $X, Y \in \mathcal{S}$, and $X \not\subseteq Y$, there exists $x \in X - Y$ such that $Y \cup x \in \mathcal{S}$.

Any set system satisfying $(A1)$ is called *accessible.*

In addition, we use the following characterization of antimatroids.

Proposition 2.2. *(Korte et al., 1991) For an accessible set system $(E, \mathcal{S})$ the following statements are equivalent:*

(i) $(E, \mathcal{S})$ is an antimatroid

(ii) $\mathcal{S}$ is closed under union $(X, Y \in \mathcal{S} \Rightarrow X \cup Y \in \mathcal{S})$

An "antimatroid with repetition" was invented by Bjorner, Lovasz and Shor (Björner et al., 1991) by studying the set of configurations of the Chip Firing Game (CFG). Further it was investigated by the name of "poly-antimatroid" as a generalization of the notion of the antimatroid for multisets. A *multiset* A over E is a function $f_A : E \rightarrow N$, where $f_A(e)$ is a number of repetitions of an element e in A. *A poly-antimatroid* is a finite non-empty multiset system $(E, \mathcal{F})$ that satisfies the antimatroid properties $(A1)$ and $(A2)$. So antimatroids may be considered as a particular case of poly-antimatroids. An example of an antimatroid $(\{x, y, z\}, \mathcal{S})$ and a poly-antimatroid $(\{x, y\}, \mathcal{F})$ is illustrated in Figure 1.

Definition 2.3. *A multiset system $(E, \mathcal{F})$ satisfies the chain property if for all $X, Y \in \mathcal{F}$, and $X \subset Y$, there exists a chain $X = X_0 \subset X_1 \subset ... \subset X_k = Y$ such that $X_i = X_{i-1} \cup x_i$ and $X_i \in \mathcal{F}$ for $0 \le i \le k$. We call the system a chain system.*

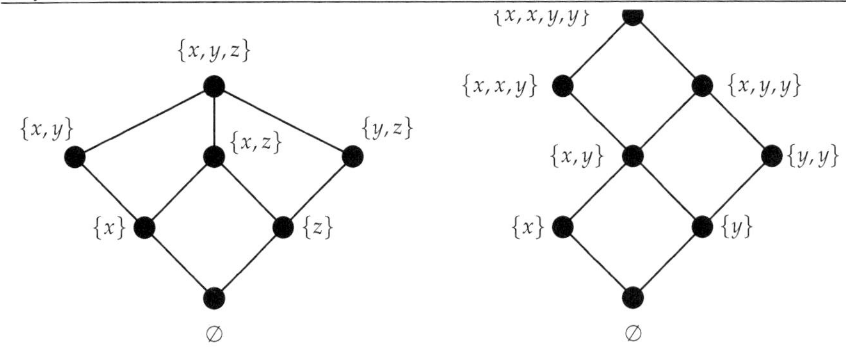

(a) (b)

Fig. 1. (a) Antimatroid. (b) Poly-antimatroid.

It is easy to see that this chain property follows from $(A2)$, but these properties are not equivalent. If $\emptyset \in \mathcal{F}$, then accessibility follows from the chain property. In general case, there are accessible set systems that do not satisfy the chain property. Indeed, consider the following example illustrated in Figure 2 (a). Let $E = \{1,2,3\}$ and $\mathcal{F} = \{\emptyset, \{1\}, \{2\}, \{2,3\}, \{1,2,3\}\})$. It is easy to check that the set system is accessible, but there are no chain from $\{1\}$ to $\{1,2,3\}$. Vice versa, it is possible to construct a system, that satisfies the chain property and it is not accessible. For example, $\mathcal{F} = \{\{1\}, \{3\}, \{1,2\}, \{2,3\}, \{1,2,3\}\}$ in Figure 2(b).

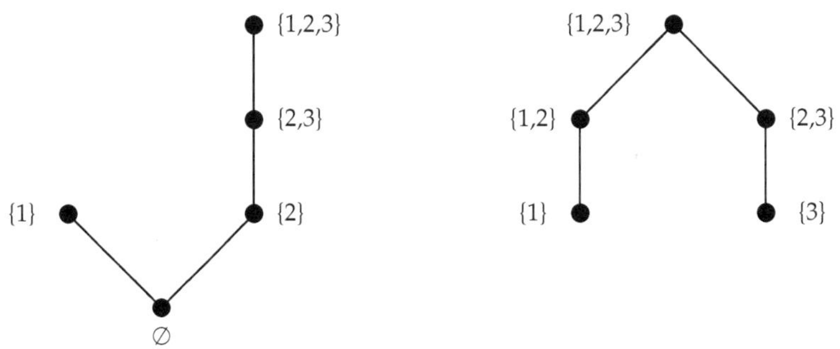

(a) (b)

Fig. 2. (a) Accessible system but not chain system. (b) Chain system but not accessible.

In fact, if we have an accessible set system satisfying the chain property, then the same system but without the empty set (or without all subsets of cardinality less then some k) is not accessible, but still satisfies the chain property.

Examples of chain systems include poly-antimatroids, convex geometries, matroids and other hereditary systems (matchings, cliques, independent sets of a graph).

Regular set systems have been defined by Honda and Grabisch (Honda & Grabisch, 2008).

Definition 2.4. *A set system $(E, \mathcal{S})$ is a regular set system if $\emptyset, E \in \mathcal{S}$ and all maximal chains have length n, where $n = |E|$.*

Equivalently, under the condition $\emptyset, E \in \mathcal{S}$, $(E, \mathcal{S})$ is a regular set system if and only if $|A - B| = 1$ for any $A, B \in \mathcal{S}$ such that A is a cover of B.

Actually, a regular set system is a chain system with an additional constraint demanding from both the empty set $\emptyset$ and the ground set E to belong to the set system $\mathcal{S}$.

An algorithmic characterization of chain systems with empty set $\emptyset$, called *strongly accessible set system*, was presented in (Boley et al., 2010).

Augmenting systems were introduced in game theory as a restricted cooperation model. The model is a weakening of the antimatroid structure and strengthening of the chain system.

Definition 2.5. *(Bilbao, 2003) A set system $(E, \mathcal{S})$ is a augmenting system if*

1. $\emptyset \in \mathcal{S}$

2. *it satisfies the chain property*

3. *for all $X, Y \in \mathcal{S}$ with $X \cap Y \neq \emptyset$, we have $X \cup Y \in \mathcal{S}$.*

An augmenting system is an antimatroid if and only if it is closed under union (Bilbao, 2003).

A comparative study of various families of set systems are given in (Grabisch, 2009).

Antimatroids have already been investigated within the framework of lattice theory by Dilworth (Dilworth, 1940). The feasible sets of an antimatroid ordered by inclusion form a lattice, with lattice operations: $X \vee Y = X \cup Y$, and $X \wedge Y$ is the maximal feasible subset of the set $X \cap Y$ called a *basis*. Since an antimatroid is closed under union, it has only one basis.

A finite lattice L is *semimodular* if whenever $x, y \in L$ both cover $x \wedge y$, $x \vee y$ covers x and y.

A finite lattice L is called *join-distributive* (Björner & Ziegler, 1992) if for any $x \in L$ the interval $[x, y]$ is Boolean, where y is the join of all elements covering x. Such lattices are appeared under several different names, e.g., locally free lattices (Korte et al., 1991) and upper locally distributive lattices (ULD) (Felsner & Knauer, 2009; Magnien et al., 2001; Monjardet, 2003).

Proposition 2.6. *(Björner & Ziegler, 1992) For an accessible set system $(E, \mathcal{S})$ the following statements are equivalent:*

(i) $(E, \mathcal{S})$ is an antimatroid.

(ii) $(\mathcal{S}, \subseteq)$ is a join-distributive lattice.

(iii) $(\mathcal{S}, \subseteq)$ is a semimodular lattice.

In fact, the two concepts - antimatroids and join-distributive lattices - are essentially equivalent.

Theorem 2.7. *((Björner & Ziegler, 1992; Korte et al., 1991) A finite lattice is join-distributive if and only if it is isomorphic to the lattice of feasible sets of some antimatroid.*

It is easy to see that feasible sets of a poly-antimatroid ordered by inclusion form a join-distributive lattice as well. This kind of findings was discussed in (Magnien et al., 2001), where it was proved that any CFG is equivalent to a simple CFG (antimatroid), i.e., the lattices of their configuration spaces are isomorphic.

3. Isometry

For each graph $G = (V, E)$ the distance $d_G(u, v)$ between two vertices $u, v \in V$ is defined as the length of a shortest path joining them.

If G and H are arbitrary graphs, then a mapping $f : V(G) \to V(H)$ is an *isometric embedding* if $d_H(f(u), f(v)) = d_G(u, v)$ for any $u, v \in V(G)$.

Let $E = \{x_1, x_2, ...x_d\}$. Define a graph $H(E)$ as follows: the vertices are the finite subsets of E, two vertices A and B are adjacent if and only if the symmetric difference $A \triangle B$ is a singleton set. Then $H(E)$ is the *hypercube* Q_n *on* E (Djokovic, 1973). The hypercube can be equivalently defined as the graph on $\{0, 1\}^d$ in which two vertices form an edge if and only if they differ in exactly one position.

The shortest path distance $d_H(A, B)$ on the hypercube $H(E)$ is the Hamming distance between A and B that coincides with the symmetric difference distance: $d_H(A, B) = |A \triangle B|$.

A graph G is called a *partial cube* if it can be isometrically embedded into a hypercube $H(E)$ for some set E.

A family of sets $\mathcal{S}$ is *well-graded* (Doignon & Falmagne, 1997) if any two sets $P, Q \in \mathcal{S}$ can be connected by a sequence of sets $P = R_0, R_1, ..., R_n = Q$ formed by single-element insertions and deletions ($|R_i \triangle R_{i+1}| = 1$), such that all intermediate sets in the sequence belong to $\mathcal{S}$ and $|P \triangle Q| = n$. This sequence of sets is called a *tight path*.

Any set system $(E, \mathcal{S})$ defines an undirected graph $G_{\mathcal{S}} = (\mathcal{S}, E_{\mathcal{S}})$, where $E_{\mathcal{S}} = \{\{P, Q\} \in \mathcal{S} : |P \triangle Q| = 1\}$.

Theorem 3.1. *(Ovchinnikov, 2008) The graph $G_{\mathcal{S}}$ defined by a set system $(E, \mathcal{S})$ is a partial cube on E if and only if the family $\mathcal{S}$ is well-graded.*

Proposition 3.2. *A family $\mathcal{S}$ of every antimatroid $(E, \mathcal{S})$ is well-graded.*

Proof. We prove that there is a tight path between each $P, Q \in \mathcal{S}$. If $P \subset Q$, then the existence of such path follows immediately from the chain property. If $P \not\subseteq Q$, then there exist chains from both P and Q to $P \cup Q$ that forms the tight path. □

Thus each antimatroid is a partial cube and may be represented as a graph $G_{\mathcal{S}}$ that is a subgraph of the hypercube $H(E)$ or as a set of points of the hypercube $\{0, 1\}^d$. For example, see an antimatroid in Figure 3. The distance in an antimatroid $(E, \mathcal{S})$ considered as a graph coincides with the Hamming distance between sets, i.e., $d_{\mathcal{S}}(A, B) = |A \triangle B|$ for any $A, B \in \mathcal{S}$.

A poly-antimatroid $(E, \mathcal{F})$ may be represented as a set of points in the digital space $\mathbb{Z}^d$, since each $A \in \mathcal{F}$ is defined by the sequence $(f_A(x_1), f_A(x_2), ..., f_A(x_d))$ that may be denoted as a point $(a_1, a_2, ..., a_d)$ in $\mathbb{Z}^d$. For example, see a two-dimensional poly-antimatroid in Figure 4.

The symmetric difference distance can be generalized to multisets by summing the absolute difference of the multiplicities of corresponding elements

$$|A \triangle B| = \sum |f_A(x_i) - f_B(x_i)|$$

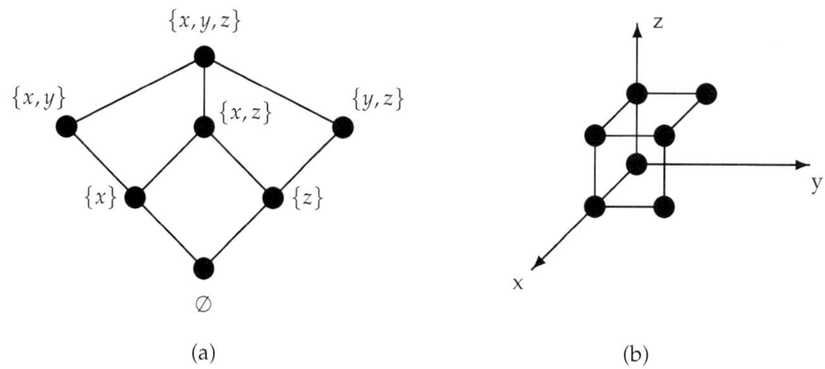

Fig. 3. Representation of an antimatroid: (a) as a graph of a family of subsets and (b) as a set of points in $\mathbb{Z}^3$.

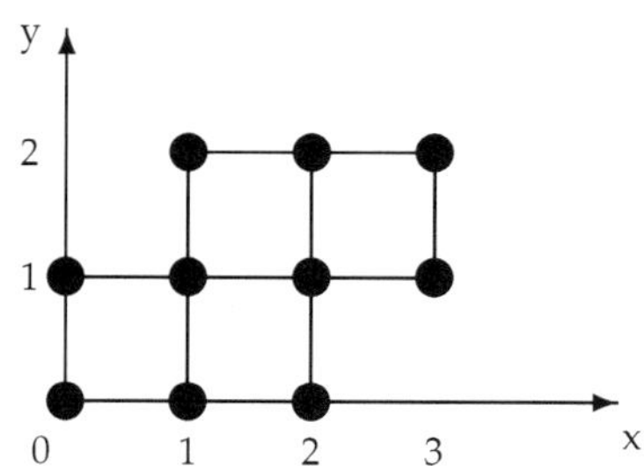

Fig. 4. A two-dimensional poly-antimatroid.

that coincides with the L_1 distance ($||A - B||_1$) on the digital space $\mathbb{Z}^d$.

A multiset system $(E, \mathcal{F})$ defines an undirected graph $G_{\mathcal{F}}$ in the same way as a set system. So each poly-antimatroid $(E, \mathcal{F})$ may be represented as a graph $G_{\mathcal{F}}$.

These representations of poly-antimatroids are isometrically isomorphic.

Proposition 3.3. *The distance in a poly-antimatroid $(E, \mathcal{F})$ considered as a graph $G_{\mathcal{F}}$ coincides with the symmetric difference distance, i.e., $d_{\mathcal{F}}(A, B) = |A \triangle B|$ for any $A, B \in \mathcal{F}$.*

Proof. For any $A, B \in \mathcal{F}$ there is a multiset $A \cup B \in \mathcal{F}$. Then there is a path in the poly-antimatroid from A to $A \cup B$ (by adding successively all the elements from $B - A$) and from $A \cup B$ to B (by removing successively all the elements from $A - B$). Therefore, $d_{\mathcal{F}}(A, B) \leq |A \triangle B|$. On the other hand, in any path from A to B every two adjacent vertices differ by only one element, and, consequently, $d_{\mathcal{F}}(A, B) \geq |A \triangle B|$. □

Thus a poly-antimatroid with the ground set of size d may be isometrically embedded into the d-dimensional lattice $\mathbb{Z}^d$.

Since each antimatroid is a poly-antimatroid, one may prove that every poly-antimatroid is isometrically isomorphic to some antimatroid.

Consider a poly-antimatroid $(E, \mathcal{F})$ given as a set of points in the digital space $\mathbb{Z}^d$. We use the Djokovic technique (Djokovic, 1973) elaborated by Eppstein (Eppstein, 2005) to embed a finite subset of the lattice $\mathbb{Z}^d$, and, therefore, a poly-antimatroid $(E, \mathcal{F})$, into a hypercube.

Let $\lambda_i = \max\{a_i | A \in \mathcal{F}\}$ and $\tau = \sum_{i=1}^{d} \lambda_i$.

Consider the following mapping $\mu : \mathbb{Z}^d \to \{0,1\}$.

Define $\mu(A) = (\mu_1(A), \mu_2(A), ..., \mu_\tau(A))$, where for each k such that $\sum_{i=1}^{j-1} \lambda_i < k \leq \sum_{i=1}^{j} \lambda_i$

$$\mu_k(A) = \begin{cases} 1 & a_j \geq k - \sum_{i=1}^{j-1} \lambda_i \\ 0 & otherwise \end{cases}.$$

It is clear that $\mu(0,0,...,0) = (0,0,...,0)$.

For example, consider the poly-antimatroid depicted in Figure 4. Mapping μ embeds the poly-antimatroid into a hypercube $\{0,1\}^5$ such that $\mu(1,0) = (1,0,0,0,0)$, $\mu(0,1) = (0,0,0,1,0)$, $\mu(2,1) = (1,1,0,1,0)$ and so on. See an isometrically isomorphic antimatroid in Figure 5.

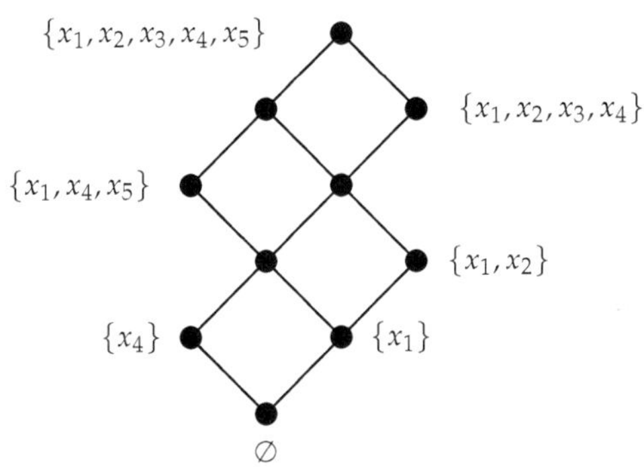

Fig. 5. An isometrically isomorphic antimatroid.

Lemma 3.4. *(Eppstein, 2005) The map μ is an isometry from a poly-antimatroid $(E, \mathcal{F})$ into a hypercube.*

Note that isometry μ is full-dimensional, i.e., each coordinate μ_i takes on both value 0 and 1 for at least one point.

It remains to show that $\mu(\mathcal{F})$ forms an antimatroid. We consider now a hypercube on some set $U = \{u_1, u_2, ..., u_\tau\}$. Then $\widehat{\mu}(A) = \{u_i | \mu_i(A) = 1\}$. Let $S = \{X \subseteq U : \exists A \in \mathcal{F}, X = \widehat{\mu}(A)\}$.

Proposition 3.5. *For every poly-antimatroid $(E, \mathcal{F})$, the set system $(U, S = \widehat{\mu}(\mathcal{F}))$ is an antimatroid.*

Proof. At first, $\emptyset \in S$. Indeed, $\emptyset \in \mathcal{F}$, i.e., $(0,0,...,0) \in \mathcal{F}$ and $\widehat{\mu}(0,0,...,0) = \emptyset$. Then S is accessible, since the map μ is distance-preserving. To see it, consider a non-empty $X \in S$. There is a set $A \in \mathcal{F}$ such that $X = \widehat{\mu}(A)$. Let $A = (a_1, a_2, ..., a_d)$. Since $(E, \mathcal{F})$ is a poly-antimatroid, there is $j \in \{1,2,...,d\}$ such that $B = (a_1, a_2, ..., a_j - 1, ..., a_d) \in \mathcal{F}$. Then $\mu(A)$ and $\mu(B)$ differs only in the position $k = \sum_{i=1}^{j-1} \lambda_i + a_j$, i.e., $\widehat{\mu}(A) - \widehat{\mu}(B) = \{u_k\}$.

Now let us prove, that the family S is closed under union, i.e., $X, Y \in S \Rightarrow X \cup Y \in S$. Since $X, Y \in S$ there are two points $A, B \in \mathcal{F}$ such that $X_1 = \widehat{\mu}(A)$ and $X_2 = \widehat{\mu}(B)$. Let $A = (a_1, a_2, ..., a_d)$ and $B = (b_1, b_2, ..., b_d)$. Then, $A \cup B = (c_1, c_2, ..., c_d)$, where $c_i = \max(a_i, b_i)$. Hence $\mu(A \cup B) = (\nu_1, \nu_2, ..., \nu_\tau)$, where $\nu_i = \max(\mu_i(A), \mu_i(B))$. So, $\widehat{\mu}(A \cup B) = \widehat{\mu}(A) \cup \widehat{\mu}(B)$, which implies $X \cup Y = \widehat{\mu}(A \cup B) \in S$. □

So we can say that the two structures - a poly-antimatroid $(E, \mathcal{F})$ and an antimatroid $(U, \widehat{\mu}(\mathcal{F}))$ are essentially identical.

4. Poly-dimension

Clearly, an antimatroid is a poly-antimatroid as well. The question is what is a minimal dimension d such that an antimatroid $(U, \mathcal{S})$ may be represented by an isomorphic poly-antimatroid $(\widehat{U}, \mathcal{F})$ in the space $\mathbb{Z}^d$.

We will call this minimal dimension $\pi(\mathcal{S})$ the *poly-dimension* of the antimatroid $(U, \mathcal{S})$.

Each antimatroid $(U, \mathcal{S})$ may be considered also as a directed graph $G = (V, E)$ with $V = \mathcal{S}$ and $(A, B) \in E \Leftrightarrow \exists c \in B$ such that $A = B - c$.

Denote *in-degree* of the vertex A as $deg_{in}(A)$, and *out-degree* as $deg_{out}(A)$, where

$$deg_{in}(A) = |\{c : A - c \in \mathcal{S}\}|, deg_{out}(A) = |\{c : A \cup c \in \mathcal{S}\}|$$

Consider antimatroids for which their maximum in-degree and maximum out-degree is at most p, and there is at least one feasible set for which in-degree or out-degree equals p. We will call such antimatroids *p-antimatroids*.

Proposition 4.1. *The poly-dimension of an 1-antimatroid is one.*

Proof. It is easy to see that 1-antimatroid is a chain $\emptyset \subseteq \{a_1\} \subseteq ... \subseteq \{a_1, a_2, ..., a_n\}$, that may be represented as a poly-antimatroid $\emptyset \subseteq \{x\} \subseteq ... \subseteq \{x, x, ..., x\}$ belonging to the axe x. The "only if" part of the proof is clear. □

To find the poly-dimension of a 2-antimatroid we show that 2-antimatroids have the special structure of "sub-grid".

A *poset antimatroid* is a particular case of antimatroid, which is formed by the lower sets of a poset (partially ordered set). The poset antimatroids can be characterized as the unique antimatroids which are closed under intersection (Korte et al., 1991).

Let us prove that any 2-antimatroid is a poset antimatroid.

An *endpoint* of a feasible set X is an element $e \in X$ such that $X - e$ is a feasible set too. A feasible set X is an *e-path* if it has a single endpoint e.

It is easy to see that an e-path is a minimal feasible set containing e.

The following lemma gives the characterization of poset antimatroids in terms of e-paths. We present a proof for the sake of completeness.

Lemma 4.2. *(Algaba et al., 2004) An antimatroid $(U, \mathcal{S})$ is a poset antimatroid if and only if every $i \in U$ has a unique i-path in $\mathcal{S}$.*

Proof. Let $(U, \mathcal{S})$ be a poset antimatroid and let $A, B, A \neq B$ be two distinct i-paths for $i \in U$. Then $i \in A \cap B \in \mathcal{S}$. Since each i-path is a minimal feasible set containing i, then $A \nsubseteq B$ and $B \nsubseteq A$. Hence the chain property implies the existence of an element $j \in A - (A \cap B)$ such that $A - j \in \mathcal{S}$. This is a contradiction with A being an i-path.

Now suppose that every $i \in U$ has a unique i-path in $\mathcal{S}$. Let $X, Y \in \mathcal{S}$. If $X \cap Y = \emptyset$ then $X \cap Y \in \mathcal{S}$ by definition of an antimatroid.

If $X \cap Y \neq \emptyset$ then for every $i \in U$ there exists an i-path $H_1^i \subseteq X$ and $H_2^i \subseteq Y$, because each i-path is a minimal feasible set containing i. By assumption $H_1^i = H_2^i = H^i$. Thus, for all $i \in X \cap Y$, an i-path $H^i \subseteq X \cap Y$, and so $X \cap Y = \bigcup_{i \in X \cap Y} H^i$. Therefore, $X \cap Y \in \mathcal{S}$, since every antimatroid is closed under union. Hence, $(U, \mathcal{S})$ is a poset antimatroid. □

Lemma 4.3. *Any 2-antimatroid $(U, \mathcal{S})$ has a unique i-path for each $i \in U$.*

Proof. Suppose the opposite. Let $A, B \in \mathcal{S}$ be two different i-paths. Note that $A \nsubseteq B$ and $B \nsubseteq A$, since each i-path is a minimal set containing i.

Consider the set $Z = A \cup B$. From the chain property it follows that there is $b \in B - A$, such that $Z - b \in \mathcal{S}$. On the other hand, there is $a \in A - B$ with $Z - a \in \mathcal{S}$. Since $(A - i) \cup (B - i) = Z - i \in S$, we have that $deg_{in}(Z) \geq 3$. □

Lemmas 4.2 and 4.3 imply the following.

Proposition 4.4. *Any 2-antimatroid is a poset antimatroid.*

Denote $C_k = \{X \in \mathcal{S} : |X| = k\}$ a family of feasible sets of cardinality k.

Definition 4.5. *A lower zigzag is a sequence of feasible sets $P_0, P_1, ..., P_{2m}$ such that any two consecutive sets in the sequence differ by a single element and $P_{2i} \in C_k$, and $P_{2i-1} \in C_{k-1}$ for all $0 \leq i \leq m$.*

In the same way we define an *upper zigzag* in which $P_{2i-1} \in C_{k+1}$.

Each zigzag $P_0, P_1, ..., P_{2m}$ is a path connecting P_0 and P_{2m}, and so the distance on the zigzag $d(P_0, P_{2m}) = 2m$ is always no less than the distance $d_S(P_0, P_{2m})$ on an antimatroid $(U, \mathcal{S})$.

In Figure 6 we can see two sets ($A = \{1,2,3,5\}$ and $B = \{1,3,4,5\}$) that are connected by an unique lower zigzag, such that the distance on the zigzag is 4, while $|A \triangle B| = 2$. Note, that the distance on the upper zigzag is indeed 2. For two sets $X = \{1,2,5\}$ and $Y = \{3,4,5\}$ both distances on the lower zigzag and on the upper zigzag are equal to 6, while $|X \triangle Y| = 4$.

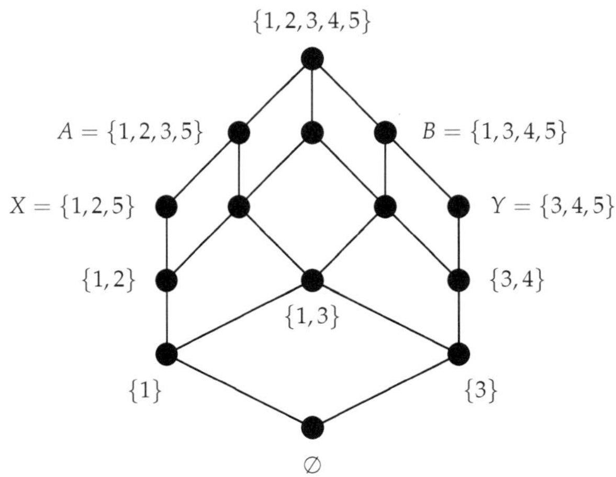

Fig. 6. An antimatroid without distance preserving zigzags.

In order to get the distance on a zigzag equal to the set distance, an antimatroid has to be a poset antimatroid.

Theorem 4.6. *In each poset antimatroid $(U, \mathcal{S})$ every two feasible sets A, B of the same cardinality k can be connected both by a lower and an upper zigzag in such a way that the distance between these sets $d_{\mathcal{S}}(A, B)$ coincides with the distance on the zigzags.*

Proof. We use induction on k. For every pair of one-element feasible sets $\{x\}$ and $\{y\}$ there is a lower zigzag (via $\varnothing$) and an upper zigzag (via $\{x, y\}$) such that the distance between these sets $d_{\mathcal{S}}(\{x\}, \{y\}) = 2$ on the antimatroid coincides with distances on the zigzags.

Assume that the hypothesis of the theorem is correct for all sets $X \in \mathcal{S}$ with $|X| < k$.

Consider two sets $A, B \in C_k$ and let $d_{\mathcal{S}}(A, B) = |A \triangle B| = 2m$. Since $(U, \mathcal{S})$ is a poset antimatroid, the set $A \cap B \in \mathcal{S}$. Hence, by the chain property, there is $a \in A - B$ such that $A - a \in \mathcal{S}$, and $b \in B - A$ with $B - b \in \mathcal{S}$. These two sets belong to C_{k-1}, so there are an upper zigzag $A - a = P_1, P_2, ..., P_{2l-1} = B - b$ connecting $A - a$ with $B - b$ (see Figure 7). Since $d_{\mathcal{S}}(A - a, B - b) = |A \triangle B| - 2 = 2m - 2$, the distance on the upper zigzag between $A - a$ and $B - b$ is $2m - 2$ by the induction hypothesis, i.e., $2l - 1 = 2m - 1$. It is easy to see that neither A nor B belongs to the upper zigzag $A - a = P_1, P_2, ..., P_{2m-1} = B - b$, because otherwise it implies that $d_{\mathcal{S}}(A, B) \leq 2m - 2$. Hence exists a lower zigzag $A = P_0, A - a = P_1, P_2, ..., P_{2m-1} = B - b, P_{2m} = B$ connecting A and B such that the distance on the zigzag between A and B equals $2m$.

Let $P^i = P_{i-1} \cup P_{i+1}$ for each $i = 1, 3, ..., 2m - 1$. All obtained sets are different, because otherwise $d_{\mathcal{S}}(A, B) < 2m$. So there is the upper zigzag by length $2m$ connecting A and B. □

Note that if for a zigzag $P_0, P_1, ..., P_{2m}$ the distance on the zigzag $d(P_0, P_{2m}) = 2m$ is equal to the distance $d_S(P_0, P_{2m}) = |P_0 \triangle P_{2m}|$ then the zigzag preserves the distance for each pair P_i, P_j, i.e., $d_S(P_i, P_j) = d(P_i, P_j) = |j - i|$.

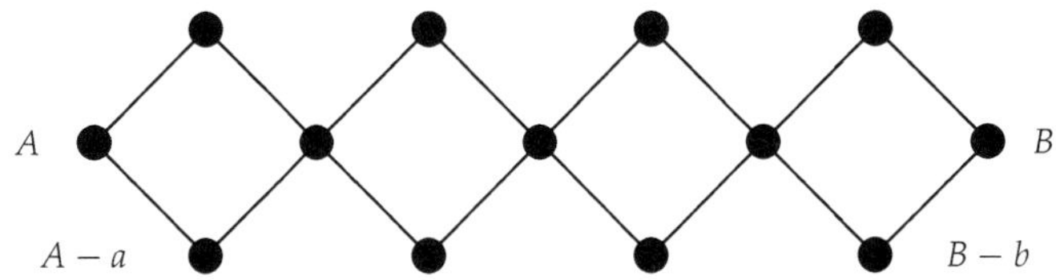

Fig. 7. Zigzags of an antimatroid.

For poset antimatroids there are distance preserving zigzags connecting two given sets, but these zigzags are not obliged to connect all feasible sets of the same cardinality. In Figure 8 we can see that there is a poset antimatroids, for which it is not possible to build two distance preserving zigzags connecting all feasible sets of the same cardinality.

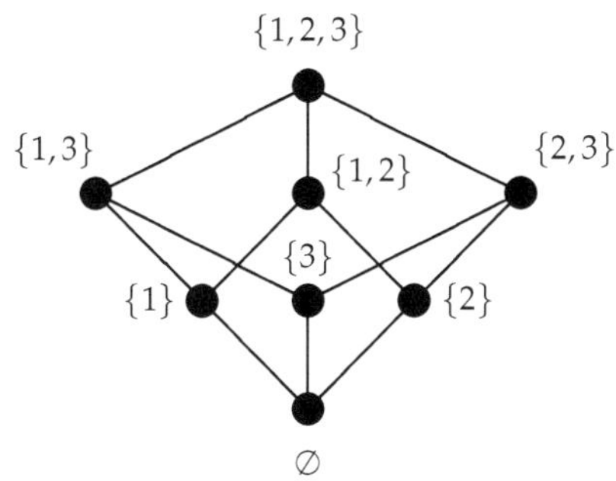

Fig. 8. A poset antimatroid without total zigzags.

It is worth mentioning that in 2-antimatroids all feasible sets of the same cardinality may be connected by one distance preserving zigzag.

Proposition 4.7. *In 2-antimatroid* $(U, \mathcal{S})$ *all feasible sets* C_k *of the same cardinality* k *can be connected both by a lower and an upper zigzag in such a way that the distance between any two sets* $d_{\mathcal{S}}(P_i, P_j)$ *belonging to the same zigzag coincides with distance on the zigzag* $d(P_i, P_j) = |j - i|$.

Proof. We proceed by induction on cardinality k. For one-elements sets it is obvious. Assume that it is correct for all sets $A \in \mathcal{S}$ with $|A| < k$.

Each set from C_k is obtained from some set of cardinality $k - 1$. Since an antimatroid is closed under union and its maximum in-degree and out-degree is 2, the $n + 1$ sets of cardinality $k - 1$ connected by an upper zigzag form n sets from C_k. In addition to these n sets, each of two extreme sets (P_0 and P_{2n}) can form one more set of cardinality k that does not belong to the upper zigzag. Since each out-degree is less than 3 there are no other sets of cardinality k. So, the set C_k is connected by a lower zigzag. Since an antimatroid is closed under union and its maximum in-degree is 2, all feasible sets of the same cardinality k are also connected by an upper zigzag.

Now prove that the distance on the zigzags coincides with the distance on the antimatroid. Since maximum in-degree and out-degree are 2, the obtained lower zigzag is only lower zigzag connecting P_0 and P_{2n}. Then from Theorem 4.6 it follows that it is a distance preserving zigzag. Similarly, we obtain that the upper zigzag preserves the distance as well. □

For each edge $(A, B) \in \mathcal{S}$ there exists a single element $c \in B$ such that $A = B - c$, and so we can label each edge by such element. Then, each 2-antimatroid consists of quadrilaterals with equal labels on opposite pairs of edges, since if it contains the vertices $X, X \cup a, X \cup b$ for some $X \in \mathcal{S}$, and $a, b \in U$, it also contains $X \cup \{a, b\}$. This property, called by $\cup$-coloring, was invented in (Felsner & Knauer, 2009) as the characterization of join-distributive lattices.

Proposition 4.8. *There exists a labeling of edges of a 2-antimatroid by two labels x or y such that opposite pairs of edges in each quadrilateral have equal labels.*

Proof. To obtain such labeling we consequently scan a 2-antimatroid by layers C_k beginning from the empty set ($k = 0$). The first zigzag of edges we mark by two labels x and y in turn, beginning from x or from y arbitrary. From the Proposition 4.7 follows that the next zigzag can be marked alternate by two labels (x, y) in such a way that the opposite pairs of edges in each quadrilateral have equal labels (see Figure 9).

If we reach the layer C_k with one element, the next zigzag is labeled alternate by two labels without dependence on the previous layers. □

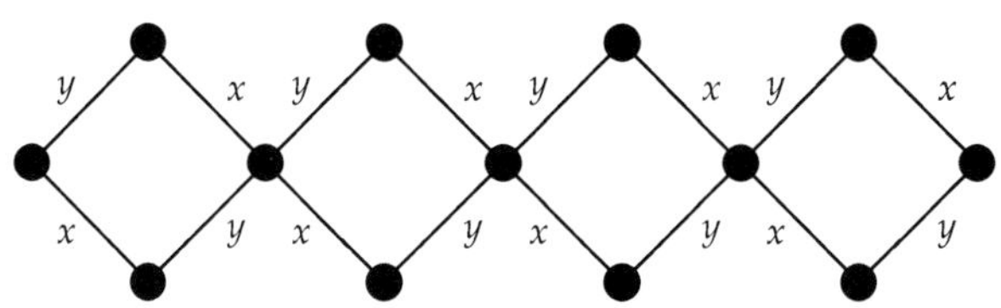

Fig. 9. A zigzag labeling.

It follows from accessibility that for each $A \in \mathcal{S}$ there is a shortest path connecting A with $\emptyset$. The length of such path is equal to the cardinality of A. Let $M(A)$ be a multiset containing all labels on this shortest path. Obviously, $M(A) \in \mathbb{Z}^2$. It is possible that there are some shortest paths between A and $\emptyset$. Prove that all such paths result in the same multiset.

Lemma 4.9. *In every 2-antimatroid $(U, \mathcal{S})$ for each $A \in \mathcal{S}$ all shortest paths connecting A with $\emptyset$ forms the same multiset $M(A)$.*

Proof. We use induction on cardinality k. For one-elements sets it is obviously. Assume it is correct for all sets $A \in \mathcal{S}$ with $|A| < k$. Consider $Y \in C_k$. If Y is obtained from only one set of cardinality $k - 1$, then $M(Y)$ is unique. If $Y = A \cup a = B \cup b$, then there is $X = A \cap B \in \mathcal{S}$ such that $A = X \cup b$ and $B = X \cup a$, since every 2-antimatroid is a poset antimatroid. Let a label of $(X, X \cup b)$ be x, and a label of $(X, X \cup a)$ be y. Thus $M(A) = M(X) \cup x$ and $M(B) = M(X) \cup y$, and so $M(Y) = M(X) \cup \{x, y\}$. Therefore, by induction hypothesis, all shortest path connecting Y with $\emptyset$ forms the same $M(Y)$. □

Proposition 4.10. *In every 2-antimatroid $(U, \mathcal{S})$ the mapping $M : (U, \mathcal{S}) \rightarrow \mathbb{Z}^2$, where each $A \in \mathcal{S}$ corresponds to $M(A)$, is an isometry.*

Proof. We have to prove that for all $A, B \in \mathcal{S}$ the distance $d_{\mathcal{S}}(A, B)$ on the antimatroid $(U, \mathcal{S})$ is equal to the distance $||M(A) - M(B)||_1$ on $\mathbb{Z}^2$, i.e., it holds

$$|A \triangle B| = |M(A) \triangle M(B)|.$$

If $A \subseteq B$, then there is a shortest path connecting B with $\emptyset$ via A, and so $|A \triangle B| = |B - A| = |M(B) - M(A)| = |M(A) \triangle M(B)|$.

Consider two incomparable sets $A, B \in \mathcal{S}$. Since a 2-antimatroid is a poset antimatroid, $A \cap B \in \mathcal{S}$. Then there are a shortest path P_A connecting A with $\emptyset$ via $A \cap B$, and a shortest path P_B connecting B with $\emptyset$ via $A \cap B$. Since $|A \triangle B| = |A - A \cap B| + |B - A \cap B|$, remain to prove that the part of P_A from A till $A \cap B$ is labeled by only one label (for example x) and the part of P_B from B till $A \cap B$ is labeled by only one but another label (y).

Indeed, from $A \cap B$ go out two different edges marked by two different labels, where one belongs to P_A and the second belongs to P_B. Let the label of the first edge was x and the label of the second edge was y. Denote obtained sets as A_1 and B_1. Note that $A_1 = (A \cap B) \cup a$ and $B_1 = (A \cap B) \cup b$, where $a \in A - B$ and $b \in B - A$. If $A_1 \neq A$ then from A_1 go out two edges. The first edge $(A_1, A_1 \cup b)$ is labeled by y and does not belong to P_A since $b \in B - A$. The second edge (A_1, A_2) is labeled by x and belongs to P_A. The same is correct for each set on path P_A from A till $A \cap B$. So the part of P_A from A till $A \cap B$ is labeled by label x only. By the same way we obtain that the part of P_B from B till $A \cap B$ is labeled by y only. □

Thus we have the following.

Theorem 4.11. *The poly-dimension of a 2-antimatroid is two.*

5. Open problems

It is clear that the poly-dimension of a d-antimatroid is at least d.

Conjecture 5.1. *The poly-dimension of an antimatroid equals d if and only if it is a d-antimatroid.*

6. References

Algaba, E.; Bilbao, J.M.; van den Brink, R. & Jimenez-Losada A. (2004). Cooperative Games on Antimatroids. *Discrete Mathematics*, Vol.282, 1-15.

Algaba, E.; Bilbao, J.M. & Slikker, M. (2010). A Value for Games Restricted by Augmenting Systems. *SIAM J. Discrete Mathematics*, Vol.24, No.3, 992-1010

Bilbao, J.M. (2003). Cooperative Games under Augmenting Systems. *SIAM J. Discrete Mathematics*, Vol.17, No.1, 122-133.

Björner, A.; Lovász, L. & Shor, P.R. (1991). Chip-firing Games on Graphs. *European Journal of Combinatorics*, Vol.12, 283-291.

Björner, A. & Ziegler, G.M. (1992). Introduction to Greedoids, In: *Matroid applications*, N. White, (Ed.), Cambridge Univ.Press, Cambridge, UK.

Boley, M; Horváth,T; Poigné,A & Wrobel,S. (2010). Listing Closed Sets of Strongly Accessible Set Systems with Applications to Data Mining. *Theoretical Computer Science - TCS* , Vol. 411, No. 3, 691-700.

Boyd, E.A. & Faigle, U. (1990). An Algorithmic Characterization of Antimatroids. *Discrete Applied Mathematics*, Vol.28, 197-205.

Cosyn, E. & Uzun, H.B. (2009). Note on Two Necessary and Sufficient Axioms for a Well-graded Knowledge Space. *Journal of Mathematical Psychology*, Vol.53, No.1, 40-42.

Dilworth, R.P. (1940). Lattices with Unique Irreducible Decomposition. *Ann. of Mathematics*, Vol.41, 771-777.

Djokovic, D.Z. (1973). Distance Preserving Subgraphs of Hypercubes. *J. Combin. Theory Ser.B*, Vol.14, 263-267.

Doignon, J.-P. & Falmagne, J.-Cl. (1997). Well-graded Families of Relations. *Discrete Mathematics*, Vol.173, 35–44.

Eppstein, D. (2005). The Lattice Dimension of a Graph. *European Journal of Combinatorics*, Vol.26, 585-592.

Eppstein, D. (2008). Upright-Quad Drawing of st-Planar Learning Spaces. *Journal of Graph Algorithms and Applications*, Vol.12, No.1, 51-72.

Eppstein, D.; Falmagne, J.-Cl. & Ovchinnikov, S. (2008). *Media Theory: Interdisciplinary Applied Mathematics*, Springer-Verlag, Berlin.

Falmagne, J.-Cl. & Doignon, J.-P., (2011). *Learning Spaces: Interdisciplinary Applied Mathematics*, Springer-Verlag, Berlin.

Felsner, S. & Knauer, K. (2009). ULD-Lattices and Δ-Bondes. *Combinatorics, Probability and Computing*, Vol.18, No.5, 707-724.

Glasserman, P. & Yao, D.D. (1994). *Monotone Structure in Discrete Event Systems*, Wiley Inter-Science, Series in Probability and Mathematical Statistics.

Grabisch, M. (2009). The Core of Games on Ordered Structures and Graphs. *4OR: A Quarterly Journal of Operations Research*, Vol.7, No.3, 207-238.

Graham, R.L. & Pollak, H.O. (1971). On the Addressing Problem for Loop Switching. *Bell System Technical Journal*, Vol.50, 2495-2519.

Honda, A. & Grabisch, M. (2008). An Axiomatization of Entropy of Capacities on Set Systems, *European Journal of Operational Research*, Vol.190 , 526-538.

Kempner, Y. & Levit, V.E. (2003). Correspondence between Two Antimatroid Algorithmic Characterizations. *The Electronic Journal of Combinatorics*, Vol.10.

Kempner, Y. & Levit, V.E. (2007). A Geometric Characterization of Poly-antimatroids, *ENDM (Electronic Notes in Discrete Mathematics)*, Vol.28, 357-364.

Kempner, Y. & Muchnik, I. (2003). Clustering on Antimatroids and Convex Geometries, *WSEAS Transactions on Mathematics*, Vol.2, No.1, 54-59.

Korte, B.; Lovász, L. & R. Schrader, R. (1991). *Greedoids*, Springer-Verlag, New York/Berlin.

Magnien, C.; Phan, H.D. & Vuillon, L. (2001). Characterization of Lattices Induced by (extended) Chip Firing Games, *Discrete Mathematics and Theoretical Computer Science Proceedings AA (DM-CCG)*, 229-244.

Monjardet, B. (2003). The Presence of Lattice Theory in Discrete Problems of Mathematical Social Sciences. Why, *Math. Social Science*, Vol.46, 103-144.

Nakamura, M. (2005). Characterization of Polygreedoids and Poly-antimatroids by Greedy Algorithms, *Oper.Res. Lett.*, Vol.33, No. 4, 389-394.

Ovchinnikov, S. (2008). Partial cubes: Structures, Characterizations, and Constructions, *Discrete Mathmatics*, Vol.308, 5597–5621.

5

A Semi-Supervised Clustering Method Based on Graph Contraction and Spectral Graph Theory

Tetsuya Yoshida
Graduate School of Information Science and Technology, Hokkaido University
Japan

1. Introduction

Semi-supervised learning is a machine learning framework where learning from data is conducted by utilizing a small amount of labeled data as well as a large amount of unlabeled data (Chapelle et al., 2006). It has been intensively studied in data mining and machine learning communities recently. One of the reasons is that, it can alleviate the time-consuming effort to collect "ground truth" labeled data while sustaining relatively high performance by exploiting a large amount of unlabeled data. (Blum & Mitchell, 1998) showed the PAC learnability of semi-supervised learning, especially in classification problem.

On the other hand, data clustering, also called unsupervised learning, is a method of creating groups of objects, or clusters, in such a way that objects in one cluster are very similar and objects in different clusters are quite distinct. Clustering is one of the most frequently performed analysis (Jain et al., 1999). For example, in web activity logs, clusters can indicate navigation patterns of different user groups. Another direct application could be clustering of gene expression data so that genes within a same group evinces similar behavior.

Although labeled data is not required in clustering, sometimes constraints on data assignment might be available as domain knowledge about the data to be clustered. In such a situation, it is desirable to utilize the available constraints as semi-supervised information and to improve the performance of clustering (Basu et al., 2008). By regarding constraints on data assignment as supervised information, various research efforts have been conducted on semi-supervised clustering (Basu et al., 2004; 2008; Li et al., 2008; Tang et al., 2007; Xing et al., 2003). Although various forms of constraints can be considered, based on the previous work (Li et al., 2008; Tang et al., 2007; Wagstaff et al., 2001; Xing et al., 2003), we deal with the following two kinds of pairwise constraints in this paper: must-link constraints and cannot-link constraints. In this chapter, the former is also called as must-links, and the latter as cannot-links.

When similarities among data instances are specified, by connecting each pair of instances with an edge with the corresponding similarity, the entire data instances can be represented as an edge-weighted graph. In this chapter we present our semi-supervised clustering method based on graph contraction in general graph theory and graph Laplacian in spectral graph theory. Graph representation enables to deal with two kinds of pairwise constraints as well as pairwise similarities over a unified representation. Then, the graph is modified by contraction in graph theory (Diestel, 2006) and graph Laplacian in spectral graph theory (Chung, 1997; von Luxburg, 2007) to reflect the pairwise constraints.

Representing the relations (both pairwise constraints and similarities) among instances as an edge-weighted graph and modifying the graph structure based on the specified constraints enable to enhancing semi-supervised clustering. In our approach, the entire data instances are projected onto a subspace which is constructed with respect to the modified graph structure, and clustering is conducted over the projected data representation of instances. Although our approach utilizes graph Laplacian as in (Belkin & Niyogi, 2002), our approach differs from previous ones since pairwise constraints for semi-supervised clustering are also utilized in our approach for constructing the projected data representation (Yoshida, 2010; Yoshida & Okatani, 2010).

We report the performance evaluation of our approach, and compare it with other state-of-the-art semi-supervised clustering methods in terms of accuracy and running time. Extensive experiments are conducted over real-world datasets. The results are encouraging and indicate the effectiveness of our approach. Especially, our approach can leverage small amount of pairwise constraints to increase the performance. We believe that this is a good property in the semi-supervised learning setting.

The rest of this chapter is organized as follows. Section 2 explains the framework of semi-supervised clustering. Section 3 explains the details of our approach for clustering under pairwise constraints. Section 4 reports the performance evaluation over various document datasets. Section 5 discusses the effectiveness of our approach. Section 6 summarizes our contributions and suggests future directions.

2. Semi-supervised clustering

2.1 Preliminaries

Let $\boldsymbol{X}$ be a set of instances. For a set $\boldsymbol{X}$, $|\boldsymbol{X}|$ represents its cardinality.

A graph $G = (\boldsymbol{V}, \boldsymbol{E})$ consists of a finite set of vertices $\boldsymbol{V}$, a set of edges $\boldsymbol{E}$ over $\boldsymbol{V} \times \boldsymbol{V}$. The set $\boldsymbol{E}$ can be interpreted as representing a binary relation over $\boldsymbol{V}$. A pair of vertices (v_i, v_j) is in the binary relation defined by a graph $G = (\boldsymbol{V}, \boldsymbol{E})$ if and only if the pair $(v_i, v_j) \in \boldsymbol{E}$.

An edge-weighted graph $G = (\boldsymbol{V}, \boldsymbol{E}, \boldsymbol{W})$ is defined as a graph $G = (\boldsymbol{V}, \boldsymbol{E})$ with a weight on each edge in $\boldsymbol{E}$. When $|\boldsymbol{V}| = n$, i.e., the number of vertices in a graph is n, the weights in $\boldsymbol{W}$ can be represented as an n by n matrix $\mathbf{W}$ [1], where w_{ij} in $\mathbf{W}$ stands for the weight on the edge for the pair $(v_i, v_j) \in \boldsymbol{E}$. $\mathbf{W}_{ij}$ also stands for the element w_{ij} in the matrix. We set $w_{ij} = 0$ for pairs $(v_i, v_j) \notin \boldsymbol{E}$. In addition, we assume that $G = (\boldsymbol{V}, \boldsymbol{E}, \boldsymbol{W})$ is an undirected, simple graph without self-loops. Thus, the weight matrix $\mathbf{W}$ is symmetric and its diagonal elements are zeros.

2.2 Clustering

In general, clustering methods can be divided into two approaches: hierarchical methods and partitioning methods. (Jain et al., 1999). Hierarchical methods construct a cluster hierarchy, or a tree of clusters (called a dendrogram), whose leaves are the data points and whose internal nodes represent nested clusters of various sizes (Guha et al., 1998). Hierarchical methods can be further subdivided into *agglomerative* and *divisive* ones. On the other hand, partitioning methods return a single partition of the entire data under a fixed parameters (number of clusters, thresholds, etc.). Each cluster can be represented by its centroid

[1] A bold italic symbol $\boldsymbol{W}$ denotes a set, while a bold symbol $\mathbf{W}$ denotes a matrix.

(k-means algorithms (Hartigan & Wong, 1979)), or by one of its instances located near its center (k-medoid algorithms (Ng & Han, 2002)). For a recent overview of various clustering methods, please refer to (Jain et al., 1999).

When pairwise similarities among instances are specified, the entire data can be represented as an edge-weighted graph. Various graph-theoretic clustering approaches have been proposed to find subsets of vertices in a graph based on the edges among the vertices. Several methods utilizes graph coloring techniques (Guënoche et al., 1991; Yoshida & Ogino, 2011). Other methods are based on the flow or cut in graph, such as spectral clustering (von Luxburg, 2007). Graph-based spectral approach is also utilized in information-theoretic clustering (Yoshida, 2011).

2.3 Semi-supervised clustering

When the auxiliary or side information for data assignment in clustering is represented as a set of constraints, the *semi-supervised clustering* problem is (informally) described as follows.

Problem 1 (Semi-Supervised Clustering). *For a given set of data* $\boldsymbol{X}$ *and specified constraints, find a partition (a set of clusters)* $\boldsymbol{T} = \{t_1, \ldots, t_k\}$ *which satisfies the specified constraints.*

There can be various forms of constraints. Based on the previous work (Li et al., 2008; Tang et al., 2007; Wagstaff et al., 2001; Xing et al., 2003), we consider the following two kinds of constraints defined in (Wagstaff et al., 2001):

Definition 1 (Pairwise Constraints). *For a given data instances* $\boldsymbol{X}$ *and a partition (a set of clusters)* $\boldsymbol{C} = \{c_1, \ldots, c_k\}$*, must-link constraints* $\boldsymbol{C}_{ML}$ *and cannot-link constraints* $\boldsymbol{C}_{CL}$ *are sets of pairs such that:*

$$\exists (x_i, x_j) \in \boldsymbol{C}_{ML} \Rightarrow \exists c \in \boldsymbol{C}, (x_i \in c \wedge x_j \in c) \tag{1}$$

$$\exists (x_i, x_j) \in \boldsymbol{C}_{ML} \Rightarrow \exists c_a, c_b \in \boldsymbol{C}, c_a \neq c_b, (x_i \in c_a \wedge x_j \in c_b) \tag{2}$$

Intuitively, must-link constraints (also called must-links in this paper) specifies the pairs of instances in the same cluster, and cannot-link constraints (also called cannot-links) specifies the pairs of instances in different clusters.

3. Graph-based semi-supervised clustering

3.1 A graph-based approach

By assuming that some similarity measure for the pairs of instances is specified, we have proposed a graph-based approach for constrained clustering problem (Yoshida, 2010; Yoshida & Okatani, 2010). Based on the similarities, the entire data instances $\boldsymbol{X}$ can be represented as an edge-weighted graph $G = (\boldsymbol{V}, \boldsymbol{E}, \boldsymbol{W})$ where w_{ij} represents the similarity between a pair (x_i, x_j). In our approach, each data instance $x \in \boldsymbol{X}$ corresponds to a vertex $v \in V$ in G. Thus, we abuse the symbol $\boldsymbol{X}$ to denote the set of vertices in G in the rest of the paper. Also, we assume that all w_{ij} is non-negative.

Definition 1 specifies two kinds of constraints. For must-link constraints, our approach utilizes a method based on graph contraction in general graph theory (Diestel, 2006) and treat it as hard constraints (Sections 3.2); for cannot-link constraints, our approach utilizes a method based on graph Laplacian in spectral graph theory (Chung, 1997; von Luxburg, 2007) and

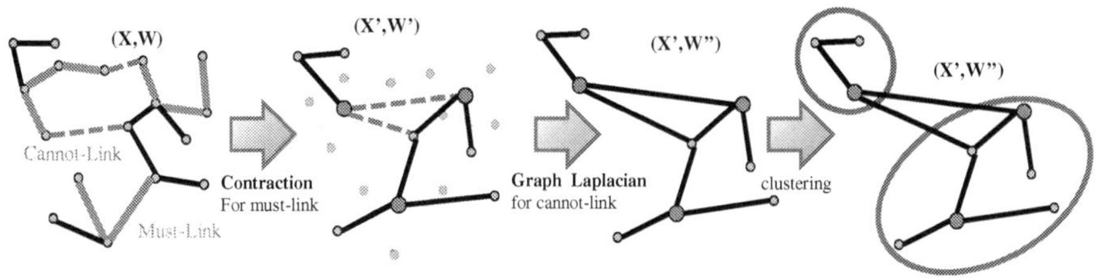

Fig. 1. Overview of our approach.

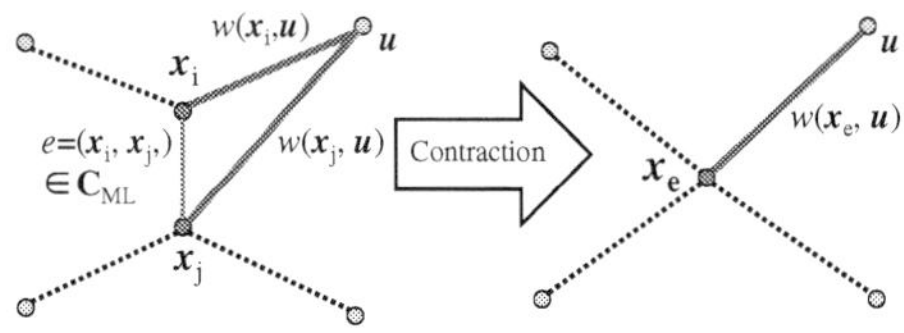

Fig. 2. Contraction for must-link constraints.

treat them as soft constraints under the optimization framework (Section 3.3). The overview of our approach is illustrated in Fig. 1.

3.2 Graph contraction for must-link constraints

When must-link constraints are treated as hard constraints, the transitive law holds among the constraints. This means that, for any two pairs (x_i, x_j) and $(x_j, x_l) \in C_{ML}$, x_i and x_l should also be in the same cluster (however, the cluster label is not known). In order to enforce the transitive law in must-links, we utilize graph contraction in general graph theory (Diestel, 2006) and modify the graph G for a data set $\mathbf{X}$ based on the specified must-links.

Definition 2 (Contraction). *Let e=(x_i, x_j) be an edge of a graph G = $(\mathbf{X}, E)$. define By G/e, we denote the graph $(\mathbf{X}',E')$ obtained from G by contracting the edge e into a new vertex x_e, where:*

$$\mathbf{X}' = (\mathbf{X} \backslash \{x_i, x_j\}) \cup \{x_e\} \tag{3}$$

$$\begin{aligned} E' &= \{(u,v) \in E | \{u,v\} \cap \{x_i, x_j\} = \phi\} \\ &\cup \{(x_e, u) | (x_i, u) \in E \backslash \{e\} \; or \; (x_j, u) \in E \backslash \{e\}\} \end{aligned} \tag{4}$$

G/e stands for the graph obtained from G by *contracting* an edge e into a new vertex x_e. The created vertex x_e becomes adjacent to all the former neighbors of x_i and x_j.

By contracting an edge e into a new vertex x_e, the newly created vertex x_e becomes adjacent to all the former neighbors of x_i and x_j. Repeated application of contraction for all the edges (pairs of instance) for must-links guarantees that the transitive law in must-links is sustained in the cluster assignment.

As described above, the entire dataset $\mathbf{X}$ is represented as an edge-weighted graph G in our approach. Thus, after contracting an edge e=$(x_i, x_j) \in C_{ML}$ into the newly created vertex x_e, it is necessary to define the weights in the contracted graph G/e. The weights in G represent the similarities among vertices. The original similarities should at least be sustained after contracting an edge in C_{ML}, since must-link constraints are for enforcing the similarities, not for reducing.

Based on the above observation, we define the weights in the contracted graph G/e as:

$$w(x_e,u)' = \max(w(x_i,u), w(x_j,u)) \quad if \ (x_i,u) \in \boldsymbol{E} \ or (x_j,u) \in \boldsymbol{E} \tag{5}$$

$$w(u,v)' = w(u,v) \quad otherwise \tag{6}$$

where $w(\cdot,\cdot)'$ stands for the weight in the contracted graph G/e. In eq.(5), the function max realizes the above requirement, and guarantees the non-decreasing properties of similarities (weights) after contraction of an edge. On the other hand, the original weight is preserved in eq.(6).

For each pair of edges in must-links, we apply graph contraction and define weights in the contracted graph based on eq.(5) and eq.(6). This results in modifying the original graph G into another graph $G^{'} = (\boldsymbol{X}^{'}, \boldsymbol{E}^{'}, \boldsymbol{W}^{'})$ (as illustrated in Fig. 2). The number of vertices in the contracted graph G' is denoted as $n^{'} = |\boldsymbol{X}^{'}|$. Note that the originally specified cannot-links also need to be modified during graph contraction with respect to must-links. The updated cannot-links over the created graph G' is denoted as $\boldsymbol{C}'_{CL}$.

3.3 Graph Laplacian for cannot-link constraints

3.3.1 Spectral clustering

The objective of clustering is to assign similar instances to the same cluster and dissimilar ones to different clusters. To realize this, we utilize spectral clustering, which is based on the minimum cut of a graph. In spectral clustering (Ng et al., 2001; von Luxburg, 2007), data clustering is realized by seeking a function f: $\boldsymbol{X} \rightarrow \mathcal{R}$ over the dataset $\boldsymbol{X}$ such that the learned function assigns similar values for similar instances and vice versa. The values assigned for the entire dataset can be represented as a vector. By denoting the assigned value for the i-th data instance as f_i, data clustering can be formalized as an optimization problem to find the vector f which minimizes the following objective function :

$$J_0 = \boldsymbol{f}^t \mathbf{L} \boldsymbol{f} \tag{7}$$

where $\boldsymbol{f}^t$ is a transpose of vector $\boldsymbol{f}$, and the matrix $\mathbf{L}$ is defined as:

$$\mathbf{D} = diag(d_1, \ldots, d_n) \quad (d_i = \sum_{j=1}^{n} w_{ij}) \tag{8}$$

$$\mathbf{L} = \mathbf{D} - \mathbf{W} \tag{9}$$

where $diag()$ in eq.(8) represents a diagonal matrix with the specified diagonal elements. The matrix $\mathbf{D}$ in eq.(8) is the degree matrix of a graph, and is calculated based on the weights in the graph. The matrix $\mathbf{L}$ in eq.(9) is called graph Laplacian (Chung, 1997; Ng et al., 2001; von Luxburg, 2007). Some clustering method, such as kmeans (Hartigan & Wong, 1979) or spherical kmeans (skmeans) (Dhillon & Modha, 2001)[2], is applied to the constructed data representation of instances (Ng et al., 2001; von Luxburg, 2007).

3.3.2 Graph Laplacian for cannot-link constraints

We utilized the framework of spectral clustering in Section 3.3.1. Furthermore, to reflect cannot-link constraints in the clustering process, we formalize the clustering under constraints

[2] skmeans is a standard clustering algorithm for high-dimensional sparse data.

as an optimization problem, and consider the minimization of the following objective function:

$$J = \frac{1}{2}\{\sum_{i,j} w'_{ij}||f_i - f_j||^2 - \lambda \sum_{u,v \in C'_{CL}} w'_{uv}||f_u - f_v||^2\} \tag{10}$$

where i and j sum over the vertices in the contracted graph G', and C'_{CL} stands for the cannot-link constraints over G'. $\lambda \in [0, 1]$ is a hyper-parameter in our approach. The first term corresponds to the smoothness of the assigned values in spectral graph theory, and the second term represents the influence of cannot-links in optimization. Note that by setting $\lambda \in [0, 1]$, the objective function in (10) is guaranteed to be a convex function.

From the above objective function in eq.(10), we can derive the following unnormalized graph Laplacian $\mathbf{L}''$ which incorporates cannot-links as:

$$J = \frac{1}{2}\{\sum_{i,j} w'_{ij}||f_i - f_j||^2 - \lambda \sum_{u,v \in C'_{CL}} w'_{uv}||f_u - f_v||^2\} = \boldsymbol{f}^t \mathbf{L}'' \boldsymbol{f} \tag{11}$$

The matrix $\mathbf{L}''$ is defined based on the following matrices:

$$(\mathbf{C}')_{uv} = \begin{cases} 1 & (x_u, x_v) \in C'_{CL} \\ 0 & \text{otherwise} \end{cases} \tag{12}$$

$$\mathbf{W}^c = \mathbf{C}' \odot \mathbf{W}', \quad \mathbf{W}'' = \mathbf{W}' - \lambda \mathbf{W}^c \tag{13}$$

$$d_i = \sum_{j=1}^{n'} w'_{ij}, \quad d_i^c = \sum_{j=1}^{n'} w_{ij}^c \tag{14}$$

$$\mathbf{D}'' = diag(d''_1, \ldots, d''_{n'}), \quad d''_i = d_i - \lambda d_i^c \tag{15}$$

$$\mathbf{L}'' = \mathbf{D}'' - \mathbf{W}'' \tag{16}$$

where $\odot$ stands for the Hadamard product (element-wise multiplication) of two matrices.

The above process amounts to modifying the representation of the contracted graph G' into another graph G'', with the modified weights $\mathbf{W}''$ in eq.(13). Thus, as illustrated in Fig. 1, our approach modifies the original graph G into the contracted graph G' with must-link constraints, and then into another graph G'' with cannot-link constraints and similarities.

It is known that some form "balancing" among clusters needs to be considered for obtaining meaningful results (von Luxburg, 2007). Based on eq.(14) and eq.(16), we utilize the following normalized objective function:

$$J_{sym} = \sum_{i,j} w''_{ij} || \frac{f_i}{\sqrt{d''_i}} - \frac{f_j}{\sqrt{d''_j}} ||^2 \tag{17}$$

over the graph G''. Minimizing J_{sym} in eq.(17) amounts to solving the generalized eigen-problem $\mathbf{L}'' f = \alpha \mathbf{D}'' f$, where α corresponds to an eigenvalue and f corresponds to the generalized eigenvector with the eigenvalue.

Algorithm 1 graph-based semi-supervised clustering (GBSSC)

Require: $G = (\boldsymbol{X}, \boldsymbol{E}, \boldsymbol{W})$; *//an edge-weighted graph*
Require: C_{ML}; *//must-link constraints*
Require: C_{CL}; *//cannot-link constraints*
Require: l; *//the number of generalized eigenvectors*
Require: k; *//the number of clusters*

1: **for** each $e \in C_{ML}$ **do**
2: contract e and create the contracted graph G/e;
3: **end for**
// Let $G^{'} = (\boldsymbol{X}^{'}, \boldsymbol{E}^{'}, \boldsymbol{W}^{'})$ *be the contracted graph.*
4: create $\mathbf{C}^{'}_{uv}, \mathbf{W}^{c}, \mathbf{W}^{''}, \mathbf{D}^{''}$ as eq.(12) $\sim$ eq.(15).
5: $\mathbf{L}^{''}_{sym} = \mathbf{I} - \mathbf{D}^{''-\frac{1}{2}}\mathbf{W}^{''}\mathbf{D}^{''-\frac{1}{2}}$
6: Find l eigenvectors $\mathbf{F} = \{f^1, \ldots, f^l\}$ for $\mathbf{L}^{''}_{sym}$, with the smallest non-zero eigenvalues.
7: Conduct clustering of data which are represented as $\mathbf{F}$ and construct clusters.
8: **return** clusters

Furthermore, the number of generalized eigenvectors can be extended to more than one. In that case, the generalized eigenvectors with positive eigenvalues are selected with ascending order of eigenvalues. The generalized eigenvectors with respect to the modified graph corresponds to the embeeded representation of the whole data instances.

3.4 Algorithm

The graph-based semi-supervised clustering method (called GBSSC) is summarized in Algorithm 1. The contracted graph $G^{'}$ is constructed from lines 1 to 3 based on the specified must-links. Lines 4 to 6 conduct the minimization of J_{sym} in eq.(17), which is represented as the normalized graph Laplacian $\mathbf{L}^{''}_{sym}$ at line 5.

These correspond to the spectral embedding of the entire data instances $\boldsymbol{X}$ onto the subspace spanned by $\mathbf{F} = \{f^1, \ldots, f^l\}$ (Belkin & Niyogi, 2002). Note that pairwise constraints for semi-supervised clustering are also utilized on the construction of the embedded representation in our approach and thus differs from (Belkin & Niyogi, 2002). Some clustering method is applied to the data at line 7 and the constructed clusters are returned. Currently spherical kmeans (skmeans) (Dhillon & Modha, 2001) is utilized at line 7.

4. Evaluations

4.1 Experimental settings

4.1.1 Datasets

Based on the previous work (Dhillon et al., 2003; Tang et al., 2007), we evaluated our approach on 20 Newsgroup dataset (hereafter, called 20NG) [3] and TREC datasets [4]. Clustering of these datasets corresponds to document clustering, and each document is represented in the standard vector space model based on the occurrences of terms. Since the number of terms are

[3] http://people.csail.mit.edu/~jrennie/20Newsgroups/. (20news-18828 was utilized)
[4] http://glaros.dtc.umn.edu/gkhome/cluto/cluto/download

dataset	included groups
Multi5	comp.graphics, rec.motorcycles,rec.sport.baseball, sci.space talk.politics.mideast
Multi10	alt.atheism, comp.sys.mac.hardware,misc.forsale, rec.autos,rec.sport.hockey, sci.crypt,sci.med, sci.electronics,sci.space,talk.politics.guns
Multi15	alt.atheism, comp.graphics, comp.sys.mac.hardware, misc.forsale, rec.autos, rec.motorcycles, rec.sport.baseball, rec.sport.hockey, sci.crypt, sci.electronics, sci.med, sci.space, talk.politics.guns, talk.politics.mideast, talk.politics.misc

Table 1. Datasets from 20 Newsgroup dataset

dataset	#attributes	#classes	#data
hitech	126372	6	2301
reviews	126372	5	4069
sports	126372	7	8580
la1	31372	6	3204
la2	31372	6	3075
la2	31372	6	6279
k1b	21839	6	2340
ohscal	11465	10	11162
fbis	2000	17	2463

Table 2. TREC datasets (original representation)

huge in general, these are high-dimensional sparse datasets. Please note that our approach is generic and not specific to document clustering.

As in (Dhillon et al., 2003; Tang et al., 2007), 50 documents were sampled from each group (cluster) in order to create a sample for one dataset, and 10 samples were created for each dataset. For each sample, we conducted stemming using porter stemmer [5] and MontyTagger [6], removed stop words, and selected 2,000 words with descending order of mutual information (Cover & Thomas, 2006).

For TREC datasets, we utilized 9 datasets in Table 2. We followed the same procedure in 20NG and created 10 samples for each dataset[7]. Since these datasets are already preprocessed and represented as count data, we did not conduct stemming or tagging.

4.1.2 Evaluation measures

For each dataset, the cluster assignment was evaluated with respect to Normalized Mutual Information (*NMI*) (Strehl & Ghosh, 2002; Tang et al., 2007). Let C, $\hat{C}$ stand for random variables over the true and assigned clusters. *NMI* is defined as

$$NMI = \frac{I(\hat{C}; C)}{(H(\hat{C}) + H(C))/2} \tag{18}$$

[5] http://www.tartarus.org/˜martin/PorterStemmer
[6] http://web.media.mit.edu/˜hugo/montytagger
[7] On fbis, 35 data were sampled for each class.

where $H(\cdot)$ is Shannon Entropy, and $I(\cdot;\cdot)$ is Mutual Information among the random variables C and $\hat{C}$. *NMI* corresponds to the accuracy of assignment. Thus, the larger *NMI* is, the better the cluster assignment is with respect to the "ground-truth" labels in each dataset.

All the compared methods first construct the representation for clustering and then apply some clustering method (e.g., skmeans). The running time (CPU time in second) for representation construction was measured on a computer with Debian/GNU Linux, Intel Xeon W5590, 36 GB memory. All the methods were implemented with R language and R packages.

4.1.3 Comparison

We compared our approach with SCREEN (Tang et al., 2007) and PCP (Li et al., 2008) (details are described in Section 5.2). Since all the compared methods are partitioning based clustering methods, we assume that the number of clusters k in each dataset is available.

SCREEN (Tang et al., 2007) conducts semi-supervised clustering by projecting the given data instances onto the subspace where the covariance with respect to the given data representation is maximized. To realize this, the covariance matrix with respect to the original data representation is constructed and their eigenvectors are utilized for projection. For high-dimensional data such as documents, this process is rather expensive, since the number of attributes (e.g., terms) gets large. To alleviate this problem, PCA (Principal Component Analysis) was first utilized as pre-processing to reduce the number of dimension in the data representation. We followed the same process in (Tang et al., 2007) and pre-processed data by PCA using 100 eigenvectors, and SCREEN was applied to the pre-processed data as in (Tang et al., 2007).

PCP (Li et al., 2008) first conducts metric learning based on the semi-definite programming, and then kernel k-means clustering is conducted over the learned metric. Some package (e.g. Csdp) is utilized to solve the semi-definite programming based on the specified pairwise constraints and similarities.

4.1.4 Parameters

The parameters under the pairwise constraints in Definition 1 are:

1) the number of constraints

2) the pairs of instances for constraints

As for **2)**, pairs of instances were randomly sampled from each dataset to generate the constraints. Thus, the main parameter is **1)**, the number of constraints, for must-links and cannot-links. We set the numbers of these two types of constrains to be the same, and varied the number of constraints.

Each data instance x in a dataset was normalized such that $x^t x = 1$, and Euclidian distance was utilized for SCREEN as in (Tang et al., 2007). With this normalization, cosine similarity, which is widely utilized as the standard similarity measure in document processing, was utilized for GBSSC and PCP, and the initial edge-weighted graph for each dataset was constructed with the similarities. The number of generalized eigenvectors l was set to the number of clusters k. In addition, following the procedure in (Li et al., 2008), m-nearest neighbor graph was constructed for PCP (m was set to 10 in the experiment). The hyper-parameter λ in eq.(10) was set to 0.5, since GBSSC is robust to this value as reported in Section 4.2.

4.1.5 Evaluation procedure

For each number of constraints, the pairwise constraints (must-links and cannot-links) were generated randomly based on the ground-truth labels in the datasets, and clustering was conducted with the generated constraints. Clustering with the same number of constraints was repeated 10 times with different initial configuration in clustering. In addition, the above process was also repeated 10 times for each number of constraints. Thus, for each dataset and the number of constraints, 100 runs were conducted. Furthermore, this process was repeated over 10 samples for each dataset. Thus, the average of 1,000 runs is reported for each dataset.

4.2 Evaluation of graph-based approach

Our approach modifies the data representation in a dataset according to the specified constraints. Especially, the similarities among instances (weights in a graph) are modified. The other possible approach would be to set the weights (similarities) as:

i) each pair $(x_i, x_j) \in C_{ML}$ to the maximum similarity
ii) each pair $(x_i, x_j) \in C_{CL}$ to the minimum similarity

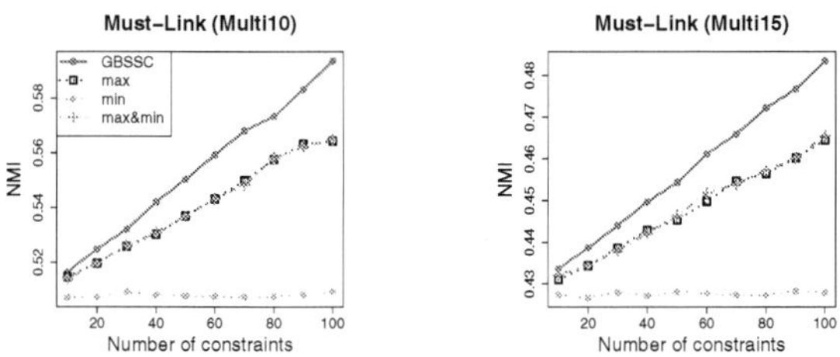

Fig. 3. Weight medication comparison.

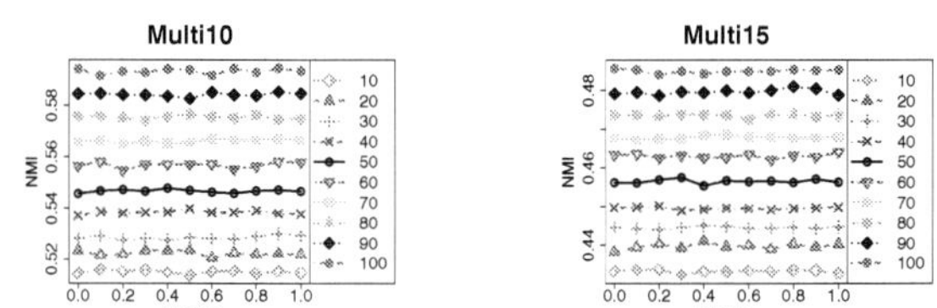

Fig. 4. Influence of λ.

First, we compared our approach for the handling of must-links in Section 3.2 with the above approaches on Multi10 and Multi15 datasets. The results are summarized in Fig. 3. In Fig. 3, horizontal axis corresponds to the number of constraints; vertical one corresponds to *NMI*. In the legend, max (black lines with boxes) stands for i), min (blue dotted lines with circles) stands for ii), and max&min (green dashed lines with crosses) stands for when both i) and ii) are employed. GBSSC (red solid lines with circles) stands for our approach.

The results in Fig. 3 show that GBSSC outperformed others and that it is effective in terms of the weight modification in a graph. One of the reasons for the results in Fig. 3 is that, when i) (max) is utilized, only the instances connected with must-links are affected, and thus they tend to be collected into a smaller "isolated" cluster. Creating rather small clusters makes the performance degraded. On the other hand, in our approach, instances adjacent to must-links are also affected via contraction.

As for ii) (min), the instances connected with cannot-links are by definition dissimilar with each other and their weights would be small in the original representation. Thus, setting the weights over must-links to the minimal value in the dataset does not affect the overall performance so much. These are illustrated in Fig. 5 and Fig. 6.

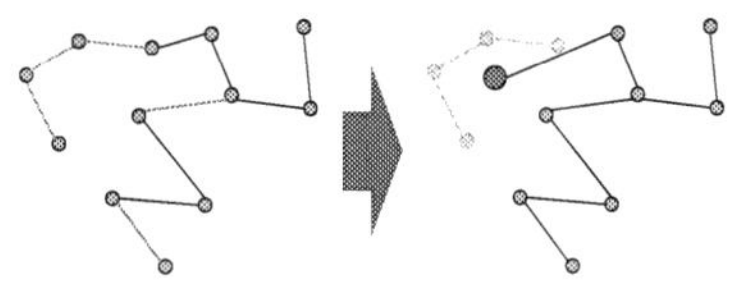

Fig. 5. Contraction of must-link constraints.

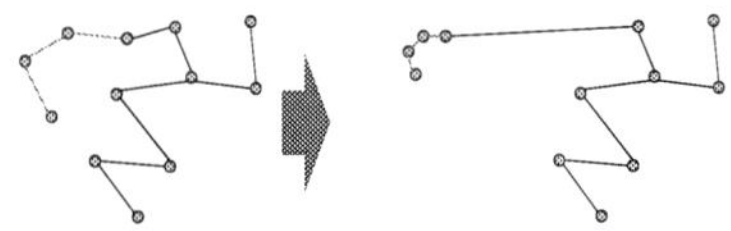

Fig. 6. Weight modification of must-link constraints.

Next, we evaluated the handling of cannot-links in Section 3.3. We varied the value of hyper-parameter λ in eq.(10) and analyzed its influence. The results are summarized in Fig. 4. In Fig. 4, horizontal axis corresponds to the value of λ, and the values in the legend corresponds to the number of pairwise constraints (e.g., 10 corresponds to the situation where the number of pairwise constraints are 10). The performance of GBSSC was not so much affected by the value of λ. Thus, our approach can be said as relatively robust with respect to this parameter. In addition, the accuracy (*NMI*) increased *monotonically* as the number of constraints increased. Thus, it can be concluded that GBSSC reflects the pairwise constraints and improves the performance based on semi-supervised information.

4.3 Evaluation on real world datasets

We report the comparison of our approach with other compared methods. In the reported figures, horizontal axis corresponds to the number of constraints; vertical one corresponds to either *NMI* or CPU time (in sec.).

In the legend in the figures, red lines correspond to our GBSSC, black dotted lines to SCREEN, green lines to PCP. Also, +PCA stands for the case where the dataset was first pre-processed by PCA (using 100 eigenvectors as in (Tang et al., 2007)) and then the corresponding method was applied. GBSSC+PCP (with purple lines) corresponds to the situation where must-links were handled by contraction in Section 3.2 and cannot-links by PCP.

4.3.1 20 Newsgroup datasets

The results for 20NG dataset are summarized in Figs. 7. These are the average of 10 datasets for each set of groups (i.e., average of 1000 runs). The results indicate that our approach outperformed other methods with respect to *NMI* (Fig. 7) when l=k[8]. For Multi5, although the

[8] The number of generalized eigenvectors l was set to the number of clusters k. Note that we did not conduct any tuning for the value of l in these experiments. (Tang et al., 2007) reports that SCREEN could be improved by tuning the number of dimensions.

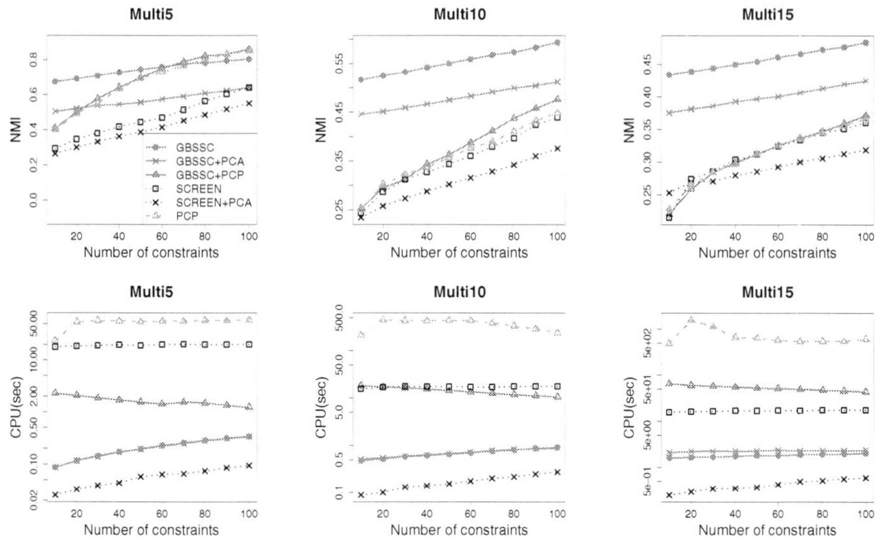

Fig. 7. Results on 20-Newsgroup

performance of PCP got close to that of GBSSC as the number of constraints increased, GBSSC was faster more than two orders of magnitude (100 times faster). Likewise, GBSSC+PCP and PCP were almost the same with respect to *NMI*, but the former was faster with more than one order (10 times faster). Although SCREEN+PCA was two to five times faster than GBSSC, it was inferior with respect to *NMI*. Utilization of PCA as the pre-processing enables this speed-up for SCREEN, in compensation for the accuracy (*NMI*).

Dimensionality reduction with PCA was effective for the speed-up of SCREEN, but it was not for GBSSC. On the other hand, it *deteriorated* their performance with respect to *NMI*. Thus, it is not necessary to utilize pre-processing such as PCA for GBSSC, and still our approach showed better performance.

4.3.2 TREC datasets

The results for TREC datasets are summarized in Fig. 8 and Fig. 9. As shown in Table 2, the number of dimensions (attributes) are huge in TREC datasets. Since calculating the eigenvalues of the covariance matrix with large number of attributes takes too much time, when SCREEN was applied to non-preprocessed data with PCA, it was too slow. Thus, SCREEN was applied only to the pre-processed data in TREC datasets. (shown as SCREEN+PCA).

On the whole, the results were quite similar to those in 20NG. Our approach outperformed SCREEN (in TREC datasets, SCREEN+PCA) with respect to *NMI*. It also outperformed PCP in most datasets, however, as the number of constraints increased, the latter showed better performance for review and sports datasets. In addition, PCP seems to improve the performance as the number of constraints increase. When GBSSC is utilized with PCP

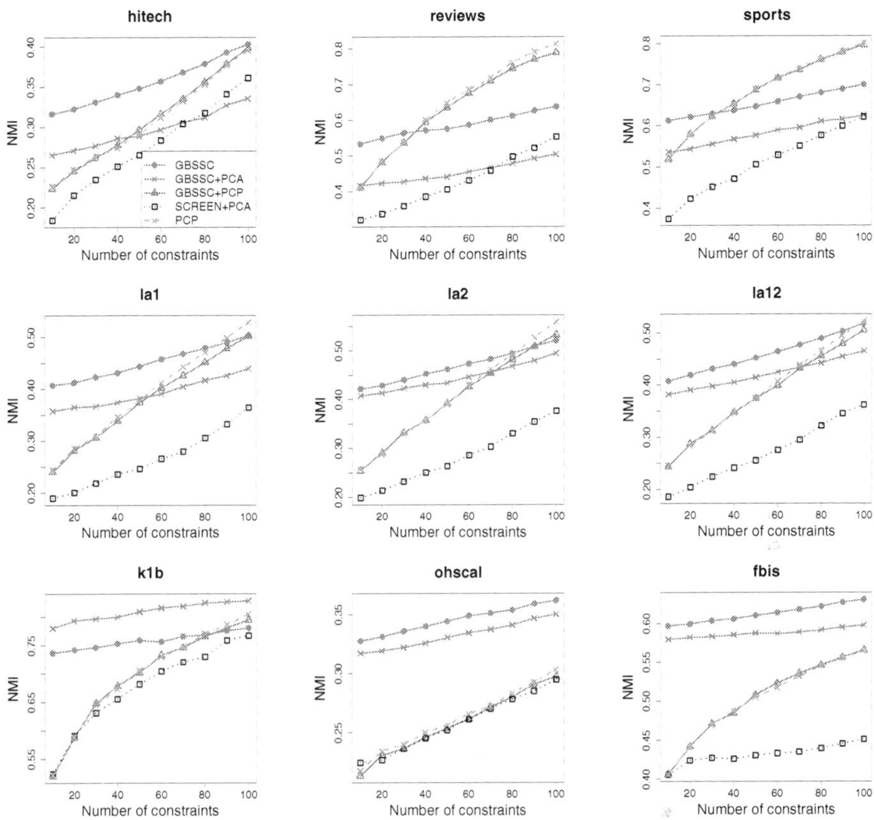

Fig. 8. Results on TREC datasets (*NMI*)

(denoted as GBSSC+PCP in the figure), it showed almost equivalent performance with respect to *NMI*, but the former was faster with more than one order.

5. Discussions

5.1 Effectiveness

The reported results show that our approach is effective in terms of the accuracy of cluster assignment (*NMI*). GBSSC outperformed SCREEN in all the datasets. Although it did not outperformed PCP in some TREC datasets with respect to *NMI*, but it was faster more than two orders of magnitude. Utilization of PCA as data pre-processing for dimensionality reduction enables the speed-up of SCREEN, in compensation for the accuracy of cluster assignment. On the other hand, PCP showed better performance in some datasets with respect to accuracy of cluster assignment, in compensation for the running time. Besides, since SCREEN originally conducts linear dimensionality reduction based on constraints, utilization

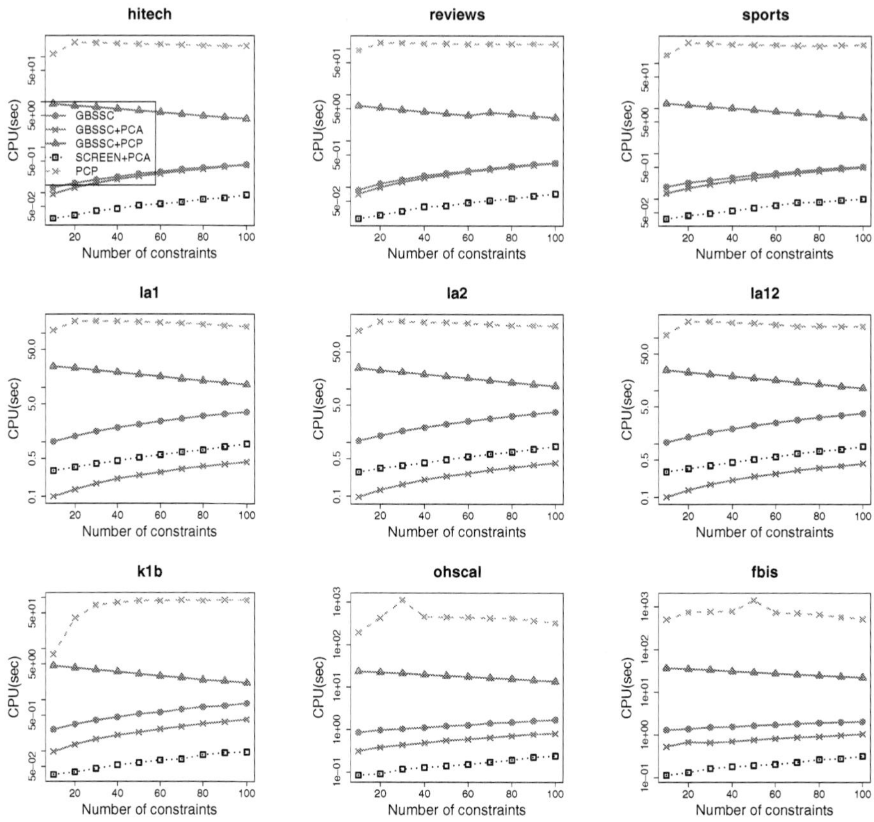

Fig. 9. Results on TREC datasets (CPU time (in seconds))

of *another* linear dimensionality reduction (such as PCA) as pre-processing might obscure its effect.

From these results, our approach can be said as effective in terms of the balance between the accuracy of cluster assignment and running time. Especially, it can leverage small amount of pairwise constraints to increase the performance. We believe that this is a good property in the semi-supervised learning setting.

5.2 Related work

Various approaches have been conducted on semi-supervised clustering. Among them are: constraint-based, distance-based, and hybrid approaches (Tang et al., 2007). The constraint-based approach tries to guide the clustering process with the specified pairwise instance constraints (Wagstaff et al., 2001). The distance-based approach utilizes metric learning techniques to acquire the distance measure during the clustering process based on the specified pairwise instance constraints (Li et al., 2008; Xing et al., 2003). The hybrid approach combines these two approaches under a probabilistic framework (Basu et al., 2004).

As for the semi-supervised clustering problem, (Wagstaff et al., 2001) proposed a clustering algorithm called COP-kmeans based on the famous kmeans algorithm. When assigning each data item to the cluster with minimum distance as in kmeans, COP-kmeans checks the constraint satisfaction and assigns each data item only to the admissible cluster (which does not violate the constraints).

SCREEN (Tang et al., 2007) first converts the data representation based on must-link constraints and removes the constraints. This process corresponds to contraction in our approach, but the weight definition is different. After that, based on cannot-link constraints, it finds out the linear mapping (linear projection) to a subspace where the variance among the data is maximized. Finally, clustering of the mapped data is conducted on the subspace.

PCP (Li et al., 2008) deals with the semi-supervised clustering problem by finding a mapping onto a space where the specified constraints are reflected. Using the specified constraints, it conducts metric learning based on the semi-definite programming and learn the kernel matrix on the mapped space. Although the explicit representation of the mapping or the data representation on the mapped space is not learned, kernel k-means clustering (Girolami, 2002) is conducted over the learned metric.

6. Conclusion

In this chapter we presented our semi-supervised clustering method based on graph contraction in general graph theory and graph Laplacian in spectral graph theory. Our approach can exploit a small amount of pairwise constraints as well as pairwise relations (similarities) among the data instances. Utilization of graph representation of instances enables to deal with the pairwise constraints as well as pairwise similarities over a unified representation. In order to reflect the pairwise constraints on the clustering process, the graph structure for the entire data instances is modified by graph contraction in general graph theory (Diestel, 2006) and graph Laplacian in spectral graph theory (Chung, 1997; von Luxburg, 2007).

We reported the performance of our approach over two real-world datasets with respect to the type of constraints as well as the number of constraints. We also compared with other state-of-the-art semi-supervised clustering methods in terms of accuracy of cluster assignment and running time. The experimental results indicate that our approach is effective in terms of the balance between the accuracy of cluster assignment and running time. Especially, it could leverage a small amount of pairwise constraints to improve the clustering performance. We plan to continue this line of research and to improve the presented approach in future.

7. Acknowledgments

The author is grateful to Mr. Okatani and Mr. Ogino for their help on implementation.

8. References

Basu, S., Bilenko, M. & Mooney, R. J. (2004). A probabilistic framework for semi-supervised clustering, *KDD-04*, pp. 59–68.

Basu, S., Davidson, I. & Wagstaff, K. (eds) (2008). *Constrained Clustering: Advances in Algorithms, Theory, and Applications*, Chapman & Hall/CRC Press.

Belkin, M. & Niyogi, P. (2002). Laplacian eigenmaps for dimensionality reduction and data representation, *Neural Computation* 15: 1373–1396.
Blum, A. & Mitchell, T. (1998). Combining labeled and unlabeled data with to-training, *Proc. 11th Computational Learning Theory*, pp. 92–100.
Chapelle, O., Schölkopf, B. & Zien, A. (eds) (2006). *Semi-Supervised Learning*, MIT Press.
Chung, F. (1997). *Spectral Graph Theory*, American Mathematical Society.
Cover, T. & Thomas, J. (2006). *Elements of Information Theory*, Wiley.
Dhillon, J., Mallela, S. & Modha, D. (2003). Information-theoretic co-clustering, *Proc. KDD'03*, pp. 89–98.
Dhillon, J. & Modha, D. (2001). Concept decompositions for large sparse text data using clustering, *Machine Learning* 42: 143–175.
Diestel, R. (2006). *Graph Theory*, Springer.
Girolami, M. (2002). Mercer kernel-based clustering in feature space, *IEEE Transactions on Neural Networks* 13(3): 780–784.
Guënoche, A., Hansen, P. & Jaumard, B. (1991). Efficient algorithms for divisive hierarchical clustering with the diameter criterion, *J. of Classification* 8: 5–30.
Guha, S., Rastogi, R. & Shim, K. (1998). Cure: An efficient clustering algorithm for large databases, *Proc. the ACM SIGMOD Conference*, pp. 73–84.
Hartigan, J. & Wong, M. (1979). Algorithm AS136: A k-means clustering algorithm, *Journal of Applied Statistics* 28: 100–108.
Jain, A., Murty, M. & P.J., F. (1999). Data clustering: A review, *ACM Computing Surveys* 31: 264–323.
Li, Z., Liu, J. & Tang, X. (2008). Pairwise constraint propagation by semidefinite programming for semi-supervised classification, *ICML-08*, pp. 576–583.
Ng, A. Y., Jordan, M. I. & Weiss, Y. (2001). On Spectral Clustering: Analysis and an algorithm, *Proc. NIPS 14*, pp. 849–856.
Ng, R. & Han, J. (2002). Clarans: a method for clustering objects for spatial data mining, *IEEE Transactions on Knowledge and Data Engineering* 14(5): 1003–1016.
Strehl, A. & Ghosh, J. (2002). Cluster Ensembles -A Knowledge Reuse Framework for Combining Multiple Partitions, *J. Machine Learning Research* 3(3): 583–617.
Tang, W., Xiong, H., Zhong, S. & Wu, J. (2007). Enhancing semi-supervised clustering : A feature projection perspective, *Proc. KDD'07*, pp. 707–716.
von Luxburg, U. (2007). A tutorial on spectral clustering, *Statistics and Computing* 17(4): 395–416.
Wagstaff, K., Cardie, C., Rogers, S. & Schroedl, S. (2001). Constrained k-means clustering with background knowledge, *In ICML01*, pp. 577–584.
Xing, E. P., Ng, A. Y., Jordan, M. I. & Russell, S. (2003). Distance metric learning, with application to clustering with side-information, *NIPS 15*, pp. 505–512.
Yoshida, T. (2010). Performance Evaluation of Constraints in Graph-based Semi-Supervised Clustering, *Proc. AMT-2010, LNAI 6335*, pp. 138–149.
Yoshida, T. (2011). A graph model for mutual information based clustering, *Journal of Intelligent Information Systems* 37(2): 187–216.
Yoshida, T. & Ogino, H. (2011). A re-coloring approach for graph b-coloring based clustering, *International Journal of Knowledge-Based & Intelligent Engineering Systems* . accepted.
Yoshida, T. & Okatani, K. (2010). A Graph-based projection approach for Semi-Supervised Clustering, *Proc. PKAW-2010, LNAI 6232*, pp. 1–13.

6

Visibility Algorithms: A Short Review

Angel M. Nuñez, Lucas Lacasa, Jose Patricio Gomez and Bartolo Luque
Universidad Politécnica de Madrid, Spain
Spain

1. Introduction

1.1 Motivation

Disregarding any underlying process (and therefore any physical, chemical, economical or whichever meaning of its mere numeric values), we can consider a time series just as an ordered set of values and play the naive mathematical game of turning this set into a different mathematical object with the aids of an abstract mapping, and see what happens: which properties of the original set are conserved, which are transformed and how, what can we say about one of the mathematical representations just by looking at the other... This exercise is of mathematical interest by itself. In addition, it turns out that time series or signals is a universal method of extracting information from dynamical systems in any field of science. Therefore, the preceding mathematical game gains some unexpected practical interest as it opens the possibility of analyzing a time series (i.e. the outcome of a dynamical process) from an alternative angle. Of course, the information stored in the original time series should be somehow conserved in the mapping. The motivation is completed when the new representation belongs to a relatively mature mathematical field, where information encoded in such a representation can be effectively disentangled and processed. This is, in a nutshell, a first motivation to map time series into networks.

This motivation is increased by two interconnected factors: first, although a mature field, time series analysis has some limitations, when it refers to study the so called complex signals. Beyond the linear regime, there exist a wide range of phenomena (not exclusive to physics) which are usually embraced in the field of the so called Complex Systems. Under this vague definition lies a common feature: the relevant effect of nonlinearities in their mathematical representation. This feature can be reflected in the temporal evolution of (at least one of) the variables describing the system and necessitates the use of specific tools for nonlinear analysis [1]. Dynamical phenomena such as chaos, long-range correlated stochastic processes, intermittency, multifractality, etc... are examples of complex phenomena where time series analysis is pushed to its own limits. Nonlinear time series analysis develops from techniques such as nonlinear correlation functions, embedding algorithms, multrifractal spectra, projection theorems... tools that increase in complexity parallel to the complexity of the process/series under study. New approaches, new paradigms to deal with complexity are not only welcome, but needed. Approaches that deal with the intrinsic nonlinearity

[1] We should note that nonlinearity is not the only feature that characterize a complex system; many interacting parts, randomness and emergence could also be cited but, as we are going to see later, nonlinearity will be sufficient for our purposes in this chapter

by being intrinsically nonlinear, that deal with the possible multiscale character of the underlying process by being designed to naturally incorporate multiple scales. And such is the framework of networks, of graph theory. Second, the technological era brings us the possibility of digitally analyze myriads of data in a glimpse. Massive data sets can nowadays be parsed, and with the aid of well suited algorithms, we can have access and filter data from many processes, let it be of physical, technological or even social garment. It is now time to develop new approaches to filter such plethora of information.

It is in this context that the network approach for time series analysis was born. The family of visibility algorithms constitute one of other possibilities to map a time series into a graph and subsequently analyze the structure of the series through the set of tools developed in the graph /complex network theory. In this chapter we will review some of its basic properties and show some of its first applications.

1.2 Different methods to map time series into graphs

The idea of mapping time series into graphs seems attractive because it lays a bridge between two prolific fields of modern science as Nonlinear Signal Analysis and Complex Networks Theory, so much so that it has attracted the attention of several research groups which have contributed to the topic with different strategies of mapping. While an exhaustive list of such strategies is beyond the scope of this work, we shall briefly outline some of them.

Zhang & Small (2006) developed a method that mapped each cycle of a pseudoperiodic time series into a node in a graph. The connection between nodes was established by a distance threshold in the reconstructed phase space when possible or by the linear correlation coefficient between cycles in the presence of noise. Noisy periodic time series mapped into random graphs while chaotic time series did it into scale-free, small-world networks due to the presence of unstable periodic orbits. This method was subsequently applied to characterize cardiac dynamics.

Xu et al. (2008) concentrated in the relative frequencies of appearance of four-node motifs inside a particular graph in order to classify it into a particular superfamily of networks which corresponded to specific underlying dynamics of the mapped time series. In this case, the method of mapping consisted in embedding the time series in an appropiated phase space where each point corresponded to a node in the network. A threshold was imposed not only in the minimum distance between two neighbours to be eligible (temporal separation should be greater than the mean period of the data) but also to the maximum number of neighbours a node could have. Different superfamilies were found for chaotic, hyperchaotic, random and noisy periodic underlying dynamics, unique fingerprints were also found for specific dynamical systems within a family.

Donner et al. (2010; 2011) presented a technique which was based on the properties of recurrence in the phase space of a dynamical system. More precisely, the recurrence matrix obtained by imposing a threshold in the minimum distance between two points in the phase space (as in Xu et al. (2008)) was interpreted as the adjacency matrix of an undirected, unweighted graph. Properties of such graphs at three different scales (local, intermediated and global) were presented and studied on several paradigmatic systems (Hénon map, Rossler system, Lorenz system, Bernoulli map). The variation of some of the properties of the graphs with the distance threshold was analyzed, the use of specific measures like the local clustering coefficient was proposed as a way for detecting dynamically invariant objects (saddle points or unstable periodic orbits) and studying the graph properties dependent on the embedding dimension was suggested as a means to distinguish between chaotic and stochastic systems.

Campanharo et al. (2011) contributed with an idea along the lines of Shirazi et al. (2009), Strozzi et al. (2009) and Haraguchi et al. (2009) of a surjective mapping which admits an inverse opperation. This approach opens the reciprocal possibility of benefiting from time series analysis to study the structure and properties of networks. Time series are treated as Markov processes, values are grouped in quantiles which will correspond to nodes in the associated graph. Weighted and directed connections are stablished between nodes as a function of the probability of transition between quantiles. An inverse operation can be defined without any a priori knowledge of the correspondance between nodes and quantiles just by imposing a continuity condition in the time series by means of a cost function defined on the weighted adjacency matrix of the graph. A random walk is performed on the network and a time series with properties equivalent to the original one is recovered. This method was applied to a battery of cases which included a periodic-to-random family of processes parametrized by the probability of transition p, a pair of chaotic systems (Lorentz and Rossler attractors) and two human heart rate time series. Reciprocally, the inverse map was applied to the metabolic network of Arabidopsis Thaliana and to the '97 year Internet Network. Time series obtained were demostrated to exhibit different dynamics.

Among all these methods of mapping, in this chapter we are going to concentrate our attention on the one developed in Lacasa et al. (2008) and subsequent works. To cite some of its most relevant features, we will stress its intrinsic nonlocality, its low computational cost, its straightforward implementation and its quite 'simple' way of inherit the time series properties in the structure of the associated graphs. These features are going to make it easier to find connections between the underlying processes and the networks obtained from them by a direct analysis of the latter. In what follows we will firstly present different versions of the algorithm along with its most notable properties, that in many cases can be derived analytically (theorems are reported when possible). Based on these latter properties, several applications are addressed.

2. Visibility algorithms: Theory

2.1 Natural visibility algorithm: definition

Let $\{x(t_i)\}_{i=1..N}$ be a time series of N data. The natural visibility algorithm (Lacasa et al., 2008) assigns each datum of the series to a node in the natural visibility graph (from now on NVg). Two nodes i and j in the graph are connected if one can draw a straight line in the time series joining $x(t_i)$ and $x(t_j)$ that does not intersect any intermediate data height $x(t_k)$ (see figure 1 for a graphical illustration). Hence, i and j are two connected nodes if the following geometrical criterion is fulfilled within the time series:

$$x(t_k) < x(t_i) + (x(t_j) - x(t_i))\frac{t_k - t_i}{t_j - t_k}. \tag{1}$$

It can easily checked that by means of the present algorithm, the associated graph extracted from a time series is always:

(*i*) connected: each node sees at least its nearest neighbors (left-hand side and right-hand side).
(*ii*) undirected: the way the algorithm is built up, there is no direction defined in the links.
(*iii*) invariant under affine transformations of the series data: the visibility criterium is invariant under rescaling of both horizontal and vertical axis, as well as under horizontal and vertical translations.
(*iv*) "lossy": some information regarding the time series is inevitably lost in the mapping from the fact that the network structure is completely determined in the (binary) adjacency matrix. For instance, two periodic series with the same period as $T1 = ..., 3, 1, 3, 1, ...$ and $T2 = ..., 3, 2, 3, 2, ...$ would have the same visibility graph, albeit being quantitatively different.

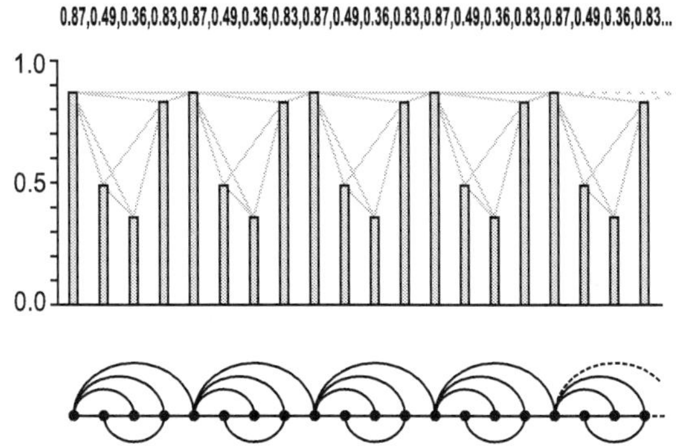

Fig. 1. Illustrative example of the visibility algorithm. In the upper part we plot a periodic time series and in the bottom part we represent the graph generated through the visibility algorithm. Each datum in the series corresponds to a node in the graph, such that two nodes are connected if their corresponding data heights fulfill the visibility criterion of equation 1. Note that the degree distribution of the visibility graph is composed by a finite number of peaks, much in the vein of the Discrete Fourier Transform of a periodic signal. We can thus interpret the visibility algorithm as a geometric transform.

One straightforward question is: what does the visibility algorithm stand for? In order to deepen on the geometric interpretation of the visibility graph, let us focus on a periodic series. It is straightforward that its visibility graph is a concatenation of a motif: a repetition of a pattern (see figure 1). Now, which is the degree distribution $P(k)$ of this visibility graph? Since the graph is just a motif's repetition, the degree distribution will be formed by a finite number of non-null values, this number being related to the period of the associated periodic series. This behavior reminds us the Discrete Fourier Transform (DFT), which for periodic series is formed by a finite number of peaks (vibration modes) related to the series period. Using this analogy, we can understand the visibility algorithm as a geometric (rather than integral) transform. Whereas a DFT decomposes a signal in a sum of (eventually infinite) modes, the visibility algorithm decomposes a signal in a concatenation of graph's motifs, and the degree distribution simply makes a histogram of such 'geometric modes'. While the time series is defined in the time domain and the DFT is defined on the frequency domain, the visibility graph is then defined on the 'visibility domain'. At this point we can mention that whereas a generic DFT fails to capture the presence of nonlinear correlations in time series (such as the presence of chaotic behavior), we will see that the visibility algorithm can distinguish between stochastic and chaotic series. Of course this analogy is, so far, a simple metaphor to help our intuition (this transform is not a reversible one for instance).

2.2 Horizontal visibility algorithm: definition

An alternative criterion for the construction of the visibility graph is defined as follows: let $\{x_i\}_{i=1..N}$ be a time series of N data. The so called horizontal visibility algorithm (Luque et al., 2009) assigns each datum of the series to a node in the horizontal visibility graph (from now on HVg). Two nodes i and j in the graph are connected if one can draw a horizontal line in the time series joining x_i and x_j that does not intersect any intermediate data height (see figure 2 for a graphical illustration). Hence, i and j are two connected nodes if the following geometrical criterion is fulfilled within the time series:

$$x_i, x_j > x_n \text{ for all } n \text{ such that } i < n < j \tag{2}$$

This algorithm is a simplification of the NVa. In fact, the HVg is always a subgraph of its associated NVg for the same time series (see figure 2). Beside this, the HVg graph will also be (*i*) connected, (*ii*) undirected, (*iii*) invariant under affine transformations of the series and (*iv*) "lossy". Some concrete properties of these graphs can be found in Gutin et al. (2011); Lacasa et al. (2010); Luque et al. (2009; 2011). In the next sections we are going to focus on properties of this particular method as it is a quite more analytically tractable version.

2.3 Topological properties of the HVg associated to periodic series: mean degree

Theorem 2.1. *The mean degree of an horizontal visibility graph associated to an infinite periodic series of period T (with no repeated values within a period) is*

$$\bar{k}(T) = 4\left(1 - \frac{1}{2T}\right) \tag{3}$$

A proof can be found in Núñez et al. (2010).

An interesting consequence of the previous result is that every time series extracted from a dynamical system has an associated HVG with a mean degree $2 \leq \bar{k} \leq 4$, where the lower bound is reached for constant series, whereas the upper bound is reached for aperiodic (random or chaotic) series (Luque et al., 2009).

2.4 Topological properties of the HVg associated to random time series

Let $\{x_i\}$ be a bi-infinite sequence of independent and identically distributed random variables extracted from a continous probability density $f(x)$, and consider its associated HVg. In the following sections we outline some theorems regarding the topological properties of these graphs.

2.4.1 Degree distribution of the visibility graph associated to a random time series

Theorem 2.2. *The degree distribution of its associated horizontal visibility graph is*

$$P(k) = \frac{1}{3}\left(\frac{2}{3}\right)^{k-2}, \; k = 2, 3, 4, \ldots \tag{4}$$

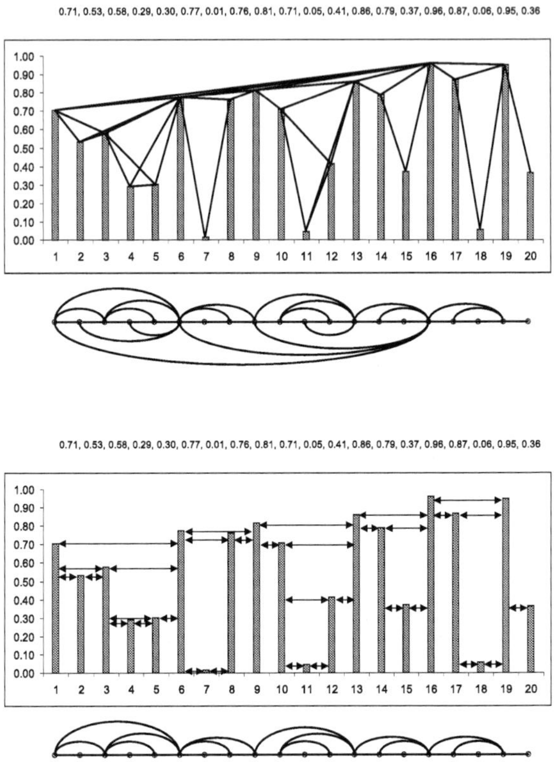

Fig. 2. Illustrative example of the natural and horizontal visibility algorithms. We plot the same time series and we represent the graphs generated through both visibility algorithms below. Each datum in the series corresponds to a node in the graph, such that two nodes are connected if their corresponding data heights fulfill respectively the visibility criteria of equations 1 and 2 respectively.

A lengthy constructive proof can be found in Luque et al. (2009) and alternative, shorter proofs can be found in Núñez et al. (2010).

Observe that the mean degree $\bar{k}$ of the horizontal visibility graph associated to an uncorrelated random process is then:

$$\bar{k} = \sum kP(k) = \sum_{k=2}^{\infty} \frac{k}{3}\left(\frac{2}{3}\right)^{k-2} = 4 \tag{5}$$

in good agreement with the prediction of eq. 3 in the limit $T \to \infty$, i.e. an aperiodic series.

2.4.2 Degree versus height

An interesting aspect worth exploring is the relation between data height and the node degree, that is, to study whether a functional relation between the height of a datum and the degree of its associated node holds. In this sense, let us define $P(k|x)$ as the conditional probability that a given node has degree k provided that it has height x. $P(k|x)$ is easily deduced in Luque et al. (2009), resulting in

$$P(k|x) = \sum_{j=0}^{k-2} \frac{(-1)^{k-2}}{j!(k-2-j)!}[1-F(x)]^2 \cdot [\ln(1-F(x))]^{k-2} \tag{6}$$

The average value of the degree of a node associated to a datum of height x, $K(x)$, in then

$$K(x) = \sum_{k-2}^{\infty} kP(k|x) = 2 - 2\ln(1-F(x)) \tag{7}$$

where $F(x) = \int_{-\infty}^{x} f(x')dx'$.

Since $F(x) \in [0,1]$ and $\ln(x)$ are monotonically increasing functions, $K(x)$ will also be monotonically increasing. We can thus conclude that graph hubs (that is, the most connected nodes) are the data with largest values, that is, the extreme events of the series.

2.4.3 Local clustering coefficient distribution

The local clustering coefficient C (Boccaletti et al., 2006; Newmann, 2003) of an horizontal visibility graph associated to a random series can be easy deduced by means of geometrical arguments (Luque et al., 2009):

$$C(k) = \frac{k-1}{\binom{k}{2}} = \frac{2}{k} \tag{8}$$

what indicates a so called hierarchical structure (Ravasz et al., 2002). This relation between k and C allows us to deduce the local clustering coefficient distribution $P(C)$:

$$P(k) = \frac{1}{3}\left(\frac{2}{3}\right)^{k-2} = P(2/C)$$

$$P(C) = \frac{1}{3}\left(\frac{2}{3}\right)^{2/C-2} \tag{9}$$

2.4.4 Long distance visibility, mean degree and mean path length

The probability $P(n)$ that two data separated by n intermediate data be two connected nodes in the graph can be demostrated to be (see Luque et al. (2009))

$$P(n) = \left(\frac{1}{n} - 1\right) \int_0^1 f(x_0)F^n(x_0)dx_0 + \int_0^1 f(x_0)F^{n-1}(x_0)dx_0$$

$$= \frac{2}{n(n+1)} \tag{10}$$

where $P(n)$ is independent of the probability distribution f(x) of the random variable. Notice that the latter result can also be obtained, alternatively, with a purely combinatorial argument: take a random series with $n+1$ data and choose its two largest values. This latter pair can be placed with equiprobability in $n(n+1)$ positions, while only two of them are such that the largest values are placed at distance n, so we get $P(n) = \frac{2}{n(n+1)}$ on agreement with the previous development.

2.4.5 Small World property

If we looked the adjacency matrix (Newmann, 2003) of the horizontal visibility graph associated to a random series (Luque et al., 2009), we would see that every data x_i has visibility of its first neighbors x_{i-1}, x_{i+1}, every node i will be connected by construction to nodes $i-1$ and $i+1$: the graph is thus connected. The graph evidences a typical homogeneous structure: the adjacency matrix is predominantly filled around the main diagonal. Furthermore, the matrix evidences a superposed sparse structure, reminiscent of the visibility probability $P(n) = 2/(n(n+1))$ that introduces some shortcuts in the horizontal visibility graph, much in the vein of the Small-World model (Strogatz, 2001). Here the probability of having these shortcuts is given by $P(n)$. Statistically speaking, we can interpret the graph's structure as quasi-homogeneous, where the size of the local neighborhood increases with the graph's size. Accordingly, we can approximate its mean path length $L(N)$ as:

$$L(N) \approx \sum_{n=1}^{N-1} nP(n) = \sum_{n=1}^{N-1} \frac{2}{n+1} = 2\log(N) + 2(\gamma - 1) + O(1/N) \qquad (11)$$

where we have made use of the asymptotic expansion of the harmonic numbers and γ is the Euler-Mascheroni constant. As can be seen, the scaling is logarithmic, denoting that the horizontal visibility graph associated to a generic random series is Small-World (Newmann, 2003).

2.5 Topological properties of the HVg associated to other stochastic and chaotic processes

It was proved that $P(k) = (1/3)(2/3)^{k-2}$ for uncorrelated random series. To find out a similar closed expression in the case of generic chaotic or stochastic correlated processes is a very difficult task, since variables can be long-range correlated and hence the probabilities cannot be separated (lack of independence). This leads to a very involved calculation which is typically impossible to solve in the general case. However, some analytical developments can be made in order to compare them with our numerical results. Concretely, for Markovian systems global dependence is reduced to a one-step dependence. We will make use of such property to derive exact expressions for $P(2)$ and $P(3)$ in some Markovian systems (both deterministic and stochastic).

2.5.1 Ornstein-Uhlenbeck process: degree distribution

Suppose a short-range correlated series (exponentially decaying correlations) of infinite size generated through an Ornstein-Uhlenbeck process (Van Kampen, 2007), and generate its associated HVg. Let us consider the probability that a node chosen at random has degree $k = 2$. This node is associated to a datum labelled x_0 without lack of generality. Now, this node will have degree $k = 2$ if the datum first neighbors, x_1 and x_{-1} have values larger than x_0:

$$P(k=2) = P(x_{-1} > x_0 \cap x_1 > x_0) \qquad (12)$$

In this case the variables are correlated, so in general we should have

$$P(2) = \int_{-\infty}^{\infty} dx_0 \int_{x_0}^{\infty} dx_{-1} \int_{x_0}^{\infty} dx_1 \, f(x_{-1}, x_0, x_1) \qquad (13)$$

We use the Markov property $f(x_{-1}, x_0, x_1) = f(x_{-1})f(x_0|x_{-1})f(x_1|x_0)$, that holds for an Ornstein-Uhlenbeck process with correlation function $C(t) \sim \exp(-t/\tau)$ (Van Kampen, 2007):

$$f(x) = \frac{\exp(-x^2/2)}{\sqrt{2\pi}} \qquad f(x_2|x_1) = \frac{\exp(-(x_2 - Kx_1)^2/2(1-K^2))}{\sqrt{2\pi(1-K^2)}}, \tag{14}$$

where $K = \exp(-1/\tau)$.

Numerical integration allows us to calculate $P(2)$ for every given value of the correlation time τ. A procedure to compute $P(3)$ can also be found in Lacasa et al. (2010).

2.5.2 Logistic map: degree distribution

A chaotic map of the form $x_{n+1} = F(x_n)$ does also have the Markov property, and therefore a similar analysis can be applied (even if chaotic maps are deterministic). For chaotic dynamical systems whose trajectories belong to the attractor, there exists a probability measure that characterizes the long-run proportion of time spent by the system in the various regions of the attractor. In the case of the logistic map $F(x_n) = \mu x_n(1 - x_n)$ with parameter $\mu = 4$, the attractor is the whole interval $[0, 1]$ and the probability measure $f(x)$ corresponds to the *beta* distribution with parameters $a = 0.5$ and $b = 0.5$:

$$f(x) = \frac{x^{-0.5}(1-x)^{-0.5}}{\mathrm{B}(0.5, 0.5)} \tag{15}$$

Now, for a deterministic system, the transition probability is

$$f(x_{n+1}|x_n) = \delta[x_{n+1} - F(x_n)], \tag{16}$$

where $\delta(x)$ is the Dirac delta distribution. Departing from equation 12, for the logistic map $F(x_n) = 4x_n(1 - x_n)$ and $x_n \in [0, 1]$, we have

$$\begin{aligned} P(2) = &\int_0^1 dx_0 \int_{x_0}^1 f(x_{-1})f(x_0|x_{-1})dx_{-1} \int_{x_0}^1 f(x_1|x_0)dx_1 = \\ &\int_0^1 dx_0 \int_{x_0}^1 f(x_{-1})\delta(x_0 - F(x_{-1}))dx_{-1} \int_{x_0}^1 \delta(x_1 - F(x_0))dx_1. \end{aligned} \tag{17}$$

Now, notice that, using the properties of the Dirac delta distribution, $\int_{x_0}^1 \delta(x_1 - F(x_0))dx_1$ is equal to one iff $F(x_0) \in [x_0, 1]$, what will happen iff $0 < x_0 < 3/4$, and zero otherwise. Therefore the only effect of this integral is to restrict the integration range of x_0 to be $[0, 3/4]$.

On the other hand,

$$\int_{x_0}^1 f(x_{-1})\delta[x_0 - F(x_{-1})]dx_{-1} = \sum_{x_k^*|F(x_k^*)=x_0} f(x_k^*)/|F'(x_k^*)|,$$

that is, the sum over the roots of the equation $F(x) = x_0$, iff $F(x_{-1}) > x_0$. But since $x_{-1} \in [x_0, 1]$ in the latter integral, it is easy to see that again, this is verified iff $0 < x_0 < 3/4$ (as a matter of fact, if $0 < x_0 < 3/4$ there is always a *single* value of $x_{-1} \in [x_0, 1]$ such that $F(x_{-1}) = x_0$, so the sum restricts to the adequate root). It is easy to see that the particular value is $x^* = (1 + \sqrt{1 - x_0})/2$. Making use of these piecewise solutions and equation 15, we finally have

$$P(2) = \int_0^{3/4} \frac{f(x^*)}{4\sqrt{1-x_0}} dx_0 = 1/3, \tag{18}$$

Note that a similar development can be fruitfully applied to other chaotic maps, provided that they have a well defined natural measure. Analytical and numerical developments for $P(3)$ can be found in Lacasa et al. (2010).

2.6 Directed horizontal visibility graph

So far, undirected visibility graphs have been considered, as visibility did not have a predefined temporal arrow. However, such a directionality can be made explicit by making use of directed networks or digraphs (Newmann, 2003).

Let a *directed* horizontal visibility graph (DHVg, Lacasa et al. (2011)) be a horizontal visibility graph, where the degree $k(x_i)$ of the node x_i is now splitted in an *ingoing* degree $k_{\text{in}}(x_i)$, and an *outgoing* degree $k_{\text{out}}(x_i)$, such that $k(x_i) = k_{\text{in}}(x_i) + k_{\text{out}}(x_i)$. The ingoing degree $k_{\text{in}}(x_i)$ is defined as the number of links of node x_i with other *past* nodes associated with data in the series (that is, nodes with $j < i$). Conversely, the outgoing degree $k_{\text{out}}(x_i)$, is defined as the number of links with *future* nodes ($i < j$).

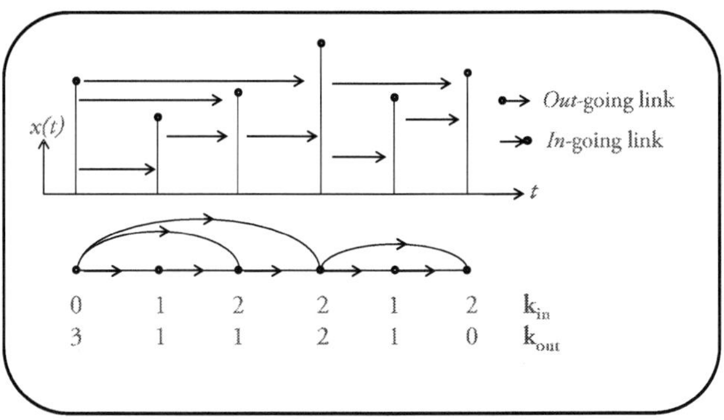

Fig. 3. Graphical illustration of the method. In the top we plot a sample time series $\{x(t)\}$. Each datum in the series is mapped to a node in the graph. Arrows, describing allowed directed visibility, link nodes. The associated directed horizontal visibility graph is plotted below. In this graph, each node has an ingoing degree k_{in}, which accounts for the number of links with *past* nodes, and an outgoing degree k_{out}, which in turn accounts for the number of links with $future$ nodes. The asymmetry of the resulting graph can be captured in a first approximation through the invariance of the outgoing (or ingoing) degree series under time reversal.

For a graphical illustration of the method, see figure 3. The degree distribution of a graph describes the probability of an arbitrary node to have degree k (i.e. k links, Newmann (2003)). We define the *in* and *out* (or ingoing and outgoing) degree distributions of a DHVg as the probability distributions of k_{out} and k_{in} of the graph which we call $P_{out}(k) \equiv P(k_{out} = k)$ and $P_{in}(k) \equiv P(k_{in} = k)$, respectively.

2.6.1 Uncorrelated stochastic series: degree distribution

Theorem 2.3. *Let $\{x_t\}_{t=-\infty,\ldots,\infty}$ be a bi-infinite sequence of independent and identically distributed random variables extracted from a continuous probability density $f(x)$. Then, both the* in *and* out *degree distributions of its associated directed horizontal visibility graph are*

$$P_{in}(k) = P_{out}(k) = \left(\frac{1}{2}\right)^k, \; k = 1, 2, 3, \ldots \tag{19}$$

Proof. (out-distribution) Let x be an arbitrary datum of the aforementioned series. The probability that the horizontal visibility of x is interrupted by a datum x_r on its right is independent of $f(x)$,

$$\Phi_1 = \int_{-\infty}^{\infty}\int_{x}^{\infty} f(x)f(x_r)dx_r dx = \int_{-\infty}^{\infty} f(x)[1 - F(x)]dx = \frac{1}{2},$$

The probability $P(k)$ of the datum x being capable of exactly seeing k data may be expressed as

$$P(k) = Q(k)\Phi_1 = \frac{1}{2}Q(k), \tag{20}$$

where $Q(k)$ is the probability of x seeing at least k data. $Q(k)$ may be recurrently calculated via

$$Q(k) = Q(k-1)(1 - \Phi_1) = \frac{1}{2}Q(k-1), \tag{21}$$

from which, with $Q(1) = 1$, the following expression is obtained

$$Q(k) = \left(\frac{1}{2}\right)^{k-1}, \tag{22}$$

which together with equation (20) concludes the proof. □

An analogous derivation holds for the *in* case. This result is independent of the underlying probability density $f(x)$: it holds not only for Gaussian or uniformly distributed random series, but for any series of independent and identically distributed (i.i.d.) random variables extracted from a continuous distribution $f(x)$.

3. Towards a graph theory of time series?

In the preceding section, specific properties of the visibility graphs (either NVg, HVg or the directed version of HVg) associated to different time series have been considered. Relying on the aforementioned dualities between time series structure and network topological features, we proceed here to make the first steps for a graph theoretical analysis of time series and dynamical systems, addressing several nontrivial problems of time series analysis through the visibility algorithm apparatus.

3.1 Estimating the Hurst exponent with NVg

Self-similar processes such as fractional Brownian motion (fBm, Mandelbrot & Van Ness (1968)) are currently used to model fractal phenomena of different nature, ranging from Physics or Biology to Economics or Engineering (see Lacasa et al. (2009) and references therein). A fBm $B_H(t)$ is a non-stationary random process with stationary self-similar increments (fractional Gaussian noise) that can be characterized by the so called Hurst exponent, $0 < H < 1$. The one-step memory Brownian motion is obtained for $H = \frac{1}{2}$, whereas time series with $H > \frac{1}{2}$ shows persistence and anti-persistence if $H < \frac{1}{2}$. While different fBm generators and estimators have been introduced in the last years, the community lacks consensus on which method is best suited for each case. This drawback comes from the fact that fBm formalism is exact in the infinite limit, i.e. when the whole infinite series of data is considered. However, in practice, real time series are finite. Accordingly, long range correlations are partially broken in finite series, and local dynamics corresponding to a particular temporal window are overestimated. The practical simulation and the estimation from real (finite) time series is consequently a major issue that is, hitherto, still open. An overview of different methodologies and comparisons can be found in Carbone (2007); Kantelhardt (2008); Karagiannis et al. (2004); Mielniczuk & Wojdyllo (2007); Pilgram & Kaplan (1998); Podobnik & Stanley (2008); Simonsen et al. (1998); Weron (2002) and references therein.

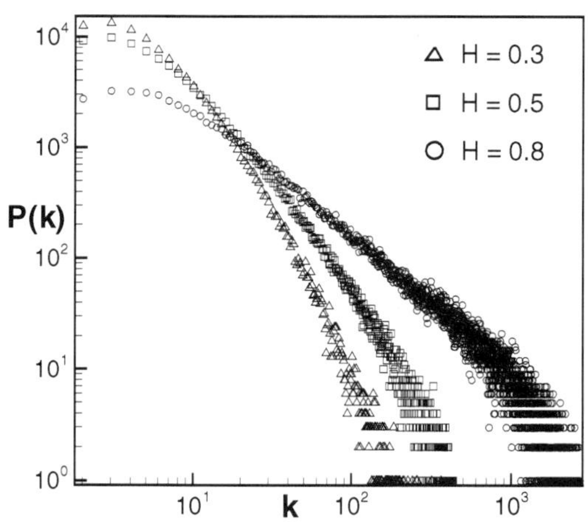

Fig. 4. Degree distribution of three visibility graphs, namely (i) triangles: extracted from a fBm series of 10^5 data with $H = 0.3$, (ii) squares: extracted from a fBm series of 10^5 data with $H = 0.5$, (iii) circles: extracted from a fBm series of 10^5 data with $H = 0.8$. Note that distributions are not normalized. The three visibility graphs are scale-free since their degree distributions follow a power law $P(k) \sim k^{-\gamma}$ with decreasing exponents $\gamma_{0.3} > \gamma_{0.5} > \gamma_{0.8}$.

Here we address the problem of estimating the Hurst exponent of a fBm series via the NVg. If we map a fBm time series by means of the NVa, what we get is a scale-free graph (Lacasa et al.,

2008; 2009), see figure 4. As a matter of fact, that fBm yields scale free visibility graphs is not that surprising; the most highly connected nodes (hubs) are the responsible for the heavy tailed degree distributions. Within fBm series, hubs are related to extreme values in the series, since a datum with a very large value has typically a large connectivity (a fact reminiscent of eq. 7). It can be proved (Lacasa et al., 2009) that the degree distribution of a NVg extracted from a fBm with Hurst exponent H shows a power law shape $P(k) \sim k^{-\gamma}$, such that

$$\gamma(H) = 3 - 2H. \tag{23}$$

Numerical analysis corroborated this theoretical relation in Lacasa et al. (2009).

It is well known that fBm has a power spectra that behaves as $1/f^{\beta}$, where the exponent β is related to the Hurst exponent of an fBm process through the well known relation

$$\beta(H) = 1 + 2H. \tag{24}$$

Now according to eqs. 23 and 24, the degree distribution of the visibility graph corresponding to a time series with $f^{-\beta}$ noise should be again power law $P(k) \sim k^{-\gamma}$ where

$$\gamma(\beta) = 4 - \beta. \tag{25}$$

The theoretical prediction eq. 25 was also corroborated numerically in Lacasa et al. (2009). Finally, eq. 24 holds for fBm processes, while for the increments of an fBm process, known as a fractional Gaussian noise (fGn), the relation between β and H turns to be

$$\beta(H) = -1 + 2H, \tag{26}$$

The relation between γ and H for a fGn (where fGn is a series composed by the increments of a fBm) can be deduced to be

$$\gamma(H) = 5 - 2H. \tag{27}$$

In order to illustrate this latter case, we address a realistic and striking dynamics where long range dependence has been recently described. Gait cycle (the stride interval in human walking rhythm) is a physiological signal that has been shown to display fractal dynamics and long range correlations in healthy young adults (Goldenberger et al., 2002; Hausdorff et al., 1996). In the upper part of fig. 5 we have plotted to series describing the fluctuations of walk rhythm of a young healthy person, for slow pace (bottom series of 3304 points) and fast pace (up series of 3595 points) respectively (data available in www.physionet.org/physiobank/database/umwdb/ (Goldberger et al., 2000)). In the bottom part we have represented the degree distribution of their visibility graphs. These ones are again power laws with exponents $\gamma = 3.03 \pm 0.05$ for fast pace and $\gamma = 3.19 \pm 0.05$ for slow pace (derived through MLE). According to eq. 25, the visibility algorithm predicts that gait dynamics evidence $f^{-\beta}$ behavior with $\beta = 1$ for fast pace, and $\beta = 0.8$ for slow pace, in perfect agreement with previous results based on a Detrended Fluctuation Analysis (Goldenberger et al., 2002; Hausdorff et al., 1996). These series record the fluctuations of walk rhythm (that is, the increments), so according to eq. 27, the Hurst exponent is $H = 1$ for fast pace and $H = 0.9$ for slow pace, that is to say, dynamics evidences long range dependence (persistence) (Goldenberger et al., 2002; Hausdorff et al., 1996).

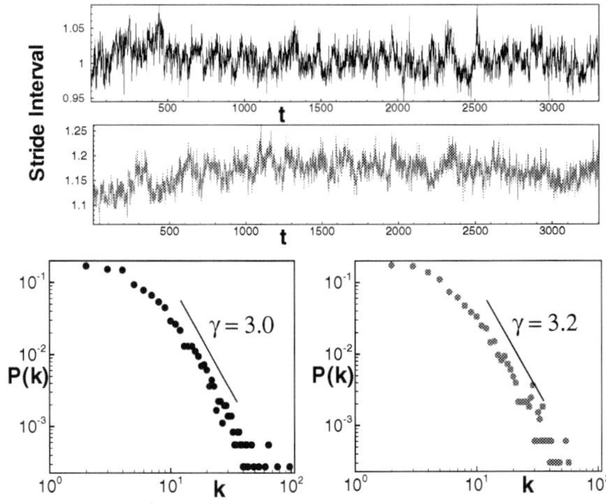

Fig. 5. Black signal: time series of 3595 points from the stride interval of a healthy person in fast pace. Red signal: time series of 3304 points from the stride interval of a healthy person in slow pace. Bottom: Degree distribution of the associated visibility graphs (the plot is in log-log). These are power laws where $\gamma = 3.03 \pm 0.05$ for the fast movement (black dots) and $\gamma = 3.19 \pm 0.05$ for the slow movement (red dots), what provides $\beta = 1$ and $\beta = 0.8$ for fast and slow pace respectively according to eq.25, in agreement with previous results (Goldenberger et al., 2002; Hausdorff et al., 1996).

3.2 Discriminating stochastic vs. chaotic series via HVg

Both stochastic and chaotic processes share many features, and the discrimination between them is indeed very subtle. The relevance of this problem is to determine whether the source of unpredictability (production of entropy) has its origin in a chaotic deterministic or stochastic dynamical system, a fundamental issue for modeling and forecasting purposes. Essentially, the majority of methods (Cecini et al., 2010; Kants H. & Schreiber, 2003) that have been introduced so far rely on two major differences between chaotic and stochastic dynamics. The first difference is that chaotic systems have a finite dimensional attractor, whereas stochastic processes arise from an infinite-dimensional one. Being able to reconstruct the attractor is thus a clear evidence showing that the time series has been generated by a deterministic system. The development of sophisticated embedding techniques (Kants H. & Schreiber, 2003) for attractor reconstruction is the most representative step forward in this direction. The second difference is that deterministic systems evidence, as opposed to random ones, short-time prediction: the time evolution of two nearby states will diverge exponentially fast for chaotic ones (finite and positive Lyapunov exponents) while in the case of a stochastic process such separation is randomly distributed. Whereas some algorithms relying on the preceding concepts are nowadays available, the great majority of them are purely phenomenological and often complicated to perform, computationally speaking. These drawbacks provide the motivation for a search for new methods that can directly distinguish, in a reliable way, stochastic from chaotic time series. We show here that the horizontal visibility algorithm offers a different, conceptually simple and computationally efficient method to distinguish between deterministic and stochastic dynamics, since the degree distribution of HVGs associated to stochastic and chaotic processes are exponential $P(k) \sim \exp(-\lambda k)$, where for stochastic dynamics $\lambda > \lambda_{un}$ and for chaotic dynamics $\lambda < \lambda_{un}$ (Lacasa et al., 2010), λ_{un} being the uncorrelated case, (theorem 2.2).

3.2.1 Correlated stochastic series

In order to analyze the effect of correlations between the data of the series, we focus on two generic and paradigmatic correlated stochastic processes, namely long-range (power-law decaying correlations) and Ornstein-Uhlenbeck (short-range exponentially decaying correlations) processes. We have computed the degree distribution of the HVg associated to different long-range and short-range correlated stochastic series (the method for generating the associated series is explained in Lacasa et al. (2010)) with correlation function $C(t) = t^{-\gamma}$ for different values of the correlation strength $\gamma \in [10^{-2} - 10^{1}]$ and with an exponentially decaying correlation function $C(t) = \exp(-t/\tau)$. In both cases the degree distribution of the associated HVG can be fitted for large k by an exponential function $\exp(-\lambda k)$. The parameter λ depends on γ or τ and is, in each case, a monotonic function that reaches the asymptotic value $\lambda = \lambda_{un} = \ln(3/2)$ in the uncorrelated limit $\gamma \to \infty$ or $\tau \to 0$, respectively. Detailed results of this phenomenology can be found in (Lacasa et al., 2010). In all cases, the limit is reached from above, i.e. $\lambda > \lambda_{un}$ (see figure 6). Interestingly enough, for the power-law correlations the convergence is slow, and there is still a noticeable deviation from the uncorrelated case even for weak correlations ($\gamma > 4.0$), whereas the convergence with τ is faster in the case of exponential correlations.

3.2.2 Chaotic maps

Poincaré recurrence theorem suggests that the degree distribution of HVgs associated to chaotic series should be asymptotically exponential (Luque et al., 2009). Several deterministic time series generated by chaotic maps have been analyzed:

(1) the α-map $f(x) = 1 - |2x - 1|^{\alpha}$, that reduces to the logistic and tent maps in their fully chaotic region for $\alpha = 2$ and $\alpha = 1$ respectively, for different values of α,
(2) the 2D Hénon map ($x_{t+1} = y_t + 1 - ax_t^2$, $y_{t+1} = bx_t$) in the fully chaotic region ($a = 1.4$, $b = 0.3$);
(3) a time-delayed variant of the Hénon map: $x_{t+1} = bx_{t-d} + 1 - ax_t^2$ in the region ($a = 1.6$, $b = 0.1$), where it shows chaotic behavior with an attractor dimension that increases linearly with the delay d (Sprott, 2006). This model has also been used for chaos control purposes (Buchner & Zebrowski, 2000), although here we set the parameters a and b to values for which we find high-dimensional chaos for almost every initial condition (Sprott, 2006);
(4) the Lozi map, a piecewise-linear variant of the Hénon map given by $x_{t+1} = 1 + y_n - a|x_t|$, $y_{t+1} = bx_t$ in the chaotic regime $a = 1.7$ and $b = 0.5$;
(5) the Kaplan-Yorke map $x_{t+1} = 2x_t \mod (1), y_{t+1} = \lambda y_t + \cos(4\pi x_t) \mod (1)$; and
(6) the Arnold cat map $x_{t+1} = x_t + y_t \mod (1), y_{t+1} = x_t + 2y_t \mod (1)$, a conservative system with integer Kaplan-Yorke dimension. References for these maps can be found in Sprott & Rowlands (2001).

We find that the tails of the degree distribution can be well approximated by an exponential function $P(k) \sim \exp(-\lambda k)$. Remarkably, we find that $\lambda < \lambda_{un}$ in every case, where λ seems to increase monotonically as a function of the chaos dimensionality [2], with an asymptotic value $\lambda \rightarrow \ln(3/2)$ for large values of the attractor dimension (see fig. 6 where we plot the specific values of λ as a function of the correlation dimension of the map (Sprott & Rowlands, 2001)). Again, we deduce that the degree distribution for uncorrelated series is a limiting case of the degree distribution for chaotic series but, as opposed to what we found for stochastic processes, the convergence flow towards λ_{un} is from below, and therefore $\lambda = \ln(3/2)$ plays the role of an effective frontier between correlated stochastic and chaotic processes.

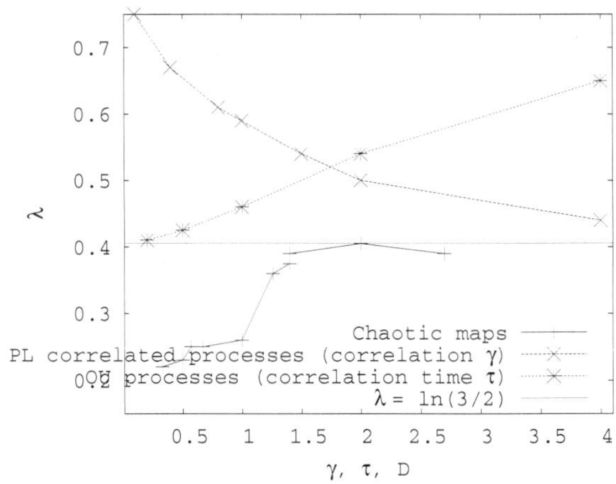

Fig. 6. Plot of the values of λ for several processes, namely: (i) for power-law correlated stochastic series with correlation function $C(t) = t^{-\gamma}$, as a function of the correlation γ, (ii) for Ornstein-Uhlenbeck series with correlation function $C(t) = \exp(-t/\tau)$, as a function of the correlation time τ, and (iii) for different chaotic maps, as a function of their correlation dimension D. Errors in the estimation of λ are incorporated in the size of the dots. Notice that stochastic processes cluster in the region $\lambda > \lambda_{un}$ whereas chaotic series belong to the opposite region $\lambda < \lambda_{un}$, evidencing a convergence towards the uncorrelated value $\lambda_{un} = \ln(3/2)$ (Luque et al., 2009) for decreasing correlations or increasing chaos dimensionality respectively.

In the following section we provide some heuristic arguments supporting our findings, for additional details, numerics and analytical developments we refer the reader to Lacasa et al. (2010).

3.2.3 Heuristics

We argue first that correlated series show lower data variability than uncorrelated ones, so decreasing the possibility of a node to reach far visibility and hence decreasing (statistically speaking) the probability of appearance of a large degree. Hence, the correlation tends to decrease the number of nodes with large degree as compared to the uncorrelated counterpart.

[2] This functional relation must nonetheless be taken in a cautious way, indeed, other chaos indicators (such as the Lyapunov spectra) may also play a relevant role in the final shape of $P(k)$ and such issues should be investigated in detail

Indeed, in the limit of infinitely large correlations ($\gamma \to 0$ or $\tau \to \infty$), the variability reduces to zero and the series become constant. The degree distribution in this limit case is, trivially,

$$P(k) = \delta(k-2) = \lim_{\lambda \to \infty} \frac{\lambda}{2} \exp(-\lambda|k-2|),$$

that is to say, infinitely large correlations would be associated to a diverging value of λ. This tendency is on agreement with the numerical simulations (figure 6) where we show that λ monotonically increases with decreasing values of γ or increasing values of τ respectively. Having in mind that in the limit of small correlations the theorem previously stated implies that $\lambda \to \lambda_{un} = \ln(3/2)$, we can therefore conclude that for a correlated stochastic process $\lambda_{stoch} > \lambda_{un}$.

Concerning chaotic series, remember that they are generated through a deterministic process whose orbit is continuous along the attractor. This continuity introduces a smoothing effect in the series that, statistically speaking, increases the probability of a given node to have a larger degree (uncorrelated series are rougher and hence it is more likely to have more nodes with smaller degree). Now, since in every case we have exponential degree distributions (this fact being related with the Poincaré recurrence theorem for chaotic series and with the return distribution in Poisson processes for stochastic series (Luque et al., 2009)), we conclude that the deviations must be encoded in the slope λ of the exponentials, such that $\lambda_{chaos} < \lambda_{un} < \lambda_{stoch}$, in good agreement with our numerical results.

3.3 Noise filtering using HVg: periodic series polluted with noise

In this section we address the task of filtering a noisy signal with a hidden periodic component within the horizontal visibility formalism, that is, we explore the possibility of using the method for noise filtering purposes (see (Núñez et al., 2010) for details). Periodicity detection algorithms (see for instance (Parthasarathy et al., 2006)) can be classified in essentially two categories, namely the time domain (autocorrelation based) and frequency domain (spectral) methods. Here we make use of the horizontal visibility algorithm to propose a third category: graph theoretical methods.

If we superpose a small amount of noise to a periodic series (a so-called *extrinsic* noise), while the degree of the nodes with associated small values will remain rather similar, the nodes associated to higher values will eventually increase their visibility and hence reach larger degrees. Accordingly, the delta-like structure of the degree distribution (associated with the periodic component of the series) will be perturbed, and an exponential tail will arise due to the presence of such noise (Lacasa et al., 2010; Luque et al., 2009). Can the algorithm characterize such kind of series? The answer is positive, since the degree distribution can be analytically calculated resulting in:

$$\begin{aligned}
&P(2) = 1/2, \\
&P(3) = 0, \\
&P(k+2) = \frac{1}{3}\left(\frac{2}{3}\right)^{k-2}, \; k \geq 2, \\
&\text{or } P(k) = \frac{1}{4}\left(\frac{2}{3}\right)^{k-3}, \; k \geq 4,
\end{aligned} \tag{28}$$

that is to say, introducing a small amount of extrinsic uncorrelated noise in a periodic signal introduces an exponential tail in the HVG's degree distribution with the same slope as the one associated to a purely uncorrelated process. The mean degree $\bar{k}$ reads

$$\bar{k} = \sum_{k=2}^{\infty} kP(k) = 4,$$

which, according to equation 3, suggests aperiodicity, as expected.

3.3.1 A graph-theoretical noise filter

Let $S = \{x_i\}_{i=1,\dots,n}$ be a periodic series of period T (where $n >> T$) polluted by a certain amount of extrinsic noise (without loss of generality, suppose a white noise extracted from a uniform distribution $U[-0.5, 0.5]$), and define the filter f as a real valued scalar such that $f \in [\min x_i, \max x_i]$. The so called filtered Horizontal Visibility Graph (f-HVg) associated to S is constructed as it follows:
(i) each datum x_i in the time series is mapped to a node i in the f-HVg, (ii) two nodes i and j are connected in the f-HVg if the associated data fulfill

$$x_i, x_j > x_n + f, \; \forall\, n \mid i < n < j\,. \tag{29}$$

The procedure of filtering the noise from a noisy periodic signal goes as follows: one generates the f-HVg associated to S for increasing values of f, and in each case proceeds to calculate the mean degree $\bar{k}$. For the proper interval $f_{min} < f < f_{max}$, the f-HVg of the noisy periodic series S will be equivalent to the noise free HVg of the pure (periodic) signal, which has a well defined mean degree as a function of the series period. In this interval, the mean degree will therefore remain constant, and from equation 3 the period can be inferred. As an example, we

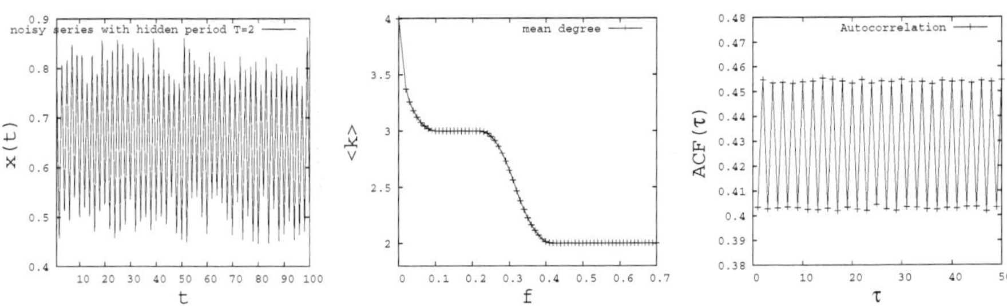

Fig. 7. *Left*: Periodic series of period $T = 2$ polluted with extrinsic noise extracted from a uniform distribution $U[-0.5, 0.5]$ of amplitude 0.1. *Middle*: Values of the HVg's mean degree $\bar{k}$ as a function of the amplitude of the graph theoretical filter. The first plateau is found for $\bar{k} = 3$, which renders a hidden period $T = (2 - \bar{k}/2)^{-1} = 2$. The second plateau corresponding to $\bar{k} = 2$ is found when the filter is large enough to screen each datum with its first neighbors, such that the mean degree reaches its lowest bound. *Right*: Autocorrelation function of the noisy periodic series, which is itself an almost periodic series with period $T = 2$, as it should.

have artificially generated a noisy periodic series of hidden period $T = 2$ (see figure 7). The results of the graph filtering technique yielded a net decreases of the mean degree, which has an initial value of 4 (as expected for the HVg ($f = 0$) of an aperiodic series such as a noisy periodic signal) and an asymptotic value of 2 (lower bound of the mean degree). The plateau is clearly found at $\bar{k} = 3$, which according to equation 3 yields a period

$$T = \left(2 - \frac{\bar{k}}{2}\right)^{-1} = 2,$$

as expected.

3.3.2 Noisy periodic versus chaotic

Let us now consider a simple case of chaotic map with disconnected attractors.The Logistic map

$$x_{t+1} = \mu x_t(1 - x_t),$$

with $x \in [0,1]$ and $\mu \in [3.6, 3.67]$ has an attractor that is partitioned in two disconnected chaotic bands, and the chaotic orbit makes an alternating journey between both bands (see fig. ̊figintro). The map is ergodic, but the attractor is not the whole interval, as there is a gap between both chaotic bands. In this situation, the chaotic series is by definition not periodic, however, an autocorrelation function analysis indeed suggests the presence of periodicity, what is reminiscent of the disconnected two-band structure of the attractor. Interestingly enough, applying the aforementioned noise filter technique, at odds with the autocorrelation function, the results suggests that the method does not find any periodic structure, as it should (see Núñez et al. (2010) for details). Furthermore, information of both the phase space structure and the chaotic nature of the map becomes accessible from an analysis of the HVg's degree distribution. First, we find $P(2) = 1/2$, that indicates that half of the data are located in the bottom chaotic band, in agreement with the alternating nature of the chaotic orbit. This is reminiscent of the misleading result obtained from the autocorrelation function. Second, the tail of the degree distribution is exponential, with an asymptotic slope smaller than the one obtained rigorously (Luque et al., 2009) for a purely uncorrelated process. This is, according to Lacasa et al. (2010), characteristic of an underlying chaotic process.

3.4 The period-doubling route to chaos via HVg: Feigenbaum graphs

In low-dimensional dissipative systems chaotic motion develops out of regular motion in a small number of ways or routes, and amongst which the period-doubling bifurcation cascade or Feigenbaum scenario is perhaps the better known and most famous mechanism (Peitgen et al., 1992; Schuster, 1988). This route to chaos appears an infinite number of times amongst the family of attractors spawned by unimodal maps within the so-called periodic windows that interrupt stretches of chaotic attractors. In the opposite direction, a route out of chaos accompanies each period-doubling cascade by a chaotic band-splitting cascade, and their shared bifurcation accumulation points form transitions between order and chaos that are known to possess universal properties (Peitgen et al., 1992; Schuster, 1988; Strogatz, 1994). Low-dimensional maps have been extensively studied from a purely theoretical perspective, but systems with many degrees of freedom used to study diverse problems in physics, biology, chemistry, engineering, and social science, are known to display low-dimensional dynamics (Marvel et al., 2009).

In this section, we offer a distinct view of the Feigenbaum scenario through the specific HVg formalism, and provide a complete set of graphs, which we call Feigenbaum graphs, that encode the dynamics of all stationary trajectories of unimodal maps. We first characterize their topology via the order-of-visit and self-affinity properties of the maps. We will additionally define a renormalization group (RG) procedure that leads, via its flows, to or from network fixed-points to a comprehensive view of the entire family of attractors. Furthermore, the optimization of the entropy obtained from the degree distribution coincides with the RG fixed points and reproduces the essential features of the map's Lyapunov exponent independently of its sign. A general observation is that the HV algorithm extracts only universal elements of the dynamics, free of the peculiarities of the individual unimodal map, but also of universality classes characterized by the degree of nonlinearity. Therefore all the results presented in this section, while referring to the specific Logistic map for illustrative reasons apply to any unimodal map.

3.4.1 Feigenbaum graphs

According to the HV algorithm, a time series generated by the Logistic map for a specific value of μ (after an initial transient of approach to the attractor) is converted into a Feigenbaum graph (Luque et al., 2011). Notice that this is a well-defined subclass of HV graphs where consecutive nodes of degree $k = 2$, that is, consecutive data with the same value, do not appear, what is actually the case for series extracted from maps (besides the trivial case of a constant series). While for a period T there are in principle several possible periodic orbits, and therefore the set of associated Feigenbaum graphs is degenerate, it can be proved that the mean degree $\bar{k}(T)$ and normalized mean distance $\bar{d}(T)$ of all these Feigenbaum graphs fulfill $\bar{k}(T) = 4(1 - \frac{1}{2T})$ and $\bar{d}(T) = \frac{1}{3T}$ respectively, yielding a linear relation $\bar{d}(\bar{k}) = (4 - \bar{k})/6$ that is corroborated in the inset of figure 8. Aperiodic series ($T \rightarrow \infty$) reach the upper bound mean degree $\bar{k} = 4$.

3.4.2 Period-doubling cascade

A deep-seated feature of the period-doubling cascade is that the order in which the positions of a periodic attractor are visited is universal (Schroeder, 1991), the same for all unimodal maps. This ordering turns out to be a decisive property in the derivation of the structure of the Feigenbaum graphs. A plot the graphs for a family of attractors of increasing period $T = 2^n$, that is, for increasing values of $\mu < \mu_\infty$ can be found in (Luque et al., 2011). This basic pattern also leads to the expression for their associated degree distributions,

$$P(n,k) = \left(\tfrac{1}{2}\right)^{k/2}, \quad k = 2,4,6,...,2n, \tag{30}$$
$$P(n,k) = \left(\tfrac{1}{2}\right)^{n}, \quad k = 2(n+1),$$

and zero for k odd or $k > 2(n+1)$. At the accumulation point μ_∞ the period diverges ($n \rightarrow \infty$) and the distribution is exponential for all even values of the degree,

$$P(\infty,k) = \left(\frac{1}{2}\right)^{k/2}, \quad k = 2,4,6,..., \tag{31}$$

and zero for k odd. Observe that these relations are independent of the order of the map's nonlinearity: the HV algorithm sifts out every detail of the dynamics except for the basic storyline.

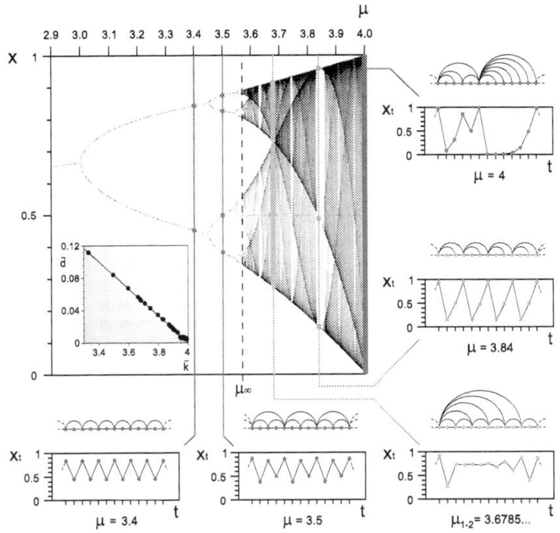

Fig. 8. Feigenbaum graphs from the Logistic map $x_{t+1} = f(x_t) = \mu x_t(1 - x_t)$. The main figure portrays the family of attractors of the Logistic map and indicates a transition from periodic to chaotic behavior at $\mu_\infty = 3.569946...$ through period-doubling bifurcations. For $\mu \geq \mu_\infty$ the figure shows merging of chaotic-band attractors where aperiodic behavior appears interrupted by windows that, when entered from their left-hand side, display periodic motion of period $T = m \cdot 2^0$ with $m > 1$ (for $\mu < \mu_\infty$, $m = 1$) that subsequently develops into m period-doubling cascades with new accumulation points $\mu_\infty(m)$. Each accumulation point $\mu_\infty(m)$ is in turn the limit of a chaotic-band reverse bifurcation cascade with m initial chaotic bands, reminiscent of the self-affine structure of the entire diagram. All unimodal maps exhibit a period-doubling route to chaos with universal asymptotic scaling ratios between successive bifurcations that depend only on the order of the nonlinearity of the map, the Logistic map belongs to the quadratic case. Adjoining the main figure, we show time series and their associated Feigenbaum graphs according to the HV mapping criterion for several values of μ where the map evidences both regular and chaotic behavior (see the text). Inset: numerical values of the mean normalized distance $\bar{d}$ as a function of mean degree $\bar{k}$ of the Feigenbaum graphs for $3 < \mu < 4$ (associated to time series of 1500 data after a transient and a step $\delta\mu = 0.05$), in good agreement with the theoretical linear relation (see the text).

3.4.3 Period-doubling bifurcation cascade of chaotic bands

We turn next to the period-doubling bifurcation cascade of chaotic bands that takes place as μ decreases from $\mu = 4$ towards μ_∞. For the largest value of the control parameter, at $\mu = 4$, the attractor is fully chaotic and occupies the entire interval $[0, 1]$ (see figure 8). This is the first chaotic band $n = 0$ at its maximum amplitude. As μ decreases in value within $\mu_\infty < \mu < 4$ band-narrowing and successive band-splittings (Peitgen et al., 1992; Schroeder, 1991; Schuster, 1988; Strogatz, 1994) occur. In general, after n reverse bifurcations the phase space is partitioned in 2^n disconnected chaotic bands, which are self-affine copies of the first chaotic band (Crutchfield et al., 1982). The values of μ at which the bands split are called Misiurewicz points (Schroeder, 1991), and their location converges to the accumulation point μ_∞ for $n \to \infty$. Significantly, while in the chaotic zone orbits are aperiodic, for reasons of continuity they visit each of the 2^n chaotic bands in the same order as positions are visited in the attractors of period $T = 2^n$ (Schroeder, 1991). A plot of the Feigenbaum graphs generated through chaotic time series at different values of μ that correspond to an increasing number of reverse bifurcations can be found in(Luque et al., 2011). Since chaotic bands do not overlap, one can derive the following degree distribution for a Feigenbaum graph after n chaotic-band reverse bifurcations by using only the universal order of visits

$$P_\mu(n,k) = \left(\tfrac{1}{2}\right)^{k/2}, \quad k = 2,4,6,...,2n,$$
$$P_\mu(n, k \geq 2(n+1)) = \left(\tfrac{1}{2}\right)^{n}, \tag{32}$$

and zero for $k = 3,5,7,...,2n+1$. We note that this time the degree distribution retains some dependence on the specific value of μ, concretely, for those nodes with degree $k \geq 2(n+1)$, all of which belong to the top chaotic band. The HV algorithm filters out chaotic motion within all bands except for that taking place in the top band whose contribution decreases as $n \to \infty$ and appears coarse-grained in the cumulative distribution $P_\mu(n, k \geq 2(n+1))$. As would be expected, at the accumulation point μ_∞ we recover the exponential degree distribution (equation 31), *i.e.* $\lim_{n\to\infty} P_\mu(n,k) = P(\infty,k)$.

3.4.4 Renormalization group

Before proceeding to interpret these findings via the consideration of renormalization group (RG) arguments, we recall that the Feigenbaum tree shows a rich self-affine structure: for $\mu > \mu_\infty$ periodic windows of initial period m undergo successive period-doubling bifurcations with new accumulation points $\mu_\infty(m)$ that appear interwoven with chaotic attractors. These cascades are self-affine copies of the fundamental one. The process of reverse bifurcations also evidences this self-affine structure, such that each accumulation point is the limit of a chaotic-band reverse bifurcation cascade. Accordingly, we label $G(m,n)$ the Feigenbaum graph associated with a periodic series of period $T = m \cdot 2^n$, that is, a graph obtained from an attractor within window of initial period m after n period-doubling bifurcations. In the same fashion, $G_\mu(n,m)$ is associated with a chaotic attractor composed by $m \cdot 2^n$ bands (that is, after n chaotic band reverse bifurcations of m initial chaotic bands). Graphs corresponding to $G(1,n)$ and $G_\mu(1,n)$ respectively can be found in (Luque et al., 2011). For the first accumulation point $G(1,\infty) = G_\mu(1,\infty) \equiv G_\infty$. Similarly, in each accumulation point $\mu_\infty(m)$, the identity $G(m,\infty) = G_\mu(m,\infty)$ is fulfilled.

In order to recast previous findings in the context of the renormalization group, let us define an RG operation $\mathcal{R}$ on a graph as the coarse-graining of every couple of adjacent nodes where one of them has degree $k = 2$ into a block node that inherits the links of the previous two nodes. This is a real-space RG transformation on the Feigenbaum graph (Newmann & Watts, 1999), dissimilar from recently suggested box-covering complex network renormalization schemes (Radicchi et al., 2008; Song et al., 2005; 2006). This scheme turns out to be equivalent for $\mu < \mu_\infty$ to the construction of an HV graph from the composed map $f^{(2)}$ instead of the original f, in correspondence to the original Feigenbaum renormalization procedure (Strogatz, 1994). We first note that $\mathcal{R}\{G(1,n)\} = G(1,n-1)$, thus, an iteration of this process yields an RG flow that converges to the (1st) trivial fixed point $\mathcal{R}^{(n)}\{G(1,n)\} = G(1,0) \equiv G_0 = \mathcal{R}\{G_0\}$. This is the stable fixed point of the RG flow $\forall \mu < \mu_\infty$. We note that there is only one relevant variable in our RG scheme, represented by the reduced control parameter $\Delta\mu = \mu_\infty - \mu$, hence, to identify a nontrivial fixed point we set $\Delta\mu = 0$ or equivalently $n \to \infty$, where the structure of the Feigenbaum graph turns to be completely self-similar under $\mathcal{R}$. Therefore we conclude that $G(1,\infty) \equiv G_\infty$ is the nontrivial fixed point of the RG flow, $\mathcal{R}\{G_\infty\} = G_\infty$. In connection with this, let $P_t(k)$ be the degree distribution of a generic Feigenbaum graph G_t in the period-doubling cascade after t iterations of $\mathcal{R}$, and point out that the RG operation, $\mathcal{R}\{G_t\} = G_{t+1}$, implies a recurrence relation $(1 - P_t(2))P_{t+1}(k) = P_t(k+2)$, whose fixed point coincides with the degree distribution found in equation 31. This confirms that the nontrivial fixed point of the flow is indeed G_∞.

Next, under the same RG transformation, the self-affine structure of the family of attractors yields $\mathcal{R}\{G_\mu(1,n)\} = G_\mu(1,n-1)$, generating a RG flow that converges to the Feigenbaum graph associated to the 1st chaotic band, $\mathcal{R}^{(n)}\{G_\mu(1,n)\} = G_\mu(1,0)$. Repeated application of $\mathcal{R}$ breaks temporal correlations in the series, and the RG flow leads to a 2nd trivial fixed point $\mathcal{R}^{(\infty)}\{G_\mu(1,0)\} = G_{\text{rand}} = \mathcal{R}\{G_{\text{rand}}\}$, where G_{rand} is the HV graph generated by a purely uncorrelated random process. This graph has a universal degree distribution $P(k) = (1/3)(2/3)^{k-2}$, independent of the random process underlying probability density (see (Lacasa et al., 2010; Luque et al., 2009)).

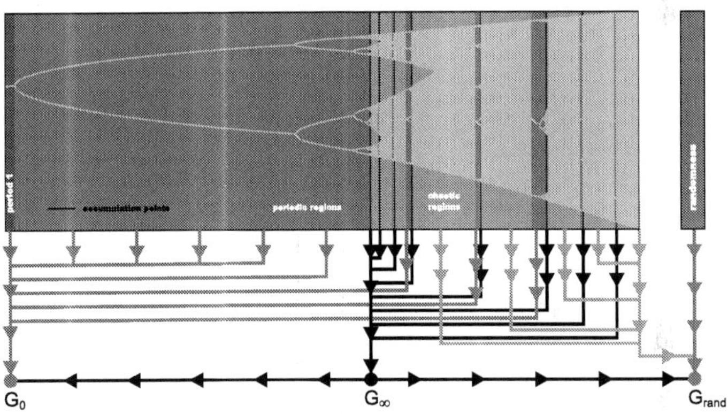

Fig. 9. Illustrative cartoon incorporating the RG flow of Feigenbaum graphs in the whole Feigenbaum diagram: aperiodic (chaotic or random) series generate graphs whose RG flow converge to the trivial fixed point G_{rand}, whereas periodic series (both in the region $\mu < \mu_\infty$ and inside windows of stability) generate graphs whose RG flow converges to the trivial fixed point $G(0,1)$. The nontrivial fixed point of the RG flow $G(\infty,1)$ is only reached through the critical manifold of graphs at the accumulation points $\mu_\infty(m)$.

Finally, let us consider the RG flow inside a given periodic window of initial period m. As the renormalization process addresses nodes with degree $k = 2$, the initial applications of $\mathcal{R}$ only change the core structure of the graph associated with the specific value m. The RG flow will therefore converge to the 1st trivial fixed point via the initial path $\mathcal{R}^{(p)}\{G(m,n)\} = G(1,n)$, with $p \leq m$, whereas it converges to the 2nd trivial fixed point for $G_\mu(m,n)$ via $\mathcal{R}^{(p)}\{G_\mu(m,n)\} = G_\mu(1,n)$. In the limit of $n \to \infty$ the RG flow proceeds towards the nontrivial fixed point via the path $\mathcal{R}^{(p)}\{G(m,\infty)\} = G(1,\infty)$. Incidentally, extending the definition of the reduced control parameter to $\Delta\mu(m) = \mu_\infty(m) - \mu$, the family of accumulation points is found at $\Delta\mu(m) = 0$. A complete schematic representation of the RG flows can be seen in figure 9.

Interestingly, and at odds with standard RG applications to (asymptotically) scale-invariant systems, we find that invariance at $\Delta\mu = 0$ is associated in this instance to an exponential (rather than power-law) function of the observables, concretely, that for the degree distribution. The reason is straightforward: $\mathcal{R}$ is not a conformal transformation (*i.e.* a scale operation) as in the typical RG, but rather, a translation procedure. The associated invariant functions are therefore non homogeneous (with the property $g(ax) = bg(x)$), but exponential (with the property $g(x+a) = cg(x)$).

3.4.5 Network entropy

Finally, we derive, via optimization of an entropic functional for the Feigenbaum graphs, all the RG flow directions and fixed points directly from the information contained in the degree distribution. Amongst the graph theoretical entropies that have been proposed we employ here the Shannon entropy of the degree distribution $P(k)$, that is $h = -\sum_{k=2}^{\infty} P(k)\log P(k)$. By making use of the Maximum Entropy formalism, it is easy to prove that the degree distribution $P(k)$ that maximizes h is exactly $P(k) = (1/3)(2/3)^{k-2}$, which corresponds to the distribution for the 2nd trivial fixed point of the RG flow G_{rand}. Alternatively, with the incorporation of the additional constraint that allows only even values for the degree (the topological restriction for Feigenbaum graphs $G(1,n)$), entropy maximization yields a degree distribution that coincides with equation 31, which corresponds to the nontrivial fixed point of the RG flow G_∞. Lastly, the degree distribution that minimizes h trivially corresponds to G_0, *i.e.* the 1st trivial fixed point of the RG flow. Remarkably, these results indicate that the fixed-point structure of the RG flow are obtained via optimization of the entropy for the entire family of networks, supporting a suggested connection between RG theory and the principle of Maximum Entropy (Robledo, 1999).

The network entropy h can be calculated exactly for $G(1,n)$ ($\mu < \mu_\infty$ or $T = 2^n$), yielding $h(n) = \log 4 \cdot (1 - 2^{-n})$. Because increments of entropy are only due to the occurrence of bifurcations h increases with μ in a step-wise way, and reaches asymptotically the value $h(\infty) = \log 4$ at the accumulation point μ_∞. For Feigenbaum graphs $G_\mu(1,n)$ (in the chaotic region), in general h cannot be derived exactly since the precise shape of $P(k)$ is unknown (albeit the asymptotic shape is also exponential (Luque et al., 2011)). Yet, the main feature of h can be determined along the chaotic-band splitting process, as each reverse bifurcation generates two self-affine copies of each chaotic band. Accordingly, the decrease of entropy associated with this reverse bifurcation process can be described as $h_\mu(n) = \log 4 + h_\mu(0)/2^n$, where the entropy $h_\mu(n)$ after n reverse bifurcations can be described in terms of the entropy associated with the first chaotic band $h_\mu(0)$. The chaotic-band reverse bifurcation process takes place in the chaotic region in the direction of decreasing μ's, and therefore leads in this case to a decrease of entropy with an asymptotic value of $\log 4$ for $n \to \infty$ at the accumulation point. These results suggest that the graph entropy behaves qualitatively as the map's Lyapunov exponent λ, with the peculiarity of having a shift of $\log 4$, as confirmed in figure 10. This unexpected qualitative agreement is reasonable in the chaotic region in view of the Pesin theorem (Peitgen et al., 1992), that relates the positive Lyapunov exponents of a map with its Kolmogorov-Sinai entropy (akin to a topological entropy) that for unimodal

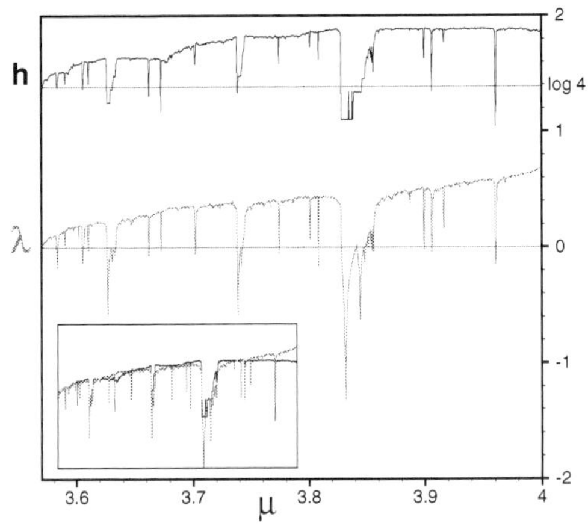

Fig. 10. Horizontal visibility network entropy h and Lyapunov exponent λ for the Logistic map. We plot the numerical values of h and λ for $3.5 < \mu < 4$ (the numerical step is $\delta\mu = 5 \cdot 10^{-4}$ and in each case the processed time series have a size of 2^{12} data). The inset reproduces the same data but with a rescaled entropy $h - \log(4)$. The surprisingly good match between both quantities is reminiscent of the Pesin identity (see text). Unexpectedly, the Lyapunov exponent within the periodic windows ($\lambda < 0$ inside the chaotic region) is also well captured by h.

maps reads $h_{KS} = \lambda, \forall \lambda > 0$, since h can be understood as a proxy for h_{KS}. Unexpectedly, this qualitative agreement seems also valid in the periodic windows ($\lambda < 0$), since the graph entropy is positive and varies with the value of the associated (negative) Lyapunov exponent even though $h_{KS} = 0$, hinting at a Pesin-like relation valid also out of chaos which deserves further investigation. The agreement between both quantities lead us to conclude that the Feigenbaum graphs capture not only the period-doubling route to chaos in a universal way, but also inherits the main feature of chaos, *i.e.* sensitivity to initial conditions.

3.5 Measuring irreversibility via HVg

A stationary process x_t is said to be statistically time reversible (hereafter time reversible) if for every n, the series $\{x_1, \cdots, x_n\}$ and $\{x_n, \cdots, x_1\}$ have the same joint probability distributions (Weiss, 1975). Roughly, this means that a reversible time series and its time reversed are, statistically speaking, equally probable. Reversible processes include the family of Gaussian linear processes (as well as Fourier-transform surrogates and nonlinear static transformations of them), and are associated with processes at thermal equilibrium in statistical physics. Conversely, time series irreversibility is indicative of the presence of nonlinearities in the underlying dynamics, including non-Gaussian stochastic processes and dissipative chaos, and are associated with systems driven out-of-equilibrium in the realm of thermodynamics (Kawai et al., 2007; Parrondo et al., 2009). Time series irreversibility is an important topic in basic and applied science. From a physical perspective, and based on the relation between statistical reversibility and physical dissipation (Kawai et al., 2007; Parrondo et al., 2009), the concept of time series irreversibility has been used to derive information about the entropy production of the physical mechanism generating the series, even if one ignores any detail of such mechanism (Roldan & Parrondo, 2011). In a more applied context, it has been suggested that irreversibility in complex physiological series decreases with aging or pathology, being maximal in young and healthy subjects (Costa et al., 2005; 2008; Yang et al., 2003), rendering this feature important for noninvasive diagnosis. As complex signals pervade natural and social sciences, the topic of time series reversibility is indeed relevant for scientists aiming to understand and model the dynamics behind complex signals.

The definition of time series reversibility is formal and therefore there is not an *a priori* optimal algorithm to quantify it in practice. Several methods to measure time irreversibility have been proposed (Andrieux et al., 2007; Cammarota & Rogora, 2007; Costa et al., 2005; Daw et al., 2000; Diks et al., 1995; Gaspard, 2004; Kennel, 2004; Wang et al., 2005; Yang et al., 2003). The majority of them perform a time series symbolization, typically making an empirical partition of the data range (Daw et al., 2000) (note that such a transformation does not alter the reversible character of the output series (Kennel, 2004)) and subsequently analyze the symbolized series, through statistical comparison of symbol strings occurrence in the forward and backwards series or using compression algorithms (Cover & Thomas, 2006; Kennel, 2004; Roldan & Parrondo, 2011). The first step requires an extra amount of *ad hoc* information (such as range partitioning or size of the symbol alphabet) and therefore the output of these methods eventually depend on these extra parameters. A second issue is that since typical symbolization is local, the presence of multiple scales (a signature of complex signals) could be swept away by this coarse-graining: in this sense multi-scale algorithms have been proposed recently (Costa et al., 2005; 2008). The *time directed* version of the horizontal visibility algorithm is proposed in this section as a simple and well defined tool for measuring time series irreversibility (see Lacasa et al. (2011) for details).

3.5.1 Quantifying irreversibility: DHVg and Kullback-Leibler divergence

The main conjecture of this application is that the information stored in the *in* and *out* distributions take into account the amount of time irreversibility of the associated series. More precisely, we claim that this can be measured, in a first approximation, as the distance (in a distributional sense) between the *in* and *out* degree distributions ($P_{\text{in}}(k)$ and $P_{\text{out}}(k)$). If needed, higher order measures can be used, such as the corresponding distance between the *in* and *out* degree-degree distributions ($P_{\text{in}}(k,k')$ and $P_{\text{out}}(k,k')$). These are defined as the *in* and *out* joint degree distributions of a node and its first neighbors (Newmann, 2003), describing the probability of an arbitrary node whose neighbor has degree k' to have degree k.

The Kullback-Leibler divergence (Cover & Thomas, 2006) is used as the distance between the *in* and *out* degree distributions. Relative entropy or Kullback-Leibler divergence (KLD) is introduced in information theory as a measure of distinguishability between two probability distributions. Given a random variable x and two probability distributions $p(x)$ and $q(x)$, KLD between p and q is defined as follows:

$$D(p||q) \equiv \sum_{x \in \mathcal{X}} p(x) \log \frac{p(x)}{q(x)}, \tag{33}$$

which vanishes if and only if both probability distributions are equal $p = q$ and it is bigger than zero otherwise.

We compare the outgoing degree distribution in the actual (forward) series $P_{k_{out}}(k|\{x(t)\}_{t=1,...,N}) = P_{out}(k)$ with the corresponding probability in the time-reversed (or backward) time series, which is equal to the probability distribution of the ingoing degree in the actual process $P_{k_{out}}(k|\{x(t)\}_{t=N,...,1}) = P_{in}(k)$. The KLD between these two distributions is

$$D[P_{out}(k)||P_{in}(k)] = \sum_k P_{out}(k) \log \frac{P_{out}(k)}{P_{in}(k)}. \tag{34}$$

This measure vanishes if and only if the outgoing and ingoing degree probability distributions of a time series are identical, $P_{out}(k) = P_{in}(k)$, and it is positive otherwise. We will apply it to several examples as a measure of irreversibility.

Notice that previous methods to estimate time series irreversibility generally proceed by first making a (somewhat *ad hoc*) local symbolization of the series, coarse-graining each of the series data into a symbol (typically, an integer) from an ordered set. Then, they subsequently perform a statistical analysis of word occurrences (where a word of length n is simply a concatenation of n symbols) from the forward and backwards symbolized series (Andrieux et al., 2007; Wang et al., 2005). Time series irreversibility is therefore linked to the difference between the word statistics of the forward and backwards symbolized series. The method presented here can also be considered as a symbolization if we restrict ourselves to the information stored in the series $\{k_{out}(t)\}_{t=1,...,N}$ and $\{k_{in}(t)\}_{t=1,...,N}$. However, at odds with other methods, here the symbolization process (i) lacks *ad hoc* parameters (such as number of symbols in the set or partition definition), and (ii) it takes into account *global* information: each coarse-graining $x_t \rightarrow (k_{in}(t), k_{out}(t))$ is performed using information from the whole series, according to the mapping criterion of fig. 3. Hence, this symbolization naturally takes into account multiple scales, which is desirable if we want to tackle complex signals (Costa et al., 2005; 2008).

3.5.2 Results for correlated stochastic series

The first example of a reversible series with $D[P_{out}(k)||P_{in}(k)] = 0$ are uncorrelated stochastic series which were considered in 2.6.1. As a further validation, linearly correlated stochastic processes have also been considered as additional examples of reversible dynamics (Weiss, 1975). An explanation of the method employed to generate the series can be consulted in (Lacasa et al., 2010), and results are summarized in table 1.

3.5.3 Results for a discrete flashing ratchet

A discrete flashing ratchet is an example of thermodynamic system which can be smoothly driven out of equilibrium by modifying the value of a physical parameter (the peak value V of an asymmetric potencial). We make use of a time series generated by a discrete flashing ratchet model introduced in (Roldan & Parrondo, 2010). For $V = 0$ detailed balance condition is satisfied, the system is in equilibrium and trajectories are statistically reversible. In this case both $D[P_{out}(k)||P_{in}(k)]$ and $D[P_{out}(k,k')||P_{in}(k,k')]$ using degree distributions and degree-degree distributions vanish. On the other hand, if V is increased, the system is driven out of equilibrium, what introduces a net statistical irreversibility which increases with V (Roldan & Parrondo, 2010). The amount of irreversibility estimated with KLD increases with

V for both measures, therefore the results produced by the method are qualitatively correct (see (Lacasa et al., 2011) for details). Interestingly enough, the tendency holds even for high values of the potential, where the statistics are poor and the KLD of sequences of symbols usually fail when estimating irreversibility (Roldan & Parrondo, 2010). However the values of the KLD obtained are far below the KLD per step between the forward and backward trajectories, which is equal to the dissipation as reported in (Roldan & Parrondo, 2010).

The degree distributions capture the irreversibility of the original series but it is difficult to establish a quantitative relationship between eq. (34) and the KLD between trajectories. The

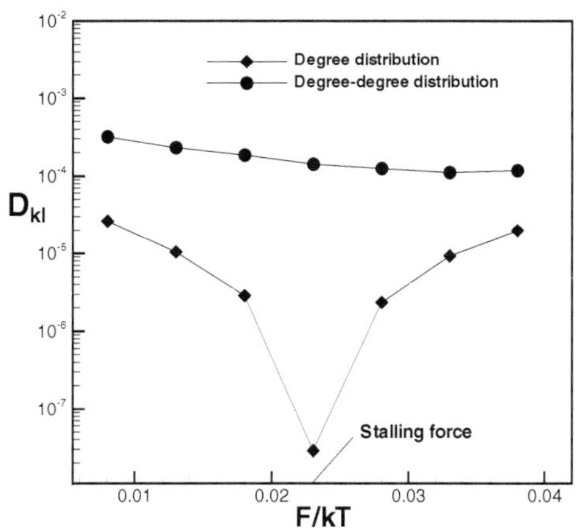

Fig. 11. Irreversibility measures $D[P_{\text{out}}(k)||P_{\text{in}}(k)]$ and $D[P_{\text{out}}(k,k')||P_{\text{in}}(k,k')]$ in the flashing ratchet ($r = 2, V = 2kT$) as a function of FL/kT. Here, F is the applied force and L is the spatial period of the ratchet, which in this case is equal to 1. For each value of the force, we make use of a single stationary series of size $N = 10^6$ containing partial information (the state information is removed).

measure based on the degree-degree distribution $D[P_{\text{out}}(k,k')||P_{\text{in}}(k,k')]$ takes into account more information of the visibility graph structure than the KLD using degree distributions, providing a closer bound to the physical dissipation as it is expected by the chain rule (Cover & Thomas, 2006), $D[P_{\text{out}}(k,k')||P_{\text{in}}(k,k')] \geq D[P_{\text{out}}(k)||P_{\text{in}}(k)]$. The improvement is even qualitatively significant in some situations. For instance, when a force opposite to the net current on the system is present (Roldan & Parrondo, 2010), the current vanishes for a given value of the force usually termed as *stalling force*. When the force reaches this value, the system is still out of equilibrium ($V > 0$) and it is therefore time irreversible, but no current of particles is observed if we describe the dynamics of the ratchet with partial information given by the position x. $D[P_{\text{out}}(k)||P_{\text{in}}(k)]$ tends to zero when the force approaches to the stalling value (see figure 11). Therefore, our measure of irreversibility (34) fails in this case, as do other KLD estimators based on local flows or currents (Roldan & Parrondo, 2010). However, $D[P_{\text{out}}(k,k')||P_{\text{in}}(k,k')]$ captures the irreversibility of the time series, and yields a positive value at the stalling force(Roldan & Parrondo, 2011).

Series description	$D[P_{\text{out}}(k)\|\|P_{\text{in}}(k)]$	$D[P_{\text{out}}(k,k')\|\|P_{\text{in}}(k,k')]$
Reversible Stochastic Processes		
$U[0,1]$ uncorrelated	$3.88 \cdot 10^{-6}$	$2.85 \cdot 10^{-4}$
Ornstein-Uhlenbeck ($\tau = 1.0$)	$7.82 \cdot 10^{-6}$	$1.52 \cdot 10^{-4}$
Long-range correlated stationary process ($\gamma = 2.0$)	$1.28 \cdot 10^{-5}$	$2.0 \cdot 10^{-4}$
Dissipative Chaos		
Logistic map ($\mu = 4$)	0.377	2.978
α map ($\alpha = 3$)	0.455	3.005
α map ($\alpha = 4$)	0.522	3.518
Henon map ($a = 1.4, b = 0.3$)	0.178	1.707
Lozi map	0.114	1.265
Kaplan Yorke map	0.164	0.390
Conservative Chaos		
Arnold Cat map	$1.77 \cdot 10^{-5}$	$4.05 \cdot 10^{-4}$

Table 1. Values of the irreversibility measure associated to the degree distribution $D[P_{\text{out}}(k)||P_{\text{in}}(k)]$ and the degree-degree distribution $D[P_{\text{out}}(k,k')||P_{\text{in}}(k,k')]$ respectively, for the visibility graphs associated to series of 10^6 data generated from reversible and irreversible processes. In every case chain rule is satisfied, since $D[P_{\text{out}}(k,k')||P_{\text{in}}(k,k')] \geq D[P_{\text{out}}(k)||P_{\text{in}}(k)]$. Note that that the method correctly distinguishes between reversible and irreversible processes, as KLD vanishes for the former and it is positive for the latter.

3.5.4 Results for chaotic series

This method was applied to several chaotic series and found that it is able to distinguish between dissipative and conservative chaotic systems. Dissipative chaotic systems are those that do not preserve the volume of the phase space, and they produce irreversible time series. This is the case of chaotic maps in which entropy production via instabilities in the forward time direction is quantitatively different to the amount of past information lost. In other words, those whose positive Lyapunov exponents, which characterize chaos in the forward process, differ in magnitude with negative ones, which characterize chaos in the backward process (Kennel, 2004). Several chaotic maps have been analyzed and the degree of reversibility of their associated time series has been estimated using using KLD, showing that for dissipative chaotic series it is positive while it vanishes for an example of conservative chaos. A summary of results cann be checked in table 1. In every case, we find an asymptotic positive value, in agreement with the conjecture that dissipative chaos is indeed time irreversible.

Finally, we also consider the *Arnold cat map*: $x_{t+1} = x_t + y_t \mod(1), y_{t+1} = x_t + 2y_t \mod(1)$. At odds with previous dissipative maps, this is an example of a *conservative* (measure-preserving) chaotic system with integer Kaplan-Yorke dimension (Sprott & Rowlands, 2001). The map has two Lyapunov exponents which coincide in magnitude $\lambda_1 = \ln(3+\sqrt{5})/2 = 0.9624$ and $\lambda_2 = \ln(3-\sqrt{5})/2 = -0.9624$. This implies that the amount of information created in the forward process (λ_1) is equal to the amount of information created in the backwards process ($-\lambda_2$), therefore the process is time reversible. $D[P_{\text{out}}(k)||P_{\text{in}}(k)]$ for a time series of this map asymptotically tends to zero with series size, and the same happens with the degree-degree distributions (see table 1). This correctly suggests that albeit chaotic, the map is statistically time reversible.

3.5.5 Robustness: Irreversible chaotic series polluted with noise

Standard time series analysis methods evidence problems when noise is present in chaotic series. Even a small amount of noise can destroy the fractal structure of a chaotic attractor and mislead the calculation of chaos indicators such as the correlation dimension or the Lyapunov exponents (Kostelich & Schreiber, 1993). In order to check if our method is robust, we add an amount of white noise (measurement noise) to a signal extracted from a fully chaotic Logistic map ($\mu = 4.0$). The results for the KLD of the signal polluted with noise is significantly greater than zero, as it exceeds the one associated to the noise in four orders of magnitude, even when the noise reaches the 100% of the signal amplitude (Lacasa et al., 2011). Therefore our method correctly predicts that the signal is irreversible even when adding a large amount of noise.

4. Summary, perspectives and open problems

In this chapter a review on the state of the art of visibility algorithms as a method to make time series analysis through network theory has been presented. We have reported the properties of natural and horizontal visibility algorithms, and have explored their ability in several problems such as the estimation of Hurst exponent in self-similar (fractal series), the discrimination between uncorrelated, correlated stochastic and chaotic processes, the problem of noise filtering, the problem of determining the amount of irreversibility (i.e. entropy production) of a system, or the generic study of nonlinear systems as they undergo a period-doubling route to chaos.

Before commenting on the plethora of applications and challenging open problems to be faced, a few words on how to be cautious and make good science should be stated. The simplicity and straightforwardness of a method can be tricky, since they could convey the wrong impression to directly produce results when applied to concrete problems. From a physical point of view, the practical interest of this method lies in its ability to reveal properties of the system under study, i.e. to reveal hidden structures in a given series. But this capacity is intimately linked to the strength and extent of the theory behind the method. That is why, before venturing to study complex systems in nature, a method should provide a sufficient theoretical support. In the case under study, it should be clearly stated what information and which properties we are mapping into what and how, before attempting to measure all kind of features in a visibility graph.

According to this, the first general open problem lies just there: to generate a mathematically sound, rigorous theory that explains and shows how time series/dynamical systems properties are mapped into the associated visibility graph. In this review we have outlined the first steps in this direction, but a broad and general theory is still to be completely developed. This theory should deal with questions such as (i) what concrete information are the algorithms mapping? and (ii) how they do so? Once we know this, we can understand what network features are behind multifractality, spatio-temporal chaos, intermittency, quasi-periodicity, and many other complex dynamical processes.

Only when these questions have been rigorously responded, this tool could be ready to be unambigously used by practitioners, since visibility algorithms will be a new and universal method to extract information from complex signals. Moreover, the possibility of defining mesoscale measures, which are typically network-based (for instance, modularity, community structure, etc), could be of interest to analyze non-local / multiscale dynamics. The potentials of the method could then apply to study long standing problems in Physics and Society, such as turbulence, stock market dynamics, or physiological signals such as electro-encephalogram, electro-cardiograms, and so on. On this respect, the initial naive approaches in those directions (turbulence (Liu et al., 2009), financial series (Liu et al., 2009; Yang et al., 2009), cardiac series (Shao, 2010)) are nowadays inconclusive because the theory behind the method is not fully developed. Eventually.

5. References

D. Andrieux, P. Gaspard, S. Ciliberto, N. Garnier, S. Joubaud, and A. Petrosyan, Entropy production and time asymmetry in nonequilibrium fluctuations, *Phys. Rev. Lett.* 98, 150601 (2007).

Boccaletti S, Latora V, Moreno Y, Chavez M, & Hwang DU (2006) Complex networks: Structure and dynamics. Phys. Rep. 424, 175.

Buchner T. and Zebrowski J.J., Logistic map with a delayed feedback: Stability of a discrete time-delay control of chaos. *Phys. Rev. E* 63, 016210 (2000).

C. Cammarota and E. Rogora, Time reversal, symbolic series and irreversibility of human heartbeat *Chaos, Solitons and Fractals* 32 (2007) 1649-1654.

Campanharo, Andriana S. L. O., Sirer, M. Irmak, Malmgren, R. Dean, Ramos, Fernando M. & Amaral, Luís A. Nunes (2011). Duality between Time Series and Networks. *PLoS ONE*, Vol. 6, No. 8, e23378.

A. Carbone, *Phys. Rev. E* 76, 056703 (2007).

Cencini M., Cecconi F., and Vulpiani A., *Chaos: From Simple Models to Complex Systems*, World Scientific (2010).

M. Costa, A.L. Goldberger, and C.-K. Peng, Broken Asymmetry of the Human Heartbeat: Loss of Time Irreversibility in Aging and Disease, *Phys. Rev. Lett.* 95, 198102 (2005).

M.D. Costa, C.K. Peng and A.L. Goldberger, Multiscale Analysis of Heart Rate Dynamics: Entropy and Time Irreversibility Measures, *Cardiovasc Eng* 8, (2008)

T.M. Cover and J.A. Thomas, *Elements of Information Theory* (Wiley, New Jersey, 2006).

Crutchfield JP, Farmer JD & Huberman BA (1982) Fluctuations and simple chaotic dynamics. Phys. Rep. 92, 2.

C.S. Daw, C.E.A. Finney, and M.B. Kennel, Symbolic approach for measuring temporal 'irreversibility', *Phys. Rev. E* 62, 2 (2000).

C. Diks, J.C. van Houwelingen, F. Takens, and J. DeGoede, Reversibility as a criterion for discriminating time series, *Phys. Lett. A* 201 (1995), 221-228.

Donner, R. V., Zou, Y., Donges, J. F., Marwan, N. & Juergen Kurths (2010). Recurrence networks - A novel paradigm for nonlinear time series analysis. *New Journal of Physics*, 12, 033025.

Donner, R. V., Small, M., Donges, J. F., Marwan, N., Zou, Y., Xiang, R. & Juergen Kurths (2010). Recurrence-based time series analysis by means of complex network methods. *International Journal of Bifurcation and Chaos*, Vol. 21, No. 4, 1019–1046.

P. Gaspard, Time-reversed dynamical entropy and irreversibility in markovian random processes, *J. Stat. Phys.* 117 (2004).

A.L. Goldberger *et al.*, *Circulation* 101, 23 (2000) 215-220.

A.R. Goldenberger *et al.*, *Proc. Natl. Acad. Sci. USA* 99, 1 (2002), 2466-2472.

Gutin, G., Mansour, T. & Severini, S. (2011). A characterization of horizontal visibility graphs and combinatorics on words. *PHYSICA A*, Vol. 390 (12), 2421–2428.

Haraguchi, Y., Shimada, Y., Ikeguchi, T. & Aihara, K. (2009). Transformation from complex networks to time series using classical multidimensional scaling, *Proceedings of the 19th International Conference on Artificial Neural Networks*, Heidelberg, Berlin, ICANN 2009, Springer-Verlag.

J.M. Hausdorff *et al.*, *J. App. Physiol.* 80 (1996) 1448-1457.

J. W. Kantelhardt, Fractal and multifractal time series, in: *Springer encyclopaedia of complexity and system science* (in press, 2008) preprint arXiv:0804.0747.

Kants H. and Schreiber T. *Nonlinear Time Series Analysis*, (Camdrige University Press, 2003).

T. Karagiannis, M. Molle and M. Faloutsos, *IEEE internet computing* 8, 5 (2004) 57-64.

R. Kawai, JMR Parrondo and C Van den Broeck, Dissipation: the phase-space perspective, *Phys. Rev. Lett.* 98, 080602 (2007).

MB Kennel, Testing time symmetry in time series using data compression techniques, *Phys. Rev. E* 69, 056208 (2004).

E.J. Kostelich and T. Schreiber, *Phys. Rev. E* 48, 1752 (1993).

Lacasa L., Luque B., Ballesteros F., Luque J. & Nuño J.C. (2008). From time series to complex networks: the visibility graph. *Proc. Natl. Acad. Sci. USA* 105, 13, 4972-4975.

Lacasa L., Luque B., Nuño J.C. & Luque J. (2009). The Visibility Graph: a new method for estimating the Hurst exponent of fractional Brownian motion. *EPL* 86, 30001 (2009).

Lacasa, L. & Toral, R. (2010). Description of stochastic and chaotic series using visibility graphs. *Phys. Rev. E* 82, 036120 (2010).

Lacasa, L., Núñez, A. M., Roldan, E., Parrondo, J.M.R., & Luque, B. (2011).Time series irreversibility: a visibility graph approach. *arXiv:1108.1691* 2011.

Liu, C., Zhou, W-T. & Yuan, W-K. (2009). Statistical properties of visibility graph of energy dissipation rates in three-dimensional fully developed turbulence. *Physics Letters A*, Vol. 389 (13), 7.

Luque B., Lacasa L., Balleteros F., & Luque J. (2009). Horizontal visibility graphs: exact results for random time series. *Phys Rev E* 80, 046103 (2009).

B. Luque, L. Lacasa, F.J. Ballesteros & A. Robledo (2011). Feigenbaum graphs: a complex network perspective of chaos *PLoS ONE* 6, 9 (2011).

B.B Mandelbrot & J.W Van Ness (1968). Fractional Brownian Motions, Fractional Noises and Applications. *SIAM Review* 10, 4 (1968) 422-437.

Marvel, S.A., Mirollo, R.E. & Strogatz, S. H. (2009) Identical phase oscillators with global sinusoidal coupling evolve by Möbius group action. Chaos 19, 043104.

J. Mielniczuk and P. Wojdyllo, *Comput. Statist. Data Anal.* 51 (2007) 4510-4525.

Núñez, A. M., Lacasa, L., Valero, E., Gómez, J.P. & Luque, B. (2010). Detecting series periodicity with horizontal visibility graphs. *International Journal of Bifurcation and Chaos*, in press, 2010.

Newmann MEJ & Watts DJ (1999) Renormalization group analysis of the small-world network model. Phys. Lett. A 263:341-346.

M.E.J. Newmann, The structure and function of complex networks, *SIAM Review* 45, 167-256 (2003).

JMR Parrondo, C Van den Broeck and R Kawai, Entropy production and the arrow of time, *New. J. Phys.* 11 (2009) 073008.

Parthasarathy S, Mehta S., and Srinivasan S. (2006). Robust Periodicity Detection Algorithms, Proceedings of the 15th ACM international conference on Information and knowledge management.

Peitgen H.O., Jurgens H., and Saupe D. *Chaos and Fractals: New Frontiers of Science*, Springer-Verlag, New York.(1992).

B. Pilgram and D.T. Kaplan, *Physica D* 114 (1998) 108-112.

B. Podobnik, H.E. Stanley, *Phys. Rev.Lett.* 100, 084102 (2008).

Radicchi F, Ramasco JJ, Barrat A, & Fortunato S (2008) Complex Networks Renormalization: Flows and Fixed Points. Phys. Rev. Lett. 101, 148701.

E. Ravasz, A.L. Somera, D.A. Mongru, Z.N. Oltvai, A.-L. Barabasi, *Science* 297, 1551 (2002).

Robledo, A. (1999) Renormalization group, entropy optimization, and nonextensivity at criticality. Phys. Rev. Lett. 83, 12.

E. Roldan and JMR Parrondo, Estimating dissipation from single stationary trajectories, *Phys. Rev. Lett.* 105, 15 (2010).

E. Roldan and JMR Parrondo, Dissipation and relative entropy in discrete random stationary states, *in preparation.*

Schroeder M (1991) Fractals, chaos, power laws: minutes from an infinite paradise. Freeman and Co., New York.

Schuster, H.G. (1988) Deterministic Chaos. An Introduction. 2nd revised ed, Weinheim: VCH.

Shao, Z-G. (2010). Network analysis of human heartbeat dynamics. *Applied Physics Letters*, Vol. 96 073703 (2010).

A. H. Shirazi, G. Reza Jafari, J. Davoudi, J. Peinke, M. Reza Rahimi Tabar & Muhammad Sahimi (2011).Mapping stochastic processes onto complex networks. *Journal of Statistical Mechanics: Theory and Experiment*, Vol. 2009, No. 07, P07046.

I. Simonsen, A. Hansen and O.M. Nes, *Phys. Rev.E* 58, 3 (1998).

Song C, Havlin S, & Makse HA (2005) Self-similarity of complex networks. Nature 433, 392.

Song C, Havlin S, & Makse HA (2006) Origins of fractality in the growth of complex networks. Nat. Phys. 2.

Sprott J.C., and Rowlands G., Improved correlation dimension calculation, *International Journal of Bifurcation and Chaos* 11, 7 (2001) 1865-1880.

Sprott J.C., High-dimensional dynamics in the delayed Hénon map. *EJTP* 12 (2006) 19-35.

Strogatz, S.H. (1994) Nonlinear dynamics and chaos. Perseus Books Publishing, LLC.

Strogatz, S.H. (2001) Exploring complex networks. Nature 410:268-276.

Strozzi, F., Zaldívar, J. M., Poljansek, K., Bono, F. & Gutiérrez, E. (2009). From complex networks to time series analysis and viceversa: Application to metabolic networks. *JRC Scientific and Technical Reports*, EUR 23947, JRC52892.

Van Kampen N.G., *Stochastic processes in Physics and Chemistry*, Elsevier, The Netherlands (2007).

Q. Wang, S. R. Kulkarni and S. Verdú, Divergence estimation of continuous distributions based on data-dependent partitions, *IEEE Transactions on Information Theory*, 51, 9 (2005).

G. Weiss, Time-reversibility of linear stochastic processes, *J. Appl. Prob.* 12, 831-836 (1975).

R. Weron, *Physica A* 312 (2002) 285-299.

Xu, X., Zhang, J. & Small, M. (2008). Superfamily phenomena and motifs of networks induced from time series. *PNAS*, Vol. 105, No. 50, 19601–19605.

A.C. Yang, S.S. Hseu, H.W. Yien, A.L. Goldberger, and C.-K. Peng, Linguistic analysis of the humean heartbeat using frequency and rank order statistics, *Phys. Rev. Lett.* 90, 10 (2003).

Yang, Y., Jianbo, W., Yang, H. & Mang, J. (2009). Visibility graph approach to exchange rate series. *PHYSICA A*, Vol. 388 (20), 4431–4437.

Zhang, J. & Small, M. (2006).Complex Network from Pseudoperiodic Time Series: Topology versus Dynamics. *PRL*, Vol. 96, 238701.

7

A Review on Node-Matching Between Networks

Qi Xuan[1], Li Yu[1], Fang Du[2] and Tie-Jun Wu[3]
[1]*Zhejiang University of Technology*
[2]*Johns Hopkins University*
[3]*Zhejiang University*
[1,3]*China*
[2]*USA*

1. Introduction

The relationships between individuals in various systems are always described by networks. Recently, the quick development of computer science makes it possible to study the structures of those super-complex networks in many areas including sociology (Xuan et al., 2009; Xuan, Du & Wu, 2010a), biology (Barabási & Oltvai, 2004; Eguíluz et al., 2005), physics (Dorogovtsev et al., 2008; Rozenfeld et al., 2010), etc., by the tools in graph theory. Interestingly, it was revealed that many of these complex networks in various areas present several similar topological properties, such as small-world (Watts & Strogatz, 1998), scale-free (Barabási & Albert, 1999), self-similarity (Motter et al., 2003), symmetry (Xiao et al., 2008), etc. In order to explain these properties, a large number of models have been proposed (Barabási & Albert, 1999; Li & Chen, 2003; Mossa et al., 2002; Watts & Strogatz, 1998; Xiao et al., 2008; Xuan, Du, Wu & Chen, 2010; Xuan et al., 2006; 2007; 2008). However, most of current researches still focus on understanding the relationships between individuals in a single system, while the inter-system relationships are always ignored.

One of such inter-system relationships may be caused by the fact that an individual may be active in different systems with different identities (Xuan & Wu, 2009), and this type inter-system relationships may further lead to the similar structures of different complex networks. For instance, an ancient protein may evolve into various homologous proteins in different species, a concept may be expressed by different words in different languages, and a person may be active in different communication networks with different identities represented by telephone numbers (Onnela et al., 2007) and email addresses (Newman et al., 2002), etc. Therefore, revealing the different identities of an individual in several different systems has practical significance in many areas (Xuan, Du & Wu, 2010b), e.g., revealing homogeneous proteins, auto-translating languages, inter-network filtrating information, and so on. Through describing complex systems by networks, these different tasks can be transferred to a common node-matching problem between different complex networks, and thus can be solved in the same framework.

However, since many real-world complex networks are always highly symmetric (Xiao et al., 2008), i.e., there are always large numbers of nodes sharing the same neighbors in a network, it seems quite difficult to distinguish them in one network only by comparing their topological properties (Costa et al., 2007), such as degrees, clustering coefficient and so on, not to mention matching them between different complex networks. Fortunately, the researchers of different areas can use their own dedicated methods, such as chemical (Cootes et al., 2007; Kelley et al., 2003), semantic (Giunchiglia & Shvaiko, 2004) and others, to reveal a part of matched nodes, although their high economical or computational cost makes it almost impossible to examine and compare each pair of nodes between different large-scale networks. Such extra information are certainly very useful in solving the node-matching problem between complex networks. Based on these findings, we first introduced two kinds of co-evolving models (Xuan, Du & Wu, 2010b; Xuan & Wu, 2009) to create interacting networks, which can help better understand the co-evolution of different systems. Such co-evolution results in some structural similarity between complex networks, which made it possible to design node-matching algorithms by adopting the structural information. With the reason that the selection of the pairwise matched nodes revealed a priori by the dedicated methods is somewhat controllable, we then proposed several revealed matched nodes selecting strategies to improve the performances of node-matching algorithms. Finally, based on the similarities between nodes of different networks calculated by their connections to several pairs of preliminarily revealed matched nodes, we provided three different node-matching algorithms, including the classical optimal matching algorithm (Kuhn, 2005; Munkres, 1957; Xuan & Wu, 2009) in graph theory, one-to-one and one-to-many iterative node-matching algorithms (Du et al., 2010; Xuan, Du & Wu, 2010b) to solve artificial and real-world node-matching problems.

This chapter will review the overall process that we defined and solved the node-matching problems between different networks. In the next section, the node-matching problem is defined, and two co-evolving network models as well as a real-world node-matching data set are introduced. In Section 3, several revealed matched nodes selecting strategies are provided in order to improve the performances of the subsequent node-matching algorithms. Then in Section 4, the similarities between nodes of different networks are defined and several node-matching algorithms are introduced and the experiments are implemented. Finally, the chapter is concluded in Section 5.

2. Definitions and data sets

2.1 Definitions

The node matching problem between two different networks are described as follows (Xuan, Du & Wu, 2010b; Xuan & Wu, 2009): the two networks under study are denoted by $G_1 = (V_1, E_1)$ and $G_2 = (V_2, E_2)$, where $V_i = v_1^i, \ldots, v_M^i$ and E_i represent the node set and the link set of network $i (i = 1, 2)$, respectively. Assume that there are $M(M \leqslant \min\{N_1, N_2\})$ pairs of matched nodes $v_j^1 \leftrightarrow v_j^2$ defined by $\{v_1^i, \ldots, v_M^i\} \subseteq V_i (i = 1, 2)$, while $P_r (P_r < M)$ pairs of them have been already revealed, named as revealed matched nodes and denoted by $\{v_1^i, \ldots, v_{P_r}^i\} \subset V_i (i = 1, 2)$. Then the problem is: can we design a method to find the other $M - P_r$ pairs of matched nodes in these two distinct networks by using the structural information of G_1 and G_2 and the revealed matched nodes? If we can design such a method and finally $P_c (Pc \leqslant M - Pr)$ pairs of them are revealed correctly, the matching precision ϕ then can be calculated by

$$\phi = \frac{P_c}{M - P_r}. \tag{1}$$

2.2 Co-evolution network models

In order to better understand the interactions between different systems and test the subsequent node matching algorithms, two co-evolution network models need to be first introduced, where the parameters are set to be $N_1 = N_2 = M = N$ for convenience. Generally, there are two ways to create a pair of interactional networks, as is shown in Fig. 1 (a) and (b), respectively, both of which may work in reality. Inspired by the evolution of organisms, the first way is that the pair of interactional networks G_1 and G_2 are evolved from a common original network; in other words, they are derived from the same network (obtained by some model) through random rewiring processes. And the other way is that the pair of interactional networks are derived from two independent networks by a random interacting process composed of the following two steps (Xuan & Wu, 2009):

- **Networks initialization:** Two networks G_1 and G_2 with N nodes respectively are created by the same rule, where all the nodes are randomly matched, i.e., N pairs of randomly matched nodes $v_i^1 \leftrightarrow v_i^2$ are provided.
- **Interaction:** if v_i^1 (or v_i^2) and v_j^1 (or v_j^2) is connected in G_1 (or G_2) while v_i^2 (or v_i^1) and v_j^2 (or v_j^1) is not connected in G_2 (or G_1), then connect v_i^2 (or v_i^1) and v_j^2 (or v_j^1) with probability η_1 (or η_2).

Here, the second way will be adopted to create pairs of tested artificial interactional networks.

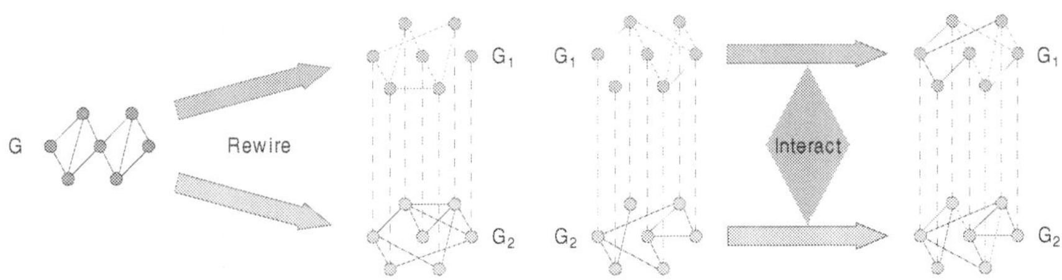

(a) Rewiring model (b) Interacting model

Fig. 1. Two ways to create a pair of interactional networks (Xuan & Wu, 2009). (a) The pair of interactional networks G_1 and G_2 are derived from the same original network through random rewiring. The corresponding nodes are matched and connected by brown dashed lines. (b) The pair of interactional networks G_1 and G_2 are derived from a pair of independent networks by random interacting, i.e., two non-linked nodes in the network G_1 are connected by a green line with probability η_2 if their corresponding matched nodes in G_2 were linked while two non-linked nodes in G_2 are connected by a red line with probability η_1 if their corresponding matched nodes in G_1 were linked. η_1 and η_2 are named as interactional degree.

2.3 Real-world interactional networks

In reality, when two strangers chat with each other for some reason, e.g., demand of business, common interests, curiosity, warmheart, etc., they may be friends one day in the future if they enjoy with each other, in other words, the chat network may influence the evolution of the friendship network. On the other hand, there is also a natural trend that one prefers to chat with his friends or acquaintances rather than strangers, i.e., the friendship network determines the chat network to a certain extent. Therefore, chat network and friend network can be considered as a pair of real-world interactional networks, which can be figured on a quite large scale by advanced communication technologies and thus used to test the subsequent node matching algorithms.

As an example, we collected the communication records and the contact lists in a week from the database of *Alibaba trademanager* (an instant messenger (IM) mainly used for electronic commerce). We mainly focus on 14,800 employees of the *Alibaba* company and construct the chat network G_1 and the friendship network G_2 among them by these records. The two networks were then preprocessed by the following two steps (Du et al., 2010; Xuan, Du & Wu, 2010b):

- **Extract the giant cluster (GC):** Extract the GCs of G_1 and G_2, denoted by $G_1^g = (V_1^g, E_1^g)$ and $G_2^g = (V_2^g, E_2^g)$ where V_i^g and E_i^g represent the node set and the link set of the GC G_i^g respectively.
- **Calculate the intersection:** A pair of matched nodes in the networks correspond to the same *Alibaba* user. Select those users appearing in both the G_1^g and G_2^g, denoted by $V^c = V_1^g \cap V_2^g$, and get the sub-networks $G_1^c = (V^c, E_1^c)$ and $G_2^c = (V^c, E_2^c)$ where $E_i^c \subseteq E_i^g$ represents the set of links between nodes in V^c. Set $G_1 = G_1^c$ and $G_2 = G_2^c$, and terminate the preprocessing if both the networks G_1^c and G_2^c are connected, otherwise, turn to the first step.

After the preprocessing, both the networks G_1 and G_2 have 9859 nodes and are one-to-one matched, i.e., each node in G_1 has a matched node in G_2 and vice versa. Moreover, if there is a link between two nodes in G_1, we can find a link between their matched nodes in G_2 with probability 80.8%, and the probability is 18.4% from G_2 to G_1. Their basic topological properties, such as the number of nodes N, the average degree $\langle k \rangle$, the average clustering coefficient $\langle C \rangle$, and the average shortest path length $\langle L \rangle$ are presented in Table 1.

Networks	N	$\langle k \rangle$	$\langle C \rangle$	$\langle L \rangle$
Chat	9859	39.4	0.218	3.37
Friendship	9859	172	0.313	2.55

Table 1. The basic properties, i.e., the number of vertices N, the average degree $\langle k \rangle$, the average clustering coefficient $\langle C \rangle$, and the average shortest path length $\langle L \rangle$ for the chat network and the friendship network derived from *Alibaba trademanager* database (Du et al., 2010; Xuan, Du & Wu, 2010b).

3. Revealed matched nodes selecting strategies

Since the interactional networks under study are usually not completely identical (Xuan & Wu, 2009), it seems unpractical to match nodes between different networks just by their local structural properties. As a result, a few pairs of matched nodes would be better revealed as references before the node-matching algorithms are implemented.

Recent studies on real-world networks reveals that many of them have similar heterogeneous structure characterized by a power-law degree distribution (Barabási, 2009; Barrat et al., 2004; Eguíluz et al., 2005; Xuan et al., 2009). This property, first modeled by Barabási and Albert (BA) (Barabási & Albert, 1999), indicates that the connection of a heterogeneous network highly depends on hub nodes with quite large degrees, i.e., once these hub nodes are attacked, the average shortest path length of the network will increase quickly (Albert et al., 2000; Crucitti et al., 2004; Motter & Lai, 2002), as a result, the communication efficiency of the network will be largely weakened. For the node matching problem introduced here, we proved that (Xuan & Wu, 2009) such hub nodes can provide more structural information than those normal nodes and thus are more suitable to be revealed matched nodes. Based on the interactional model introduced in Fig. 1 (b), denoting the degree of v_i^1 by d_i^1 and the degree of v_j^2 by d_j^2, if they are randomly selected as a pair of matched nodes, then, averagely speaking, there are $d_i^1 d_j^2/N$ other pairs of matched nodes around them before the interaction. And after the interaction, the degree of v_i^1 and that of v_j^2 can be calculated by Eq. (2) and Eq. (3) respectively,

$$\widetilde{d_i^1} = d_i^1 + d_j^2(1 - \frac{d_i^1}{N})\eta_2, \tag{2}$$

$$\widetilde{d_j^2} = d_j^2 + d_i^1(1 - \frac{d_j^2}{N})\eta_1. \tag{3}$$

And the number of pairs of other matched nodes around the matched nodes v_i^1 and v_j^2 after the interaction can be calculated by Eq. (4),

$$F_{ij} = d_j^2(1 - \frac{d_i^1}{N})\eta_2 + d_i^1(1 - \frac{d_j^2}{N})\eta_1 + \frac{d_i^1 d_j^2}{N}. \tag{4}$$

Since real-world complex networks always have a very huge number of nodes and a relatively small average degree, Eq. (2)-Eq. (4) can be further simplified to Eq. (5)-Eq. (7) respectively,

$$\widetilde{d_i^1} \approx d_i^1 + \eta_2 d_j^2, \tag{5}$$

$$\widetilde{d_j^2} \approx d_j^2 + \eta_1 d_i^1, \tag{6}$$

$$F_{ij} \approx \eta_1 d_i^1 + \eta_2 d_j^2. \tag{7}$$

Then we get Eq. (8) as

$$F_{ij} \approx \begin{cases} \frac{\eta_1(1-\eta_2)}{1-\eta_1\eta_2}\widetilde{d_i^1} + \frac{\eta_2(1-\eta_1)}{1-\eta_1\eta_2}\widetilde{d_j^2}, & \eta_1\eta_2 < 1; \\ \frac{1}{2}\widetilde{d_i^1} + \frac{1}{2}\widetilde{d_j^2}, & \eta_1\eta_2 = 1. \end{cases} \tag{8}$$

With the reason that the matched nodes are supposed unknown beforehand in reality, it seems unpractical to sort all the pairs of matched nodes by F_{ij} in descending order in order to improve the final matching precision ϕ, although larger F_{ij} corresponds to more pairs of unrevealed matched nodes around a pair of revealed matched nodes v_i^1 and v_j^2. Fortunately, Eq. (8) suggests a substitute way, i.e., selecting nodes with larger degree in the reference network, revealing their matched nodes in the other network by some dedicated methods, then these pairs of matched nodes are set to the revealed matched nodes.

3.1 Large degree priority strategies

Based on this principle, we proposed large degree priority strategies (Xuan & Wu, 2009) for the optimal node matching algorithm, as described by

- **Large Degree Priority in G_1 (LDP1)**: G_1 is selected as the reference network, where the nodes are sorted by their degrees in descending order, and the top P_r of them as well as their matched nodes in G_2 are selected as the revealed matched nodes.
- **Large Degree Priority in G_2 (LDP2)**: G_2 is selected as the reference network, where the nodes are sorted by their degree in descending order, and the top P_r of them as well as their matched nodes in G_1 are selected as the revealed matched nodes.

But which of them can bring higher matching precision? Can we answer this question just by comparing the structural properties (in particular, the degree sequences) of the two interactional networks? Without loss of generality, for a pair of interactional networks, suppose G_1 has larger average degree than G_2, i.e., $\langle \widetilde{d^1} \rangle > \langle \widetilde{d^2} \rangle$. Multiply Eq. (5) by η_1 and minus Eq. (6), we get

$$\eta_1 \langle \widetilde{d^1} \rangle - \langle \widetilde{d^2} \rangle = (\eta_1 \eta_2 - 1) \langle d^2 \rangle. \tag{9}$$

Since $\eta_1 \eta_2 \leqslant 1$, the value of η_1 can be roughly estimated by

$$\eta_1 \leqslant \frac{\langle \widetilde{d^2} \rangle}{\langle \widetilde{d^1} \rangle}, \tag{10}$$

while the value of η_2 cannot be estimated just by comparing the structural properties of the interactional networks. Suppose that the nodes are sorted by their degrees in descending order, denote by $R^i (i = 1, 2)$ the set of top P_r nodes in G_i, then from Eq. (8), we can see that more structural information may be provided when G_2 is selected as the reference network, if it is satisfied that

$$\eta_1 \sum_{v_i^1 \in R^1} \widetilde{d_i^1} + (1 - \eta_1) P_r \langle \widetilde{d^2} \rangle < \eta_1 P_r \langle \widetilde{d^1} \rangle + (1 - \eta_1) \sum_{v_i^2 \in R^2} \widetilde{d_i^2}, \tag{11}$$

which is equivalent to

$$\eta_1 \Big(\sum_{v_i^1 \in R^1} \widetilde{d_i^1} - P_r \langle \widetilde{d^1} \rangle \Big) + (1 - \eta_1) \Big(P_r \langle \widetilde{d^2} \rangle - \sum_{v_i^2 \in R^2} \widetilde{d_i^2} \Big) < 0. \tag{12}$$

Because it is always satisfied that

$$\sum_{v_i^1 \in R^1} \widetilde{d_i^1} \geqslant P_r \langle \widetilde{d^1} \rangle, \quad \sum_{v_i^2 \in R^2} \widetilde{d_i^2} \geqslant P_r \langle \widetilde{d^2} \rangle, \tag{13}$$

Eq. (12) must be satisfied if we have

$$\frac{\langle \widetilde{d^2} \rangle}{\langle \widetilde{d^1} \rangle} \Big(\sum_{v_i^1 \in R^1} \widetilde{d_i^1} - P_r \langle \widetilde{d^1} \rangle \Big) + \Big(1 - \frac{\langle \widetilde{d^2} \rangle}{\langle \widetilde{d^1} \rangle}\Big) \Big(P_r \langle \widetilde{d^2} \rangle - \sum_{v_i^2 \in R^2} \widetilde{d_i^2} \Big) < 0. \tag{14}$$

where all the parameters are known when two interactional networks are provided. That is, only when Eq. (14) is satisfied, we can say that LDP2 may be superior to LDP1.

3.2 Centralized large degree priority strategies

The above LDP strategies are designed for optimal node-matching algorithms, while for iterative node-matching algorithms, these strategies need to be further modified. Because in this case, the revealed pairwise matched nodes would better be centralized to a local world in the networks so as to improve the matching precision in the first round, then the second round and so on. Correspondingly, we propose two centralized large degree priority strategies specially for iterative node-matching algorithms (Xuan, Du & Wu, 2010b):

- **Centralized Large Degree Priority in G_1 (CLDP1).** G_1 is selected as the reference network, where a set R_1 ($|R_1| = P_r$) of nodes are picked up according to their degrees by following process. The node of the largest degree in G_1 is firstly selected as the only member of R_1. Denoting the neighbor set of R_1 as U_1 ($U_1 \cap R_1 = \emptyset$), i.e., each node in U_1 (but none of the nodes in $V_1 \setminus (U_1 \cup R_1)$) is at least connected to one node in R_1, at each time the nodes in $V_1 \setminus R_1$ are sorted by the number of neighbors belonging to U_1 in descending order and the top one is selected to join in R_1. Update R_1 and U_1 and repeat the selecting process until the set R_1 contains exactly P_r nodes. Then the set R_1 of nodes in G_1 as well as their matched nodes in G_2 are selected as the revealed pairwise matched nodes.
- **Centralized Large Degree Priority in G_2 (CLDP2).** G_2 is selected as the reference network, where a set R_2 ($|R_2| = P_r$) of nodes are picked up according to their degrees by following process. The node of the largest degree in G_2 is firstly selected as the only member of R_2. Denoting the neighbor set of R_2 as U_2 ($U_2 \cap R_2 = \emptyset$), i.e., each node in U_2 (but none of the nodes in $V_2 \setminus (U_2 \cup R_2)$) is at least connected to one node in R_2, at each time the nodes in $V_2 \setminus R_2$ are sorted by the number of neighbors belonging to U_2 in descending order and the top one is selected to join in R_2. Update R_2 and U_2 and repeat the selecting process until the set R_2 contains exactly P_r nodes. Then the set R_2 of nodes in G_2 as well as their matched nodes in G_1 are selected as the revealed pairwise matched nodes.

4. Node-matching algorithms

4.1 Similarities between nodes of interactional networks

Name	Definition
Common Neighbors (Newman, 2001)	$S_{ij} = n_M(v_i^1, v_j^2)$
Salton Index (Salton & McGill, 1983)	$S_{ij} = \frac{n_M(v_i^1,v_j^2)}{\sqrt{n_L(v_i^1)\times n_L(v_j^2)}}$
Jaccard Index (Jaccard, 1901)	$S_{ij} = \frac{n_M(v_i^1,v_j^2)}{n_L(v_i^1)+n_L(v_j^2)-n_M(v_i^1,v_j^2)}$
Sørensen Index (Sørensen, 1948)	$S_{ij} = \frac{2n_M(v_i^1,v_j^2)}{n_L(v_i^1)+n_L(v_j^2)}$
Hub Promoted Index (Ravasz et al., 2002)	$S_{ij} = \frac{n_M(v_i^1,v_j^2)}{\min\{n_L(v_i^1),n_L(v_j^2)\}}$
Hub Depressed Index (Lü & Zhou, 2011)	$S_{ij} = \frac{n_M(v_i^1,v_j^2)}{\max\{n_L(v_i^1),n_L(v_j^2)\}}$

Table 2. Several definitions of similarities between nodes of interactional networks based on their local structural information.

The similarity between two nodes belonging to different networks can be measured by the number of pairs of revealed matched nodes around them, e.g., the number of common friends they contact with in different communication networks, where a common friend is denoted by a pair of revealed matched nodes in corresponding communication networks. Denote by $n_L(v_i^1)$ and $n_L(v_j^2)$ the numbers of links connected to the node v_i^1 and v_j^2 in the networks G_1 and G_2, respectively, and by $n_M(v_i^1, v_j^2)$ the number of pairs of revealed matched nodes (v_k^1, v_k^2) where v_i^1 and v_j^2 are mutually connected, i.e., v_i^1 is connected to v_k^1 and v_j^2 is connected to v_k^2, in the corresponding networks. Then the similarity between v_i^1 and v_j^2 can be calculated by a number of methods (Jaccard, 1901; Lü & Zhou, 2011; Newman, 2001; Ravasz et al., 2002; Salton & McGill, 1983; Sørensen, 1948), as presented in Table. 2. Here, we adopt Jaccard Index to calculate the similarities between nodes of interactional networks.

4.2 Optimal node-matching algorithm

When revealed pairwise matched nodes are selected by LDP strategies, the similarity of each pair of the remaining nodes from different interactional networks can be calculated by Jaccard Index. Then, reviewing the definitions in Section 2.1, the node-matching problem between G_1 and G_2 can be transferred to a maximum matching problem for the bipartite graph $G_b = (U_1, U_2, W)$ where $U_i = \{v^i_{P_r+1}, v^i_{P_r+2}, \ldots, v^i_N\}$ $(i = 1, 2)$, and W denotes the set of links weighted by the similarities between these two groups of nodes. Without loss of generality, under the assumption $N_1 \leqslant N_2$, the task is to find a set of nonadjacent weighted links $\{w_1, w_2, \ldots, w_{N_1-P_r}\}$ to maximize the sum of their weights $\sum_{i=1}^{N_1-P_r} s_i$, which can be solved by the classical KM algorithm (Kuhn, 2005; Munkres, 1957). Note that, although the KM algorithm was developed for the case $N_1 = N_2$, it could be also feasible in the case $N_1 < N_2$ through factitiously adding $N_2 - N_1$ isolated nodes in G_1. For this reason we supposed $N_1 = N_2 = N$ for simplicity.

Since the KM algorithm has relatively high complexity $O(N^3)$, the sizes of the test networks cannot be very large. Here the two interactional networks G_1 and G_2 are both created by the BA model with $N = 100$ nodes and average degree $\langle k \rangle = 8$. Then they interact with each other with different interactional degrees $\eta_1 = 0.9$ and $\eta_2 = 0.1$ by the model shown in Fig. 1 (b). Denote the sample ratio by $\gamma = P_r/N$, the matching results are shown in Fig. 2, where we can see that, in most cases, LDP1 is prior to LDP2. This result is reasonable because when $\eta_1 \gg \eta_2$, Eq. (8) suggests that larger F_{ij} can be expected when select those nodes with large degrees in G_1 and their correspondences in G_2 as the revealed matched nodes. Note that, in this experiment, we set $M = N$ for simplicity, that is, every node in one network has its correspondence in the other network. In reality, M may be smaller than N, i.e., some individuals may be active in only one of the interactional networks. In this case, we need further select $M - P_r$ pairs of matched nodes from $N - P_r$ pairs of matched nodes obtained by the node-matching algorithm. If the value of M is known a priori, we can simply sort $N - P_r$ pairs of matched nodes by their attached similarities, then select the top $M - P_r$ pairs with larger similarities as the final pairs of matched nodes. However, if M is unknown, we have to set a threshold $\theta \in [0, 1)$ beforehand, and those pairs of matched nodes with similarities larger than θ then are selected as the final pairs of matched nodes, which will not be further discussed here. That is, in the following studies, we always set $M = N_1 = N_2 = N$ for simplicity.

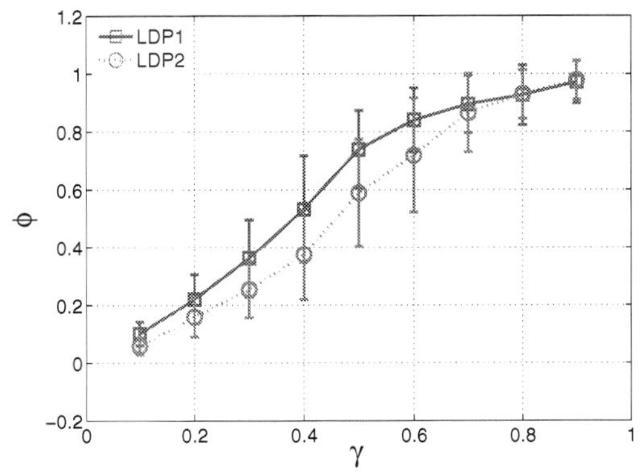

Fig. 2. The matching precision ϕ as the function of the sample ratio γ by adopting the two revealed matched nodes selection strategies, i.e., LDP1 and LDP2, for scale-free networks created by the BA model with $N = 100$ and $\langle k \rangle = 8$ and different interactional degrees $\eta_1 = 0.9$ and $\eta_2 = 0.1$ (Xuan & Wu, 2009). For each γ and each selection strategy, the experiment is implemented on 100 different pairs of scale-free networks, then the average matching precision as well as the error bar is recorded.

4.3 Iterative node-matching algorithm

As we can see in Fig. 2, the optimal node-matching algorithm fails to achieve acceptable results when there are only a relatively small number of pairwise matched nodes revealed beforehand, e.g., in order to achieve a matching precision of 80%, we have to reveal as many as 60% correspondences between nodes of the two networks in advance, which, as well as its long running time, hinders its efficient application in node-matching between real-world networks of quite large size. Based on the CDLP revealed matched nodes selecting strategies and Jaccard similarities between nodes of different networks, the iterative node-matching algorithm is simply composed of the following two steps (Xuan, Du & Wu, 2010b):

- **Node matching.** At each time, a pair of unmatched nodes belonging to different networks with the largest similarity are selected as a pair of matched nodes. Then this pair of matched nodes are considered as a pair of newly revealed matched nodes, then recalculate the similarities between the remaining nodes, and so forth.
- **Termination.** The iterative process is terminated when all of the nodes in the interactional networks have been matched.

The time complexity of the above node-matching algorithm mainly depends on the recalculation of the similarities. Generally, once a pair of nodes from different networks are matched at $(\tau - 1)$th round, we need to recalculated the similarities of about $k_\tau^1 k_\tau^2$ pairs of nodes mutually connected to that pair of matched nodes at τth round, where k_τ^i $(i = 1, 2)$ represents the degree of the matched node in G_i at $(\tau - 1)$th round. Provided $N_1 = N_2 = M = N$, the running time of the algorithm, denoted by Γ, can be calculated by Eq. (15) statistically,

$$\Gamma \sim E\left(\sum_{\tau=1}^{N} k_\tau^1 k_\tau^2\right). \tag{15}$$

If the two networks under study are strongly dependent each other, i.e., extremely G_1 and G_2 are identical and a node in one network only can be matched to the node of equal degree in the other network, Eq. (15) can be replaced by Eq. (16),

$$\Gamma \sim \sum_{\tau=1}^{N} E((k_\tau^1)^2). \tag{16}$$

For scale-free networks generated by the BA model, the degree distribution follows $p(k) \sim k^{-3}$, thus the running time can be simplified by Eq. (17),

$$\Gamma \sim N \int_1^N k^2 k^{-3} dk \sim N \ln N. \tag{17}$$

However, if the two target networks are relatively independent from each other, i.e., a node with large degree in one network can be matched to a node with small degree in the other network, which is more common in reality, Eq. (15) can be approximatively transferred to Eq. (18),

$$\Gamma \sim \sum_{\tau=1}^{N} E(k_\tau^1)E(k_\tau^2) \sim N\langle k^1\rangle\langle k^2\rangle, \tag{18}$$

where $\langle k^i\rangle$ represents the average degree of the network G_i. In most cases, $\langle k^i\rangle$ can be considered as a constant, therefore, Eq. (18) suggests a linear time complexity $O(N)$ of the algorithm (Xuan, Du & Wu, 2010b). Eqs. (17) and (18) mean that the iterative node-matching algorithm has much lower complexity than the optimal node-matching algorithm.

In order to compare to the optimal node-matching algorithm, here we take the same example to test the iterative node-matching algorithm. Since the iterative algorithm is able to solve node-matching problems between networks of quite large size, the two interactional networks G_1 and G_2 here are also created by the BA model with same average degree $\langle k\rangle = 8$, but much larger network size $N = 500$. Then these two networks interact with each other with different interactional degrees $\eta_1 = 0.9$ and $\eta_2 = 0.1$ by the same model shown in Fig. 1 (b). The matching results are show in Fig. 3 (a). At this time, in order to correctly reveal most of matched nodes in the networks (e.g., $\phi \geqslant 80\%$), we only need to have a very small percentage of matched nodes revealed beforehand (1% for CLDP1 and 1.6% for CLDP2), i.e., the iterative node-matching algorithm is far more efficient than the optimal node-matching algorithm on interactional artificial scale-free networks.

However, when we test this iterative node-matching algorithm on the real-world interactional chat network and friendship network introduced in Section 2.3, the matching results, as shown in Fig. 3 (b), are not that satisfactory, i.e. the final matching precision between the pair of real-world networks is much lower than that between the artificial networks generated by the BA model when adopting the same proportion of pairwise revealed matched nodes. For example, only about 40% matched nodes are revealed correctly, even though there are as many as 10% matched nodes are revealed beforehand. This phenomenon may be caused by the relatively high symmetry of the chat network and the friendship network. Generally, the local symmetry between the two non-linked nodes v_i and v_j in a network is defined by (Xuan, Du & Wu, 2010b)

$$\omega_{ij} = \frac{\chi_{ij}^c}{\chi_{ij}^t}, \tag{19}$$

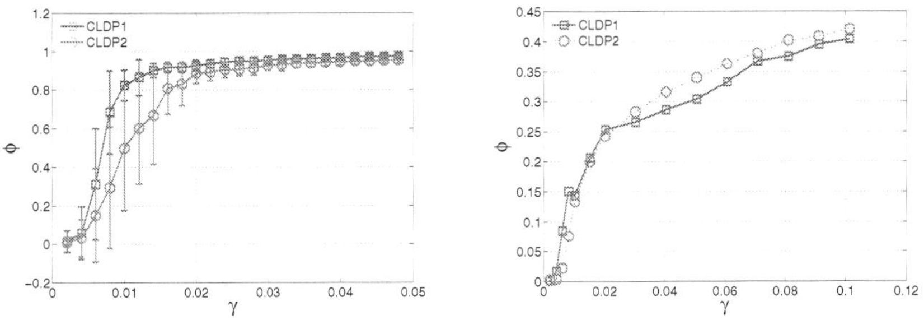

(a) Matching results on artificial networks (b) Matching results on real-world networks

Fig. 3. The matching precision ϕ as the function of the sample ratio γ by adopting the two revealed matched nodes selection strategies, i.e., CLDP1 and CLDP2, for (a) the interactional scale-free networks created by the BA model with $N = 500$ and $\langle k \rangle = 8$ and different interactional degrees $\eta_1 = 0.9$ and $\eta_2 = 0.1$, and (b) the interactional real-world chat network and friendship network (Xuan, Du & Wu, 2010b). For artificial networks, the experiment is implemented on 100 different pairs of scale-free networks for each γ and each selection strategy, then the average matching precision as well as the error bar is recorded.

where χ_{ij}^c and χ_{ij}^t are the numbers of their common and total neighbors, respectively. If nodes v_i and v_j are connected, release the link and then calculate the symmetry between them following Eq. (8). Since it is impossible to distinguish two nodes v_i and v_j in a network with the symmetry $\chi_{ij} = 1$ (i.e. they share the same neighbors excluding themselves) just by adopting their topological information, those highly symmetric nodes in one network may be wrongly matched to the nodes in the other network with quite a high probability, and thus one-to-one node-matching algorithms may produce poor results in such situations.

4.4 One-to-many iterative node-matching algorithms

In order to overcome the above limitation of one-to-one node-matching algorithms, we proposed one-to-many node matching (Du et al., 2010) through expanding the number of nodes in each matching step. In fact, one-to-many node matching has its practical significance because it can help to quickly narrow down the searching range of a target individual in different complex systems. Particularly, a 1-to-M algorithm should output $N - P_r$ correspondences as defined by Eq. (20),

$$v_i^1 \to Q_i^2 = \{v_{i_1}^2, v_{i_2}^2, \ldots, v_{i_M}^2\}, \quad (20)$$

where v_i^1 $(i = P_r + 1, P_r + 2, \ldots, N)$ is a node in G_1, and Q_i^2 is a node set including the top M most likely matched nodes of v_i^1 in G_2. It should be noted that here 1-to-M match is just a natural generalization of 1-to-1 match, therefore, Eq. (20) also provides a consistent 1-to-1 match, i.e., $v_i^1 \leftrightarrow v_{i_1}^2$, satisfying that $v_{i_1}^2$ and $v_{j_1}^2$ represent two different nodes in G_2 if $i \neq j$. For a 1-to-M matching algorithm, a node v_i^1 in G_1 is considered correctly matched if its real matched node v_i^2 is contained in Q_i^2, i.e., $v_i^2 \in Q_i^2$. Denoting P_M $(P_M \leqslant N - P_r)$ as the number of nodes in G_1 that are correctly matched, the matching precision ϕ_M for the 1-to-M node matching algorithm can be calculated by Eq. (21), and naturally Eq. (22) is always satisfied.

$$\phi_M = \frac{P_M}{N - P_r}, \tag{21}$$

$$\phi_M \geq \phi_{M-1}. \tag{22}$$

Next, we will introduce two different one-to-many iterative node-matching algorithms (Du et al., 2010).

1) **A1: Local mapping**. Since the similarity between each pair of nodes may change as the one-to-one iterative algorithm is implemented step by step, it is possible to correct some initially wrongly matched nodes by recalculating their similarities after the one-to-one node matching algorithm is terminated. This fact leads to the first one-to-many node matching algorithm based on local mapping. In particular, the Algorithm A1 is defined by the following two steps (Du et al., 2010):

- **Iterative 1-to-1 node matching**. $N - P_r$ pairs of nodes, i.e., $v_i^1 \leftrightarrow Q_i^2 = \{v_{i_1}^2\}$ $(i = P_r + 1, P_r + 2, \ldots, N)$, are firstly matched by the iterative 1-to-1 node matching algorithm.
- **Candidate nodes selection**. Denote by X_i^1 the neighbor set of node v_i^1 in G_1, which has a matched node set X_i^2 in G_2 where the nodes are 1-to-1 matched to those in X_i^1, then denote by Y_i^2 the neighbor set of X_i^2, including all the nodes directly connected to those in X_i^2. Based on the definition of similarity, only the similarities between node v_i^1 $(i = P_r + 1, P_r + 2, \ldots, N)$ and the nodes in Y_i^2 can be larger than 0 and thus are recalculated. Then the top $M - 1$ nodes with largest similarities are selected as the candidate corresponding nodes of v_i^1. It should be noted that $v_{i_1}^2$ is not reconsidered here, and if Y_i^2 only contains fewer than $M - 1$ nodes, other $M - 1 - |Y_i^2|$ nodes can be randomly selected from G_2 to be consistent with Eq. (20).

2) **A2: Ensembling**. In the area of machine learning, it is a common way to improve the generalization performance of an algorithm by combining the results of many different predictors (Breiman, 1996; Freund & Schapire, 1997; Krogh & Sollich, 1997; Miyoshi et al., 2005). However, the above iterative one-to-one node matching algorithm is totally deterministic, i.e., for a given pair of target networks and certain revealed matched nodes, the algorithm must produce the same matching result. Therefore, it cannot be directly used for ensemble, and thus a new statistical iterative one-to-one node matching algorithm have to be introduced first, where a pair of newly revealed matched nodes is adopted only with probability $p(p < 1)$ to calculate the similarities between those unrevealed nodes of different networks in the succeeding iterative process. Then a group of different one-to-one matching results can be obtained by implementing such a statistical iterative one-to-one node matching algorithm for several rounds, and the obtained results can be merged into a unique one-to-many matching result by a voting strategy. In particular, the algorithm A2 is defined by the following three steps (Du et al., 2010):

- **Iterative 1-to-1 node matching**. $N - P_r$ pairs of nodes, i.e., $v_i^1 \leftrightarrow Q_i^2 = \{v_{i_1}^2\}$ $(i = P_r + 1, P_r + 2, \ldots, N)$, are firstly matched by the deterministic iterative 1-to-1 node matching algorithm.
- **Implement and vote**. The statistical 1-to-1 node matching algorithm with parameter $p(p < 1)$ is implemented for B $(B \gg M)$ rounds and a group of B different 1-to-1 matching results are obtained. All of the correspondences in G_2 of v_i^1 in G_1 are grouped by a node set Z_i^2

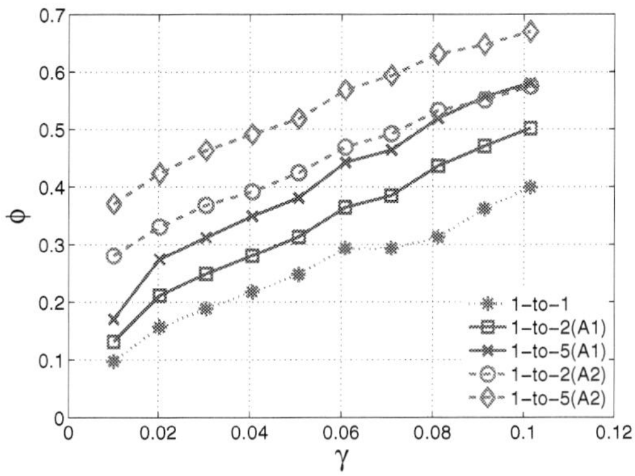

Fig. 4. The matching precision ϕ as the function of the sample ratio γ for $M = 1, 2, 5$ ($M = 1$ means the one-to-one matching result) between the friendship network and the chat network obtained from the database of *Alibaba trademanager* (Du et al., 2010). Here, the chat network is taken as the reference network.

with its size (the number of nodes) satisfying $|Z_i^2| \leq B$. It should be noted that each node in Z_i^2 is attached by a positive integer as its weight representing the times that it is matched to v_i^1 in the total B rounds, and similarly $v_{i_1}^2$ is excluded here.

- **Candidate nodes selection**. The top $M - 1$ nodes with largest weights in Z_i^2 are selected as the $M - 1$ candidate corresponding nodes of v_i^1. Sometimes, there may be only fewer than $M - 1$ nodes in Z_i^2, i.e., $|Z_i^2| \leq M - 1$, in such a situation, other $M - 1 - |Z_i^2|$ nodes can be randomly selected from G_2 to be consistent with Eq. (20).

Similarly, these two one-to-many iterative node matching algorithms are tested on the real-world interactional chat network and friendship network introduced in Section 2.3, and the matching results are shown in Fig. 4. As we can see, both the proposed one-to-many algorithms (especially the random algorithm A2) can significantly improve the matching precision, and thus can be considered to partially overcome the limitation of one-to-one node-matching algorithms.

5. Conclusion

Since an individual may appear in different systems with different identities, many real-world complex systems are considered to be interacted with each other all the time. Revealing these identities of the same individual is a common task in many areas such as sociology, linguistics, biology, etc, by their dedicated methods. When these complex systems are described by networks, this common task can be changed to a node matching problem between different complex networks, and thus can be solved in the framework of graph theory.

In this chapter, we reviewed the overall process to solve such node-matching problems between different networks: We first calculated the similarities between nodes of different networks through their connections to several pairs of preliminarily revealed matched nodes and transferred the node matching problem between two different networks to a maximum weighted bipartite matching problem; then we proposed several node-matching algorithms to solve such problem. By comparison, the iterative node-matching algorithm has approximately linear complexity and behaves much better than the traditional KM algorithm in graph theory. However, it seems that almost all of the network structure-based one-to-one node-matching algorithms lose their efficiencies when the target networks are highly symmetric, e.g., the iterative node-matching results are not that good on real-world chat network and friendship network obtained from the database of *Alibaba trademanager*. Such limitation can be partially overcome by the proposed one-to-many node-matching algorithms, which mainly focus on quickly narrowing down the searching range, rather than revealing exact one-to-one mapping between nodes of different networks. Meanwhile, we also introduced several degree-based revealed matched nodes selecting strategies for optimal and iterative node-matching algorithms, respectively, in order to further improve the matching results. In the future, more information about individuals and connections may be adopted to create more efficient node-matching algorithms.

6. References

Albert, R., Jeong, H., & Barabási, A.-L. (2000). Error and attack tolerance of complex networks, *Nature* 6794(406): 378–382.

Barabási, A.-L. (2009). Scale-free networks: A decade and beyond, *Science* 325(5939): 412–413.

Barabási, A.-L. & Albert, R. (1999). Emergence of scaling in random networks, *Science* 286(5439): 509–512.

Barabási, A.-L. & Oltvai, Z. N. (2004). Network biology: Understanding the cell's functional organization, *Nature* 5(2): 101–113.

Barrat, A., Barthélemy, M., Satorras, R. P. & Vespignani, A. (2004). The architecture of complex weighted networks, *Proceedings of the National Academy of Sciences U.S.A* 101(11): 3747–3752.

Breiman, L. (1996). Bagging predictors, *Machine Learning* 26(2): 123–140.

Cootes, A. P., Muggleton, S. H. & Sternberg, M. J. E. (2007). The identification of similarities between biological networks: Application to the metabolome and interactome, *Journal of Molecular Biology* 369(4): 1126–1139.

Costa, L. D. F., Rodrigues, F. A., Travieso, G. & Boas, P. R. V. (2007). Characterization of complex networks: A survey of measurements, *Advances in Physics* 56(1): 167–242.

Crucitti, P., Latora, V., Marchiori, M. & Rapisarda, A. (2004). Error and attack tolerance of complex networks, *Physica A: Statistical Mechanics and Its Applications* 340(1-3): 388–394.

Dorogovtsev, S. N., Goltsev, A. V. & Mendes, J. F. F. (2008). Critical phenomena in complex networks, *Review of Modern Physics* 80(4): 1275–1335.

Du, F., Xuan, Q. & Wu, T.-J. (2010). One-to-many node matching between complex networks, *Advances in Complex Systems* 13(6): 725–739.

Eguíluz, V. M., Chialvo, D. R., Cecchi, G. A., Baliki, M. & Apkarian, A. V. (2005). Scale-free brain functional networks, *Physical Review Letters* 94(1): 018102.

Freund, Y. & Schapire, R. E. (1997). A decision-theoretic generalization of on-line learning and an application to boosting, *Journal of Computer and System Sciences* 55(1): 119–139.

Giunchiglia, F. & Shvaiko, P. (2004). Semantic matching, *The Knowledge Engineering Review* 18: 265–280.

Jaccard, P. (1901). Étude comparative de la distribution florale dans une portion des alpes et des jura, *Bulletin de la Société Vaudoise des Science Naturelles* 37: 547–579.

Kelley, B. P., Sharan, R., Karp, R. M., Sittler, T., Root, D. E., Stockwell, B. R. & Ideker, T. (2003). Conserved pathways within bacteria and yeast as revealed by global protein network alignment, *Proceedings of the National Academy of Sciences U.S.A* 100(20): 11394–11399.

Krogh, A. & Sollich, P. (1997). Statistical mechanics of ensemble learning, *Physical Review E* 55(1): 811–825.

Kuhn, H. W. (2005). The hungarian method for the assignment problem, *Naval Research Logistics* 52(1): 7–21.

Li, X. & Chen, G. (2003). A local-world evolving network model, *Physica A: Statistical Mechanics and Its Applications* 328(1-2): 274–286.

Lü, L. & Zhou, T. (2011). Link prediction in complex networks: A survey, *Physica A: Statistical Mechanics and Its Applications* 390(6): 1150–1170.

Miyoshi, S., Hara, K. & Okada, M. (2005). Analysis of ensemble learning using simple perceptrons based on online learning theory, *Physical Review E* 71(3): 036116.

Mossa, S., Barthélémy, M., Stanley, H. E. & Amaral, L. A. N. (2002). Truncation of power law behavior in scale-free network models due to information filtering, *Physical Review Letters* 88(13): 138701.

Motter, A. E. & Lai, Y.-C. (2002). Cascade-based attacks on complex networks, *Physical Review E* 66(6): 065102.

Motter, A. E., Nishikawa, T. & Lai, Y.-C. (2003). Large-scale structural organization of social networks, *Physical Review E* 68(3): 036105.

Munkres, J. (1957). Algorithms for the assignment and transportation problems, *Journal of the Society for Industrial and Applied Mathematics* 5(1): 32–38.

Newman, M. E. J. (2001). Clustering and preferential attachment in growing networks, *Physical Review E* 64(2): 025102.

Newman, M. E. J., Forrest, S. & Balthrop, J. (2002). Email networks and the spread of computer viruses, *Physical Review E* 66(3): 035101.

Onnela, J.-P., Saramäki, J., Hyvönen, J., Szabó, G., Lazer, D., Kaski, K., Kertész, J. & Barabási, A.-L. (2007). Structure and tie strengths in mobile communication networks, *Proceedings of the National Academy of Sciences U.S.A* 104(18): 7332–7336.

Ravasz, E., Somera, A. L., Mongru, D. A., Oltvai, Z. N. & Barabási, A.-L. (2002). Hierarchical organization of modularity in metabolic networks, *Science* 297(5586): 1551–1555.

Rozenfeld, H. D., Song, C. & Makse, H. A. (2010). Small-world to fractal transition in complex networks: A renormalization group approach, *Physical Review Letters* 104(2): 025701.

Salton, G. & McGill, M. J. (1983). *Introduction to Modern Information Retrieval*, MuGraw-Hill, Auckland.

Sørensen, T. (1948). A method of establishing groups of equal amplitude in plant sociology based on similarity of species content and its application to analyses of the vegetation on danish commons, *Biologislce Skrifler* 5(4): 1–34.

Watts, D. J. & Strogatz, S. H. (1998). Collective dynamics of 'small-world' networks, *Nature* 393(6684): 440–442.

Xiao, Y., Xiong, M., Wang, W. & Wang, H. (2008). Emergence of symmetry in complex networks, *Physical Review E* 77(6): 066108.

Xuan, Q., Du, F. & Wu, T.-J. (2009). Empirical analysis of internet telephone network: From user id to phone, *Chaos* 19(2): 023101.

Xuan, Q., Du, F. & Wu, T.-J. (2010a). Partially ordered sets in complex networks, *Journal of Physics A: Mathematical and Theoretical* 43(18): 185001.

Xuan, Q., Du, F. & Wu, T.-J. (2010b). Partially ordered sets in complex networks, *Journal of Physics A: Mathematical and Theoretical* 43(39): 395002.

Xuan, Q., Du, F., Wu, T.-J. & Chen, G. (2010). Emergence of heterogeneous structures in chemical reaction-diffusion networks, *Physical Review E* 82(4): 046116.

Xuan, Q., Li, Y. & Wu, T.-J. (2006). Growth model for complex networks with hierarchical and modular structures, *Physical Review E* 73(3): 036105.

Xuan, Q., Li, Y. & Wu, T.-J. (2007). A local-world network model based on inter-node correlation degree, *Physica A: Statistical Mechanics and Its Applications* 378(2): 561–572.

Xuan, Q., Li, Y. & Wu, T.-J. (2008). Does the compelled cooperation determine the structure of a complex network?, *Chinese Physics Letters* 25(2): 363–366.

Xuan, Q. & Wu, T.-J. (2009). Node matching between complex networks, *Physical Review E* 80(2): 026103.

8

Path-Finding Algorithm Application for Route-Searching in Different Areas of Computer Graphics

Csaba Szabó and Branislav Sobota
Technical University of Košice
Slovak Republic

1. Introduction

Common graphical notations for graphs use a set of points interconnected by lines. Points are called vertices. The lines called edges can also have in some cases a direction (orientation) specified.

Paths are sequences of vertices and edges between them. Path-finding between two locations in a graph is used in many areas like GPS navigation, CAD systems (auto-routing in design of circuit boards), and applications of artificial intelligence, computer games, virtual reality, military forces or robotics. The main aim of path-finding is to avoid collisions with obstacles and safely pass through the virtual world (or the real one) along the path found by the selected algorithm. Examples of this need are autonomous robots on distant planets without the possibility to be controlled in real time because of latencies in signal sending, or automatic vehicles control presented in (Simon et al., 2006) and (Kuljić et al., 2009). Another examples of path-finding are strategic computer games, mostly with computer opponent. Path-finding is also widely used in finding best routers interconnection for data transmission in many kinds of computer networks.

To be successful in path-finding, the need of reliable algorithm and reliable implementation of that algorithm is enormous. Another important thing is the need of some user-friendly visualization of results of path-finding, which is realized by application of computer graphics techniques (Vokorokos et al., 2010).

A geographical information system (GIS) as defined in (Tuček, 1998) is an information system (IS) designed to work with data that represent geographical or spatial coordinates. These data can be further analyzed and statistically evaluated.

Another way to specify a GIS is that it is a specialized IS defined as a collection of computer hardware (as noted by (Vokorokos et al., 2004)) and software and geographical data designed for effective gathering, retaining, editing, processing, analysis and visualization of all kinds of geographical information. Generally, it is an IS designed as specialized for spatial data, or an IS developed to such specialization during its life cycle by extensions and/or refactoring steps presented by (Szabó & Sobota, 2009).

Being an IS, GIS has to provide information in graphical (e.g. location of the hotel on the map) and non-graphical (e.g. fees, room equipment) way that supports fast searching and actualization of data. Nowadays, graphical information are stored as vector graphics (two-dimensional), but the trends are clearly forecasting the second generation GIS as an IS working with 3D objects and surfaces as in (Szabó et al., 2010).

It is useful to extend the implementation of the above-mentioned searching of objects by route-searching between two selected objects. As the map is the core of any GIS, a possible way of implement path-finding on graphs within such a system is the mapping of these maps onto search-able graphs that will be shown in next sections of this chapter.

Section 2 presents the theoretical background needed in algorithm descriptions in the other following sections. In Sections 3–4, terms such as map and route are defined. Blind-search and A* algorithms are introduced in Section 5. Next section (Section 6) presents the test cases and results: results on static two-dimensional maps, results from tests where three-dimensional (city) maps were used, results of testing with dynamics in the maps. Tests also demonstrate the tested 3D city information system, especially its user interface, and hardware configurations of host computers used during testing. Section 7 ends the chapter by concluding it and pointing out future work.

2. Graph theory basics

Leonhard Euler is considered the founder of graph theory, since he solved the problem known as the Seven Bridges of Königsberg in 1736. Graph theory as a science discipline started with first graph theory monographs written by mathematicians (Kőnig, 1936) and (Berge, 1958). The next part of this section relies on definitions in (Bučko & Klešč, 1999).

Let V be a final non-empty set, i.e. the set of vertices, and let E be the set of edges defined as:

$$E = \{e | e = \{v_1, v_2\}; v_{1,2} \in V\} . \tag{1}$$

Obviously, $E \subseteq \binom{V}{2}$, where $\binom{V}{2}$ is a set of all two-element subsets of V:

$$\binom{V}{2} = \{A | A \subset V \wedge |A| = 2\} . \tag{2}$$

Considering these two sets presented in Equation 2 and Equation 1, the couple $G = (V, E)$ defines graph G with the corresponding vertices and edges.

Path is a sequence of vertices where an edge exists for any two consecutive vertices of this sequence. Degree of a vertex is the count of edges outgoing from this vertex, e.g. the degree of any internal vertex in a path is not less than two, the end vertices have a degree at least one.

The graph G is a coherent graph if all vertices are reachable, i.e. for all vertices exists at least one path to any other vertex.

Let $G = (V, E)$ be a coherent graph. Distance $d(u, v)$ between vertices u and v of graph G is the length of shortest route linking vertices u, v, i.e. the shortest path. Vertices distance $d(u, v)$ of graph G has the following properties:

$$\begin{aligned} d(u,v) &\geq 0; d(u,v) = 0 \Leftrightarrow u = v \\ d(u,v) &= d(v,u) \\ \forall z \in V : d(u,v) &\leq d(u,z) + d(z,v) \end{aligned} \tag{3}$$

These properties are metrics axioms; so ordered pair (V, d) is a metrical space. Nevertheless V is a vertical set of graph $G = (V, E)$, d is a metric – vertices distance in graph G. The advantage of these properties is the fact that they consist even after isomorphism is done. One result of this is the fact, that also notions defined by metric have the same advantage.

Let $G = (V, E)$ be a coherent graph, then:

1. For every vertex $u \in V$ the number $e(u, G) = \max d(u, v)$, $v \in V$ is called eccentricity of vertex u.
2. Number $P(G) = \max e(v, G)$, $v \in V$ is average of graph G.
3. Number $r(G) = \min e(v, G)$, $v \in V$ is radius of graph G.
4. The center of graph G is every vertex u of graph G with eccentricity equal to radius $e(u, G) = r(G)$.

Graph diameter can also be defined as $P(G) = \max d(u, v); u, v \in V$.

Graph $G = (V, E)$ is an Eulerian graph, if this graph is coherent and every one of its vertices has even degree. Graph can be covered by a single enclosed stroke (i.e. Eulerian circuit) only if it is an Eulerian graph. Graph $G = (V, E)$ can be covered by a single unenclosed stroke only if it is a coherent graph with two vertices of degree 2 (opened stroke starts in one of these vertices and ends in another).

Let $G = (V, E)$ be a graph, $|V| = n, n \geq 3$. Let the degree of every vertex of graph G be at least $n/2$. Then G is a Hamilton graph. If graph $G = (V, E)$ is a Hamilton graph, this graph has to be terminal, non-empty, coherent and may not consist of bridges. Nevertheless fulfillment of these conditions does not guarantee existence of Hamilton graph.

Oriented graph G is defined as ordered pair (V, E), where V is the set of vertices and E is set of ordered element pairs of set V. Elements of V are called graph vertices and elements of E are called oriented graph edges.

3. Maps

The core element of any GIS is the map. All objects have spatial coordinates defining their placement on this map. On other hand, maps are also basic elements if it comes to path-finding or animations. Architecture of such a system for animations based on drawing objects on a 2D map is shown on Fig. 1, its output is presented on Fig. 2.

The specifics and role of maps in the selected domain areas are presented in the following subsections.

3.1 Maps in virtual reality

Simulations use 2D and 3D maps that are dynamically changing due simulation state changes. This type of maps is also used in any interactive graphics such virtual reality city walkthroughs or computer games.

Dynamic of the maps' change is expressed by structural changes in the maps, i.e. at least one object's spatial coordinates have been changed. Changes near found paths might indicate the need of re-running the path-finding algorithm on the new map segments.

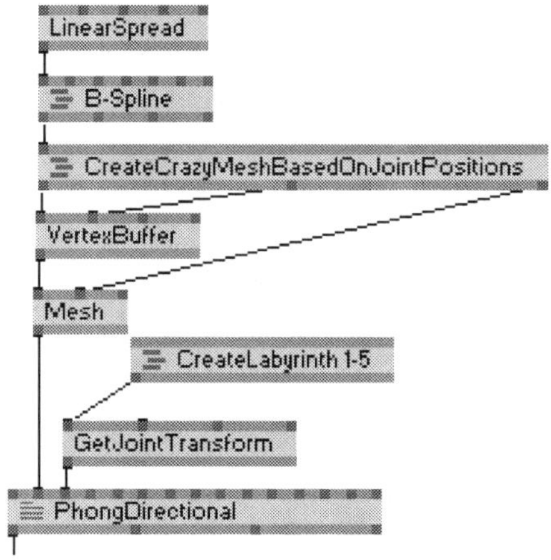

Fig. 1. Architecture of example system for 3D maze drawing using a 2D map

Fig. 2. Example system output with animated actor

3.2 Maps in GIS

Geographical information systems mainly use static maps. These maps could be both 2D or 3D or combined. Mostly, these maps are segments of cadastral maps, where the most important factor is the proper positioning of the segment root (see Fig. 3) that could be achieved by manual operation or using image filters (Póth, 2007).

3.3 Circuit boards as maps

Printed Circuit Boards (PCB) are well tested and proven technology. A manufacturer of electronics cannot imagine manufacturing of electronic equipment without this technology. Reliable operation of the current integrated circuits with high operating frequencies requires a minimum length of printed circuit conductors. Therefore, it is necessary to pay close attention to the PCB design mainly in the case of the optimal length of the printed circuit conductors. The conductive pattern may be on one side or both sides of the board and might be linked

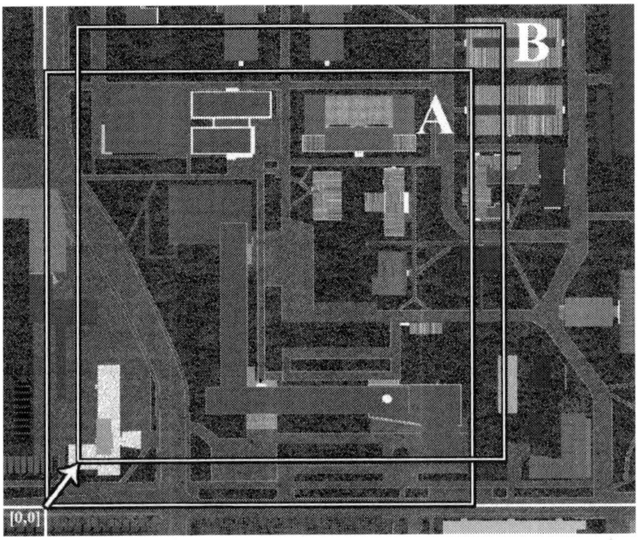

Fig. 3. Correct (A) and incorrect (B) position of a segment of the city map designated for GIS internal map creation

in various ways. In the case of multilayer PCB, it might be between a few plates of copper conductive patterns. The creation and routing of conductors on PCB is the key of PCB design. In principle, the addressed issues are the issues discussed in this chapter.

The algorithm used in PCB design applications is the principal factor of their success. The most used algorithms in this area are heuristic algorithms, channel algorithm, rip-up algorithm (rip and reroute) and maze algorithms. These algorithms include, for example Lee router or also algorithms such as Blind search or A* described and compared later in this chapter.

In short, Lee router was first published more than 40 years ago and it was successfully implemented 20 years ago as a maze algorithm (Brown & Zwolinsky, 1990). In its simplest form, this router represents the algorithm to find a path between two points in 2D area with various obstacles. Its main features are ability to found always a path between the points, if any, within the limits of the work area size (PCB size) and this path is always the shortest route between two points.

However, it is very slow and, moreover, cannot organize its data structure to minimize gaps, and so it is being replaced by above mentioned algorithms now. Lee router organizes PCB space to the network of points. All unfilled points in the basic network are unmarked during algorithm initialization. The algorithm consists of two phases: an exploratory phase and a processing phase. Exploratory phase is similar with seed-fill algorithm used in computer graphics. The target point is on last place in the list and we travel back over the list of unfilled points to the original seeds in the subsequent processing phase. This original seed represents a starting point. Very simple and efficient improvement is the possibility to use 45 degrees angles too.

3.4 From map to graph representation

The basic working structure of algorithms is the map, which is represented as a set $M = N \times N$ (two-dimensional quadratic grid). Square is a member of set M. Every square represents position in map and has its own coordinates $[x, y]$ according to beginning P_m. Squares $[x1, y1]$ and $[x2, y2]$ are neighbors, if $(|x1 - x2| = 1$ and $|y1 - y2| <= 1)$ or $(|x1 - x2| <= 1$ a $|y1 - y2| = 1)$ (they are neighbors geometrically). The beginning in map P_m is a defined square. This representation is called map representation.

Next, a function is defined:

$$w_m : M \rightarrow \mathbb{R}^+ \cup \{+\infty\}. \tag{4}$$

This function assigns regress (e.g. weight, terrain cost) to every square. This function determines the difficulty of input for each square (or square traversing). If the regress is $+\infty$ then the square is impassable and contains an obstacle (black color nodes in Fig. 4, white color indicates passable vertices). This function is simple only if it contains a two-element set 1 and $+\infty$. In the map, the start square of the route is marked A, the target square is marked B.

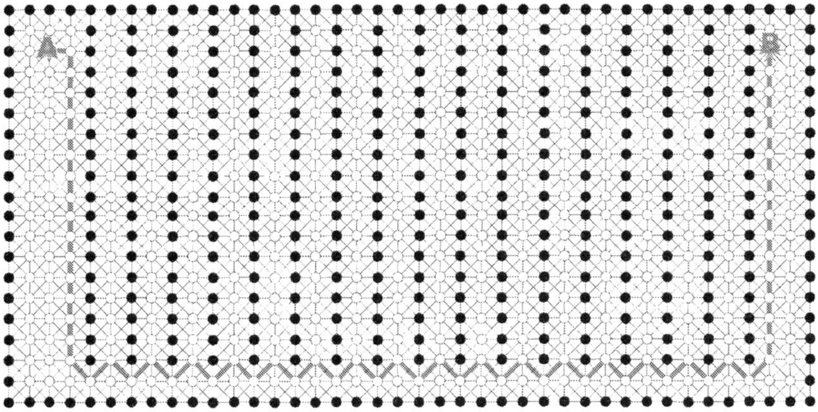

Fig. 4. Example graph of a maze with walls (black color), lanes (white color) and a route (red color)

4. Routes

Route in map is a sequence of map squares $(m_1, m_2, \ldots, m_n)$ in which every next square is neighbor to previous square on the route. There are no squares on the route that are included more than once. The route length is the sum of regresses of all route squares:

$$d = \sum_i w_m(m_i). \tag{5}$$

5. Algorithms

The algorithm task is to find the shortest route in map from the start to the target, i.e. from A to B.

The map representation is a special graph example. Vertices correspond to squares. The bijection transforming the graph to squares will be called *map*. Transition between neighbor squares corresponds to graph edge and initial vertex in graph P_g corresponds to initial vertex in map P_m. Next function to define is w, which will perform weight calculation on the graph. Function w_g is defined as representation from set of edges to set of non-negative real numbers with $+\infty$:

$$w_g : E \rightarrow \mathbb{R}^+ \cup \{+\infty\}. \tag{6}$$

For edge $e = (p, q)$, function w_g is defined as:

$$w_g(e) = w_m(map(q)). \tag{7}$$

Heuristics is defined as function $h : V \rightarrow \mathbb{R}^+ \cup \{+\infty\}$, which assigns the expected distance to target to vertex v. It estimates the length of shortest route from vertex v to the target.

The most common heuristics used for path-finding in 2D static maps are:

- Euclidean distance or Euclidean metric,
- Manhattan method that uses $\mathrm{d}x + \mathrm{d}y$, and
- the method of the maximum that uses $\max(\mathrm{d}x, \mathrm{d}y)$ as heuristics value.

There are several algorithms for route-searching in static maps:

- blind-search
- divide & conquer
- breadth-first search
- bidirectional breadth-first search
- depth-first search
- iterative depth-first search
- Dijkstra's algorithm
- best-first search
- Dijkstra's algorithm with heuristics (A*)

In our tests, the blind-search algorithm and Dijkstra's algorithm with Manhattan method of heuristics (A*) were used.

5.1 Blind-search algorithm

The blind-search algorithm (example results are shown in Fig. 5(a)–5(c)) is based on progress to the target, until it collides with obstacle, then the direction of movement is changed and the algorithm tries to move along nearest to get around the obstacle. This algorithm works with aim on one square and usually does not take into consideration the whole evaluation function w, but only its two states represented by values $+\infty$ or 1 (i.e. other than $+\infty$). So it works only with simple evaluating function and does not count with regress. This algorithm does not guarantee the finding of shortest route and can be used on special maps because of its speed, low memory requirements and simple implementation.

The evaluation process is as follows:

$$abs\left[(e_x - t_x) + (e_y - t_y)\right], \tag{8}$$

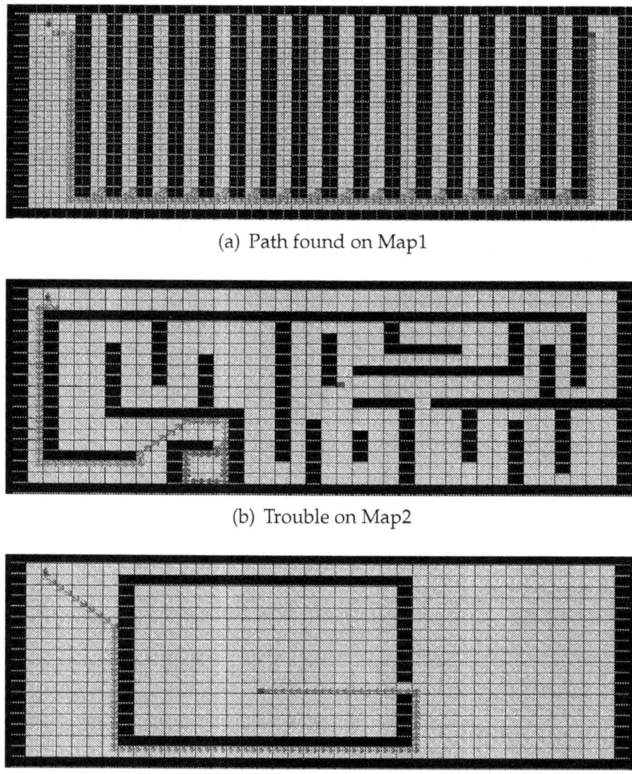

(a) Path found on Map1

(b) Trouble on Map2

(c) Path found on Map3

Fig. 5. Example paths found by the blind-search algorithm

where $e_{x,y}$ are the $[x, y]$ coordinates of the actually evaluated square and $t_{x,y}$ are coordinates of target square on the map.

The square with the lowest evaluation is chosen and set as new starting square for the next iteration. Continuing using this mechanism, the algorithm moves to target with the fastest possible approach. Because of the use of a simple evaluation, this algorithm is one of the fastest algorithms for path-finding.

Problem occurs when the evaluated square is impassable. If this situation occurs, the algorithm stops to evaluate squares and remembers the obstacle direction and then tries to avoid this obstacle. The avoid process is done by choosing the nearest available square, which is gained by turning the movement direction into right. This square is the new starting square, which is not evaluated but only checked if the direction with obstacle is not released. If yes, then the square in this direction is set as new starting square and the evaluation process starts again. If not, then the algorithm continues with new direction and tests first route. By this movement the algorithm can collide with new obstacles. It remembers again only the direction with obstacle and sets new course. This new course is tested and if it is released, then the original direction is tested. If the algorithm collides with obstacle it stops to evaluate squares and tests transitivity of only one square. This can fasten the algorithm but can also become the algorithm into endless loop (see Fig. 5(b)).

5.2 A* algorithm

The A* algorithm (test results on Fig. 6(a)–6(c)) is a natural generalization of Dijkstra's algorithm and the scanning is based only on heuristics. In A* the element classification process is done by a binary heap. All square near the evaluated square are also evaluated in eight directions. Function g(x) is evaluated from the starting square. To work with integer values, a modification is made to the representation of Euclidean distance as follows:

- If the evaluated square is in the diagonal, then the number 14 is assigned to this square, and
- if not, then number 10 is assigned to this square.

As heuristics, the Manhattan method is used:

$$10 * \left[abs(e_x - t_x) + abs(e_y - t_y)\right], \tag{9}$$

i.e. the distance between $dx + dy$ is computed. Sequence function is defined as $f(x) = g(x) + h(x)$. The algorithm description follows.

Assume that graph $G = (V, E)$ has already evaluated edges, i.e. the mapping and weight computation is already done. Two values for every already processed vertex will be stored: $d[v]$ will store the length of the shortest path to the vertex, $p[v]$ will be the vertex before v on the path. The algorithm also uses two sets: $OPEN$ and $CLOSED$. $OPEN$ is the set of vertices to process, $CLOSED$ includes vertices already processed as presented in (Sobota, Szabó & Perháč, 2008):

1. At the beginning, the starting vertex is inserted into $OPEN$.
2. The iteration cycle starts with the choose of the vertex n with best value of $f(n)$. This vertex will be inserted into set $CLOSED$ and all from n reachable vertices v are selected, and if they are not in set $OPEN$, they will be inserted with value $p[v] = n$ and the corresponding value of $d[v] = d[n] + l(n, v)$, where $l(n, v) = w_g(v)$ is the cost function for the selected edge from n. If v was already a member of $OPEN$, a test is needed if the new path is shorter than the old one by comparing $d[v] < d[n] + l(n, v)$. If the comparison fails, update of the values $p[v]$ and $d[v]$ is performed.
3. The presented cycle continues until the target is found or the set $OPEN$ is empty.
4. After the algorithm had finished, the path is reconstructed using values of $p[v]$.

Fig. 6(a)–6(c) show examples of usage of the A* algorithm on 2D static maps to compare with the results of the blind-search algorithm from the previous section.

There are possible modifications to this algorithm that can decrease memory usage and fasten the A* algorithm. The most common techniques optimize the number of vertices within the sets $OPEN$ and $CLOSED$ by discarding the less useful ones. This technique limits the count of the elements of each set separately to get best performance but do not miss some possible paths. The common problem is the grid resolution selection: high resolution rapidly slows down the algorithm execution; low resolution may cause loss on important information as smaller buildings and/or gates. The maximum sizes of sets $OPEN$ and $CLOSED$ were

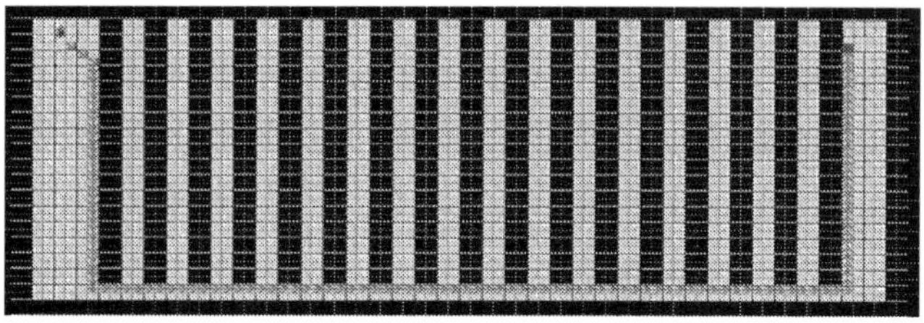

(a) Path found on Map1

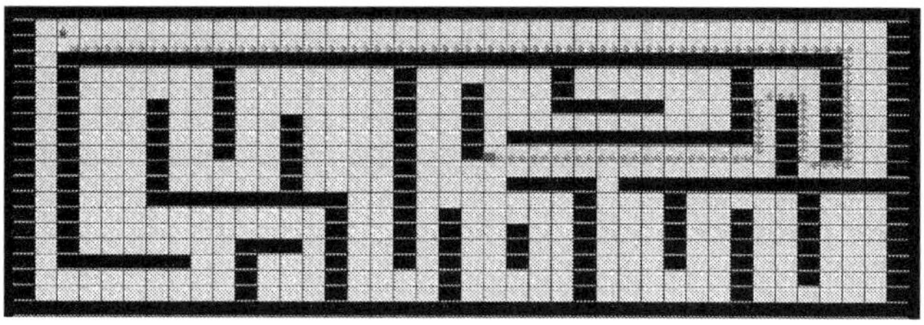

(b) Path found on Map2

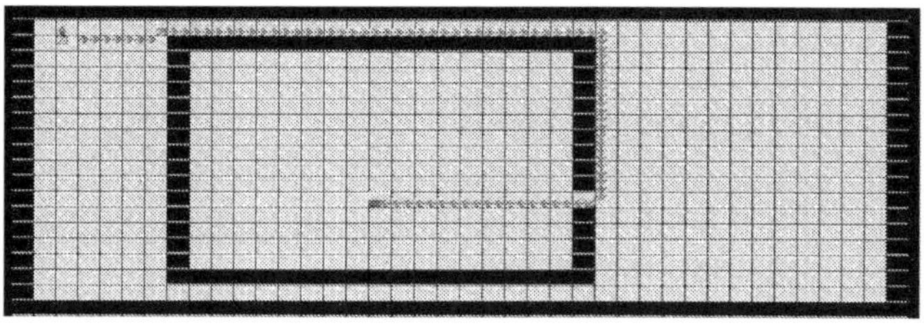

(c) Path found on Map3

Fig. 6. Example paths found by the A* algorithm

examined and experimentally defined in (Sobota, Szabó & Perháč, 2008) and (Vlasova, 2008) as 1000 and 3000.

6. Algorithm use cases and evaluation results

6.1 Test results for static 2D maps - the maze example continued

A couple of tests have been run on two-dimensional static maps to compare the blind-search and A* algorithms, which implementations were based on (Adams, 2003; Barron, 2003). Ten (10) maps were tested.

Routes found differ in length (compare results on Fig. 5(c) and Fig. 6(c)). The route always starts with red arrow. If the route is returning by the same route backward, then the arrow is changed to yellow and the route continues with yellow arrow. If the route crosses itself (blind-search algorithm), then it is in cycle and the arrow will be marked by boxed blue color (see 5(b)). Yellow square is start square, blue square is target square.

The efficiency of blind-search algorithm is only 40% because it found a route only in four of 10 maps. A* algorithm searched in all maps 14 895 squares together. Blind-search needed to search 83 928 squares, because it used to cycle itself (see Fig. 5(b)) and the condition of cycle detection was at 10000 cycles. The blind-search algorithm searched 5.64 times more squares than A* algorithm. Considering only those maps, where both algorithms succeeded, blind-search algorithm would be the better one in speed and number of squares searched, respectively.

We present the test results of both algorithms on Fig. 7. It is obvious that blind-search was not so effective like the A* algorithm when compared the count of squares searched on all maps. The speeds on all maps are not comparable due to the low efficiency of the blind-search algorithm.

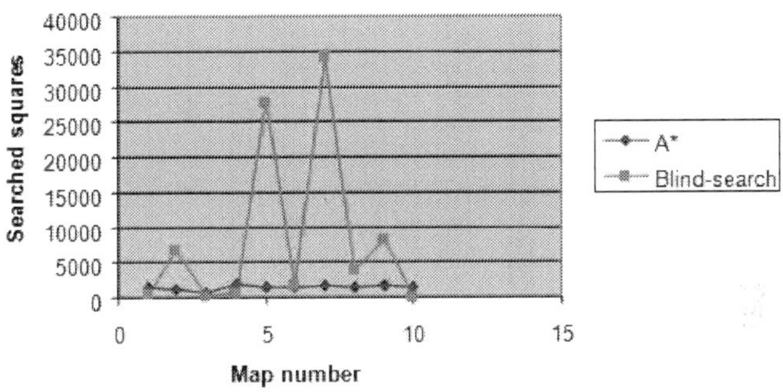

Fig. 7. Statistical results comparison for both algorithms gathered on 10 maps

6.2 Testing with static 3D city maps

Two-dimensional maps, as presented above, are a good testing tool, but in real systems three-dimensional ones are more frequently asked. Representing higher fidelity to real world, virtual reality techniques help to build more user-friendly and more precise information systems.

Dealing with geographical information, a three-dimensional map (or more precisely, the visualization of it) introduces a few new problems into the path-finding by extending the amount of information to be searched.

Therefore, tests on more complicated surfaces and maps with building objects, hills etc. were also run. The result is shown on Fig. 8 in the form of a route found from point *A* to point *B* between the buildings of a randomly generated city.

Tests on optimizing of sizes for sets *OPEN* and *CLOSED* were also performed. As already mentioned, in (Vlasova, 2008) were made some experiments under the supervision of the authors. The testing conditions were as follows:

- each test case was run separately on the same hardware (no sequences etc.),
- visualization (rendering) speed was set to minimum, and
- each test case was run ten times and results were averaged.

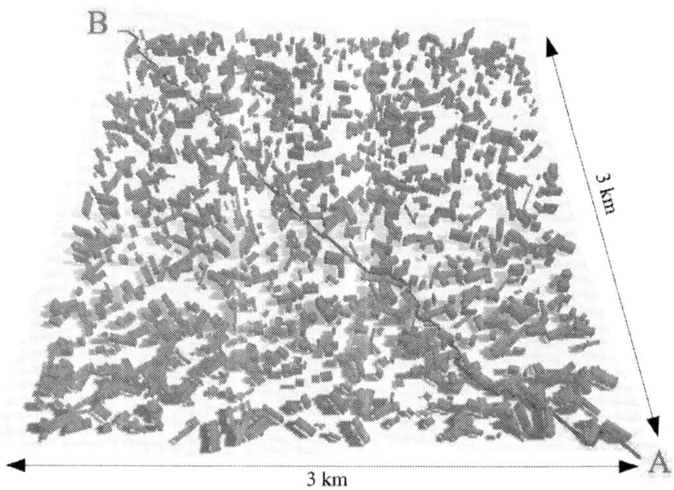

Fig. 8. Path found by A* algorithm on a random 9km^2 city map

Optimization technique	Average execution time [s]
none	489
CLOSED	458
OPEN	368
OPEN & *CLOSED*	346

Table 1. Speed test results for A* algorithm optimization

The test results are shown on Table 1 and Table 2. The best performance was achieved by dual optimizing (i.e. using both limits), but the optimization of size of set *OPEN* had stronger effect on execution speed than the size optimization of set *CLOSED*.

Optimization technique	Path length [m]	$\|OPEN\|$	$\|CLOSED\|$
none	5210	6022	5210
CLOSED	5210	6022	3000
OPEN	5210	1000	5263
OPEN & *CLOSED*	5210	1000	3000

Table 2. Set sizes and path lengths during A* algorithm optimization

6.2.1 The 3D City IS test case

The tested A* algorithm was implemented within a GIS called the 3D city IS, details of the system can be found in (Sobota et al., 2010; Sobota, Korečko & Perháč, 2009; Sobota, Perháč & Petz, 2009; Sobota, Szabó, Perháč & Ádám, 2008; Sobota, Szabó & Perháč, 2008).

Fig. 9(a) shows the main screen of the tested GIS. There are a few building objects shown on the base map. In the upper right corner are navigation buttons (ref. no. 3 for minimize, ref.

no. 4 – close). Upper left corner contains also two buttons: ref. no. 1 is for opening a map; ref. no. 2 point on the options menu. 'Options' are e.g. map resolution. The ref. number 5 indicates the search button, which functionality was tested in the test cases.

(a) The main screen

(b) Path searching dialog

Fig. 9. 3D city IS test case setup

Selecting this last option, a search dialog opens that is shown on Fig. 9(b). As any classical search dialogs, it has a field for the search query (reference number ref. no. 6), results displaying area (ref. no. 7), search execution button (ref. no. 8), animation button (ref. no. 9), path display button (ref. no. 10), object display button (ref. no. 11), and close dialog button (ref. no. 12).

The testing procedure is simple:

1. Open a map, e.g. in this case each of the following maps was used:
   - a map with some known labeled objects randomly generated by other tool,
   - the real (but yet only partial) city map, and
   - the map of the university campus.
2. Type a search phrase and evaluate what has been found and displayed.
3. Now follows the test of path-finding abilities.
   - Function go-to-object only moves the camera to the selected target.
   - Function show-path opens after a few minutes the resulting route from the actual position on the map to the selected target as shown on Fig. 8.

The speed is faster with less resolution, but some narrow streets have been missed. With the campus map are nearly real-time results due to the small count of objects.

The virtual reality oriented part of the tested geographical information system is the animation function. The path-finding module was shared with the other already mentioned parts. The test case had to ensure the quality of the obstacle detection. This part offers path visualization by circles and the animated walkthrough of the scene rendered from the map and additional object information stored in the GIS database. Fig. 10 shows the animation screen. Buttons labeled 13–16 are classical navigation buttons for movement within the animation. This test case is evaluated by expressing the quality and feel by human testers; and were used in the debugging phase of development of the path animation part of the system.

Fig. 10. Walk-through animation of 3D city information system

6.3 Path-finding results in dynamic 2D maps

In virtual reality applications (also in computer simulators and games), the effect of reality is significantly achieved by dynamics of the scene.

For problem simplification, the next test case uses pseudo 3D solution, meaning that the scene is a composition of 2D (map) and 3D objects. Note that in this case path-finding algorithms have to deal with less data, i.e. weight function and final calculations could be performed faster. The same simplification could be made in the case of any type of systems listed above.

There were 10 maps created with different amount and positions of static obstacles. Tests were provided for 1, 8, 16, 24, 32, 40, 48, 56, 64, 72, 80, 88, 96, 192 and 384 active moving objects called units. Test cases were oriented on calculation time (e.g. speed of path-finding in relation to CPU) and visualization time (e.g. the role and impact of GPU) while comparing the two selected algorithms.

Tables 3 and 4 show the contrast between the algorithms during the testing process. While considering all maps as in Table 3 A* algorithm seems to be better in every case, the fact is that there are averaged values for all maps, where blind-search algorithm failure to find a path incorrectly implies being this algorithm the slower one. Considering only calculation time on maps, where both algorithms succeed shown in Table 4 reflect that blind-search algorithm is faster but less stable.

Next group of tests was designed to compare speeds of both path-finding algorithm implementations on different hardware CPUs. Table 5 shows the test configurations used.

Although the implementations should not be affected by the hardware and results are not used as CPU metrics, Tables 6–7 present the values. The only conclusion to make is that the slower A* algorithm could be evaluated faster on a fast CPU than the faster blind-search algorithm using a slower CPU.

Units	1	8	16	24	32	40	48	56
A* [s]	0.022	0.146	0.281	0.381	0.514	0.658	0.849	0.966
BS [s]	0.043	0.42	0.853	1.262	1.707	2.303	2.756	3.233
Units	64	72	80	88	96	192	384	
A* [s]	1.077	1.126	1.324	1.453	1.665	3.169	6.343	
BS [s]	3.717	4.247	4.705	5.173	5.671	11.376	23.799	

Table 3. Average time for 10 maps for A* and blind-search (BS) algorithm in relation to No. of units

Units	1	8	16	24	32	40	48	56
A* [s]	0.009	0.058	0.112	0.152	0.206	0.263	0.340	0.386
BS [s]	0.001	0.008	0.016	0.025	0.032	0.044	0.052	0.058
Units	64	72	80	88	96	192	384	
A* [s]	0.431	0.450	0.530	0.581	0.666	1.268	2.537	
BS [s]	0.065	0.075	0.081	0.087	0.097	0.189	0.390	

Table 4. Average time for A* and blind-search (BS) algorithm in relation to No. of units (for maps, where BS succeed)

Name	CPU	GPU	RAM
TConf1	AMD Duron 1200 MHz	Geforce MX400/64MB	256 MB
TConf2	AMD Athlon 1700+	Radeon 9200SE	512 MB
TConf3	AMD Athlon 2000+	Geforce MX460/64MB	512 MB
TConf4	AMD Barton 2500+	Geforce 5900	2 GB
TConf5	Intel P4 Centrino 1.7 GHz	Intel GMA 900	512 MB

Table 5. Hardware test configurations

Units	1	8	16	24	32	40	48	56
TConf1 [s]	0.000	0.016	0.031	0.047	0.047	0.062	0.094	0.094
TConf2 [s]	0.002	0.016	0.020	0.032	0.042	0.053	0.066	0.074
TConf3 [s]	0.002	0.010	0.018	0.029	0.039	0.046	0.056	0.065
TConf4 [s]	0.002	0.007	0.017	0.023	0.031	0.039	0.047	0.055
TConf5 [s]	0.000	0.016	0.015	0.016	0.031	0.031	0.047	0.047
Units	64	72	80	88	96	192	384	
TConf1 [s]	0.109	0.125	0.125	0.140	0.156	0.328	0.640	
TConf2 [s]	0.086	0.090	0.106	0.117	0.125	0.252	0.504	
TConf3 [s]	0.074	0.085	0.095	0.104	0.113	0.226	0.452	
TConf4 [s]	0.065	0.073	0.078	0.085	0.092	0.189	0.377	
TConf5 [s]	0.047	0.062	0.062	0.078	0.078	0.157	0.297	

Table 6. Average times for A* algorithm using different hardware configurations

Last group of tests was aimed to measure average time for animations of unit movement on path from A to B. In test realization, for places A and B constant locations were used. Time was measured including path-finding, but the additional condition was to achieve the same formation of the units in both locations, e.g. for 96 units a 8×12 rectangle. Test results are shown in Table 8 and Table 9.

Units	1	8	16	24	32	40	48	56
TConf1 [s]	0.000	0.000	0.000	0.016	0.031	0.031	0.031	0.031
TConf2 [s]	0.000	0.007	0.014	0.012	0.017	0.021	0.027	0.035
TConf3 [s]	0.000	0.004	0.008	0.012	0.017	0.022	0.027	0.032
TConf4 [s]	0.000	0.003	0.006	0.009	0.013	0.016	0.020	0.023
TConf5 [s]	0.000	0.000	0.000	0.000	0.000	0.000	0.000	0.015

Units	64	72	80	88	96	192	384	
TConf1 [s]	0.047	0.047	0.063	0.063	0.063	0.109	0.250	
TConf2 [s]	0.040	0.044	0.045	0.052	0.055	0.117	0.229	
TConf3 [s]	0.035	0.040	0.042	0.046	0.051	0.104	0.209	
TConf4 [s]	0.029	0.032	0.035	0.039	0.040	0.084	0.168	
TConf5 [s]	0.015	0.031	0.031	0.031	0.031	0.078	0.156	

Table 7. Average times for blind-search algorithm using different hardware configurations

Units	1	96	192	384
TConf1 [s]	39	63	84	124
TConf2 [s]	31	31	35	50
TConf3 [s]	15	19	30	35
TConf4 [s]	13	13	25	28
TConf5 [s]	22	28	43	50

Table 8. Average animation times for A* algorithm using different hardware configurations

Units	1	96	192	384
TConf1 [s]	55	92	117	167
TConf2 [s]	43	43	49	70
TConf3 [s]	21	27	42	49
TConf4 [s]	18	19	34	39
TConf5 [s]	31	39	60	68

Table 9. Average animation times for blind-search algorithm using different hardware configurations

7. Conclusion

This chapter presents a view on graph theory from point of view of virtual reality. Applications and testing of blind-search algorithm and the modified Dijkstra's A* algorithm of path-finding in graphs within a geographical information system were presented.

From the test results some conclusions can be made. The blind-search algorithm is fast but is not accurate enough. It can be used in maps with low number of obstacles only when the results have to be gained as fast as possible and the route does not have to be the shortest one.

A* algorithm is the most used algorithm and showed its qualities in our tests as well. Despite time results (the speed of this algorithm is not the fastest), this algorithm is reliable and has provided better results. The optimization techniques of set size restrictions were useful and brought higher speed into execution of path-finding.

The implementation of both algorithms showed up as useful, but the significant difference of applicability between them excludes the blind-search algorithm from the set of candidates of route-searching algorithms for a GIS.

Algorithms were implemented into a 3D city information system as a prototype of a GIS. The included functionalities except those presented include the object browser and map editor. The future plan is to interconnect the system with other systems for geographical data processing such points clouds analyzers, video or ortophoto processors etc.

The similarity to today's GPS in the case of route- searching is intentional. According to the trends in the area, future navigation systems might offer three-dimensional interfaces as well. The only difference is in the type of the map, because our system uses a static map while a good navigation system uses a dynamic one that might future GIS use too.

As mentioned in the introducing section, the use of graph theory becomes common in modern computer graphics and virtual reality systems. Collision detection is the main area of it, but, as this article implies, the information system area should follow these trends as well by implementing its algorithms into the visualization and searching modules.

8. Acknowledgements

Authors thank R. Šváby, M. Šváby (M. Vlasova) and V. Kríž for their constructive work in the implementation and debugging phase of development of the presented computer graphics software applications.

This work was supported by VEGA grant project No. 1/0646/09: "Tasks solution for large graphical data processing in the environment of parallel, distributed and network computer systems."

9. References

Adams, J. (2003). *Advanced Animation with DirectX*, Premier Press, a division of Course Technology.

Barron, T. (2003). *Strategy Game Programming with DirectX 9.0*, Wordware Publishing Inc.

Berge, C. (1958). *Théorie des graphes et ses applications*, Vol. II of *Collection Universitaire de Mathématiques*, Dunod, Paris 1958 (English edition, Wiley 1961; Methuen & Co, New York 1962; Russian, Moscow 1961; Spanish, Mexico 1962; Roumanian, Bucharest 1969; Chinese, Shanghai 1963; Second printing of the 1962 first English edition. Dover, New York 2001).

Brown, A. & Zwolinsky, M. (1990). Lee router modified for global routing, *CAD* (5): 296–300.

Bučko, M. & Klešč, M. (1999). *Discrete Mathematics, Diskrétna matematika (orig. Slovak title)*, Academic Press elfa, Košice.

Kőnig, D. (1936). *Theorie der Endlichen und Unendlichen Graphen: Kombinatorische Topologie der Streckenkomplexe*, Akad. Verlag, Leipzig.

Kuljić, B., Simon, J. & Szakáll, T. (2009). Pathfinding based on edge detection and infrared distance measuring sensor, *Acta Polytechnica Hungarica* 6(1): 103–116.

Póth, M. (2007). Comparison of convolutional based interpolation techniques in digital image processing, *Proc. of the 5th Int. Symposium on Intelligent Systems and Informatics, SISY 2007*, Subotica, Serbia, pp. 87–90.

Simon, J., Szakáll, T. & Čović, Z. (2006). Programming mobile robots in ANSI C language for PIC MCU's, *Proc. of the 4th Serbian-Hungarian Joint Symposium on Intelligent Systems, SISY 2006*, Subotica, Serbia, pp. 131–137.

Sobota, B., Hrozek, F. & Szabó, Cs. (2010). 3D visualization of urban areas, *Proc. of the 8th Int. Conf. on Emerging eLearning Technologies and Applications, ICETA 2010*, Stará Lesná, Slovakia, pp. 277–280.

Sobota, B., Korečko, Š.. & Perháč, J. (2009). 3D modeling and visualization of historic buildings as cultural heritage preservation, *Proc. of the Tenth Int. Conf. on Informatics, INFORMATICS 2009*, Herlany, Slovakia, pp. 94–98.

Sobota, B., Perháč, J. & Petz, I. (2009). Surface modelling in 3D city information system, *J. of Comp. Sci. and Control Systems* 2(2): 53–56.

Sobota, B., Szabó, Cs., Perháč, J. & Ádám, N. (2008). 3D visualisation for city information system, *Proc. of Int. Conf. on Applied Electrical Engineering and Informatics, AEI 2008*, Athens, Greece, pp. 9–13.

Sobota, B., Szabó, Cs. & Perháč, J. (2008). Using path-finding algorithms of graph theory for route-searching in geographical information systems, *SISY 2008 – Proc. of the 6th International Symposium on Intelligent Systems and Informatics*, Subotica, Serbia, pp. 1–6.

Szabó, Cs. & Sobota, B. (2009). Some aspects of database refactoring for GIS, *Proc. of the Fourth Int. Conf. on Intelligent Computing and Information Systems, ICICIS 2009*, Cairo, Egypt, pp. 352–356.

Szabó, Cs., Sobota, B. & Kiš, R. (2010). Terrain LoD in real-time 3D map visualization, *8th Joint Conference on Mathematics and Computer Science, Selected Papers*, J. Selye University, Komárno, Slovakia, pp. 395–402.

Tuček, J. (1998). *Geographical Information Systems, Geografické informační systémy (orig. Czech title)*, Computer Press, Praha.

Vlasova, M. (2008). *3D city information system*, Master's thesis, DCI FEEaI TU, Košice, Slovakia.

Vokorokos, L., Blišťan, P., Petrík, S. & Ádám, N. (2004). Utilization of parallel computer system for modeling of geological phenomena in GIS, *Metalurgy J.* 43(4): 287–291.

Vokorokos, L., Danková, E. & Ádám, N. (2010). Parallel scene splitting and assigning for fast ray tracing, *Acta Electrotechnica et Informatica* 10(2): 33–37.

9

Techniques for Analyzing Random Graph Dynamics and Their Applications

Ali Hamlili
ENSIAS, Mohamed V-Souissi University, Rabat, Morocco

1. Introduction

Graph theory is birth in 1736 with the publication of the work of the Swiss mathematician Leonhard Euler on the problem of finding a round trip path that would cross all the seven bridges of the city of Königsberg exactly once (Euler, 1736). Since then, this theory has known many important developments and has answered to a lot of practical issues. Today, the graph theory is considered as an essential component of discrete mathematics. It aims at analyzing the structure induced by interactions between a set of elements and to study the resulting fundamental properties. Graph theory occurs as a fundamental and theoretical framework for analyzing a wide range of the so-called *real-world networks* in biology, computer sciences, multi-agent systems, chemistry, physics, economy, knowledge management, and sociology. In many works, graph models are employed as constructive descriptions to represent and understand the behavior of different complexe systems (Molloy and Reed, 1998; Mieghem et al., 2000; Newman, 2003; Kawahigashi et al. 2005; Jurdak, 2007). In such models, the graph vertices stand for the components (nodes) of the network that encode information about the values of the state variables of the dynamical system and the edges represent the mutual relationships between the correspondent end-nodes. In practice, random graph theory has become increasingly important for modeling networks whose behaviors exhibit nondeterministic looks. In recent years, many significant results have used random graph models to explain, replicate and simulate the behavior of dynamic real-world networks (Hekmat and Van Mieghem, 2003; Kawahigashi et al., 2005; Durrett, 2006; Onat et al., 2008; Hewer et al., 2009; Hamlili, 2010; Trullols et al., 2010).

To provide a convenient way to represent and analyze dynamic networks by dynamic random graphs, it is very important to clarify how the model of random graphs should explain the behavior of change in the topology of the network. Thus, we introduce some stochastic processes (times of graph change, graph configurations, degree number at a chosen vertex ...) in order to attempt to account for the observed statistical properties in graph dynamics. Therefore, we will try to highlight the basic mathematical operations that transform a graph into other one to make possible describing the dynamic change of graph configurations. In this objective, different concepts and notation are introduced in the preliminary sections and will be used throughout the chapter. A reader familiar with the common topics in general graph theory may skip ahead. However, he may use it as necessary to refer to unknown definitions or unusual notations. Also, a particular attention is agreed to Erdös-Rényi's random graph model (Erdös and Rényi, 1960; Bollobàs, 2001).

2. Preliminary concepts

This section is a short introduction on graph theory. It will review the basic definitions and notation used throughout all this chapter.

2.1 Graphs

A classical graph is a static structure of a set of objects where some pairs of these objects are connected by one or several directed or undirected links. In this chapter, we assume that there is no multiple links between a pair of objects and the orientation of the links doesn't play a decisive role.

Definition 1

An undirected simple graph or simply a graph G can be defined as a pair $G=(V,E)$ *of two sets: a nonempty set V of elements called vertices, and a set* $E \subset \{(u,v)\in V^2 \,/\, v \neq u\}$ *of unordered pairs of vertices. The elements of E are called edges.*

Since the graph is undirected, (u,v) and (v,u) designate the same edge which we write simply uv. Furthermore, the assumption "simple" states the fact that between two given vertices, we cannot pass more than a single edge.

Definition 2

If $|S|$ *denotes the cardinality of a set S, the number of vertices* $N=|V|$ *and the number of edges* $M=|E|$ *of a graph* $G=(V,E)$ *define respectively the order and the size of this graph.*

Furthermore, we assume in this chapter that graphs can be finite or infinite according to their order and such that the sets of vertices and edges can't be jointly or separately empty.

Definition 2

Let $G=(V,E)$ *and* $G^*=(V^*,E^*)$ *be two graphs. We say that* G^* *is a host for G or equivalently G is a subgraph of G*, if and only if* $V \subset V^*$ *and* $E \subseteq E^*$.

Definition 3

A graph $G=(V,E)$ *is called a weighted graph if and only if a positive function (or weights) can be defined on the set of edges E.*

Depending on the underlying area of application, such weights might represent probabilities, costs, lengths, capacities, or other positive quantities having a particular meaning. In the general weighted graph version, both vertices and edges can be weighted.

2.2 Neighbors, neighborhood and connectivity

Routing problems are among the oldest problems in graph theory. They are generally based on the hypothesis of connectivity. Let us note that the concepts of neighborhood and path are the most typical ideas associated to the connectivity assumption.

Definition 4

A neighbor of a vertex u is any vertex v such that $uv \in E$.

We note $N_G(u)$ the set of direct neighbors of *u* (also called the *neighborhood* of *u*). e.g.

$$N_G(u)=\{ v \in V \mid uv \in E\} \tag{1}$$

Inversely, two vertices *u* and *v* of a graph G are said to be *adjacent*, if $v \in N_G(u)$. The *closed neighborhood* of *u* is denoted $\overline{N}_G(u)=N_G(u)\cup\{u\}$ and for a set $S \subset V$, the closed neighborhood of S can be defined as $\overline{N}_G(S)=\bigcup_{u\in S}\overline{N}_G(u)$. By analogy, two edges are called neighbors if they have an end-vertex in common. In addition, pairwise non-adjacent vertices or edges are called independent. If all vertices of a subset $S \subseteq V$ are pairwise adjacent, S is called a complete subset or a clique.

Definition 5

On a given graph $G=(V,E)$ *we can define a path* $\Pi_{u,v}$ *between a pair of vertices u and v if and only if there is a sequence of vertices (or walk)* $u_i=u, u_{i+1},\cdots,u_{j-1},u_j=v$ *such that*

$$u_k u_{k+1} \in E, \forall k = i..j-1$$

where the vertices u and v are called end-vertices of the path.

An *elementary path* is a path such that when all the vertices are sequentially visited, a same vertex is never met twice. A path such that the end-vertices coincide is called *cycle*. An *elementary cycle* is a cycle such that all the vertices have exactly two neighbors. The concept of path is behind the notion of connectivity. In the rest of this chapter, we note $\mathcal{P}_{u,v}$ the set of all paths between the vertices *u* and *v*.

Definitions 6

Let G be a simple graph,

i. *A pair of vertices* (u,v) *of G is called connected if G contains a path connecting u to v. Otherwise, they are called disconnected.*
ii. *A graph G is called connected if any pair of vertices of G is connected. Otherwise, it is called non-connected.*

To achieve a *fully connected* graph G, there must exist a path from any vertex to each other vertex in the graph.

The path between the source vertex and the destination vertex may consist of one hop when source and destination are neighbors or several hops if they aren't directly connected by an edge of G. The *hopcount* specifies the number of hops through a path between two vertices. This measure is meaningful only when there is a path between the source and the destination. The *average hopcount* of a graph is the average value of the hopcount between the end-vertices of all the possible paths.

Furthermore, in a non-connected graph there is no path between at least one source-destination pair of vertices. Hence, a non-connected graph consists of several disconnected clusters and/or vertices. Thus, routing is only possible between the different vertices of a same cluster.

Definitions 7

Consider a weighted graph G, (u,v) *a pair of vertices of G and let w be the weight function defined on G, the weight assigned to a path* $\Pi_{u,v}$ *can be computed as the sum of weights assigned to its edges. i.e.*

$$\Pi_{u,v} = \langle u_i = u, u_{i+1}, \cdots, u_{j-1}, u_j = v \rangle \Rightarrow w(\Pi_{u,v}) = \sum_{k=i}^{j-1} w(u_k u_{k+1}) \tag{2}$$

2.3 Matrix representation of graphs and degree function of vertices

The topological structure of the graph $G = (V,E)$ can alternatively be described by a $|V| \times |V|$ adjacency matrix $A_G = (a_{u,v})_{u,v \in V}$ such that each entry is either 0 or 1

$$a_{u,v} = \begin{cases} 1 & \text{if} \quad v \in N(u) \\ 0 & \text{else} \end{cases} \tag{3}$$

where $a_{u,v} = 1$ signifies that uv is an edge of G. i.e. $uv \in E$.

Definition 8

The degree of a vertex u is the number of its direct neighbors

$$d_G(u) = |N_G(u)| \tag{4}$$

Proposition 1

Consider an undirected graph $G(V,E)$ *and* $A_G = (a_{u,v})_{u,v \in V}$ *its adjacency matrix, then*

$$d_G(u) = \sum_{v \in V} a_{u,v} \tag{5}$$

The two last equations (4) and (5) are equivalent by definition of the matrix A_G. They induce a function d_G from V to **N** (the set of nonnegative integers) called the *degree function*. Particularly, a vertex of degree 0 is called an *isolated* vertex and a vertex of degree 1 is called a *leaf*.

3. Random graphs

Another theory of graphs began in the late 1950s. It was baptized *random graph theory* in several papers by Paul Erdös and Alfréd Rényi. As a real-world network model, the Erdös-

Rényi's random graph model has a number of attractive properties (Bollobàs, 2001). This model is exceptionally quantifiable; it allows an easy calculation of average values of the graph characteristics (Janson et al., 2000; Hamlili, 2010).

In this section, we want introduce in first a generalization of the concepts of the theory of random graphs. This generalization is intended to describe the issues in applicative frameworks where the number of the graph vertices can vary randomly (number of communicating entities in a wireless ad hoc network, number of routers in the Internet, etc). Also, we will show that most classical models, such as those of Erdös-Rényi random graphs and geometric random graphs can be derived as special cases of the model that we put forward as a generalized alternative.

3.1 Generalized random graph model

Intuitively, a generalized random graph representation can be defined in a simple way using the fully weighted graphs.

Definition 9

Consider a non-empty set Ω, called the set of possible vertices and $\mathbf{P}=\left(p_{u,v}\right)_{u,v\in\Omega}$ a symmetric $|\Omega|\times|\Omega|$ matrix of probabilities. We call generalized random graph a graph G where each vertex u is generated with the probability $p_{u,u}\in\left]0,1\right[$, and where for all two existing vertices u and v, the edge uv is built with a probability $p_{u,v}\in\left]0,1\right[$.

Let $\mathcal{G}_{\mathbf{P}}(\Omega)$ be the collection of all possible graphs made on the set of possible vertices Ω such that the graph vertices u are generated independently with the probabilities $p_{u,u}$ and edges uv are built independently in $\Omega\times\Omega$ with the respective probabilities $p_{u,v}$. i.e.

$$\mathcal{G}_{\mathbf{P}}(\Omega)=\left\{ G \mid \forall u\in\Omega:\Pr[u\in V]=p_{u,u}\wedge\forall u,v\in\Omega:v\neq u\Rightarrow\Pr[uv\in E]=p_{u,v}\right\}$$

This definition of random graph models is very general. We should note that, if G is a generalized random graph,

$$G=(V,E)\Rightarrow V\subseteq\Omega\wedge E\subseteq V\times V \tag{6}$$

As will be discussed later, this way of modeling a random graph will represent opportunities for characterizing complex situations where classical models such as Erdös-Rényi model are not satisfactory.

Definition 10

The extended adjacency matrix $A=\left(a_{u,v}\right)_{u,v\in\Omega}$ associated to a graph $G=(V,E)$ of the model $\mathcal{G}_{\mathbf{P}}(\Omega)$ is a $|\Omega|\times|\Omega|$ matrix such that $a_{u,v}$ is independent equal to 1 if the pair of vertices uv belongs to E knowing that u and v belong to V and 0 otherwise.

3.2 Practical examples

Different particular cases can be identified and as stated above, in different contexts it may be useful to define the term random graph with different degrees of generality. Hence, the generalized model can describe random geometric graphs (Steele, 1997; Barabasi and Albert, 1999; Penrose, 1999). It suffices to consider G such that $V = \Omega$ and the edge probabilities

$$p_{u,v} = p(\|u - v\|) = \begin{cases} 1 & \text{if } 0 < \|u - v\| \le R \\ 0 & \text{otherwise} \end{cases} \tag{7}$$

In this model, $p_{u,v}$ depends on the Euclidean distance $\|u - v\|$ between the geometric points locating the vertices u and v.

$$\mathcal{G}_R(V) = \{ G(V,E) \mid E \subseteq V \times V \wedge \forall\, u,v \in V : \Pr(vu \in E) = 1 \text{ if } \|u - v\| \le R \text{ and } \Pr(vu \in E) = 0 \text{ if } \|u - v\| > R \}$$

This model is very interesting and as such it can formalize the framework of mobile wireless ad hoc networks where the connectivity of the network depends on the geometric positions of the communicating nodes and a radio coverage range which is generally supposed the same for all the network nodes. In such networks, the random dynamics of the associated graph is induced by the mobility of nodes.

Another example is the random graph model initiated by Erdös and Rényi in the 1950s. This kind of graphs can be represented by a generalized model where the set of vertices is not random (it is constantly the same $V = \Omega$) and all the graph pairs of vertices are connected with the same probability $p_{u,v} = p$. Thus, let V a nonempty set of vertices, we can define the collection $\mathcal{G}_p(V)$ of all possible graphs made on the set of vertices V, such that the graph edges are built independently in $V \times V$ with a probability p. i.e. formally, we can write

$$\mathcal{G}_p(V) = \{ G(V,E) \mid E \subseteq V \times V \wedge \forall\, v,w \in V : v \neq w \Rightarrow \Pr[vw \in E] = p \}$$

This model was be used in most areas of science and human activities in biology, chemistry, sociology, computer networks, manufacturing, etc. In a random Erdös-Rényi graph with N vertices, the edges are independently and randomly built with a probability p between the $N(N-1)/2$ possible edges of the full mesh graph. This definition builds the binomial model $\mathcal{G}_p(V)$ of random graphs, also referred as Erdös-Rényi model (Bollobàs, 2001).

Proposition 2

Consider a nonempty set V, a real p in $]0,1[$ *and a random graph G on V. Let* $N = |V|$ *be the order of G and M be the random order of G, then*

$$\Pr\left(M = m \mid G \in \mathcal{G}_p(V)\right) = p^m (1-p)^{\binom{N}{2} - m} \tag{8}$$

and

$$E[M] = p\frac{N(N-1)}{2} \tag{9}$$

Proof

The set $\mathcal{G}_p(V)$ has $\binom{N}{2}$ random graphs with equal probabilities. In consequence, each one can be chosen with a probability equal to $\binom{N}{2}^{-1}$. Thus, on one hand,

$$\begin{aligned}\Pr\left(M = m \,|\, G \in \mathcal{G}_p(V)\right) &= \binom{N}{2}^{-1}\binom{N}{2} p^m (1-p)^{\binom{N}{2}-m} \\ &= p^m (1-p)^{\binom{N}{2}-m}\end{aligned}$$

On the other hand, the number of edges M in a random Erdös-Rényi graph is a random variable with an average value equal to

$$E[M] = \sum_{m=0}^{N(N-1)/2} m\, p^m (1-p)^{\binom{N}{2}-m} = p\,\frac{N(N-1)}{2}$$

3.3 Degree distribution

As defined above, the degree function d_G on the graph vertices returns the number of vertices directly connected to the considered vertex. Thus, the *degree distribution* measures the local connectivity relevance of the graph vertices. In a generalized random graph model, the degree distribution can be set depending on the wished point of view. Its general form is defined by

$$p_k = \Pr\left[d_G(u) = k\right] \tag{10}$$

3.3.1 Binomial model and Poisson approximation

In particular, in the Enrdös-Rényi representation $\mathcal{G}_p(V)$, the theoretical degree distribution of any vertex u is defined by a binomial distribution (Bollobàs, 2001)

$$p_k = \binom{|V|-1}{k} p^k (1-p)^{|V|-1-k} \tag{11}$$

when the number of vertices $|V|$ is small. Otherwise, from the limit central theorem (LCT), the binomial distribution is approximately Gaussian with parameters

$$\begin{cases} \mu = (|V|-1)\,p & \text{(the mean)} \\ \sigma^2 = (|V|-1)\,p\,(1-p) & \text{(the variance)} \end{cases} \tag{12}$$

But the Gaussian distribution is continuous, while the binomial distribution is discrete. Thus, sometimes when $|V|$ is large and under certain special assumptions we prefer the Poisson approximation to the LCT approximation.

Proposition 3

When the graph order is large, the degree distribution is in the order of

$$p_k \approx e^{-\varsigma} \frac{\varsigma^k}{k!} \tag{13}$$

where p is small and $|V|$ is sufficiently large.

Proof

When the graph oder $|V|$ is large, we can also write the degree density as

$$\Pr\left[d(u)=k\right] = \binom{|V|-1}{k} \left[\frac{\varsigma}{|V|-1}\right]^k \left(1-\frac{\varsigma}{|V|-1}\right)^{|V|-1-k} \approx e^{-\varsigma} \frac{\varsigma^k}{k!}$$

where p is small and $|V|$ is sufficiently large. This shows the equation (13).

More generally, this approximation is known in probability theory as the De Moivre's Poisson approximation to the Binomial distribution. Indeed, the Poisson distribution can be applied whenever it is dealing with systems with a large number of possible events such that each of which is rare.

Thus, it is in the order of things to note that the main advantage of the Enrdös–Rényi models comes from the traceability of calculations and the simplicity of parameter estimation. A form or another of this model will be applied as and when it's required.

3.3.2 Power-law models

The traditional model of Erdös and Rényi is not a universal representation for all the random graph behaviors. Sometimes, in many natural scale-free networks (such as World Wide Web pages and their links, Internet, grid computer networking, etc), despite the randomness of the resulting graphs, experimental studies have revealed that the degree distribution can have a pure power-law tail (Albert et al., 1999; Barabàsi and Albert, 1999; Faloutsos et al. 1999)

$$p_k = \alpha\, k^{-\gamma} \tag{14}$$

where $\alpha > 0$ is a scaling constant and $\gamma > 0$ is a constant scaling exponent. Scale-free Barabàsi-Albert random graphs are generally built through a growth process combined to a profile of preferential attachment to existing vertices (Barabàsi and Albert, 1999). Although such graphs have a large number of vertices, the degree distribution deviates significantly from the Poisson law expected for classical random graphs (Barabàsi and Albert, 1999). Other forms of degree distribution with a power-law tail have been studied (Amaral et al., 2000; Newman et al., 2001)

$$p_k = C\ k^{-\gamma} \exp\left(-\frac{k}{\kappa}\right);\ \text{for } k > 1 \tag{15}$$

where C is a constant fixed by the requirement of normalization, γ is the constant scaling exponent, and κ is a typical degree size from which the exponential adaptation becomes significant.

In scale-free graphs, the parameters estimation of the degree distribution has to be obviously adapted to each specific case of power-law. In general, the distribution coordinates have to be converted into the logarithmic scales and then apply a method such as least-square method.

4. Random Graph Dynamics (RGD)

In classic graph theory a graph is simply a collection of objects connected to each other in some manner. This description is very restrictive. In fact, the notions of random graph theory have been introduced in the objective to produce better models and more complete tools to represent non deterministic looks of configurations of a dynamic network. Here again, the language of random graphs is used simply to relate the graph structure of the different network situations. This language must be completed by defining a number of indispensable operations in order to introduce a basic mathematical framework for graph dynamics modeling.

Definition 11

A dynamic graph is a graph such that its configuration (or topology) is subject to dynamic changes with time.

Hence, it goes without saying that the topology changes induced by the random graph dynamics are made through a number of fundamental operations that affect only the set of edges E.

4.1 Random change process

Generally, we can define several kinds of graph dynamics. The following contexts are the basic ways of defining this kind of behavior:

- Vertex-dynamic graph model: the set of vertices varies with time. In this context vertices may be added or deleted. However, we must be careful in this case to the edges such that an end-vertex is removed. They should just be deleted too.
- Edge-dynamic graph model: the set of edges E varies with time. Thus, edges may be added or deleted from the graph. In this case, there are no consequences to fear on the set of vertices.

- Vertex-weighted dynamic graph model: the weights on the vertices vary with time.
- Edge-weighted dynamic graph model: the weights on the edges vary with time.
- Fully-weighted dynamic graph model: the weights on both vertices and edges vary with time.

Thus, we consider at first a model of dynamic graphs that combines all these aspects together. A such random dynamic graph G can be defined as a stochastic graph process i.e. a collection of independent random graphs $\mathbf{G} = \{G_t | t \in I\}$ where the parameter t is usually assumed to be time and which take values in a set I which can be continuous or countable (finite or infinite).

In the widest sense, each graph G_t can belong to a different model $\mathcal{G}_{\mathbf{P}_t}(\Omega)$. The set of all possible states is called the state space. If the state space is discrete, we deal with a discrete state stochastic graph process, which is called a chain of graphs. The state space can also be continuous; we then deal with a continuous-state stochastic process. A similar classification can be made regarding whether the index set I is continuous leading to a continuous-time stochastic process or countable leading to a discrete-time stochastic process. Thus, a dynamic graph **G** is a representation which assumes that at any time t, there exists an instance $G_t = (V_t, E_t)$ that belongs to a model $\mathcal{G}_{\mathbf{P}_t}(\Omega)$.

To explain the changes in a dynamic random graph, we must often refer to events of presence, absence, addition, deletion, birth, death and structure of objects; where the term "object" refers to both vertices and edges of the graph. The following definitions clarify what do these events really mean and how can they be mathematically defined in the context of graph dynamics.

Definition 12

The weighted graphs $(G_t;\mathbf{P}_t)$ *thus defined are called instantaneous configurations of the random dynamic graph* **G**.

The random graph dynamics can be characterized by the ordered stochastic time process $T_0 = 0 < T_1 < T_2 < \cdots < T_{k-1} < T_k < \cdots$ where the configuration changes of the random dynamic graph G are operated. Thus, a marked random graph process is defined such that, at the kth time of change $T_k = t_k$, a $|\Omega| \times |\Omega|$ symmetric matrix $\mathbf{P}_k = \left(p_{u,v}^{(k)}\right)_{u,v \in \Omega}$ of probabilities is selected and a graph (configuration) $G_k = (V_k, E_k)$ is chosen according to the random graph model $\mathcal{G}_{\mathbf{P}_k}(\Omega)$.

In this model, the diagonal entries of the matrix $\mathbf{P}_k$ represent the probabilities to select, at time t_k, the vertices of V_k individually in Ω and the off-diagonal entries of this symmetric matrix represent the probabilities to activate the edges between two given vertices of V_k. Both the sets of vertices and edges in the graph configuration process are chosen as temporary. Thus, between two existing end-vertices u and v an edge is selected with the temporary probability $p_{u,v}^{(k)}$. Both the vertices and the edges of a dynamic random graph can be seen as subject to dynamic random changes.

This type of model is very interesting for modeling dynamic networks where the parameters are all temporary. As examples, we can mention routers and links of the Internet, friends in web social networking, communicating nodes in mobile wireless mobile ad hoc networks that use essentially the methods of broadcast.

4.2 Change operations

In this section, the studied approaches are classified according to their own definition in the context of graph dynamics. The RGD is said low when only few elements (number of vertices, number of edges, building edges probability, vertices clustering ...) change over time. Otherwise, the dynamics is strong. Furthermore, there are several operations that build new graphs from old ones. They might be characterized through a number of descriptor events and basic transforms.

Definition 13 (Presence)

In a dynamic graph **G**, *an object is present at time t if it belongs to the instance* G_t *of* **G**.

Thus, a vertex u is present at time t, if and only if $u \in V_t$. Similarly, an edge uv is present at time t, if and only if $uv \in E_t$ knowing that both u and v belong to V_t.

Definition 14 (absence)

In a dynamic graph **G**, *an object is absent at time t, if it does not belong to the instance* G_t *of* **G**.

Operating dynamic changes on a random graph consists of a series of graph modifications (weight, vertex or edge adaptations). In contrast, the dynamicity analysis is more effective when all combination of additions and deletions of edges and vertices are taken into account.

Definition 15 (Addition)

An object appears in the dynamic graph **G**, *if it transits from the state absent to the state present.*

From an operational perspective, this definition should be clarified. Let u and v be two vertices of G such that uv is not an edge of G, the addition of the edge uv to the graph G is defined by the operation

$$G + uv = (V, E \cup \{uv\}) \tag{16}$$

Now, there are two ways to add a new vertex to a graph. One way is to add an isolated vertex to the graph G, i.e.

$$G \breve{\oplus} u = (V \cup \{u\}, E) \tag{17}$$

and the other is to add a new vertex u which will be connected to an existing vertex v of the graph G, i.e.

$$G \underset{v}{\bar{\oplus}} u = (V \cup \{u\}, E \cup \{uv\}) \tag{18}$$

From the algorithmic point of view this last operation (18) can be seen as a composition of the two previous ones (16) and (17). Also, note that any instance $G=(V,E)$ of the model $\mathcal{G}_{\mathrm{P}}(\Omega)$ has a host $G^{*}=(\Omega,E)$ which is defined by adding to the graph G isolated vertices taken in $\Omega-V$

$$G^{*}=G \breve{\bigoplus}_{u\in\Omega-V} u \tag{19}$$

Thus, we conceive that the adjacency matrix of G^{*} is obtained by completing the adjacency matrix of G by 0. This matrix will be called in the rest of the chapter *extended adjacency matrix of* G. The advantage of working with the host graph G^{*} can be viewed rather as freeing from the assumption that the set of vertices of a random dynamic graph varies with time. But the downside of this alternative is that the graph model can exhibit needlessly an excessively large order or incomplete information.

Proposition 4

Let $V\subset\Omega$ *be two nonempty sets such that* $G=(V,E)$ *be a graph and* $G^{*}=(\Omega,E)$ *be a host for G. Then*

$$G\hat{\underset{v}{\oplus}}u=\left(G\breve{\oplus}u\right)+uv \tag{20}$$

Proof

This property results trivially from the definitions corresponding to the operations $\hat{\oplus}$ and $\breve{\oplus}$.

Definition 16 (Deletion)

An object disappears (or is deleted) from the dynamic graph **G**, *if it transits from the state present to the state absent.*

In these terms, the edge deletion can be formalized as follow. Let u and v be two vertices of a graph $G=(V,E)$ such that uv is an edge of G, the deletion of the edge uv from the graph G is defined by the operation

$$G-uv=(V,E-\{uv\}) \tag{21}$$

On another hand, the vertex deletion can be defined

$$G\Delta u=\left(V-\{u\},E-\bigcup_{v\in N(u)}\{uv\}\right) \tag{22}$$

Indeed, the deletion of the vertex u induces the deletion of all the edges having u as end-vertex.

Definition 17 (Birth)

The birth of an object is the date of its first appearance in the dynamic graph **G**.

Formally, the birth of a vertex u is the date τ_u^+ of its first occurrence

$$\tau_u^+ = \min\{t \in \mathbf{R}+ | u \in V_t\} \tag{23}$$

and the birth of an edge e is the date τ_u^+ of its first occurrence

$$\tau_e^+ = \min\{t \in \mathbf{R}+ | e \in E_t\} \tag{24}$$

Definition 18 (Death)

Death of an element is the date for the last deletion of this element from the dynamic graph **G**.

Thus, the death of a vertex is the date τ_u^- of its last occurrence

$$\tau_u^- = \max\{t \in \mathbf{R}+ | u \in V_t\} \tag{25}$$

and the birth of an edge e is the date τ_e^- such that

$$\tau_e^- = \max\{t \in \mathbf{R}+ | e \in E_t\} \tag{26}$$

Definition 19 (Structure)

A structure S of a graph consists in a dynamical set of elements that satisfies a given property.

A path, a click and a cluster are all examples of structures. Let us note that from the random viewpoint the succession of graph transforms and structure updates that convert a configuration of the dynamic graph in another one are not known in advance.

4.3 Graph topology changes in RGD

Remark that between two consecutive changes of the graph configuration recorded at T_k and T_{k+1}, the extended adjacency matrix $A^{(k)}$ of G_k remains unchanged all through the interval $[T_k, T_{k+1}[$. Thus, the dynamicity of the graph topology can be characterized by the variation of the extended adjacency matrix between T_{k-1} and T_k

$$\Delta A^{(k)} = A^{(k)} - A^{(k-1)} \tag{27}$$

where $A^{(k)}$ is the extended adjacency matrix of the current configuration of the graph at time $T_k = t_k$ and $A^{(k-1)}$ is the extended adjacency matrix of the previous configuration at time $T_{k-1} = t_{k-1}$ (with $T_{k-1} < T_k$).

4.3.1 Characterizing the change of the number of vertices

We can define for successive configurations of the graph, the number of new vertices, the number of lost vertices and the number of maintained vertices respectively at $T_k = t_k$ by

$$\alpha^{(k)} = \sum_{u\in\Omega} \mathbf{1}_{\left\{\Delta a_{u,u}^{(k)}>0\right\}},\ \beta^{(k)} = \sum_{u\in\Omega} \mathbf{1}_{\left\{\Delta a_{u,u}^{(k)}=0\right\}} \text{ and } \gamma^{(k)} = \sum_{v\in\Omega} \mathbf{1}_{\left\{\Delta a_{u,u}^{(k)}<0\right\}} \tag{28}$$

where $\mathbf{1}_S$ indicates the characteristic function of the set S and $\Delta a_{u,u}^{(k)}$ symbolizes the diagonal term of the matrix $\Delta A^{(k)}$ associated to the eventual vertices of the dynamic graph.

Proposition 5

Let **G** *be a random dynamic graph following the model* $\mathcal{G}_{\mathbf{P}_t}(\Omega)$ *such that the configuration change is characterized by the stochastic time process* $T_0 = 0 < T_1 < T_2 < \cdots < T_{k-1} < T_k < \cdots$. *Consider the extended adjacency matrices* $A^{(k)} = \left(a_{u,v}^{(k)}\right)_{u,v\in\Omega}$ *of* $G_k = (V_k, E_k)$ *and* $\Delta A^{(k)}$ *the matrix defined by the equation (27). Then,*

$$\begin{cases} \Pr\left(\Delta a_{u,u}^{(k)} = 1\right) = p_{u,u}^{(k)}\left(1 - p_{u,u}^{(k-1)}\right) \\ \Pr\left(\Delta a_{u,u}^{(k)} = 0\right) = p_{u,u}^{(k)} p_{u,u}^{(k-1)} + \left(1 - p_{u,u}^{(k)}\right)\left(1 - p_{u,u}^{(k-1)}\right) \\ \Pr\left(\Delta a_{u,u}^{(k)} = -1\right) = \left(1 - p_{u,u}^{(k)}\right) p_{u,u}^{(k-1)} \end{cases} \tag{29}$$

Proof

Since all trials are independent, each of the three probabilities can be decomposed as follows

$$\begin{cases} \mathbf{Pr}\left(\Delta a_{u,u}^{(k)} = 1\right) = \mathbf{Pr}\left(\left\{a_{u,u}^{(k)} = 1\right\} \wedge \left\{a_{u,u}^{(k-1)} = 0\right\}\right) = \mathbf{Pr}\left(a_{u,u}^{(k)} = 1\right)\mathbf{Pr}\left(a_{u,u}^{(k-1)} = 0\right) \\ \mathbf{Pr}\left(\Delta a_{u,v}^{(k)} = 0\right) = \mathbf{Pr}\left[\left(\left\{a_{u,u}^{(k)} = 1\right\} \cap \left\{a_{u,u}^{(k-1)} = 1\right\}\right) \cup \left(\left\{a_{u,u}^{(k)} = 0\right\} \cap \left\{a_{u,u}^{(k-1)} = 0\right\}\right)\right] = \\ \qquad = \mathbf{Pr}\left(\left\{a_{u,u}^{(k)} = 1\right\} \cap \left\{a_{u,u}^{(k-1)} = 1\right\}\right) + \mathbf{Pr}\left(\left\{a_{u,u}^{(k)} = 0\right\} \cap \left\{a_{u,u}^{(k-1)} = 0\right\}\right) = \\ \qquad = \mathbf{Pr}\left(a_{u,u}^{(k)} = 1\right)\mathbf{Pr}\left(a_{u,u}^{(k-1)} = 1\right) + \mathbf{Pr}\left(a_{u,u}^{(k)} = 0\right)\mathbf{Pr}\left(a_{u,u}^{(k-1)} = 0\right) \\ \mathbf{Pr}\left(\Delta a_{u,u}^{(k)} = -1\right) = \mathbf{Pr}\left(\left\{a_{u,u}^{(k)} = 0\right\} \cap \left\{a_{u,u}^{(k-1)} = 1\right\}\right) = \mathbf{Pr}\left(a_{u,u}^{(k)} = 0\right)\mathbf{Pr}\left(a_{u,u}^{(k-1)} = 1\right) \end{cases}$$

and because $\Pr\left(a_{u,u}^{(k-1)} = 1\right) = p_{u,u}^{(k-1)}$, $\Pr\left(a_{u,u}^{(k-1)} = 0\right) = 1 - p_{u,u}^{(k-1)}$, $\Pr\left(a_{u,u}^{(k)} = 1\right) = p_{u,u}^{(k)}$ and $\Pr\left(a_{u,v}^{(k)} = 0\right) = 1 - p_{u,v}^{(k)}$ we have the result (29).

Corollary 6

Under the assumptions of the above proposition, and by supposing that the configuration process of the dynamic graph is homogeneous and that all the element of Ω *can appear with the same probability* π *in a configuration of the dynamic random graph* **G**, *the triplet* $\left(\alpha^{(k)}, \beta^{(k)}, \gamma^{(k)}\right)$ *follows a trinomial distribution of parameters*

$$\left(|\Omega|;\pi(1-\pi),\pi(1-\pi),\pi^2+(1-\pi)^2\right) \text{ i.e.}$$

$$\Pr\left(\alpha^{(k)}=n_1,\beta^{(k)}=n_2,\gamma^{(k)}=n_3\right)=\frac{|\Omega|!}{n_1!\,n_2!\,n_3!}\left[\pi(1-\pi)\right]^{n_1+n_2}\left[\pi^2+(1-\pi)^2\right]^{n_3} \tag{30}$$

Proof

On one hand, there are only three possible outcomes $\left\{\Delta a_{u,u}^{(k)}=1\right\}$, $\left\{\Delta a_{u,u}^{(k)}=0\right\}$ and $\left\{\Delta a_{u,u}^{(k)}=-1\right\}$ such that $\Pr\left(\Delta a_{u,u}^{(k)}=1\right)+\Pr\left(\Delta a_{u,u}^{(k)}=0\right)+\Pr\left(\Delta a_{u,u}^{(k)}=-1\right)=1$ and all trials are independent. On the other hand, we have $|\Omega|$ discrete trials (relating the different situations in the set Ω) and because the occurrence measures of graph vertex situations $\alpha^{(k)}$, $\beta^{(k)}$ and $\gamma^{(k)}$ are interrelated by the equation $\alpha^{(k)}+\beta^{(k)}+\gamma^{(k)}=|\Omega|$, this means that we deal with a multinomial distribution of $|\Omega|$ trials and from the previous proposition (proposition 5) three outcomes with respective probabilities

$$\begin{cases}\Pr\left(\Delta a_{u,u}^{(k)}=1\right)=\pi(1-\pi)\\ \Pr\left(\Delta a_{u,u}^{(k)}=0\right)=\pi^2+(1-\pi)^2\\ \Pr\left(\Delta a_{u,u}^{(k)}=-1\right)=(1-\pi)\pi\end{cases}$$

This shows the required result in (30).

Following this line of thinking, these results can be applied only if the number of the observed vertices varies with time. That is when the dynamicity affects the vertices of the dynamic graph. Otherwise, while the number observed vertices remain unchanged, we will show similar results in the next subsection under the assumption of dynamicity of edges. These two approaches are complementary.

4.3.2 Characterizing the change of the number of edges

First and foremost let us remain under the assumption of the general model $\mathcal{G}_{\mathbf{P}_t}(\Omega)$ of dynamic graphs. In the context of connectivity, the number of edges connected to the same vertex defines its degree. Thus, from the uncertain connectivity viewpoint of dynamic random graphs, we can define locally for each graph vertex the number of new neighbors, the number of lost neighbors and the number of maintained neighbors respectively at $T_k=t_k$ by

$$\nu_u^{(k)}=\sum_{v\in V_k}\mathbf{1}_{\left\{\Delta a_{u,v}^{(k)}>0\right\}},\quad \mu_u^{(k)}=\sum_{v\in V_k}\mathbf{1}_{\left\{\Delta a_{u,v}^{(k)}=0\right\}} \text{ and } \lambda_u^{(k)}=\sum_{v\in V_k}\mathbf{1}_{\left\{\Delta a_{u,v}^{(k)}<0\right\}} \tag{31}$$

where $\mathbf{1}_S$ indicates the characteristic function of the set S and $\Delta a_{u,v}^{(k)}$ indicates a generic entry of the matrix $\Delta A^{(k)}$. Essentially, the knowledge, step by step, of the evolution of the local metrics $\nu_u^{(k)}$ and $\lambda_u^{(k)}$ will allow us to determine a propagation equation of degree function at each vertex of the observed dynamic graph.

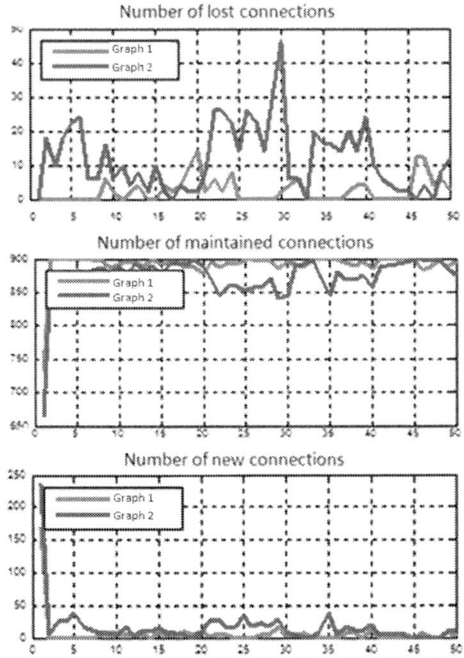

Fig. 1. Connectivity metrics change for two simulated random dynamic graphs

Proposition 7

Let $\mathbf{G}$ *be a random dynamic graph following the model* $\mathcal{G}_{\mathbf{P}_t}(\Omega)$ *and consider the configurations* $(G_k)_{k\in\mathbf{N}}$ *of* $\mathbf{G}$ *associated to the stochastic time process* $T_0 = 0 < T_1 < T_2 < \cdots < T_{k-1} < T_k < \cdots$. *If* d_{G_k} *denotes the underlying degree function to* G_k

$$\forall u \in \Omega:\ d_{G_k}(u) = d_{G_{k-1}}(u) + \nu_u^{(k)} - \lambda_u^{(k)} \tag{32}$$

Proof

The proof of (32) results directly from the definitions of $\nu_u^{(k)}$ and $\lambda_u^{(k)}$.

We can also define global graph indices which reflect the global configuration changes of the dynamic random graph (see figure 1)

$$\nu^{(k)} = \sum_{v \in V_k} \nu_u^{(k)}, \ \mu^{(k)} = \sum_{v \in V_k} \mu_u^{(k)} \text{ and } \lambda^{(k)} = \sum_{v \in V_k} \lambda_u^{(k)} \tag{33}$$

Under the condition of conservation of the number of vertices from a configuration to a successor one, we can establish a number of results for dynamic graphs under Erdös-Rényi model constrains.

Proposition 8

Let **G** *be a random dynamic graph following the model* $\mathcal{G}_p(V)$ *such that the configuration change is characterized by the stochastic time process* $T_0 = 0 < T_1 < T_2 < \cdots < T_{k-1} < T_k < \cdots$. *Consider the extended adjacency matrices* $A^{(k)} = \left(a_{u,v}^{(k)}\right)_{u,v \in V_k}$ *of* $G_k = (V, E_k)$ *and* $\Delta A^{(k)}$ *the matrix defined by the equation (27) and such that all the terms of its principal diagonal are equal to zero, then*

$$\begin{cases} \Pr\left(\Delta a_{u,v}^{(k)} = 1\right) = p(1-p) \\ \Pr\left(\Delta a_{u,v}^{(k)} = 0\right) = p^2 + (1-p)^2 \\ \Pr\left(\Delta a_{u,v}^{(k)} = -1\right) = (1-p)p \end{cases} \tag{34}$$

Proof

Since all trials are independent, each of the three probabilities can be decomposed such as follows

$$\begin{cases} \Pr\left(\Delta a_{u,v}^{(k)} = 1\right) = \Pr\left(\left\{a_{u,v}^{(k)} = 1\right\} \cap \left\{a_{u,v}^{(k-1)} = 0\right\}\right) = \Pr\left(a_{u,v}^{(k)} = 1\right)\Pr\left(a_{u,v}^{(k-1)} = 0\right) \\ \Pr\left(\Delta a_{u,v}^{(k)} = 0\right) = \Pr\left[\left(\left\{a_{u,v}^{(k)} = 1\right\} \cap \left\{a_{u,v}^{(k-1)} = 1\right\}\right) \cup \left(\left\{a_{u,v}^{(k)} = 0\right\} \cap \left\{a_{u,v}^{(k-1)} = 0\right\}\right)\right] = \\ \qquad = \Pr\left(\left\{a_{u,v}^{(k)} = 1\right\} \cap \left\{a_{u,v}^{(k-1)} = 1\right\}\right) + \Pr\left(\left\{a_{u,v}^{(k)} = 0\right\} \cap \left\{a_{u,v}^{(k-1)} = 0\right\}\right) = \\ \qquad = \Pr\left(a_{u,v}^{(k)} = 1\right)\Pr\left(a_{u,v}^{(k-1)} = 1\right) + \Pr\left(a_{u,v}^{(k)} = 0\right)\Pr\left(a_{u,v}^{(k-1)} = 0\right) \\ \Pr\left(\Delta a_{u,v}^{(k)} = -1\right) = \Pr\left(\left\{a_{u,v}^{(k)} = 0\right\} \cap \left\{a_{u,v}^{(k-1)} = 1\right\}\right) = \Pr\left(a_{u,v}^{(k)} = 0\right)\Pr\left(a_{u,v}^{(k-1)} = 1\right) \end{cases}$$

and because $\Pr\left(a_{u,v}^{(k)} = 1\right) = \Pr\left(a_{u,v}^{(k-1)} = 1\right) = p$ and $\Pr\left(a_{u,v}^{(k)} = 0\right) = \Pr\left(a_{u,v}^{(k-1)} = 0\right) = 1-p$, we have the result (34).

Corollary 9

Under the assumptions of the above proposition, and by supposing that the random dynamic graph belongs to the $\mathcal{G}_p(V)$ *model, the triplet* $\left(\nu^{(k)}, \mu^{(k)}, \lambda^{(k)}\right)$ *follows a trinomial distribution of parameters* $\left(|V|(|V|-1)/2; p(1-p), p(1-p), p^2 + (1-p)^2\right)$. *i.e.*

$$\Pr\left(\nu^{(k)} = n_1, \mu^{(k)} = n_2, \lambda^{(k)} = n_3\right) = \frac{\binom{|V|}{2}!}{n_1!\, n_2!\, n_3!} \left[p\left(1-p\right)\right]^{n_1+n_2} \left[p^2 + \left(1-p\right)^2\right]^{n_3} \tag{35}$$

Proof

First, note that all pairs of vertices u and v, there are only three possible independent outcomes $\left\{\Delta a_{u,v}^{(k)} = 1\right\}$, $\left\{\Delta a_{u,v}^{(k)} = 0\right\}$ and $\left\{\Delta a_{u,v}^{(k)} = -1\right\}$. Furthermore, we have

$$\Pr\left(\Delta a_{u,v}^{(k)} = 1\right) + \Pr\left(\Delta a_{u,v}^{(k)} = 0\right) + \Pr\left(\Delta a_{u,v}^{(k)} = -1\right) = 1$$

and all trials are independent. Subsequently, we have $|V|$ discrete trials and since there are no other situations than those described above, the three measures of occurrence of graph edges $\nu^{(k)}$, $\mu^{(k)}$ and $\lambda^{(k)}$ are interrelated and verify

$$\nu^{(k)} + \mu^{(k)} + \lambda^{(k)} = |V|\left(|V|-1\right)/2 \tag{36}$$

Each of the $|V|\left(|V|-1\right)/2$ trials (off-diagonal generic entries of the symmetric matrix $\Delta A^{(k)}$) matches to one of the three possible outcomes with respective probabilities

$$\Pr\left(\Delta a_{u,v}^{(k)} = 1\right) = p\left(1-p\right),\ \Pr\left(\Delta a_{u,v}^{(k)} = 0\right) = p^2 + \left(1-p\right)^2 \text{ and } \Pr\left(\Delta a_{u,v}^{(k)} = -1\right) = \left(1-p\right)p \tag{37}$$

Thus, by taking into account the results established by the equation (36) and the system (37), we can conclude that, *the triplet* $\left(\nu^{(k)}, \mu^{(k)}, \lambda^{(k)}\right)$ *follows a trinomial distribution of parameters* $\left(|V|\left(|V|-1\right)/2; p\left(1-p\right), p\left(1-p\right), p^2 + \left(1-p\right)^2\right)$.

Corollary 10

Under the assumptions of the proposition 8, the off-diagonal entries of the correlation matrix associated to $\left(\nu^{(k)}, \mu^{(k)}, \lambda^{(k)}\right)$ *are such that*

$$\rho\left(\nu^{(k)}, \mu^{(k)}\right) = \rho\left(\lambda^{(k)}, \mu^{(k)}\right) = -\sqrt{\frac{\left(1-p\right)^2 + p^2}{2\left[\left(1-p\right)^2 + p\right]}} \text{ and } \rho\left(\lambda^{(k)}, \nu^{(k)}\right) = -\frac{p\left(1-p\right)}{\left(1-p\right)^2 + p} \tag{38}$$

Proof

The corollary results from the general properties of the correlation matrix of a trinomial distribution of parameters $\left(|V|\left(|V|-1\right)/2; p\left(1-p\right), p\left(1-p\right), p^2 + \left(1-p\right)^2\right)$.

Note that the graph order $|V|\left(|V|-1\right)/2$ drop out of the off-diagonal entries of the correlation matrix associated to $\left(\nu^{(k)}, \mu^{(k)}, \lambda^{(k)}\right)$.

5. Parameter estimation of the random dynamic graph model

The ultimate objective in random graph dynamics analysis is the estimation of the graph model parameters. In some respects, nearly all types of dynamic changes can be interpreted in this way. In the empirical study, for reasons of traceability of the calculations, we restrict ourselves to an homogeneous model $\mathcal{G}_{\mathbf{P}_t}(\Omega)$ such that, there exists a non-negative real $p \in]0,1[$, for all existing pair of vertices u and v $p_{u,v}^{(k)} = p$.

Furthermore, we assume that by some means a vertex may deduct its neighborhood set directly from information exchanged as part of edge sensing. This section aims to show how the model parameters of the random dynamic graph can be estimated.

5.1 Dynamic graphs with known number of vertices and unknown edge probability

The main goal here is to find the maximum-likelihood estimate (MLE) of the edge probability p when the number of the graph vertices $N = |V|$ is known.

Proposition 11

Let **G** *be a random dynamic graph following the model* $\mathcal{G}_p(V)$ *and note* $\zeta = p|V|$ *when p is small and* $|V|$ *is large. Consider D the random variable counting the degree in a fixed vertex u of* **G** *and let* $D_1, D_2, \cdots, D_s$ *be a s-sample formed by the degrees of u for s different configurations of the random dynamic graph at the graph change times* $T_1 < T_2 < \cdots < T_s$. *Then*

$$\begin{cases} \hat{p}_{MLE} = \dfrac{1}{N-1}\bar{D} & \text{if } N \text{ is small} \\ \hat{\zeta}_{MLE} = \bar{D} & \text{if } N \text{ is large} \end{cases} \tag{39}$$

Proof

If the graph order $N = |V|$ is small, from equation (11), the log-likelihood function of the degree distribution in a given vertex u is

$$\ell(p, N; D_1, \cdots, D_s) = \sum_{i=1}^{s} \log\binom{N-1}{D_i} + \log\left(\frac{p}{1-p}\right) \sum_{i=1}^{s} D_i + s\ (N-1)\ \log(1-p)$$

The MLE of p is obtained by solving the partial differential equation $\dfrac{\partial \ell(p, N; D_1, \cdots, D_s)}{\partial p} = 0$

i.e.

$$\hat{p}_{MLE} = \frac{\sum_{i=1}^{s} D_i}{s(N-1)} = \frac{1}{N-1}\bar{D}$$

Now, if N is large, from equation (13), the log-likelihood function of the degree distribution in a given vertex u is $\ell(\zeta;D_1,\cdots,D_s) = \log(\zeta)\sum_{i=1}^{s} D_i - \sum_{i=1}^{s}\log(D_i!) - s\,\zeta$

The MLE of p is obtained by solving the partial differential equation $\frac{\partial\,\ell(\zeta;D_1,\cdots,D_s)}{\partial\,\zeta} = 0$ i.e.

$$\hat{\zeta}_{MLE} = \frac{\sum_{i=1}^{s} D_i}{s} = \overline{D}$$

When s observations of the change of the random dynamic graph topology are accomplished, the variations of $\hat{p}_{MLE}$ and $\hat{\zeta}_{MLE}$ displayed in one vertex or another relates the local knowledge on the values of these parameters taking into account the observed neighborhood behavior at u.

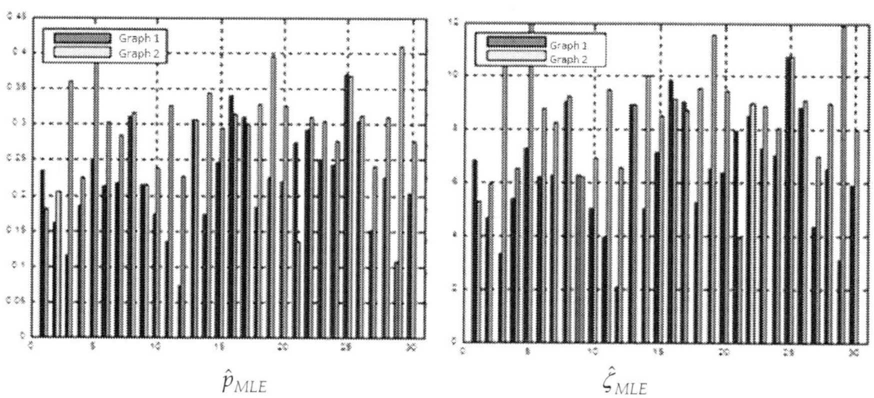

Fig. 2. $\hat{p}_{MLE}$ and $\hat{\zeta}_{MLE}$ evaluations for two simulated random graphs of order 30 vertices

Indeed, since $\hat{p}_{MLE}$ depends only on the observed number of neighbors of a selected vertex for different configurations of the random dynamic graph, this quantity is estimated differently in each vertex (see figure 2).

5.2 Dynamic graphs with unknown number of vertices and edge probability

In the statistical common sense, when the graph order is unknown the method proposed in the previous paragraph cannot be applied. Another resourceful method of point estimation called method of moments (Lehmann E. L. and Casella G., 1998) can be used when the number N of the graph vertices and the edge density parameter p are both unknown. Likewise, these parameters should be estimated on the basis of an s-sample $D_1, D_2, \cdots, D_s$ of the degree of a vertex u for s different instances of the random dynamic graph topology.

Proposition 12

Let **G** *be a random dynamic graph following the model* $\mathcal{G}_p(V)$ *and suppose that* $N = |V|$ *is small. Consider D the random variable counting the degree in a fixed vertex u of* **G** *and let* $D_1, D_2, \cdots, D_s$ *be a s-sample formed by the degrees of u for s different configurations of the random dynamic graph at the graph change times* $T_1 < T_2 < \cdots < T_s$. *Then the estimates of moments of the graph parameters are respectively*

$$\begin{cases} \hat{p}_{ME} = 1 - \dfrac{S^2}{\bar{D}} \\ \hat{N}_{ME} = 1 + \dfrac{\bar{D}^2}{\bar{D} - S^2} \end{cases} \tag{40}$$

Proof

In this case, the method of moments supposes that the empirical moment $\bar{D}$ is a natural estimate of the theoretical moment of order 1 $E(D)$ and the theoretical centralized moments of order k $\mu_k = E\left[D - (D)\right]^k$ can be estimated by their respective empirical centralized moments $M_k = \frac{1}{s}\sum_{i=1}^{s}\left(D_i - \bar{D}\right)^k$. When $N = |V|$ is small, the degree follows a binomial distribution of parameters p an $(N-1)$ and the method of moments in terms of the average and the variance of the observed degrees leads to the system of equations

$$\begin{cases} (N-1)\,p = \bar{D} \\ (N-1)\,p\,(1-p) = S^2 \end{cases} \tag{41}$$

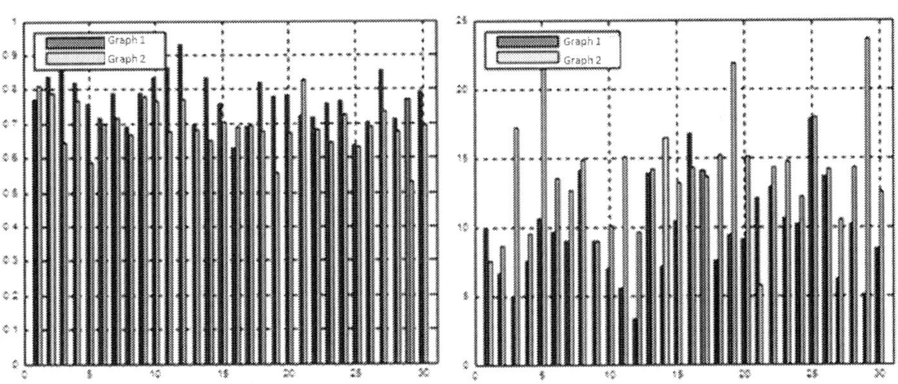

$\hat{p}_{ME}$ $\hat{N}_{ME}$

Fig. 3. $\hat{p}_{ME}$ and $\hat{N}_{ME}$ evaluations for two simulated dynamic random graphs

It results from the resolution of the system of equations (41) that the moment estimates of the unknown graph parameters

$$\begin{cases} \hat{p}_{ME} = 1 - \dfrac{S^2}{\overline{D}} \\ \hat{N}_{ME} = 1 + \dfrac{\overline{D}^2}{\overline{D} - S^2} \end{cases}$$

Depending on the neighbors met by each of the random dynamic graph vertices, the evaluation of the estimated parameters will be different.

5.3 Expected degree number of vertices in wide random dynamic graphs

Various random dynamic graph problems (Internet, out vehicle networks, wide ad hoc networks ...) are analyzed and interpreted under the assumption that the order of the resulting graph may be relatively large (with some tens, hundreds or even thousands of vertices). Let ζ be the average degree number

$$\zeta = E(D) \tag{42}$$

As a result of scaling, since we use an approximation of the degree distribution, it is very important to work with good estimates. This shows that the resulting computed values are most likely not due merely to chance.

Proposition 13

Let **G** *be a random dynamic graph following the model* $\mathcal{G}_p(V)$ *and suppose that* $N = |V|$ *is large. Consider D the random variable counting the degree in a fixed vertex u of* **G** *and let* $D_1, D_2, \cdots, D_s$ *be a s-sample formed by the degrees of u for s different configurations of the random dynamic graph at the graph change times* $T_1 < T_2 < \cdots < T_s$. *Let* ζ *be the Poisson distribution parameter of the degree. Then, the empirical moment of order 1* $\hat{\zeta} = \overline{D}$ *is a good estimate of the average degree. i.e.*

i. $\hat{\zeta}$ *is unbiased.*

ii. $\hat{\zeta}$ *realizes the maximum of the likelihood function.*

iii. $\hat{\zeta}$ *is an efficient estimate of* ζ.

Proof

The first property results from

$$E(\overline{D}) = \frac{1}{s} E\left(\sum_{i=1}^{s} D_i\right) = \frac{1}{s} \sum_{i=1}^{s} E(D_i) = E(D) = \zeta$$

because $D_1, D_2, \cdots, D_s$ are independent and identically distributed to D.

Furthermore, the log-likelihood function of a sample $D_1, D_2, \cdots, D_s$ representing the degrees of a given vertex *u* of *G* for *s* different configurations of the random dynamic graph is given by

$$\ell(\zeta\, ; D_1, \cdots, D_s) = -\sum_{i=1}^{s} \log D_i! + \sum_{i=1}^{s} D_i \log \zeta - s\,\zeta$$

The MLE is obtained by solving the partial differential equation $\frac{\partial\, \ell(\zeta\, ; D_1, \cdots, D_s)}{\partial\, \zeta} = 0$ i.e

$$\hat{\zeta} = \frac{\sum_{i=1}^{s} D_i}{s} = \overline{D}$$

which shows the proposition *ii*. It follows, on one hand,

$$\operatorname{var}(\hat{\zeta}) = \frac{1}{s^2} \sum_{i=1}^{s} \operatorname{var}(D_i) = \frac{1}{s} \operatorname{var}(D) \quad \text{(because are independent and identically distibuted to } D\text{)}$$

$$= \frac{\zeta}{s} \quad \text{(because } D \text{ is Poisson distributed with parameter } \zeta\text{)}$$

and on the other hand,

$$\frac{\partial\, \ell(\zeta\, ; D_1, \cdots, D_s)}{\partial\, \zeta} = -s + \frac{\sum_{i=1}^{s} D_i}{\zeta} \quad \text{and} \quad \frac{\partial^2\, \ell(\zeta\, ; D_1, \cdots, D_s)}{\partial\, \zeta^2} = -\frac{\sum_{i=1}^{s} D_i}{\zeta^2}$$

Thus, the Fisher information quantity of the parameter ζ is such that

$$I(\zeta) = E\left[-\frac{\partial^2\, \ell(\zeta\, ; D_1, \cdots, D_s)}{\partial\, \zeta^2} \right] = \frac{\sum_{i=1}^{s} E(D_i)}{\zeta^2} = \frac{s}{\zeta} = \frac{1}{\operatorname{var}(\hat{\zeta})} \tag{43}$$

which is the lower bound of the Fréchet-Darmois-Cramer-Rao (FDCR) inequality.

Then, since $\hat{\zeta}$ is unbiased and verifies the lower bound of the FDCR inequality, it is an efficient estimate.

5.4 Routing performance metrics evaluation

5.4.1 Average hopcount estimation

Proposition 14

Let **G** *be a random dynamic graph following the model* $\mathscr{G}_p(V)$ *and suppose that* $|V|$ *is large and known. Consider D the random variable counting the degree in a fixed vertex u of* **G** *and let* $D_1, D_2, \cdots, D_s$ *be a s-sample formed by the degrees of u for s different configurations of the random dynamic graph at the graph change times* $T_1 < T_2 < \cdots < T_s$. *Then, the average hopcount MLE is approximately*

$$\hat{\eta}_{MLE} \approx \frac{\log |V|}{\log \bar{D}} \tag{44}$$

Proof

Let ζ be the average degree number. As each vertex in the random graph is connected to about ζ other nodes, after η hops, we expect that ζ^{η} vertices must be reached. Thus all the vertices are reached for the value η_V such that $\zeta^{\eta_V} \approx |V|$. Since $|V|$ and ζ are both known constant parameters, the average hopcount $E[\eta_V] \approx \frac{\log |V|}{\log \zeta}$ in large random graphs is

$$E[\eta_V] \approx \frac{\log |V|}{\log \zeta} \tag{45}$$

From the proposition 11 and the equation (45), and because the MLE of a function of a parameter is equal to the function of the MLE of this parameter, the average hopcount MLE is made by

$$\hat{\eta}_{MLE} \approx \frac{\log |V|}{\log \bar{D}}$$

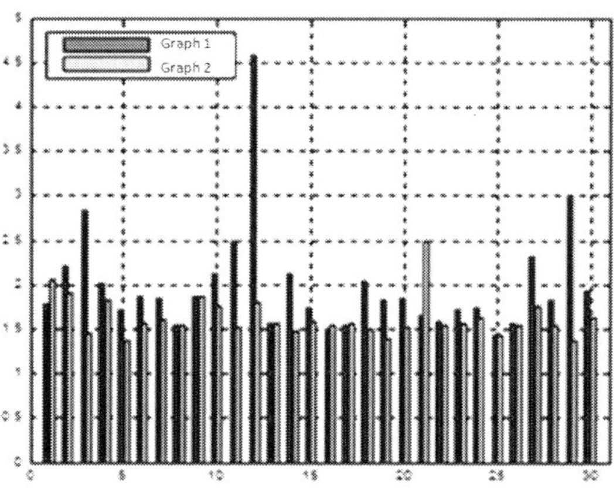

Fig. 4. Hopcount MLE evaluation for two simulated dynamic random graphs

This approximation holds because $\bar{D}$ is a good estimate of ζ in the strict sense of the proposition 13. Under other assumptions than those suggested in this paragraph, different authors have led to further forms of the approximation of the average hopcount number (Mieghem et al., 2000; Bhamidi et al., 2010).

5.4.2 Giant component size estimation

Let us consider **G** a random dynamic graph following the model $\mathcal{G}_p(V)$ and suppose that the graph order $|V|$ is large and known. From the theory of Erdös-Rényi graphs, we know (Molloy and Reed, 1998) that the graph will almost surely have a unique giant component containing a positive fraction of the graph vertices if $p > 1/|V|$ (see figure 5) i.e. the average degree numbet $\zeta > 1$.

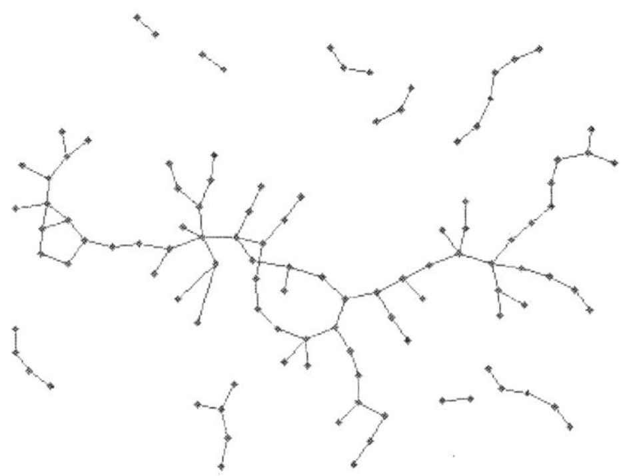

Fig. 5. Existence of the giant component of a graph

Proposition 15

Let **G** *be a random dynamic graph following the model* $\mathcal{G}_p(V)$ *and suppose that* $|V|$ *is large and known. Consider* D *the random variable counting the degree in a fixed vertex* u *of* **G** *and let* $D_1, D_2, \cdots, D_s$ *be a s-sample formed by the degrees of* u *for* s *different configurations of the random dynamic graph at the graph change times* $T_1 < T_2 < \cdots < T_s$*. Then, the average size MLE of the giant component is approximately*

$$\hat{\Theta} = 1 + \frac{1}{\bar{D}} \text{LambertW}\left[-\bar{D}\exp\left(-\bar{D}\right)\right] \tag{46}$$

Proof

Let Θ be the giant component size, for large order random graphs, Θ is a solution of the equation

$$\Theta = 1 - \exp(-\zeta\,\Theta) \tag{47}$$

But, it is well known that there are two possible solutions to this equation

$$\begin{cases} \Theta_1 = 0 \\ \Theta_2 = 1 + \frac{1}{\zeta}\text{LambertW}\left[-\zeta\exp(-\zeta)\right] \end{cases} \tag{48}$$

where LambertW is the classic "Lambert W " function. Since only the non-zero solution is adequate, the giant component size increases as a function of the average degree ζ of the graph vertices G following the curve $\vartheta : z \mapsto 1 + \frac{1}{z}\text{LambertW}\left[-z\exp(-z)\right]$.

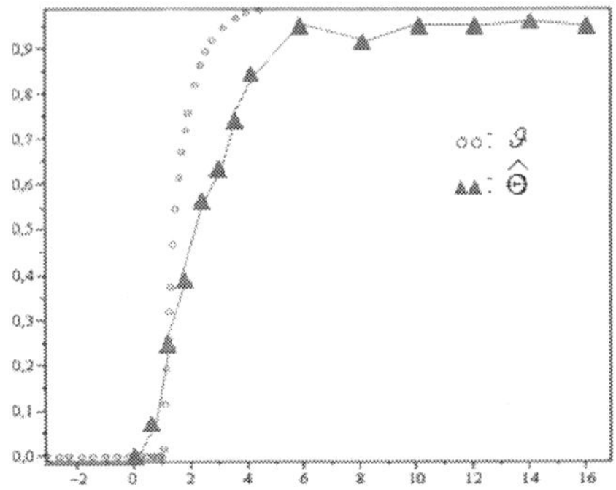

Fig. 6. Comparison of theoretic and empiric solutions ϑ and $\hat{\Theta}$

Thus, from the proposition 11 and because the MLE of a function of an unknown parameter is equal to the function of the MLE of this parameter, when $|V|$ is large the part of the graph occupied by the giant component can be estimated by

$$\hat{\Theta} = 1 + \frac{1}{\bar{D}}\text{LambertW}\left[-\bar{D}\exp\left(-\bar{D}\right)\right]$$

Elementary dissimilarities exist between random graph models and real-world graphs. Real-world graphs show strong clustering, but Erdös and Rényi's model does not. Many of the graphs, including Internet and World-Wide Web graphs, show a power-law degree distribution (Albert et al., 1999). This means that only a small part of the graph vertices can have a large degree. In fact, Erdös-Rényi assumptions can imply strong consequences on the behavior of the graph (Newman, 2003).

6. Conclusions

In this chapter we have illustrated several basic tools for representing and analyzing dynamic random graph in a general context and a practical approach to estimate the parameters of classical models of such behaviors. The generalized model that we have proposed can describe not only classical real-world networks models but also situations with more complex constraints. In this model, random graph dynamics is outlined by introducing a random time process where the dynamic graph topology changes are recorded. Among the advantages of this model is the possibility to generate successive independent random graphs with potentially different sets of vertices but all belonging to the same basic set of vertices. Otherwise, the fact that the generalized model allows to consider probabilities which are not necessarily all equal gives the possibility to favor the establishment of certain connections over others. This kind of behavior is often observed in wireless mobile networks and social networks. Here, there are ways to implement in the generalized model the ability to prioritize connections to closest vertices. These advantages of modeling are generally not possible through the traditional random graphs of Erdös-Rényi. Also, we have described the global behavior between two consecutive configurations by calculating the probability of change. This is done in the case where the dynamic change concerns only the graph edges, as well as in the case where the dynamic change affects also the graph vertices.

At the end of this chapter we have shown how the parameters of a dynamic random graph can be estimated under the assumptions of the Erdös-Rényi model. Thus, the estimation of these parameters has led to the estimates of the average degree of vertices, the average hopcount and the size of the giant component in large dynamic graphs.

7. References

Albert R., Jeong H., and Barabàsi A.L. (1999). Diameter of the Worldwide Web. Nature, vol. 401, pp.130–131.

Amaral L.A.N., Scala A., Barthélémy M., and Stanley H.E. (2000). Classes of small-world networks. Proc. of Nat. Acad. Sci. USA 97, pp. 11149–11152. http://polymer.bu.edu/hes/articles/asbs00.pdf

Bollobàs B. (2001). Random Graphs. Cambridge studies in advanced mathematics.

Barabàsi A. L. and Albert R. (1999). Emergence of scaling in random networks, Science, vol. 286, pp. 509–512.

Bhamidi S., van der Hofstad R. and Hooghiemstra G., (2010). First passage percolation on random graphs with finite mean degrees. The Annals of Applied Probability, Vol. 20, No. 5, pp. 1907-1965, DOI: 10.1214/09-AAP666

Durrett R. (2006). Random Graph Dynamics. Cambridge University Press. Cambridge, U.K.

Euler, L. (1736). Solutio problematis ad geometriam situs pertinentis. (The solution of a problem relating to the geometry of position). Commentarii Academiae Scientiarum Imperialis Petropolitanae, vol. 8, pp. 128–140.

Erdös P. and Rényi A. (1960). On the evolution of random graphs. Publications of the Mathematical Institute of the Hungarian Academy of Sciences, vol. 5, pp. 17–61.

Faloutsos M., Faloutsos P., Faloutsos C. (1999). On the power-law relationship of the internet topology. Proceedings of SIGCOMM '99, New York, USA, pp 251–262 http://www.cis.upenn.edu/~mkearns/teaching/NetworkedLife/power-internet.pdf

Hamlili A. (2010). Adaptive Schemes for Estimating Random Graph Parameters in Dynamic Random Networks' Modeling, Proceedings of IEEE/IFP Wireless days, Venice-Italy, 20 - 22 October, 2010.

Hekmat R. and Van Mieghem P. (2003). Degree distribution and hopcount in wireless ad-hoc networks. Proceedings of the 11th IEEE International Conference on Networks (ICON 2003), Sydney, Australia, pp. 603–609, Sept. 28-Oct. 2003.

Hewer T., Nekovee M. and Coveney P. V. (2009). Parameter exploration in parallel for dynamic vehicular network efficiency, International Conference on Advances in Computational Tools for Engineering Applications Proceedings (ACTEA '09), pp. 16 - 20, 15-17 July 2009.

Janson S., Lucak T., and Rucinski A. (2000). Random Graphs, John Wiley and Sons, New York.

Jurdak R. (2007). Wireless Ad Hoc and Sensor Networks: A Cross-Layer Design Perspective, Springer.

Kawahigashi H., Terashima Y., Miyauchi N. and Nakakawaji T. (2005). Modeling ad hoc sensor networks using random graph theory, Proceedings of Consumer Communications and Networking Conference (CCNC'05), pp.104 - 109.

Lehmann E. L. and Casella G. (1998). Theory of Point Estimation. Second Edition, Springer.

Mieghem P.V., Hooghiemstra G., van der Hofstadh R. (2000). A Scaling Law for the Hopcount, Report 2000125. Delft University of Technology, Delft, The Netherlands. http://wwwtvs.et.tudelft.nl/people/piet/telconference.html

Molloy M. and Reed B. (1998). The size of the giant component of a random graph with a given degree sequence, Combinatorics, Probability and Computing, vol. 7, pp. 295–305.

Newman M. E. J., Strogatz S. H., Watts D. J. (2001). Random graphs with arbitrary degree distributions and their applications. Physical Review E 64, 026118. http://arxiv.org/PS_cache/cond-mat/pdf/0007/0007235v2.pdf

Newman M. E. J. (2003). Random graphs as models of networks, in Handbook of Graphs and Networks, Bornholdt S. and Schuster H. G. (eds.), Wiley-VCH, Berlin.

Onat F. A., Stojmenovic I. and Yanikomeroglu H. (2008). Generating random graphs for the simulation of wireless ad hoc, actuator, sensor, and internet networks, Pervasive and Mobile Computing, Vol. 4, Issue 5, pp. 597-615.

Penrose M. D. (1999). On *k*-connectivity for a geometric random graph, Random Structures and Algorithms, vol. 15, pp. 145–164.

Steele M. (1997). Probability theory and combinatorial optimization. Vol. 69, SIAM.

Trullols O., Fiore M., Casetti C., Chiasserini C. F., and Barcelo Ordinas J. M. (2010). Planning Roadside Infrastructure for Information Dissemination in Intelligent Transportation Systems. Comput. Commun., 33(4):432-442.

10

The Properties of Graphs of Matroids*

Ping Li[1] and Guizhen Liu[2,†]
[1]Department of Mathematics, West Virginia University, Morgantown, WV
[2]School of Mathematics and System Science, Shandong University, Jinan
[1]USA
[2]China

1. Introduction

Let E be a finite set of elements. For $S_1, S_2 \subseteq E$, set $S_1 - S_2 = \{x | x \in S_1 \text{ and } x \notin S_2\}$. Let $\mathcal{C}$ be a collection of non-null subsets of E which satisfies the following two axioms.

(C1) A proper subset of a member of $\mathcal{C}$ is not a member of $\mathcal{C}$.

(C2) If $a \in C_1 \cap C_2$ and $b \in C_1 - C_2$ where $C_1, C_2 \in \mathcal{C}$ and $a, b \in E$, then there exists a $C_3 \in \mathcal{C}$ such that $b \in C_3 \subseteq (C_1 \cup C_2) - \{a\}$.

Then $M = (E, \mathcal{C})$ is called a matroid on E. We refer to the members of $\mathcal{C}$ as circuits of matroid M. The set of bases of a matroid M is a nonempty collection $\mathcal{B}$ of subsets of E such that the following condition is satisfied. For any $B, B' \in \mathcal{B}$, $|B| = |B'|$ and for any $e \in B \setminus B'$, there exists $e' \in B' \setminus B$ such that $(B \setminus \{e\}) \cup \{e'\} \in \mathcal{B}$, We also write as $M = (E, \mathcal{B})$. Each member of $\mathcal{B}$ is called a base of M. The rank r of a matroid is the number of elements in a base and the co-rank r^* is the number of its basic circuits. If $e \in E \setminus B$, then $B \cup \{e\}$ contains a unique basic circuit and denoted by $C(e, B)$. For a given base B of M, the set of basic circuits with respect to B is denoted by $\mathcal{C}_B$. We use $\mathcal{B}_e$ and $\overline{\mathcal{B}_e}$ to denote the set of bases containing e and avoiding e, respectively. Let $M = (E, \mathcal{C})$ be a matroid. If $X \subseteq E$, then the matroid on $E - X$ whose circuits are those of M which are contained in $E - X$ is called the restriction of M to $E - X$ (or the matroid obtained by deleting X from M) and is denoted by $M \backslash X$ or $M|(E - X)$. There is another derived matroid of importance. If $X \subseteq E$, then the family of minimal non-empty intersections of $E - X$ with circuits of M is the family of circuits of a matroid on $E - X$ called the contraction of M to $E - X$. If $X = \{e\}$, we use $M \backslash e$ and M/e to denote the matroid obtained from M by deleting and contracting e, respectively. A matroid obtained from M by limited times of contractions and limited times of deletions is called a minor of M. A subset S of E is called a separator of M if every circuit of M is either contained in S or $E - S$. Union and intersection of two separators of M is also a separator of M. If $\emptyset$ and E are the only separators of M, then M is said to be connected. The minimal non-empty separators of M are called the

*This research was supported by NNSF(61070230) of China.
†Corresponding Author

components of M. The base graph of matroid M is a graph $G_B(M)$ with vertex set $V(G_B)$ and edge set $E(G_B)$ such that $V(G_B) = \mathcal{B}$ and $E(G_B) = \{BB' \mid B, B' \in \mathcal{B}, \mid |B - B'| = 1\}$.

Let G be a graph. The vertex set and edge set of a graph G are denoted by $V(G)$ and $E(G)$, respectively. If $A \subseteq V(G)$, then $G[A]$ denotes the induced subgraph of G by A. A k-path is a path of k-edges and denoted by P_k. A k-circuit is a circuit of k-edges and denoted by C_k. K_n denotes the complete graph of order n. A graph is *Hamiltonian connected* if for any two vertices there is a Hamilton path connects them. A graph is *Hamiltonian* if it contains a Hamilton circuit. A graph G is positively Hamiltonian, written $G \in H^+$, if for every edge of G, there is a Hamilton circuit containing it. G is negatively Hamiltonian, written $G \in H^-$, if for every edge of G, there is a Hamilton circuit avoiding it. When $G \in H^+$ and $G \in H^-$, we say that G is *uniformly Hamiltonian*. If for every edge e of G, there is a k-circuit containing it for any $k, 3 \leq k \leq |V(G)|$, then G is called edge-pancyclic. A graph G is called E_2-Hamiltonian if every two edges of G are contained in a Hamilton cycle of G. Let G be a simple graph of order at least 3 vertices. Then graph G is called p_3-Hamilton, if for any path P with 3 vertices, there exists a Hamilton cycle of G which contains P. If for any two vertices v_1 and v_2 and any edge v_2v_3 where $v_1 \neq v_3$, graph G has a Hamilton path from v_1 to v_2 and such that edge v_2v_3 in this path, then we say that graph G is 1-Hamilton connected. Terminology and notations not defined here can be found in [1] and [2].

Maurer defined the base graph of a matroid , and discussed the graphical properties of the base graph of a matroid [3-4]. Cummins showed that every matroid base graph with at least three vertices has a Hamilton circuit [5]. Holzmann and Harary showed that for every edge in a base graph there is a Hamilton circuit containing it and another Hamilton circuit avoiding it [6]. Alspach and Liu studied the properties of paths and circuits in base graphs of matroids [7]. The connectivity of the base graph of matroids is investigated by Liu [8]. The other graphical properties of the base graphs of matroid have also been investigated by Liu [9-16].

Now we give a new concept as follows. The circuit graph of a matroid M is a graph $G_C = G(M)$ with vertex set $V(G_C)$ and edge set $E(G_C)$ such that $V(G_C) = \mathcal{C}$ and $E(G_C) = \{CC' \mid C, C' \in \mathcal{C}, \mid C \cap C' \mid \neq 0\}$, where the same notation is used for the vertices of G and the circuits of M. We give another new graph related to the bases of matroids as follows. The intersection graph of bases of matroid $M = (E, \mathcal{B})$ is a graph $G_I(M)$ with vertex set $V(G_I)$ and edge set $E(G_I)$ such that $V(G_I) = \mathcal{B}$ and $E(G_I) = \{BB' : |B \cap B'| \neq 0, B, B' \in \mathcal{B}(M)\}$, where the same notation is used for the vertex of G_I and the base of M. The properties of paths , cycles and the connectivity of circuit graphs of matroids are discussed in this chapter. In particular, some new results obtained by us are given.

2. Preliminary results

To prove the main theorem we need the following preliminary results.

Lemma 2.1. [17] A matroid M is connected if and only if for every pair e_1, e_2 of distinct elements of E, there is a circuit containing both e_1 and e_2.

Lemma 2.2. [17] If M is a connected matroid, then for every $e \in E$, either M/e or $M \backslash e$ is also connected.

Lemma 2.3. [17] Let C and $C^\star$ be any circuit and co-circuit of a matroid M. Then $|C \cap C^\star| \neq 1$.

Lemma 2.4. [1] If $a \in C_1 \cap C_2$ and $b \in C_1 - C_2$ where $C_1, C_2 \in \mathcal{C}$, then there exists a $C_3 \in \mathcal{C}$ such that $b \in C_3 \subseteq (C_1 \cup C_2) - \{a\}$.

Let $M = (E, \mathcal{C})$ be a connected matroid. An element e of E is called an essential element if $M \backslash e$ is disconnected. Otherwise it is called an inessential element. A connected matroid each of whose elements is essential is called a critically connected matroid or simply a critical matroid.

Lemma 2.5. [17] A critical matroid of rank 2 contains a co-circuit of cardinality two.

A matroid M is trivial if it has no circuits. In the following matroids will be nontrivial. Next we will discuss the properties of the matroid circuit graph. To prove the main results we firstly present the following result which is clearly true.

Lemma 2.6. [17] Let M be any nontrivial matroid on E and $e \in E$. If G_C and G_{Ce} are circuit graphs of M and $M \backslash e$, respectively, then G_{Ce} is a subgraph of G induced by V_1 where $V_1 = \{C \mid C \in \mathcal{C}, e \notin C\}$.

Obviously the subgraph G_{C2} of G induced by $V_2 = V - V_1$ is a complete graph. By Lemma 2.6 G_{C1} and G_{C2} are induced subgraphs of G and $V(G_{C1})$ and $V(G_{C2})$ partition $V(G)$.

Lemma 2.7. [17] For any matroid $M = (E, \mathcal{C})$ which has a 2-cocircuit $\{a, b\}$, the circuit graph of M is isomorphic to that of M/a.

Proof. Since $|C \cap \{a, b\}| \neq 1$ for any circuit C, by Lemma 2.3, the circuits of M can be partitioned into two classes, those circuits containing both a and b and those circuits containing neither a nor b. Likewise, the circuits of M/a can be partitioned into two classes: those containing b and those not containing b, clearly there is a bijection between $\mathscr{C}(M)$ and $\mathscr{C}(M/a)$. Hence $G(M) \cong G(M/a)$, the lemma is proved.

Lemma 2.8. [17] Suppose that $M = (E, \mathcal{C})$ is a connected matroid with an element e such that the matroid $M \backslash e$ is connected and $G = G_C(M)$ is the circuit graph of matroid M. Let $G_1 = G(M \backslash e)$ be the circuit graph of $M \backslash e$ and G_2 be the subgraph of G induced by V_2 where $V_2 = \{C \mid C \in \mathcal{C}, e \in C\}$. If the matroid $M \backslash e$ has more than one circuit, then for any edge $C_1C_2 \in E(G)$, there exists a 4-cycle $C_1C_2C_3C_4$ in graph G such that one edge of the 4-cycle belongs to $E(G_1)$ and one belongs to $E(G_2)$ and C_1, C_2 are both adjacent to C_3.

Proof. By Lemma 2.6, $V(G_1)$ and $V(G_2)$ partition $V(G)$. There are three cases to distinguish.

Case 1. $e \in E - (C_1 \cup C_2)$. Thus C_1C_2 is an edge of $M \backslash e$. By Lemma 2.1, there are at least three vertices in $G(M \backslash e)$. There is an element e_1 such that $e_1 \in C_1 \cap C_2$. Let G_1 and G_2 be the graphs defined as above. Note that G_2 is a complete graph. By Lemma 2.1, there is a vertex C_3 in G_2 containing both e_1 and e. Thus in G, C_3 is adjacent to both C_1 and C_2. Since $C_1 \not\subset C_3$, there exists e_2 such that $e_2 \in C_1$, but $e_2 \notin C_3$. By Lemma 2.1, there is a circuit C_4 in G_2 containing e_2 and e and $C_3 \neq C_4$. Thus C_4 is adjacent to C_1.

Case 2. $e \in C_1 - C_2$ or $e \in C_2 - C_1$. Suppose that $e \in C_2 - C_1$, $e_1 \in C_1 \cap C_2$. By Lemma 2.4, there is a circuit $C_3 \subseteq (C_1 \cup C_2) - \{e_1\}$ containing e. We assume that $e_2 \in C_1 \cap C_3$, $e_3 \in E - (C_1 \cup \{e\})$. Note that e_3 exists because, by hypothesis, $M \backslash e$ has more than one circuit. By Lemma 2.1, in $G_1 = G(M \backslash e)$ there is a circuit C_4 containing e_2 and e_3. $C_1C_2C_3C_4$ is the 4-cycle we wanted. C_1 and C_2 are both adjacent to C_3.

Case 3. $e \in C_1 \cap C_2$. C_1 and C_2 are both in G_2. If there are only two circuits containing e, it is easy to see that $C_1 \cup C_2 = E(M)$ by Lemma 2.6. We prove that $C_1 \cap C_2 = \{e\}$. If $C_1 \cap C_2 = \{e, e'\}$, then $\{e, e'\}$ is a co-circuit of M because by Lemma 2.4, if there is a circuit containing e' does not contain e, then there is a circuit containing e does not contain e'; which is a contradiction to the hypothesis. Thus $C_1 \cap C_2 = \{e\}$. Then there is only one circuit $C_3' = (C_1 \cup C_2) - \{e\}$ in $M \backslash e$. For if there is a circuit $C_4' \neq C_3'$ in $M \backslash e$, then there exists $e_1 \in E(M) - (\{e\} \cup C_4')$ and $e_1 \in C_1 - C_2$ or $e_1 \in C_2 - C_1$. We assume that $e_1 \in C_1 - C_2$. By Lemma 2.4, there is a circuit C_5 such that $e \in C_5 \subseteq (C_2 \cup C_4') - \{e_2\}$ where $e_2 \in C_2 \cap C_4'$. $e_1 \notin C_5$, $C_5 \neq C_1$, thus there are at least three circuits containing e, a contradiction. So there are more than two circuits containing e, we assume that $e_3 \in C_1 - C_2$. By Lemma 2.4, there is C_3 in G_1 such that $e_3 \in C_3 \subseteq (C_1 \cup C_2) - \{e\}$. By Lemma 2.1, there is a vertex C_4 in G_1 containing e_3 and e_4 where $e_4 \in E - (C_3 \cup \{e\})$. We get the 4-cycle $C_1C_2C_3C_4$. The proof is completed.

Lemma 2.9. [17] Suppose that $M = (E, \mathcal{C})$ is a connected matroid with an element e such that the matroid $M \backslash e$ is connected and $G = G(M)$ is the circuit graph of matroid M. Let $G_1 = G(M \backslash e)$ be the circuit graph of $M \backslash e$ and G_2 be the subgraph of G induced by V_2 where $V_2 = \{C \mid C \in \mathcal{C}, e \in C\}$. If $C_1 \in V(G_1)$, $C_2 \in V(G_2)$ and $d(C_1, C_2) = 2$, there exists a 3-path $C_1C_3C_4C_2$ in graph G such that $C_3 \in V(G_1)$, $C_4 \in V(G_2)$ and C_1, C_2 are both adjacent to C_3 and C_4.

Proof. By Lemma 2.6, $V(G_1)$ and $V(G_2)$ partition $V(G)$. By assumption, $|C_1 \cap C_2| = 0$. We assume that $e_1 \in C_1$, $e_2 \in C_2$. By Lemma 2.1, there is C_4 in G_2 containing both e_1 and e. Thus in G, C_4 is adjacent to C_1 and C_2. By Lemma 2.1, there is C_3 in G_1 containing both e_1 and e_2. Thus in G, C_3 is adjacent to C_1, C_2 and C_4

Let P_4 be the Hamilton path connecting C_1 and C_2 in $G(M \backslash e)$ which traverses $C_1'C_2'$ and P_2 be the m-path connecting C_3 and C_4 in G_2 ($1 \leq m \leq n_2 - 1$), respectively. $P_3 + C_1'C_3 + C_3C_2' + P_4$ is a n_1-path of $G(M)$ that joins C_1 and C_2. $P_3 + C_1'C_4 + P_2 + C_3C_2' + P_4$ is a $n_1 + m$-path of $G(M)$ that joins C_1 and C_2.

Subcase 1.2. $e \in C_1 - C_2$ or $e \in C_2 - C_1$. Suppose that $e \in C_2 - C_1$. Thus $C_1 \in V(G_1)$, $C_2 \in V(G_2)$. If $d(C_1, C_2) = 1$, by Lemma 2.8, there is a 4-cycle $C_1C_2C_3C_4$ in G such that $C_3 \in V(G_2)$ and $C_4 \in V(G_1)$ and $C_1C_2C_3$ is a 3-cycle of G. By induction, for any k_1, $1 \leq k_1 \leq n_1 - 1$, there is a k_1-path in G_1 connecting C_4 and C_1. Note that G_2 is a complete graph. For any k_2, $1 \leq k_2 \leq n_2 - 1$, there is a k_2-path in G_2 connecting C_2 and C_3. Let P_1 be the k_1-path in G_1 connecting C_1 and C_4 and P_2 be the k_2-path in G_2 connecting C_3 and C_2, respectively. $P_1 + C_4C_3 + P_2$ is a $k_1 + k_2 + 1$-path of $G(M)$ that connects C_1 and C_2. If $d(C_1, C_2) = 2$ and $e \in C_2 - C_1$, by Lemma 2.9, there is a 3-path $C_1C_3C_4C_2$ in G such that $C_3 \in V(G_1)$ and $C_4 \in V(G_2)$ and $C_1C_3C_2$ is a 2-path of G. Then the proof is similar to the case when $d(C_1, C_2) = 1$.

Subcase 1.3. $e \in C_1 \cap C_2$. Thus $d(C_1, C_2) = 1$. If there are only two circuits containing e, then there is only one circuit in $M \backslash e$. The result holds obviously because $G = K_3$. Assume that there are more than two circuits containing e. Note that G_2 is a complete graph. For any m, $1 \leq m \leq n_2 - 1$, there is a path of length m connecting C_1 and C_2. Choose $C_3 \in V(G_2)$

such that $C_3 \neq C_1$ and $C_3 \neq C_2$. By Lemma 2.8, there is a 4-cycle $C_1C_3C_4C_5$ in G such that $C_4C_5 \in E(G_1)$ and $C_1C_3C_4$ is a 3-cycle of G. By induction, for any k, $1 \leq k \leq n_1 - 1$, there is a k-path in G_1 connecting C_4 and C_5. Note that G_2 is a complete graph. Let P_1 be the k-path in G_1 connecting C_4 and C_5 and P_2 be the Hamilton path in G_2 connecting C_1 and C_2 which traverses the edge C_1C_3. Let $P_2 = C_1C_3 + P_3$. $C_1C_4 + C_4C_3 + P_3$ is a n_2-path that connects C_1 and C_2. $C_1C_5 + P_1 + C_4C_3 + P_3$ is the $n_2 + k$-path we wanted.

Case 2. The matroid M is critically connected. By Lemma 2.2, for any element e in M, M/e is connected. By Lemma 2.5, M has a 2-cocircuit $\{a, b\}$. By Lemma 2.7, the circuit graph of M/a is isomorphic to that of M. By induction hypothesis, the result holds.

Thus the theorem follows by induction.

Lemma 2.10. [2] A graph G is k-edge-connected if and only if any two distinct vertices of G are connected by at least k edge- disjoint paths.

3. The properties of circuit graphs of matroids

We have known that a matroid M is connected if and only if for every pair e_1, e_2 of distinct elements of E, there is a circuit containing both e_1 and e_2. The following results are the new results obtained by Li and Liu.

Theorem 3.1. [17] For any connected matroid $M = (E, \mathcal{C})$ which has at least three circuits, the circuit graph $G = G(M)$ is positively Hamiltonian, that is, for every edge of G, there is a Hamilton circuit containing it.

We shall prove the theorem by induction on $|E|$. When $|E| = 3$, each element in M is parallel to another. It is easy to see that $G = K_3$. The theorem is clearly true. Suppose that the result is true for $|E| = n - 1$. We prove that the result is also true for $|E| = n > 3$. Let C_1C_2 be any edge in G.

There are two cases to distinguish.

Case 1. There is an element e in M such that $M\backslash e$ is connected. Let G_1 and G_2 be the graphs defined as above. We assume that $|V(G_1)| = n_1$ and $|V(G_2)| = n_2$.

There are three subcases to distinguish.

Subcase 1.1. $e \in E - (C_1 \cup C_2)$. Thus C_1C_2 is an edge of $M\backslash e$. By Lemma 2.4, there are at least three vertices in $G(M\backslash e)$. By induction, $G(M\backslash e)$ is edge-pancyclic. For any m, $3 \leq m \leq n_1$, there is a cycle of length m containing C_1C_2. By Lemma 2.8, for any edge $C_1'C_2'$ in the Hamilton cycle of $G(M\backslash e)$ containing C_1C_2 where $C_1'C_2' \neq C_1C_2$, there is a 4-cycle $C_1'C_2'C_3C_4$ in G such that $C_3C_4 \in E(G_2)$ and $C_1'C_2'C_3$ is a 3-cycle in G. If there are only three vertices in $G(M\backslash e)$, let $C_1 = C_1'$. Note that G_2 is a complete graph. Let P_1 be the Hamilton path connecting C_1' and C_2' in $G(M\backslash e)$ which traverses C_1C_2 and P_2 be the k-path connecting C_3 and C_4 in G_2 ($1 \leq k \leq n_2 - 1$), respectively. $P_1 + C_2'C_3 + C_3C_1'$ is a $n_1 + 1$-cycle of $G(M)$ that contains C_1C_2. $P_1 + C_2'C_3 + P_2 + C_4C_1'$ is a $n_1 + k + 1$-cycle of $G(M)$ that contains C_1C_2.

Subcase 1.2. $e \in C_1 - C_2$ or $e \in C_2 - C_1$. Suppose that $e \in C_2 - C_1$. Thus $C_1 \in V(G_1)$, $C_2 \in V(G_2)$. By Lemma 2.8, there is a 4-cycle $C_1C_2C_3C_4$ in G such that $C_3 \in V(G_2)$ and $C_4 \in V(G_1)$ and $C_1C_2C_3$ is a 3-cycle of G. By induction, for any k_1, $1 \leq k_1 \leq n_1 - 1$, there is a k_1-path in G_1 connecting C_4 and C_1. Note that G_2 is a complete graph. For any k_2, $1 \leq k_2 \leq n_2 - 1$, there is a k_2-path in G_2 connecting C_2 and C_3. Let P_1 be the k_1-path in G_1 connecting C_1 and C_4 and P_2 be the k_2-path in G_2 connecting C_3 and C_2, respectively. $P_1 + C_4C_3 + P_2 + C_2C_1$ is a $k_1 + k_2 + 2$-cycle of $G(M)$ that contains C_1C_2.

Subcase 1.3. $e \in C_1 \cap C_2$. If there are only two circuits containing e, then there is only one circuit in $M \backslash e$. The result holds obviously because $G = K_3$. Assume that there are more than two circuits containing e. Note that G_2 is a complete graph. For any m, $3 \leq m \leq n_2$, there is a cycle of length m containing C_1C_2. Choose $C_3 \in V(G_2)$ such that $C_3 \neq C_1$ and $C_3 \neq C_2$. By Lemma 2.8, there is a 4-cycle $C_1C_3C_4C_5$ in G such that $C_4C_5 \in E(G_1)$ and $C_1C_3C_4$ is a 3-cycle of G. By induction, for any k, $1 \leq k \leq n_1 - 1$, there is a k-path in G_1 connecting C_4 and C_5. Note that G_2 is a complete graph. Let P_1 be the k-path in G_1 connecting C_4 and C_5 and P_2 be the Hamilton path in G_2 connecting C_3 and C_1 which traverses the edge C_2C_1. $C_4C_3 + P_2 + C_1C_4$ is a $n_2 + 1$-cycle that contains C_1C_2. $P_1 + C_4C_3 + P_2 + C_1C_5$ is the $n_2 + k + 1$-cycle we wanted.

Case 2. The matroid M is critically connected. By Lemma 2.2, for any element e in M, M/e is connected. By Lemma 2.5, M has a 2-cocircuit $\{a, b\}$. By Lemma 2.7, the circuit graph of M/a is isomorphic to that of M. By induction hypothesis, the result holds.

Thus the theorem follows by induction.

Theorem 3.2. [21] Let M be any connected matroid which has at least four circuits and let $G = G(M)$ be the circuit graph of M. Then for each edge of $G = G(M)$ there is a Hamilton cycle avoiding it. that is, the circuit graph $G = G(M)$ is negatively Hamiltonian.

Proof. We prove the theorem by induction on $|E|$. It is easy to see that $|E| \geqslant 4$. When $|E| = 4$ and $r(M) = 1$, $M = U_{1,4}$ [1]. It is easy to see that $G(M) \in H^-$. When $|E| = 4$ and $r(M) = 2$, M has at most three circuits except when $M = U_{2,4}$. Obviously $G(U_{2,4}) = K_4$ and $K_4 \in H^-$. Then suppose that the theorem is true for $|E| = n - 1$. We shall prove the theorem holds for $|E| = n > 4$. Let C_1C_2 be any edge of G. There are two cases to consider.

Case 1. There exists an element e such that $M \backslash e$ is connected. Let G_1 and G_2 be the graphs defined as above.

There are three subcases to consider.

Subcase 1.1. If $e \in E - (C_1 \cup C_2)$, then C_1C_2 is an edge of $G(M \backslash e)$. By Theorem 3.1, there is a Hamilton cycle in $G(M \backslash e)$ containing C_1C_2. By the proof of Lemma 2.8, there is a 4-cycle $C_1C_2C_3C_4$ in G such that $C_3C_4 \in E(G_2)$. As in the proof of Theorem 3.1, let P_1 be a Hamilton path in G_1 connecting C_1 and C_2 and P_2 be a Hamilton path in G_2 connecting C_3 and C_4, respectively. Then the cycle $P_1 + C_2C_3 + P_2 + C_4C_1$ is a Hamilton cycle of G avoiding C_1C_2.

Subcase 1.2. Let $e \in C_1 - C_2$ or $e \in C_2 - C_1$. It is easy to see that there are more than two vertices in $G(M \backslash e)$, and there are at least three vertices in G_2. We assume that $e \in C_2 - C_1$ and $e_1 \in C_1 - C_2$. By Lemma 2.1, there is C_3 in G_2 containing e and e_1. By the proof of Lemma 2.8, in G there is a 4-cycle $C_1C_3C_4C_5$ such that $C_4 \in V(G_2)$, $C_5 \in V(G_1)$. Let P_1 be a Hamilton path in $G(M \backslash e)$ connecting C_1 and C_5 and P_2 be a Hamilton path in G_2 connecting C_4 and C_3, respectively. $P_1 + C_5C_4 + P_2 + C_3C_1$ is a Hamilton cycle avoiding C_1C_2.

Subcase 1.3. If $e \in C_1 \cap C_2$, as in the proof of subcase 1.3 in Theorem 3.1, let $C_2 = C_3$ and P_2 be a Hamilton path connecting C_1 and C_2 in G_2, then $P_1 + C_4C_2 + P_2 + C_1C_5$ is a Hamilton cycle we wanted.

Case 2. For every $e \in E(M)$, $M\backslash e$ is disconnected. Then the matroid M is critically connected. By Lemma 2.2, for any element e in M, M/e is connected. By Lemma 2.5, M has a cocircuit $\{a,b\}$. By Lemma 2.7, $G(M) \cong G(M/a)$. By induction hypothesis, the result holds.

The proof of the theorem is completed.

Corollary 3.3. For any connected matroid M, the circuit graph $G_C(M)$ is uniformly Hamilton whenever $G_C(M)$ contains at least four vertices. That is for any edge e of $G_C(M)$, there is a Hamilton containing e and there is another Hamilton cycle excluding e.

Theorem 3.4. [20] Let $G = G(M)$ be the circuit graph of a connected matroid $M = (E, \mathcal{C})$. If $|V(G)| = n$ and $C_1, C_2 \in V(G)$ with $d(C_1, C_2) = r$, then there is a path of length k joining C_1 and C_2 for any k satisfying $r \leq k \leq n-1$.

Proof. We shall prove the theorem by induction on $|E|$. When $|E| = 3$, each element in M is parallel to another. It is easy to see that $G = K_3$. The theorem is clearly true. Suppose that the result is true for $|E| = n-1$. We prove that the result is also true for $|E| = n > 3$. It is easy to see that for any vertices C_1, C_2 in $V(G)$, we have $d(C_1, C_2) = r$ where $r = 1$ or $r = 2$ by the definition of the circuit graph of a matroid.

There are two cases to distinguish.

Case 1. There is an element e in M such that $M\backslash e$ is connected. Let G_1 and G_2 be the graphs defined as above. We assume that $|V(G_1)| = n_1$ and $|V(G_2)| = n_2$.

There are three subcases to distinguish.

Subcase 1.1. $e \in E - (C_1 \cup C_2)$. Thus $C_1 \in V(G_1), C_2 \in V(G_1)$. Clearly, there are at least three vertices in $G(M\backslash e)$. By induction, for any $k, r \leq k \leq n_1 - 1$, there is a path of length k joining C_1 and C_2 in $G(M\backslash e)$. By Lemma 2.8, for any edge $C_1'C_2'$ in the Hamilton path connecting C_1 and C_2 in $G(M\backslash e)$, there is a 4-cycle $C_1'C_2'C_3C_4$ in G such that $C_3C_4 \in E(G_2)$ and $C_1'C_2'C_3$ is a 3-cycle in G. If there are only three vertices in $G(M\backslash e)$, let $C_1 = C_1'$. Note that G_2 is a complete graph. Let $P_1 = P_3 + C_1'C_2' + P_4$ be the Hamilton path connecting C_1 and C_2 in $G(M\backslash e)$ which traverses $C_1'C_2'$ and P_2 be the m-path connecting C_3 and C_4 in G_2 $(1 \leq m \leq n_2 - 1)$, respectively. $P_3 + C_1'C_3 + C_3C_2' + P_4$ is a n_1-path of $G(M)$ that joins C_1 and C_2. $P_3 + C_1'C_4 + P_2 + C_3C_2' + P_4$ is a $n_1 + m$-path of $G(M)$ that joins C_1 and C_2 .

Subcase 1.2. $e \in C_1 - C_2$ or $e \in C_2 - C_1$. Suppose that $e \in C_2 - C_1$. Thus $C_1 \in V(G_1), C_2 \in V(G_2)$. If $d(C_1, C_2) = 1$, by Lemma 2.8, there is a 4-cycle $C_1C_2C_3C_4$ in G such that $C_3 \in V(G_2)$ and $C_4 \in V(G_1)$ and $C_1C_2C_3$ is a 3-cycle of G. By induction, for any k_1, $1 \leq k_1 \leq n_1 - 1$, there is a k_1-path in G_1 connecting C_4 and C_1. Note that G_2 is a complete graph. For any k_2, $1 \leq k_2 \leq n_2 - 1$, there is a k_2-path in G_2 connecting C_2 and C_3. Let P_1 be the k_1-path in G_1 connecting C_1 and C_4 and P_2 be the k_2-path in G_2 connecting C_3 and C_2, respectively. $P_1 + C_4C_3 + P_2$ is a $k_1 + k_2 + 1$-path of $G(M)$ that connects C_1 and C_2.

If $d(C_1, C_2) = 2$ and $e \in C_2 - C_1$, by Lemma 2.9, there is a 3-path $C_1C_3C_4C_2$ in G such that $C_3 \in V(G_1)$ and $C_4 \in V(G_2)$ and $C_1C_3C_2$ is a 2-path of G. Then the proof is similar to the case when $d(C_1, C_2) = 1$.

Subcase 1.3. $e \in C_1 \cap C_2$. Thus $d(C_1, C_2) = 1$. If there are only two circuits containing e, then there is only one circuit in $M\backslash e$. The result holds obviously because $G = K_3$. Assume that there are more than two circuits containing e. Note that G_2 is a complete graph. For any m, $1 \leq m \leq n_2 - 1$, there is a path of length m connecting C_1 and C_2. Choose $C_3 \in V(G_2)$ such that $C_3 \neq C_1$ and $C_3 \neq C_2$. By Lemma 2.8, there is a 4-cycle $C_1C_3C_4C_5$ in G such that $C_4C_5 \in E(G_1)$ and $C_1C_3C_4$ is a 3-cycle of G. By induction, for any k, $1 \leq k \leq n_1 - 1$, there is a k-path in G_1 connecting C_4 and C_5. Note that G_2 is a complete graph. Let P_1 be the k-path in G_1 connecting C_4 and C_5 and P_2 be the Hamilton path in G_2 connecting C_1 and C_2 which traverses the edge C_1C_3. Let $P_2 = C_1C_3 + P_3$. $C_1C_4 + C_4C_3 + P_3$ is a n_2-path that connects C_1 and C_2. $C_1C_5 + P_1 + C_4C_3 + P_3$ is the $n_2 + k$-path we wanted.

Case 2. The matroid M is critically connected. By Lemma 2.2, for any element e in M, M/e is connected. By Lemma 2.5, M has a 2-cocircuit $\{a, b\}$. By Lemma 2.7, the circuit graph of M/a is isomorphic to that of M. By induction hypothesis, the result holds.

Thus the theorem follows by induction.

Theorem 3.5. [20] Suppose that $G = G_C(M)$ is the circuit graph of a connected matroid M and C_1 and C_2 are distinct vertices of G. Then C_1 and C_2 are connected by $d = min\{d(C_1), d(C_2)\}$ edge -disjoint paths where $d(C_1)$ and $d(C_2)$ denote the degree of vertices C_1 and C_2 in G, respectively.

Proof. We shall prove the theorem by induction on $|E|$. When $|E| = 3$, each element in M is parallel to another. It is easy to see that $G = K_3$. The theorem is clearly true. Suppose that the result is true for $|E| = n - 1$. We prove that the result is also true for $|E| = n > 3$. Let C_1 and C_2 be any two vertices in G.

There are two cases to distinguish.

Case 1. $(C_1 \cup C_2) = E$. It is easy to see that C_1 and C_2 are both adjacent to any circuit in $\mathscr{C} - \{C_1 \cup C_2\}$ and the conclusion is obviously true.

Case 2. $(C_1 \cup C_2) \neq E$.

There are two subcases to distinguish.

Subcase 2.1. There is an element $e \in E - (C_1 \cup C_2)$ such that $M\backslash e$ is connected. Let $G_1 = G(M\backslash e)$ be the circuit graph of $M\backslash e$ and G_2 be the subgraph of G induced by V_1 where $V_1 = \{C \mid C \in \mathscr{C}, e \in C\}$. Thus C_1 and C_2 are in G_1. By induction, in G_1, C_1, C_2 are connected by $d_1 = min\{d_1(C_1), d_1(C_2)\}$ edge-disjoint paths where $d_1(C_1)$ and $d_1(C_2)$ denote the degree of vertices C_1 and C_2 in G_1, respectively. Let $\mathscr{P}_1 = \{P_1, P_2, \cdots, P_{d_1}\}$ be the family of shortest edge-disjoint paths connecting C_1 and C_2 in G_1. Without loss of generality, we may assume that $d_1(C_1) \geq d_1(C_2)$. There are two subcases to distinguish.

Subcase 2.1 a. $d_1(C_1) = d_1(C_2)$. Thus $d_1 = min\{d_1(C_1), d_1(C_2)\} = d_1(C_1) = d_1(C_2)$. We assume that there are m vertices $A_1, A_2, \cdots, A_m$ in G_2 that are adjacent to C_1 and n vertices $D_1, D_2, \cdots, D_n$ in G_2 that are adjacent to C_2 where m, n are integers. G_2 is a complete graph, so A_i is adjacent to $D_j(i = 1,2,\cdots,m; j = 1,2,\cdots,n)$. Here maybe $A_i = D_j$ for some $1 \leq i \leq m; 1 \leq j \leq n$. Let $q = min\{m,n\}$. $C_1A_iD_iC_2(i = 1,2,\cdots,q)$ are q edge-disjoint paths in G. It is easy to see that $d(C_1) = d_1(C_1) + m, d(C_2) = d_1(C_2) + n$ and $d = min\{d(C_1), d(C_2)\} = min\{d_1(C_1) + m, d_1(C_2) + n\} = d_1(C_1) + min\{m,n\} = d_1(C_1) + q$. $\mathscr{P} = \mathscr{P}_1 \cup \{C_1A_1D_1C_2, C_1A_2D_2C_2, \cdots, C_1A_qD_qC_2\}$ are d edge-disjoint paths connecting C_1 and C_2 in G.

Subcase 2.1 b. $d_1(C_1) > d_1(C_2)$. By induction, in G_1 there are $d_1 = min\{d_1(C_1), d_1(C_2)\} = d_1(C_2)$ edge -disjoint paths connecting C_1 and C_2. Let $\mathscr{P}_1 = \{P_1, P_2, \cdots, P_{d_1(C_2)}\}$ be the family of shortest edge-disjoint paths connecting C_1 and C_2 in G_1. It is obvious that each $P_i(i = 1,2,\cdots,d_1(C_2))$ contains exactly one vertex adjacent to C_1 and one vertex adjacent to C_2. Let $A_1, A_2, \cdots, A_{d_1(C_1)-d_1(C_2)}$ be the vertices in G_1 that are adjacent to C_1 but not contained in d_1 edge-disjoint paths. By Lemma 2.1, for any element e' in A_i $(i = 1,2,\cdots,d_1(C_1) - d_1(C_2))$ there is a circuit A_i' in G_2 containing e and e', thus A_iA_i' is an edge in $G(M)$. Let $D_1, D_2, \cdots, D_m$ denote the vertices in G_2 that is adjacent to C_2. G_2 is a complete graph, so A_i' is adjacent to $D_j(i = 1,2,\cdots,d_1(C_1) - d_1(C_2); j = 1,2,\cdots,m)$. If $m \leq d_1(C_1) - d_1(C_2)$, $C_1A_iA_i'D_iC_2$ are m edge-disjoint paths connecting C_1 and C_2 where A_i' can be D_i $(i = 1,2,\cdots,m)$. Here it is possible that $A_i' = A_j'(i \neq j; i,j = 1,2,\cdots,d_1(C_1) - d_1(C_2))$. But it is forbidden that $D_i = D_j(i \neq j; i,j = 1,2,\cdots,m)$. $d(C_2) = d_1(C_2) + m \leq d_1(C_1) < d(C_1)$, thus $d = min\{d(C_1), d(C_2)\} = d(C_2)$. $\mathscr{P} = \mathscr{P}_1 \cup \{C_1A_1A_1'D_1C_2, C_1A_2A_2'D_2C_2, \cdots, C_1A_mA_m'D_mC_2\}$ are d edge-disjoint paths connecting C_1 and C_2 in G. If $m > d_1(C_1) - d_1(C_2)$, let $\mathscr{P}_2 = \{C_1A_1A_1'D_1C_2, C_1A_2A_2'D_2C_2, \cdots, C_1A_{d_1(C_1)-d_1(C_2)}A'_{d_1(C_1)-d_1(C_2)}D_{d_1(C_1)-d_1(C_2)}C_2\}$ be $d_1(C_1) - d_1(C_2)$ edge-disjoint paths connecting C_1 and C_2 where A_i' can be D_i $(i = 1,2,\cdots,d_1(C_1) - d_1(C_2))$. Let $L_1, L_2, \cdots, L_n$ denote the vertices in G_2 that is adjacent to C_1. G_2 is a complete graph, so L_i is adjacent to $D_j(i = 1,2,\cdots,n; j = d_1(C_1) - d_1(C_2) + 1, d_1(C_1) - d_1(C_2) + 2, \cdots, m)$. If $m > n + d_1(C_1) - d_1(C_2)$, $d(C_1) = d_1(C_1) + n \leq d_1(C_2) + m < d(C_2)$, thus $d = min\{d(C_1), d(C_2)\} = d(C_1)$. $\mathscr{P}_3 = C_1L_iD_{d_1(C_1)-d_1(C_2)+i}C_2$ are n edge-disjoint paths connecting C_1 and C_2 where L_i can be $D_{d_1(C_1)-d_1(C_2)+i}$ $(i = 1,2,\cdots,n)$. Thus $\mathscr{P} = \mathscr{P}_1 \cup \mathscr{P}_2 \cup \mathscr{P}_3$ are $d = d(C_1)$ edge-disjoint paths in G. If $d_1(C_1) - d_1(C_2) < m \leq n + d_1(C_1) - d_1(C_2)$, $\mathscr{P}_3' = C_1L_iD_{d_1(C_1)-d_1(C_2)+i}C_2$ are $m - (d_1(C_1) - d_1(C_2)$ edge-disjoint paths connecting C_1 and C_2 where L_i can be $D_{d_1(C_1)-d_1(C_2)+i}$ $(i = 1,2,\cdots,m - (d_1(C_1) - d_1(C_2))$ but $D_{d_1(C_1)-d_1(C_2)+i} \neq D_{d_1(C_1)-d_1(C_2)+j}$ $(i \neq j; i,j = 1,2,\cdots,m - (d_1(C_1) - d_1(C_2))$. $d(C_2) = d_1(C_2) + m \leq d_1(C_1) + n = d(C_1)$, thus $d = min\{d(C_1), d(C_2)\} = d(C_2)$. $\mathscr{P} = \mathscr{P}_1 \cup \mathscr{P}_2 \cup \mathscr{P}_3'$ are $d = d(C_2)$ edge-disjoint paths connecting C_1 and C_2 in G. The conclusion holds.

Subcase 2.2. There is no element $e \in E - (C_1 \cup C_2)$ such that $M\backslash e$ is connected. If $E - (C_1 \cup C_2) = \{e\}$ and $M\ e$ is disconnected, it is easy to see that $C_1 \cap C_2 = \emptyset$ and C_1, C_2 are the two components of $M\backslash e$. Thus any circuit of M intersecting both C_1 and C_2 contains e. Then C_1 and C_2 are both adjacent to any circuit in $\mathscr{C} - \{C_1 \cup C_2\}$ and the conclusion is obviously true. Suppose that $|E - (C_1 \cup C_2)| \geq 2$ and for any $e \in E - (C_1 \cup C_2)$, $M\backslash e$ is disconnected. By Lemma 2.5, M has a 2-cocircuit $\{a, b\}$. By Lemma 2.7, the circuit graph of M/a is isomorphic to that of M. By induction hypothesis, the result holds. Thus the theorem follows by induction.

By Theorem 3.5, we can get the following corollary.

Corollary 3.6. Suppose that $G = G(M)$ is the circuit graph of a connected matroid M with minimum degree $\delta(G)$. Then the edge connectivity $\kappa'(G) = \delta(G)$.

Proof. By Theorem 3.5, we know that $\kappa'(G) \geq \delta(G)$. Since for any graph G, we have $\kappa'(G) \leq \delta(G)$, then $\kappa'(G) = \delta(G)$.

Theorem 3.7. [20] Let G be the circuit graph of a connected matroid $M = (E, \mathscr{C})$. If $|V(G)| = n$ and $k_1 + k_2 + \cdots + k_p = n$ where k_i is an integer, $i = 1, 2, \ldots, p$, then there is a partition of $V(G)$ into p parts $V_1, V_2, \ldots, V_p$ such that $|V_i| = k_i$ and the subgraph H_i induced by V_i contains a k_i -cycle when $k_i \geq 3$, H_i is isomorphic to K_2 when $k_i = 2$, H_i is a single vertex when $k_i = 1$.

Proof. We shall prove the theorem by induction on $|E|$. When $|E| = 3$ and $|V(G)| = 1$, the result holds clearly. When $|E| = 3$ and $|V(G)| = 3$, $M = U_{1,3}[1]$. It is easy to see that $G = K_3$. The theorem is clearly true. Suppose that the result is true for $|E| = m - 1$. We prove that the result is also true for $|E| = m > 3$.

Case 1. There is an element e in M such that $M \backslash e$ is connected. Let G_1 and G_2 be the graphs defined as above. We assume that $|V(G_1)| = n_1$ and $|V(G_2)| = n_2$. There exists an q such that $k_1 + k_2 + \cdots + k_{q-1} < n_1$ and $k_1 + k_2 + \cdots + k_q \geq n_1$. By induction, the vertices of $G(M \backslash e)$ can be partitioned into q parts $V_1, V_2, \ldots, V_q'$ such that $|V_1| = k_1, |V_2| = k_2, \ldots, |V_{q-1}| = k_{q-1}, |V_q'| = n_1 - (k_1 + k_2 + \cdots + k_{q-1}) = k_q'$ and the subgraph H_i (H_q') induced by V_i ($i = 1, 2, \ldots, q-1$) (V_q') contains a k_i (k_q') -cycle when $k_i \geq 3$ ($k_q' \geq 3$), H_i (H_q') is isomorphic to K_2 when $k_i = 2$ ($k_q' = 2$), H_i (H_q') is a single point when $k_i = 1$ ($k_q' = 1$). When $k_q = k_q'$, the result holds clearly because G_2 is a complete graph. When $k_q > k_q'$, there are three subcases to consider.

Subcase 1.1. $k_q' = 1$. Suppose that C_1 is the subgraph in $G(M \backslash e)$ induced by V_q'. When $k_q = 2$, obviously there is a vertex in G_2 that is adjacent to C_1. When $k_q \geq 3$, we prove that there is a 3-cycle $C_1C_2C_3$ in G such that $C_2C_3 \in E(G_2)$. For any $e_1 \in C_1$, by Lemma 2.1, there is a circuit $C_2 \in G_2$ containing e_1 and e. Let $e_2 \in C_1 - C_2$. There is a circuit $C_3 \in G_2$ containing e_2 and e. We get the 3-cycle $C_1C_2C_3$. Note that G_2 is a complete graph. In G_2 there is a $k_q - 2$ path P connecting C_2 and C_3. $C_1C_2 + P + C_3C_1$ is a k_q -cycle in G. Because G_2 is a complete graph, the subgraph induced by $V(G_2) - V(P)$ is also a complete graph. Thus the vertices of the subgraph induced by $V(G_2) - V(P)$ can be partitioned into $p - q$ parts $V_{q+1}, V_{q+2}, \ldots, V_p$ such that $|V_i| = k_i$, $i = q+1, q+2, \ldots, p$, and the subgraph H_i induced by V_i contains a k_i -cycle when $k_i \geq 3$, H_i is isomorphic to K_2 when $k_i = 2$, H_i is a single point when $k_i = 1$. The result holds.

Subcase 1.2. $k_q' = 2$. Suppose that C_1C_2 is the subgraph in $G(M \backslash e)$ induced by V_q'. When $k_q = 3$, by Lemma 2.8, the result holds. When $k_q \geq 4$, by Lemma 2.8, there is a 4-cycle $C_1C_2C_3C_4$ in G such that $C_3 \in V(G_2)$ and $C_4 \in V(G_2)$ and $C_1C_2C_3$ is a 3-cycle of G. In G_2 there is a $k_q - 3$ -path P connecting C_3 and C_4. $C_1C_2 + C_2C_3 + P + C_4C_1$ is a k_q -cycle in G. Because G_2 is a complete graph, the subgraph induced by $V(G_2) - V(P)$ is also a complete graph. Thus the result holds.

Subcase 1.3. $k_q' > 2$. The subgraph H_q' in $G(M \backslash e)$ induced by V_q' contains a k_q' -cycle. Let C_1C_2 be any edge in this cycle and P_1 be the Hamilton path in H_q' connecting C_1 and C_2. By Lemma 2.8, there is a 4-cycle $C_1C_2C_3C_4$ in G such that $C_3C_4 \in E(G_2)$ and $C_1C_2C_3$ is a 3-cycle of G. When $k_q - k_q' = 1$, $P_1 + C_2C_3 + C_3C_1$ is a k_q -cycle in G. When $k_q - k_q' \geq 2$, in G_2 there is a $k_q - k_q' - 1$ -path P_2 connecting C_3 and C_4. $P_1 + C_2C_3 + P_2 + C_4C_1$ is a k_q -cycle in G. Note that

G_2 is a complete graph. The subgraph induced by $V(G_2) - V(P_2)$ is also a complete graph. Thus the result holds.

Case 2. The matroid M is critically connected. By Lemma 2.2, for any element e in M, M/e is connected. By Lemma 2.5, M has a 2-cocircuit $\{a, b\}$. By Lemma 2.7, the circuit graph of M/a is isomorphic to that of M. By induction hypothesis, the result holds.

Thus the theorem follows by induction.

From Theorem 3.7 we have the following theorem holds.

Theorem 3.8. Let $G = G(M)$ be the circuit graph of a connected matroid $M = (E, \mathcal{C})$. If $|V(G)| = n$ and $k_1 + k_2 + \cdots + k_p = n$ where k_i is an integer and $k_i \geq 3, i = 1, 2, \ldots, p$, then G has a 2-factor F containing p vertex-disjoint cycles $D_1, D_2, \ldots, D_p$ such that the length of D_i is k_i $(i = 1, 2, \ldots, p)$.

By the similar methods we can prove that the above theorems also holds for the intersection graph of bases of matroids.

Finally, We present the following open problems to be considered.

Problem 1. Let $G = G(M)$ be the circuit graph of a connected matroid $M = (E, \mathcal{C})$. If $|V(G)| = n$ and $C_1, C_2 \in V(G)$ with $d(C_1, C_2) = r$, how many Hamilton paths connect C_1 and C_2 in G? Furthermore, how many k-paths connect C_1 and C_2 in G $(r \leq k \leq n-1)$?

Problem 2. Let $G = G(M)$ be the intersection graph of bases of matroid $M = (E, \mathcal{B})$. If $|V(G)| = n$ and $B_1, B_2 \in V(G)$ with $d(B_1, B_2) = r$, how many Hamilton paths connect B_1 and B_2 in G? Furthermore, how many k-paths connect B_1 and B_2 in G $(r \leq k \leq n-1)$?

Other related results of graphs on matroids can be found in [22-60].

4. References

[1] J. G. Oxley, Matroid theroy, Oxford University Press, New York, 1992.

[2] J. A. Bondy, U. S. R. Murty, Graph Theory With Applications, American Elsevier, New York, 1976.

[3] S. B. Maurer, Matroid basis graphs I, *J.Comb. Theory B*, 14 (1973), 216-240.

[4] S. B. Maurer, Matroid basis graphs II, *J. Comb. Theory B*, 15 (1973) 121-145.

[5] R. L. Cummins, Hamilton circuits in tree graphs. *IEEE Trans Circuit theory*, 1 (1966), 82-90.

[6] C. A. Holzmann, P. G. Norton and M. D. Tobey. A graphical representation of matroids. *SIAM J Appl Math.*, 29 (1973), 618-672.

[7] B. Alspach and G. Liu. Paths and cycles in matroid base graphs, *Graphs and combinatorics*, 1989, 5(3), 207-211.

[8] G. Liu. The connectivities of matroid base graphs, *J. Operations Research*, 3(1) (1984), 67-68.

[9] G. Liu, Matroids complexes–geometrical representations on matroids. *Acta Math. Scientia*, 5 (1985), 35-42.

[10] G. Liu, The Connectivities of Adjacent Tree Graphs. *Acta Mathematicae Applicatae Sinica*, 3(4) (1987), 313-317.
[11] G. Liu. A lower bound on connectivities of matroid base graphs, *Discrete Math.*, 69(1) (1988), 55-60.
[12] G. Liu. On connectivities of base graph of some matroids, *J. Sys. Sci. and Math. Scis.*, 1(1) (1988), 18-21.
[13] G. Liu, On connectivities of tree graphs, *J. Graph Theory*, 12(3) (1988), 453-459.
[14] G. Liu, The proof of a conjecture on matroid basis graphs. *Scince Sinica*, 1990: 593-599.
[15] Liu Guizhen and Chen Qinghua, Matroids, Publishing House of National University Defense Technology, Changsha, (in chinese) 1994.
[16] Guizhen Liu and L. Zhang, Forest graphs of graphs, Chinese Journal of Engineering Mathmatics, 22 (6) (2005), 1100-1109.
[17] P. Li, Guizhen Liu, Cycles in circuit graphs of matroids, *Graphs and Combinatorics* 23 (2007), 425-431.
[18] Yinghao Zhang and Guizhen Liu, On Properties of the intersection graphs of matroids, to appear in *Frontiers of Mathematics.*
[19] H. Deng and F. Xia. The P_3-Hamiltonian property of matroid base graphs. *Jour Nat Sci Hunan Norm Uni.*, 1 (2000), 5-8.
[20] D. Deng and R. Li. The 1-Hamiltonian property of matroid base graphs. *Acta. Scinat Univ. Norm. Hunan.*, 22 (3) (1999), 1-5..
[21] L. Li, Matroids and Graphs, Ph.D. Dissertation, Shandong University, (2005).
[22] Ping Li, Guizhen Liu , Hamilton cycle in circuit graphs of matroids, Computer and mathematics with Applications 55 (2008), 654-659
[23] Ping Li, Some Properties of Circuit Graphs of Matroids, Doctoral Dissertation, Shandong University, (2010)
[24] B. Bollobas, A lower bound for the number of nonisomorphic Matroids, *J. Comb. Theory*, 1969, 7, 366-368.
[25] J. A. Bondy, Transversal matroids, base orderable matroids and graphs, *Quart. J. Math.*, 1972, 23, 81-89.
[26] J. A. Bondy, A.W. Ingleton, Pancyclic graph II, *J.Comb. Theory*, B20,1976, 41-46
[27] R. A. Brualdi, On foundamental transversal matroids, *Proc. Amer. Math. Soc.*, 45 (1974), 151-156.
[28] R. A. Brualdi, G. W. Dinolt, Characterization of transversal matroids and their presentations, *J. Comb. Theory*, 12 (1972), 268-286.
[29] M. Cai, A solution of Chartand's problem on spanning trees, *Acta Mathematicae Applicatae Sinica* (English Ser.), 1:2 (1984), 97-98.
[30] P. A. Catlin, J. W. Grossman, A. M. Hobbs, and H. J. Lai. Fractional arboricity, strength, and principal partitions in graphs and matroids. *Disc. Appl. Math.*, 40(1992), 285-302.
[31] H. H. Crapo, Single element extensions of Matroids, *J. Res. Nat. Bur. Stand.*, 69B (1965), 57-65.
[32] J. Donald, C. Holzmann and M. Tobey. A characterization of complete matroid base graphs, *J. Comb. Theory Ser.*, 22B (1977), 139-193.
[33] J. R. Edmonds, Minimum partition of a matroid into indedent subsets. *J.Res. Natl. Bur. Stand.*, 69B(1965), 67-72.

[34] J. R. Edmonds, Matroids and the greedy algorithm, *Math Programming*, 1, (1971), 127-136.
[35] V. Estivill-Castro, M. Noy and J. Urrutia, On the chromatic number of tree graphs. *Discrete Math.*, 223 (2000), 363-366.
[36] J. Gao, Quasi-1-Hamilton connectedness of tree graphs. *Math. Res. and Exposition*, 7(3) (1987), 498.
[37] J. Gao, 1-Hamilton connectedness of tree graphs. *Mathematica Applicata.*, 6(2) (1993), 136-144.
[38] H. Harary, R. J. Mokken and M. J. Plantholt, Interpolation theorem for diameters of spanning trees. *IEEE Trans Circuits and System*, 30 (1983), 429-432.
[39] F. Harary and M. J. Plantholt, Classification of interpolation theorems for spanning trees and other families of spanning subgraphs. *J. Graph Theory*, 13(6)(1989), 703-712.
[40] R. Rado, A theorem on independence relations. *Quart. J. Math. Oxford Ser.*, 13 (1942), 83-89.
[41] C. A. Holzmann, F. Harary, On the tree graph of a matroid. *SIAM J. Appl. Math.*, 22 (1972), 187-193.
[42] A. W. Ingleton, Gammoids and transversal matroids, *J. Comb. Theory*, 15 (1973), 51-68.
[43] T. Kamae. The existence of Hamilton circuit in a tree graph. *IEEE Trans Circuit theory*, 14 (1967), 279-283.
[44] G. Kishi and Y. Kajitani. On Hamilton circuits in a tree graphs. *IEEE Trans Circuit theory*, 15 (1968), 42-50.
[45] E. Lawler. Combinatorial Optimization. *John Wiley, New York*, 1972.
[46] L. Li, The Hamilton properties of tree graphs. *J. Shandong Unv. of Technology*, 27 (3) (1997), 261-263.
[47] L. Li and G. Liu, The connectivities of the adjacency leaf exchange forest graphs, *J. Shandong University*, 39 (6) (2004), 49-51.(in Chinese)
[48] L. Li, Q. Bian and G. Liu, The matroid incidence graphs, *J. Shandong University*, 40 (2) (2005), 24-40.(in Chinese)
[49] L. Li, Matroids and Graphs, Ph.D. Dissertation, Shandong University, (2005).
[50] X. Li. The connectivities of the *SEE*-graph and the *AEE*-graph for the connected spanning *k*-edge subgraphs of a graph *Discete Math.*, 183 (1998), 237-245.
[51] X. Li, V. Neumann-Lara and E. Rivera-Campo, Two Approaches for the Generalization of Leaf Edge Exchange Graphs on Spanning Trees to Connected Spanning k-Edge Subgraphs of a Graph. *Ars. combin.*, 75 (2005), 257-265.
[52] L. Lovasz, A. Recski, On the sum of Matroids, *Acta Math. Acad. Sci. Hung*, 24 (1973), 329-333.
[53] S. B. Maurer, Intervals in matroid basis graphs. *Discrete Math.*, 11 (1975), 147-159.
[54] U. S. R. Murty, On the number of bases of matroid, *Proc. Second Louisiana Conference on Combinatorics*, (1971), 387-410.
[55] U.S.R. Murty, Extremal critically connected matroids, *Discrete Math.*, 8 (1974), 49-58.
[56] D. Naddef and W. R. Pulleyblank. Hamiltonicity and combinatorial polyhedra. *J. Combin. theory B*, 31 (1981), 279-312.
[57] C. St. J. A. Nash-Williams, Edge-disjiont spanning trees of finite graphs. *J. London Math. Soc.*, 36 (1961), 445-450.

[58] C. St. J. A. Nash-Williams, Decompositions of finite graphs. *J. London Math. Soc.*, 39 (1964), 12.

[59] J. G. Oxley, Matroid Theory, Oxford University Press, New York, 1992.

[60] M. J. Piff, An upper bound for the number of matroids. *J. Comb. Theory,* 13 (1973), 241-245.

11

Symbolic Determination of Jacobian and Hessian Matrices and Sensitivities of Active Linear Networks by Using Chan-Mai Signal-Flow Graphs

Georgi A. Nenov
Higher School of Transport "T. Kableshkov", Sofia, Bulgaria

1. Introduction

Every network synthesis procedure normally includes a first-order or (more rarely) second-order network sensitivity analysis. The main problem here is the evaluation of the corresponding first- or second-order derivatives of network functions with respect to the circuit element values. These derivatives form the network Jacobian (**J**) and Hessian (**H**) matrices, respectively. A variety of methods exist for such an evaluation but most of them are intended for the sensitivity of one network transfer function only. Besides this in many cases it is desirable to find the symbolic expressions of the sensitivities because such a presentation facilitates the element value influence determination. An other useful and important application of the matrices **J** and **H** is in the tasks for optimization of synthesized networks with respect to their sensitivities or other parameters (Korn & Korn, 1968; Wilde,1978).

As it is well known all linear active networks can be modeled by using passive elements and nullator-norator pairs (nullors). The presented paper deals with the application of Chan-Mai signal-flow graphs (CMG) to the determination of the matrices **J** and **H** elements, having in mind the peculiarities of nullors and their influence on the passive element network admittance matrix and on the corresponding CMG. The method developed here is an improved and enlarged version of the approach in (Nenov, 2004). One demonstrates that the method reduces to the obtaining of two (for the elements of **J**) or four (for the elements of **H**) isomorphic Chan-Mai signal-flow graphs.

2. Chan-Mai signal flow graph

It was introduced in graph theory in 1967 (Chan & Mai, 1967). Compared with other kinds of oriented graphs (especially Mason and Coates graphs) the Chan-Mai graph (CMG) holds out a simplest way to the representation the relationships between the dependent and independent quantities in an algebraic equation set. In order to make easier the understanding of the following sections of the paper further we give the procedure for drawing of CMG and the basic formulae related.

Assume the algebraic set

$$\mathbf{A.X} = \mathbf{Y} \tag{1}$$

is given, where

$$\mathbf{A} = \begin{bmatrix} a_{11} & a_{12} & \dots & a_{1n} \\ a_{21} & a_{22} & \dots & a_{2n} \\ . & . & . & . \\ a_{n1} & a_{n2} & . & a_{nn} \end{bmatrix} \tag{2}$$

is a square matrix with real or complex entries and

$$\left.\begin{aligned} \mathbf{X} &= \begin{bmatrix} x_1 & x_2 & \dots & x_n \end{bmatrix}_t; \\ \mathbf{Y} &= \begin{bmatrix} y_1 & y_2 & \dots & y_n \end{bmatrix}_t \end{aligned}\right\} \tag{3}$$

are the vectors of the dependent and of the independent variables, respectively. The CMG consists of n vertices with sink signals $y_1, y_2, \dots, y_n$, n vertices with source signals $x_1, x_2, \dots, x_n$ and maximum n^2 edges with transmission coefficients a_{ji} directed from the vertex x_i toward the vertex y_j ; $i,j = 1, 2, \dots, n$ - Fig. 1. The calculations on the base of a CMG are connected with the following definitions (Chan & Mai, 1967, Donevsky & Nenov, 1979):

i. By removing all outgoing from the vertex x_i edges and by adding the edges with transmission coefficients y_j from the vertex x_i directed toward the vertices y_j , $j=1, 2, \dots, n$ one obtains the *graph* CMG,*i*;
ii. A *separation (S)* contains all vertices of CMG and a part of edges so that every vertex is incident to only one incoming and one only outgoing edge. The product of the transmission coefficients of all edges in a separations represents the corresponding *separation product (SP)*;
iii. Two edges with transmission coefficients a_{ij} and a_{ji} form a *symmetrical pair.*
iv. An edge which does not belong to a symmetrical pair is an *asymmetrical edge.*

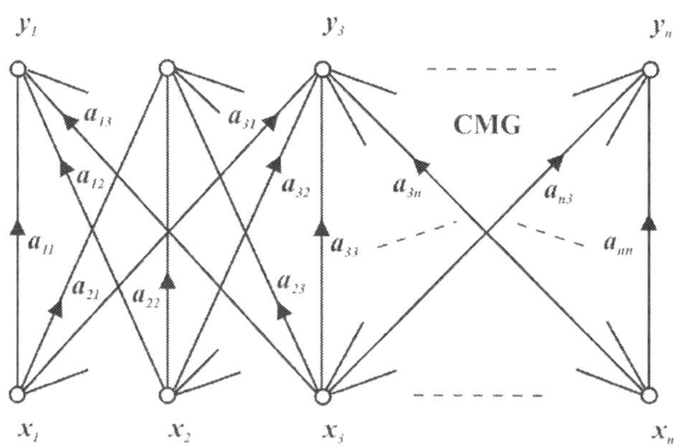

Fig. 1. Chan-Mai Signal-Flow Graph

An arbitrary unknown quantity x_i in $\mathbf{X}$ can be evaluated according to the expression

$$x_i = \frac{\sum_{q=1}^{m} (signSP_q) SP_q(CMG,i)}{\sum_{k=1}^{r} (signSP_k) SP_k(CMG,_k)}, \tag{4}$$

where

$$signSP_l = \begin{cases} (-1)^{N_{s,l}+N_{a,l}-1} & \text{for } N_{a,l} \neq 0 \\ (-1)^{N_{s,l}} & \text{for } N_{a,l} = 0 \end{cases} \tag{5}$$
$$l = q \text{ or } k$$

In (4) and (5) r is the number of the separations in CMG, m is the number of the separations in CMG,$_i$, $N_{a,k}$ is the number of all asymmetrical edges in k-th separation of CMG, $N_{s,k}$ is the number of all symmetrical pairs in k-th separation of CMG, N_{aq} is the number of the asymmetrical edges in q-th separation of CMG,i, $N_{s,q}$ is the number of the symmetrical pairs in q-th separation of CMG,i, whereas $SP_q(CMG,i)$ and $SP_k(CMG)$ are the separation products of q-th separation of CMG,i and the separation products of k-th separation of CMG, respectively.

3. Nullor network Chan-Mai signal-flow graph

Suppose that an equivalent nullor network N with $m+1$ nodes, r passive branches and g nullors is given and the nodal equation of its passive part N_p (the part of N which is obtained by removing all nullors) is

$$\mathbf{Y}_p \mathbf{V}_p = \mathbf{I}_p \tag{6}$$

where

$$\mathbf{Y} = \begin{bmatrix} Y_{p,11} & \cdots & Y_{p,1m} \\ . & . & . \\ Y_{p,m1} & \cdots & Y_{p,mm} \end{bmatrix} \tag{7}$$

is the nodal matrix of N_p and

$$\left.\begin{aligned} \mathbf{V}_p &= \begin{bmatrix} V_{p,1} & V_{p,2} & \cdots & V_{p,m} \end{bmatrix}_t; \\ \mathbf{I}_p &= \begin{bmatrix} I_{p,1} & I_{p,2} & \cdots & I_{p,m} \end{bmatrix}_t \end{aligned}\right\} \tag{8}$$

are the nodal voltage and the nodal current vectors of N_p, respectively. Additionally we assume that between the nodes of all node pairs in N only one element or more than one but parallel connected elements exist.

The equation (1) can be represented graphically by using a CMG G_p (Chan & Mai, 1967). Further, taking into account the peculiarities of the nullators and the norators (Davies, 1966) the graph G_p can be transformed into the graph G of the actual network N according to the following

Rule 1:

i. When a nullator is connected between the node k in N and the ground node $m+1$ one removes all vertices going out from the vertex V_k of G_p;
ii. When a norator is connected between the node k in N and the ground node $m+1$ one removes all vertices coming into the vertex I_k of G_p;
iii. When a nullator is connected between the nodes k and l in N one unites the vertices V_k and V_l in G_p;
iv. When a norator is connected between the nodes k and l in N one unites the vertices I_k and I_l in G_p.

The so obtained graph CMG G corresponds to the matrix equation

$$\mathbf{YV} = \mathbf{I} \tag{9}$$

where $\mathbf{Y}$ is an $(n \times n)$ nodal admittance matrix of N, $\mathbf{V}$ is the nodal voltage vector of N and $\mathbf{I}$ is the nodal current vector of for $n=m-g$.

4. Jacobian matrix determination

The matrices in (9) have the form:

$$\left.\mathbf{Y} = \begin{bmatrix} Y_{11} & .. & Y_{1i} & .. & Y_{1n} \\ . & . & . & . & . \\ Y_{j1} & .. & Y_{ji} & .. & Y_{jn} \\ . & . & . & . & . \\ Y_{n1} & .. & Y_{nj} & .. & Y_{nn} \end{bmatrix}; \ \mathbf{V} = \begin{bmatrix} V_1 & V_2 & \dots & V_n \end{bmatrix}_t; \ \mathbf{I} = \begin{bmatrix} I_1 & I_2 & \dots & I_n \end{bmatrix}_t \right\} \tag{10}$$

In the common case every element Y_{ji} in (7) is an algebraic admittance sum

$$Y_{ji} = \sum_s y_s; \ j,i \in \{1,2,...,n\}; s \in \{1,2,...,r\}, \tag{11}$$

where y_s is the admittance of s-th branch of the network N_p.

The vectors $\mathbf{V}$ and $\mathbf{I}$ correspond to the unknown (dependent) variables and to independent variables of N, respectively and consequently

$$\mathbf{V} = \mathbf{Y}^{-1}\mathbf{I}. \tag{12}$$

Let us suppose that the admittance y_s changes its value to

$$y_s' = y_s + dy_s. \tag{13}$$

Usually the admittance y_s takes part in several (but no more then four) elements of (7) and then all these elements change their values (Nenov, 2004)

$$\left.\begin{aligned} & Y_{ji}^{'} = Y_{ji} + dY_{ji} = Y_{ji} + \frac{\partial Y_{ji}}{\partial y_s} dy_s; \\ & j,i \in \{1,2,...,n\}; s \in \{1,2,...,r\} \end{aligned}\right\} \tag{14}$$

and

$$\mathbf{Y}^{'} = \mathbf{Y} + d\mathbf{Y}. \tag{15}$$

In a common case the admittance y_s influences the admittances Y_{ji}, Y_{jl}, Y_{ki} and Y_{kl}; $i,j,k,l \in \{1, 2, \ldots, n\}$. Then one obtains

$$\left.\begin{aligned} & d\mathbf{Y} = dy_s \mathbf{K}_s; \\ & \mathbf{K}_s = \begin{bmatrix} 0 & . & 0 & . & 0 & . & 0 \\ . & . & . & . & . & . & . \\ 0 & . & \dfrac{\partial Y_{ji}}{\partial y_s} & . & \dfrac{\partial Y_{jl}}{\partial y_s} & . & 0 \\ . & . & . & . & . & . & . \\ 0 & . & \dfrac{\partial Y_{ki}}{\partial y_s} & . & \dfrac{\partial Y_{kl}}{\partial y_s} & . & 0 \\ . & . & . & . & . & . & . \\ 0 & . & 0 & . & 0 & . & 0 \end{bmatrix}; \ i,j,k,l \in \{1,2,...,n\} \end{aligned}\right\}. \tag{16}$$

Note that the values of the derivatives in (16) are 1 or –1 because every admittance y_s takes part in (11) only once. Hence

$$\mathbf{V}^{'} = \mathbf{V} + d\mathbf{V} \tag{17}$$

for

$$d\mathbf{V} = \left(\frac{\partial \mathbf{V}}{\partial Y_{ji}} \frac{\partial Y_{ji}}{\partial y_s} + \frac{\partial \mathbf{V}}{\partial Y_{jl}} \frac{\partial Y_{jl}}{\partial y_s} + \frac{\partial \mathbf{V}}{\partial Y_{ki}} \frac{\partial Y_{ki}}{\partial y_s} + \frac{\partial \mathbf{V}}{\partial Y_{kl}} \frac{\partial Y_{kl}}{\partial y_s} \right) dy_s, \tag{18}$$

or:

$$\left.\begin{aligned} & d\mathbf{V} = dy_s \sum_{pq} \frac{\partial \mathbf{V}}{\partial Y_{pq}} \frac{\partial Y_{pq}}{\partial y_s}; \\ & p,q \in \{1,2,...,n\}. \end{aligned}\right\} \tag{19}$$

By substituting $\mathbf{Y}'$ and $\mathbf{V}'$ in (9) instead $\mathbf{Y}$ and $\mathbf{V}$, respectively, it follows

$$[\mathbf{Y} + d\mathbf{Y}].[\mathbf{V} + d\mathbf{V}] = \mathbf{I}. \tag{20}$$

Having in mind that

$$d\mathbf{Y}d\mathbf{V} \to 0 \tag{21}$$

the equation (20) yields

$$\mathbf{Y}d\mathbf{V} = -d\mathbf{Y}\mathbf{V} \tag{22}$$

or

$$d\mathbf{V} = -\mathbf{Y}^{-1}d\mathbf{Y}\mathbf{V} . \tag{23}$$

Then we obtain

$$\frac{\partial \mathbf{V}}{\partial y_s} dy_s = -dy_s.\mathbf{Y}^{-1}\mathbf{K}_s\mathbf{V} \tag{24}$$

and the Jacobian matrix (Korn & Korn, 1968). for the change of the admittance y_s is

$$\mathbf{J} = \begin{bmatrix} \frac{\partial V_1}{\partial y_1} & \frac{\partial V_1}{\partial y_2} & .. & \frac{\partial V_1}{\partial y_s} & .. & \frac{\partial V_1}{\partial y_r} \\ \frac{\partial V_2}{\partial y_1} & \frac{\partial V_2}{\partial y_2} & .. & \frac{\partial V_2}{\partial y_s} & .. & \frac{\partial V_2}{\partial y_r} \\ . & . & .. & . & .. & . \\ \frac{\partial V_n}{\partial y_1} & \frac{\partial V_n}{\partial y_2} & .. & \frac{\partial V_n}{\partial y_s} & .. & \frac{\partial V_n}{\partial y_r} \end{bmatrix} = \begin{bmatrix} \mathbf{J}_1 & \mathbf{J}_2 & .. & \mathbf{J}_s & .. & \mathbf{J}_r \end{bmatrix} , \tag{25}$$

where

$$\mathbf{J}_s = \begin{bmatrix} \frac{\partial V_1}{\partial y_s} & \frac{\partial V_2}{\partial y_s} & .. & \frac{\partial V_n}{\partial y_s} \end{bmatrix}_t . \tag{26}$$

Taking into account (24) and (25) one obtains

$$\left.\begin{aligned} &\mathbf{J}_s = -\mathbf{Y}^{-1}\mathbf{K}_s\mathbf{Y}^{-1}\mathbf{I} = -\mathbf{Y}^{-1}\mathbf{K}_s\mathbf{V} = -\mathbf{Y}^{-1}\mathbf{V}_s; \\ &\mathbf{V}_s = \mathbf{K}_s\mathbf{V}. \end{aligned}\right\} \tag{27}$$

and according to (20) ÷ (22)

$$\mathbf{J} = -\mathbf{Y}^{-1}\begin{bmatrix} \mathbf{K}_1 & .. & \mathbf{K}_s & .. & \mathbf{K}_r \end{bmatrix}\mathbf{V} . \tag{28}$$

The expressions (22) show that in order to find the vector $\mathbf{J}_s$ it is necessary to follow the *Rule 2:*

i. Find the vector $\mathbf{V}$ by using the CMG G;
ii. Evaluate the vector $\mathbf{V}_s$;
iii. Draw a new CMG G_s where the source vertices are the elements of the vector $\mathbf{J}_s$ and the sink vertices are the elements of the vector $\mathbf{V}_s$;
iv. Find the source vertex variables in G_s.

Example A

The network N in Fig. 2 is given, where m=6; r=9; g=2. Here obviously $V_2=V_3=V_{23}$; $V_6=0$ and we wish to find the vector

$$\mathbf{J}_3=\begin{bmatrix}\dfrac{\partial V_1}{\partial(sC_3)} & \dfrac{\partial V_{23}}{\partial(sC_3)} & \dfrac{\partial V_4}{\partial(sC_3)} & \dfrac{\partial V_5}{\partial(sC_3)}\end{bmatrix}_t. \tag{29}$$

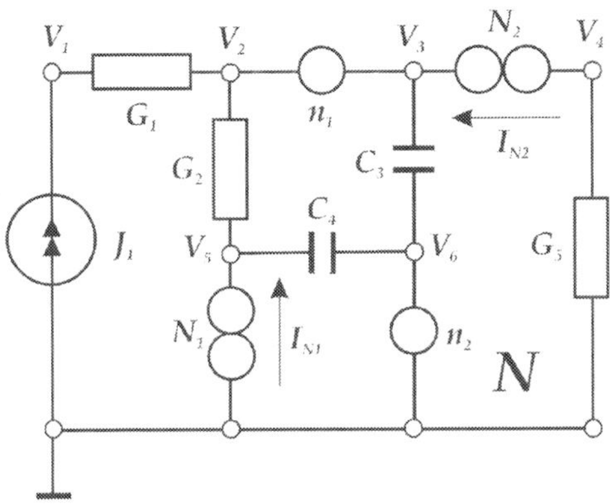

Fig. 2. Nullor Network N

In Fig. 3 the CMG $\mathbf{G}_\mathrm{p}$ of the passive part of N is drawn (Nenov, 2004). Further following the ***Rule*** 2 we reach to the graph $\mathbf{G}$ in Fig. 4 for

$$\left.\begin{aligned}&\mathbf{Y}=\begin{bmatrix}G_1 & -G_1 & 0 & 0\\ -G_1 & G_1+G_2 & 0 & -G_2\\ 0 & sC_3 & G_5 & 0\\ 0 & -sC_3 & 0 & -sC_4\end{bmatrix};\\ &\mathbf{V}=\begin{bmatrix}V_1 & V_2=V_3=V_{23} & V_4 & V_5\end{bmatrix}_t;\mathbf{I}=\begin{bmatrix}J_1 & 0 & 0 & 0\end{bmatrix}_t.\end{aligned}\right\} \tag{30}$$

Because $Y_{32}=sC_3$; $Y_{42}=-sC_3$ and

$$\frac{\partial Y_{32}}{\partial(sC_3)}=1;\ \frac{\partial Y_{32}}{\partial(sC_3)}=-1. \tag{31}$$

from (16) and (31) we have

$$\left.\begin{aligned}&\mathbf{K}_3=\begin{bmatrix}0&0&0&0\\0&0&0&0\\0&1&0&0\\0&-1&0&0\end{bmatrix};\\ &\mathbf{V}_3=\mathbf{K}_3\mathbf{V}=\begin{bmatrix}0 & 0 & V_{23} & -V_{23}\end{bmatrix}_t\end{aligned}\right\} \tag{32}$$

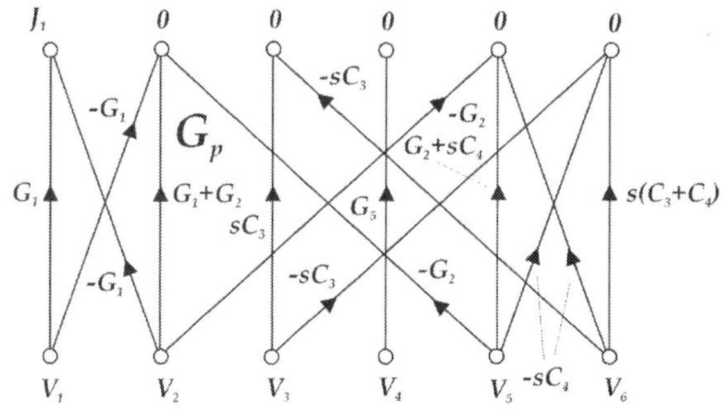

Fig. 3. CM Signal-Flow Graph $\boldsymbol{G}_p$

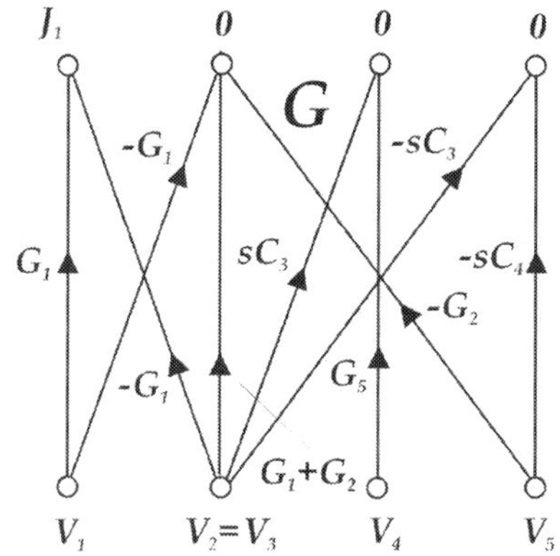

Fig. 4. CM Signal-Flow Graph $\boldsymbol{G}$

Obviously, in the case we have to find the voltage V_{23} only. For this purpose a CM graph $\boldsymbol{G}_{23}$ is drawn (Fig. 5).

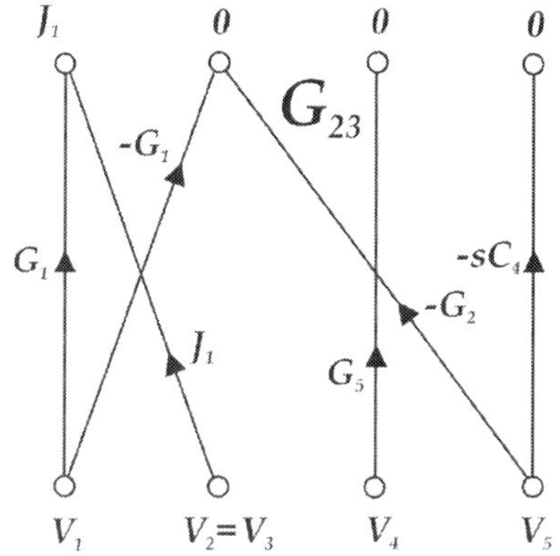

Fig. 5. CM Signal-Flow Graph $\boldsymbol{G}_{23}$

According to (4) and (5) for the separations of the graph **G** (Fig. 6) we obtain

$$\left.\begin{array}{l} SP_1 = -G_1 sC_4 G_5 (G_1 + G_2); N_{a,1} = 4; N_{s,1} = 0; \\ SP_2 = -G_1^2 sC_4 G_5; N_{a,2} = 2; N_{s,2} = 1; \\ SP_3 = G_2 sC_3 G_5 : N_{a,3} = 2; N_{s,3} = 1 \end{array}\right\} \tag{33}$$

and for the unique separation of the graph $\mathbf{G}_{23}$ (Fig. 7):

$$SP_{23,1} = J_1 G_1 sC_4 G_5; N_{a,23,1} = 2; N_{s,23,1} \tag{34}$$

Then the formulae (4) and (5) yield

$$V_{23} = \frac{J_1 C_4}{G_2 (C_3 + C_4)}. \tag{35}$$

Having in mind (26) ÷ (29) we have

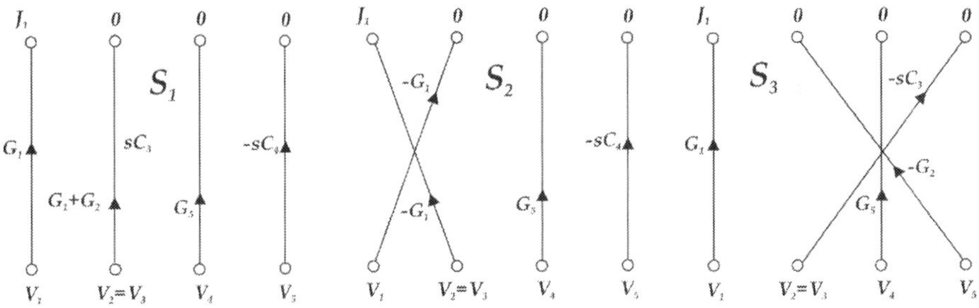

Fig. 6. Separations S_1, S_2 and S_3 of CM Graph **G**

$$\mathbf{J}_3 = -\mathbf{Y}^{-1}\mathbf{V}_3 = \mathbf{Y}^{-1}(-\mathbf{V}_3) \tag{36}$$

and following ***Rule 2*** one draws the CM graph $\mathbf{G}_{J3}$ (Fig. 8). Obviously, the graphs **G** and $\mathbf{G}_{J3}$ have one and the same structure and consequently the expressions (33) hold for the source vertex quantities in (29) also. But for the nominator polynomials in (4) we have to draw according the ***Rule 2*** four new CM graphs – $\mathbf{G}_{J3,1}$, $\mathbf{G}_{J3,23}$, $\mathbf{G}_{J3,4}$ and $\mathbf{G}_{J3,5}$ – Fig. 9.

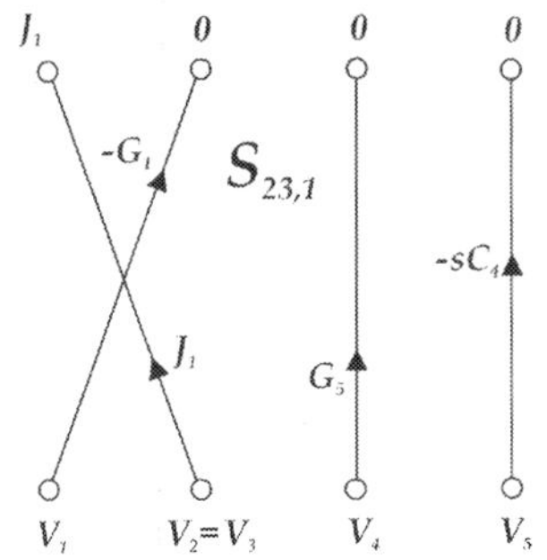

Fig. 7. Separation $S_{23,1}$ of CM Graph $\mathbf{G}_{23}$

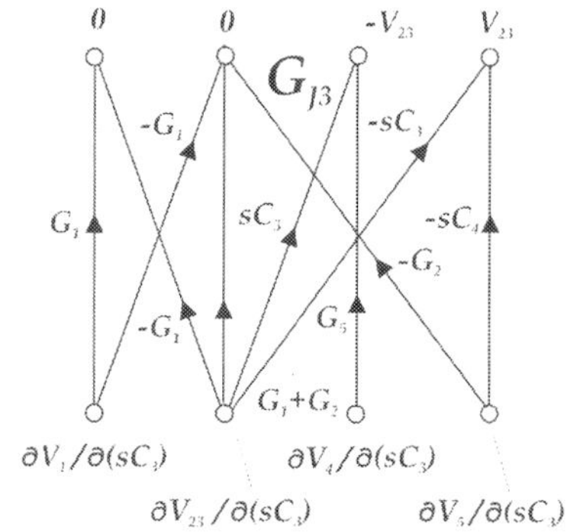

Fig. 8. CM Graph G_{J3}

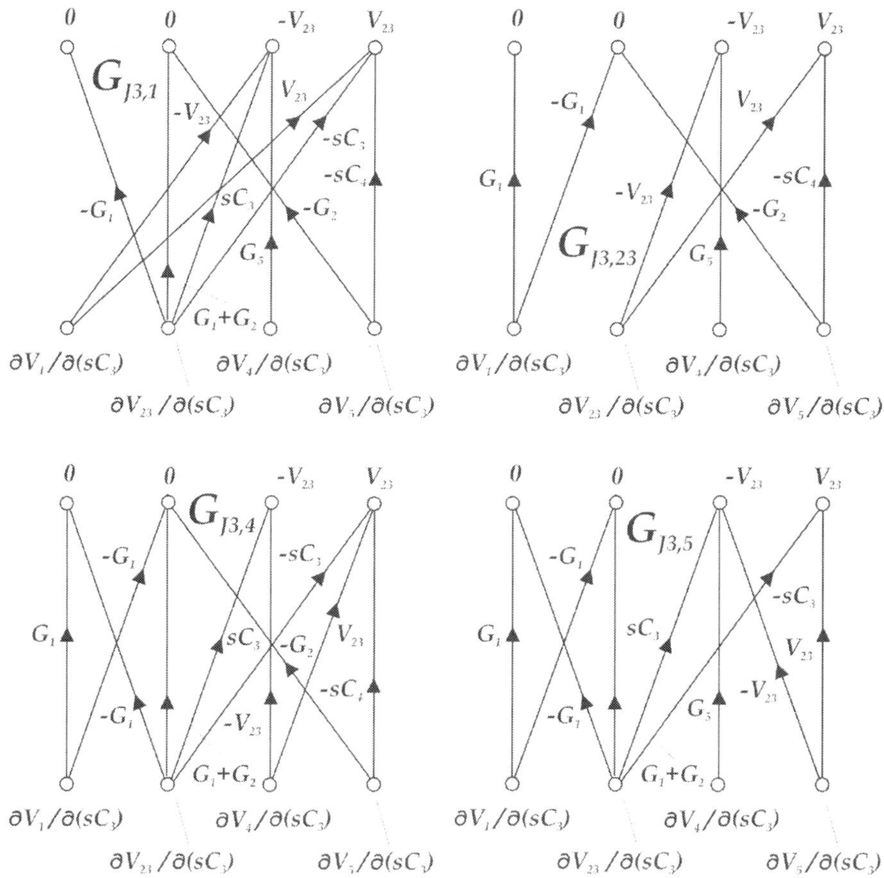

Fig. 9. CM Graphs $G_{J3,1}$, $G_{J3,23}$, $G_{J3,4}$ and $G_{J3,5}$

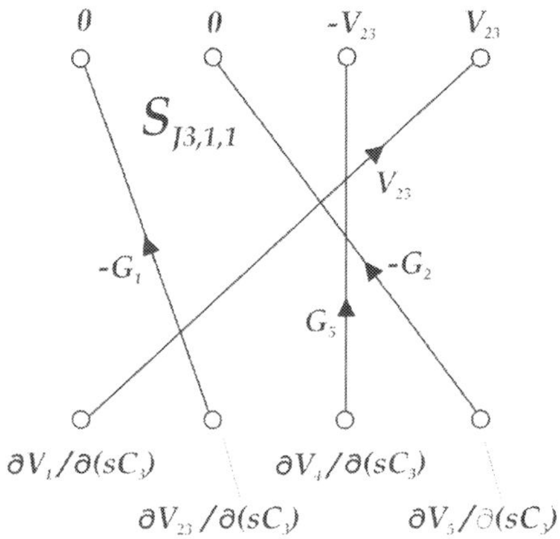

Fig. 10. Separation $S_{J3,1,1}$ of CM Graph $G_{J3,1}$

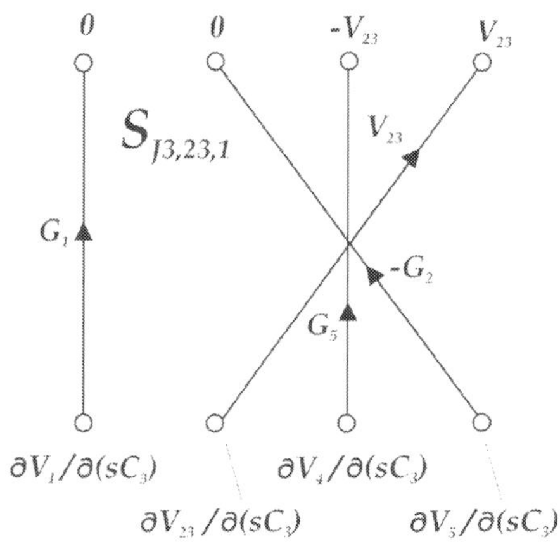

Fig. 11. Separation $S_{J3,23,1}$ of CM Graph $G_{J3,23}$

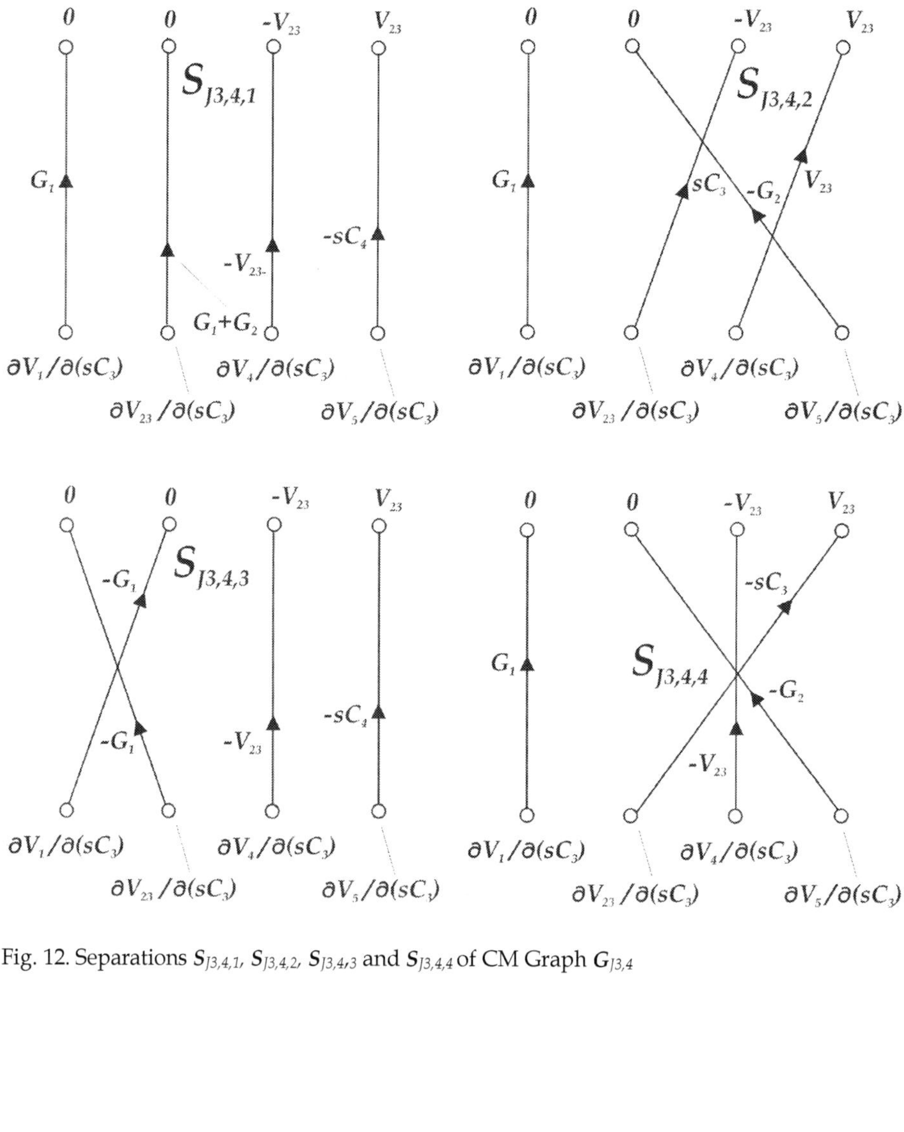

Fig. 12. Separations $S_{J3,4,1}$, $S_{J3,4,2}$, $S_{J3,4,3}$ and $S_{J3,4,4}$ of CM Graph $G_{J3,4}$

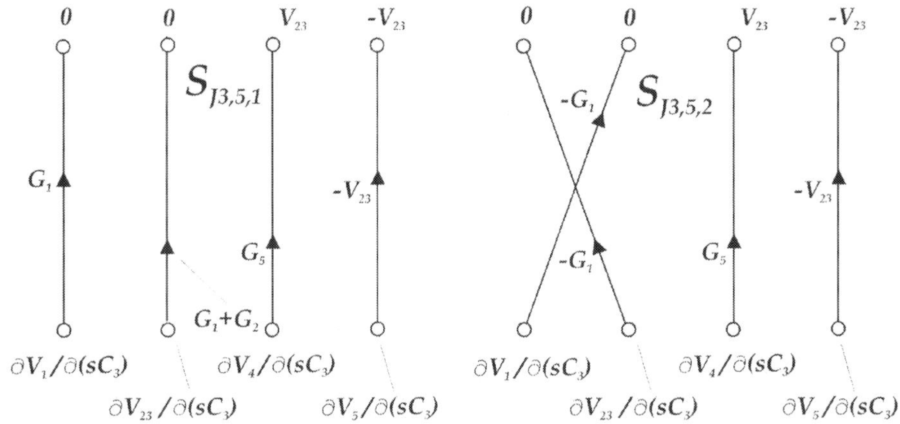

Fig. 13. Separations $S_{J3,5,1}$ *and* $S_{J3,5,2}$ of CM Graph $G_{J3,5}$

From Fig. 9 ÷ Fig. 13 it follows

$$\left.\begin{array}{l}
SP_{J3,1,1}=G_1G_2G_5V_{23};\ N_{a,J3,1,1}=4;\ Ns,_{J3,1,1}=0;\\
SP_{J3,23,1}=-G_1G_2G_5V_{23};\ N_{a,J3,23,1}=4;\ Ns,_{J3,23,1}=1;\\
SP_{J3,4,1}=G_1(G_1+G_2)sC_4V_{23};\ N_{a,J3,4,1}=4;\ Ns,_{J3,4,1}=0;\\
SP_{J3,4,2}=-G_1G_2sC_3V_{23};\ N_{a,J3,4,2}=4;\ N_{s,J3,4,2}=0;\\
SP_{J3,4,3}=G_1^2sC_4V_{23};\ N_{a,J3,4,3}=2;\ N_{s,J3,4,3}=1;\\
SP_{J3,4,4}=-G_1G_2sC_3V_{23};\ N_{a,J3,4,4}=2;\ N_{s,J3,4,4}=1;\\
SP_{J3,5,1}=G_1(G_1+G_2)C_5V_{23};\ N_{a,J3,5,1}=4;\ N_{s,J3,5,1}=0;\\
SP_{J3,5,2}=G_1^2G_5V_{23};\ N_{a,J3,5,2}=2;\ N_{s,J3,5,2}=1;
\end{array}\right\} \qquad (37)$$

Than by substituting (35) in (36) and by taking into consideration (33) from (4) and (5) we obtain the vector $\mathbf{J}_3$:

$$\mathrm{J}_3=\left[\frac{J_1C_4}{G_2s(C_3+C_4)^2}\quad\frac{J_1C_4}{G_2s(C_3+C_4)^2}\quad\frac{J_1C_4^2}{G_2G_5(C_3+C_4)^2}\quad\frac{J_1C_4}{G_2s(C_3+C_4)^2}\right]_t \qquad (38)$$

5. Hessian matrix determination

In many practical cases it is necessary and useful to find not only the first-order derivatives of a network function or variable (for example voltage V_w) among n variables with respect to some parameter (for example y_s) but their second-order derivatives with respect to the same or to an other parameter (for example y_t), too.

The matrix formed from all possible second-order derivatives of V_w with respect to the simultaneous changes of two parameters

$$\mathbf{H}_w = \begin{bmatrix} \frac{\partial^2 V_w}{\partial y_1^2} & \frac{\partial^2 V_w}{\partial y_1 \partial y_2} & \cdots & \frac{\partial^2 V_w}{\partial y_1 \partial y_n} \\ \frac{\partial^2 V_w}{\partial y_2 \partial y_1} & \frac{\partial^2 V_w}{\partial y_2^2} & \cdots & \frac{\partial^2 V_w}{\partial y_2 \partial y_n} \\ \cdot & \cdot & \cdot & \cdot \\ \frac{\partial^2 V_w}{\partial y_n \partial y_1} & \frac{\partial^2 V_w}{\partial y_n \partial y_2} & \cdots & \frac{\partial^2 V_w}{\partial y_n{}^2} \end{bmatrix} \tag{39}$$

is the Hessian matrix or briefly Hessian (Korn & Korn, 1968, Wilde, 1978). Obviously for a network one exists a variety of Hessian matrices - every one matrix corresponds to a definite network function or variable.

The results obtained in section 3. can be applied to the derivation of a Hessian matrix as it will be explained below. By differentiating the vector $\mathbf{J}_s$ in (27) with respect to the admittance y_t one obtains

$$\left.\begin{array}{l} \frac{\partial \mathbf{J}_s}{\partial y_t} = \frac{\partial^2 \mathbf{V}}{\partial y_s \partial y_t} = -\left[\frac{\partial \mathbf{Y}^{-1}}{\partial y_t} \mathbf{K}_s \mathbf{Y}^{-1} + \mathbf{Y}^{-1} \frac{\partial}{\partial y_t} \left(\mathbf{K}_s \mathbf{Y}^{-1} \right) \right] \mathbf{I}; \\ s,t \in \{1,2,...,n\}. \end{array}\right\} \tag{40}$$

Because the elements in $\mathbf{Y}$ depend linearly on the network element admittances and their derivatives with respect to the parameter y_s equal 1, -1 or 0 it holds

$$\frac{\partial \mathbf{K}_s}{\partial y_t} = 0; \forall s; \frac{\partial \mathbf{Y}}{\partial y_t} = \mathbf{K}_t \tag{41}$$

and from (40) it follows

$$\left.\begin{array}{l} \frac{\partial^2 \mathbf{V}}{\partial y_s \partial y_t} = \mathbf{Y}^{-1} \left(\mathbf{K}_t \mathbf{Y}^{-1} \mathbf{K}_s + \mathbf{K}_s \mathbf{Y}^{-1} \mathbf{K}_t \right) \mathbf{Y}^{-1} \mathbf{I} = \\ = \mathbf{Y}^{-1} \mathbf{K}_{st} \mathbf{V} = \mathbf{Y}^{-1} \mathbf{V}_{st}; \\ \mathbf{K}_{st} = \mathbf{K}_t \mathbf{Y}^{-1} \mathbf{K}_s + \mathbf{K}_s \mathbf{Y}^{-1} \mathbf{K}_t; \\ \mathbf{V}_{st} = \mathbf{K}_{st} \mathbf{V}. \end{array}\right\} \tag{42}$$

The last result compared with the formulae (27) and (28) shows that we can find the vector $\partial^2\mathbf{V}/\partial y_s \partial y_t$ in principle by using the same approach as for $\partial \mathbf{V}/\partial y_s$ in section 3.

However here we must pay attention to the obtaining of the matrix $\mathbf{K}_{st}$: In the common case the matrices $\mathbf{K}_s$ and $\mathbf{K}_t$ contain more than one nonzero element (1 or –1). Hence we can expressed each of them as a sum of no more then four addends

$$\mathbf{K}_s = \sum_a \mathbf{K}_{s,a}; \ \mathbf{K}_t = \sum_b \mathbf{K}_{t,b}; \ a,b \le 4 , \tag{43}$$

where each of the matrices $\mathbf{K}_{s,a}$ and $\mathbf{K}_{t,b}$ has only one nonzero element. Then as a result the expression of $\mathbf{K}_{st}$ in (42) is a sum of products of the kind

$$\mathbf{K}_{s,a}\mathbf{Y}^{-1}\mathbf{K}_{t,b} \text{ and } \mathbf{K}_{t,b}\mathbf{Y}^{-1}\mathbf{K}_{s,a};\ \forall a,b. \quad (44)$$

The products in (44) are square matrices with only one nonzero element which is a definite element of $\mathbf{Y}^{-1}$. Let, for example, the nonzero element for the left-side matrix in (44) is on i-th row and on j-th column and the similar element for the right-side matrix is on k-th row and on l-th column. Then it is easy to see that the corresponding product in (44) contains the element $\pm z_{u,v}$; $u, v \in \{1, 2, \ldots, n\}$ on i-th row and on l-th column, where $z_{u,v}$ is an element of $\mathbf{Y}^{-1}$. The upper (lower) sign of this element holds for equal (non equal) signs of nonzero elements of $\mathbf{K}_{s,a}$ and $\mathbf{K}_{t,b}$ in (44), respectively.

The matrix $\mathbf{Y}^{-1}$ can be evaluated by using an auxiliary CM graph $\boldsymbol{G_0}$ too. For this purpose let us consider the equation

$$\mathbf{X} = \mathbf{Y}^{-1}\mathbf{E}, \quad (45)$$

where

$$\left.\mathbf{Y}^{-1} = \begin{bmatrix} z_{11} & z_{12} & \cdot & z_{1n} \\ z_{21} & z_{22} & \cdot & z_{2n} \\ \cdot & \cdot & \cdot & \cdot \\ z_{n1} & z_{n2} & \cdot & z_{nn} \end{bmatrix};\ \mathbf{X} = \begin{bmatrix} x_1 & x_2 & \cdot & x_n \end{bmatrix}_t;\ \mathbf{E} = \begin{bmatrix} e_1 & e_2 & \cdot & e_n \end{bmatrix}_t. \right\}. \quad (46)$$

After multiplying in (45) for $\mathbf{X}$ one follows

$$\mathbf{X} = \begin{bmatrix} z_{11}e_1 + z_{12}e_2 + \ldots + z_{1n}e_n \\ z_{21}e_1 + z_{22}e_2 + \ldots + z_{2n}e_n \\ \cdot \\ z_{n1}e_1 + z_{n2}e_2 + \ldots + z_{nn}e_n \end{bmatrix}. \quad (47)$$

This means that if the CM graph $\boldsymbol{G_0}$ corresponds to (45) the multipliers of $e_1, e_2, \ldots, e_n$ for every element of $\mathbf{X}$ are elements of $\mathbf{Y}^{-1}$. Note that in real cases a limited number of the elements of $\mathbf{Y}^{-1}$ are necessary only. Hence for determination of an element of the Hessian matrix $\mathbf{H}_{st}$ we can form the following:

Rule 3:

i. Draw the CM graph $\boldsymbol{G_p}$ of the nullor network under consideration;
ii. Transform the graph $\boldsymbol{G_p}$ into the graph $\boldsymbol{G}$, according to the *Rule 1* in section 2. and compose the vectors $\mathbf{V}$ and $\mathbf{I}$;
iii. Determine the vector $\mathbf{V}$ from $\boldsymbol{G}$;
iv. Write the matrices $\mathbf{K}_s$ and $\mathbf{K}_t$;
v. Determine the matrix $\mathbf{Y}^{-1}$ by using the auxiliary CM graph $\boldsymbol{G_0}$;
vi. Determine the matrix $\mathbf{K}_{st}$;
vii. Determine the matrix $\mathbf{V}_{st}$;
viii. Draw a CM graph $\boldsymbol{G_{st}}$ in accordance with $\mathbf{V}_{st}$;
ix. Determine the elements of the vector $\partial^2\mathbf{V}/\partial y_s\partial y_t$ from $\boldsymbol{G_{st}}$.

Note that by following the above sequence we obtain $2n$ elements of n Hessian matrices simultaneously, *because* $\partial^2\mathbf{V}/\partial y_s\partial y_t = \partial^2\mathbf{V}/\partial y_t\partial y_s$ - Fig. 14.

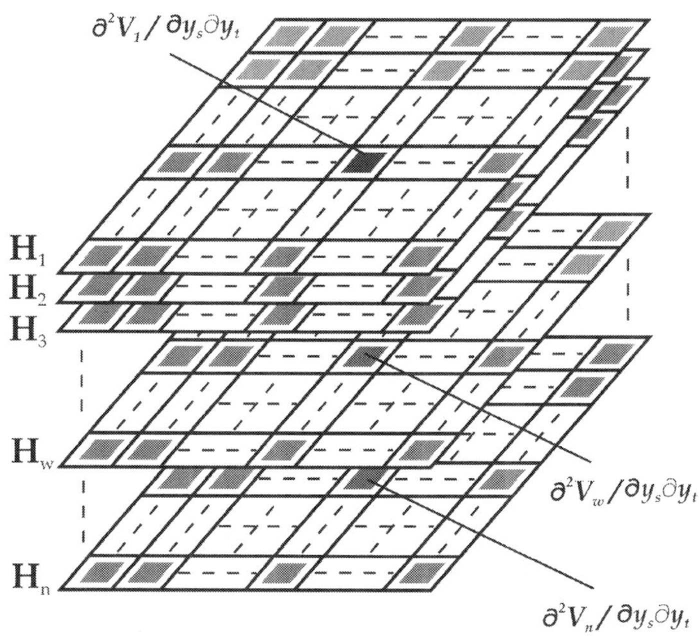

Fig. 14. A Set of n Hessian Matrices

Example B

Suppose that we want to determine the vector $\partial^2\mathbf{V}/\partial(sC_3)\partial(sC_4)$ for the network N in Fig.2. Because the items **i**, **ii** and **iii** of the ***Rule 3*** were fulfilled in the **Example A** we have to continue further: Here the matrices $\mathbf{K}_3$ and $\mathbf{K}_4$ are

$$\left.\begin{array}{l}
\mathbf{K}_{31} = \begin{bmatrix} 0 & 0 & 0 & 0 \\ 0 & 0 & 0 & 0 \\ 0 & 1 & 0 & 0 \\ 0 & 0 & 0 & 0 \end{bmatrix}; \ \mathbf{K}_{32} = \begin{bmatrix} 0 & 0 & 0 & 0 \\ 0 & 0 & 0 & 0 \\ 0 & 0 & 0 & 0 \\ 0 & -1 & 0 & 0 \end{bmatrix}; \\
\mathbf{K}_3 = \mathbf{K}_{31} + \mathbf{K}_{32}; \ \mathbf{K}_4 = \begin{bmatrix} 0 & 0 & 0 & 0 \\ 0 & 0 & 0 & 0 \\ 0 & 0 & 0 & 0 \\ 0 & 0 & 0 & -1 \end{bmatrix}
\end{array}\right\} \tag{48}$$

and from (42) ÷ (46) it follows

$$\mathbf{K}_{34} = \begin{bmatrix} 0 & 0 & 0 & 0 \\ 0 & 0 & 0 & 0 \\ 0 & 0 & 0 & -z_{24} \\ 0 & -z_{43}+z_{44} & 0 & z_{24} \end{bmatrix}. \tag{49}$$

We can find the nonzero elements of $\mathbf{K}_{34}$ by using the auxiliary CM graph $\boldsymbol{G}_0$ drawn in Fig. 15. By comparing (47) with (49) one settles we need only these addends of elements x_2 and x_4 in (47) that content the quantities e_4 and e_3, e_4, respectively. According to the Chan-Mai procedure we draw the graphs $\boldsymbol{G}_{0,2}$ and $\boldsymbol{G}_{0,4}$ - Fig. 16 and Fig. 17.

$$z_{24} = z_{44} = -\frac{1}{s(C_3 + C_4)}; z_{43} = 0. \tag{50}$$

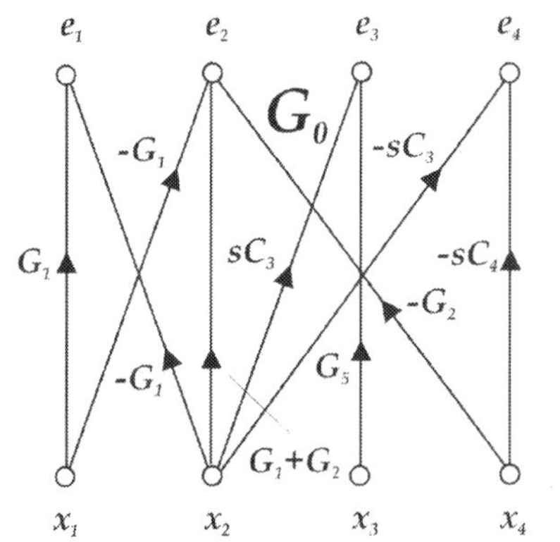

Fig. 15. The auxiliary CM graph $\boldsymbol{G}_0$

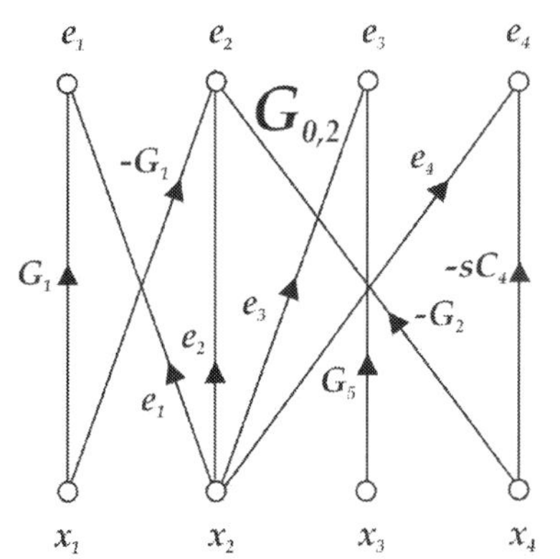

Fig. 16. The CM graph $\boldsymbol{G}_{0,2}$

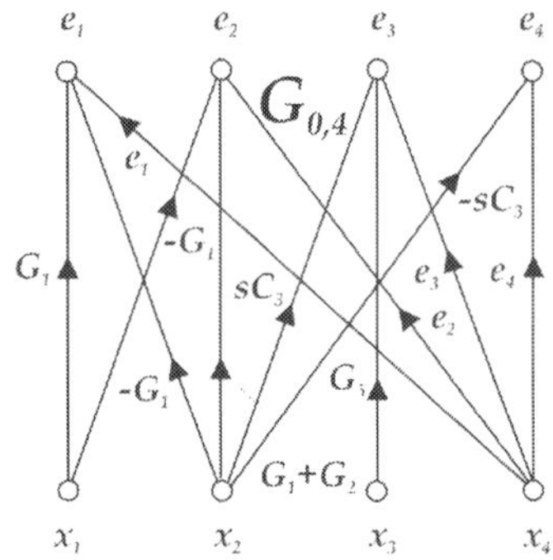

Fig. 17. The CM graph $\boldsymbol{G_{0,4}}$

From Fig. 18 ÷ Fig. 19 we obtain the products

$$\left.\begin{array}{l} SP_{0,2,1} = -G_1sC_4G_5e_2;\ N_{a,0,2,1} = 4;\ N_{s,0,2,1} = 0; \\ SP_{0,2,2} = G_1sC_4G_5e_1;\ N_{a,0,2,2} = 2;\ N_{s,0,2,2} = 1; \\ SP_{0,2,3} = -G_1G_2G_5e_4;\ N_{a,0,2,3} = 2;\ N_{s,0,2,3} = 1; \\ SP_{0,4,1} = G_1(G_1+G_2)G_5e_4;\ N_{a,0,4,1} = 4;\ N_{s,0,4,1} = 0; \\ SP_{0,4,2} = G_1^2G_5e_4;\ N_{a,0,4,2} = 2;\ N_{s,0,4,2} = 1; \\ SP_{0,4,3} = -G_1sC_3G_5e_2;\ N_{a,0,4,3} = 2;\ N_{s,0,4,3} = 1; \end{array}\right\}. \tag{51}$$

Note that with the exception of the sink and source quantities the graph $\boldsymbol{G_0}$ is isomorphic to the graph $\boldsymbol{G}$ in Fig. 4. That is why the expressions (33) remain valid for the denominator in (4) also. Than for the elements of the vector (47) from (51) and (33) it follows:

$$\left.\begin{array}{l} x_2 = \dfrac{G_1sC_4G_5e_1 + G_1sC_4G_5e_2 - G_1G_2G_5e_4}{G_1G_2G_5s(C_3+C_4)}; \\ x_4 = \dfrac{-G_1sC_3G_5e_2 - G_1G_2G_5e_4}{G_1G_2G_5s(C_3+C_4)} \end{array}\right\} \tag{52}$$

or taking into consideration (46) and (47)

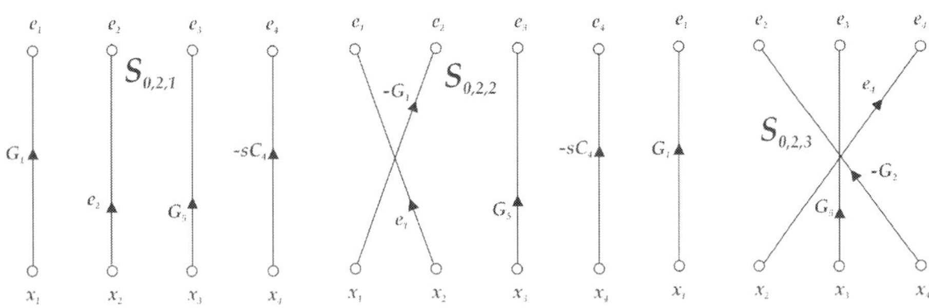

Fig. 18. Separations $\boldsymbol{S_{0,2,1}}$, $\boldsymbol{S_{0,2,2}}$ and $\boldsymbol{S_{0,2,3}}$ of CM graph $\boldsymbol{G_{0,2}}$

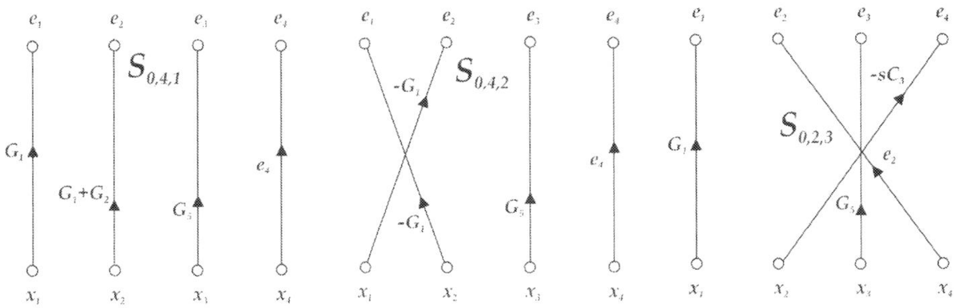

Fig. 19. Separations $S_{0,4,1}$, $S_{0,4,2}$ and $S_{0,4,3}$ of CM graph $G_{0,4}$

$$\left.z_{24} = z_{44} = -\frac{1}{s(C_3 + C_4)};\ z_{43} = 0\right\}. \tag{53}$$

Now we return to (42) and (49) and obtain

$$\left.\mathbf{K}_{34} = \begin{bmatrix} 0 & 0 & 0 & 0 \\ 0 & 0 & 0 & 0 \\ 0 & 0 & 0 & \frac{1}{s(C_3+C_4)} \\ 0 & -\frac{1}{s(C_3+C_4)} & 0 & -\frac{1}{s(C_3+C_4)} \end{bmatrix};\ \mathbf{V}_{34} = \mathbf{K}_{34}\mathbf{V} = \mathbf{K}_{34}\begin{bmatrix} V_1 \\ V_{23} \\ V_4 \\ V_5 \end{bmatrix} = \begin{bmatrix} 0 \\ 0 \\ \frac{V_5}{s(C_3+C_4)} \\ -\frac{V_{23}+V_5}{s(C_3+C_4)} \end{bmatrix}\right\}. \tag{54}$$

$$\left.\begin{aligned}
&SP_{H,34,1,1} = -G_1G_2G_5\frac{V_{23}+V_5}{s(C_3+C_4)};\ N_{a,J3,1,1} = 4;\ Ns,_{J3,1,1} = 0;\\
&SP_{H,34,23,1} = G_1G_2G_5\frac{V_{23}+V_5}{s(C_3+C_4)};\ N_{a,J3,23,1} = 4;\ Ns,_{J3,23,1} = 1;\\
&SP_{H,34,4,1} = -G_1(G_1+G_2)sC_4\frac{V_5}{s(C_3+C_4)};\ N_{a,J3,4,1} = 4;\ Ns,_{J3,4,1} = 0;\\
&SP_{H,34,4,2} = G_1G_2sC_3\frac{V_{23}+V_5}{s(C_3+C_4)};\ N_{a,J3,4,2} = 4;\ N_{s,J3,4,2} = 0;\\
&SP_{H,34,4,3} = -G_1^2sC_4\frac{V_5}{s(C_3+C_4)};\ N_{a,J3,4,3} = 2;\ N_{s,J3,4,3} = 1;\\
&SP_{H,34,4,4} = G_1G_2sC_3\frac{V_5}{s(C_3+C_4)};\ N_{a,J3,4,4} = 2;\ N_{s,J3,4,4} = 1;\\
&SP_{H,34,5,1} = -G_1(G_1+G_2)C_5\frac{V_{23}+V_5}{s(C_3+C_4)};\ N_{a,J3,5,1} = 4;\ N_{s,J3,5,1} = 0;\\
&SP_{H,34,5,2} = -G_1^2G_5\frac{V_{23}+V_5}{s(C_3+C_4)};\ N_{a,J3,5,2} = 2;\ N_{s,J3,5,2} = 1;
\end{aligned}\right\}. \tag{55}$$

In order to determine the second derivatives of the vector $\partial^2\mathbf{V}/\partial(sC_3)\partial(sC_4)$ and having in mind (42) one draws the CM graph $G_{H,34}$ shown in Fig. 20. In the case we have a simplification of the analysis on the base of the graph $G_{H,34}$ because the substantial difference between $G_{H,34}$ and G_{J3} consists in the sink and source vertex signal expressions – instead of $-V_{23}$ and V_{23} in G_{J3} the corresponding signals in $G_{H,34}$ are $V_5/s(C_3+C_4)$ and $-(V_{23}+V_5)/s(C_3+C_4)$. Owing to this peculiarity further we use directly (37) after substituting sink vertex signals, namely:

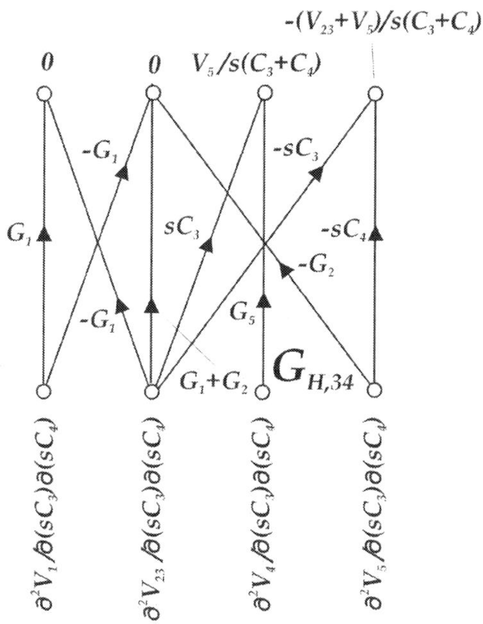

Fig. 20. CM Graph $G_{H,34}$

The voltage V_5 can be find similarly to V_{23} from CM graph **G** and it is:

$$V_5 = -\frac{C_3 J_1}{s(C_3+C_4)}. \tag{56}$$

Then by using (33), (35), (55) and (56) one obtains the vector

$$\frac{\partial^2\mathbf{V}}{\partial(sC_3)\partial(sC_4)} = \left[\frac{J_1(C_4-C_3)}{G_2 s^2(C_3+C_4)^3} \quad \frac{J_1(C_4-C_3)}{G_2 s^2(C_3+C_4)^3} \quad -2\frac{J_1 C_3 C_4}{sG_2G_5(C_3+C_4)^3} \quad \frac{J_1(C_4-C_3)}{G_2 s^2(C_3+C_4)^3}\right]_t, \tag{57}$$

Its elements are a part of elements in the Hessian matrices $\mathbf{H}_1$, $\mathbf{H}_{23}$, $\mathbf{H}_4$ and $\mathbf{H}_5$ with respect to the admittances sC_3 and sC_4.

6. First and second-order quadratic sensitivity sums

The sensitivity is an important parameter for the evaluation of practical suitability of electrical networks. For this purpose usually one uses the first-order sensitivity and the second-order sensitivity, defined by the well known formulae (Cederbaum, 1984; Chua & Lin, 1975)

$$S_x^F = \frac{\partial F}{\partial x} \cdot \frac{x}{F}; \tag{58}$$

and

$$S_{x,y}^F = \frac{\partial^2 F}{\partial x \partial y} \cdot \frac{xy}{F}, \tag{59}$$

respectively and where F is a network function or variable and x, y are changeable network element parameters.

Obviously, the derivatives in these expressions can be determined according to the above described method based on Chan-Mai signal-flow graphs. Besides very often we are interested in a global index as a quadratic sum of sensitivities (first- or second-order):

$$\sum_i (S_x^{F_i})^2 = \sum_i \left(\frac{\partial F_i}{\partial x} \cdot \frac{x}{F_i} \right)^2 \tag{60}$$

and

$$\sum_i (S_{x,y}^{F_i})^2 = \sum_i \left(\frac{\partial^2 F_i}{\partial x \partial y} \cdot \frac{xy}{F_i} \right)^2, \tag{61}$$

where i ϵ {1, 2, ..., n} .

Without loss of generality further we assume that the functions F_i are the elements of the voltage vector **V**. Then the sum (60) can be derived with the help of the expressions of the corresponding Jacobian matrix subvectors $\mathbf{J}_i$ and of the voltage vector **V**:

$$\left. \begin{aligned} &\sum_i (S_x^{V_i})^2 = x^2 \mathbf{J}_{i,t} (\mathbf{M}^{-1})^2 \mathbf{J}_i; \\ &\mathbf{M} = diag\{V_1, V_2, ..., V_i, ..., V_n\} \end{aligned} \right\}. \tag{62}$$

If from the elements of the Hessian matrices $\mathbf{H}_i$ one forms the vector

$$\mathbf{h}_{xy} = \begin{bmatrix} h_{1,xy} & h_{2,xy} & \cdots & h_{i,xy} & \cdots & h_{n,xy} \end{bmatrix}_t ; \; h_{i,xy} = \frac{\partial^2 V_i}{\partial x \partial y} \tag{63}$$

the sum (61) can be rewritten as

$$\sum_i (S_{xy}^{V_i})^2 = x^2 y^2 \mathbf{h}_{i,t} (\mathbf{M}^{-1})^2 \mathbf{h}_i \,. \tag{64}$$

7. Conclusions

A topological method for obtaining the Jacobian and Hessian matrices and their use for quadratic first- or second-order sensitivity sums calculation of active networks is presented. It is based on the replacement of the investigated network N by using a nullor equivalent circuit and on the representation of the circuit passive part N_p by a Chan-Mai signal-flow graph G_p. The Jacobian and the Hessian matrix elements of the nullor network can be obtained by means of the some dependent variables of some Chan-Mai graphs derived from G. The substantial advantage of the method consists in the use mainly of isomorphic graphs. Two examples illustrate the proposed method.

8. Acknowledgement

The author would like to thank Higher School of Transport "Todor Kableshkov", Sofia, Bulgaria for the financial support for the publishing this work.

9. References

Cederbaum, I. (1984). "Some Applications of Graph Theory to Network Analysis and Synthesis", *IEEE Tr. on Circuits and Systems,* vol. CAS-31, 1, 1984, pp. 64-68

Chan, S.P., Mai, H.N. (1967). "A Flow-Graph Method for the Analysis of Linear Systems", *IEEE Tr. on Circuit Theory*, 9, 1967, pp. 350-354

Chua, L.O., Lin, P.-M. (1975). *"Computer-Aided Analysis of Electronic Circuits"*, Prentice-Hall Inc. Englewood Clifs, New Jersey, 1975

Davies, A. C. (1966). "Matrix Analysis of Network Containing Nullators and Norators", *Electronics Letters*, vol. 2, ,2, 1966, pp. 48 -49

Donevsky, B.D., Nenov,G.A. (1979). *"Application of Graphs for the Analysis and Synthesis of Electronic Circuits"*, "Technica", Sofia, 1979 (in Bulgarian)

Korn, G., A., Korn, T.M. (1968). *"Mathematical Handbook"*, Mc Graw-Hill Co. New York. 1968

Nenov, G. A. (2004). "Evaluation of Nullor Nertwork Jacobian Matrix by using Chan-Mai Signal-Flow Graphs", *Proceedings of the SMACD'04*, Wroclaw, 2004, Poland, pp. 79-82

Wilde, D.J. (1978). *"Globally Optimal Design"*, John Wiley & Sons, New York, 1978

12

Application of the Graph Theory in Managing Power Flows in Future Electric Networks

P. H. Nguyen[1], W. L. Kling[1], G. Georgiadis[2],
M. Papatriantafilou[2], L. A. Tuan[2] and L. Bertling[2]
[1]*Eindhoven University of Technology,*
[2]*Chalmers University of Technology,*
[1]*The Netherlands*
[2]*Sweden*

1. Introduction

Electrical power system is one of the largest and most crucial engineering systems which spreads everywhere in countries to supply electricity for hundreds of millions of consumers from hundreds of thousands of producers. In its more than one century history, the development of the power system proceeded through evolutional stages from local isolated networks with small-scale load and generation to large interconnected networks with myriads of consumers vertically fed by centralized generation, such as coal, hydro, or nuclear power plants. System stability and reliability have been continuously improved along this development of the power systems.

Nowadays, the society not only demands a high level of reliability of electricity supply but also concerns with the environmental impacts from the electrical power system. To achieve a reliable and sustainable electricity supply, there is an increasing need to use energy from renewable sources such as wind, solar, or biomass. The development of many intermittent and inverter-connected Renewable Energy Sources (RES) will require having new ways of planning, operating, and managing the entire process. In other words, the power system is moving into a new development era.

Due to the expected large-scale deployment of distributed generation (DG), the electrical power system is changing gradually from a vertically controlled and operated structure to a horizontally one. Fig. 1 illustrates one of the expected changes in the power system with the large penetration of DG. The integration of RES related to both large-scale production (e.g., wind and solar farms) and massively distributed production (e.g., micro combined heat and power plants and photovoltaic systems at residential and tertiary buildings) causes a number of challenges in fluctuating/unpredictable and bidirectional power flows in distribution networks. Future electrical power systems must be able to manage these bidirectional power flows, and has to deal with the uncertainties of renewable power generation. Power flow management will be needed in order to cope with these challenges.

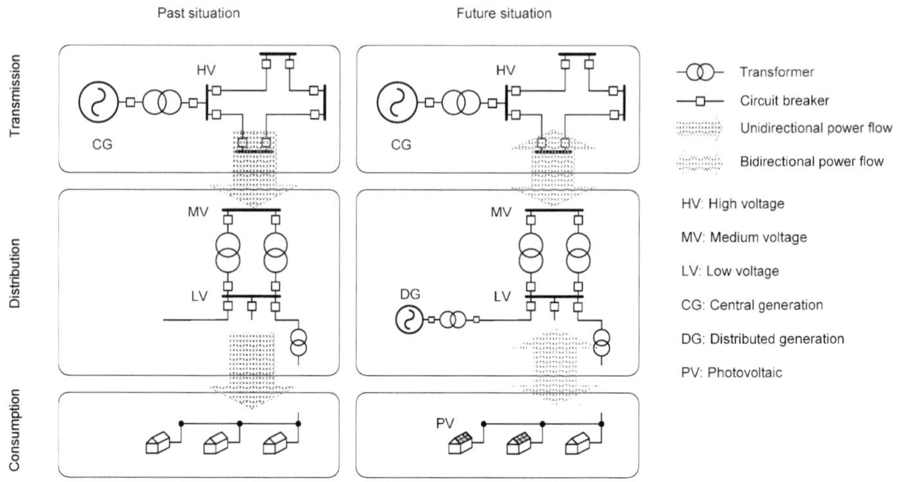

Fig. 1. Past and future situation of the power system

In this chapter, applications of the graph theory to handle the function of power flow management will be introduced. Detail descriptions of these methods can be found in (Nguyen et al., 2010(a); Nguyen et al., 2010(b)).

2. Power flow management

The use of the Optimal Power Flow (OPF) framework is a common practice for managing power flow within the electric transmission network, where the algorithm is centralized and deployed at the economic dispatch stage (Huneault & Galiana, 1991). The mathematical model of the OPF problem can be presented as follows:

$$\text{Minimize } f(x,u) \tag{1}$$

subject to:

$$g(x,u) = 0 \tag{2}$$

$$h(x,u) \leq 0 \tag{3}$$

where $f(x,u)$ is the objective function that can be formulated to represent different operational goals, e.g., minimization of total power production cost or total power loss. The vector of independent variables u represents the state of the system, i.e., the phase angles and voltage magnitudes. The vector of dependent variables x represents the control variables, for example, power generations or tap ratios of On-Load Tap Changer (OLTC) of transformers. The equality constraint represents the power balance between supply and demand while the inequality constraint shows the operational limits of the network components.

The OPF requires a large-scale control overview of the whole network that is difficult to implement in the future situation with high penetrations of DG units. Although some distributed OPF techniques have been proposed, they need complex input information and take relatively long processing times (Kim & Baldick, 2000). Along with OPF, stability constraints and congestion problems can implicitly be investigated (Gan et al., 2000; Bompard et al., 2003). However, those procedures are most suitable for the transmission networks which have a limited number of network components, e.g., generators, transmission lines, and substations.

Since the electric networks of the future are expected to include numerous DGs dispersed over wide areas, other solutions for power flow management must be founded. A price-based control method, which can also be considered as a distributed OPF solution, has been proposed for systems with high level of DG penetration (Jokic, 2007). By converting the power system parameters into desired market signals, the solution yields nodal prices for generators that help to mitigate the network congestion problem and also contribute to other so called ancillary services. This can be presented in a mathematical model as follows:

$$\text{Minimize } \sum_{i=1}^{n} f(P_i, P_i^{ex}, A_i, A_i^{ex}) \quad (4)$$

subject to:

$$P_i - P_i^{ex} - P_i^{load} = 0 \quad (5)$$

$$A_i - A_i^{ex} - A_i^{req} \geq 0 \quad (6)$$

$$g(P_i, A_i) \leq 0 \quad (7)$$

where $f(P_i, P_i^{ex}, A_i, A_i^{ex})$ is the aggregated cost function of an autonoumous network part i; P_i and A_i are the generated power and the provided ancillary service respectively in the network i, and P_i^{ex} and A_i^{ex} present the generation and services coming from outside of the network i; the equality constraint represents for power balance; the upper bound condition denotes requirements of ancillary services while the lower bound condition shows the operational limits of network components.

The method, however, concerns only the supply and demand of the system in which actors can be influenced by price signals. Other controllable devices of the system, e.g., electronic-based power flow controllers, are not considered. In (Dolan et al., 2009), the power flow management is represented as constraint satisfaction. Algorithms in that research determine the level of DG curtailment because of loading constraints in a small test network. Based on a local information network, a distributed two-level control scheme was proposed to adjust power output from clusters of photovoltaic (PV) generators when disturbances occur (Xin et al., 2011).

3. Power routing – A new way for power flow management

The function of distributed power routing is to fully exploit the potential of the local resources in managing the power flow. The function deals with transport optimization related to the actual load and generation schedules of the market parties. Price signals yielded by the market clearing conditions can be used as an input for the routing algorithms to achieve certain operational objectives, e.g., relief of network congestion, maximization of the reliability of the network, minimization of losses and if desired minimization of the production cost and maximization of serving high-priority customers.

In this section, the function of distributed power routing is proposed for the future electric network as a new way to manage power flows. Basically, the function of power routing is the same as the optimization of the power flow which can be formulated in a mathematical model as follows:

$$\text{Minimize } \mathcal{F} = \sum_{i\in\mathcal{G}}(\omega_{Gi}^{+}\Delta P_{Gi}^{+} + \omega_{Gi}^{-}\Delta P_{Gi}^{-}) + \sum_{(i,j)\in\mathcal{T}}(\omega_{Tij}^{+}\Delta P_{Tij}^{+} + \omega_{Tij}^{-}\Delta P_{Tij}^{-}) + \sum_{k\in\mathcal{D}}(\omega_{Dk}^{+}\Delta P_{Dk}^{+} + \omega_{Dk}^{-}\Delta P_{Dk}^{-}) \quad (8)$$

subject to:

$$\sum_{i\in\mathcal{G}} P_{Gi} = \sum_{(i,j)\in\mathcal{T}} P_{Tij} + \sum_{k\in\mathcal{D}} P_{Dk} \quad (9)$$

$$P_{Gi}^{min} \le P_{Gi} \le P_{Gi}^{max}, \quad \forall i \in \mathcal{G} \quad (10)$$

$$|P_{Tij}| \le P_{Tij}^{max}, \quad \forall(i,j) \in \mathcal{T} \quad (11)$$

$$|P_{Tij}| \pounds P_{Tij}^{max}, \quad "(i,j)\hat{I}T \quad (12)$$

where

$$P_{Gi} = P_{Gi}^{0} + \Delta P_{Gi}^{+} - \Delta P_{Gi}^{-}, \quad \forall i \in \mathcal{G} \quad (13)$$

$$P_{Tij} = P_{Tij}^{0} + \Delta P_{Tij}^{+} - \Delta P_{Tij}^{-}, \quad \forall(i,j) \in \mathcal{T} \quad (14)$$

$$P_{Dk} = P_{Dk}^{0} + \Delta P_{Dk}^{+} - \Delta P_{Dk}^{-}, \quad \forall k \in \mathcal{D} \quad (15)$$

The objective function (8) is the total cost for re-routing power when a disturbance occurs in the system. As the power routing function might change power generation at each bus i (ΔP_{Gi}^{+}, ΔP_{Gi}^{-}), power flow through each network device i-j (ΔP_{Tij}^{+}, ΔP_{Tij}^{-}), and demand at each bus k (ΔP_{Dk}^{+}, ΔP_{Dk}^{-}) different from the original market clearing conditions (P_{Gi}^{0}, P_{Tij}^{0}, P_{Dk}^{0}), the objective function takes these representative costs into account. Due to the fact that most of the renewable generation can participate only in down regulation (with cost ω_{Gi}^{-}), integration of storage devices becomes important to give the power routing function flexibility in up regulation (with cost ω_{Gi}^{+}) of generation. Power flow change on network devices influences the total power losses and reliability of the system. However, the associated transmission costs ($\omega_{Tij}^{+}, \omega_{Tij}^{-}$) as considered to be low compared to the other costs. Since the demand side becomes more active with mechanisms of Demand Side Management (DSM) and Demand Response (DR), its potential in regulating demand up (with cost ω_{Dk}^{+}) and down (with cost ω_{Dk}^{-}) are considered in the objective function.

The power balance condition is represented in the equality constraint (9). The inequality constraints in (10) and (11) show the generation and consumption boundaries. The transmitted power needs to be within the device's thermal limits in the inequality constraint (12). This optimization model assumes that voltage is autonomously controlled and reactive power is not considered in the formulation.

4. Graph-based algorithms

Graph theory has been utilized in some power system applications, such as wholesale cross-border trading by using a shortest path algorithm (Wei et al., 2001), and achieving maximum power transmission with FACTS devices (Armbruster et al., 2005). This section will focus on solving minimum cost flow problem by using successive shortest path and scaling cost-relabel algorithm.

The power system, firstly, is converted to a graph $G(V,E)$, where V represents the set of vertices (buses in the network) and E represents arcs (interconnection lines among buses in the network). The arc length (arc cost) c_{ij} and residual (available) capacity r_{ij} associated with each arc (i, j) are derived from the transmission costs $(\omega_{Tij}^{+}, \omega_{Tij}^{-})$ and the transmission line capacity P_{Tij}^{max}. Two additional vertices are then added to trigger algorithms: a virtual source node s and a sink node t. For each bus i with generation, a pair of arcs is connected to the source node s with residual capacities equivalent to generation capacities $(P_{Gi}^{max}, P_{Gi}^{min})$ and arc costs equivalent to generation costs $(\omega_{Gi}^{+}, \omega_{Gi}^{-})$. For each bus k with load demand, a pair of arcs is connected to the sink node t with residual capacities equivalent to the bounds of power demand $(P_{Dk}^{max}, P_{Dk}^{min})$ and arc costs equivalent to demand costs $(\omega_{Dk}^{+}, \omega_{Dk}^{-})$.

Fig. 2 shows an example of a 3-bus system and its representative directed graph. It is assumed in this example that there is no difference between costs for up and down power regulation and flow. Values of parameters of the system are given in table 1.

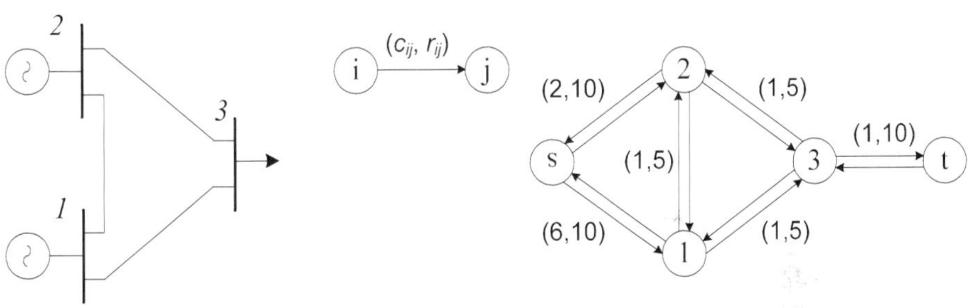

Fig. 2. Single-line diagram and representative directed graph of the 3-bus k network

Components	Cost [p.u.]	Capacity [MW]
Generator at bus 1	$\omega_{G1}^{+} = \omega_{G1}^{-} = 6$	$P_{G1}^{max} = 10;\ P_{G1}^{min} = 0$
Generator at bus 2	$\omega_{G1}^{+} = \omega_{G1}^{-} = 2$	$P_{G2}^{max} = 10;\ P_{G2}^{min} = 0$
Load at bus 3	$\omega_{D3}^{+} = \omega_{D3}^{-} = 1$	$P_{D3}^{max} = P_{D3}^{min} = 10$
Transmission lines	$\omega_{Tij}^{+} = \omega_{Tji}^{-} = 1$	$P_{Tij}^{max} = 5$

Table 1. Data for the 3-bus test network

By representing the electric network as a directed graph, the function of power flow management can be considered as a minimum cost flow problem. In this chapter, the Successive Shortest Path (SSP) and the Scaling Push-Relabel (SPR) algorithm are used to solve the minimum cost flow.

4.1 Successive Shortest Path algorithm

Successive Shortest Path (SSP) is one of the basic algorithms to deal with the minimum cost flow problem in graph theory. The algorithm starts by searching for the shortest path to augment the flow from the source node *s* to the sink node *t*. A node potential, $(\pi_j \geq \pi_i - c_{ij};\ \forall(i,j) \in E)$, associated with each node and a reduced cost, $(c_{ij}^{\pi} = c_{ij} - \pi_i + \pi_j)$, associated with each arc (*i*, *j*) are used to find the shortest path. After augmenting the flow and updating the information, the process is repeated until there is no possible path anymore from *s* to *t*.

Regarding the above example of the 3-bus network, SSP initially finds the shortest path to be *s*-2-3-*t*, as shown in Fig. 3. The flow along this shortest path is augmented until the rated capacity of arc 2-3 (5 MW) is reached. When the information is updated, the algorithm searches again for a new shortest path *s*-2-1-*t*.

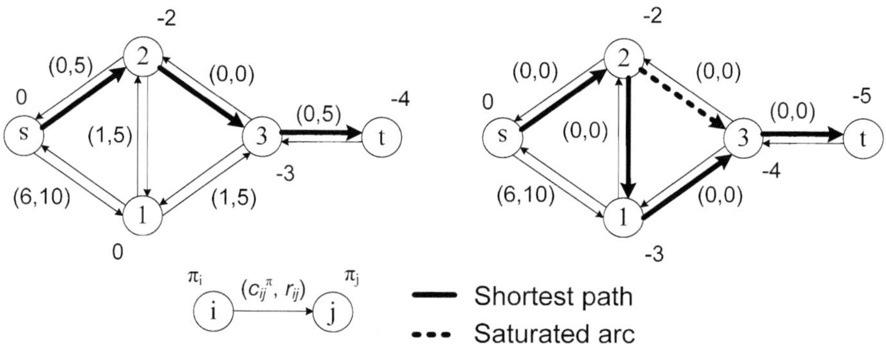

Fig. 3. Illustration of the successive shortest path algorithm for the 3-bus network

4.2 Scaling Push-Relabel algorithm

Scaling Push-Relabel (SPR) belongs to the set of the polynomial-time algorithms to solve the minimum cost flow problem in complex networks. It is different from capacity scaling which is a scaled version of the SSP algorithm.

The algorithm includes two main processes: cost scaling and push-relabel. The cost scaling step determines a boundary for the ε-optimal condition in which the scaling factor ε is initially set at the maximum cost of the graph. The boundary will gradually approach the optimal solution by scaling $\varepsilon \leftarrow \varepsilon/2$ after each iterative loop. Within the procedure of cost scaling, the push-relabel step is used. This step aims to push as much excess flow *e* as possible from a higher node to a lower node. The height of each node is computed from the node potential π_i. Since there is an excess in node *i* $(e_i > 0)$ while it is lower than its neighbors, the node will be relabeled $(\pi_i = \pi_i + \varepsilon/2)$ to be higher than at least one neighbor node to push the excess.

In Fig. 4, the push-relabel procedure is illustrated by displaying the first steps of the SPR algorithm in the above example of the 3-bus network. As the source node *s* is the first active node, it will be relabelled before it pushes flows down to node 1 and 2. When there is no excess at node s anymore, node 2 as the next active node initiates the push-relabel procedure. However, it needs to be relabeled to be higher than at least one neighbor. After relabeling, node 2 can push flow to nodes 1 and 3. A similar step occurs at node 1.

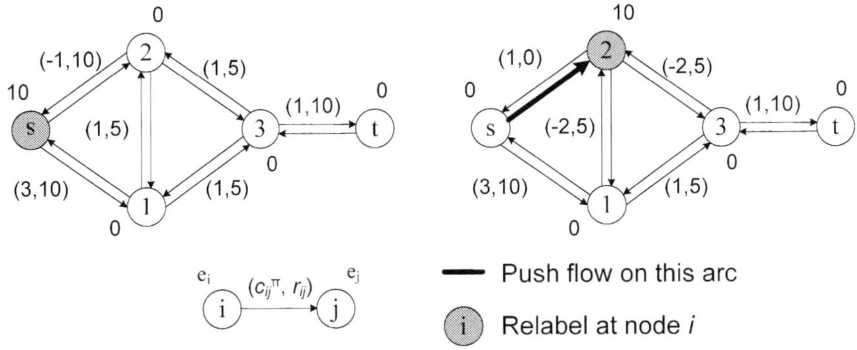

Fig. 4. Illustration of the push-relabel procedure for the 3-bus network

4.2.1 Decentralized and self-healing extensions of SPR

This section presents an extension of the SPR algorithm. In particular, we show that it is possible to implement the SPR method in a distributed way by using only local information and coordination (in contrast to the widely used centralized methods). This property of the algorithm has the additional benefit of allowing the grid operation to recover/react autonomously and faster from changes in demand/supply, cost or capacity. Note that the implementation used in the remaining of this chapter has certain centralized characteristics, since it was used for the comparison between SPR and SSP.

The SPR algorithm described above consists of two main phases: an initial phase to calculate feasible flows and a subsequent phase to convert the initial flow into a minimum cost flow (refinements). It is identified in (Goldberg & Tarjan, 1988) a variety of methods (centralized, parallel or distributed) which can be used in these two phases. Specifically for the refinement phase, a completely distributed Goldberg Tarjan (DGT) scheme that uses the concept of blocking flows and travelling atoms has been developed in (Goldberg & Tarjan, 1989). A flow is called blocking when every path from source to destination contains at least one saturated arc, while an atom at some point in time is defined as a maximal quantity of excess that has travelled as a whole up to that point. The DGT refinement scheme starts with an initialization phase, where the arcs leaving the source are saturated with atoms, and pushes atoms forward until no more pushes are possible.

Lemma 1: The DGT refinement scheme converges under the presence of changes in demand/supply of nodes or capacity of arcs, within $O(n)$ steps after the last change occurs.

Proof: Changes in the demand/supply of nodes affects the initial saturation of the outgoing arcs of the source and load content of nodes, and as a result more atoms are being created at the source or fewer atoms are being accepted at the destination. In the first case, the new atoms are being propagated forward and the algorithm proceeds normally. In the second case, the nodes at the destination become blocked and some atoms are being returned backwards, again resuming the normal operation of the algorithm. In addition, changes in the capacity of arcs affect their residual capacities. As a result, increased (decreased) residual capacity in an arc may unblock (block) the end-node closer to the source. In both cases, the algorithm resumes its normal course, sending atoms forward or backward accordingly.

Since the normal operation of the DGT algorithm is resumed after the last change, in the worst case it will terminate in the same number of steps, which is $O(\mathrm{n})$ for the distributed case.

Using the above refinement scheme along with a distributed maximum flow (DMF) algorithm that can tolerate changes in node demand/supply and arc capacities as proposed in (Ghosh et al., 1995) for the initial phase, it is easy to see that the resulting algorithm has certain self-healing properties since it can tolerate these changes.

Theorem 1: Consider a minimum cost flow algorithm that consists of an initial phase of a feasible flow calculation using the DMF algorithm and subsequent refinement phases using the DGT algorithm. This algorithm can be implemented in a completely distributed way and can converge under the presence of changes in demand/supply of nodes or capacity of arcs, within a certain number of steps after the last change occurs.

Note that the initial and refinement phases must be separated in order to tolerate changes, thus some form of synchronization between nodes is required. This is discussed in (Goldberg & Tarjan, 1988) since it is also a challenge for the original algorithm, and the proposed termination conditions there can also be applied here. Note also that the amount of steps needed for the algorithm to converge under the presence of changes depends on the implementation of this synchronization.

4.3 Complexity of the algorithms

Though the SSP algorithm is straightforward to be implemented, its computational complexity is $O(n^2 mB)$ (Ahuja et al., 1993), where n is the number of the network nodes, m is the number of network arcs and B is the upper bound on the largest supply (demand) of any node. In the worst case, each augmentation phase carries a very small amount of flow, resulting in a fairly large number of iterations. A modification of the scaling algorithm can reduce the number of iterations to $O(m\, log\, B)$.

The SPR algorithm can be implemented in a variety of methods (centralized, parallel or distributed) for both the initial and subsequent refinement phases. The scheme followed in this chapter for both phases is distributed with centralized characteristics, i.e., all active nodes are kept in set S, which is passed from node to node and controls the activation sequence. This corresponds to a sequential variant of the algorithm, which yields $O(n^2 m\, log\, nC)$ convergence time, where C is the maximum cost of an arc (Ahuja et al., 1993). However, other distributed variants are also possible, and the previously mentioned refinement scheme based on blocking flows and travelling atoms achieves $O(n^2\, log\, n\, min\{log\, n\, C, m\, log\, n\})$ total convergence time (Goldberg & Tarjan, 1988).

5. Agent-based implementation

For the power routing function it is important to implement the graph-based algorithms in a distributed environment. This section introduces Multi-Agent System (MAS) as a suitable platform for that because it can facilitate distributed control and perform monitoring functions in the power system.

5.1 Multi-agent system technology

Agent-oriented programming is a relatively new technique to implement artificial intelligence into distributed system operation (Ahuja et al., 1993). An agent can be created by a short program (software entity) to operate autonomously with its environment. Moreover, the agent can interact with each other to form a Multi-Agent System. With characteristics of reactivity, proactiveness, and social ability, the MAS technology can offer numerous benefits in distributed power networks.

Actually, a part of the agent's features has been revealed in some applications of the power system before. As an example, an Intelligent Electronic Device (IED) performs various control and protection functions according to changes in their environment, e.g., voltage drop and current increase. Recently, applications of MAS in power systems have been explored in many aspects such as disturbance diagnosis, restoration, protection, and power flow and voltage control. Several research projects have begun to investigate MAS as an approach to manage distributed generation, virtual power plants and micro grids.

5.2 Algorithm implementation

To utilize the discussed graph-based algorithms in the power routing function, it is assumed that agents are available representing nodes (buses) of an active distribution network (ADN). Each agent A_i can obtain current state variables of bus i from the power network such as power flow in incoming (outgoing) feeders P_{Tij}^0 with $\forall(i,j) \in \mathcal{T}$, power generation P_{Gi}^0, and load demand P_{Dk}^0. The limits of power generation, transport, and load demands can be pre-defined or updated during a communication period of A_i. In addition, A_i is provided with information about the costs for adjusting power production $(\omega_{Gi}^+, \omega_{Gi}^-)$, consumption $(\omega_{Dk}^+, \omega_{Dk}^-)$ as well as transmission costs $(\omega_{Tij}^+, \omega_{Tij}^-)$. Besides managing autonomous control actions, A_i can route messages to communicate with same-level agents via the MAS platform. Two additional agents, A_s and A_t, are created to represent the source node s and the sink node t of the graph $G(V,E)$ respectively. By using the MAS platform, the SSP and SPR algorithms can be implemented in a distributed environment.

5.2.1 Implementation of the SSP algorithm

Fig. 5 illustrates a simplified agent sequence diagram for the above example of the 3-bus network using the SSP algorithm. There are three main types of actions, which are defined for each agent as follows:

- Update information: Node agents (A_1, A_2, and A_3) update information from the power network and market conditions. By using *Information()* messages, they share the information with agents A_s and A_t.

- Update node potential: After updating information, A_s initiates to an update of the node potential. A message of *Get_label()* is sent to its neighbors (A_1, A_2). When receiving the *Get_label()* command, a node agent compares the proposal with its node potential to get the cheapest (smallest) one and its predecessor. The shortest path is determined when A_t updates its node potential.
- Augmentation: A_t starts augmenting flow along the new shortest path. An *Augment_flow()* message is sent from node agent to its predecessor which is to track back the shortest path. When A_s receives the message, it begins looking for a new shortest path by repeating the above action of updating node potentials.

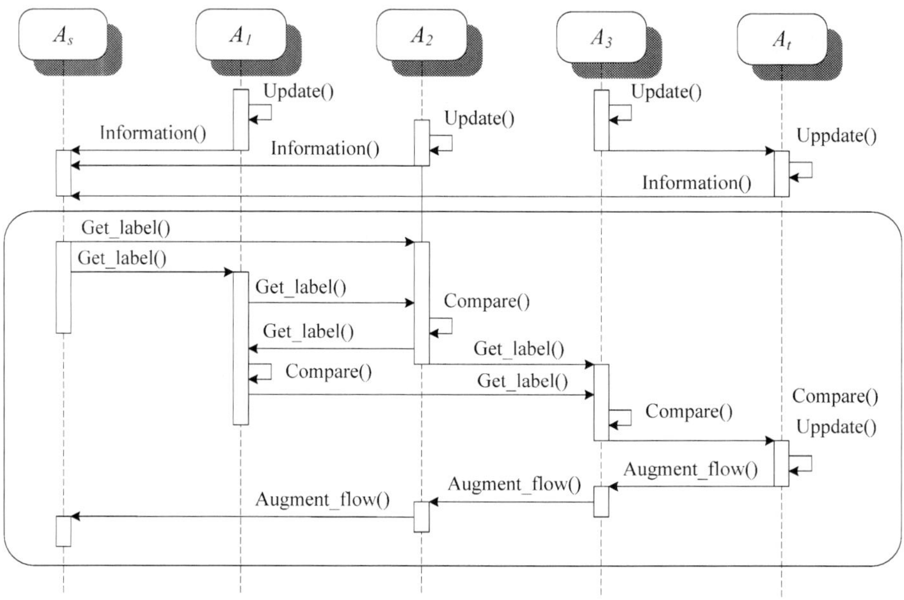

Fig. 5. A simplified agent sequence diagram for deploying the SSP algorithm

5.2.2 Implementation of the SPR algorithm

A simplified agent sequence diagram for deploying the SPR algorithm is shown in Fig. 6. Main types of actions for each agent are described as follows:

- Update information: The procedure is similar to the case of the SSP algorithm. A slight difference is the information that A_s uses for initiating the SPR algorithm. It is the total generated power instead of total load demand, as in the SSP algorithm.
- Cost scaling: The scaling factor ε is initial set by the maximum value of the costs updated from the power network. When the function *Cost_Scaling()* is called, it transformers ε-optimal flow into a $^1/_2\,\epsilon$-optimal flow.
- Relabel node potential: The relabel phase is called by each agent when it has flow excess and its height is lower than its neighbors. The function adds a value of $^1/_2\,\epsilon$ to the height.

- Push flow: When the node agent finds a feasible neighbor in which to push flow, it increases as much as possible the power with respect to its flow excess and the connecting arc's residual capacity.

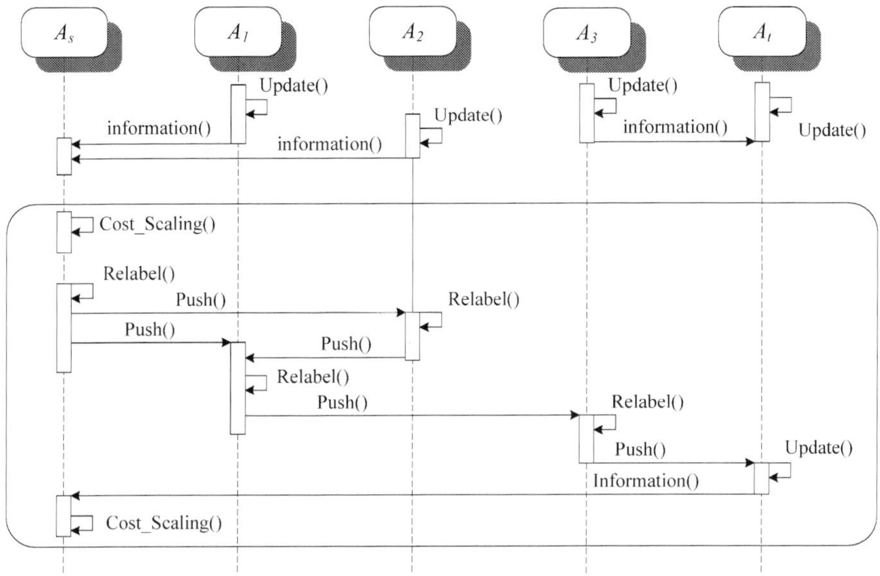

Fig. 6. A simplified agent sequence diagram for deploying the SPR algorithm

6. Simulation results and discussions

This section investigates the performance of the power routing function of the two algorithms in the simulation cases. The power network is simulated in MATLAB/Simulink environment while Java Agent Development Framework (JADE) (Telecom Italia S.p.A., 2010) is used for creating a Multi-Agent System (MAS) platform. The protocol for communication between two environments is based on client/server socket communication.

6.1 Typical radial distribution network

A simulation example is implemented to investigate the performances of the algorithms on a typical radial medium voltage (MV) network. This test network includes two feeders with 10 buses on each feeder, connected to the same substation. The two ends of the feeders can be connected through a normally open point (NOP). Parameters of the test network are given as follows:

- Line section: π-equivalent circuit, line section parameters: $Z = 0.25 + j0.178\,\Omega$; $B = 1\mu S$; $P_{Tij}^{max} = 10$ MW.
- Base load: Each bus has a base load of 1 MW + $j0.48$ MVAr.
- Distributed generation: DG units are available at bus 1, 3, and 5 of feeder 1 and 16, 18, and 20 of feeder 2.

Fig. 7 shows a single-line diagram and the representative directed graph of the radial test network. In the representative graph, the square symbols show nodes having DG units which are connected to the virtual source node *s*. The remaining nodes have only load demand.

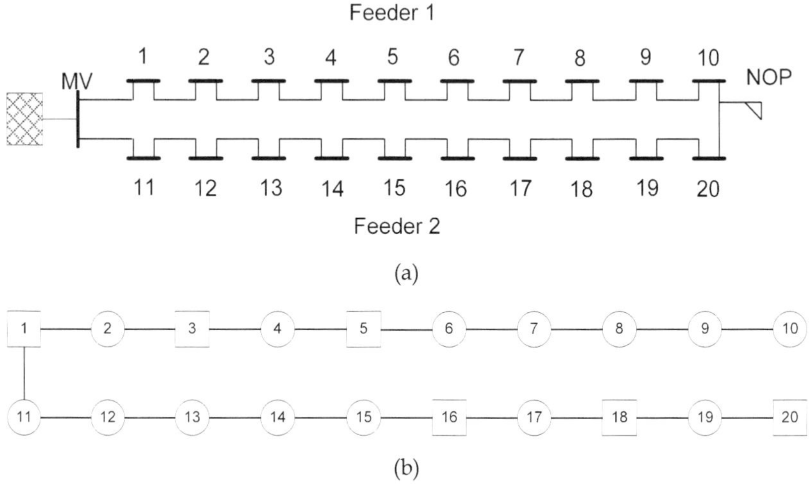

Fig. 7. Single-line diagram and representative directed graph of the radial test network

6.1.1 Case 1 - Update information and start up algorithms

The simulation starts with an initial state as shown in table 2. The three DG units of feeder 1 provide more power than the ones connected to feeder 2, but with higher marginal costs.

Generator	$\omega_{Gi}^{+} = \omega_{Gi}^{-}$ [p.u.]	P_{Gi}^{0} [MW]	P_{Gi}^{min} [MW]	P_{Gi}^{max} [MW]
1	15	11	0	15
3	11	3	0	10
5	9	3	0	10
16	5	2	0	3
18	5	2	0	3
20	5	2	0	3

Table 2. Initial state of the radial test network

At $t = 5\,s$, each agent starts collecting and sharing information across the MAS platform. At $t = 10\,s$, new reference values are set for the DG units. The goal in this case is to minimize generation cost. Fig. 8 shows the behaviour of the DG units before and after receiving new set points from MAS using the SPR algorithm. In this case, P_{gen2} and P_{gen3} increases from 3 MW to 4 MW and 10 MW respectively, while the other generators of feeder 2 increases from 2 MW to 3 MW. These controls are implemented to avoid the most expensive generation from bus 1 (P_{gen1} = 0 MW).

The total saving cost in money-based unit before and after utilizing the power routing function is also shown in Fig. 8. A major part of the total cost (76.97 p.u.) is saved from changes of power generation mentioned above while the contribution from the power transmission on the total cost is 4.02 p.u.

The SSP algorithm gives almost the same results as the SPR algorithm. Minor differences are the set points for P_{gen2} set to 4.3 MW and P_{gen3} set to 9.7 MW. These come from the fact that SSP is based on the total load demand which is smaller than the total generation capacity used in the SPR algorithm.

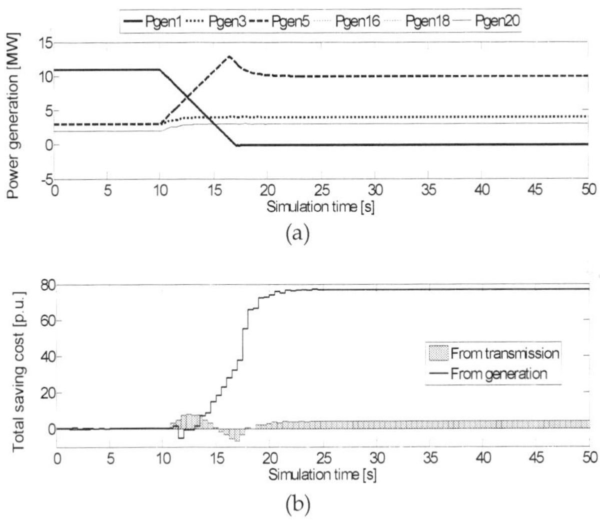

Fig. 8. Case of optimal generation dispatch for the radial test network using the SPR algorithm

6.1.2 Case 2 – Load demand increases

After settling at this new optimal operation mode, the simulation is continued by increasing the demand by 2 MW + j0.2 MVAr at bus 2, 4, 17, and 19. Fig. 9 shows the dynamic operations of the test network. At t = 1s, the load demand increases 20%. It is assumed that the generator at bus 1 will be responsible for the primary control to compensate initially for the amount of load increase. After receiving information from the power network at t = 15 s, MAS gives back the new set points at t = 30 s. Because of the increase in demand, all generators at bus 3, 5, 16, 18, and 20 operate at their maximum capacities while the generator at bus 1 is set to 2 MW.

In this case, the total saving cost is referred to the cost value before applying the power routing function, in period from 25 s to 30 s. Therefore, the prior state of the system with lower load demand has a lower operating cost (with high total saving cost, 120 p.u.). This saving cost starts decreasing when the primary control of the generator at bus 1 imitates.

After $t = 30\ s$, the change of power generation contributes to decreasing the total cost 23.85 p.u. Meanwhile, the charge for the power transmission increases 4.42 p.u.

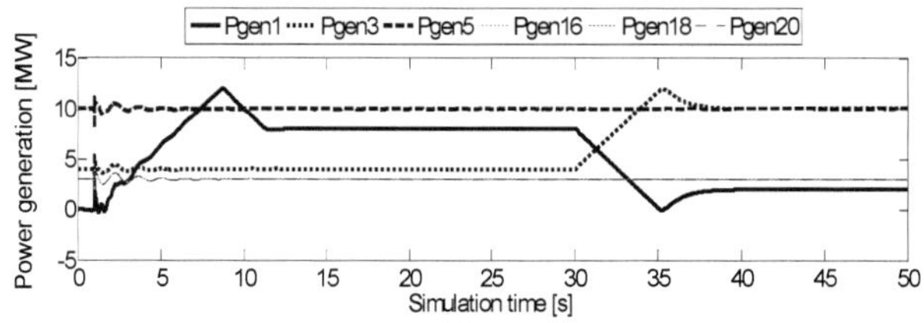

(a)

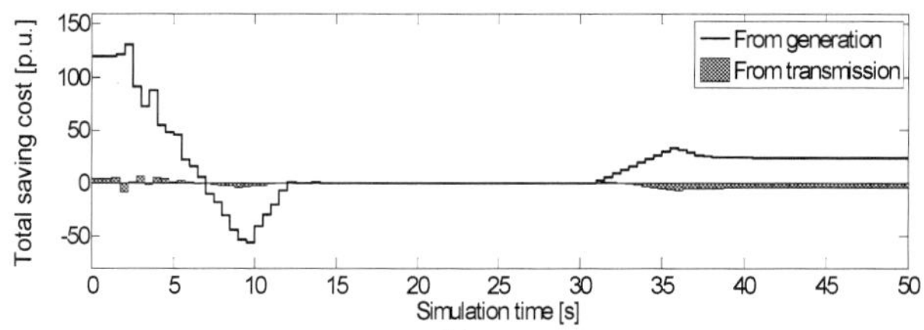

(b)

Fig. 9. Case of load demand increases for the radial test network using the SPR algorithm

6.1.3 Case 3 – Network configuration change

In this case, a contingency is considered where line section 5-6 is taken out of service. To supply power to the rest of feeder 1, the NOP will be closed. The new configuration of the network is shown in Fig. 10. Stand-by storages are enabled at bus 16, 18 and 20 which increases their capacities up to 5 MW, 7 MW and 9 MW respectively.

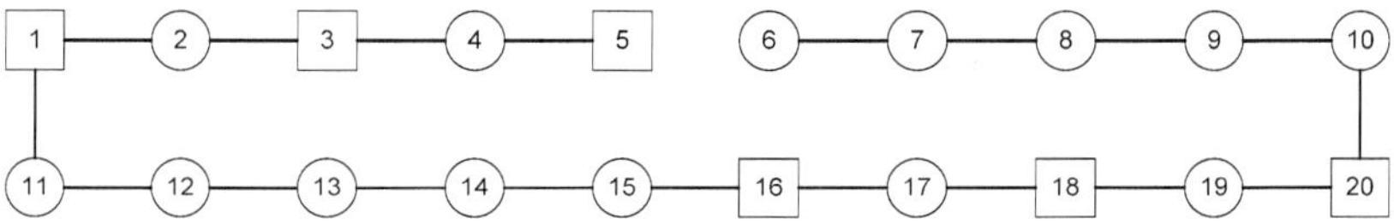

Fig. 10. Representative directed graph for the new configuration of the radial test network

Fig. 11 shows the changes of power generation and power flow, as well as the total operating cost in this case. In feeder 2, the power generation at bus 16, 18, and 20 are increased to their new maximum capacity (5 MW, 7 MW, and 9 MW). While P_{gen3} is constant, P_{gen1} and P_{gen5} are decreased to limit the exchanged flow below 10 MW. The total saving cost in this case has relatively equal contributions from the power generation and power transmission, 48.62 p.u. and 48.59 p.u. respectively.

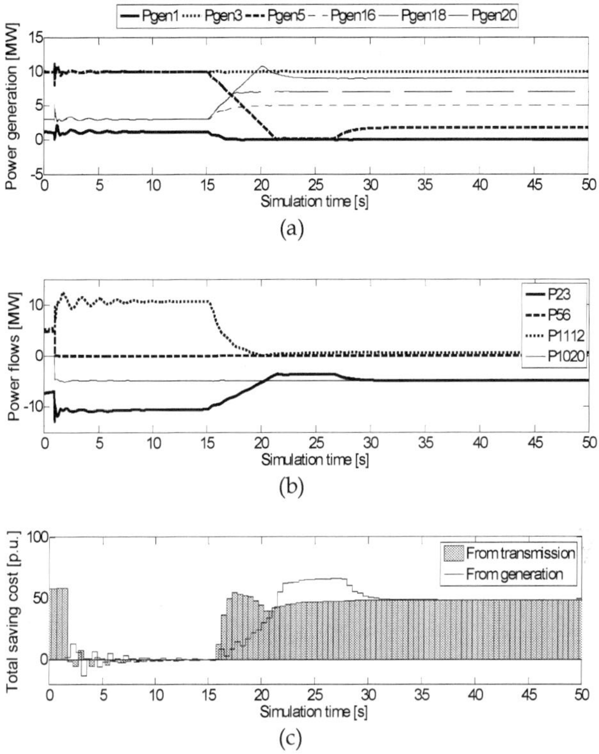

Fig. 11. Case of network configuration change for the radial test network using the SPR algorithm

7. Conclusion

This chapter has presented an application of the graph theory in power systems for the function of power routing. The performance of the power routing function using Successive Shortest Path (SSP) and Scaling Push Relabel (SPR) algorithms are investigated on a simulation of a radial network. Simulation results show that the algorithm has self-stabilizing and self-healing properties in response to changes in the cost and capacity for power demand/supply. Simulations reveal also the ability of the power routing function to deal with issues of network variations and constraints. Moreover, the function can be implemented in an online, real-time environment which is emerging in the development of the future power systems.

8. References

Ahuja, R.K., Magnanti, T.L., & Orlin, J.B. (1993) *Network flows: theory, algorithms, and applications*, Prentice Hall.

Armbruster, A. et al., 2005. Power transmission control using distributed max-flow. In *29th Annual International Computer Software and Applications Conference, COMPSAC*, Vol. 2, pp. 256-263

Bompard, E. et al. (2003). Congestion-management schemes: a comparative analysis under a unified framework. *IEEE Transactions on Power Systems*, Vol. 18, No. 1, pp. 346-352.

Dolan, M. et al. (2009). Techniques for managing power flows in active distribution networks within thermal constraints. *Proceeding of the 20th International Conference and Exhibition on Electricity Distribution - CIRED 2009*, Prague, Czech Republic, June 18-11, 2009.

Gan, D., Thomas, R.J. & Zimmerman, R.D. (2000). Stability-constrained optimal power flow. *IEEE Transactions on Power Systems*, Vol. 15, No. 2, pp. 535-540.

Ghosh, S., Gupta, A., & Pemmaraju, S.V. (1995). A self-stabilizing algorithm for the maximum flow problem. *Proceeding of the IEEE Fourteenth Annual International Phoenix Conference on Computers and Communications*, pp. 8-14.

Goldberg, A.V. & Tarjan, R.E. (1988). A new approach to the maximum-flow problem. *Journal of the ACM*, Vol. 35, pp. 921-940.

Goldberg, A.V. & Tarjan, R.E. (1989). A parallel algorithm for finding a blocking flow in an acyclic network. *Information Processing Letters*, Vol. 31, pp. 265-271.

Huneault, M. & Galiana, F.D. (1991). A survey of the optimal power flow literature. *IEEE Transactions on Power Systems*, Vol. 6, No. 2, pp. 762-770.

Jokic, A. (2007). *Price-based optimal control of electrical power systems*. Technische Universiteit Eindhoven, ISBN 978-90-386-1574-5, Eindhoven, The Netherlands.

Kim, B.H. & Baldick, R. (2000). A comparison of distributed optimal power flow algorithms. *Power Systems, IEEE Transactions on*, Vol. 15, No. 2, pp. 599-604.

Nguyen, P.H., Kling, W.L., & Myrzik, J.M.A. (2010). An application of the successive shortest path algorithm to manage power in multi-agent system based active networks. *European Transactions on Electrical Power*, Vol. 20, No. 8, pp. 1138-1152.

Nguyen, P. H., Kling, W.L., Georgiadis, G., Papatriantafilou, M., Anh-Tuan, L. & Bertling, L. (2010). Distributed routing algorithms to manage power flow in agent-based active distribution network. *Proceedings of the 2010 IEEE PES Conference on Innovative Smart Grid Technologies Conference Europe (ISGT Europe)*, 11-13 October 2010, Gothenburg, Sweden. (pp. 1-7).

Telecom Italia S.p.A., 2010. Java Agent Development Framework. Available from http://jade.tilab.com/index.html [Accessed May 2010].

Wei, P. et al., 2001. A decentralized approach for optimal wholesale cross-border trade planning using multi-agent technology. *Power Systems, IEEE Transactions on*, Vol. 16, No. 4, pp. 833-838.

Xin, H. et al. (2011). A Self-Organizing Strategy for Power Flow Control of Photovoltaic Generators in a Distribution Network. *IEEE Transactions on Power Systems*, Vol. 26, No. 3, pp. 1462-1473.

13

Research Progress of Complex Electric Power Systems: Graph Theory Approach

Yagang Zhang, Zengping Wang and Jinfang Zhang
State Key Laboratory of Alternate Electrical Power System with Renewable Energy Sources (North China Electric Power University), China

1. Introduction

Electric power system is one of the most complex artificial systems in this world, which safe, steady, economical and reliable operation plays a very important part in guaranteeing socioeconomic development, even in safeguarding social stability. In early 2008, the infrequent disaster of snow and ice that occurred in the south of China had confirmed it again. The complexity of electric power system is determined by its characteristics about constitution, configuration, operation, organization, etc., which has caused many disastrous accidents, such as the large-scale blackout of America-Canada electric power system on August 14, 2003, the large-scale blackout of Italy electric power system on September 28, 2003. In order to resolve this complex and difficult problem, some methods and technologies that can reflect modern science and technology level have been introduced into this domain, such as computer and communication technology, control technology, superconduct and new materials technology and so on. Obviously, no matter what we adopt new analytical method or technical means, we must have a distinct recognition of electric power system itself and its complexity, and increase continuously analysis, operation and control level (Yuan, 2007; Ye, 2003; Xue, 2002).

A fault is defined as a departure from an acceptable range of an observed variable or calculated parameter associated with systems. It may arise in the basic technological components or in its measurement and control instruments, and may represent performance deterioration, partial malfunctions or total breakdowns. Fault analysis implies the capability of determining, either actively or passively, whether a system is functioning as intended or as modeled. The goal of fault analysis is to ensure the success of the planned operations by recognizing anomalies of system behavior. A system with faults does not necessarily imply that the system is not functioning. Detecting a fault involves identifying a characteristic of the system, which when a fault occurs, can be distinguished from other characteristics of the system. According to nonlinear complex systems, we have carried out large numbers of basic researches (Zhang et al., 2010; Zhang et al., 2006; Zhang et al., 2007; Zhang & Wang, 2008). In this chapter, basing on graph theory and multivariate statistical analysis theory, we will discuss the complexity in electric power system.

The fault in electric power system can not be completely avoided. When electric power system operates from normal state to failure or abnormal operates, its electric quantities (current, voltage and their angles, etc.) may change significantly. In our researches, after some accidents, utilizing real-time measurements of phasor measurement unit (PMU) (Phadke & Thorp, 2008; Wang et al., 2007; Rakpenthai et al., 2005; Peng et al., 2006), basing on graph theory and multivariate statistical analysis theory, we are using mainly Breadth-first search (BFS), Depth-first search (DFS) and cluster analysis technology (Arifin & Asano, 2006; Otazu & Pujol, 2006; Park & Baik, 2006; Tola et al., 2008; Zhao et al., 2008; Templ et al., 2008), and seeking after for the uniform laws of electrical quantities' marked changes. Then we can carry out fast and exact analysis of fault component. Finally we can accomplish fault isolation.

2. Electric circuit theory

Let's consider a circuit with resistors(R), inductors (L), and capacitors(C), which has one element of each connected in a loop (Robinson, 2004). The part of the circuit containing one element is a branch. The points where the branches connect are nodes. There are three branches and nodes in Figure. 1.

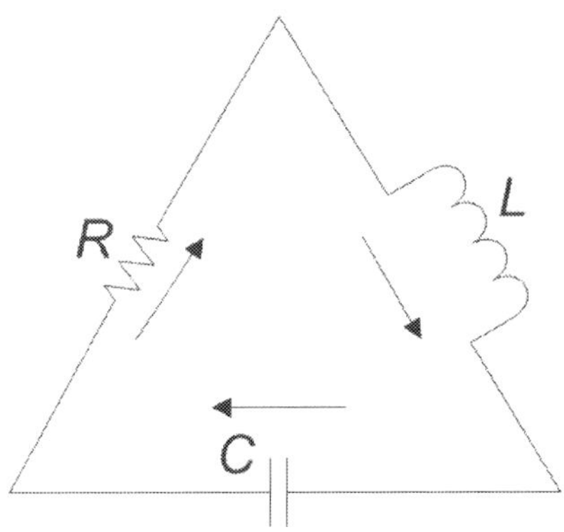

Fig. 1. RLC electric circuit

Let i_R , i_L and i_C be the current in the resistor, inductor and capacitor respectively, and let v_R , v_L and v_C be the voltage drop across the three branches of the circuit. Kirchhoff's voltage law states that the sum of the voltage drops around any loop is zero, that is, $v_R + v_L + v_C = 0$. Kirchhoff's current law states that the total current flowing into a node must equal the current flowing out of that node, namely, $|i_R| = |i_L| = |i_C|$ with the correct choice of signs.

A resistor is determined by a relationship between the current i_R and voltage v_R . Here, a linear resistor given by $v_R = R\, i_R$, where $R > 0$ is a constant, which is determined by Ohm's law. An inductor is characterized by giving the time derivative of the current $\frac{di_L}{dt}$, Faraday's law has proved that,

$$L\frac{di_L}{dt} = v_L \tag{1}$$

where the constant $L > 0$ is called the inductance. A capacitor is characterized by giving the time derivative of the voltage $\frac{dv_C}{dt}$, in terms of the current i_C,

$$C\frac{dv_C}{dt} = i_C \tag{2}$$

where the constant $C > 0$ is called the capacitance.

Furthermore, let's define two variables $x = i_R = i_L = i_C$, $y = v_C$, and $v_R = R\,x$, $v_L = -v_C - v_R = -y - R\,x$. So, this system can be expressed as,

$$\frac{d}{dt}\begin{pmatrix} x \\ y \end{pmatrix} = \begin{pmatrix} -\frac{R}{L} & -\frac{1}{L} \\ \frac{1}{C} & 0 \end{pmatrix}\begin{pmatrix} x \\ y \end{pmatrix} \tag{3}$$

Its characteristic equation is,

$$\lambda^2 + \frac{R}{L}\lambda + \frac{1}{LC} = 0 \tag{4}$$

which has two roots:

$$\lambda = -\frac{R}{2L} \pm \sqrt{\frac{R^2C - 4L}{4L^2C}} \tag{5}$$

Actually this system always has eigenvalues with negative real parts. If $R^2 \geq \frac{4L}{C}$, then the eigenvalues are real; else $R^2 < \frac{4L}{C}$, they are complex.

3. Search principles in graph theory

Many real world situations can conveniently be described by means of a diagram consisting of a set of points together with lines joining certain pairs of these points. In mathematics and computer science, graph theory is the study of graphs: mathematical structures used to model conjugated relations between objects from a certain collection. A graph is an abstract notion of a set of nodes and connection relations between them, that is, a collection of vertices or nodes and a collection of edges that connect pairs of vertices. A graph may be undirected, meaning that there is no distinction between the two vertices associated with each edge, or its edges may be directed from one vertex to another.

Applications of graph theory are primarily, but not exclusively, concerned with labeled graphs and various specializations of these. Structures that can be represented as graphs are ubiquitous, and many problems of practical interest can be represented by graphs. For example, in electric circuit theory, the Kirchhoff's voltage law and Kirchhoff's current law are only concerned with the structures and properties of the electric circuit. Then, any concrete electric circuit can be abstracted as a graph (Bondy & Murth, 1976). Here, let's give a simple electric circuit (See Figure 2), and its structure can be expressed as a graph (See Figure 3).

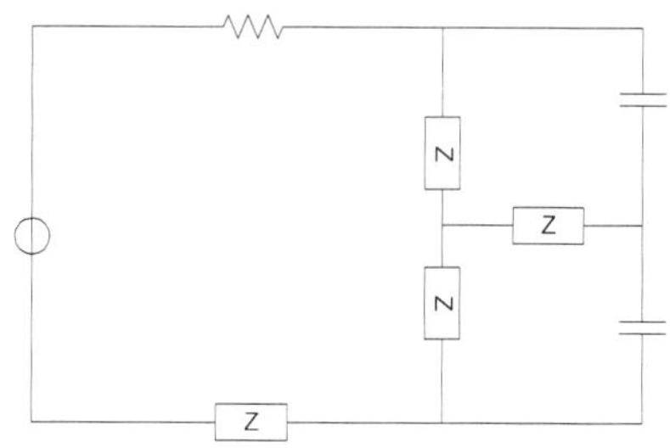

Fig. 2. A simple electric circuit

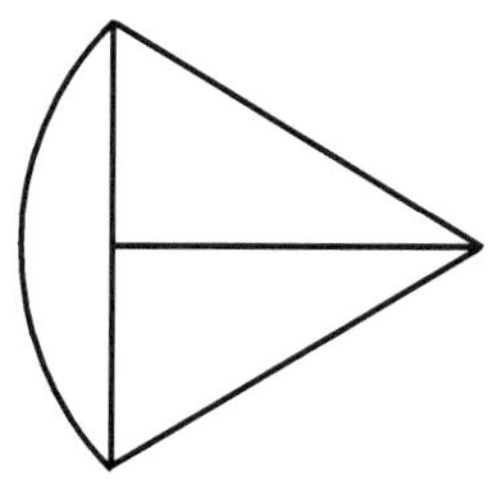

Fig. 3. A graph based on the simple electric circuit

Graph theory can be used to model many different physical and abstract systems such as transportation and communication networks, models for business administration, political science, and psychology and so on. Efficient storage and algorithm design techniques based on the graph representation make it particularly useful for utilizing computer. There are many algorithms that can be applied to resolve different kinds of problems, such as Breadth-first search, Depth-first search, Bellman-Ford algorithm, Dijkstra's algorithm, Ford-Fulkerson algorithm, Kruskal's algorithm, Nearest neighbor algorithm, Prim's algorithm, etc. Hereinto, Breadth-first search (BFS) is a graph search algorithm that begins at the root node and explores all the neighboring nodes. Then for each of those nearest nodes, it explores their unexplored neighbor nodes, and so on, until it finds the goal.

BFS is an uninformed search method that aims to expand and examine all nodes of a graph or combinations of sequence by systematically searching through every solution. In other words, it exhaustively searches the entire graph or sequence without considering the goal until it finds it. From the standpoint of the algorithm, all child nodes obtained by expanding a node are added to a first-in, first-out (FIFO) queue. In typical implementations, nodes that have not yet been examined for their neighbors are placed in some container (such as a queue or linked list) called "open" and then once examined are placed in the container "closed" (Knuth, 1997).

BFS can be used to solve many problems in graph theory, for example:

- Testing whether graph is connected, and finding all connected components in a graph;
- Computing a spanning forest of graph;
- Computing, for every vertex in graph, a path with the minimum number of edges between start vertex and current vertex or reporting that no such path exists;
- Computing a cycle in graph or reporting that no such cycle exists.

The Depth-first search (DFS) is an algorithm for traversing or searching a tree, tree structure, or graph. One starts at the root and explores as far as possible along each branch before backtracking (Thomas et al., 2001).

In formal way, DFS is an uninformed search that progresses by expanding the first child node of the search tree that appears and going deeper and deeper until a goal node is found, or until it reaches a node which has no child node. Then the search backtracks, and it will return to the most recent node that it has not finished exploring. The space complexity of DFS is much lower than BFS. It also lends itself much better to heuristic methods of choosing a likely-looking branch. Time complexity of both algorithms is proportional to the number of vertices plus the number of edges in the graphs they traverse.

4. Cluster analysis

Theories of classification come from philosophy, mathematics, statistics, psychology, computer science, linguistics, biology, medicine, and other areas. Cluster analysis can also be named classification, which is concerned with researching the relationships within a group of objects in order to establish whether or not the data can be summarized validly by a small number of clusters of similar objects. That is, cluster analysis encompasses the methods used to:

- Identify the clusters in the original data;
- Determine the number of clusters in the original data;
- Validate the clusters found in the original data.

Cluster analysis is commonly applied for statistical analyses of large amounts of experimental data exhibiting some kind of redundancy, which allows for compression of data to amount feasible for further exploration. This permits further mining of each cluster independently or, alternatively, constructing a high level view of the data set by replacing each cluster with its best single representative. Cluster analysis has great strength in data analysis and has been applied successfully to the researches of various fields. The effectiveness of a cluster approach depends on many choices. These include the choice of a cluster algorithm, an appropriate feature subspace, and a similarity metric defined over this subspace. In addition, cluster algorithms typically have a set of tunable parameters inherent to them that can heavily influence their performance. For example, many algorithms require the number of clusters desired, the maximum number of iterations, learning rate, its change schedule, etc. While some of these choices are obvious for simple artificial datasets. The most common clustering algorithm choices are hierarchical cluster analysis.

5. Fault analysis based on BFS and DFS

Now let us consider IEEE9-Bus system, Figure 4 is presents the IEEE 9-Bus system electric diagram. In the structure of electric power system, Bus1 appears single-phase to ground fault. Through simulation experiments, using these actual measurement data of corresponding variables, we can carry through fault analysis of fault component and non-fault component.

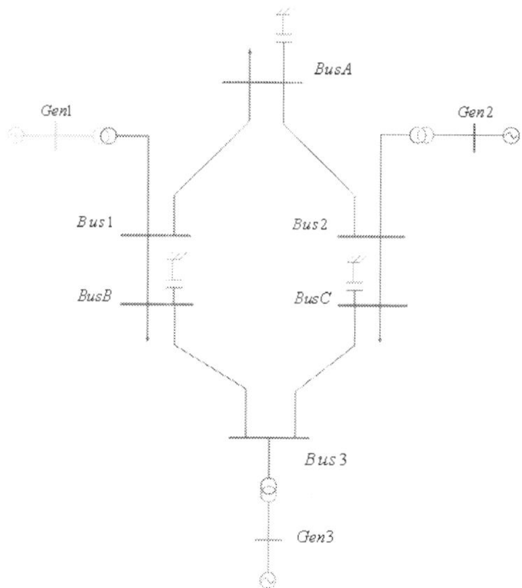

Fig. 4. Electric diagram of IEEE 9-Bus system

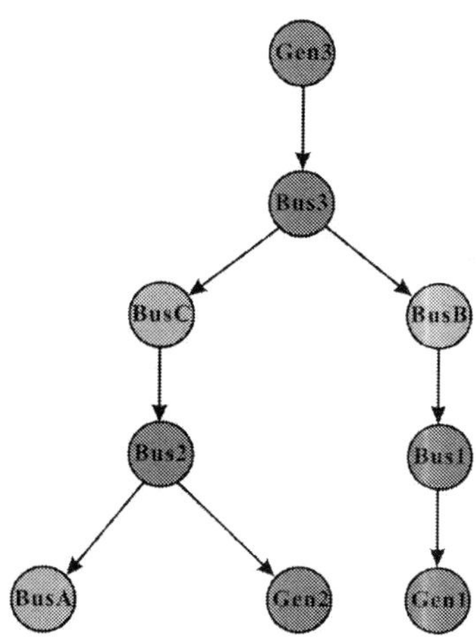

Fig. 5. BFS diagram of IEEE 9-Bus system

The adjacency matrix of IEEE9-Bus system can be expressed as follows,

	Bus1	Bus2	Bus3	BusA	BusB	BusC	Gen1	Gen2	Gen3
Bus1	0	0	0	1	1	0	1	0	0
Bus2	0	0	0	1	0	1	0	1	0
Bus3	0	0	0	0	1	1	0	0	1
BusA	1	1	0	0	0	0	0	0	0
BusB	1	0	1	0	0	0	0	0	0
BusC	0	1	1	0	0	0	0	0	0
Gen1	1	0	0	0	0	0	0	0	0
Gen2	0	1	0	0	0	0	0	0	0
Gen3	0	0	1	0	0	0	0	0	0

By the simulation experiments, we can get node phase voltage at T_{-1}, T_0 (Fault), T_1, T_2 and T_3 five times, see Table 1.

Bus	T_{-1}	T_0(Fault)	T_1	T_2	T_3
Gen1	1.0100	0.7275	0.6924	0.6814	0.6747
Gen2	1.0100	0.8762	0.8476	0.8327	0.8134
Gen3	1.0100	0.8449	0.8071	0.7909	0.7710
Bus1	1.0388	0	0	0	0
Bus2	1.0430	0.7622	0.7350	0.7217	0.7049
Bus3	1.0534	0.7600	0.7275	0.7134	0.6960
BusA	1.0319	0.7540	0.7248	0.7114	0.6944
BusB	1.0222	0.2512	0.2404	0.2356	0.2294
BusC	1.0061	0.2470	0.2381	0.2336	0.2276

Table 1. The Node Phase Voltage At T_{-1}, T_0 (Fault), T_1, T_2 And T_3 Five Times

Figure.5 is the BFS process of IEEE9-Bus system. In this diagram, Gen1 is the first generator node, it is also one of the terminals of BFS, and Bus1 is just the only node that connects with it. Combined the information characters of electrical measurements that have marked changes, the difference of Bus1 and other Buses is distinct. At the beginning, Bus1 has just been set as single-phase to ground, which is a typical bus-bar fault. In the final analysis, both of these two aspects are consistent, and we can identify effectively fault location based on BFS.

Figure.6 is the DFS process of IEEE9-Bus system. In this diagram, the difference of Bus1 and other Buses is more distinct. Gen1 is the terminal of DFS, and Bus1 is just the only node that connects with it. In the beginning, we have set the Bus1 as single-phase to ground fault. Both of these two aspects are consistent. So, we can also identify effectively fault location based on DFS.

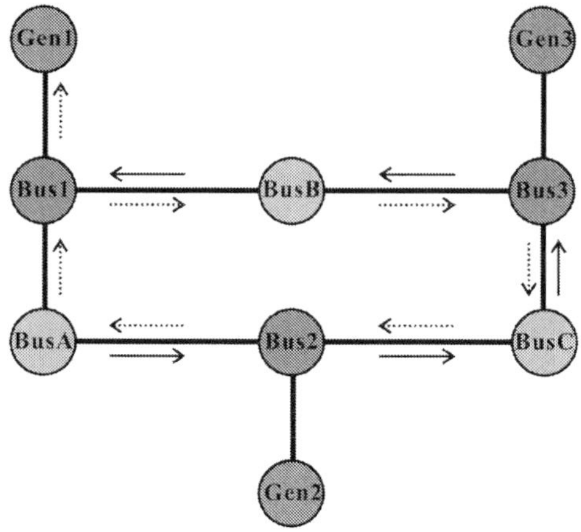

Fig. 6. DFS diagram of IEEE 9-Bus system

6. Fault analysis based on hierarchical cluster analysis

The hierarchical cluster analysis does not require us to specify the desired number of clusters *K*, instead affording a cluster dendrogram. In practice, the choice can be based on some domain specific and often have subjective components. There are three steps to hierarchical cluster analysis. First, we must identify an appropriate proximity measure. Second, we need to identify the appropriate cluster method for the data. Finally, an appropriate stopping criterion is needed to identify the number of clusters in the hierarchy. The distance or similarity metric used in cluster is crucial for the success of the cluster method. Euclidean distance and Pearson correlation are among the most frequently used.

Now let us continue to consider IEEE9-Bus system. According to the results of the simulation experiments (Table 1), basing on node phase voltage, we carry out hierarchical cluster analysis. Figure.7 is the dendrogram of hierarchical cluster analysis based on node phase voltage.

Let us explain the entire process of cluster analysis in detail. The entire cluster analysis process is carried out according to the principle of similarity from high to low (distance from near to far), the order is,

Steps 1: BusC is combined with BusB to form the new BusB;
Steps 2: Bus3 is combined with Bus2 to form the new Bus2;
Steps 3: BusA is combined with Bus2 to form the new Bus2;
Steps 4: Bus2 is combined with Gen1 to form the new Gen1;
Steps 5: Gen3 is combined with Gen2 to form the new Gen3;
Steps 6: Gen2 is combined with Gen1 to form the new Gen1;
Steps 7: BusB is combined with Bus1 to form the new Bus1;
Steps 8: Gen1 is combined with Bus1 to form the new Bus1.

From the entire hierarchical cluster process analysis, Bus1 has the lowest similarity to other nodes (the farthest distance to other nodes). It can also be found easily out from Figure.7

that Bus1 has remarkable difference with other buses, and the fault characteristic is obvious. These results are entirely identical to the fault location set in advance, so we can also confirm exactly fault location by the hierarchical cluster analysis.

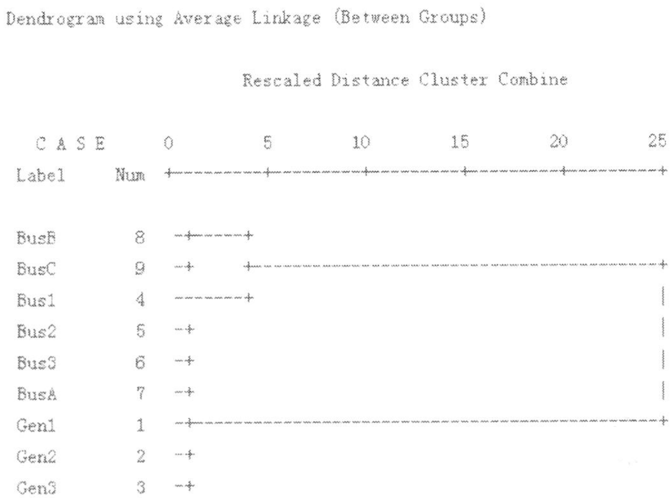

Fig. 7. The dendrogram of hierarchical cluster analysis based on node phase voltage

7. New approach for finding connected routes of power network

The connectivity analysis is the essence of the power system topology analysis, which is also playing the basic function in many kinds of advanced application software for power system analysis and calculation (Monticelli, 1999). The actual power network structures are shown by the result of the power system topology analysis processor, as the bus/branch model. Hence, the aim of topology analysis is to map the bus-section/switching-device model in the physical equipments level into the bus/branch model for a number of advanced functions in Energy Management System (EMS) or Distribution Management System (DMS) (Monticelli, 1999), such as power flow calculation, state estimation, dispatcher training simulator (DTS) and so on.

The main methods used in connectivity analysis of power system are based on the Graph theory, including tree-search based method and matrix-based method (Zhu et al., 2002). The former one can also be classified into two algorithms according to the different search patterns, named as Depth First Search (DFS) and Breadth First Search (BFS). By now, this topology analysis method has a widely application in power system analysis software (e.g. EMS or DMS). However, if the loop structure exists in the current network, the efficiency of tree-search based method will be low (Zhu et al., 2002). Matrix-based method is a systematic method based on adjacent matrix (Goderya et al., 1980), which can clearly depict the connected relationship between the two nodes belonged to the same branch. As the aim of connectivity analysis, whether any two nodes is connected or not and how many connected pieces all nodes could be mapped into will be the ultimate target of topology analysis. Therefore, the complete connected matrix will be needed to gain a global connectivity information among nodes, which can be obtained by the self-multiplying of the above mentioned adjacent matrix with the number of operations no more than $n-1$ (where, the n is the total number of the nodes). Obviously, the calculation burden of the matrix-based method will increase sharply as the expanding of the network scale. So in the substation or plants of power system where the number of nodes is not large, the matrix-based one also can play the role in grouping the connected physical nodes and then mapping the connected pieces into buses. Substation configuration has taken the most part of the total time needed in topology analysis (Zhang et al., 2010). Therefore, the substation configuration will be paid more attention in this paper.

The basic object of the above two methods is the vertexes/edges model mapped from the physical connections, in which the edges are corresponding to the switch devices, and the vertex will be the electrical connected points or physical buses. Therefore, once the state of the switches is changed, the connectivity analysis process will be restarted. Neither in tree-search based method nor in matrix-based method, the repeat search and calculation can not be avoided, which seriously effects the efficiency of the tracking of the status change happened in switch devices. In order to reduce the on-line topology analysis burden, the reference (Zhang et al., 2010) has established one method based on the graphic characteristic of the main connections, in which the each element of the complete connected matrix is represented by a set of connected routes with the open-close state of edges as variables. If the status of the each edge is determined, the value of these connected routes could be gained and the relationship between the mentioned nodes is confirmed. Hence, the large amount of repeat calculation is avoided. However, the connected routes finding algorithm is based on the type of electrical main connections used as the rule-based method, which is not systematic method and not suit for the irregular connections.

In this section, a new connected routes finding algorithm is proposed based on the adjoint matrix of the symbolic adjacent matrix, and a simplifying method is also applied to extract the connected routes information readily. Compare to the graphic feature based method, the new finding algorithm is an systematic one, which is suitable for various network connection structures.

8. The new connected routes finding algorithm

According to the Graph Theory (Diestel, 2000), the matrix could be used as the representation of one special graph, which is easily be analyzed and calculated by the computer. The two kinds of matrix usually used in analysis are incident matrix A_{inc} and adjacent matrix A_{adj} respectively. The A_{inc} depicts the connected relationship between the nodes and edges, and the A_{adj} gives a description of the relationship between two nodes. The aim of connectivity analysis is to group the nodes into different connected pieces, A_{adj} could meet this requirement and usually be used to do connectivity analysis.

For a special simple network structure as shown in Figure.8, the vertex set is $V(G)=[v1,v2,v3,v4,v5,v6]$, and the edge set is $E(G)=[e1,e2,e3,e4,e5,e6]$. The mapping relationship set between the vertexes and edges is $\varphi(G): E \to V \times V$, such as $\varphi(e1)=\{v1,v2\}$, $\varphi(e2)=\{v2,v3\}$, $\cdots$, $\varphi(e6)=\{v5,v6\}$.

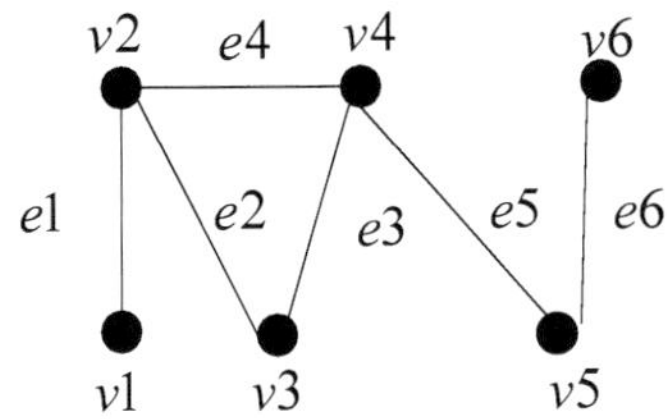

Fig. 8. A simple graph G with six vertexes and six edges

The adjacent matrix A_{adj} of graph G in Figure.8 is following:

$$A_{adj} = \begin{bmatrix} 1 & 1 & 0 & 0 & 0 & 0 \\ 1 & 1 & 1 & 1 & 0 & 0 \\ 0 & 1 & 1 & 1 & 0 & 0 \\ 0 & 1 & 1 & 1 & 1 & 0 \\ 0 & 0 & 0 & 1 & 1 & 1 \\ 0 & 0 & 0 & 0 & 1 & 1 \end{bmatrix} \tag{6}$$

Where, if there is a edge between vertex i and vertex j, the value of $A_{adj}(i,j)$ is equal to 1; otherwise, $A_{adj}(i,j)=0$. Especially, the diagonal element of A_{adj} is set to 1. Obviously, this matrix A_{adj} can not describe the relationship between any two nodes, which are not incident to the same edge. Therefore, the completed connected matrix A is needed, which can depict the connected relationship between any two nodes in one graph. Corresponding to connected graph G in Figure. 8, the elements of matrix A are equal to 1, as following:

$$A = \begin{bmatrix} 1 & 1 & 1 & 1 & 1 & 1 \\ 1 & 1 & 1 & 1 & 1 & 1 \\ 1 & 1 & 1 & 1 & 1 & 1 \\ 1 & 1 & 1 & 1 & 1 & 1 \\ 1 & 1 & 1 & 1 & 1 & 1 \\ 1 & 1 & 1 & 1 & 1 & 1 \end{bmatrix} \tag{7}$$

In a summary, the matrix-based method for the connectivity analysis is to find the completed connected matrix A from original adjacent matrix A_{adj}. According to the Graph Theory, the matrix A is obtained from the formulation (8):

$$A = A_{adj}^{n-1} \tag{8}$$

where, n is the number of vertexes in the graph G. In this process, the computation burden centers on the square of the matrix. It is worth to point out that the repeat calculation has taken the most part of the total time for the determination process of connected relationship among nodes.

8.1 The basic principle of new algorithm

Different from the traditional matrix-based method, the edges in the graph G are treated as the independent variables with the open-close two statuses; that is, if the edge is opened, the value of this corresponding variable is set to 0, otherwise, the value is equal to 1. Therefore, the adjacent matrix A_{adj} is the function of the current edge status, as following based on the Figure. 8.

$$A_{adj}(E) = \begin{bmatrix} 1 & e1 & 0 & 0 & 0 & 0 \\ e1 & 1 & e2 & e4 & 0 & 0 \\ 0 & e2 & 1 & e3 & 0 & 0 \\ 0 & e4 & e3 & 1 & e5 & 0 \\ 0 & 0 & 0 & e5 & 1 & e6 \\ 0 & 0 & 0 & 0 & e6 & 1 \end{bmatrix} \tag{9}$$

where, E is organized as a vector, such as $[e1,e2,e3,e4,e5,e6]$. Once the state of the each edge is determined, the vector E will be established and the matrix $A_{adj}(E)$ is also formed by substituting the current edge status. Take Figure.8 as an example, all the edges are closed and the current edge status vector E is equal to $[1,1,1,1,1,1]$.

The adjoint matrix of A_{adj} is defined as A^*_{adj}, and corresponding to formulation (9), the detailed element representations in the first row of A^*_{adj} are extracted for the in-depth analysis, which are as following:

$$\begin{aligned} A^*_{adj}(1,1) &= e2^2e5^2 + e2^2e6^2 - e2^2 - 2e2e3e6^2e4 \\ &\quad + 2e4e3e2 + e3^2e6^2 - e6^2 + e6^2e4^2 \\ &\quad - e3^2 - e5^2 + 1 - e4^2 \\ A^*_{adj}(1,2) &= e1e3^2 - e1e3^2e6^2 + e1e5^2 + e1e6^2 - e1 \\ A^*_{adj}(1,3) &= -e1e2e5^2 - e1e2e6^2 + e1e2 - e1e4e3 \\ &\quad + e1e3e6^2e4 \\ A^*_{adj}(1,4) &= e1e6^2e2e3 - e1e2e3 - e1e6^2e4 + e1e4 \\ A^*_{adj}(1,5) &= e1e5e2e3 - e1e5e4 \\ A^*_{adj}(1,6) &= -e1e6e5e2e3 + e1e6e5e4 \end{aligned} \tag{10}$$

The detailed analysis of the above representations in (10) is:

As to non-diagonal element, the representation has included all the routes between the two nodes indexed by the column and row number. For instance, in Figure.8, there is only one route between node $v1$ and node $v2$, which is $e1$. Comparing to the $A^*_{adj}(1,2)$, the route $e1$ is included in this element's representation as one individual term stamped by one rectangle,

$$A^*_{adj}(1,2) = e1e3^2 - e1e3^2e6^2 + e1e5^2 + e1e6^2 - \boxed{e1} \tag{11}$$

Similarly, there are two connected routes between node $v1$ and $v4$, respectively which are $e1e4$ and $e1e2e3$. As a result in the representation of $A^*_{adj}(1,4)$, these two routes are playing the roles as two terms signed by two rectangles,

$$A^*_{adj}(1,4) = e1e6^2e2e3 - \boxed{e1e2e3} - e1e6^2e4 + \boxed{e1e4} \tag{12}$$

As to diagonal element, there is not route between the node and itself. As shown in $A^*_{adj}(1,1)$, the representation is very complicated. However, in the practical analysis, the value of the diagonal element is set to 1. Obviously, this term is also existing in the $A^*_{adj}(1,1)$ as

$$\begin{aligned} A^*_{adj}(1,1) = {} & e2^2e5^2 + e2^2e6^2 - e2^2 - 2e2e3e6^2e4 \\ & + 2e4e3e2 + e3^2e6^2 - e6^2 + e6^2e4^2 \\ & - e3^2 - e5^2 + \boxed{1} - e4^2 \end{aligned} \tag{13}$$

In a summary, the non-diagonal element of the adjoint matrix A_{adj} has contained all the routes between the relevant two nodes. However, it is very low efficient to finding all the connected routes between the nodes just by the observation method. Therefore, in the next subsection, one simplifying method is proposed to make a rapidly and accurately finding.

8.2 Simplifying method

Having taken many different network structures cases into consideration, the needed terms which represent the connected routes between the mentioned two nodes can be extracted by the following three steps:

As to one special representation of the element in adjoint matrix A^*_{adj},

Step1: Firstly, if the highest power of one term in the polynomial is not less than 2, this term should be removed;
Step2: Secondly, if the absolute value of coefficient of one term is not equal to 1, this term also should be removed;
Step3: Thirdly, the coefficient of all the left terms is set to its absolute value, which is 1 in fact.

After the above mentioned three steps, the representation of element in adjoint matrix A_{adj} can be simplified into the needed connected routes formation. In order to make a detailed depiction, the $A^*_{adj}(1,2)$ is picked and taken as example.

For $A^*_{adj}(1,2) = e1e3^2 - e1e3^2e6^2 + e1e5^2 + e1e6^2 - e1$:

These terms such as $e1e3^2$, $-e1e3^2e6^2$, $e1e5^2$, $e1e6^2$ will be removed in the first step, because the highest power of them are equal to 2 respectively; and the simplified result $A^*_{adj}(1,2)\_s1$ in this step is as following:

$$A_{adj}^{*}(1,2)\_s1 = s_1(A_{adj}^{*}(1,2)) = -e1 \tag{14}$$

In the second step, no term will be removed, because the left term $-e1$ does not meet the condition that absolute value of coefficient is not equal to 1. Hence, there is:

$$A_{adj}^{*}(1,2)\_s2 = s_2(A_{adj}^{*}(1,2)\_s1) = -e1 \tag{15}$$

In the final step, the coefficients of terms in $A_{adj}^{*}(1,2)\_s2$ are substituted by their absolute values, and ultimate organization formation of connected routes is obtained as following:

$$A_{adj}^{*}(1,2)\_s3 = s_3(A_{adj}^{*}(1,2)\_s2) = e1 \tag{16}$$

Similarly, the first row in the adjoint matrix A_{adj} can be transformed into the connected routes formation as following

$$\begin{aligned}
&A_{adj}^{*}(1,1)_s3 = 1\\
&A_{adj}^{*}(1,2)_s3 = e1\\
&A_{adj}^{*}(1,3)_s3 = e1e2 + e1e4e3\\
&A_{adj}^{*}(1,4)_s3 = e1e2e3 + e1e4\\
&A_{adj}^{*}(1,5)_s3 = e1e5e2e3 + e1e5e4\\
&A_{adj}^{*}(1,6)_s3 = e1e6e5e2e3 + e1e6e5e4
\end{aligned} \tag{17}$$

According to the above simplifying method, the elements in the other rows of the adjoint matrix A_{adj} also can be simplified and organized as the connected routes form. When the matrix A_{adj}_s3 is formed as the ultimate result, the current edge statuses can be substituted as individual variables and the completed connected matrix A also can be obtained equally. Obviously, the following formulation will be established:

$$A = A_{adj}\_s3(E) \tag{18}$$

9. The application for substation configuration of power system topology analysis

In substation configuration, the network structure is more complicated than the network connection among substations or plants. The number of nodes in one substation or plants is not large, so the matrix-based method can be adopted for the operation of low dimension matrix. Generally, one electrical connection can be mapped into a graph, in which the switch device is corresponding to the edge, and the physical bus and electrical connected point are transformed into vertexes.

In this part, the more complicated electrical main connection—angle connection with four angles is taken as an example. One typical connection of this type is show in Figure. 9.

The corresponding adjacent matrix A_{adj} is:

$$A_{adj}=\begin{bmatrix}1 & e1 & 0 & e2\\ e1 & 1 & e3 & 0\\ 0 & e3 & 1 & e4\\ e2 & 0 & e4 & 1\end{bmatrix} \tag{19}$$

As the adjoint matrix of the symmetrical matrix A_{adj}, the upper triangular of A^{*}_{adj} is:

$$A^{*}_{adj}=\begin{bmatrix}-e4^2+1-e3^2 & e1e4^2-e1-e4e3e2 & e1e3+e2e4 & -e1e3e4-e2+e3^2e2\\ & -e4^2+1-e2^2 & -e3-e2e1e4+e2^2e3 & e4e3+e2e1\\ & & -e2^2+1-e1^2 & -e4+e1^2e4-e1e2e3\\ & & & -e3^2+1-e1^2\end{bmatrix} \tag{20}$$

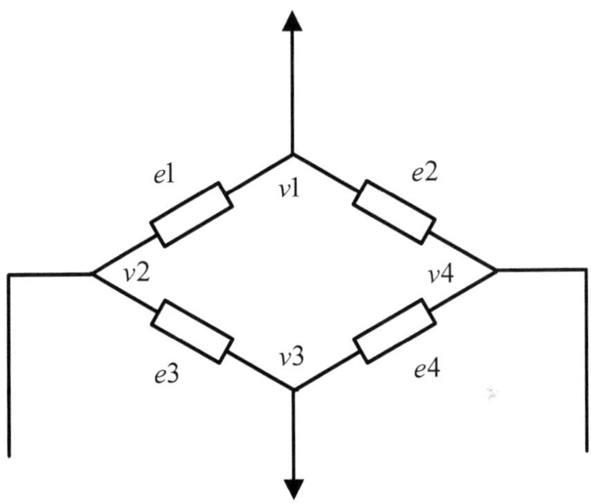

Fig. 9. A typical angle connection with four angles

After the treatment of the simplifying method proposed in Section II, the final connected routes matrix is represented by the upper triangular as following:

$$A^{*}_{adj}\_s3=\begin{bmatrix}1 & e1+e4e3e2 & e1e3+e2e4 & e1e3e4+e2\\ & 1 & e3+e2e1e4 & e4e3+e2e1\\ & & 1 & e4+e1e2e3\\ & & & 1\end{bmatrix} \tag{21}$$

Hence, the completed connected matrix A can be determined according to matrix $A^{*}_{adj}\_s3$ with the current edges status vector E.

If the $e1$ and $e4$ are opened with the other two edges closed, the current edge status vector $E = [1,0,0,1]$, then

$$A = A^{*}_{adj}\_s3(E) = \begin{bmatrix} 1 & 1 & 0 & 0 \\ 1 & 1 & 0 & 0 \\ 0 & 0 & 1 & 1 \\ 0 & 0 & 1 & 1 \end{bmatrix} \tag{22}$$

Therefore, the vertex $v1$ and $v2$ are grouped into one connected pieces, and the left two vertexes are mapped into the second bus.

Sometimes, the edge $e4$ is opened from closed, and the edge $e2$ and $e3$ are closed, the current edge status vector has become as $E = [1,1,1,0]$; therefore, the complete connected matrix A is equal to:

$$A = A^{*}_{adj}\_s3(E) = \begin{bmatrix} 1 & 1 & 1 & 1 \\ 1 & 1 & 1 & 1 \\ 1 & 1 & 1 & 1 \\ 1 & 1 & 1 & 1 \end{bmatrix} \tag{23}$$

In other words, all the four vertexes are connected with each, and only one connected piece is formed with the current edge statuses. In this way, this connection is mapped into one bus.

10. Conclusion

Electric power system is one of the most complex artificial systems in this world, which safe, steady, economical and reliable operation plays a very important part in guaranteeing socioeconomic development, even in safeguarding social stability. The complexity of electric power system is determined by its characteristics about constitution, configuration, operation, organization, etc. However, no matter what we adopt new analytical method or technical means, we must have a distinct recognition of electric power system itself and its complexity, and increase continuously analysis, operation and control level.

The characteristic of the adjoint matrix has been given an in-depth analysis, which is deduced from the adjacent matrix represented as the function of current edge status in the network. By the use of the simplifying method, the needed connected routes information could be extracted readily and accurately. Combination the original analysis of the adjoint marix and the connected routes extracting process, a novel connected routes finding algorithm is established. In this way, the complete connected matrix is finally formed as the function of the edge state, and each element could be represented by a set of connected routes provided by the proposed new algorithm. Once the status of each edge is determined, the connectivity between any two nodes is easily to be confirmed by substituting the current statuses into the corresponding connected routes set. These connected routes set could be found in the off-line way based on the novel routes finding algorithm, which will be able to save the on-line analysis time, especially for the topology analysis of power system. Finally, the case study on the angle connection in substation has validated the efficiency of the established novel routes finding algorithm.

The fault in electric power system can not be completely avoided. When electric power system operates from normal state to failure or abnormal operates, its electric quantities (current, voltage and their angles, etc.) may change significantly. In our researches, utilizing real-time measurements of PMU, we are using mainly graph theory and multivariate statistical analysis theory to seek after for the uniform laws of electrical quantities' marked changes. Then we can carry out fast and exact analysis of fault component. Finally we can accomplish fault isolation.

These researches have proven that the complexity of electric power system can be explored successfully by analysis and calculation based on graph theory and multivariate statistical analysis theory.

11. Acknowledgements

This research was supported partly by the National Natural Science Foundation of China (50837002), the Fundamental Research Funds for the Central Universities (11MG37), the Natural Science Foundation of Hebei Province and the Training Plan of Top-notch Doctoral Candidates in "211 Project" of NCEPU.

12. References

Arifin, A.Z. & Asano, A. (2006). Image segmentation by histogram thresholding using hierarchical cluster analysis. *Pattern Recognition Letters*, Vol. 27, 1515-1521, ISSN: 0167-8655

Bondy, J.A. & Murth, U.S.R. (1976). *Graph Theory with Applications*, Elsevier Science Publishing Co., Inc., ISBN: 978-0-444-19451-0, New York

Diestel, R. (2000). *Graph Theory*, Springer-Verlag, ISBN: 978-3-642-14278-9, NewYork

Goderya, F., Metwally, A.A & Mansour, O. (1980). Fast detection and identification of islands in power networks. *IEEE Transactions on Power Apparatus and Systems*, Vol. PAS-99(1), 217-221, ISSN: 0018-9510

Knuth, D.E. (1997). *The Art Of Computer Programming*, Third Edition, Addison-Wesley, ISBN: 978-0-201-89684-8, Boston

Monticelli, A. (1999). *State Estimation in Electric Power Systems: A Generalized Approach*, Kluwer Academic Publisher, ISBN: 978-0-792-38519-6, Massachusetts

Otazu, X. & Pujol, O. (2006). Wavelet based approach to cluster analysis. Application on low dimensional data sets. *Pattern Recognition Letters*, Vol. 27, 1590-1605, ISSN: 0167-8655

Park, H.S. & Baik, D.K. (2006). A study for control of client value using cluster analysis. *Journal of Network and Computer Applications*, Vol.29, 262-276, ISSN: 1084-8045

Peng, J.N., Sun, Y.Z. & Wang, H.F. (2006). Optimal PMU placement for full network observability using Tabu search algorithm. *International Journal of Electrical Power & Energy Systems*, Vol. 28, 223-231, ISSN: 0142-0615

Phadke, A.G. & Thorp, J.S. (2008). *Synchronized Phasor Measurements and Their Applications*, Springer verlag, ISBN: 978-0-387-76535-8

Rakpenthai, C., Premrudeepreechacharn, S., Uatrongjit, S. & Watson, N.R. (2005). Measurement placement for power system state estimation using decomposition technique. *Electric Power Systems Research*, Vol. 75, 41-49, ISSN: 0378-7796

Robinson, R.C. (2004). *An Introduction to Dynamical Systems: Continuous and Discrete*, Pearson Education, ISBN: 978-0-131-43140-9, New Jersey

Templ, M., Filzmoser, P. & Reimann, C. (2008). Cluster analysis applied to regional geochemical data: Problems and possibilities. *Applied Geochemistry*, Vol. 23, 2198-2213, ISSN: 0883-2927

Thomas, H.C., Charles, E.L., Ronald, L.R. & Clifford, S. (2001). *Introduction to Algorithms*, Second Edition, MIT Press and McGraw-Hill, ISBN: 978-0-262-03293-3, Cambridge

Tola, V., Lillo, F., Gallegati, M. & Mantegna, R.N. (2008). Cluster analysis for portfolio optimization. *Journal of Economic Dynamics and Control*, Vol.32, 235-258, ISSN: 0165-1889

Wang, C., Dou, C.X., Li, X.B. & Jia, Q.Q. (2007). A WAMS/PMU-based fault location technique. *Electric Power Systems Research*, Vol. 77, 936-945, ISSN: 0378-7796

Xue, Y.S. (2002). Interactions between power market stability and power system stability. *Automation of Electric Power Systems*, Vol. 26, 1-6, ISSN: 1000-1026.

Ye, L. (2003). Study on sustainable development strategy of electric power in China in 2020. *Electric Power*, Vol. 36, 1-7, ISSN: 1004-9649

Yuan, J.X. (2007). *Wide Area Protection and Emergency Control to Prevent Large Scale Blackout*, China Electric Power Press, ISBN : 978-7-508-35182-7, Beijing

Zhang, J.F., Wang, Z.P. & Zhang, Y.G. (2010). A new substation configuration algorithm based on the graphic characteristic of the main electrical connection. *Proc. 2010 5th International Conference on Critial Infrastructure(CRIS 2010)*

Zhang, J.F., Wang, Z.P., Zhang, Y.G. & Ma, J. (2010). A novel method of substation configuration based on the virtual impedance. *Proc. 2010 Asia-Pacific Power and Energy Engineering Conf. (APPEEC 2010)*

Zhao, W.X., Hopke, P.K. & Prather, K.A. (2008). Comparison of two cluster analysis methods using single particle mass spectra. *Atmospheric Environment*, Vol. 42, 881-892, ISSN: 1352-2310

Zhang, Y.G. & Wang, C.J. (2007). Multiformity of inherent randomicity and visitation density in n-symbolic dynamics. *Chaos, Solitons and Fractals*, Vol. 33, 685-694, ISSN: 0960-0779

Zhang, Y.G., Wang, C.J. & Zhou, Z. (2006). Inherent randomicity in 4-symbolic dynamics. *Chaos, Solitons and Fractals*, Vol. 28, 236-243, ISSN: 0960-0779

Zhang, Y.G. & Wang, Z.P. (2008). Knot theory based on the minimal braid in Lorenz system. *International Journal of Theoretical Physics*, Vol. 47, 873-880, ISSN: 0020-7748

Zhang, Y.G., Xu, Y. & Wang, Z.P. (2010). Dynamical randomicity and predictive analysis in cubic chaotic system. *Nonlinear Dynamics*, Vol.61, 241-249, ISSN: 0924-090X

Zhu, Y.L., Sidhu, T.S., Yang, M.Y. & Huo, L.M. (2002). An AI-based automatic power network topology processor. *Electric Power Systems Research*, Vol. 61, 57-65, ISSN: 0378-7796

14

Power Restoration in Distribution Network Using MST Algorithms

T. D. Sudhakar
St Joseph's College of Engineering, Chennai, India

1. Introduction

In this new era electric power has become a fundamental part of the infrastructure of modern society, with most of daily activity is based on the assumption that the desired electric power is readily available for utilization. In the near future, electric supply to houses, offices, schools and factories is taken for granted. The complex power distribution system provides the required electricity to the customers.

The transfer of power from the generating stations to the consumers is known as an electric supply system (figure 1). It consists of three principal components, namely the generating station, transmission lines and distribution networks. The power is generated at favorable places which are quite far away from the customers. The power is produced and transmitted using a 3 phase 3 wire alternating current (A.C.) system and it is distributed using a 3 phase 4 wire A.C. system.

The distribution network components are the distribution substation, the primary feeder, distribution transformers, secondary distribution transformers, sectionalizing switches, tie switches and the services.

The network carries electricity from the transmission systems and delivers it to consumers at the load centres through a number of power lines (branches). Switching on and off of these power lines makes the power to flow in the power distribution network.

2. Power restoration in distribution system

The power distribution network can undergo outages, which may be forced or scheduled. Forced outages take place due to any faults in the network, whereas scheduled outages happen because of maintenance work. The various outages that occur in the distribution network are :

- Outage of the primary feeders
- Outage of the distribution transformers
- Outage of the distribution line

During outages, the supply of power is either partially or completely isolated from the feeder to the load centres. This deficit of power supply has to be the minimized. To achieve

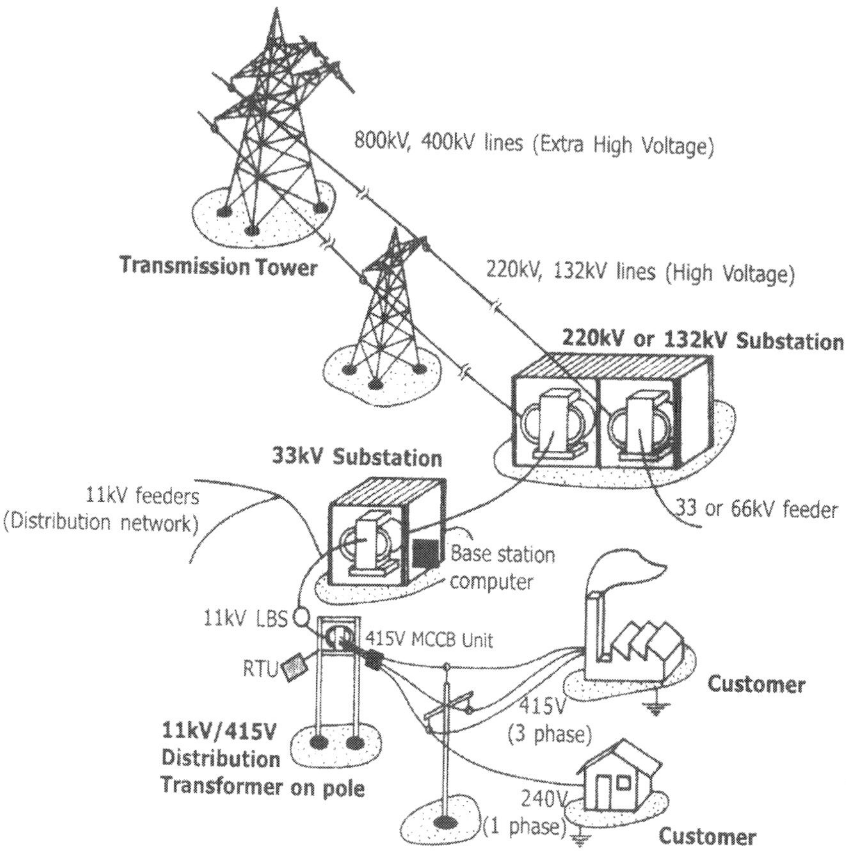

Fig. 1. Basic Electric Supply System

this goal, a proper switching sequence of power lines in the power distribution network is required. Sometimes, the load cannot be served to the customers; in which case, the loads are shed for the least priority customers.

The power distribution network in general, is built as an interconnected mesh network as shown in figure 2. Bus1, bus2 and bus3 indicate the feeder buses and the number in the circle indicates the load buses. The marking Si indicates the distribution branch i, that is used to transfer the power from one bus to another. Feeders in a distribution system have a mixture of types of loads, such as Very Important Person (VIP) & essential, industrial, commercial and domestic consumer loads. The peak load on feeders occurs at different times of the day, depending upon the type of load, making certain feeders to get heavily loaded and certain others to get lightly loaded. In such a practical situation, the reconfiguration based redistribution of the load amongst the feeders should attempt to evenly distribute the loads in the feeder.

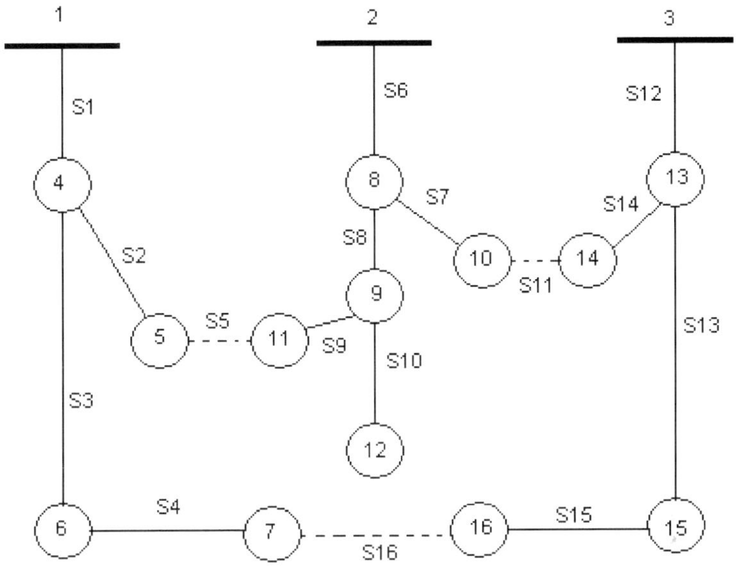

Fig. 2. Basic Power Distribution System

The branches in the power distribution network are normally configured radially for the effective coordination of their protective systems and such radiality is considered here. These networks are divided into a number of subsystems, which contain a number of normally closed switches (sectional switches) and normally open switches (tie line switches). These switches are operated during conditions of maintenance, dispatch and abnormalities. The aim of this switching operation is to reschedule the loads more effectively and improve the reliability of the distribution network. By changing the status of the switches, the topology of the power distribution network is reconfigured, and the resulting line currents and losses are redistributed, with a change in the bus voltage. These parameters of the network are obtained using Backward Sweep Power Flow algorithm.

In the case of an outage in any part of the system, it is imperative to restore the power system to an optimal target of the network configuration. The problem of obtaining a target network by switching is referred to as power system restoration. Power restoration after an outage usually refers to an emergency situation and the resultant plan should meet the following requirements:

- Restore as many loads as possible while considering priority customers
- Not cause violations in either engineering or operating constraints
- Outline a feasible sequence of operations to reach the final configuration
- Power balancing should be done
- Reached in a short time
- Radial network structure. This requirement is based on the feeder design for ease in fault location, isolation and protective device coordination.
- No components must be overloaded

The implementation of power restoration in a vast distribution system is thus a complicated combinatorial optimization problem because there are a great number of switches in the distribution system. It may take a long time using combinatorial optimization algorithm to reach a feasible restoration plan satisfying all practical constraints. An efficient way of achieving this would be to operate those switches that cause minimum loss and satisfy the voltage, current and other constraints. The major constraints to be satisfied in the distribution network are :

- Load allocation of the Feeder
- Voltage fluctuation
- Customer priority
- Reliability of the network
- Security of the network
- Distributed generation
- Harmonics due to intermittent switching
- Capacitor switching,
- Sudden increase of load and
- Failure of automated communication technology

Therefore, the dispatchers at many utilities tend to use their experience to narrow down and reach a proper restoration plan in a short period. This area has received a lot of attention by the researchers in the past three decades as evidenced by the number of publications (Sudhakar et. al 2011)

With the fast-paced changing technologies in the power industry, novel references addressing new technologies are being published. The automation of restoration of distribution power gained significance in the late eighties (Adibi and Kafka 1991). The state of the art methods used to solve the power system restoration for distribution system problems include Heuristic search (Morelato and Monticelli 1989), Expert system (Hotta et al 1990), and Knowledge based system (Matsumoto et al 1992). Due to the advancement in mathematics, new algorithms were developed to solve the restoration problem in distribution network. It mainly consisted of Artificial Neural Networks (Hoyong Kim et al 1993), Fuzzy Logic control (Han-Ching kuo and Yuan Yih Hsu 1993), Genetic Algorithm (Gregory Levitin et al 1995), Artificial Intelligence (Rahman 1993), Petri net (Fountas et al 1997), Tabu search (Toune 1998), Optimization (Nagata and Sasaki 2002), Ant colony search algorithm (Mohanty et al 2003) and Particle Swarm Optimization (Si-Qing Sheng et al 2009).

The main drawback faced in using the above methods, was the difficulty in identifying all the distribution branches used for the power to flow, after an outage for which predefined rules were used. To overcome this drawback, hybrid models such as fuzzy GA model (Ying-Tung Hsiao and Ching-Yang Chien 2000), was tried. To solve a complex combinatorial problem, the time required for solving the restoration problem using any of the above said methods is high. Now if hybrid models are used then the time required to obtain a solution is still higher. As a result it has become mandatory to identify the radial path of power flow with least mathematical efforts.

Most of the work reported focused on constraints like voltage limits, radiality and feeder capacity as the time required to obtain a restoration plan is more. To maintain these constraints, load shedding is done immediately. Load shedding option would imply loss of supply to essential loads such as medical facilities. If the time consumed is less; then the line losses and feeder capacity based on internal load division priority can be considered. To obtain the solution of the restoration problem without any iterative procedure, a graph theory based minimum spanning tree (MST) methodology proposed.

3. Graph theory

Graphs, the basic subject studied by the graph theory are abstract representations of a set of objects, where some pairs of objects are connected by links. The interconnected objects are represented mathematically as vertices, and the links that connect some pairs of vertices are called edges. Typically, a graph is depicted in a diagrammatic form as a set of dots for the vertices, joined by lines or curves called the edges. The vertices are also called nodes or points, and the edges are called lines.

A graph can be classified into two types namely an undirected and directed graph. A graph may be undirected, meaning that there is no distinction between the two vertices associated with each line, or its lines; or directed, meaning there is a distinction between one node and another. Table 1 shows the terminology for proceeding through the graph theory.

Term	Meaning
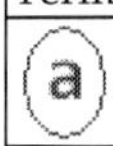	Vertex or node
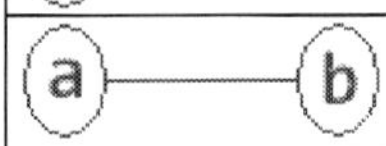	The line joining two nodes or vertices is called an line. Since the line doesn't show the direction it is an undirected graph.
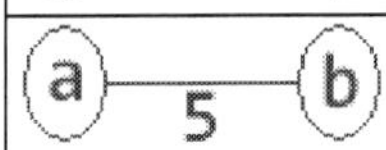	An line having a weight 5 being connected between the node 1 and node 2

Table 1. Symbols used in minimum spanning tree

Fig. 3. shows an example network with 6 nodes and 10 lines, which have their respective weights.

3.1 Minimum spanning tree

In the mathematical field of the graph theory, a spanning tree T of a connected, undirected graph G is a tree composed of all the vertices and some (or perhaps all) of the lines of G. That is, every node lies in the tree, but no cycles (or loops) are formed. A spanning tree of a connected graph G can also be defined as a maximal set of lines of G that contains no cycle, or as a minimal set of lines that connect all the vertices. For a connected graph with V nodes, any spanning tree will have the V-1 lines.

Given a connected, undirected graph, a spanning tree of that graph is a subgraph, which is a tree and connects all the vertices together. A weight is assigned to each line, whose value represents how unfavorable it is for the considered task. Individual weights of lines in a spanning tree decide its weight. The total sum of all the weights of the lines in a particular spanning tree is its weight.

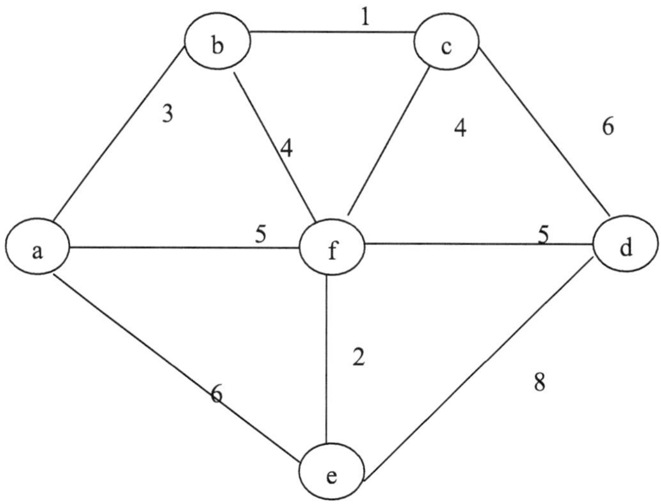

Fig. 3. Example network for MST problem

A minimum spanning tree (MST) or minimum weight spanning tree is then a spanning tree with a weight less than or equal to the weight of every other spanning tree. This concept is often used in routing. The algorithms to find MST, a graph search algorithm that solves the single-source shortest path problem for a graph with non-negative line path weights, produces a shortest path tree. For a given source node in the graph, the algorithm finds the path with the lowest weight (i.e., the shortest path) between that node and every other node. For example, if the nodes of the graph represent cities, and the line path weights represent the driving distances between pairs of cities connected by a direct road then MST can be used to find the shortest route between one city and all other cities. The main advantage of using the MST is that the optimum solution is obtained in a single stage.

3.2 Algorithms for finding MST

This section presents the proposed MST algorithm. Each algorithm is explained with a common example. A single graph can have many different spanning trees. If an exhaustive search approach to construct an MST is tried, two serious drawbacks arise. First, the number of spanning trees grows exponentially with the graph size; second, generating all the spanning trees for a given graph is not easy. To overcome these drawbacks the MST algorithms are proposed. The MST algorithms are further classified as line based MST algorithms and node based MST algorithms. They are

1. Line based MST algorithms
   i. Kruskal's algorithm
   ii. Reverse Delete algorithm
2. Node based MST algorithms
   i. Prim's algorithm
   ii. Dijkstra's algorithm

3.3 Kruskal's algorithm

Kruskal's algorithm is an algorithm in graph theory presented in 1956 (Anany Levitin (2009)) that finds a minimum spanning tree for a connected weighted graph. This means that it finds a subgraph of the lines that form a tree. It includes every node of the network and the total weight of all the lines in the tree is minimized. To implement the Kruskal's algorithm, two conditions have to be satisfied. First the weight of the lines in a graph is arranged in the increasing order. Second an empty subgraph T (called Traversal matrix) is created.

Then, the algorithm considers a line, based on the order of increasing weight. If a line (u, v) (u, v are the starting & ending node of a line) does not form a cycle along with the existing lines in the subgraph (T) then the line (u, v) is added to the subgraph (T). Then the line (u, v) is discarded. If a line is added to the subgraph then the counter is incremented. It is checked that the counter value is equal to V–1, where V is the number of nodes. If it is true, the procedure is stopped; otherwise, the process continues.

The Kruskal's algorithm is applied to the example network as shown in figure 3. The step by step procedure of the algorithm is discussed by Sudhakar et al (2011). The resultant traversal matrix with a weight of 15 is

T = [b c

f e

b a

b f

f d]

At the termination of the algorithm, the traversal matrix forms a MST of the graph. Based on this process, a pseudo code of the algorithm is developed and is as follows,

Pseudocode for the Kruskal's algorithm:

Sort E in increasing order of edge weights and the sorted edges are in A.

- Initialize the set of tree edges and its size, T.
- Counter ←0
- While counter < |V|-1
- If T U (u, v) is acyclic
- T ← T U (u, v)
- Counter ← Counter+1

Return T

3.4 Reverse Delete algorithm

The Reverse-Delete algorithm is an algorithm in graph theory used to obtain a minimum spanning tree from a given connected, line-weighed graph. The Reverse-Delete algorithm starts with the original graph and deletes lines from it. The Reverse-Delete algorithm ensures connectivity in the graph before deletion. Since the algorithm only deletes lines when it does not disconnect the graph, any line removed by the algorithm forms a cycle prior to the deletion. Since the algorithm starts from the maximum weighted line and continues in descending order, the line removed from any cycle is the maximum weighted line in that cycle. Therefore, according to the definition of a minimum spanning tree, the lines removed by the algorithm are not in any minimum spanning tree.

The Reverse-Delete algorithm is applied to the example network as shown in figure 3. The step by step procedure of the algorithm is discussed by Sudhakar et al (2011). Thus, the minimum weight for traversing the graph is 15 and the resultant network is shown in figure 4.

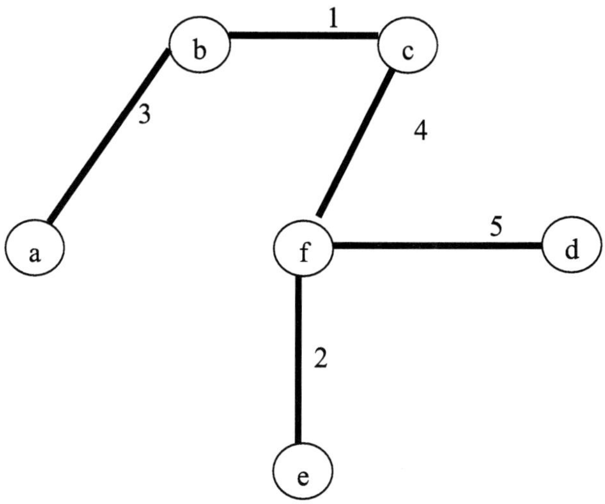

Fig. 4. Final Result of Reverse-Delete algorithm

Based on this procedure a pseudo code of the algorithm is formed as follows :

```
Pseudocode for the Reverse-Delete algorithm:
Function Reverse Delete (edges [T])
Sort T in decreasing order
Define an index i ← 0
   while i < size(T)
    Define edge temp ←T[i]
    delete T[i]
  if temp.v1 and  temp.v2 are not connected to the tree
          T[i] ← temp
        i ← i+1
return edges[T]
```

3.5 Prim's algorithm

The algorithm was developed in 1930 by the Czech mathematician, Vojtech Jarnik, and later independently, by the computer scientist, Robert C. Prim, in 1957 (Anany Levitin (2009)).

This algorithm finds a subset of the nodes that form a tree that includes every node, where the total weight of all the lines in the tree is minimized.

The Prim's algorithm constructs an MST through a sequence of expanding subtrees. The initial subtree in such a sequence consists of a single node selected arbitrarily from the set $V-V_T$ of the graph's nodes. In the following steps, the current tree expands, by simply getting attached to a nearer node with less weight. The algorithm stops, after all the graph's nodes have been included in the tree being constructed. Since the algorithm expands a tree by exactly one node on each of its steps, the total number of such steps is $V-1$, where V is the number of nodes in the graph.

The nature of the Prim's algorithm makes it necessary to provide two data values for every other unselected node. The data values are provided through two arguments : first will be the unselected node's ($V-V_T$) connectivity to the currently selected node (V_T). It will be nil '-' if no connectivity exists. The second entry (distance label) will be the respective weight. If there is no connection then the value will be ∞. With such labels, the smallest distance label in the set $V - V_T$, is selected and added in the selected nodes list.

After a node e^* is identified which is to be added to the tree, the following operations have to be performed:

- Move e^* from the set $V-V_T$ to the set of selected nodes V_T.
- Based on the nodes in set V_T, the weights of the node in $V-V_T$ are updated.
- For each remaining node u in $V-V_T$, e^* is selected which has the minimum weight
- The e^* is the next node to be added to the current tree T and the node e^* is added in V_T

The Prim's algorithm is applied to the example network as shown in figure 3. The step by step procedure of the algorithm is discussed by Sudhakar et al (2011). Thus, the minimum weight for traversing the graph is 15 and the resultant network is shown in figure 5.

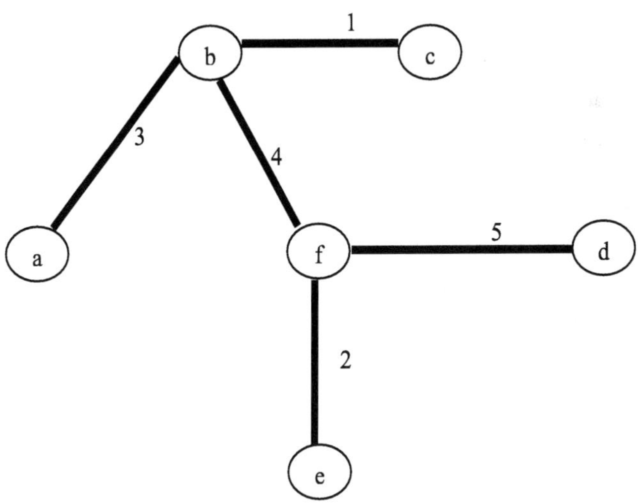

Fig. 5. Result of Prim's algorithm

Based on this procedure a pseudo code of the algorithm is formed as follows :

ALGORITHM *Prim(G)*

//Prim's algorithm for constructing an MST
//Input: A weighted connected graph G = *(V, E)* // V is node; E is line
//Output: E_T, the set of lines composing the MST of *G*
//the set of tree nodes can be initialized with any node
$E_T \leftarrow \emptyset$
for i=1 to (V-1) do
find a minimum-weight line $e^* = (v^*, u^*)$ among all the lines (v,u)
such that v is in V_T and u is in $V - V_T$
$V_T \leftarrow V_T \cup \{u\}$
$E_T \leftarrow E_T \cup \{v\}$
return E_T

3.6 Dijkstra's algorithm

The Dijkstra's algorithm, was conceived by the Dutch computer scientist Edsger Dijkstra in 1959 (Anany Levitin (2009)). This algorithm uses traversal matrix [T]. It indicates the distance from a single node to all the other nodes including it. In the considered example of figure 3, when node 'a' is considered first, its distance from it and all nodes from a through f will form the initial entries of [T]. The same procedure is repeated till all the nodes are selected and the final network with a total weight of 20 as shown in figure 6. algorithm is applied to the example network as shown in figure 3. The step by step procedure of the algorithm is discussed by Sudhakar et al (2010). Thus, the minimum weight for traversing the graph is 20 and the resultant network is shown in figure 6.

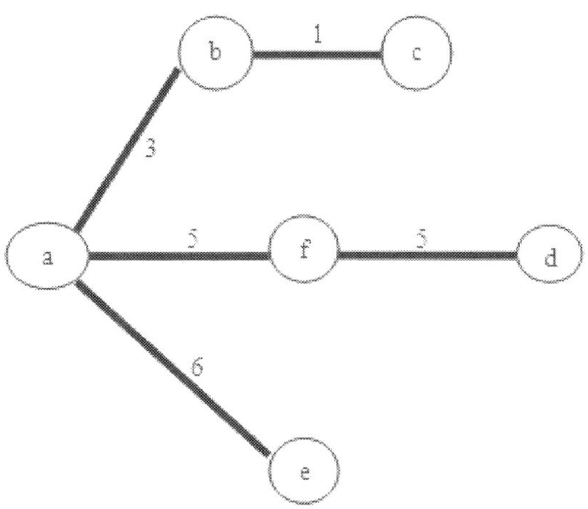

Fig. 6. Resultant network of Dijkstra's algorithm

Based on this modus operandi, a pseudo code of the algorithm is developed as follows,

Pseudocode for the Dijkstra's algorithm:

```
function Dijkstra(Graph, source):
// Initializations
for each node v in Graph:
// Unknown distance function from s to v
 dist[v] := infinity  previous[v] := undefined
// Distance from s to s
 dist[source] := 0
// Set of all unvisited vertices
 Q := copy(Graph)
// The main loop
while Q is not empty:
// Remove best node from the priority queue;
 // returns to the source after first step
  u := extract_min(Q)
  for each neighbor v of u:
    alt = dist[u] + length(u, v)
// Relax (u,v)
     if alt < dist[v]
      dist[v] := alt
      previous[v] := u
```

3.7 Comparison of the results

The four algorithms are applied to the example network of figure 3, and the results are tabulated in table 2.

Algorithm	Total weight
Prim's algorithm	15
kruskal's algorithm	15
Dijkstra's algorithm	20
Reverse Delete algorithm	15

Table 2. Comparison of MST algorithms for example network

In the case of the Dijkstra's algorithm, the total weight of the resultant network is more than that of the other three algorithms; but for the case of node 'f' from the starting node 'a' the total weight using the Dijkstra's algorithm is 5 which is smaller than the value 7 obtained using the other three algorithms. As a result we cannot neglect the Dijkstra's algorithm as an inefficient method.

3.8 MST applications

Graph theory based on MST approach has been discussed in various papers for various applications. Lin Ming Jin & Shu Park Chan (1989) presents an algorithm for finding the shortest path for power routing (DC) between two nodes in an electrical network used in the airlines. Hiroyuki Mork, Senji Tsuzuki (1991) presents mathematically MST for network topological observability analysis. Shun Lin Su et al (1994) dealt with application of the MST for finding the connectivity in VLSI circuits. Cavellucci & Lyra (1997), presented the minimization of energy losses in distribution systems by applying a general search method to a Brazilian power network. Here outages were not considered as an important factor. Michel Barbehenn (1998) discusses about the application of Dijkstra's algorithm for various applications like airline electrical networks. Ali Shatnawi et al (1999) indicates the use of Floyd - Warshall's based MST to find the time scheduling in the data flow graph of a DSP. Partricia Amancio Vargas (2002) uses the learning classifier system for loss minimization in a power system. Kaigui Xie (2003) calculates the reliability index of radial network using forward search method of MST. TianTian CAi & Qian Ai (2005) discusses the depth first search method used to find the MST for the optimal placement of the PMU devices in the power system. Distribution reconfiguration algorithm, named Core Schema Genetic Shortest-path Algorithm (CSGSA) proposed by Yixin Yu & Jianzhong Wu (2002) is based on the weights calculation method for each load condition based on line losses.

The above survey highlighted the extension of the application of graph theory for MV power distribution AC system, which has been attempted at this juncture. Here, the mathematical formulation of Yixin Yu has been applied to a PDN wherein distribution branch outages have been fully addressed. Thus to obtain the restoration plan quickly without any iterative procedure, a graph theory based methodology using MST algorithms is proposed here. Four algorithms based on graph theory are used to restructure the PDN by considering the distribution branch outage which forms the major contribution of this work.

The MST algorithm identifies all the possible paths for the power to flow and obtains only one solution. In a single iteration the MST algorithm overcome the radiality constraint. Since, MST algorithm gives a path of minimum impedance, the line losses will be minimum with the result no separate loss minimization procedure is required here. The solution of MST algorithm minimizes the solution time and as a result loss minimization and load shedding with internal priorities are included in the proposed work. Thus, in a minimum time a power system restoration solution is obtained, which will not lead to cascaded outage.

4. Restoration problem

An outage degrades the most important function of an electrical system, that of supplying the customers, and thus has a radical influence on the operating objectives. Whenever power supply interruption occurs in distribution systems due to an outage, it is imperative to bring back the system promptly to its initial state or to an optimal target network, by switching operations. The problem of obtaining a target network is called as power system restoration, has two prime objectives (a) the number of customers with a restored supply should be the largest possible and (b) the restoration should be accomplished as quickly as possible.

In this section, the network reconfiguration problem for service restoration is discussed in detail. The system is represented on a per phase basis and the load along a feeder section is represented as constant P, Q loads placed at the end of the lines. It is assumed that every switch is associated with a line in the system. The network reconfiguration problem for loss reduction involves the load transfer between the feeders or substations by changing the position of the switches. The radial configuration corresponds to a 'spanning tree' of a graph representing the network topology.

Given a graph, find a spanning tree such that the problem formulation of the restoration problem is given here

Objective Function is to

Find the Optimal Power Path

With the following constraints:

i. Maximize the power restored to the isolated area,

$$\max f = \sum_{K \in B} L_K X_K \tag{1}$$

Where L_K is the load at bus K

B is the total number of buses

X_K is the decision variable

The position of the sectional and tie line switches is considered here as the binary decision variable. This variable decides whether the switch is open or closed. The binary decision variable, X_K is defined as

$$X_K = 1 \text{ (if the } K^{th} \text{ switch is closed)}$$

$$= 0 \text{ (if the } K^{th} \text{ switch is open)} \tag{2}$$

If there are m switches in the initial network, there will be 2^m on / off switching options. That is, for a two switch network, 2^2 switching options are possible [(0,0), (0,1), (1,0), (1,1)]. The resultant decision vector is given by

$$X = [X_1, X_2, X_3 \ldots\ldots\ldots\ldots\ldots\ldots X_m]. \tag{3}$$

For the two switch network the decision vector can be represented as X = (0,0), X = (0,1), X = (1,0) and X = (1,1).

ii. Voltage limits : For each bus bar, the voltage constraints have upper and lower limits. A general expression for voltage constraints would be

$$|V_{\min j}| \le |V_j| \le |V_{\max j}| \tag{4}$$

where $|V_j|$ is the voltage at j node, $|V_{\min j}|$ is the minimum permitted voltage at node j, $|V_{\max j}|$ is the maximum permitted voltage at node j, and j belongs to a set of buses where voltage constraints are observed.

iii. Radiality : It is a condition in power distribution network that only one feeder bus feeds a load bus.

iv. Loading constraints : A general expression for loading constraints would be

$$L_i < L_{MP\,i} \tag{5}$$

where L_i is the loading of the network element i, $L_{MP\ i}$ is the maximum permitted loading of the network element i, and i belongs to a set of protected network elements. These protected network elements, are normally lines and feeders that can be protected by actual protection devices, or can be algorithmically protected. However, the fact is that, the considered feeder is not capable of supplying the whole load and hence, cannot be used further for problem solving.

v. Line losses: The total power losses of the network should be minimum.
vi. Feeder capacity: The total capacity of the feeder should not be violated. and
vii. Priority of customers: As the priority of each service zone is determined in advance, which customers would be restored can be determined according to the $L_{MP\ i}$.

This is a combinatorial optimization problem, since the solution involves the consideration of all possible spanning trees.

5. Application of the proposed MST algorithms for restoration problem

MST algorithm is a graph search algorithm that solves the single-source shortest path problem for a graph with non-negative weights, producing a shortest path tree. For a given source vertex (node) in the graph, the algorithm finds the path with lowest impedance (i.e. the shortest path) between the source node and every other node.

In order to achieve a maximum amount of power restored in a radial distribution system, the aim is to identify the appropriate switching options, which consists of all the buses in the network. In the proposed method, the distribution system is considered with all its laterals simultaneously, instead of determining the switching options on loop by loop basis. In applying the graph theory the buses and the feeders are considered as the node, the distribution line is considered as line and the impedance of the distribution line is considered as weight of the line. With this consideration the proposed graph theory based algorithm for the distribution system is :

Step 1. Initial power flow path is stored
Step 2. Get the input data about the amount of loads at each bus, the feeder capacity and the current status of all the lines
Step 3. In case of any outage remove those data from the input data file
Step 4. Check for multi feeder or single feeder
Step 5. If it is single feeder go for step 7
Step 6. If it is multi feeder, then enter the number of feeders
Step 7. Get the MST for the feeders
Step 8. Perform the load flow for the resultant network
Step 9. Check for multi feeder or single feeder
Step 10. If it is single feeder go to step 13
Step 11. Check for feeder overloading condition. If the feeders are overloaded, then load transferring can be done. If load transferring is not possible then perform load shedding. Otherwise if the feeders are not overloaded proceed to step 13.
Step 12. Perform the load flow for the modified conditions
Step 13. Check for over voltage condition. If the voltage limits are violated then perform load shedding otherwise proceed to step 15.
Step 14. Perform the load flow for the modified conditions

Step 15. Check for over current condition. If the current capacity are violated then perform load shedding otherwise proceed to step 17.
Step 16. Perform the load flow for the modified conditions
Step 17. If all the constraints are satisfied then display the optimal switching sequence

By applying this methodology objective function is solved and the constraints are satisfied. The result of step 7 finds a path for the power to flow after an outage, which satisfies the objective function. This step also satisfies the constraints viz., maximize the power restored to the isolated area, radiality and line losses. The power restored to the isolated area is maximum as the MST obtained after step 7 has all the possible buses available in the network. So all the loads connected to these buses will receive the power. The MST does not allows any closed loop in the network, as a result the MST obtained after step 7 will not have any closed loops, so the radiality constraint is satisfied. The MST network will have a minimum impedance value because the MST is obtained by considering the impedance value of each distribution line. Then the losses of the network will be minimum.

The feeder capacity constraint is mainly applicable for the multi feeder networks. In the case of the single feeder network, the loads are rearranged in the same network whereas in the multi feeder network there are some conditions that the loads of a feeder are transferred to the next feeder nearby. This condition is checked in the step 10. If there is any feeder overloading then load transferring is done. If load transferring is also not possible then load shedding is done based on the priority of the customer's constraint.

Step 13 checks the voltage limit condition and step 15 checks the loading constraint of the network. The maximum allowable limits are based on the network considered. Thus the proposed methodology satisfies all the above said objective function and the constraint.

The proposed methodology is not an iterative procedure, it calculates the amount of the load to be shed at each bus or load transferring between feeder (in the case of multi feeders) three times to satisfy the constraints. The load shed or load transferring has to be performed three times because the MST obtained by step 7 is based on the impedance minimization; it means the load has no influence on the solution. To bring in the effect of the load conditions only the load shedding or load transferring is done. Each time the amount of load to be shed is calculated at each bus and finally all the loads are shed simultaneously.

6. Results of the proposed MST algorithms for restoration problem

The original configuration of 33-bus test distribution network shown in figure 7 has a total load capacity of 3.525 MW and 2.3 Mvar. The network consists of 33 buses and 37 branches, where branches S1-S32 and S33-S37 indicate the sectional and tie lines switch respectively. The total impedance of the network for the original configuration having sectional lines is 21.8744+ j 18.1456 and the loss of the network 0.1869MW and 0.1240Mvar.

For the given network, the proposed methodology using the four MST algorithms is applied and the switch that should be kept open under normal conditions is tabulated in Table 3. The table indicates the switches those act as tie switches, their total impedance of the resultant network, loss of the network after applying the Kruskal's algorithm, Reverse delete algorithm, Prim's algorithm & Dijkstra's algorithm and minimum p.u. voltage of the network.

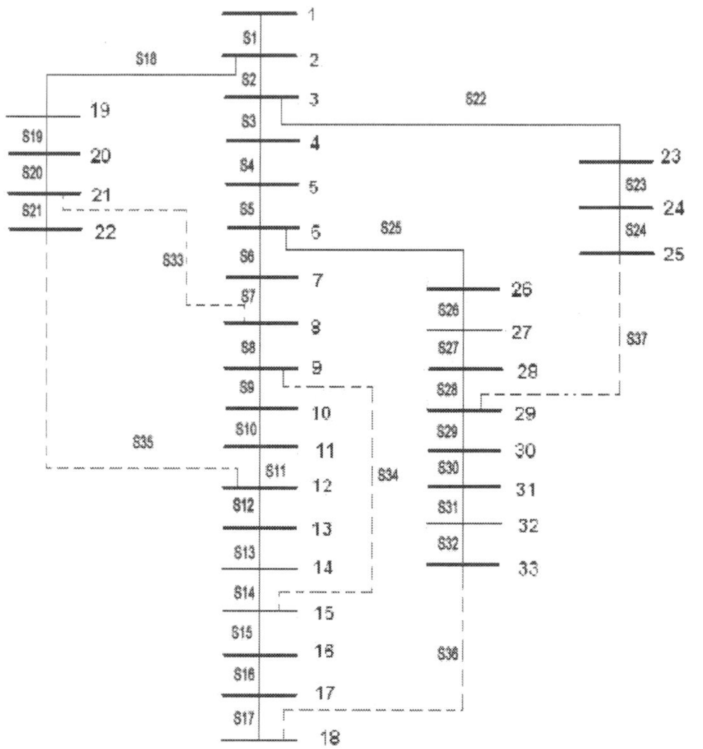

Fig. 7. Thirty three bus single feeder distribution network

Algorithm	Tie Switches					Total Impedance		Real power loss	Reactive power loss	Minimum bus Voltage
						R	X			
						Ω	Ω	MW	Mvar	p.u.
KRUSKAL'S	S16	S27	S33	S34	S35	20.52	16.49	0.1780	0.1230	0.922
REVERSE DELETE	S16	S27	S33	S34	S35	20.52	16.49	0.1780	0.1230	0.922
PRIM'S	S16	S27	S33	S34	S35	20.52	16.49	0.1780	0.1230	0.922
DIJKSTRA'S	S9	S14	S16	S28	S33	26.15	22.46	0.1671	0.1192	0.928

Table 3. Switches that are open and the impedance of the network

From the table it is observed that the resultant losses of the network obtained using the MST algorithms for the normal condition are less when compared to that of the original configuration. In the case of Dijkstra's algorithm it is noted that the impedance value is higher than the total impedance obtained using other three MST algorithm and the initial configuration. The value of the loss is less when compared to other minimum spanning tree algorithms and the initial network.

For the same network hybrid GA (Jizhong Zhu and Chang (1998)) and heuristic search method (Shirmohammadi and Hong (1989)) are applied and their results are tabulated in Table 4.

Algorithm	Tie Switches					Total Impedance (Ω)		Real power loss	Reactive power loss	Minimum bus Voltage
						R	X	MW	Mvar	p.u.
REFINED GA	S7	S10	S14	S36	S37	25.38	22.31	0.2007	0.1776	0.883
HEURISTIC METHOD	S7	S9	S14	S32	S37	24.39	21.61	0.1984	0.1760	0.887

Table 4. Switches that are open and the impedance of the network

Using the proposed methodology for a single line outage in 33 - bus network, the results are obtained and tabulated in Table 5.

OUTAGE IN LINE	SWITCHES THAT ARE OPEN				
S1	Power system cannot be restored				
S2	S2	S8	S24	S32	S34
S3	S3	S7	S9	S14	S16
S4	S4	S7	S9	S14	S16
S5	S5	S7	S9	S14	S16
S6	S6	S9	S13	S16	S28
S7	S7	S9	S16	S28	S34
S8	S8	S15	S28	S33	S34
S9	S9	S14	S16	S28	S33
S10	S10	S14	S16	S28	S33
S11	S11	S14	S16	S28	S33
S12	S12	S9	S16	S28	S33
S13	S13	S9	S16	S28	S33
S14	S14	S9	S16	S28	S33
S15	S15	S9	S14	S28	S33
S16	S16	S9	S14	S28	S33
S17	S17	S9	S14	S28	S33
S18	S18	S13	S16	S28	S35
S19	S19	S13	S16	S28	S35
S20	S20	S13	S16	S28	S35
S21	S21	S14	S16	S28	S33
S22	S22	S9	S14	S16	S33
S23	S23	S9	S14	S16	S33
S24	S24	S9	S14	S16	S33
S25	S25	S9	S14	S16	S33
S26	S26	S9	S14	S16	S33
S27	S27	S9	S14	S16	S33
S28	S28	S9	S14	S16	S33
S29	S29	S9	S14	S28	S33
S30	S30	S9	S14	S28	S33
S31	S31	S9	S14	S28	S33
S32	S32	S9	S14	S28	S33

Table 5. Result for single line outage in 33 bus network

6.1 Hardware implementation of the proposed MST algorithms for restoration problem

For the real time application in the automated world the developed program has to be used with hardware. So the developed methodology is implemented using Verilog HDL. Verilog is a hardware description language (HDL). A HDL is a language used to describe a digital system, for example, a network switch, or any memory or a single flip flop. This means that by using a HDL, one can describe any hardware at any level.

The proposed methodology indicates the ON and OFF status of the switch. In this hardware the ON and OFF status of a line is denoted by LOGIC 1 and LOGIC 0 respectively. The status of all the lines is denoted through on-board LEDs which is interfaced with the FPGA kit. The I/O pins of the FPGA chip are configured and port mapped accordingly. The Verilog program for 33 - bus single feeder system is implemented in Verilog through SPARTAN 3 FPGA (Field Programmable Gate Array) kit (Figure 8). It uses a XILINX XC3S400 chip for processing. The XC3S400 FPGA chip is embedded in a kit with peripheral ICs and components for research and development purpose.

Fig. 8. XILINX SPARTAN3 FPGA Kit

A Verilog program is written using XILINX ISE software to program the FPGA and display the status of lines as output based on the outage line which is given as input. The chip is programmed using XILINX ISE navigator tool. The FPGA kit used in this project consists of sixteen input switches and sixteen output LEDs (Figure 9). In addition the kit also has a 34 pin FRC and 60 pin FRC connector for 94 I/Os. Using these additional pins, the status of other switches (S17 - S37) are indicated in a bread board (Figure 10).

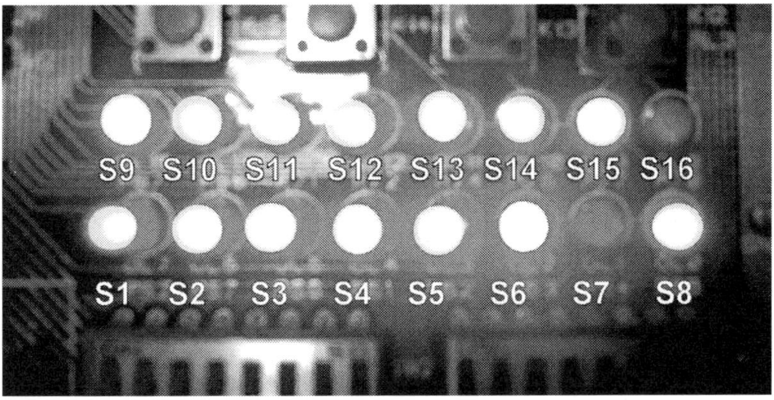

Fig. 9. Onboard LEDs displaying status of lines S1 to S16

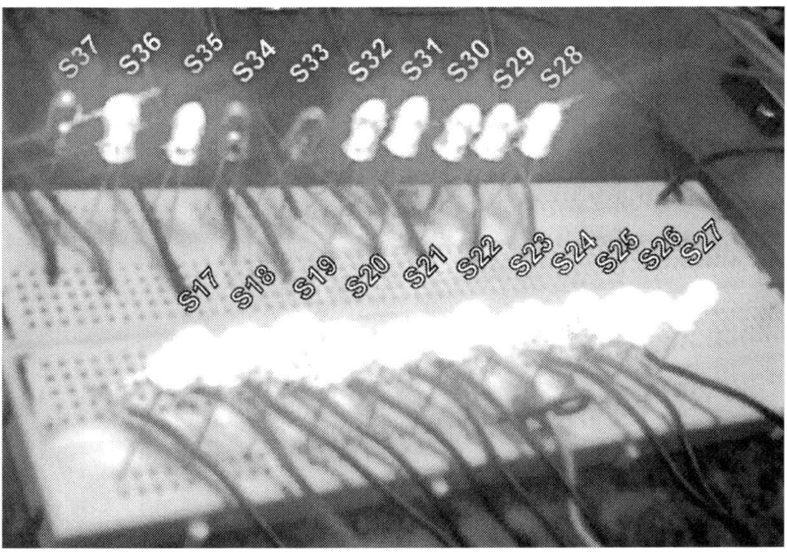

Fig. 10. Additional LEDs displaying status of lines S17 to S37

7. Conclusion

A feeder reconfiguration method using MST for service restoration of radial distribution system is presented. From the important observations of the present study it could be concluded that:

- The out-of-service area is reduced to the maximum by the developed MST methodology
- The power losses of distribution systems are reduced by proper feeder reconfiguration.

- In addition to power-loss reduction, the voltage profile is improved by the proposed method.
- Based on the methodology the feeder loads and load flow are performed each time, so that the effect of unbalanced power distribution network is also considered.
- It can be applied to distribution network of any size.

Test results obtained indicate that, this method results in better restoration plan when compared to other reference papers.

8. References

Adibi, M. M. and Kafka, R. J. (1991). *Power System Restoration Issues*, IEEE Computer Applications in Power, Vol. 4, No. 2, pp. 19-24.

Ali Shatnawi, M O Ahmad and M N Swamy, (1999) *Scheduling of DSP data flow graphs onto multiprocessor for maximum throughput*, IEEE 1999, pp 386 - 389.

Cavellucci and Lyra, (1997), *Minimization of energy losses in electric power distribution system by intelligent search strategies*, International transaction in operational research, vol. 4, no. 1, pp 23 - 33.

Fountas, N. A. Hatziargyriou, N. D. and Valavanisl, K. P. (1997). *Hierarchical Time Extended Petri Nets As A Generic Tool For Power System restoration*, IEEE Transactions on Power Systems, Vol. 12, No. 2, pp. 837-843.

Gregory Levitin, Shmuel Mazal-Tov and David Elmakis, (1995). *Genetic algorithm for optimal sectionalizing in radial distribution systems with alternative supply*, Electric Power Systems Research, Vol. 35, pp. 149-155.

Han - Ching kuo and Yuan Yih Hsu, (1993). *Distribution System Load Estimation and Service Restoration using a Fuzzy Set Approach*, IEEE Transactions on Power Delivery, Vol. 8, No. 4, pp. 1950-1957.

Hiroyuki Mork and Senji Tsuzuki, (1991), *A fast method for topological observability analysis using minimum spanning tree technique*, IEEE Transaction on power system vol. 6, no. 2, May 1991, pp 491 - 500.

Hotta, K., Nomura, H., Takemoto, H., Suzuki, K., Nakamura, S. and Fukui, S. (1990). *The Implementation of a Real-Time Expert System for a Restoration Guide in a Dispatching Center*, IEEE Transactions on Power Systems, Vol. 5, No. 3, pp. 1032-1038.

Hoyong Kim, Yunseok ko and Kyung-Hee Jung, (1993), *Artificial Neural-Network based Feeder Reconfiguration for Loss Reduction in Distribution Systems*, IEEE Transactions on Power Systems, Vol. 8, No. 3, pp. 1356-1366.

Kaigui Xie, Jiaqi Zhou and R Billinton, (2003), *Reliability evaluation algorithm for complex medium voltage electrical distribution networks based on the shortest path*, IEE Proc.-Gener. Transm. Distrib., vol. 150, no. 6, November 2003, pp 686 - 690

Lin Ming Jin and Shu Park Chan, (1989), *An electrical method for finding suboptimal routes*, ISCAS'89 IEEE pp 935 - 938.

Matsumoto, K., Sakaguchi, T., Kafka, R. J. and Adibi, M. M., (1992), *Knowledge-Based Systems as Operational Aids in Power System Restoration*, Proceedings of the IEEE, Vol. 80, No. 5, pp. 689-697.

Michel Barbehenn, (1998), *A note on the complexity of Dijkstra's algorithm for graphs with weighted vertices*, IEEE Transactions on computers, vol. 41, no 2, feb 1998, pp 263.

Mohanty, I., Kalita, J., Das, S., Pahwa, A. and Buehler, E., (2003), *Ant algorithms for the optimal restoration of distribution feeders during cold load pickup,* Proceedings of the 2003 Swarm Intelligence Symposium, SIS '03, IEEE, pp. 132-137.

Morelato, A. L. and Monticelli, A. (1989) *Heuristic Search Approach to Distribution System Restoration*, IEEE Transactions on Power Delivery, Vol. 4, No. 4, pp. 2235-2241.

Nagata, T. and Sasaki, H., (2002), *A Multi-Agent Approach to Power System Restoration*, IEEE transactions on power systems, Vol. 17, No. 2, pp. 457- 462.

Partricia Amancio Vargas, Christiano Lyra Filho and Fernanado J Von Zuben, (2002), *On line approach for loss reduction in electric power distribution networks using learner classifier systems*, Springer, pp 181 - 196.

Rahman, S., (1993), *Artificial intelligence in electric power systems – a survey of the Japanese industry*, IEEE Transactions on Power System, Vol. 8, No. 3, pp. 1211-1218.

Shun Lin Su, Charles H Barry and Chi Yuan Lo, (1994) *A space efficient short finding algorithms*, IEEE Transactions on computer aided design of integrated circuit & systems, vol. 13, no. 8, August 1994, pp 1065 - 1068.

Si - Qing Sheng, Yun Cao and Yu Yao, (2009), *Distribution Network Reconfiguration Based on Particle Swarm Optimization and Chaos Searching"*, Asia-Pacific Power and Energy Engineering Conference, APPEEC 2009, IEEE, pp. 1-4

Sudhakar T D, et. Al, (2010), "*Prim's Algorithm for Loss Minimization and Service Restoration in Distribution Networks*", International Journal of Electrical and Computer Engineering (IJEC), Volume 2, Number 1 (2010), pp. 43 - 62

Sudhakar T D, et. Al, (2010), "*A Graph Theory - Based Distribution Feeder Reconfiguration for Service Restoration*", International Journal of Power and Energy Systems, Vol. 30, No. 3, 2010, pp 161 - 168

Sudhakar T D, et. Al, (2011), "*Power System Reconfiguration based on Kruskal's Algorithm*" IEEE conference ICEES 2011 Volume 1 Page No 234 - 240

Sudhakar T D, et. Al, (2011), "*Power System Restoration using Reverse Delete Algorithm Implemented in FPGA*", Second IET International Conference on Sustainable Energy and Intelligent System, Page : 373 - 378

Sudhakar T D, et. Al, (2011), "*Restoration of Power Distribution Network – A Bibliographical Survey*", European Transactions on Electrical Power, Vol. 21, pp 635 - 655

TianTian CAi and Qian Ai, (2005), *Research of PMU optimal placement in power systems", International conference on system theory and scientific computation*, pp 38 - 43, ISBN 960-845735-1

Toune, S., Fudo, H., Genji, T., Fukuyama, Y. and Nakanishi, Y., (1998), *A reactive tabu search for service restoration in electric power distribution systems"* The 1998 IEEE International Conference on Evolutionary Computation Proceedings, IEEE World Congress on Computational Intelligence, pp. 763-768.

Ying - Tung Hsiao and Ching - Yang Chien, (2000), *Enhancement of Restoration Service in Distribution Systems Using a Combination Fuzzy – GA Method*, IEEE Transactions On Power Systems, Vol. 15, No. 4, pp. 1394-1400.

Yixin Yu, and Jianzhong Wu, (2002), *Loads Combination Method Based Core Schema Genetic Shortest-path Algorithm For Distribution Network Reconfiguration*, 2002 IEEE, pp 1729 - 1733.

15

Applications of Graphical Clustering Algorithms in Genome Wide Association Mapping

K.J. Abraham[1*] and Rohan Fernando[2]
[1]*Programa de Pós Graduação em Genética, Faculdade de Medicina de Ribeirão Preto, Universidade de São Paulo*
[2]*Dept. of Animal Science, Iowa State Univ*
[1]*Ribeirão Preto SP, Brazil*
[2]*Ames IA USA*

1. Introduction

The field of statistical genetics has been the area of a great deal of active research in recent years; due in part to dramatic advances in sequencing technology which has led to vast amounts of genomic data becoming available at lower and lower costs. The data from these sequencing efforts is not only copious, but is also characterized by significant levels of experimental noise. Processing data of this nature to draw statistically significant inferences requires dealing with a number of challenges, both statistical and algorithmic. In this chapter we will not discuss the very substantial statistical issues which arise in extracting genome sequences, but rather will focus on computational and algorithmic issues which arise in drawing biological inferences once the sequence is known. Event though our discussion will be oriented more towards applications of graph theory, it is worth keeping in mind that statistical considerations will still play a role due the intrinsically probabilistic nature of Mendelian Genetics as well as finite sample sizes. We will first begin by reviewing earlier well known work which will serve to illustrate the utility of graph theoretical concepts in dealing with genomic data. The data at our disposal are assumed to consist of observations of at a large number of locations (tens of thousands or possibly much more) on multiple chromosomes for a collections of individuals, or plants or animals; for now we assume that these individuals are related with known parent offpsring information. We restrict our attention to species which have just two chromosomes, but much of what we will discuss can be generalized to species with more than two chromosomes although the computational implementation could be challenging. At any locus (precise location on a specified chromosome) we assume that there are two or more possible alleles in the population, the precise number is assumed to differ from locus to locus. The number of possible observable genotypes at each locus will thus also vary from locus to locus. In a population of related individuals with known parent offspring relations between individuals (*i.e.* pedigree) it is possible to predict the probability for an offspring to receive a given allele from a parent based on Mendelian Genetics. If we represent a given locus for a given individual by a vertex, we can assign multiple possible states to each vertex depending on how many genotypes are possible. Since genetic information flows from parents to offspring

*Bolsista CAPES/Brasil

we can construct a directed graph where the arrows flow from parental vertices to offspring vertices. The indegree of each vertex is maximally two, while the outdegree will depend on how many offspring an individual has. We thus have a directed graph where each vertex has multiple states (genotypes or alleles) associated with it. Since individuals cannot be their own ancestors, the graph is acyclic as well as being directed. With each edge we can associate a transmission probability which is determined by Mendelian Genetics; in addition there is a Markov Field Property involved as conditional on parental genotypes offspring genotypes are independent of all other ancestral genotypes and sib genotypes. We thus have all the ingredients of a Bayesian Network. Many important problems relating to genetic inference from data on pedigrees have been formulated in the language of Bayesian Networks (Fishelson & Geiger, 2002); (Fishelson & Geiger, 2004); finding exact and approximate solutions to these problems particulary on large data sets has led to the development of very sophisticated algorithms which we will not discuss here. The key feature underlying the data is that it consists of a potentially large but discrete number of observations. These observations have a very complex correlational structure, some of the observations are heavily correlated (*eg.* the genotypes of parents and offspring at the same locus) while others may be very loosely correlated (*eg.* the genotypes of individuals and ancestors going back several generations). The discrete nature of the data points permits us to assign a vertex in a graph to each data point while the edge structure (which arises from the pedigree structure) is a reflection of the association between data points; seen in this light the use of a graph theoretical formulation is quite natural. In what follows, the data under consideration will have the same features, suggesting the use of graphical models but our discussion will focus more on the use of undirected graphical models.

In order to motivate the application of undirected graphical models, we consider two fixed loci on the same chromosome in a population of individuals. It is frequently observed that the joint distribution of alleles at loci which are in close physical proximity on the same chromosome, is not uniform. More specifically, if there are two alleles at one locus A or a and B or b at another locus, then the probability of finding allele B in some arbitrary individual in a population may depend on the which allele (A or a) is present at the other locus. In the language of probabilities $\mathcal{P}(A,B) \neq \mathcal{P}(A)\mathcal{P}(B)$ for certain pairs of loci; this is the phenomenon of linkage disequilibrium (LD) (Weir, 1996). The extent and statistical significance of the non-randomness of the alleleic association can be quantified by analyzing a (3×3) contingency table whose entries are genotype counts. If there are just two of the three possible genotypes present, or if the population from which the unrelated individuals are sampled is subject to certain other constraints, it becomes possible to estimate the linkage disequilibrium between each pair of distinct markers using just a (2×2) contingency table, alternatively the non-randomness in the asociation between the alleles depends one just one function of the allele counts. What is actually computed is just the sample LD, the standard errors on the LD will depend inversely on the size of the population. The magnitude of the observed LD can vary quite dramatically depending on which loci are being compared, large LD is very much more common among loci close together than loci on different chromosomes. Furthermore, while LD tends to decrease as the distance between loci increases, the decrease is often neither uniform nor monotonic. This discussion can be extended to multiple loci by considering larger contingency tables, more sophisticated multivariate discrete probability distributions and also multiple coefficients of association. Our data once again consists of a large number of discretized observations with a possibly complex correlation structure between the observations; suggesting the use of a graph theoretical formulation. If we represent each locus by a vertex, the LD structure can be captured graphically by introducing an undirected edge between a pair of vertices whenever the LD between the vertices in the pair is statistically significantly different from zero. It is assumed that there is a user defined significance threshold. The edge is undirected because the statment of statistical association between loci relates only to correlation, and does not carry any implications of causality. This defines an undirected graph whose edge structure is indicative of the LD patterns between the loci under consideration. Unlike in (Fishelson & Geiger, 2002); (Fishelson & Geiger, 2004); we do not associate states with a vertex in a graph, all that information has been averaged over all indviduals in determining the LD between markers. The use of graphical models to elucidate the LD structure between loci is well established (Thomas & Camp, 2004) as is the connection between graphical models and discrete multivariate probability distributions (Lauritzen, 1996). To summarize, datasets in statistical genetics consist of a vast collection of discretized observations with potentially very complex correlations between the observations; graph theoretical methods can be adopted for describing and analyzing data of this nature. In the rest of this chapter, we will discuss some applications of this nature, some open problems and possible solutions.

2. Graphical methods in association mapping

2.1 Population stratification

Understanding the LD structure is of considerable interest not only from the viewpoint of population genetics, but is vital for deducing the location of genes influencing traits in populations by Genetic Association Mapping. The Case Control design is a popular design for Genetic Association Mapping (Thomas, 2004). Here the data are assumed to consist of a large number of genotypes at fixed loci observed on two distinct groups of individuals, healthy controls and diseased cases, and we assume that the individuals are unrelated to each other. We assume that the genotypes are observed at marker loci, *i.e.* locations on the chromosome where there are no genes directly influencing the disease. Nonethless, if genotypes are observed at a large number of sufficiently closely spaced markers , there may be some markers physically close to the gene influencing the disease and which are potentially in strong LD with the diesease gene leading to a statisticaly significant association between certain genotypes and disease status. The goal of Case Control studies is to discover which markers (if any) show statistically significant associations with disease status and then draw conclusions about the physical location of a gene causing the disease with relation to these markers. As the association is statistical in nature it is important to understand potential causes of false positives in order to minimize Type I error. Two very important causes of Type I error in Case Control studies are population stratification and multiple testing artifacts. As we will see, undirected graphical models can be used to acquire new insights on both these problems. We begin with an analysis of population stratification; population stratification can be understood in terms of a difference in genetic content between cases and controls over and above any differences at loci in high LD with the disease gene. For example, if all the diseased cases are from one ethnic group, and all the healthy controls are from another ethnic group, then there will be statistically significant associations between case/control status and genotypes at loci which reflect differences in ethnicity *i.e.* population structure , in addition to loci which are possibly liked to the disease. This is an example of population stratification, and will lead to false positive associations at loci reflecting the ethnic differences between cases and controls but unrelated to the disease under study. In this very simple instance we just considered two ethnic groups, with all the cases drawn from one group and all the controls from the other, in more typical instances, both the cases and controls will themselves be mixtures of two or more ethnic groups. In these more realistic scenarios population stratification will be a problem when the proportions of various distinct groups are different in cases and controls and when genotypes are observed at loci where the frequencies of the various genotypes are different in the various ethnic groups represented in the case and control samples. The effects of population stratification can be ameliorated by carefully matching ethnicities between cases and controls but this is not always possible or feasible. In real life situations, it is safer to assume that population stratification exists, which then must be taken into account before testing any markers for association with disease status. There are two broad approaches to correcting for population stratification in genetic association studies, non-parametric and parametric. The most popular parametric method for dealing with population structure is using the program *Structure* (Pritchard, 2000) ;(Falush, 2003) in which specific scenarios for population admixture are assumed. *Structure* attempts to assign the individuals to specific clusters based on a specific model, the genotypes are the feature vectors used to decide how to assign individuals to clusters. In addition to the genotype data the number of populations present in the data must be supplied by the user, this is analogous to specifying the number of clusters in k-means or other clustering methods. In the most sophisticated scenario (the Linkage Model) the genotypes for any individual reflect a mixture of different populations with different chromosomal segments possibly arising from different populations. The number of populations however is not specified and must be supplied by the user. The precise assignment of individuals to different populations frequently arises only after a long MCMC simulation which uses genotypes for all individuals at all loci as input. Any LD between the loci is corrected for in the process of assigning individuals to constituent sub-populations. Since it is not uncommon to have genotypes at tens of thousands (frequently more) of loci implementing the methodology of *Structure* can be time consuming partly due to the sheer size of the data set and partly due the overhead of correcting for LD between the loci which is typically present when there are a large number of loci under consideration. The presence of LD between the loci also suggests that even though the number of loci may be large, the various loci do not necessarily contribute additional independent information on population stratification. This suggests that with a judicious choice of mutually independent loci, population stratification can be analyzed with a smaller and more manageable subset of the data in less CPU time. We will next explain how exactly this can be done using graph theoretical ideas and mention an application to real data.

An optimal set of loci for discerning population structure should be sufficiently large so that loci characteristic of populations whose frequency in the sample is relatively small, are nonetheless included, while ensuring a high degree of statistical independence between the loci. The requirement of statistical independence between the loci can be made more precise by ensuring that the loci are in low LD with one another. What we are then looking for is the largest possible subset of loci such that the LD between any arbitrary pair of loci is low. We will recast the problem in the language of graph theory using the correspondence between vertices in a graph and loci on a chromosome we discussed earlier and show a correspondence between a well known combinatorial optimization problem, that of finding the maximum independent set on an undirected graph. As there is no known polynomial time solution for this problem, a randomized heuristic algorithm will be described along with its performance on a real data set.

The input to the algorithm is $\mathcal{N}$, a set of N markers, an $N \times N$ symmetric matrix $\mathcal{M}$ with positive off diagonal values, and a positive constant c. The precise value of the diagonal matrix elements of $\mathcal{M}$ are not relevant as long as they are smaller than c . If we denote the elements of $\mathcal{N}$ by N_j $(1 \leq j \leq N)$ then each row of $\mathcal{M}$ corresponds to a unique marker; with this assignment $\mathcal{M}_{ij}(i \neq j)$ is simply the magnitude of the association between markers N_i and N_j. All the different M_{ij} can be easily computed given a rectangular data matrix of genotypes in which individuals are indexed by rows and each column contains the genotypes for one particular marker. As mentioned earlier we assign to each marker a vertex in an undirected graph $\mathcal{G}$. Thus $\mathcal{G}$ has a set of vertices $\mathcal{V}$ with N elements denoted by $V_i \in \mathcal{V}$, where $1 \leq i \leq N$. Since each marker is assigned to a unique row of $\mathcal{M}$, we can now uniquely associate to each row of $\mathcal{M}$ a vertex $V_i \in \mathcal{V}$, where $1 \leq i \leq N$. Let the set of edges of $\mathcal{G}$ be denoted by $\mathcal{E}$. An undirected edge E_{ij} exists between any two elements V_i and V_j of $\mathcal{V}$ if $\mathcal{M}_{ij} > c$. This condition is adequate to define all the elements of $\mathcal{E}$. There can clearly be no edges from any vertex to itself due to the choice of the diagonal matrix elements of $\mathcal{M}$. By a suitable choice of c, any two unlinked vertices in $\mathcal{G}$ can be made to correspond to two unassociated markers in $\mathcal{N}$. The precise value of c needed to achieve this correspondence will depend on some user specified threshold for defining significant association. Thus given a subset of vertices $\{V_i, V_j, V_k, V_m\}$ with no edges connecting any of the six possible pairs of vertices that can be formed from this subset, we can find a corresponding subset of markers $\{N_i, N_j, N_k, N_m\}$ which are mutually unassociated. This argument can be extended to any $\mathcal{V}_s \subset \mathcal{V}$ which gives rise to a corresponding $\mathcal{N}_s \subset \mathcal{N}$ of mutually unassociated markers. Furthermore, each unique $\mathcal{N}_s \subset \mathcal{N}$ corresponds to a unique $\mathcal{V}_s \subset \mathcal{V}$. However, any $\mathcal{V}_s$ corresponds to a clique on $\mathcal{G}^c$, the complement graph of $\mathcal{G}$. If we want the largest possible $\mathcal{N}_s \subset \mathcal{N}$ of mutually unassociated markers we must find the maximum independent set of vertices in $\mathcal{G}$.

We have thus transformed the problem of finding the largest possible set of mutually unassociated markers to a well known problem in graph theory that of finding the maximum independent subset of vertices in an undirected graph, (or equivalently the clique of largest size on the complement graph) a problem for which there is no known efficient solution. Thus we are forced to resort to heuristics which yield only approximate solutions, more precisely a subset of vertices which may be smaller in size than the true maximum independent subset. As a cross-check on any given solution it would be useful to have a different solution for the sake of comparision. This motivates the use of a stochastic greedy heuristic which can generate multiple solutions, rather than use of one of the many well known published heuristic algorithms for this problem. The graph that we have is unweighted, although we could have considered a weighted graph with the LD between markers playing the role of weights. Although the precise LD information has been ignored in the construction of the graph and in our heuristic algorithm, this does not matter. LD represents a statistical correlation and all that matters for our purposes is whether the correlation is significant or not. One complication we have ignored here is that the presence or absence of edges is determined by comparing sample LD values with some threshold; in a more sophisticated scheme the standard errors on the sample LD values could also be used to assign probabilities for the presence of edges in the graph where the corresponding sample LD values are close to the significance threshold.

We will next describe a stochastic greedy heuristic for finding the clique of maximum size on an undirected graph, which due to the exact corespondence between maximum cliques and maximum independent sets can readily be applied to our maximum independent set problem.

• Description of Algorithm

As before we assume we have an undirected graph $\mathcal{G}$ in which $\mathcal{V}$ is the set of vertices and $\mathcal{E}$ is the set of edges. $\mathcal{G}$ is not assumed related to any genetic marker map so the algorithm is at this stage perfectly general. The algorithm also requires as input a positive parameter γ which is a measure of how far the algorithm deviates from a deterministic greedy heuristic. The larger the value of γ the closer the algorithm resembles a deterministic heuristic. We define L_i the set of neighbors of V_i and n_i size of L_i, and assume $n_i > 0 \; \forall \; V_i \in \mathcal{V}$. We define sets of vertices $CandSet$, $TempSet$ as well as $ReturnSet$ which is the output from the program.

Informally, the algorithms starts by picking a seed vertex which has a relatively large number of neighbors, relatively large being defined with respect to the number of neighbors of all the vertices in the graph. This seed vertex V_s is inserted into $ReturnSet$. $CandSet$ is initialized by the set of neighbors V_s, while $TempSet$ is initialized by the empty set. An element V_n of $CandSet$ is chosen on the basis of having a relatively large number of neighbors and $TempSet$ is the set of neighbors of V_n not already included in $ReturnSet$. Next $CandSet \leftarrow (CandSet \cap TempSet)$, which has the effect of ensuring that all all surviving elements of $CandSet$ are elements of both V_s and V_n, *i.e.* all elements of $CandSet$ are connected to all elements of $ReturnSet$. Once this step is carried out, it is safe to pick another element from $CandSet$ and repeat the cycle untill $CandSet$ is the null set. At this stage $ReturnSet$ cannot be further augmented and the algorithm halts. A more precise description of the algorithm is given below.

• Initialization

1. Compute $norm = \sum_{i=1}^{N} n_i^{\gamma}$.
2. Evaluate $p_i = (n_i^{\gamma}/norm) \;\; \forall \, i \; 1 \leq i \leq N$.
3. Pick some j with probability p_j.
4. Insert V_j in $ReturnSet$.
5. $CandSet \leftarrow L_j$.
6. $TempSet \leftarrow \emptyset$.

• Main Loop

while $CandSet \neq \emptyset$ do

1. Evaluate $n_i^{\gamma} \; \forall \; V_i \in CandSet$
2. Compute $norm = \sum n_i^{\gamma}$
 with the summation restricted to elements of $CandSet$
3. Compute $p_k = (n_k^{\gamma}/norm) \; \forall \; V_k \in CandSet$
4. Select $V_n \in CandSet$ with probability p_n.
5. Insert V_n in $ReturnSet$.
6. $TempSet \leftarrow \{V_m \in L_n : V_m \notin ReturnSet \text{ where } 1 \leq m \leq N\}$
7. $CandSet \leftarrow (CandSet \cap TempSet)$
8. $TempSet \leftarrow \emptyset$

If $CandSet \equiv \emptyset$ return $ReturnSet$.

It is also possible to define a deterministic greedy heuristic in which the vertices selected in step 3 of the initialization and step 4 of the main loop are just those with the largest number of neighbors. If the parameter γ is made larger and larger, then the output from the program will increasingly resemble that from a deterministic greedy heuristic. It is worth pointing out that our algorithm does not make use of the relative location of markers with respect to each other along the chromosome, thus the methodology we outline is applicable whether the LD decays rapidly or slowly as a function of the distance between markers on the chromosome. The output from the algorithm returns a subset of markers which is not necessarily the largest subset of independent markers, nontheless the number of markers returned could still be large enough to get an accurate handle on population stratification. We now briefly discuss the application of of this to real data, more details are available in (Hamblin, 2010).

In conjunction with the Barley Coordinated Agricultural Project (www.BarleyCAP.org), 1816 Barley lines (treated as individuals for our purposes) were genotyped at 1415 markers. Five initial attempts to run *Structure* with 500,000 iterations and 100,000 burn in steps taking into account the association between markers and allowing for admixture between populations were unsuccessfull due to non-convergence of the MCMC iterations. At this stage, our algorithm was used to identify a subset of markers with linkage disequilibrium r^2 between any two markers in the subset to be less than 0.25, a criteria used to decide when to consider markers unlinked. A subset of 486 markers was identified and used as input for *Structure* allowing for admixture between individuals but no association between markers. Eight runs of *Structure* with 100,000 burn in and 200,000 analysis iterations all converged with consistent likelihood estimates, illustrating the utility of selecting unassociated markers as opposed to using the entire set and allowing for association between markers. It is worth pointing out that constituent populations identified by *Structure* have differing linkage disequilibrium structure at both short and large distances, with some SNPs in a few but not all of the subpopulations in high LD even when 50cM apart. As mentioned earlier, our algorithm does not use map distances in selecting markers, neither the presence of significant LD between unlinked markers nor the very different patterns of LD in the subpopulations is an issue. This feature gives rise to a complex edge structure on the graph, similar to the examples considered in (Thomas & Camp, 2004).

We next turn our attention to the relevance of the maximum independent set problem to non-parametric methods for analyzing population stratification. The most widely used non-parametric approach for analyzing population stratification is Principal Componets Analysis, a number of popular implementations such as EIGENSTRAT (Price, 2006) and EIGENSOFT (Patterson, 2006) are available. We will discuss the relevance of the apparoaches just described to EIGENSOFT and then show how some of the statistical methodology in EIGENSOFT might have applications to machine learning problems outside of statistical genetics. The input data for EIGENSOFT is a rectangular data matrix where the rows correspond to individuals and there is one column for each marker, the entries of the data-matrix correspond to the genotypes suitably parametrized and standardized. The key idea behind the implementation in (Patterson, 2006) is the realization that in the absence of population stratification, the largest Singular Value of the data matrix is distributed according to the Tracy Widom distribution (Tracy & Widom, 1994). However, even in the absence of stratification, deviations from the Tracy Widom distribution are possible if there is LD between the markers. One way to avoid false signals of population stratification is to choose a set of markers which are mutually uncorrelated, preferrably as large an unrelated set of markers as possible. As we have seen in the discussion of model dependent population stratification, choosing this set is tantamount to solving an instance of a maximum independent set on an undirected graph defined by the LD matrix. In practical instances, alternative methods have been used to find a set of unrelated markers, for example by exploiting special features of the LD structure or by other approximations(Heerwarden, 2010). It is not clear that these approaches will find the largest possible set of uncorrelated markers which is required for putting the most stringent bounds on the extent of population stratification. Very few (if any) attempts have been made to use the methodology previously described to identify as large a subset of unrelated markers as possible, such an analysis could be fruitful. This concludes our discussion on the application of graph theoretical methods for analyzing population stratification. The key point of our discussion is the relevance of the problem of finding the maximum independent set to understanding population stratification. This connection has not been established before (to the best of our knowledge) and can be exploited to speed up the the analysis of population stratification in real data sets. Before going on to discuss the application of graph theoretical methods to multiple testing, it is worth mentioning how the methodology developed in EIGENSOFT could possibly be used to address a long standing problem in cluster analysis, *i.e.* how to identify the number of distinct groupings in a dataset. As mentioned in our discussion of *Structure* the number of constituent populations to fit in *Structure* is user defined, in (Patterson, 2006) the authors point out how this number might be reliably estimated using the sample singular values of the data matrix and the details of the Tracy Widom Distribution. What this amounts to is computing a non-parametric statistic of the dataset which is then used to estimate the number of distinct groupings in the dataset. Since the methodology is very general and model independent it could conceivably be applied to a whole range of problems far removed from statistical genetics.

2.2 Multiple testing

Another major source of Type-I error in Genome Wide Association studies (GWAS) is false positives arising from multiple testing, and as mentioned earlier these can arise even if population stratification between cases and controls is fortuitously negligible or has been controlled for in some manner. Before we discuss the relevance of graph theoretical methods for understanding multiple testing artefacts, it is worth outlining the root of the problem and some common remedies. A large number of markers (N) are tested one after another for association with the trait or disease of interest. Under H_0 none of the markers are associated with the trait, and in addition the p-values for the test statistic are distributed like $\sim U(0,1)$. For a significance level α the expected number of significant tests under H_0 will be $\sim N\alpha$, since N in modern GWAS can be $\mathcal{O}(10^6)$ this leads to a sizeable number of false positives even if α is small. One way to ensure that there are no false positives with N independent tests is by choosing α so that $N\alpha \ll 1$ (the Bonferroni correction). However this leads to such stringent significance thresholds that only markers with very strong effects are picked up and many markers associated with the trait are ignored because their effects are not large enough to survive the stringent significance threshold, *i.e* there are is a large Type II error rate. Furthermore, if all the tests are not independent due to correlations between the markers the correction is excessively conservative. This problem can be avoided by permutation testing which leads to a non-parametric estimate of the number of significant test under H_0 given the correlation structure between the markers. While this approach certainly works it can become computationally very intensive when there are hundreds of thousands of markers to be tested. A less computationally intensive method to lower the number of Type II errors at the cost of allowing a certain number of false positives is by controlling the False Discovery Rate (FDR)(Benjamini & Hochberg, 1995); variants on this idea have also been considered. It has been suggested by (Nyholt, 2004) that the Bonferroni corrections be modified by replacing N with N^*, the number of independent tests, where hopefully N^* is very much smaller than N. With this replacement, the significance threshold can be made less stringent lowering the Type II error rate. We will next examine this sugestion in the language of graph theory, more specifically we will consider the problem of finding a suitable subset of independent markers, the size of this subset is the number of independent markers. One key observation is that restricting ourselves to a subset of markers is most meaningfull if it is possible to choose that subset of markers not only to be statistically independent also to be serve as surrogates for all the markers under consideration. If the latter condition is fulfilled, then testing only the markers in the independent subset can be regarded as testing each and every marker. If this condition is not fulfilled, we run the risk of skipping association tests on some markers which are part of the panel. It is worth pointing out that the idea that a limited subset of markers can be used as surrogates for an entire panel is well established; this is the notion underlying the use of tag SNPs in GWAS (Carlson, 2004). Identifying an optimal tag SNPs in a marker panel given the LD matrix between the markers can be reformulated as a variety of different well known graph theoretical problem, including the search for a dominating set of smallest size (Li & Wang, 2011). In order not to underestimate the number of independent tests it is necessary that the subset of markers be as large as possible; from our earlier discussion of population stratification it is clear than once again we are dealing with finding a maximum independent set on a undirected graph defined by the LD structure between the markers and a user defined specification of statistical independence between markers. The condition that the markers we select be proxies for all the markers in the panel can be fulfilled by requiring that each vertex be connected by an edge to at least one of the markers in the maximum independent set. In other words, the maximum independent set should be a dominating set for the graph. Since any maximal independent set is a dominating set (Foulds, 1992) the maximum independent set satisfies this condition. If the heuristic used to find the maximum independent set only returns a maximal independent set, this attractive feature will be preserved. Thus estimating the number of independent tests via maximum independent set heuristics seems to have some advantages. One can also approach the problem of estimating N^* in terms of the the size of the smallest dominating set on the graph. If the smallest dominating set turns out not to be an independent set, then the resulting estimate of N^* would be smaller than what we would obtain from analyzing independent sets, but not easy to estimate precisely, given the dependence of the markers. This point is illustrated in Fig. 1. where $\{A, B, E, F\}$ is the maximum independent set, but all markers can be tested by considering just two (not independent) markers C and D. In situations such as these, it is not clear what to value use for N^*.

Fig. 1. Ambuguity in N^*

In practise implementing the prescription of (Nyholt, 2004) has been shown to be problematic in real and simulated datasets (Dudbridge & Koeleman, 2004);(Salyakina, 2005);(Coneely & Boehnke, 2007), but there has been no general model independent analysis as to why these difficulties arise. Our graph theoretical analysis sheds light on possible ambiguities in the prescription of (Nyholt, 2004) which may be at part of the reason for its observed limitations. Before concluding our discussion on the applications of the maximum independent set it worth recalling that all that heuristics can deliver is a lower bound on the size of the maximum complete set. What is missing is some means using the data to obtain an estimate of the upper bound, such an estimate could potentially improve the performance and applicability of the heuristics. One feature of the data which has not been exploited is that the $N \times N$ matrix of correlation values is obtained from a data matrix with dimensionality $N_{ind} \times N$, where N_{ind} is the number of individuals and typically $N_{ind} < N$. Thus both the data matrix and the correlation matrix can be expected to have rank less than N. The redundancy in the rows of the correlation matrix due to the reduced rank could possibly be exploited in order to obtain an upper bound on the size of the maximum independent set. As has been shown in (Li & Li, 2005) this redundancy can be used to obtain an alternative estimate for the number of independent tests; combining the approach of (Li & Li, 2005) with the maximum independent set heuristic we describe here could be a fruitfull line of future research.

3. Blocking Gibbs

In the remainder of this chapter we will focus on possible applications of graph theoretical methodology to analysing pedigree data; more precisely we will consider individuals with known parent offspring relations and genotypic information at a possibly large number of loci. As was mentioned earlier, the pedigree structure and the genotypes can be combined to form a Bayesian Network where the conditional probabilities along the edges are defined by Mendelian Genetics. Since there are known genotypes there are vertices in the Bayesian networks where evidence is available. From the standpoint of genetic linkage analysis one of the most important quantities to be computed from a pedigree and associated genotypic data is the Likelihood (Ott, 1999). Computing the Likelihood involves evaluating a very complex series of nested sums and products of conditional probabilities over expressions such as the one shown below:

$$\cdots P(g^G \mid g^F, g^E)\, P(g^H \mid g^F, g^E)\, P(g^E \mid g^A, g^B) P(g^I \mid g^C, g^D) P(g^C \mid g^A, g^B)\, P(g^D \mid g^A, g^B) \cdots \tag{1}$$

g^A, g^B, *etc.* are discrete random variables representing either genotypes or alleles, and the $\cdots$ indicate the presence of many more such conditional probabilities. The conditional probabilities shown above are typical of the factors that would appear in the Joint Probability Distribution defined by the Bayesian Network, however realistic pedigrees often contain far more factors than can be written down. Computing the Likelihood involves summing over all allowed values of all the random variables, (*i.e.* all consistent genotypes), and in realistic situations where there are huge numbers of conditional probabilities, this is analytically intractable. Numerical solutions are hypothetically possible due to the local structure of the computations (Lauritzen & Spiegelhalter, 1988). The computational effort involved depends critically on the order in which the summations are performed (Jordan, 2004) and determining the lowest cost summation order is $\mathcal{NP}$ Hard (Arnborg, 1987). If no good heuristic algorithm for determining the most efficient summation order can be found the multiple sum cannot be performed exactly, and must be approximated by sampling the most significant terms.

This provides the motivation for introducing Markov Chain Monte Carlo (MCMC) methods which have been used extensively in linkage analysis (Thompson, 2005). The simplest form of MCMC sampler to implement is the Gibbs sampler, which however can be very tricky to implement on a large pedigree with many known genotypes. One of the key conceptual difficulties in implementing the Gibbs Sampler can be illustrated on a very simple situation involving just four individuals as shown in the following figure.

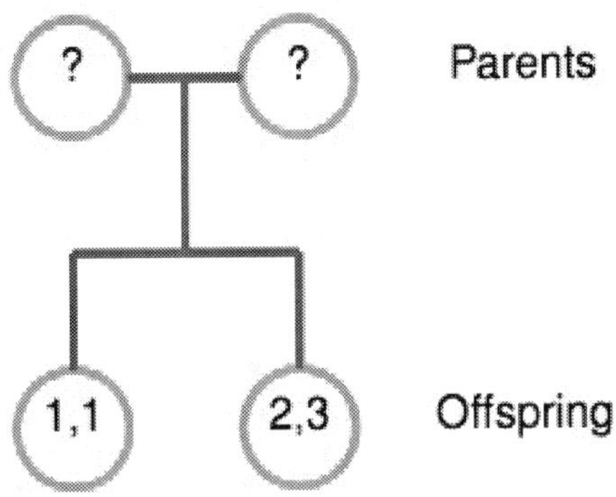

Fig. 2. Trouble with Gibbs

The two offspring have observed genotypes, and the laws of Mendelian Inheritance dictate that the two parental genotypic combinations are either $\{\{1,2\},\{1,3\}\}$ or $\{\{1,3\},\{1,2\}\}$ in obvious notation. In order for the sampler to be irreducible transitions between configurations should be possible, and in keeping with textbook Gibbs sampling one parental genotype would be updated at a time keeping the other fixed. Let us begin from the configuration$\{\{1,2\},\{1,3\}\}$ with a view to reaching $\{\{1,3\},\{1,2\}\}$. If we sample conditional on any one parent and the known genotypes, there is no way in which we can update the genotype of the other parent; *i.e.* the sampler gets stuck in the starting configuration. Thus a single site update is problematic and it is easy to see that the root of the problem lies in the stringent constraints arising from Mendelian Genetics which lead to strong correlations between the variables to be updated. A possible solution within the framework of Gibbs sampling is to update both parental genotypes simultaneously, *i.e.* use a blocking Gibbs sampler where a block consists of multiple stochastic variables which are strongly correlated and must be updated simultaneously. The idea of updating multiple strongly correlated variables during a single MCMC update in order to improve convergence is well established and outperforms standard Gibbs sampling in statistical genetics (Totir, 2003) and other applications. (Swendsen & Wang, 1987); (Roberts & Sahu, 1997). Furthermore, this approach has been applied in Bayesian Networks arising not only in Statistical Genetics (Jensen & Kong, 1999);(Thomas, 2000), but also in expert systems (Jensen, 1995). For our purposes the optimal choice of blocks is not only crucial for ensuring the irreducibility of the sampler but also for improving the mixing and convergence properties of the sampler. In the rest of this chapter we will study the issue of block definition and relate this problem to a well known problem in machine learning, that of partitioning data sets into semi-autonomous clusters. Before doing so we will briefly mention another aspect of likelihood computations on large pedigrees which has attracted recent attention, *i.e.* the relation to constraint satisfaction. The problem of finding assignments of unknown genotypes consistent with known genotypes, the pedigree structure and the laws of Mendelian Inheritance can be viewed as finding the solution of a constraint satisfaction problem, and is known to be computationally hard (Aceto, 2001). There is however one additional complication which arises in dealing with pedigrees, each solution can be assigned a posterior probability and what is required are the solutions with higher posterior probabilities. What an irreducible ergodic MCMC sampler should do is not only find solutions to a very complex contraint satisfaction problem, but also assign the correct posterior probability to the various solutions. Seen in this light it is easy to see why the MCMC sampling on pedigrees can be so challenging.

The key difficulty in constructing blocks is correctly grouping strongly correlated variables together, followed by updating them simultaneously in a manner consistent with the known genotypes. In simple instances like Fig. 2, grouping variables is easy, but in more complicated cases such as the pedigree in Fig. 3 it can be highly non-trivial.

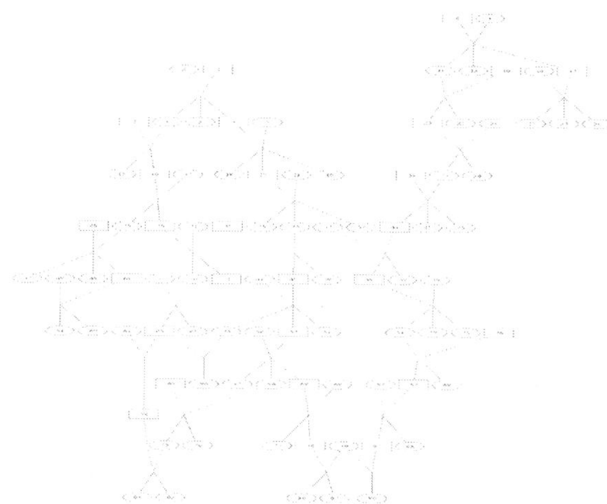

Fig. 3. Large pedigree

A moments reflection will suggest that the difficulty in partitioning the pedigree of Fig. 3 into blocks arises because of the large number of cycles in the graph. A more general analysis of the difficulties has been undertaken in (Jensen & Sheehan, 1998), the presence of cycles is indeed a problem and no general solution for dividing an arbitrary pedigree into blocks is known. However, a few features of a well motivated Blocking Scheme can be identified

- The assignment of blocks should be such that all the variables are assigned to at least one block. If this condition is not satisfied, some variables may not be updated leading to biased MCMC estimates.
- All strongly correlated variables must be contained in the same block, if not the irreducubility issues mentioned earlier will arise
- Within a given block variables should be more strongly correlated with each other than with variables outside the block.

It is easy to understand the relevance of these criteria, the last two criteria are not only relevant for pedigree analysis but are also similar to what might expected from an optimal partitioning of a data set into clusters. Note that we have not specified the number of partitions in advance; if this scheme were to be implemented on an arbitrary dataset it would not only assign all the elements of the dataset to clusters but could also return the number of partitions. Thus any heuristic solution for finding optimal blocks could be very useful in a number of machine learning applications. One important distinction between pedigree analysis and other applications is the requirement that the sampler mix rapidly, this was the motivation for the use of overlapping blocks. The relevance to data partitioning problems of a more general nature is greatest when the clusters are expected to overlap. The other important distinction is that many genotypes in pedigrees may be unknown, corresponding to vertices with no information. Missing or ambiguous data are not as widely considered in other data sets, so the analogy works better when there are not too many unknown genotypes.

One outline of a Blocking Gibbs scheme was made in (Abraham, 2007) where the problem of Block Identification and consistent assignment of genotypes were addressed simultaneously. The algorithmic insight exploited in (Abraham, 2007) was that the genotypes of any given individual are strongly dependent by just a handfull of close relatives; in the language of the pedigree graph the state of a vertex is influenced by just a handfull of neighbouring vertices. This is because the edge structure in the graph reflects a combination of either relatedness between individuals or physical distance between loci. The notion of neighbouring vertices can be made more precise by defining distances between vertices in terms of a breadth first search. Due to the underlying Markov Field Property, vertices which are far apart as defined by the breadth first search are expected to be roughly independent. Once there is a guideline for deciding which vertices can be expected to be independent of other vertices, it becomes possible to partition the graph into overlapping blocks in which consistent genotype assignments in a block can be made with little input from the evidence from other blocks. The dataset used in (Abraham, 2007) is very complex and has many of the features discussed in (Jensen & Sheehan, 1998) which are known to lead to difficulties, nonetheless it was possible to generate a consistent set of genotypes using the scheme just outlined. Furthermore, it was checked that the posterior probabilities of the genotypes found in this manner were consistent with those that would have been obtained in the absence of any approximations. This suggests that separation of vertices on the graph is a useful guideline for assessing the approximate independence of the corresponding random variables. Criteria similar to these have been successfully used to construct blocks and mcmc samplers in other complex examples, (Habier, 2009);(Habier, 2010) indicating that the basic idea may have a broad general applicability.

If we consider the problem in a more general light, what we have done is to use the known correlations in a data set containing many discrete observations to identify subsets of variables which have strong correlations with each other but weaker correlations with the other variables. If this methodology were to be applied to cluster a general data set with a a known matrix of correlation values it would be first necesary to define graph and identify edges between the vertices (datapoints). Identifying edges could be acchieved through a user defined threshold which could be defined independent of the data values as described in our discussion of population stratification , or could be defined in terms of some suitable number of sample standard deviations above the sample mean of all the correlation values. Once the edges are specified in this manner, the procedure used in (Abraham, 2007) could be used to define blocks which in a more general case would correspond to a cluster in the data set. One advantage of this procedure is that it has been shown to work in the context of pedigree graphs where inaccurate assignment of vertices to clusters will often be penalized by poor

MCMC convergence or in extreme cases by a lack of irreducibility of the sampler. Adapting the blocking methodologies in (Abraham, 2007);(Habier, 2009) and (Habier, 2010) to other cluster identification in general ohmics data sets could prove to be fruitful.

We next consider a long standing issue which is relevant in both block assignment in blocking gibbs and cluster assignment in general, *i.e.* the problem of determining the number of independent subgroups in the data set making as few model dependent assuptions as possible. As was mentioned in our discussion of non-parametric population stratification , the authors of (Patterson, 2006) suggest that from the elements of a suitably constructed correlation matrix a test statistic can be obtained which can be used to decide on the appropriate number of populations to use as input for parametric population stratification analysis. The treatment of this issue in (Patterson, 2006) is so general that it would appear to be the basis for a model-free approach that could be used to estimate the number of subgroups in an arbitrary ohmics data set given a matrix of correlation values. As applied to blocking gibbs, the matrix of correlation values could be substituted by the distance matrix used in (Abraham, 2007) or some more sophisticated variant thereof. In this regard it is worth recalling that number zero eigenvalues of the Laplacian of an undirected graph is the number of connected components, which supplies a lower bound on the number of clusters. Thus the connection between the entries of a suitable correlation matrix and the number of clusters is well established, by applying the results of (Patterson, 2006) it might be possible to extract more detailed information on the number of clusters present in a dataset.

4. Conclusions

In this chapter we have discussed the relevance and applications of graph theoretical methods to a number of problems in statistical genetics. In particular, some novel applications of the maximum independent set on an undirected graph to population stratification were presented. Some key issues in the construction of Blocking Gibbs Samplers on complex pedigrees were discussed along with their relevance outside of statistical genetics.

5. Acknowledgments

RLF and KJA both received supprot from the United States Department of Agriculture, National Research Iniative Grant USDA NRI-2009-03924. KJA also acknowledges financial support of the program Professor Visitante do Exterior of Coordenação de Aperfeiçoamento de Pessoal de Nível Superior (CAPES) , Brasil. KJA thanks Prof. Jean-Eudes Dazard and members of the Department of Computation and Mathematics, University of São Paulo (Ribeirão Preto) for valuable discussions.

6. References

Abraham, K.J., *et.al.*. (2007). Improved techniques for sampling complex pedigrees with the gibbs sampler, *Genetics, Selection and Evolution* 39: 27–38.

Aceto, L., *et. al.*. (2001). The complexity of checking consistency of pedigree information and related problems, *The Journal of Computer Science and Technology* 19(1): 42–59.

Arnborg, S., *et.al.*. (1987). Complexity of finding embeddings in a k-tree, *SIAM Journal on Algebraic and Discrete Methods* 8: 277–284.

Benjamini, Y. & Hochberg, Y. (1995). Controlling the false discovery rate a practical and powerful approach to multiple testing, *Journal of the Royal Statistical Society B* 57: 289–300.

Carlson, C.S., *et.al.*. (2004). Selecting a maximally informative set of single-nucleotide polymorphisms for association analysis using linkage disequilibrium, *American Journal of Human Genetics* 74: 106–120.

Coneely, K. & Boehnke, M. (2007). So many correlated tests, so little time! rapid adjustments of p values for multiple correlated tests, *American Journal of Human Genetics* 81(6): 2074–2093.

Dudbridge, F. & Koeleman, B. (2004). Efficient computation of significance levels for multiple associations in large studies of correlated data, including genomewide association studies, *American Journal of Human Genetics* 75(3): 424–435.

Falush, D., *et.al.*. (2003). Inference of population structure using multilocus genotype data: Linked loci and correlated allele frequencies, *Genetics* 164: 1567–1587.

Fishelson, M. & Geiger, D. (2002). Exact genetic linkage computations for general pedigrees, *Bioinformatics* 18 Suppl. 1: S189–S198.

Fishelson, M. & Geiger, D. (2004). Optimizing exact genetic linkage computations, *Journal of Computational Biology* 11(2-3): 263–275.

Foulds, L. (1992). *Graph Theory Applications*, Springer Verlag.

Habier, D., *et.al.*. (2009). Genomic selection using low density marker panels, *Genetics* 182: 343–353.

Habier, D., *et.al.*. (2010). A two-stage approximation for analysis of mixture genetic models in large pedigrees, *Genetics* 185: 655–670.

Hamblin, M.T., *et.al.*. (2010). Population structure and linkage disequilibrium in us barley germplasm: Implications for association mapping, *Crop Science* 50(2): 556–566.

Heerwarden, J. V., *et.al.*. (2010). Fine scale genetic structure in the wild ancestor of maize zea mays ssp parviglumis, *Molecular Ecology* 19: 1162–1163.

Jensen, C. & Kong, A. (1999). Blocking gibbs sampling for linkage analysis in large pedigrees, *American Journal of Human Genetics* 65(3): 885–901.

Jensen, C. & Sheehan, N. (1998). Problem with determination of noncommunicating classes for markov chain monte carlo applications in pedigree analysis, *Biometrics* 54: 416–425.

Jensen, C.S., *et.al.*. (1995). Blocking gibbs sampling in very large probabilistic expert systems, *International journal of human computer studies* 42(6): 573–704.

Jordan, M. (2004). Graphical models, *Statistical Science* 19(1): 140–155.

Lauritzen, S. L. (1996). *Graphical Models*, Oxford University Press.

Lauritzen, S. & Spiegelhalter, D. (1988). Local computations with probabilities on graphical structures and their application to expert systems, *Journal of the Royal Statistical Society Series B* 50: 157–224.

Li, J. & Li, K. (2005). Adjusting multiple testing in multilocus analyses using the eigenvalues of a correlation matrix, *Human Heredity* 95: 221–227.

Li, J. & Wang, W.-B. (2011). Tag snp selection, *in* E. Zeggini & A. Morris (eds), *Analysis of Complex Disease Association Studies, A Practical Guide*, Academic Press, pp. 49–65.

Nyholt, D. (2004). A simple correction for multiple testing for single nucleotide polymorphisms in linkage disequilibrium with each other, *American Journal of Human Genetics* 74(2): 765–769.

Ott, J. (1999). *Statistical Methods in Genetic Epidemiology*, The Johns Hopkins University Press.

Patterson, N. *et.al.*. (2006). Population structure and eigenanalysis, *PLoS Genetics* 2(12): 2074–2093.

Price, A.L., *et.al.*. (2006). Principal components analysis corrects for stratification in genome-wide association studies, *Nature Genetics* 38: 904–909.

Pritchard, J.K., *at.al.*. (2000). Inference of population structure using multilocus genotype data, *Genetics* 155(2-3): 945–959.

Roberts, G. & Sahu, S. (1997). Updating schemes, correlation structure, blocking and parameterization for the gibbs sampler, *Journal of the Royal Statistical Society Series B* 59(6): 573–704.

Salyakina, D., *et.al.*. (2005). Evaluation of nyholt's procedure for multiple testing correction, *Human Heredity* 60: 19–25.

Swendsen, R. & Wang, J.-S. (1987). Nonuniversal critical dynamics in monte carlo simulations, *Physical Review Letters* 58: 86–88.

Thomas, A. & Camp, N. (2004). Graphical modelling of the joint distributions of alleles at associated loci, *American Journal of Human Genetics* 74: 1088–1101.

Thomas, A., *et.al.*. (2000). Multilocus linkage analysis by blocked gibbs sampling, *Statistics and Computing* 10: 259–269.

Thomas, D. T. (2004). *Statistical Methods in Genetic Epidemiology*, Oxford University Press.

Thompson, E. A. (2005). Mcmc in the analysis of genetic data on pedigrees, *in* W. S. Kendall, F. Liang & J.-S. Wang (eds), *Markov Chain Monte Carlo Innovations and Applications*, World Scientific Publishing, pp. 183–217.

Totir, L.R., *et.al.*. (2003). A comparison of alternative methods to compute conditional genotype probabilities for genetic evaluation with finite locus models, *Genetics,Selection and Evolution* 35: 585–604.

Tracy, C. & Widom, H. (1994). Level spacing distribution and the airy kernel, *Communications in Mathematical Physics* 159: 151–174.

Weir, B. S. (1996). *Genetic Data Analysis II*, Sinauer Associates, Sunderland MA 01375 USA.

16

Centralities Based Analysis of Complex Networks

Giovanni Scardoni and Carlo Laudanna
Center for BioMedical Computing (CBMC), University of Verona
Italy

1. Introduction

Characterizing, describing, and extracting information from a network is by now one of the main goals of science, since the study of network currently draws the attention of several fields of research, as biology, economics, social science, computer science and so on. The main goal is to analyze networks in order to extract their emergent properties (Bhalla & Iyengar (1999)) and to understand functionality of such complex systems. Two possible analysis approaches can be applied to a complex network: the first based on the study of its topological structure, the second based on the dynamic properties of the system described by the network itself. Since "always structure affects function" (Strogatz (2001)), the topological approach wants to understand networks functionality through the analysis of their structure. For instance, the topological structure of the road network affects critical traffic jam areas, the topology of social networks affects the spread of information and disease and the topology of the power grid affects the robustness and stability of power transmission. Remarkable results have been reached in the topological analysis of networks, concerning the study and characterization of networks structure, and even if far from being complete, several key notions have been introduced. These unifying principles underly the topology of networks belonging to different fields of science. Fundamental are the notions of scale-free network (Barabasi & Albert (1999); Jeong et al. (2000)), cluster (Newman (2006)), network motifs (Milo et al. (2002); Shen-Orr et al. (2002)), small-world property (Watts & Strogatz (1998); Watts (1999); Wagner & Fell (2001)) and centralities. Particularly, centralities have been initially applied to the field of social science (Freeman (1977)) and then to biological networks (Wuchty & Stadler (2003)). Usually, works regarding biological networks rightly consider global properties of the network and when centralities are used, they are often considered from a global point of view, as for example analyzing degree or centralities distribution (Jeong et al. (2000); Wagner & Fell (2001); Wuchty & Stadler (2003); Yamada & Bork (2009); Joy et al. (2005)). A node-oriented approach have been used analyzing attack tolerance of network, where consequences of central nodes deletion are studied (Albert et al. (2000); Crucitti et al. (2004)). But also in this case the analysis have been concentrate on global properties of the network and not on the relevance of the single nodes in the network. Similarly, available software for network analysis is usually oriented to global analysis and characterization of the whole networks. To identify relevant nodes of a biological network, protocols of analysis integrating centralities analysis and lab experimental data are needed and the same for software allowing this kind of analysis. Cytoscape is an excellent visualization and analysis tool with the analysis features greatly enhanced by plug-ins. Plug-in such as NetworkAnalyzer (Assenov et al. (2008)) computes some node centralities but does not allow direct integration with experimental data. Applications such as VisANT

(Hu et al. (2005)), and Centibin (Junker et al. (2006)) calculate centralities, although they either calculate fewer centralities or are not suitable to integration with experimental data. Starting from these general considerations, the first part of this chapter concern the application of network centralities analysis to complex networks from a perspective oriented to identify relevant nodes, with a particular attention to biological networks. Necessary steps to do this are illustrated above through an example of protein-protein interaction network analysis. The aim of the first part of this chapter is to face the centralities analysis of a protein interaction network from a node oriented point of view. The same approach can then be extended to several kinds of complex networks. We want to identify nodes that are relevant for the networks for both centralities analysis and lab experiments. To do this, the following steps have been done:

- Some centralities that we consider significant have been detected. A biological meaning of these centralities have been hypothesized.
- A protocol of analysis for a protein network based on integration of centralities analysis and data from lab experiments (activation level) have been designed.
- A software (CentiScaPe) for computing centralities and integrating topological analysis results with lab experimental data set is presented.
- A human kino-phosphatome network have been extracted from a global human protein interactome data-set, including 11120 nodes and 84776 unique undirected interactions obtained from public data-bases.
- CentiScaPe have been applied to this human kino-phosphatome network and activation level (in threonine and thyrosine) of each protein obtained performeing lab experiments have been related to centrality values.
- Proteins important from both topological analysis and activation level have been easily identified: the attention of successive experiments and analysis should be focused on these proteins.

A further step have been introduced. Once we have identified relevant proteins in a network, we are interested in identifying non-obvious relation between these and other proteins in the network. In any network structure, the role of a node depends, not only on the features of the node itself, but also on the topological structure of the network and on the other nodes features. So even if centralities are node properties, they depend also on other nodes. We know that in a protein network nodes can be added or deleted because of different reasons as for example gene duplication (adding) or gene deletion or drug usage (deleting). More generally, If we delete a relevant node in a complex network, the effects of the deletion have impact not only on the single node and its neighbors, but also on other part of the network. For instance, if you are close friend of an important politician of your town, you have a central role in the social network of the town, and consequently your friends have a central role. But if this politician looses his central role, or if he is completely excluded from the political life of the town, for instance because they put him in prison (this correspond to a deletion on the social network), also you loose your central role in the network and the same for those people related to you. The idea is that the impact of an adding or deletion of a node can be measured through the variation of centrality values of the other nodes in the network. Such notion we introduced have been called "network centralities interference". It allows to identify those nodes that are more sensitive to deletion or adding of a particular node in the network. The Interference Cytoscape plugin have been released to allow this kind of analysis (Scardoni & Laudanna (2011)).

Section 2 consists in a review of some centralities considered important with particular consideration for biological networks. For each centrality a possible biological meaning have been treated and some examples illustrate their significance. Section 3 introduce the CentiScaPe software, the Cytoscape plug-in we implemented for computing network centralities. Main feature of the software is the possibility of integrating experimental data-set with the topological analysis. In CentiScaPe, computed centralities can be easily correlated between each other or with biological parameters derived from the experiments in order to identify the most significant nodes according to both topological and biological properties. In section 4 the protocol of analysis is introduced through an example of analysis of a human kino-phosphatome network. Most relevant kinases and phosphatases according to their centralities values have been extracted from the network and their phosphorylation level in threonine and tyrosine have been obtained through a lab experiment. Centrality values and activation (phosphorylation) levels have been integrated using CentiScaPe and most relevant kinases and phosphatases according to both centrality values and activation levels have been easily identified. Section 5 introduce the Interference software to measure the changes in the topological structure of complex networks.

2. Node centralities: definition and description

In this section, some of the classical network centralities are introduced. For each centrality, we present the mathematical definition, a brief description with some examples, and a possible biological meaning in a protein network. A good and complete description of network centralities can be found in (Koschützki et al. (2005)), where also some algorithms are presented. For many centralities indices it is required that network is connected, i.e. each node is reachable from all the others. If not, some centralities can results in infinity values or some other not properly correct computation. Besides some centralities are not defined for directed graph (except of trivial situation), so we will consider here only connected undirected graph.

Preliminary definitions

Let $G = (N, E)$ an undirected graph, with $n = |N|$ vertexes. $deg(v)$, indicate the degree the vertex. $dist(v, w)$ is the shortest path between v and w. σ_{st} is the number of shortest paths between s and t and $\sigma_{st}(v)$ is the number of shortest paths between s and t passing through the vertex v. Notably:

- Vertex = nodes; edges = arches;
- The "distance" between two nodes, $dist(v, w)$ is the shortest path between the two nodes;
- All calculated scores are computed giving to "higher" values a "positive" meaning, where positive does refer to node proximity to other nodes. Thus, independently on the calculated node centrality, higher scores indicate proximity and lower scores indicate remoteness of a given node v from the other nodes in the graph.

2.1 Degree ($deg(k)$)

Is the simplest topological index, corresponding to the number of nodes adjacent to a given node v, where "adjacent" means directly connected. The nodes directly connected to a given node v are also called "first neighbors" of the given node. Thus, the degree also corresponds to the number of adjacent incident edges. In directed networks we distinguish in-degree, when the edges target the node v, and out-degree, when the edges target the adjacent neighbors of v. Calculation of the degree allows determining the "degree distribution" $P(k)$, which gives the probability that a selected node has exactly k links. $P(k)$ is obtained counting the number of nodes $N(k)$ with $k = 1, 2, 3 \ldots$ links and dividing by the total number of nodes N. Determining the degree distribution allows distinguishing different kind of graphs. For instance, a graph with a peaked degree distribution (Gaussian distribution) indicates that the system has a characteristic degree with no highly connected nodes. This is typical of random, non-natural, networks. By contrast, a power-law degree distribution indicates the presence of few nodes having a very high degree. Nodes with high degree (highly connected) are called "hubs" and hold together several nodes with lower degree. Networks displaying a degree distribution approximating a power-law, $P(k) \approx k^{-\gamma}$, where γ is degree exponent, are called scale-free networks (Barabasi & Albert (1999)). Scale-free networks are mainly dominated by hubs and are intrinsically robust to random attacks but vulnerable to selected alterations (Albert et al. (2000); Jeong et al. (2001)). Scale-free networks are typically natural networks.

In biological terms

The degree allows an immediate evaluation of the regulatory relevance of the node. For instance, in signaling networks, proteins with very high degree are interacting with several other signaling proteins, thus suggesting a central regulatory role, that is they are likely to be regulatory "hubs". For instance, signaling proteins encoded by oncogenes, such as HRAS, SRC or TP53, are hubs. Depending on the nature of the protein, the degree could indicate a central role in amplification (kinases), diversification and turnover (small GTPases), signaling module assembly (docking proteins), gene expression (transcription factors), etc. Signaling networks have typically a scale-free architecture.

2.2 Diameter (Δ_G)

ΔG is the maximal distance (shortest path) amongst all the distances calculated between each couple of vertexes in the graph G. The diameter indicates how much distant are the two most distant nodes. It can be a first and simple general parameter of graph "compactness", meaning with that the overall proximity between nodes. A "high" graph diameter indicates that the two nodes determining that diameter are very distant, implying little graph compactness. However, it is possible that two nodes are very distant, thus giving a high graph diameter, but several other nodes are not (see figure 1). Therefore, a graph could have high diameter and still being rather compact or have very compact regions. Thus, a high graph diameter can be misleading in term of evaluation of graph compactness. In contrast a "low" graph diameter is much more informative and reliable. Indeed, a low diameter surely indicates that all the nodes are in proximity and the graph is compact. In quantitative terms, "high" and "low" are better defined when compared to the total number of nodes in the graph. Thus, a low diameter of a very big graph (with hundreds of nodes) is much more meaningful in term of compactness than a low diameter of a small graph (with few nodes). Notably, the diameter enables to measure the development of a network in time.

In biological terms

The diameter, and thus the compactness, of a biological network, for instance a protein-signaling network, can be interpreted as the overall easiness of the proteins to communicate and/or influence their reciprocal function. It could be also a sign of functional

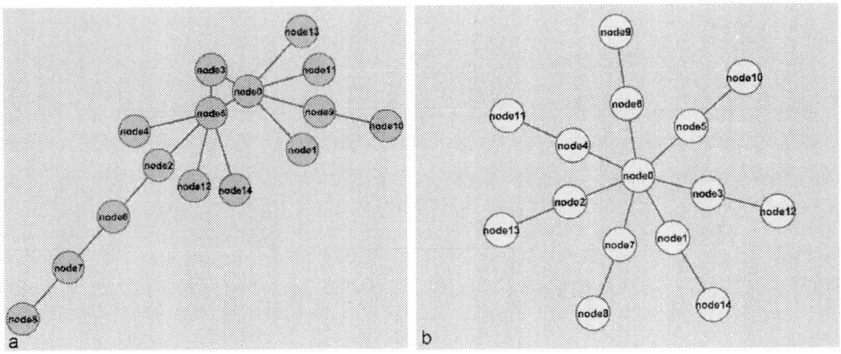

Fig. 1. a. A network where high diameter is due to a low number of nodes. b. A network with low diameter and average distance. The network is "compact".

convergence. Indeed, a big protein network with low diameter may suggest that the proteins within the network had a functional co-evolution. The diameter should be carefully weighted if the graph is not fully connected (that is, there are isolated nodes).

2.3 Average distance (AvD_G)

$$AvD_G = \frac{\sum_{i,j \in N} dist(i,j)}{n(n-1)}$$

where n is the number of nodes in G. The average distance (shortest path) of a graph G, corresponding to the sum of all shortest paths between vertex couples divided for the total number of vertex couples. Often it is not an integer. As for the diameter, it can be a simple and general parameter of graph "compactness", meaning with that the overall tendency of nodes to stay in proximity. Being an average, it can be somehow more informative than the diameter and can be also considered a general indicator of network "navigability". A "high" average distance indicates that the nodes are distant (disperse), implying little graph compactness. In contrast a "low" average distance indicates that all the nodes are in proximity and the graph is compact (figure **??**). In quantitative terms, "high" and "low" are better defined when compared to the total number of nodes in the graph. Thus, a low average distance of a very big graph (with hundreds of nodes) is more meaningful in term of compactness than a low average distance of a small graph (with few nodes).

In biological terms

The average distance of a biological network, for instance a protein-signaling network, can be interpreted as the overall easiness of the proteins to communicate and/or influence their reciprocal function. It could be also a sign of functional convergence. Indeed, a big protein network with low average distance may suggest that the proteins within the network have the tendency to generate functional complexes and/or modules (although centrality indexes should be also calculated to support that indication).

2.4 Eccentricity ($C_{ecc}(v)$)

$$C_{ecc}(v) := \frac{1}{max\{dist(v,w) : w \in N\}}$$

The eccentricity is a node centrality index. The eccentricity of a node v is calculated by computing the shortest path between the node v and all other nodes in the graph, then the "longest" shortest path is chosen (let (v, K) where K is the most distant node from v). Once this path with length $dist(v, K)$ is identified, its reciprocal is calculated $(1/dist(v, K))$. By doing that, an eccentricity with higher value assumes a positive meaning in term of node proximity. Indeed, if the eccentricity of the node v is high, this means that all other nodes are in proximity. In contrast, if the eccentricity is low, this means that there is at least one node (and all its neighbors) that is far form node v. Of course, this does not exclude that several other nodes are much closer to node v. Thus, eccentricity is a more meaningful parameter if is high. Notably, "high" and "low" values are more significant when compared to the average eccentricity of the graph G calculated by averaging the eccentricity values of all nodes in the graph.

In biological terms

The eccentricity of a node in a biological network, for instance a protein-signaling network, can be interpreted as the easiness of a protein to be functionally reached by all other proteins in the network. Thus, a protein with high eccentricity, compared to the average eccentricity of the network, will be more easily influenced by the activity of other proteins (the protein is subject to a more stringent or complex regulation) or, conversely could easily influence several other proteins. In contrast, a low eccentricity, compared to the average eccentricity of the network, could indicate a marginal functional role (although this should be also evaluated with other parameters and contextualized to the network annotations).

2.5 Closeness ($C_{clo}(v)$)

$$C_{clo}(v) := \frac{1}{\sum_{w \in N} dist(v,w)}$$

The closeness is a node centrality index. The closeness of a node v is calculated by computing the shortest path between the node v and all other nodes in the graph, and then calculating the sum. Once this value is obtained, its reciprocal is calculated, so higher values assume a positive meaning in term of node proximity. Also here, "high" and "low" values are more meaningful when compared to the average closeness of the graph G calculated by averaging the closeness values of all nodes in the graph. Notably, high values of closeness should indicate that all other nodes are in proximity to node v. In contrast, low values of closeness should indicate that all other nodes are distant from node v. However, a high closeness value can be determined by the presence of few nodes very close to node v, with other much more distant, or by the fact that all nodes are generally very close to v. Likewise, a low closeness value can be determined by the presence of few nodes very distant from node v, with other much closer, or by the fact that all nodes are generally distant from v. Thus, the closeness value should be considered as an "average tendency to node proximity or isolation", not really informative on the specific nature of the individual node couples. The closeness should be always compared to the eccentricity: a node with high eccentricity + high closeness is very

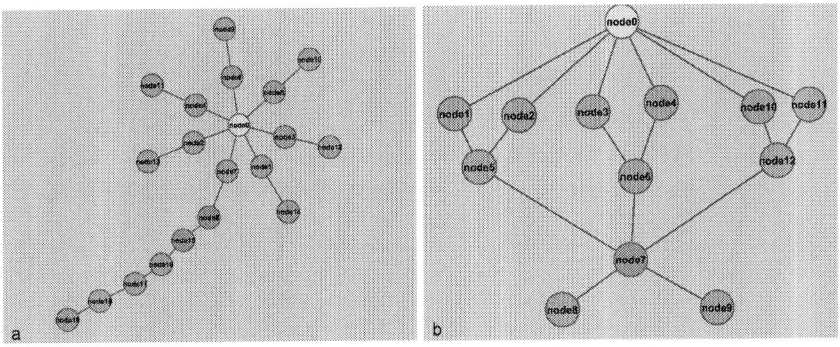

Fig. 2. a. The network shows the difference between eccentricity and closeness. The values of eccentricity are node0=0.14, node8=0.2, node15=0.2. The closeness values are node0=0.021, node8=0.017, node15=0.014. In this case node0 is closer than node8 and node15 to the most of nodes in the graph. Eccentricity value of node0 is smaller than value of node8 and node15, but this is due only to few nodes. If they are proteins this probably mean that node0 is fundamental for the most of reaction in the network, and that node8 and node15 are important only in reactions between few proteins. b. The network shows the difference between centroid and closeness. Here node0 has highest centroid value (centroid=1, closeness=0,04) and node7 has highest closeness value (centroid=-1, closeness= 0,05).

likely to be central in the graph. Figure 2 shows an example of difference between closeness and eccentricity.

In biological terms

The closeness of a node in a biological network, for instance a protein-signaling network, can be interpreted as a measure of the possibility of a protein to be functionally relevant for several other proteins, but with the possibility to be irrelevant for few other proteins. Thus, a protein with high closeness, compared to the average closeness of the network, will be easily central to the regulation of other proteins but with some proteins not influenced by its activity. Notably, in biological networks could be also of interest to analyze proteins with low closeness, compared to the average closeness of the network, as these proteins, although less relevant for that specific network, are possibly behaving as intersecting boundaries with other networks. Accordingly, a signaling network with a very high average closeness is more likely organizing functional units or modules, whereas a signaling network with very low average closeness will behave more likely as an open cluster of proteins connecting different regulatory modules.

2.6 Radiality ($C_{rad}(v)$)

$$C_{rad}(v) := \frac{\sum_{w \in N}(\Delta_G + 1 - dist(v,w))}{n-1}$$

The radiality is a node centrality index. The radiality of a node v is calculated by computing the shortest path between the node v and all other nodes in the graph. The value of each path is then subtracted by the value of the diameter $+1$ $(\Delta G + 1)$ and the resulting values are summated. Finally, the obtained value is divided for the number of nodes -1 $(n-1)$. Basically, as the diameter is the maximal possible distance between nodes, subtracting systematically from the diameter the shortest paths between the node v and its neighbors will give high values if the paths are short and low values if the paths are long. Overall, if the radiality is high this means that, with respect to the diameter, the node is generally closer to the other nodes, whereas, if the radiality is low, this means that the node is peripheral. Also here, "high" and "low" values are more meaningful when compared to the average radiality of the graph G calculated by averaging the radiality values of all nodes in the graph. As for the closeness, the radiality value should be considered as an "average tendency to node proximity or isolation", not definitively informative on the centrality of the individual node. The radiality should be always compared to the closeness and to the eccentricity: a node with high eccentricity + high closeness+ high radiality is a consistent indication of a high central position in the graph.

In biological terms

The radiality of a node in a biological network, for instance a protein-signaling network, can be interpreted as the measure of the possibility of a protein to be functionally relevant for several other proteins, but with the possibility to be irrelevant for few other proteins. Thus, a protein with high radiality, compared to the average radiality of the network, will be easily central to the regulation of other proteins but with some proteins not influenced by its activity. Notably, in biological networks could be also of interest to analyze proteins with low radiality, compared to the average radiality of the network, as these proteins, although less relevant for that specific network, are possibly behaving as intersecting boundaries with other networks. Accordingly, a signaling network with a very high average radiality is more likely organizing functional units or modules, whereas a signaling network with very low average radiality will behave more likely as an open cluster of proteins connecting different regulatory modules. All these interpretations should be accompanied to the contemporary evaluation of eccentricity and closeness.

2.7 Centroid value ($C_{cen}(v)$)

$$C_{cen}(v) := min\{f(v,w) : w \in N\{v\}\}$$

Where $f(v,w) := \gamma_v(w) - \gamma_w(v)$, and $\gamma_v(w)$ is the number of vertex closer to v than to w. The centroid value is the most complex node centrality index. It is computed by focusing the calculus on couples of nodes (v,w) and systematically counting the nodes that are closer (in term of shortest path) to v or to w. The calculus proceeds by comparing the node distance from other nodes with the distance of all other nodes from the others, such that a high centroid value indicates that a node v is much closer to other nodes. Thus, the centroid value provides a centrality index always weighted with the values of all other nodes in the graph. Indeed, the node with the highest centroid value is also the node with the highest number of neighbors (not only first) if compared with all other nodes. In other terms, a node v with the highest centroid value is the node with the highest number of neighbors separated by the shortest path to v. The centroid value suggests that a specific node has a central position within a graph region characterized by a high density of interacting nodes. Also here, "high" and "low" values are more meaningful when compared to the average centrality value of the graph G calculated by averaging the centrality values of all nodes in the graph.

In biological terms

The centroid value of a node in a biological network, for instance a protein-signaling network, can be interpreted as the "probability" of a protein to be functionally capable of organizing discrete protein clusters or modules. Thus, a protein with high centroid value, compared to the average centroid value of the network, will be possibly involved in coordinating the activity of other highly connected proteins, altogether devoted to the regulation of a specific cell activity (for instance, cell adhesion, gene expression, proliferation etc.). Accordingly, a signaling network with a very high average centroid value is more likely organizing functional units or modules, whereas a signaling network with very low average centroid value will behave more likely as an open cluster of proteins connecting different regulatory modules. It can be useful to compare the centroid value to algorithms detecting dense regions in a graph, indicating protein clusters, such as, for instance, MCODE (Bader & Hogue (2003)).

2.8 Stress ($C_{str}(v)$)

$$C_{str}(v) := \sum_{s \neq v \in N} \sum_{t \neq v \in N} \sigma_{st}(v)$$

The stress is a node centrality index. Stress is calculated by measuring the number of shortest paths passing through a node. To calculate the "stress" of a node v, all shortest paths in a graph G are calculated and then the number of shortest paths passing through v is counted. A "stressed" node is a node traversed by a high number of shortest paths. Notably and importantly, a high stress values does not automatically implies that the node v is critical to maintain the connection between nodes whose paths are passing through it. Indeed, it is possible that two nodes are connected by means of other shortest paths not passing through the node v. Also here, "high" and "low" values are more meaningful when compared to the average stress value of the graph G calculated by averaging the stress values of all nodes in the graph.

In biological terms

The stress of a node in a biological network, for instance a protein-signaling network, can indicate the relevance of a protein as functionally capable of holding together communicating nodes. The higher the value the higher the relevance of the protein in connecting regulatory molecules. Due to the nature of this centrality, it is possible that the stress simply indicates a molecule heavily involved in cellular processes but not relevant to maintain the communication between other proteins.

2.9 S.-P. Betweenness ($C_{spb}(v)$)

$$C_{spb}(v) := \sum_{s \neq v \in N} \sum_{t \neq v \in N} \delta_{st}(v)$$

where

$$\delta_{st}(v) := \frac{\sigma_{st}(v)}{\sigma_{st}}$$

The S.-P. Betweenness is a node centrality index. It is similar to the stress but provides a

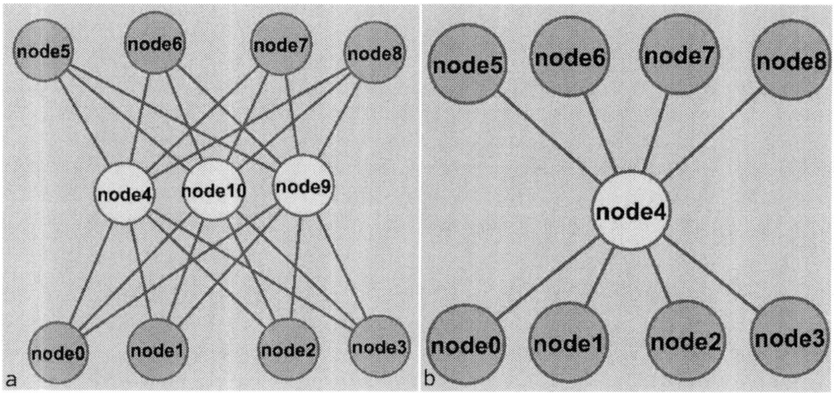

Fig. 3. Betweenness vs Stress. In fig. a node4, node10, and node9 present high value of stress (= 56), and the same value of betweenness (=18.67). In fig.b, node4 presents the same value of stress of fig.a and higher value of betweenness(=56). This is because the number of shortest paths passing through node4 is the same in the two network. But in the second network node4 is the only node connecting the two parts of the network. In this sense betweenness is more precise than stress giving also information on how the node is fundamental in the network. If we remove node4 in fig.a, the connection between the node in the network don't change so much. If we remove node 4 from fig.b the network is completely disconnected.

more elaborated and informative centrality index. The betweenness of a node n is calculated considering couples of nodes $(v1, v2)$ and counting the number of shortest paths linking $v1$ and $v2$ and passing through a node n. Then, the value is related to the total number of shortest paths linking $v1$ and $v2$. Thus, a node can be traversed by only one path linking $v1$ and $v2$, but if this path is the only connecting $v1$ and $v2$ the node n will score a higher betweenness value (in the stress computation would have had a low score). Thus, a high S.-P. Betweenness score means that the node, for certain paths, is crucial to maintain node connections. Notably, to know the number of paths for which the node is critical it is necessary to look at the stress. Thus, stress and S.-P. Betweenness can be used to gain complementary information. Further information could be gained by referring the S.-P. Betweenness to node couples, thus "quantifying" the importance of a node for two connected nodes. Also here, "high" and "low" values are more meaningful when compared to the average S.-P. Betweenness value of the graph G calculated by averaging the S.-P. Betweenness values of all nodes in the graph.

In biological terms

The S.-P. Betweenness of a node in a biological network, for instance a protein-signaling network, can indicate the relevance of a protein as functionally capable of holding together communicating proteins. The higher the value the higher the relevance of the protein as organizing regulatory molecule. The S.-P. Betweenness of a protein effectively indicates the capability of a protein to bring in communication distant proteins. In signaling modules, proteins with high S.-P. Betweenness are likely crucial to maintain functionally and coherence of signaling mechanisms.

2.10 Normalization and relative centralities

Once centralities have been computed, the question that arise immediately is what does it means to have a centrality of, for example, 0.4 for a node? This clearly depends on different parameters as the number of nodes in the network, the maximum value of the centrality and on the topological structure of the network. In order to compare centrality scores between the elements of a graph or between the elements of different graphs some kind of normalization of centrality values is needed. Common normalizations applicable to most centralities are to divide each value by the maximum centrality value or by the sum of all values. We will use the second defining it as the relative centralities value. So, given a centrality C, $C(G,n)$ is the value of the centrality of node n in the network G. We define the relative centrality value of node n as:

$$relC(G,n) = \frac{C(G,n)}{\sum_{i \in N} C(G,i)}$$

So a relative centrality of 0.4 means that the node has the 40% of the total centrality of the network.

2.11 Conclusions

A review of nodes centralities have been presented. The centralities introduced have been chosen for their biological relevance, and a possible biological meaning for each centrality have been hypothesized. Normalization of centralities, useful for comparison between nodes in a network and between nodes of different networks have also been considered.

3. CentiScaPe a software for network centralities

In this section we describe the CentiScaPe software (Scardoni et al. (2009)), a Cytoscape (Cline et al. (2007); Shannon et al. (2003)) plugin we implemented to calculate centralities values and integrating topological analysis of networks with lab experimental data. Main concepts of this section have been published on (Scardoni et al. (2009)).

The vast amount of available experimental data generating annotated gene or protein complex networks has increased the quest for visualization and analysis tools to understand individual node functions masked by the overall network complexity. Cytoscape is an excellent visualization and analysis tool with the analysis features greatly enhanced by plug-ins. Plug-in such as NetworkAnalyzer (Assenov et al. (2008)) computes some node centralities but does not allow direct integration with experimental data. Applications such as VisANT (Hu et al. (2005)), and Centibin (Junker et al. (2006)) calculate centralities, although they either calculate fewer centralities or are not suitable to integration with experimental data. Figure 1 shows a comparative evaluation of CentiScaPe and other applications. CentiScaPe is the only Cytoscape plug-in that computes several centralities at once. In CentiScaPe, computed centralities can be easily correlated between each other or with biological parameters derived from the experiments in order to identify the most significant nodes according to both topological and biological properties. Functional to this capability is the scatter plot by value options, which allows easy correlating node centrality values to experimental data defined by the user. Particularly this feature allows a new way to face the analysis of biological network, integrating topological analysis and lab experimental data. This new approach is described in section 4. At present version 1.2 is available and it is downloaded with a rate of about hundred downloads for month (see Cytoscape

Feature	Centiscape	Network analyzer	Visant	Centibin
Degree	Yes	Yes	Yes	Yes
Radiality	Yes	Yes	No	Yes
Closeness	Yes	Yes	No	Yes
Stress	Yes	Yes	No	Yes
Betweenness	Yes	Yes	No	Yes
Centroid value	Yes	No	No	Yes
Eccentricity	Yes	Yes	No	Yes
Scatter plot between centralities	Yes	No	No	No
Scatter plot with experimental data	Yes	No	No	No
Plot by node	Yes	No	No	No
Highlighting filter	Yes	No	No	No

Table 1. Features of CentiScaPe versus Network Analyzer, Visant, Centibin

website for download statistics). Several results using CentisCaPe have been published in Arsenio Rodriguez (2011); Sengupta et al. (2009a); Lepp et al. (2009); Sengupta et al. (2009b); Biondani et al. (2008); Sengupta et al. (2009c); Feltes et al. (2011); Schokker et al. (2011); Ladha et al. (2010); Choura & Rebaï (2010); Venkatachalam et al. (2011); Webster et al. (2011).
Availability: CentiScaPe can be downloaded via the Cytoscape web site:
http://chianti.ucsd.edu/cyto_web/plugins/index.php.
Tutorial, centrality descriptions and example data are available at:
http://www.cbmc.it/%7Escardonig/centiscape/centiscape.php

3.1 System overview

CentiScaPe computes several network centralities for undirected networks. Computed parameters are: Average Distance, Diameter, Degree, Stress, Betweenness, Radiality, Closeness, Centroid Value and Eccentricity. Plug-in help and on-line files are provided with definition, description and biological significance for each centrality (see section 2). Min, max and mean values are given for each computed centrality. Multiple networks analysis is also supported. Centrality values appear in the Cytoscape attributes browser, so they can be saved and loaded as normal Cytoscape attributes, thus allowing their visualization with the Cytoscape mapping core features. Once computation is completed, the actual analysis begins, using the graphical interface of CentiScaPe.

3.2 Algorithm and implementation

To calculate all the centralities the computation of the shortest path between each pair of nodes in the graph is needed. The algorithm for the shortest path is the well known Dijkstra algorithm (Dijkstra (1959)). There are no costs in our network edges, so in our case the algorithm keeps one as the cost of each edge. To compute Stress and Betweenness we need all the shortest paths between each pair of nodes and not only a single shortest path between each pair. To do this the Dijkstra algorithm has been adjusted as follows. Exploring the graph when calculating the shortest path between two nodes s and t, the Dijkstra algorithm keep for each node n a predecessor node p. The predecessor node is the node that is the predecessor of n in one of the shortest paths between s and t. So in case of the Dijkstra algorithm, only one predecessor for each node is needed. To have all the shortest paths, we replace the predecessor p with a set of predecessors for each node n. The set of predecessors of the node n is the set of all the predecessors of the node n in the shortest paths set between s and t, i.e. one node is in the set of predecessors of n if it is a predecessor of n in one of the shortest paths between s and t containing n. Once the predecessors set of each node n has been computed, also the tree of all the shortest paths between s and t can be easily computed. Once we have computed all the shortest paths between each pairs of nodes of our network, the algorithm of each centralities comes directly from the formal definition of each centrality. Computational complexity for each centrality value is shown in table 2. A well done description of this and

Centrality	Computational complexity
Diameter	$O(mn + n^2)$
Average distance	$O(mn + n^2)$
Degree (deg(v))	$O(n)$
Radiality (rad(v))	$O(mn + n^2)$
Closeness (clo(v))	$O(mn + n^2)$
Stress (str(v))	$O(mn + n^2)$
Betweenness (btw(v))	$O(n^3)$
Centroid Value (cen(v))	$O(mn + n^2)$
Eccentricity (ecc(v))	$O(mn + n^2)$

Table 2. Computational complexity for each centrality value. n is the number of nodes and m is the number of edges in the network.

other centralities algorithms can be found in (Koschützki et al. (2005)). CentiScaPe is written in Java as a Cytoscape plugin, in order to exploit all the excellent features of Cytoscape and to reach the larger number of users. The Java library JFreechart (Gilbert (n.d.)) has been used for some graphic features.

3.3 Using CentiScaPe

Once CentiScaPe have been started, the main menu will appear as a panel on the left side of the Cytoscape window as shown in figure 4. The panel shows to the user the list of centralities and the user can select all the centralities or some of them. A banner and a node worked count appear during the computation to show the computation progress. The numerical results are saved as node or network attributes in the Cytoscape attributes browser, depending on the kind of parameters, so all the Cytoscape features for managing attributes are supported: after the computation the centralities are treated as normal Cytoscape attributes. The value of each centrality is saved as an attribute with name "CentiScaPe" followed by the name of the centrality. For example the eccentricity is saved in the Cytoscape attributes browser as "CentiScaPe Eccentricity". Since the Cytoscape attributes follow the alphabetical order this make it easy to find all the centralities in the attributes browser list. There are two kind of centralities: network centralities, and node centralities.

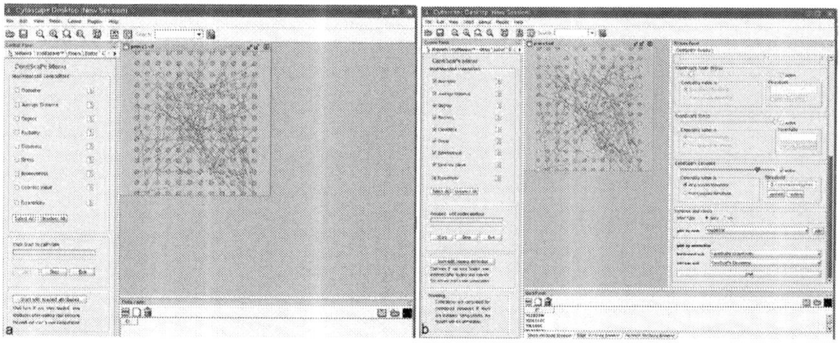

Fig. 4. a. CentiScaPe starting panel. On the left side the main menu appears, to select the centralities for computation. b. A computation results of CentiScaPe. All nodes having centrality values more/equal than the corresponding threshold (AND operator) are highlighted.

Network centralities

The network centralities concern the entire network and not the single nodes. They are the Diameter and the Average Distance. They will appear on the data panel selecting the Cytoscape network attribute browser.

Node centralities

All other centralities are node parameters and refer to the single nodes. So they will appear on the attribute browser as node attributes. Using the Node attribute browser the user can select one or more of them as normal attributes. CentiScaPe also calculates the min, max and mean value for each centrality. Since they are network parameters they appear on the Network attribute browser. As for the other attributes the user can save and load network and node parameters to/from a file. If an attribute is already loaded or calculated and the user try to recalculate it, a warning message will appear.

CentiScaPe results panel

If one or more node centralities have been selected, a result panel will appear on the right side of the Cytoscape window (figure 4b). The first step of the analysis is the Boolean logic-based result panel of CentiScaPe (figure 4b). It is possible, by using the provided sliders in the Results Panel of Cytoscape, to highlight the nodes having centralities values that are higher, minor or equal to a threshold value defined by the user. The slider threshold is initialized to the mean value of each centrality so all the nodes having a centrality value less or equal to the threshold are highlighted by default in the network view with a color depending on the selected visual mapper of Cytoscape (yellow in figure 4b). So if one centrality has been selected, all the nodes having a value less or equal the threshold for that centralities are highlighted. If more than one centralities has been selected they can be joined with an AND or an OR operator. If the AND operator is selected, the nodes for which all the values are less or equal the corresponding threshold are highlighted. If the OR operator is selected the nodes for which at least one value is less or equal the corresponding threshold are highlighted. The possibility of highlighting also the nodes that are more/equal than the threshold is supported. So the user can select the more/equal option for some centralities, the less/equal option for others and can join them with the AND or the OR operator. If necessary, one or more centralities can be deactivated. This feature can immediately answer to questions as: "Which are the nodes having high Betweenness and Stress but low Eccentricity?" Notably, the threshold can also be modified by hand to gain in resolution. In figure **??** are highlighted all the nodes having centralities values more/equal than the corresponding threshold (AND operator). Once the nodes have been selected according to their node-specific values, the corresponding subgraph can be extracted and displayed using normal Cytoscape core features.

Graphic output

Two kind of graphical outputs are supported: plot by centrality and plot by node, both allowing analysis that are not possible with other centralities tools. The user can correlate

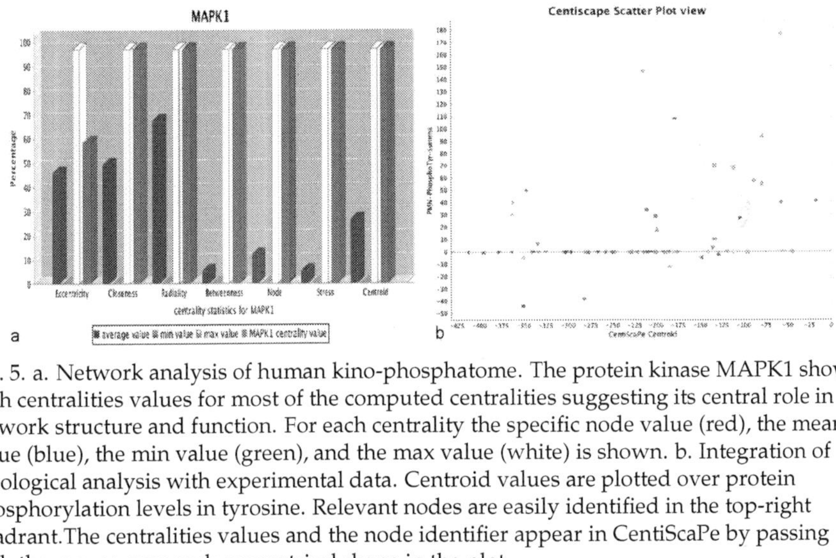

Fig. 5. a. Network analysis of human kino-phosphatome. The protein kinase MAPK1 shows high centralities values for most of the computed centralities suggesting its central role in the network structure and function. For each centrality the specific node value (red), the mean value (blue), the min value (green), and the max value (white) is shown. b. Integration of topological analysis with experimental data. Centroid values are plotted over protein phosphorylation levels in tyrosine. Relevant nodes are easily identified in the top-right quadrant.The centralities values and the node identifier appear in CentiScaPe by passing with the mouse over each geometrical shape in the plot.

centralities between them or with experimental data, such as, for example, gene expression level or protein phosphorylation level (plot by centrality), and can analyze all centralities values node by node (plot by node). Example of plot by node and plot by centrality are shown in figure 5. Graphics can be saved to a jpeg file.

Plot by centrality

The plot by centrality visualization is an easy and convenient way to discriminate nodes and/or group of nodes that are most relevant according to a combination of two selected parameters. It shows correlation between centralities and/or other quantitative node attributes, such as experimental data from genomic and/or proteomic analysis. The result of the plot by centrality option is a chart where each individual node, represented by a geometrical shape, is mapped to a Cartesian axis. In the horizontal and vertical axis, the values of the selected attributes are reported. Most of the relevant nodes are easily identified in the top-right quadrant of the chart. Figure 5b shows a plot of centroid values over intensity of protein tyrosine phosphorylation in the human kino-phosphatome network derived from the analysis of human primary polymorphonuclear neutrophils (PMNs) stimulated with the chemoattractant IL-8 (see section 4). The proteins having high values for both parameters likely play a crucial regulatory role in the network. The user can plot in five different ways: centrality versus centrality, centrality versus experimental data, experimental data versus experimental data, a centrality versus itself and an experimental data versus itself. Notably, a specific way to use the plot function is to visualize the scatter plot of two experimental data attributes. This is an extra function of the plug-in and can be used in the same way of the centrality/centrality option and centrality/experimental attribute option. If the plot by centrality option is used selecting the same centrality (or the same experimental attribute) for both the horizontal and the vertical axis, result is an easy discrimination of nodes having low values from nodes having high values of the selected parameter (figure 6a) Thus, the main use of the "plot by centrality" feature is to identify group of nodes clustered according to combination of specific topological and/or experimental properties, in order to extract sub-networks to be further analyzed. The combination of topological properties with experimental data is useful to allow more meaningful predictions of sub-network function to be experimentally validated.

Plot by node

The plot by node option, another unique feature of CentiScaPe, shows for every single node the value of all calculated centralities represented as a bar graph. The mean, max and min values are represented with different colors. To facilitate the visualization, all the values in the graph are normalized and the real values appear when pointing the mouse over a bar. Figure 5a shows, as an example, the values for the MAPK1 calculated from the global human kino-phosphatome (see section 4).

3.4 Conclusions

CentiScaPe is a versatile and user-friendly bioinformatic tool to integrate centrality-based network analysis with experimental data. CentiScaPe is completely integrated into Cytoscape and the possibility of treating centralities as normal attributes permits to enrich the analysis with the Cytoscape core features and with other Cytoscape plug-ins. The analysis obtained with the Boolean-based result panel, the "plot by node" and the "plot by centrality" options give meaningful results not accessible to other tools and allow easy categorization of nodes in large complex networks derived from experimental data.

4. A new protocol of analysis. Centralities in the human kino-phosphatome

In this section a new protocol of analysis of protein interaction network is introduced through an example of analysis of the human kino-phosphatome (Scardoni et al. (2009)). The analysis starts with the extraction of known interaction from a protein interactome. In our case we consider kinases and phosphatases interaction i.e. those interaction regarding activation and inhibition of proteins in the network. Kinases and phosphatases are enzymes involved in the phosphorilation process: they transfer or remove phosphate groups to/from a protein regulating in this way its activity. Substantially kinases and phosphatases activate or inhibit other proteins. In a kino-phosphatome network this process generates a cascade of activations and inhibitions of proteins corresponding to the transmissions of signals and to the control of complex processes in cells. The approach to the kino-phosphatome network is to identify the most important proteins for their centrality values and then to analyze with a lab experiment their activation level. After this, using the CentiScaPe feature of integrating topological analysis and data from lab experiments, those values are integrated and those nodes important for both centralities value and activation level are easily identified. This introduce a new way of facing the analysis of a protein interaction network based on the Strogatz assertion that in a biological network "Structure always affects function" (Strogatz (2001)). Instead of concentrating the analysis, as usual, on the global properties of the network (such degree distribution, centralities distribution, and so on) we consider in a cause-effect point of view single nodes of the network relating their centrality values (cause) with activation level (effects). Most of the contents of this section have been published on (Scardoni et al. (2009)).

4.1 Centralities analysis

The protocol used for the analysis of the human kino-phosphatome network is the following:

- The nodes of interest are extracted from the global network, resulting in a subnetwork to analyze (in our example the subnetwork of human kinases and phosphatases have been extracted from a human proteins interactome).
- The centralities values are computed with CentiScaPe. A subnetwork of proteins with all centrality values over the average is extracted.
- The lab experiment identifies which of these proteins present high phosphorilation level (in our example in tyrosine and threonine)
- Using CentiScaPe, lab experimental data and centrality values are integrated, so proteins with high level of activation and high centralities values are easily identified.
- Next experiments and analysis should be focused on these proteins.

This protocol have been applied as follows. A global human protein interactome data-set (Global Kino-Phosphatome network), including 11120 nodes and 84776 unique undirected interactions (IDs = HGNC), was complied from public data-bases (HPRD, BIND, DIP, IntAct, MINT, others; see (Scardoni et al. (2009)) on-line file GLOBAL-HGNC.sif) between human protein kinases and phosphatases. The resulting sub-network, a kino-phosphatome network, consisted of 549 nodes and 3844 unique interactions (see (Scardoni et al. (2009)) on-line files Table S4 and Kino-Phosphatome.sif), with 406 kinases and 143 phosphatases. The kino-phosphatome network did not contain isolated nodes. We used CentiScaPe to calculate centrality parameters. A first general overview of the global topological properties of the kino-phosphatome network comes from the min, max and average values of all computed centralities along with the diameter and the average distance of the network (table 3). These data provide a general overview of the global topological properties of the kino-phosphatome network. For instance, an average degree equals to 13.5 with an average distance of 3 may suggest a highly connected network in which proteins are strongly functionally interconnected. Computation of network centralities allowed a first ranking of human kinases and phosphatases according to their central role in the network (see (Scardoni et al. (2009)) on-line files Table S6 reporting all node-by-node values of different centralities). To facilitate the identification of nodes with the highest scores we applied the "plot by centrality" feature of CentiScaPe. A first plotting degree over degree generated a linear distribution, as expected (see fig. 6). However, it is evident that the distribution is

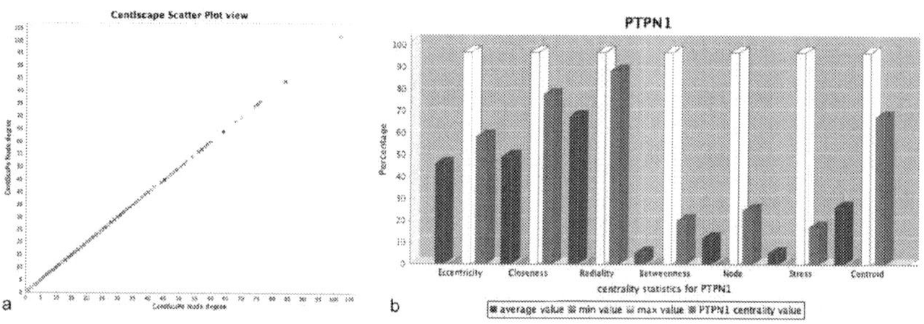

Fig. 6. a. A scatter plot degree over degree. As expected this generate a linear distribution. Notably the distribution is not uniform: many nodes display low degree and only few nodes with high degree, according to the scale-free architecture of biological network. b. The "plot by node" representation for PTPN1. The phosphatase PTPN1 presents the highest degree between all the phosphatases and a rather high score for other centralities. This suggests that PTPN1 may play a central regulatory role in the network. For each centrality the specific node value (red), the mean value (blue), the min value (green), and the max value (white) is shown.

not uniform, with the majority of nodes having a similar low degree and very few having very high degree. This is consistent with the known scale-free architecture of biological networks (Jeong et al. (2000)). The scale-free topology of the kino-phosphatome network was also confirmed with Network Analyzer (Assenov et al. (2008)). A total of 186 nodes (164 kinases and 22 phosphatases) displayed a degree over the average. The top 10 degrees (64 to 102) were all kinases, with MAPK1 showing the highest degree (102). Notably, MAPK1 displayed the highest score for most of the computed centralities (fig. 5a), suggesting its central regulatory role in the kino-phosphatome. In contrast, PTPN1 had the highest degree, 46, between all phosphatases (top 31 among all nodes) and had a rather high score also for other centralities Thus, degree analysis suggests that MAPK1 and PTPN1 are the most central kinase and phosphatase, respectively. To further support this suggestion we analyzed the centroid. Average centroid was -393. 242 nodes (206 kinases and 36 phosphatases) displayed a centroid over the average. The top 10 centroid (-79 to 8) were all kinases, with MAPK1 showing the highest centroid value (18). PTPN1 had the highest centroid value, -154, between all phosphatases (top 22 among all nodes). Thus, as for the degree, also the centroid value analysis suggests a possible scale-free distribution, with MAPK1 and PTPN1 being the most central kinase and phosphatase, respectively. This conclusion is also easily evidenced by plotting the degree over the centroid (fig. 7). Here MAPK1 appears at the top right of the plot and PTPN1 is present in the top most dispersed region of the plot, thus suggesting their higher scores. Interestingly, from the analysis is evident a non-linear distribution of nodes, with few dispersed nodes occupying the top right quadrant of the plot (i.e. high degree and high centroid): these nodes can potentially represent particularly important regulatory kinases and phosphatases. This kind of analysis can be iterated by evaluating all other centralities. To extract the most relevant nodes according to all centrality values we used CentiScaPe to select all nodes having all centrality values over the average. Upon filtering we obtained a kino-phosphatome sub-network (fig.**??**) consisting of 97 nodes (82 kinases and 15 phosphatases) and 962 interactions (see (Scardoni et al. (2009)) on-line files Table S7, and K-P sub-network.sif).

CentiScaPe Average Distance	3.0292037280789224
CentiScaPe Betweenness Max value	20159.799011925716
CentiScaPe Betweenness mean value	1112.0036429872616
CentiScaPe Betweenness min value	0.0
CentiScaPe Centroid Max value	18.0
CentiScaPe Centroid mean value	-393.07285974499086
CentiScaPe Centroid min value	-547.0
CentiScaPe Closeness Max value	8.771929824561404E-4
CentiScaPe Closeness mean value	6.175318530305184E-4
CentiScaPe Closeness min value	3.505082369435682E-4
CentiScaPe Diameter	8.0
CentiScaPe Eccentricity Max value	0.25
CentiScaPe Eccentricity mean value	0.18407494145199213
CentiScaPe Eccentricity min value	0.125
CentiScaPe Radiality Max value	6.91970802919708
CentiScaPe Radiality mean value	5.970796271921072
CentiScaPe Radiality min value	3.7937956204379564
CentiScaPe Stress Max value	210878.0
CentiScaPe Stress mean value	11537.009107468124
CentiScaPe Stress min value	0.0
CentiScaPe degree Max value	102.0
CentiScaPe degree mean value	13.5591985428051
CentiScaPe degree min value	1.0

Table 3. Global values of the kino-phosphatome network computed using CentiScaPe. The table includes min, max and mean value for each centrality and also the global parameter Diameter and Average Distance.

This sub-network possibly represents a group of highly interacting kinases and phosphatases displaying a critical role in the regulation of protein phosphorylation in human cells. Further analysis with CentiScaPe or other analysis tools, such as MCODE (Bader & Hogue (2003)) or Network Analyzer (Assenov et al. (2008)), performing a Gene Ontology database search (Ashburner et al. (2000)), or adding functional annotation data, may allow a deeper functional exploration of this sub network. The regulatory role of proteins belonging to the kino-phosphatome network may be also experimentally tested in a context-selective manner. Indeed, the centrality analysis by CentiScaPe can be even more significant by superimposing experimental data. To test this possibility, we focused the analysis on human polymorphonuclear neutrophils (PMNs).

4.2 Phosphoproteomic analysis of chemoattractant stimulated human PMNs

Human primary polymorphonuclear cells isolation

Human primary polymorphonuclear cells (PMNs) were freshly isolated form whole blood of healthy donors by ficoll gradient sedimentation. Purity of PMN preparation was evaluated by flow cytometry and estimated to about 95% of neutrophils. Isolated PMNs were kept in culture at 37^oC in standard buffer (PBS, $1mM$ $CaCl_2$, $1mM$ $MgCl_2$, 10% FCS, $pH7.2$) and used within 1 hour. Viability before the assays was more than 90%.

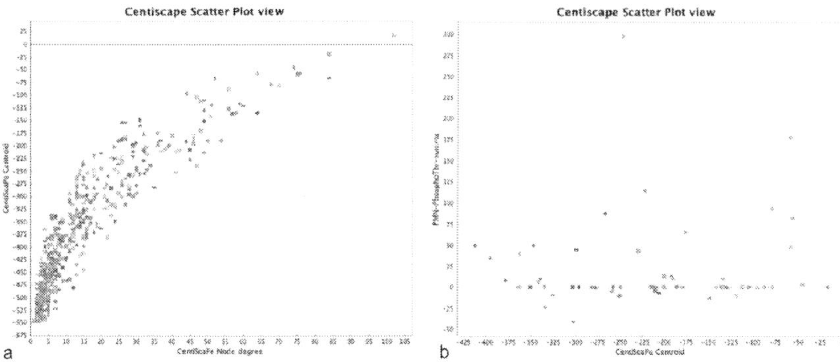

Fig. 7. a. A "plot by centralities" representation of degree over centroid. In the top right of the plot appear the nodes having high values of both degree and centroid (including MAPK1). b. Integration of topological analysis with experimental data. Centroid values are plotted over protein phosphorylation levels in threonine, experimentally determined as described in the text.

Human primary polymorphonuclear cell stimulation

Human neutrophils were resuspended in standard buffer at $10^7/ml$ and stimulated under stirring at $37^o C$ for 1 min. with the classical chemoattractant fMLP ($100nM$). Stimulation was blocked by directly disrupting the cells for 10 min. in ice-cold lysis buffer containing: $20mM$ MOPS, $pH7.0$, $2mM$ EGTA, $5mM$ EDTA, $30mM$ sodium fluoride, $60mM$ β-glycerophosphate, $20mM$ sodium pyrophosphate, $1mM$ sodium orthovanadate, $1mM$ phenylmethylsulfonylfluoride, $3mM$ benzamidine, $5\mu M$ pepstatin A, $10\mu M$ leupeptin, 1% Triton X-100. Lysates were clarified by centrifugation at $12.000xg$ for 10 min. and kept at $80^o C$ until further processing.

Evaluation of protein phosphorylation

Protein phosphorylation was evaluated both qualitatively and quantitatively by using the Kinexus protein array service (Kinexus (n.d.)). Kinexus provides a complete service for high throughput proteomic and phosphoproteomic high sensitive analysis of cell lysed samples, allowing detection of more than 800 proteins, including about 200 phosphorylated proteins (about 350 phospho-sites) by means of in-house validated antibody microarrays (Kinexus (n.d.)). $100\mu l$ of frozen samples of lysed PMNs (about $1mg/ml$ protein concentration) have been sent to Kinexus for the analysis. Phosphoproteomic antibody microarray data have been delivered by email and subsequently elaborated to extract values of protein phosphorylation of control versus agonist-triggered samples. (phosphorylation data files are available on-line: see (Scardoni et al. (2009)) PMN-PhosphoSer.NA, PMN-PhosphoTyr.NA, PMN-PhosphoThr.NA).

4.3 Combining topological analysis and experimental data

Data about protein phosphorylation were used as bioinformatic probes and node attributes to extract, from the Global Kino-Phosphatome network, subnetworks of protein phosphorylation, to be analyzed with CentiScaPe Experimental data were loaded as node attributes in Cytoscape and the computed centrality values were plotted over values of protein phosphorylation. Here, every node is represented with two coordinates consisting of a computed centrality and of experimental data regarding protein phosphorylation induced in PMNs by fMLP. In figures 5b and 7b are shown plots of centroid values over intensity of protein phosphorylation in threonine or tyrosine residues induced by fMLP triggering in human PMNs. Notably, in the plot are shown only those proteins whose phosphorylation level was experimentally determined. The two plots allow immediately evidencing that proteins phosphorylated in threonine (fig. 5b) or in tyrosine (fig. 7b) have different topological position in the network, with proteins phosphorylated in tyrosine showing a higher centrality values. This could suggest that tyrosine phosphorylation induced in PMNs by chemoattractants involves signaling proteins regulating clusters of proteins, as the centroid value may suggest. Besides, the top/left quadrant is empty in both figures 5b and 7b. So there are no nodes having low centroid value and high phosphorylation in threonine or tyrosine. This may suggest that centroid value and activation level are strictly related. Further hypotheses can be formulated by expanding the analysis to other centralities and by adding more phopshorylation data. From this type of plotting it is possible to further identify relevant nodes not only according to topological position but also to experimental outputs. Thus, groups of nodes whose regulatory relevance is suggested by centrality analysis are further characterized by the corresponding data of biological activity.

4.4 Conclusions

In this section a protocol of analysis for protein network have been proposed. The key idea is that of identify most important proteins from both topological and biological point of view. Through the example of the kino-phosphatome network, we have seen how CentiScaPe can integrate the two kinds of analysis allowing an easy characterization of most relevant proteins. The topological analysis and experimental data do confirm each other's regulatory relevance and may suggest further, more focused, experimental verifications. Combination of CentiScaPe with other bioinformatics tools may help to analyze high throughput genomic and/or proteomic experimental data and may facilitate the decision process.

5. A further step in centralities analysis: node centralities interference

As seen in the previous section, network centralities allow us to understand the role and the importance of each single node in a protein network. Next step we introduce in this section is to understand and measure changes to the topological structure of the network. The effects of mutation in the network structure, have been studied from a global point of view: nodes are removed from the network and the effects on some global parameters, as for example diameter, average distance or global efficiency are evaluated (Barabasi & Oltvai (2004); Jeong et al. (2001); Albert et al. (2000); Crucitti et al. (2004)). Our approach wants to answer to this question: "we remove or add one node in the network, how do other nodes modify their functionality because of this removal?" Since centrality indexes allow categorizing nodes in complex networks according to their topological relevance (see CentiScaPe plugin), in a node-oriented perspective, centralities are very useful topological parameters to compute in order to quantify the effect of individual node(s) alteration. We introduced the notion of interference and developed the Cytoscape plugin **Interference** (Scardoni & Laudanna (2011)) to evaluate the topological effects of single or multiple nodes removal from a network. In this perspective, interference allows virtual node knock-out experiments: it is possible to remove one or more nodes from a network and analyze the consequences on network structure, by looking to the variations of the node centralities values. As the centrality value of a node is strictly dependent on the network structure and on the properties of other nodes in the network, the consequences of a node deletion are well captured by the variation on the centrality values of all the other nodes. The interference approach can model common situations where real nodes are removed or added from/to a physical network:

- Biological networks, where one or more nodes (genes, proteins, metabolites) are possibly removed from the network because of gene deletion, pharmacological treatment or protein degradation. Interference can be used to:
  - Simulate pharmacological treatment: one can potentially predict side effects of the drug by looking at the topological properties of nodes in a drug-treated network, meaning with that a network in which a drug-targeted node (protein) was removed. To inhibit a protein (for instance a kinases) corresponds to removing the node from the network
  - Simulate gene deletion: gene deletion implies losing encoded proteins, thus resulting in the corresponding removal of one or more nodes from a protein network
- Social and financial networks, where the structure of the network is naturally modified over time
- Power grid failures
- Traffic jam or work in progress in a road network
- Temporary closure of an airport in an airline network

5.1 How Interference plugin works

The Interference plug-in allows you identifying the area of influence of single nodes or group of nodes. Specifically, Interference:

- Compute the centralities value of the network
- Remove the node(s) of interest
- Recompute the centralities in the new network (the one where the node(s) have been removed)
- Evaluate the differences between the centralities in the two networks.

This allows identifying the differences between the two networks: the one with the node(s) of interest still present and the one where the node(s) have been removed. Some nodes will increase, whereas others will reduce, their individual centrality values. This may suggest hints on the functional, regulatory, relevance of specific node(s).

Example

Consider the two networks in figure 8 and observe the role of node1 and node5. Network B is obtained by network A removing node5. Interference notion is based on measuring the effects of such remotion: in the table 4 are reported the betweenness values of the two networks (in percentage). Consider node1: in the network A, node1 has the 27% of the total value of betweenness. In the network B (where node5 has been removed) node1 has the 64% of the total value. The betweenness interference of node5 with respect to node1 is: Betwennes of node1 in the network A - Betwennes of node1 in the network = -37% It means that the topological relevance measured by the betweenness centrality of node1 increase of the 37% of the total betweenness if we remove node5 from the network. The presence of node5 negatively interferes with the central role of node1 measured by the betweennes centrality.

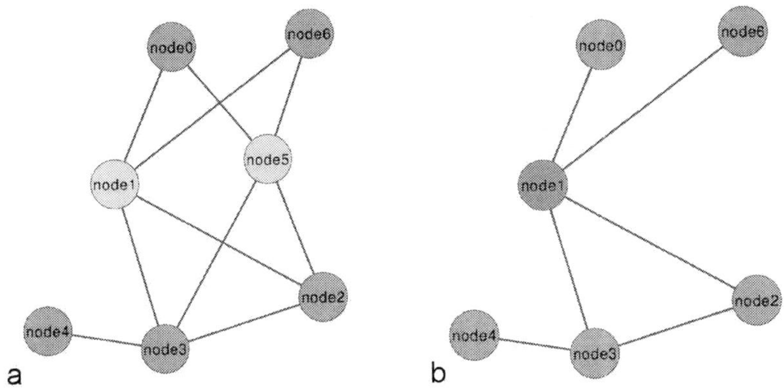

Fig. 8. Network b is obtained by network a removing node5. In this case node1 remains the only node connecting the top of the network with the bottom. Its betweenness values will increase.

Node	Network A (with node5) Betweenness (%)	Network B (no node5) Betweenness (%)	Interference value
node1	27%	64%	-37%
node4	0%	0%	0%
node0	2%	0%	2%
node2	2%	0%	2%
node6	2%	0%	2%
node3	40%	36%	4%
node5	27%		

Table 4. Betweenness and interference values expressed as percentage of the total value for the networks in figure 8. Node1 is the most sensitive to the deletion of node5.

The interference values of node5 with respect to the overall network are reported in the table. Node1 is the node mostly affected by the presence of node5 in the network. If we are considering real networks we expect that the activity of node5 strongly affects the activity of node 1.

Positive interference

If a node (A), upon removal from the network of a specific node (B) or of a group of nodes, decreases its value for a certain centrality index, its interference value is positive. This means that this node (A), topologically speaking, takes advantage (is positively influenced) by the presence in the network of the node (B) or of that group of nodes. Thus, "removal" of node (B) or of that group of nodes from the network, negatively affects the topological role of the node (A). This is called positive interference.

Negative interference

If a node (A), upon removal from the network of a specific node (B) or of a group of nodes, increases its value for a certain centrality index, its interference value is positive. This means that this node (A), topologically speaking, is disadvantaged (is negatively influenced) by the presence in the network of the node (B) or of that group the nodes. Thus, "removal" of node (B) or of that group of nodes from the network, positively affects the topological role of node (A). This is called negative interference.

5.2 Conclusions

As argued above, interference naturally induces cluster of proteins that are similar for their interference values due to the same node. A new clusterization algorithm can be derived if we group nodes depending on their interference value: given a node we compute its interference value and we put all the nodes having high interference in the same cluster. This interference-based modular decomposition of a network characterizes nodes for their answer to the inhibition (or adding) of a certain node in the network. If deletion of the node in a protein network is due to drug usage, the cluster of nodes having high interference value is the set of proteins where the drug has its greatest effects. In pharmacology this should permit to predict which proteins are more affected from the inhibition of another protein in the network. We can so prevent side effects of the inhibition of a node due to a drug usage.

6. References

Albert, R., Jeong, H. & Barabasi, A.-L. (2000). Error and attack tolerance of complex networks, *Nature* 406(6794): 378–382.

Arsenio Rodriguez, D. I. (2011). Characterization in silico of flavonoids biosynthesis in theobroma cacao l., *Network Biology* 1: 34–45.

Ashburner, M., Ball, C. A., Blake, J. A., Botstein, D., Butler, H., Cherry, J. M., Davis, A. P., Dolinski, K., Dwight, S. S., Eppig, J. T., Harris, M. A., Hill, D. P., Issel-Tarver, L., Kasarskis, A., Lewis, S., Matese, J. C., Richardson, J. E., Ringwald, M., Rubin, G. M. & Sherlock, G. (2000). Gene ontology: tool for the unification of biology. the gene ontology consortium., *Nature genetics* 25(1): 25–29.

Assenov, Y., Ramirez, F., Schelhorn, S.-E., Lengauer, T. & Albrecht, M. (2008). Computing topological parameters of biological networks, *Bioinformatics* 24(2): 282–284.

Bader, G. D. & Hogue, C. W. (2003). An automated method for finding molecular complexes in large protein interaction networks., *BMC Bioinformatics* 4(1).

Barabasi, A.-L. & Albert, R. (1999). Emergence of scaling in random networks, *Science* 286(5439): 509–512.

Barabasi, A.-L. & Oltvai, Z. N. (2004). Network biology: understanding the cell's functional organization, *Nature Reviews Genetics* 5(2): 101–113.

Bhalla, U. S. & Iyengar, R. (1999). Emergent properties of networks of biological signaling pathways, *Science* 283.

Biondani, Viollet, Foretz, Laudanna, Devin-Leclerc, Scardoni & Franceschi, D. (2008). Identification of new functional targets of $ampk\alpha 1$ in mouse red cells., *48th annual meeting of American society for cell biology*.

Choura, M. & Rebaï, A. (2010). Application of computational approaches to study signalling networks of nuclear and Tyrosine kinase receptors., *Biology direct* 5: 58+.

Cline, M. S., Smoot, M., Cerami, E., Kuchinsky, A., Landys, N., Workman, C., Christmas, R., Avila-Campilo, I., Creech, M., Gross, B., Hanspers, K., Isserlin, R., Kelley, R., Killcoyne, S., Lotia, S., Maere, S., Morris, J., Ono, K., Pavlovic, V., Pico, A. R., Vailaya, A., Wang, P.-L. L., Adler, A., Conklin, B. R., Hood, L., Kuiper, M., Sander, C., Schmulevich, I., Schwikowski, B., Warner, G. J., Ideker, T. & Bader, G. D. (2007). Integration of biological networks and gene expression data using cytoscape., *Nature protocols* 2(10): 2366–2382.

Crucitti, P., Latora, V., Marchiori, M. & Rapisarda, A. (2004). Error and attack tolerance of complex networks, *Physica A: Statistical Mechanics and its Applications* 340(1-3): 388 – 394. News and Expectations in Thermostatistics.

Dijkstra, E. W. (1959). A note on two problems in connexion with graphs, *Numerische Mathematik* 1: 269–271.

Feltes, B., de Faria Poloni, J. & Bonatto, D. (2011). The developmental aging and origins of health and disease hypotheses explained by different protein networks, *Biogerontology* 12: 293–308. 10.1007/s10522-011-9325-8.

Freeman, L. C. (1977). A set of measures of centrality based on betweenness, *Sociometry* 40(1): 35–41.

Gilbert, D. (n.d.). http://www.jfree.org/jfreechart/.

Hu, Z., Mellor, J., Wu, J., Yamada, T., Holloway, D. & DeLisi, C. (2005). VisANT: data-integrating visual framework for biological networks and modules, *Nucl. Acids Res.* 33(suppl_2): W352–357.

Jeong, H., Mason, S. P., Barabasi, A. L. & Oltvai, Z. N. (2001). Lethality and centrality in protein networks, *Nature* 411(6833): 41–42.

Jeong, H., Tombor, B., Albert, R., Oltvai, Z. N. & Barabasi, A. L. (2000). The large-scale organization of metabolic networks, *Nature* 407(6804): 651–654.

Joy, M. P., Brock, A., Ingber, D. E. & Huang, S. (2005). High-betweenness proteins in the yeast protein interaction network., *J Biomed Biotechnol* 2005(2): 96–103.

Junker, B., Koschutzki, D. & Schreiber, F. (2006). Exploration of biological network centralities with centibin, *BMC Bioinformatics* 7(1): 219+.

Kinexus (n.d.). http://www.kinexus.ca.

Koschützki, D., Lehmann, K. A., Peeters, L., Richter, S., Podehl, D. T. & Zlotowski, O. (2005). Centrality indices, *in* U. Brandes & T. Erlebach (eds), *Network Analysis: Methodological Foundations*, Springer, pp. 16–61.

Ladha, J., Donakonda, S., Agrawal, S., Thota, B., Srividya, M. R., Sridevi, S., Arivazhagan, A., Thennarasu, K., Balasubramaniam, A., Chandramouli, B. A., Hegde, A. S., Kondaiah, P., Somasundaram, K., Santosh, V. & Rao, S. M. R. (2010). Glioblastoma-specific protein interaction network identifies pp1a and csk21 as connecting molecules between cell cycle-associated genes., *Cancer Res* 70(16): 6437–47.

Lepp, Z., Huang, C. & Okada, T. (2009). Finding Key Members in Compound Libraries by Analyzing Networks of Molecules Assembled by Structural Similarity, *Journal of Chemical Information and Modeling* 0(0): 091030094710018+.

Milo, R., Shen-Orr, S., Itzkovitz, S., Kashtan, N., Chklovskii, D. & Alon, U. (2002). Network motifs: Simple building blocks of complex networks, *Science* 298(5594): 824–827.

Newman, M. E. J. (2006). Modularity and community structure in networks, *Proceedings of the National Academy of Sciences* 103(23): 8577–8582.

Scardoni, G. & Laudanna, C. (2011). Interference: a tool for virtual experimental network topological analysis.
URL: *http://www.cbmc.it/ scardonig/interference/Interference.php*

Scardoni, G., Petterlini, M. & Laudanna, C. (2009). Analyzing biological network parameters with CentiScaPe, *Bioinformatics* 25(21): 2857–2859.

Schokker, D., de Koning, D.-J., Rebel, J. M. J. & Smits, M. A. (2011). Shift in chicken intestinal gene association networks after infection with salmonella., *Comp Biochem Physiol Part D Genomics Proteomics* .

Sengupta, U., Ukil, S., Dimitrova, N. & Agrawal, S. (2009a). Expression-based network biology identifies alteration in key regulatory pathways of type 2 diabetes and associated risk/complications., *PloS one* 4(12): e8100+.

Sengupta, U., Ukil, S., Dimitrova, N. & Agrawal, S. (2009b). Expression-based network biology identifies alteration in key regulatory pathways of type 2 diabetes and associated risk/complications., *PloS one* 4(12): e8100+.

Sengupta, U., Ukil, S., Dimitrova, N. & Agrawal, S. (2009c). Identification of altered regulatory pathways in diabetes type ii and complications through expression networks, *Genomic Signal Processing and Statistics, 2009. GENSIPS 2009. IEEE International Workshop on*, pp. 1 –4.

Shannon, P., Markiel, A., Ozier, O., Baliga, N. S., Wang, J. T., Ramage, D., Amin, N., Schwikowski, B. & Ideker, T. (2003). Cytoscape: a software environment for integrated models of biomolecular interaction networks., *Genome research* 13(11): 2498–2504.

Shen-Orr, S., Milo, R., Mangan, S. & Alon, U. (2002). Network motifs in the transcriptional regulation network of escherichia coli, *Nature Genetics* 31.

Strogatz, S. H. (2001). Exploring complex networks, *Nature* 410(6825): 268–276.

Venkatachalam, G., Kumar, A. P., Sakharkar, K. R., Thangavel, S., Clement, M.-V. & Sakharkar, M. K. (2011). Pparγ; disease gene network and identification of therapeutic targets for prostate cancer., *J Drug Target* .
URL: *http://www.biomedsearch.com/nih/PPAR-disease-gene-network-identification/21780947.html*

Wagner, A. & Fell, D. A. (2001). The small world inside large metabolic networks., *Proceedings. Biological sciences / The Royal Society* 268(1478): 1803–1810.

Watts, D. J. (1999). *Small worlds: the dynamics of networks between order and randomness*, Princeton University Press, Princeton, NJ, USA.

Watts, D. J. & Strogatz, S. H. (1998). Collective dynamics of 'small-world' networks, *Nature* 393(6684): 440–442.

Webster, Y. W., Dow, E. R., Koehler, J., Gudivada, R. C. & Palakal, M. J. (2011). Leveraging Health Social Networking Communities in Translational Research., *Journal of biomedical informatics* .
URL: *http://dx.doi.org/10.1016/j.jbi.2011.01.010*

Wuchty, S. & Stadler, P. F. (2003). Centers of complex networks., *J Theor Biol* 223(1): 45–53.

Yamada, T. & Bork, P. (2009). Evolution of biomolecular networks: lessons from metabolic and protein interactions., *Nature reviews. Molecular cell biology* 10(11): 791–803.

17

Simulation of Flexible Multibody Systems Using Linear Graph Theory

Marc J. Richard
Department of Mechanical Engineering,
Laval University, Québec (Québec)
Canada

1. Introduction

This chapter provides a general description of a variational graph-theoretic formulation for simulation of flexible multibody systems (FMS) which includes a brief review of linear graph principles required to formulate this algorithm. The system is represented by a linear graph, in which nodes represent reference frames on flexible bodies, and edges represent components that connect these frames. To generate the equations of motion with elastic deformations, the flexible bodies are discretized using two types of finite elements. The first is a 2 node 3-D beam element based on *Mindlin* kinematics with quadratic rotation. This element is used to discretize unidirectional bodies such as links of flexible systems. The second, consists of a triangular thin shell element based on the discrete *Kirchhoff* criterion and can be used to discretize bidirectional bodies such as high speed lightweight manipulators, deployable space structures and micro-nano electro-mechanical systems (MEMS).

Realistic dynamic simulation of industrial mechanisms that requires tracking accuracy at high operational speed is becoming increasingly important for engineers. Hence, to accurately describe such motions, the effects of flexibility and damping must be included in the dynamic model. Since the equations governing the motion of FMS are highly non-linear and dynamically coupled, one must exploit some kind of linear graph principles (Andrews, 1971; Behzad & Chartrand, 1971; Christofides, 1975; Even, 1979; Koenig & Blackwell, 1960) to properly define the interconnection between the bodies. By combining linear graph theory (Andrews & Kesavan, 1975; Koenig et al., 1967; Richard, 1985) with the principle of virtual work (Richard et al., 2011; Shi & McPhee, 2000; Shi et al., 2001) and finite elements, a dynamic formulation is obtained that extends graph-theoretic (GT) modelling methods to the analysis of 3-D beams and shell surfaces of FMS. The widespread interest in flexible multibody systems (FMS) is evidenced by the existence of a large number of algorithms (Wasfy & Noor, 2003). It has been shown (McPhee & Redmond, 2006; Richard et al., 2004; Shi & McPhee, 1997) that for multibody systems, a graph-theoretic formulation can generate a minimal set of equations. GT-based approaches explicitly separate the linear topological equations for the entire system from the non-linear constitutive equations for individual components, resulting in very modular and efficient algorithms.

To be applicable to a wide range of spatial mechanical systems containing both open and closed kinematic chains, a flexible multibody formulation must incorporate general mathematical methods for representing both the system topology as well as the time-varying configuration. The representation of topology is naturally handled using elements of graph theory. It has also been shown (McPhee, 1998) that a proper "tree" with a set of coordinates called "branch coordinates" encompasses both sets of Cartesian and joint coordinates as special cases. Also, the use of virtual work has been proposed and validated as a new graph-theoretic variable. In order to create a system graph that results in correct kinematic and flexible dynamic equations for any choice of spanning tree, it is necessary to introduce a dependent virtual work element. Hence, by combining linear graph theory and the principle of virtual work, it is possible to develop a variational graph-theoretic formulation in terms of branch coordinates capable of automatically generating the motion equations for FMS.

2. System representation by linear graph

Many researchers have studied the theory of graphs (Arczewski, 1990; Baciu et al., 1990; Chou et al., 1986; Roberson, 1984) and bond-graphs (Bos, 1986; Hu, 1988) mainly due to the fact that among all the fields of human interest, there are few where graph theory cannot be applied to the process of analyzing or synthesizing problems. In order to extract the kinetic properties resting within mechanical systems, it is convenient to discretize the system into a schematic diagram composed of nodes or vertices representing points of interconnection in the system and oriented edges identifying system elements. Combination of all the vertices delimiting the network of elements with the total set of spanning edges between appropriate nodes will result in a diagram which is a simple isomorphism of the mechanical system.

One of the most appealing features of graph-theoretic methods lies in the geometric and pictorial aspect of the method. Given a spatial mechanical system, one can construct the system's diagram by a simple mapping of the mechanism. For instance, the vertices would correspond to rigid or flexible bodies, points on bodies to which forces are applied or joints are connected, and a ground node that represents the origin of an inertial reference frame. Each element is represented by a line segment and each joint or connection by an appropriate point such that a user can associate the network diagram to the mechanical system in a direct fashion. The technique is very methodical and well suited for computer implementation.

Much of the simplicity and efficiency of graphical methods lie in the use of a "tree" to assist in arranging the order of computation. By definition, a tree is a subgraph where every vertex of the graph is connected by exactly one chord. This connotes that the subgraph is connected and contains all the nodes of a given system graph, but has no closed loops. A tree is considered a minimal connected graph in which the deletion of a single branch would separate the subgraph. The set of vectors that complement the tree are called "cotree". It has been shown (McPhee, 1998) that the components necessary to generate an optimum tree for branch coordinates should be selected in the following order: N_1 rigid or flexible arms; N_2 position drivers (function of time); N_3 spherical or revolute joints; N_4 cylindrical or prismatic joints; N_5 rigid or deformable bodies, N_6 force actuators and N_7 virtual work elements.

The linear graph representation of a mechanical system is most easily described by means of an example. Consider the simple planar dynamic system, shown in figure 1(a), which consists of a body with center of gravity located at C.G. acted upon by two springs and a dashpot. Assuming negligible weight, the vector-network diagram, including the body traced in dashed lines to make the network easier to identify, is depicted in figure 1(b) and portrays a linear graph with six vertices and eight edges.

The edge e_1 is the inertial displacement vector representing the center of gravity, e_2 and e_3 define rigid or flexible arm elements, e_4 and e_5 specify displacement drivers while e_6 and e_7

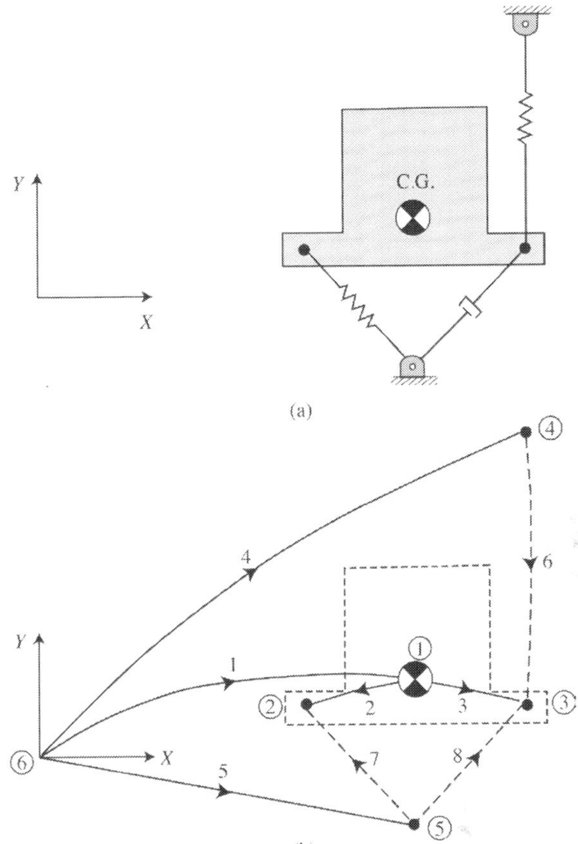

Fig. 1. a) Simple planar mechanical system and b) graph representation of the system

represent the springs and e_8 the dashpot. All vectors such as e_1, e_4 and e_5, the properties of which are established from an inertial frame, must emanate from the single ground node (*datum*) since that node is the only absolute fixed reference in the diagram, as compared to e_2 and e_3 which are defined relative to the body. Visibly, edges e_6, e_7 and e_8 span their respective two points of interconnection in the system.

It is possible to determine the number of branches and chords in a given graph $Graph(\nu, \epsilon)$ by applying basic theorems of graph theory (Andrews, 1977). Intuitively, a connected graph with ν vertices will have $(\nu - 1)$ branches in its tree since a tree is a minimally connected graph. Consequently, by subtracting the number of branches from the total set of edges ϵ, there will be $(\epsilon - \nu + 1)$ chords in the cotree.

Given a graph with ν vertices and ϵ edges, the order of interconnection of a system can be summarized in a ν by ϵ incidence matrix. It is easy to construct since each edge is adjacent to exactly two vertices. The incidence matrix of $Graph(\nu, \epsilon)$ is denoted by $[\kappa]$ and is defined as follows: (1) each of the ν rows corresponds to a vertex of $Graph(\nu,\epsilon)$, (2) each of the ϵ columns corresponds to an edge of $Graph(\nu,\epsilon)$, and (3) entries $\kappa_{ij} = -1$ if the ith node is the initial vertex of the jth edge, $\kappa_{ij} = +1$ if the ith node is the final vertex of the jth edge, and $\kappa_{ij} = 0$ otherwise. All columns contain exactly two non-zero entries and $(\nu - 2)$ zero entries. The incidence matrix can always be compiled from inspection of the graph. As an illustration, the graph of figure 1(b) has the following incidence matrix:

$$[\kappa] = \begin{bmatrix} 1 & -1 & -1 & 0 & 0 & 0 & 0 & 0 \\ 0 & 1 & 0 & 0 & 0 & 0 & 1 & 0 \\ 0 & 0 & 1 & 0 & 0 & 1 & 0 & 1 \\ 0 & 0 & 0 & 1 & 0 & -1 & 0 & 0 \\ 0 & 0 & 0 & 0 & 1 & 0 & -1 & -1 \\ -1 & 0 & 0 & -1 & -1 & 0 & 0 & 0 \end{bmatrix} \tag{1}$$

From the incidence matrix, one can generate a cutset matrix. A cutset is a disconnecting set of edges such that after removal of that set of edges, the graph is divided into two or more components. A fundamental cutset (f-cutset) is considered a minimal cutset. A f-cutset reduces a connected graph into exactly two components. The selection of a tree branch will always identify one f-cutset associated to the branch and if a single cotree chord of the f-cutset is re-introduced into the graph, it unites the two residual subgraphs into a connected graph. As opposed to trees which represent a minimal set of edges which connect all the vertices of $Graph(\nu,\epsilon)$, a f-cutset is a minimal set of edges which disconnect some vertices from others.

Since a f-cutset exists for each tree branch, there will be $(\nu - 1)$ f-cutsets in a graph with ν vertices. Therefore, all f-cutsets can be assembled in a $(\nu - 1)$ by ϵ cutset matrix $[D]$ identifying all cotree terminal graphs acting through each vertex. For example, the cutset matrix of the diagram sketched in figure 1(b) can be obtained by simple row operations (Andrews, 1971) performed on the $(\nu - 1)$ rows of the incidence matrix. In this case, rows (2) and (3) are added to row (1) leading to the five branches cutset matrix,

$$[U_t \;\; D] = \left[\begin{array}{c|ccc} 1\,0\,0\,0\,0 & 1 & 1 & 1 \\ 0\,1\,0\,0\,0 & 0 & 1 & 0 \\ 0\,0\,1\,0\,0 & 1 & 0 & 1 \\ 0\,0\,0\,1\,0 & -1 & 0 & 0 \\ 0\,0\,0\,0\,1 & 0 & -1 & -1 \end{array}\right] \tag{2}$$
$$\text{tree} \qquad\qquad \text{cotree}$$

where $[U_t]$ is a $(\nu - 1)$ by $(\nu - 1)$ unit sub-matrix associated with tree branches and $[D]$ is a $(\nu - 1)$ by $(\epsilon - \nu + 1)$ sub-matrix associated with cotree chords. Since a f-cutset isolates a part of the system, its application to dynamic systems will become obvious when solving the relationship among forces which requires the construction of a "free-body diagram".

From the cutset matrix, one can generate a circuit matrix. A circuit is a connected subgraph in which exactly two edges are incident with each vertex. This concept will be molded into graph-networks through the use of a fundamental-circuit (f-circuit) which is defined as a subgraph which contains a single cotree chord, forming a closed chain, with tree branches. Following this definition, each chord of the cotree will form a f-circuit, thereby producing an independent set of closed chains since at least one edge will not be found in any other circuit. Earlier, the exact number of cotree chords in a $Graph(\nu,\epsilon)$ was found to be $(\epsilon - \nu + 1)$.

Combining this result with the fact that for each chord there is a corresponding f-circuit, the total number of independent circuits in a $Graph(\nu, \epsilon)$ is $(\epsilon - \nu + 1)$. The total set of f-circuits can be generated in a $(\epsilon - \nu + 1)$ by ϵ circuit matrix $[E]$ specifying each inertial terminal graph compatible with each circuit. The circuit matrix can be obtained by applying another basic theorem (Andrews, 1971) of graph theory which proves that the cutset and circuit matrices are **orthogonal**. This orthogonal relationship states that the scalar product of the cutset matrix and circuit matrix must vanish. Hence, in matrix notation, the submatrices $[D]$ and $[E]$ are related by the negative transpose principle of orthogonality (Andrews & Kesavan, 1975; Richard, 1985) (not well-known in dynamics):

$$[E] = -[D]^T \ or \ [D] = -[E]^T. \tag{3}$$

This liaison regulates the entire structure of this GT formulation. This principle can be demonstrated by using the sample graph of figure 1(b). Relation (3) can now be exploited to automatically transform the cutset matrix into the three chords circuit matrix,

$$[E \ U_c] = \underbrace{\begin{bmatrix} -1 & 0 & -1 & 1 & 0 \\ -1 & -1 & 0 & 0 & 1 \\ -1 & 0 & -1 & 0 & 1 \end{bmatrix}}_{\text{tree}} \left| \underbrace{\begin{matrix} 1\,0\,0 \\ 0\,1\,0 \\ 0\,0\,1 \end{matrix}}_{\text{cotree}} \right. \tag{4}$$

where $[U_c]$ is a $(\epsilon - \nu + 1)$ by $(\epsilon - \nu + 1)$ unit sub-matrix associated with cotree chords and $[E]$ is a $(\epsilon - \nu + 1)$ by $(\nu - 1)$ sub-matrix associated with tree branches. In mechanical systems, the limitations to the freedom of movement of a body are specified by certain compatibility criteria which can be extricated from the circuit matrix. This matrix will prove to be a necessary mathematical tool in the resolution of dynamic systems since it provides some internal information relevant to the geometry of contact between terminal graphs.

At this point, one must introduce a physical meaning to these matrices. Unlike the traditional approach to dynamics in which Newton's second law is the basic postulate, in the graphical method there are two equally-important fundamental postulates: the vertex and circuit postulates. The vertex postulate states that the algebraic sum of through-variables $\{\mathbf{TV}\}$, symbolizing quantities such as force $\mathbf{F}$, torque $\mathbf{T}$ and virtual work δW, corresponding to all the vectors incident with any vertex of the graph is, identically, zero. Essentially, this is recognizable as the dynamic force-balance law or d'Alembert's principle which requires that force summation upon each body, including d'Alembert's inertial variable, must be equal to zero. However, in this form it is more general, since it applies to any physical system; for example, in electrical systems, it is equivalent to Kirchhoff's current law. A **cutset** isolates a part of the system and is equivalent to the construction of a free-body-diagram. It has been shown earlier that these cutset equations are obtainable by simple row operations on the incidence matrix, and can be written in the form:

$$[U_t \ \ D]\{\mathbf{TV}\} = \mathbf{0} \tag{5}$$

where $[D_{ij}]$ is a sub-matrix containing +1, -1 and 0 depending whether element N_j is incident to N_i and sub-matrix U_t is a unit matrix associated tree elements. The column matrix $\{\mathbf{TV}\}$ represents the through-variables ($\mathbf{F}_i$, $\mathbf{T}_i$ or δW_i) applied by element N_i. For the example depicted in figure 1(a), by combining equations (2) and (5), the vertex equation for node 1 representing the center of mass of the body is

$$\mathbf{F}_1 + \mathbf{F}_6 + \mathbf{F}_7 + \mathbf{F}_8 = 0. \tag{6}$$

In this case, conventional through variables, such as force vectors, are introduced in equation (6) (where $\mathbf{F}_1 = -m\,\ddot{\mathbf{r}}$ represents the inertial force).

The other governing postulate is the **circuit** postulate which states that the algebraic sum of across-variables $\{\mathbf{AV}\}$, representing those quantities such as displacements $\mathbf{r}$, velocities $\mathbf{v}$, accelerations $\dot{\mathbf{v}}$, virtual angular displacement $\delta\boldsymbol{\theta}$, angular velocities $\boldsymbol{\omega}$ and angular accelerations $\dot{\boldsymbol{\omega}}$, corresponding to all the vectors included in any circuit is, identically, zero. Basically, this postulate represents the geometrical relations guiding the motion of mechanical systems. To be precise, each circuit equation alludes to a closed vector polygon respecting the geometric fit or compatibility law of rigid body dynamics. From graph theory, it can be shown that these kinematic constraint equations can be obtained from the cutset equations and are usually written in the form:

$$[E \;\; U_c]\{\mathbf{AV}\} = \mathbf{0} \tag{7}$$

where sub-matrix $[E_{ji}]$ specifies which element N_i is included in the closed loop N_j and sub-matrix U_c is a unit matrix associated with cotree elements. The column matrix $\{\mathbf{AV}\}$ represents the across-variables ($\mathbf{r}_i$, $\mathbf{v}_i$, $\dot{\mathbf{v}}_i$, $\delta\boldsymbol{\theta}_i$, ω_i and $\dot{\omega}_i$) for element N_i. Since there is one independent circuit equation for each chord in the graph, the circuit equation for edge e_8 is

$$-\mathbf{r}_1 - \mathbf{r}_3 + \mathbf{r}_5 + \mathbf{r}_8 = 0 \tag{8}$$

where $\mathbf{r}$ represents the translational displacement of the corresponding element.

Consider the planar four-bar mechanism shown in figure 2(a). The system consists of three moving bodies (plus one fixed link) and four revolute joints. The link OA that is connected to the power source is called the input link (or crank). A driving torque causes the crank to rotate with angular velocity ω.The output link connects the moving pivot B to the ground pivot C. The coupler link connects the two moving pivots, A and B. The linear graph representation of the planar flexible four-bar linkage is depicted in figure 2(b) where the edges shown in bold comprise the spanning tree.

In this GT model, nodes (or vertices) are used to represent reference frames in the system while edges (lines) represent physical elements that connects these frames. Edges e_{51}, e_{52} and e_{53} represent the bodies in the system and e_{11}, e_{12}, both rigid arm elements, representing the body-fixed locations of the revolute joints at O and A, respectively. Edges e_{13} and e_{14} model the flexible links. The four revolute joints are modelled with joint edges e_{3i} ($i = 1, ..., 4$). Edge e_{21} represents a position driver and e_{61} is the driving torque. Finally, seven edges e_{7i} ($i = 1, ..., 7$) corresponding to dependent virtual work elements are automatically added to the system graph to complete the virtual topological equations.

Since we can also use virtual work δW as a through variable, the cutset equation for the tree joint element e_{34}, for example, is

$$\delta W_{33} + \delta W_{75} + \delta W_{76} + \delta W_{53} + \delta W_{34} = 0 \tag{9}$$

where each term corresponds directly to a physical component. Since edge e_{33} represents only relative displacements, it is necessary to introduce the dependent virtual work elements e_{74} and e_{75} to correctly capture the virtual works done by joint B on the coupler and output links. In general, whenever two bodies are connected by a component, two dependent virtual

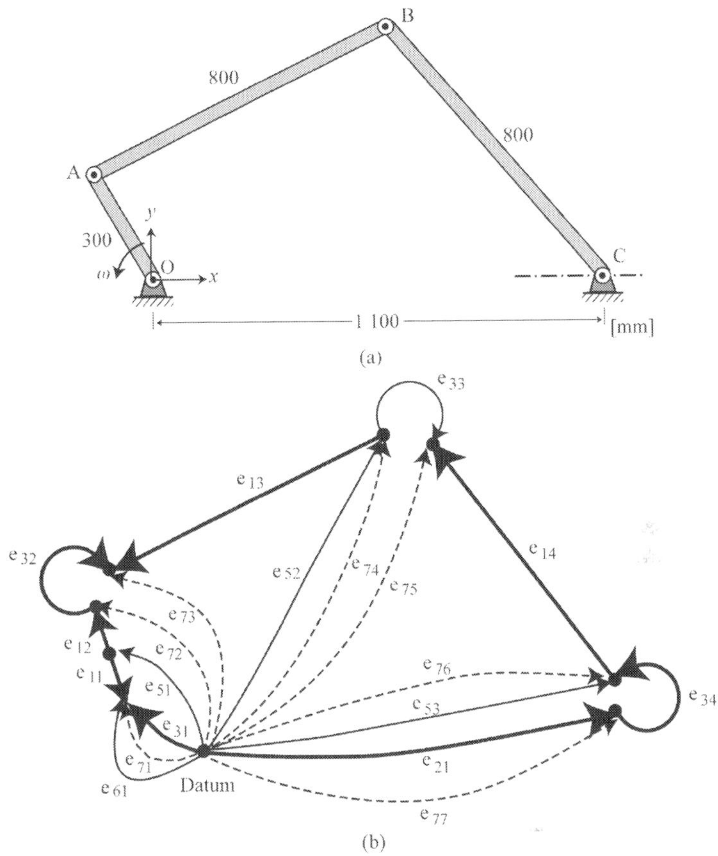

Fig. 2. a) Planar four-bar mechanism and b) graph representation of the system

work elements should automatically be included in the diagram model. Note that $\delta W_{33}=0$, since a frictionless joint cannot add or remove energy from a system. Furthermore, the sum of the virtual works done by joint B must also be zero, hence, $\delta W_{74} + \delta W_{75} = 0$. This fact can be exploited in this GT formulation to eliminate all joint reactions from the constitutive equations. Later, it will be shown that joint reactions can be retained in the GT algorithm by means of Lagrange multipliers.

The second set of topological equations, the circuit equations, can be generated automatically from the cutset equations. As an example, the circuit equation for cotree edge e_{33} is

$$\mathbf{r}_{33} - \mathbf{r}_{14} - \mathbf{r}_{34} - \mathbf{r}_{21} + \mathbf{r}_{31} - \mathbf{r}_{11} + \mathbf{r}_{12} + \mathbf{r}_{32} - \mathbf{r}_{13} = 0 \tag{10}$$

Clearly, this linear equation represents the vector loop closure condition for the circuit containing e_{33} where $\mathbf{r}_{31} = \mathbf{r}_{32} = \mathbf{r}_{33} = \mathbf{r}_{34} = 0$. Thus, the circuit equation (7) represent a set of linearly independent equations, one for each chord in the cotree.

3. Virtual work terminal equations for rigid bodies

The basic premise of the graphical approach is that each system element is modelled separately by defining its characteristics, independent of the other system elements, in the form of a "virtual terminal" (or constitutive) equation. Associated with every edge is one or more terminal equations that define the generalized force Q of an element corresponding to its branch coordinate q. These terminal equations are written in terms of the system through and across variables. In this formulation, a translational and rotational network is required in order to ensure consistency in the initial theory. Hence, these equations are functions of virtual displacements and virtual work.

In this formulation a rigid-arm element is used to represent the relative position and orientation of two reference frames on the same body. This second reference frame may be needed to locate a point of application for some other element. The terminal equations, in terms of virtual displacements, for a rigid-arm element are

$$\delta\boldsymbol{\theta}_1 = 0 \tag{11}$$

$$\delta\mathbf{r}_1 = \delta\boldsymbol{\theta}_5 \times \mathbf{r}_1 \tag{12}$$

where $\mathbf{r}_1$ is the rigid-arm position vector which is function of rotational body-fixed frame $\boldsymbol{\theta}_5$ since the direction of $\mathbf{r}_1$ varies as the rigid body rotates.

If the virtual work is the work done by specified forces on virtual displacements which are consistent with the constraints, with all other coordinates being kept constant, then the virtual work of force $\mathbf{F}$ is

$$\delta W = \delta\mathbf{r}^T\mathbf{F} \tag{13}$$

Now, let us consider a system whose kinematics are parameterized by a branch coordinate vector $\mathbf{q}$ where $\mathbf{r} = \mathbf{r}(\mathbf{q})$, then a virtual displacement $\delta\mathbf{r}$ is related to a branch coordinate variation $\delta\mathbf{q}$ by

$$\delta\mathbf{r} = \mathbf{r}_{\mathbf{q}}\delta\mathbf{q} \tag{14}$$

where the subscript $\mathbf{q}$ indicates a partial derivative with respect to vector $\mathbf{q}$. Then the virtual work of a force may be obtained by substituting equation (14) in equation (13),

$$\delta W = \delta\mathbf{q}^T\mathbf{r}_{\mathbf{q}}^T\mathbf{F} \tag{15}$$

Equation (13) may be interpreted as the scalar product of a branch variation $\delta\mathbf{q}$ and its generalized force $\mathbf{Q}$,

$$\delta W = \delta\mathbf{q}^T\mathbf{Q} \tag{16}$$

where the generalized force is defined as $\mathbf{Q} \equiv \mathbf{r}_{\mathbf{q}}^T\mathbf{F}$. In this formulation, one may separate forces into applied forces $\mathbf{F}^A$ and constraint forces $\mathbf{F}^C$ such that,

$$\delta W = \delta\mathbf{q}^T(\mathbf{Q}^A + \mathbf{Q}^C) = \delta W^A + \delta W^C \tag{17}$$

If branch coordinates are consistent with constraints, then $\mathbf{q}$ is a vector with independent coordinates. Note that if constraints that act on the system are workless and if the branch coordinates $\mathbf{q}$ must satisfy constraint equations of the form

$$\boldsymbol{\Phi}(\mathbf{q}, t) = 0, \tag{18}$$

they are dependent. Thus branch coordinate variations must satisfy

$$\mathbf{\Phi}_{\mathbf{q}}\delta\mathbf{q} = 0. \tag{19}$$

where $\mathbf{\Phi}_{\mathbf{q}}$ is the Jacobian matrix of the constraint equation (18). If constraint forces are workless, it can be proven that

$$\delta W^{C} = \delta\mathbf{q}^{T}\mathbf{Q}^{C} = \delta\mathbf{q}^{T}\mathbf{\Phi}_{\mathbf{q}}^{T}\lambda \tag{20}$$

where the Lagrange multiplier λ represents vector-generalized constraint forces.

Up to now, we have assumed that the reaction forces due to constraints neither produce nor consume work. This restriction has prohibited us from analyzing systems with non-rigid links (like elastic bodies which will be treated in the next section) or systems with energy-dissipating devices such as viscous or Coulomb dampers. The effect of such constraints is to produce certain pairs of internal forces which may be treated exactly as we would any other applied forces. Hence, the new form of terminal equations for applied forces has been written in the first part of equation (17). For elements containing physical constraints the terminal equation (20) is introduced. Care must be taken when applying the constraint generalized force because the physical constraints do no work and its Lagrange multiplier form must be introduced in the initial cutset equations at the beginning of the substitution procedure.

Spring and gravitational forces belong to the wider class of so-called conservative forces for which the generalized force can be efficiently calculated from the potential energy. Thus, if forces that act on a system can be expressed as the gradient of a scalar function of generalized coordinates, the virtual work may be written as the negative of a variation in potential energy V and the new terminal equation for conservative forces becomes

$$\delta W^{cons} = \delta\mathbf{q}^{T}\mathbf{Q}^{cons} = -\delta\mathbf{q}^{T}V_{\mathbf{q}}^{T} \tag{21}$$

Now, let us consider a moving system defined by a set of branch coordinates. If between these branch coordinates and time t there exists some relation of the form of equation (18), it is said that the system is moving under constraint. This means that the functions of constraints are geometric or kinematic conditions which restrain the possibilities of motion of the system. For a spatial mechanical system there is a limited number of types of functions of constraint, represented by the joints between the bodies. Figure 3 presents the four most common types of ideal joints which can be found in multibody systems.

A spherical joint shown in figure 3(a) is defined by the condition that the center of the ball coincides with the center of the socket. The terminal equations are, then, 3 scalar constraint equations that restricts the relative positions between the bodies,

$$[\,\mathbf{e}^{x}\ \mathbf{e}^{y}\ \mathbf{e}^{z}\,]^{T}\delta\mathbf{r}_{3} = [0\ \ 0\ \ 0]^{T} \tag{22}$$

where $\mathbf{e}^{x}, \mathbf{e}^{y}, \mathbf{e}^{z}$ are unit vectors and $\delta\mathbf{r}_{3}$ represents the relative virtual displacement between the bodies. Essentially, the three constraining equations (22) impose that there is no relative displacements at the joint in the $x-y-z$ directions.

A revolute joint, shown in figure 3(b), is constructed with bearings that allow relative rotation about a common axis in a pair of bodies, but precludes relative translation along this axis. The

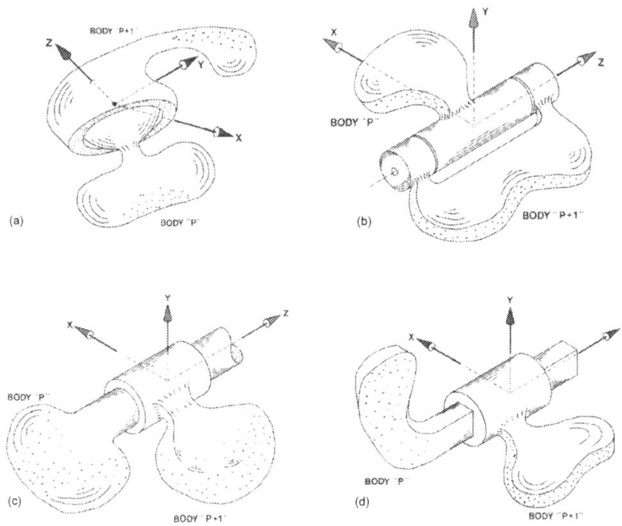

Fig. 3. Ideal kinematic joints a) spherical, b) revolute, c) cylindrical and d) prismatic

five terminal constrained equations are

$$[\,\mathbf{e}^x\ \mathbf{e}^y\ \mathbf{e}^z\,]^T\delta\mathbf{r}_3 = [0\ \ 0\ \ 0]^T \quad ; \quad [\,\mathbf{e}^x\ \mathbf{e}^y\,]^T\delta\boldsymbol{\theta}_3 = [0\ \ 0]^T \tag{23}$$

where $\delta\boldsymbol{\theta}_3$ represents the relative virtual angular rotation between the bodies.

A cylindrical joint between a pair of bodies is shown in figure 3(c). It permits relative translation and relative rotation between bodies about a common axis. The four terminal constrained equations are

$$[\,\mathbf{e}^x\ \mathbf{e}^y\,]^T\delta\mathbf{r}_4 = [0\ \ 0]^T \quad ; \quad [\,\mathbf{e}^x\ \mathbf{e}^y\,]^T\delta\boldsymbol{\theta}_4 = [0\ \ 0]^T \tag{24}$$

A prismatic joint, shown in figure 3(d), allows relative translation along a common axis between a pair of bodies, but precludes relative rotation about this axis. The five terminal constrained equations are

$$[\,\mathbf{e}^x\ \mathbf{e}^y\,]^T\delta\mathbf{r}_4 = [0\ \ 0]^T \quad ; \quad [\,\mathbf{e}^x\ \mathbf{e}^y\ \mathbf{e}^z\,]^T\delta\boldsymbol{\theta}_4 = [0\ \ 0\ \ 0]^T \tag{25}$$

At this point, one can represent these kinematic joints in a (6×6) Boolean matrix,

$$\mathbf{E}^k = diag(\mathbf{e}^k) = \begin{bmatrix} \mathbf{E}_t^k & 0 \\ 0 & \mathbf{E}_r^k \end{bmatrix} \tag{26}$$

where $\mathbf{E}_t^k$ and $\mathbf{E}_r^k$ are two diagonal (3×3) tensors which define the translational and rotational connexions between bodies.

Let us now consider rigid body elements N_5. The graph for this type of element consists of an edge e_5 from the datum node to a local reference frame on the body. The use of the variational form of Lagrange's equation relies upon a correct formulation of the kinetic energy of the multibody system in terms of branch coordinates. If the system is composed of n_b rigid bodies, the kinetic energy of the ith body is defined as

$$T_i = \frac{1}{2} m_i \mathbf{v}_i^T \mathbf{v}_i + \frac{1}{2} \omega_i'^T [I_i'] \omega_i' \tag{27}$$

where m_i is the mass of body i, $\mathbf{v}_i$ is the velocity vector of the centre of mass of the body in inertial space, $[I_i']$ is the inertia tensor of the body expressed in a body-fixed $'$ coordinate system and ω_i' is the angular velocity vector of the body in inertial space and expressed in the inertia $'$ tensor coordinate system. Note that absolute or inertial-space velocities must be used although they may be expressed in any convenient (inertial or non-inertial) coordinate system. Then, the virtual work terminal equation for the ith body becomes

$$\delta W_{5i} = \delta \mathbf{q}^T \left\{ \left[\frac{d}{dt} \left(\frac{\partial T_i}{\partial \dot{\mathbf{q}}} \right) - \frac{\partial T_i}{\partial \mathbf{q}} \right]^T \right\} \tag{28}$$

It is assumed at this point that the velocities $\{\mathbf{v}_i\}$ and $\{\omega_i\}$ have been found in symbolic form for each body component in terms of branch coordinates and their derivatives. In order to apply the variational form of Lagrange's equation, the terms $\frac{d}{dt}\left(\frac{\partial T_i}{\partial \dot{\mathbf{q}}}\right)$ and $\frac{\partial T_i}{\partial \mathbf{q}}$ will be required for each branch coordinates. By partial differentiation of equation (27),

$$\frac{\partial T_i}{\partial \mathbf{q}} = \left(m_i \mathbf{v}_i^T \mathbf{v}_{i\mathbf{q}} + \omega_i'^T [I_i'] \omega_{i\mathbf{q}}' \right) \tag{29}$$

and similarly,

$$\frac{\partial T_i}{\partial \dot{\mathbf{q}}} = \left(m_i \mathbf{v}_i^T \mathbf{v}_{i\dot{\mathbf{q}}} + \omega_i'^T [I_i'] \omega_{i\dot{\mathbf{q}}}' \right) \tag{30}$$

The time derivative of equation (30) is

$$\frac{d}{dt}\left(\frac{\partial T_i}{\partial \dot{\mathbf{q}}} \right) = \left(m_i \dot{\mathbf{v}}_i^T \mathbf{v}_{i\dot{\mathbf{q}}} + m_i \mathbf{v}_i^T \dot{\mathbf{v}}_{i\dot{\mathbf{q}}} + \dot{\omega}_i'^T [I_i'] \omega_{i\dot{\mathbf{q}}}' + \omega_i'^T [I_i'] \dot{\omega}_{i\dot{\mathbf{q}}}' \right) \tag{31}$$

Substituting equations (29) and (31) into the variational form of Lagrange's equation (28) gives

$$\delta W_{5i} = \delta \mathbf{q}^T \left\{ \left[m_i \dot{\mathbf{v}}_i^T \mathbf{v}_{i\dot{\mathbf{q}}} + \dot{\omega}_i'^T [I_i'] \omega_{i\dot{\mathbf{q}}}' + m_i \mathbf{v}_i^T \mathbf{P}_{i/\mathbf{q}}^{v} + \omega_i'^T [I_i'] \mathbf{P}_{i/\mathbf{q}}^{\omega'} \right]^T \right\} \tag{32}$$

where

$$\mathbf{P}_{i/\mathbf{q}}^{v} = \dot{\mathbf{v}}_{i\dot{\mathbf{q}}} - \mathbf{v}_{i\mathbf{q}} \tag{33}$$

$$\mathbf{P}_{i/\mathbf{q}}^{\omega'} = \dot{\omega}_{i\dot{\mathbf{q}}}' - \omega_{i\mathbf{q}}' \tag{34}$$

The quantity $\mathbf{P}_{i/\mathbf{q}}^{v}$ can be shown to be equal to zero. Since $\mathbf{r}_i = \mathbf{r}_i(\mathbf{q}, t)$, we have

$$\mathbf{v}_i = \dot{\mathbf{r}}_i = \mathbf{r}_{i\mathbf{q}} \dot{\mathbf{q}} + \mathbf{r}_{it} \tag{35}$$

From equation (35), form the partial derivative of $\mathbf{v}_i$ with respect to $\dot{\mathbf{q}}$

$$\mathbf{v}_{i\dot{\mathbf{q}}} = \mathbf{r}_{i\mathbf{q}} \tag{36}$$

Take the time derivatives of both sides of equation (36) to get

$$\dot{\mathbf{v}}_{i\dot{\mathbf{q}}} = \dot{\mathbf{r}}_{i\mathbf{q}} = \mathbf{v}_{i\mathbf{q}} \tag{37}$$

Substitute equation (37) into equation (33) to show that $\mathbf{P}^{v}_{i/\mathbf{q}} = 0$. When the angular velocity vector is the exact derivative of another vector function of branch coordinates and time, the preceding argument will show that $\mathbf{P}^{\omega'}_{i/\mathbf{q}} = 0$. This is always the case for problems formulated in one or two-dimensional space where angular velocities are simply the time derivatives of angular coordinates. In problems which must be formulated in three dimensions, finite rotations cannot be represented as vectors and $\mathbf{P}^{\omega'}_{i/\mathbf{q}}$ is generally non-zero.

The virtual equation (32) is now simplified to

$$\delta W_{5i} = \delta \mathbf{q}^T \left\{ \left[m_i \dot{\mathbf{v}}_i^T \mathbf{v}_{i\dot{\mathbf{q}}} + \dot{\omega}_i'^T [I_i'] \omega'_{i\dot{\mathbf{q}}} + \omega_i'^T [I_i'] \mathbf{P}^{\omega'}_{i/\mathbf{q}} \right]^T \right\} \tag{38}$$

The right hand side of equation (38) can be separated into terms containing branch accelerations $\ddot{\mathbf{q}}$ and terms containing products of branch velocities $\dot{\mathbf{q}}\dot{\mathbf{q}}$. This is necessary in order to place the coefficients of the terms $\ddot{\mathbf{q}}$ into an augmented mass matrix $\hat{\mathbf{M}}_i$ and the product terms into a generalized force $\mathbf{Q}_i^K$. Write the time-derivatives of the velocity vectors as

$$\dot{\mathbf{v}}_i = \mathbf{v}_{i\dot{\mathbf{q}}} \ddot{\mathbf{q}} + \dot{\mathbf{v}}_i^p \tag{39}$$

$$\dot{\omega}_i = \omega'_{i\dot{\mathbf{q}}} \ddot{\mathbf{q}} + \dot{\omega}_i'^p \tag{40}$$

The terms superscripted ^{p} contain all products of generalized velocities. Then, exploit equations (39) and (40) to rewrite equation (38) into the final terminal equation for rigid bodies as follows

$$\delta W_{5i} = \delta \mathbf{q}^T \left\{ \left[\hat{\mathbf{M}}_i \, \ddot{\mathbf{q}} + \mathbf{Q}_i^K \right]^T \right\} \tag{41}$$

where

$$\hat{\mathbf{M}}_i = \left(m_i \mathbf{v}_{i\dot{\mathbf{q}}}^T \mathbf{v}_{i\dot{\mathbf{q}}} + \omega'^T_{i\dot{\mathbf{q}}} [I_i'] \omega'_{i\dot{\mathbf{q}}} \right) \tag{42}$$

and

$$\mathbf{Q}_i^K = \left(m_i \dot{\mathbf{v}}_i^{pT} \mathbf{v}_{i\dot{\mathbf{q}}} + \dot{\omega}_i'^{pT} [I_i'] \omega'_{i\dot{\mathbf{q}}} + \omega_i'^T [I_i'] \mathbf{P}^{\omega'}_{i/\mathbf{q}} \right) \tag{43}$$

The elements of the coefficient matrix $\hat{\mathbf{M}}_i$ are the coefficient of $\ddot{\mathbf{q}}$ appearing in the differential equation corresponding to the branch coordinate $\mathbf{q}$. The forcing vector $\mathbf{Q}_i^K$ shown in equation (43) is made up of all the terms in the equations of motion which do not contain second derivatives. This vector contains part of the contribution of the kinetic energy to the equations of motion. Substituting the general form of virtual work terminal equations for each element in the cutset equation for this tree body constraint or joint, one gets

$$\delta \mathbf{q}^T \left\{ \hat{\mathbf{M}} \, \ddot{\mathbf{q}} + \mathbf{Q}^K + \mathbf{Q}^C + \mathbf{Q}^{cons} - \mathbf{Q}^A \right\} = 0 \tag{44}$$

This variational equation of motion holds for arbitrary virtual displacement $\delta \mathbf{q}$, so it is equivalent to the Lagrange multiplier form of constrained equations of motion.

Together, the cutset, circuit and terminal equations form a necessary and sufficient set of motion equations for determining the time response of multibody systems. However, an efficient approach to this problem consists in reducing the number of equations that need to be solved simultaneously by using branch transformation equations for a tree selection. The first step consists in defining the problem by creating a proper spanning tree and generating the branch transformation equations for all the elements in the cotree. These transformations will be used to replace the across-variables for cotree elements as function of branch coordinates.

Depending on the topology of the mechanical system and the specified tree, the branch coordinates may not be independent quantities. If the number of coordinates n is greater than the degrees of freedom f, then $(c = n - f)$ constraint equations are required to express the dependency between coordinates. The constraint equations are obtained directly from the joints and motion drivers in the cotree, by projecting their circuit equations onto the joint reaction space (McPhee, 1998). Upon substitution of the branch transformation equations into these circuit equations, the constraint equations are obtained in the form of equation (18) which constitutes a set of c nonlinear algebraic equations. Differentiating twice equation (18), using the chain rule of differentiation, yields the c constraint acceleration equations

$$\boldsymbol{\Phi}_{\mathbf{q}}\ddot{\mathbf{q}} = -\left[(\boldsymbol{\Phi}_{\mathbf{q}}\dot{\mathbf{q}})_{\mathbf{q}}\dot{\mathbf{q}} + 2\boldsymbol{\Phi}_{\mathbf{q}t}\dot{\mathbf{q}} + \boldsymbol{\Phi}_{tt}\right] \equiv \boldsymbol{\Lambda} \tag{45}$$

In general, the n branch coordinates are not independent, but are related by the c kinematic constraint equations (18). Thus, these constraint acceleration equations must be appended to the set of dynamic equations (44), giving $(n + c)$ equations to solve for branch coordinates $\mathbf{q}$ and the c reaction loads $\boldsymbol{\lambda}$. Substituting equation (18) into equation (44) and combining with equation (45) finally yields the classical system differential-algebraic equations of motion for rigid multibody systems in matrix form,

$$\begin{bmatrix} \hat{\mathbf{M}} & \boldsymbol{\Phi}_{\mathbf{q}}^T \\ \boldsymbol{\Phi}_{\mathbf{q}} & 0 \end{bmatrix} \begin{Bmatrix} \ddot{\mathbf{q}} \\ \lambda \end{Bmatrix} = \begin{Bmatrix} \mathbf{Q}^{total} \\ \boldsymbol{\Lambda} \end{Bmatrix} \tag{46}$$

where $\hat{\mathbf{M}}$ is a symmetric augmented $(n \times n)$ mass matrix, $\boldsymbol{\Phi}_{\mathbf{q}}$ is a $(c \times n)$ constraint Jacobian matrix and the total generalized force $\mathbf{Q}^{total} = \mathbf{Q}^A - \mathbf{Q}^K - \mathbf{Q}^{cons}$. Using equation (42) it is easy to form symbolically the coefficient matrix $\hat{\mathbf{M}}$, element by element, from partial derivatives of the velocity vectors. Non-linearities have been preserved throughout the formulation as each element may contain branch coordinates and quantities which vary with time. Note that the global matrix coefficient is symmetric. This requires only that the inertia tensor be symmetric, which it is. The off-diagonal mass sub-matrices represent coupling effects between adjacent bodies. The fundamental form of these equations and physical properties of kinetic energy guarantee that a unique solution of the constrained equations of motion exists.

4. Flexible multibody systems (FMS)

This variational graph-theoretical approach is based on the flexible models developped by (Shabana, 1986) and (Tennich, 1994). In this formulation a flexible arm element, as shown in figure 4, is used to represent the relative position and orientation of two reference frames on the same body. This second reference frame may be needed to locate a point of application for some other element.

A flexible arm element is defined as being made up of a continuum of particles that can move relative to one another. Since actual bodies are never perfectly rigid, small deformation effects are often added and can have great influence on the motion of mechanisms that are made up of multiple bodies. A flexible arm element can be located by defining the position vector $\mathbf{R}$ of the origin of its body-fixed frame $\Re'(X', Y', Z')$, relative to the global reference frame $\Re(XYZ)$.

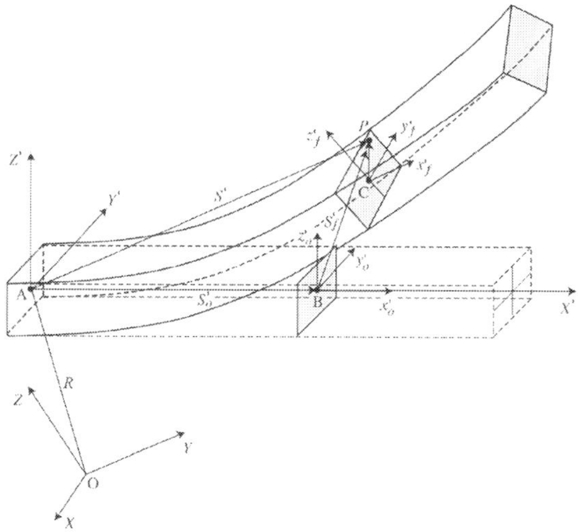

Fig. 4. Flexible arm element

The global location of an arbitrary point P on a flexible body can be described as

$$\mathbf{r} = \mathbf{R} + \mathbf{\Pi}\,\mathbf{s}' = \mathbf{R} + \mathbf{\Pi}\,(\mathbf{s}'_o + \mathbf{s}'_f) \tag{47}$$

where $\mathbf{\Pi}$ represents an Euler parameter transformation matrix (Wittenburg, 1977) from the structure $\Re'(X', Y', Z')$ coordinate system to the global reference frame $\Re(XYZ)$. The vector $\mathbf{s}'_o$ is the initial undeformed position of point p with respect to the body-fixed reference frame, $\mathbf{s}'_f$ represents the flexible displacement of point p and $\mathbf{s}'(= \mathbf{s}'_o + \mathbf{s}'_f)$ represents a flexible arm element N_1.

Since the body-fixed frame $\Re'(x', y', z')$ translates and rotates relative to the global frame, the vector $\mathbf{R}$ and Euler transformation matrix $\mathbf{\Pi}$ are functions of time. Both sides of eq.(47) may be differentiated twice with respect to time to obtain the acceleration equation,

$$\ddot{\mathbf{r}} = \ddot{\mathbf{R}} + \mathbf{\Pi}\,(\ddot{\mathbf{s}}' + \tilde{\dot{\omega}}\,\mathbf{s}' + \tilde{\omega}\,\tilde{\omega}\,\mathbf{s}' + 2\,\tilde{\omega}\,\dot{\mathbf{s}}') \tag{48}$$

where $\dot{\omega}$ and $\ddot{\mathbf{s}}'$ are, respectively, the angular acceleration of the body and the second derivative of the elastic displacement of point p and $\tilde{\omega}$ represents a 3×3 skew-symmetric matrix which performs a cross-product multiplication and represents the angular velocity vector of the body-fixed frame $\Re'$.

To describe the deformation of a flexible body, one can discretize the structure into finite elements. If a reference frame $\Re(e_1, e_2, e_3)$ is attached to the jth element, the displacement of point p on a flexible body can be given by

$$\mathbf{s}' = \mathbf{N}^j\,(\mathbf{s}'_{on} + \mathbf{s}'_{fn}) = \mathbf{N}^j\,\mathbf{s}'^j_n \tag{49}$$

with

$$\mathbf{N}^j = \mathbf{Q}^j\,\mathbf{N}^{je}\,\mathbf{T}^{j^T}$$

where $\mathbf{s}'_{on}$ and $\mathbf{s}'_{fn}$ are the non-deformed and the nodal visco-elastic displacement of point p and $\mathbf{s}'^{j}_{n}$ is the total displacement nodal vector of the jth element. Note that $\mathbf{N}^j$ is a finite element spatial interpolation function from the jth element to the body frame $\Re'$ where $\mathbf{Q}^j$ represents a transformation matrix from the frame $\Re(e_1, e_2, e_3)$ to the body reference frame $\Re(\bar{x}, \bar{y}, \bar{z})$ and $\mathbf{T}^j$ is a transfert matrix assembled with the $\mathbf{Q}^j$ matrices.

Figures 5(a) and 5(b) represent the 3-D beam and the triangular shell elements, respectively. For the 3-D beam element, the two spatial interpolation function is given

$$N_1^{je} = \frac{1}{2}(1 - \xi) \quad and \quad N_2^{je} = \frac{1}{2}(1 + \xi) \tag{50}$$

where ξ is an adimensional variable mesured along each beam element, with $\xi = -1$ at node 1 and $\xi = 1$ at node 2. For the triangular shell element, the three spatial interpolation functions are given by

$$N_1^{je} = 1 - \xi - \eta \quad ; \quad N_2^{je} = \xi \quad ; \quad N_3^{je} = \eta \tag{51}$$

where ξ and η are adimensional variables mesured along the triangular element.

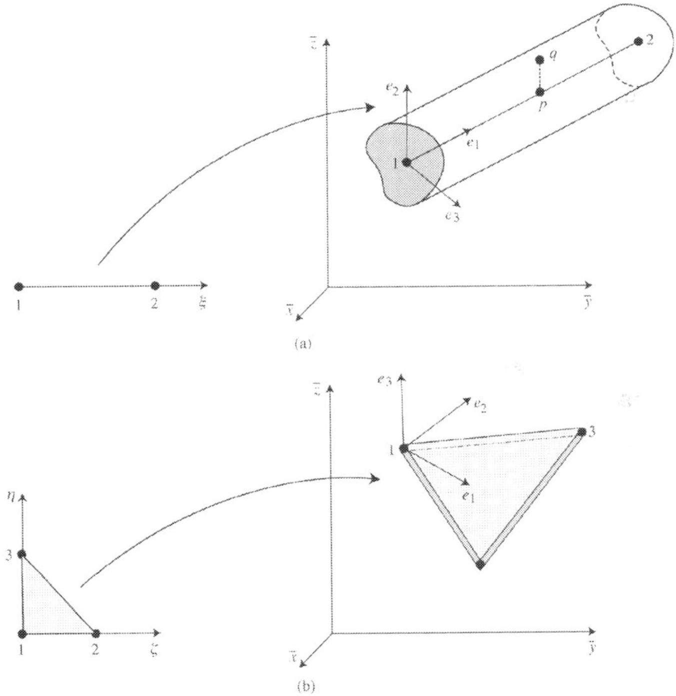

Fig. 5. a) Flexible beam linear finite element b) Flexible shell triangular finite element

Vectors $\mathbf{e}_1^j$, $\mathbf{e}_2^j$ and $\mathbf{e}_3^j$, in figure 5, form a reference surface base for the jth element which is independent of the nodal numbering. Hence, the transfert matrix between the frame $\Re(e_1, e_2, e_3)$ to the body reference frame $\Re(\bar{x}, \bar{y}, \bar{z})$ can be written as $\mathbf{Q}^j = (e_1, e_2, e_3)^j$. Then, the diagonal transfert matrix $\mathbf{T}^j$ between the element local frame $\Re(e_1, e_2, e_3)^j$ and the deformable body frame $\Re(\bar{x}, \bar{y}, \bar{z})$ can be written with six rotation tensors $\mathbf{Q}^j$ (of dimension 3×3).

Finally, the acceleration expression of point p on the flexible body can then be rewritten from the discretized form of $\mathbf{s}'$, from eq.(48),

$$\ddot{\mathbf{r}} = \ddot{\mathbf{R}} - \mathbf{\Pi}\,\tilde{\mathbf{s}}'\,\mathbf{\Lambda}\,\ddot{\theta} + \mathbf{\Pi}\,N^j\,\ddot{\mathbf{s}}_n'^j + \mathbf{\Pi}\,(\tilde{\omega}\,\tilde{\omega}\,N^j\,\mathbf{s}_n'^j + 2\,\tilde{\omega}\,N^j\,\dot{\mathbf{s}}_n'^j) \tag{52}$$

where $\omega = \mathbf{\Lambda}\,\dot{\boldsymbol{\theta}}$ with $\mathbf{\Lambda}$ representing an Euler transformation matrix for the angular velocity of the body with respect to the body reference frame $\Re'$. The generalized coordinate vector $\mathbf{q}$ for a flexible body can then be assembled from the position vector $\mathbf{R}$, orientation $\boldsymbol{\theta}$ of the origin of the body reference frame $\Re'$ and the nodal coordinate vector $\mathbf{s}_n'$ with $\mathbf{q} = \{\,\mathbf{R},\ \boldsymbol{\theta},\ \mathbf{s}_n'\}^T$.

Consider a volume element $dv = dx\,dy\,dz$ near point p on a deformable body. The constitutive virtual work equation of this volume element dv can be separated in three different virtual work components (Shi et al., 2001; Tennich, 1994),

$$\delta W_5 = \delta W_5^{inertial} - \delta W_5^{forces} + \delta W_5^{internal} = 0 \tag{53}$$

with

$$\delta W_5^{inertial} = \int_V \delta\mathbf{r}^T\,\rho\,\ddot{\mathbf{r}}\,dv \tag{54}$$

$$\delta W_5^{forces} = \int_V \delta\mathbf{r}^T\,\mathbf{f}_v\,dv \tag{55}$$

$$\delta W_5^{internal} = \int_V \delta\boldsymbol{\epsilon}^T\,\sigma\,dv \tag{56}$$

where $\delta\epsilon$ is the column matrix of varied strain components in the local frame; $(\rho\,\ddot{\mathbf{r}})$ is the inertial force per unit volume; σ contains the corresponding internal stress components and $\mathbf{f}_v$ is the body volume forces including gravity.

For a deformable body, the virtual work of all inertial forces can be written from equation (54) under the following general form,

$$\delta W_5^{inertial} = \delta\mathbf{q}^T\,\mathbf{M}\,\ddot{\mathbf{r}} - \delta\mathbf{q}^T\,\mathbf{Q}^q \tag{57}$$

where $\mathbf{M}$ and $\mathbf{Q}^q$ represent the global mass matrix and the quadratic velocity vector including Coriolis term, respectively. The global mass matrix of the jth finite element of the flexible body can be assembled from the elementary mass matrices,

$$\mathbf{M}^j = \int_{V^j} \rho^j \begin{bmatrix} I & -\mathbf{\Pi}\,\tilde{\mathbf{s}}'\,\mathbf{\Lambda} & \mathbf{\Pi}\,N^j \\ & \mathbf{\Lambda}^T\,\tilde{\mathbf{s}}'^T\,\tilde{\mathbf{s}}'\,\mathbf{\Lambda} & -\mathbf{\Lambda}^T\,\tilde{\mathbf{s}}'^T\,N^j \\ Sym. & & N^{j^T}\,N^j \end{bmatrix} dv = \begin{bmatrix} \mathbf{M}_{RR} & \mathbf{M}_{R\theta} & \mathbf{M}_{Rf} \\ & \mathbf{M}_{\theta\theta} & \mathbf{M}_{\theta f} \\ Sym. & & \mathbf{M}_{ff} \end{bmatrix}^j \tag{58}$$

where ρ^j and V^j are, respectively, the mass density and the volume of the jth element. The elements of the mass matrix $\mathbf{M}$ are the coefficient of $\ddot{\mathbf{q}}$ appearing in the differential equation corresponding to the branch coordinate $\mathbf{q}$. Using equation (53), it is easy to assemble the coefficient matrix $\mathbf{M}$, element by element, from the transformation matrices between reference frames. The formulation of the time-invariant matrices $\mathbf{M}_{RR}$ and $\mathbf{M}_{ff}$

is straight-forward. The matrix $\mathbf{M}_{RR}$ is a diagonal matrix whose elements are equal to the mass of the element. The matrix $\mathbf{M}_{ff}$ is the conventional mass matrix that arises in any finite element analysis. Non-linearities have been preserved throughout the formulation as each element may contain branch coordinates and quantities which vary with time. The off-diagonal mass sub-matrices represent coupling effects between translational, rotational and flexible elements. The matrices $\mathbf{M}_{Rf}$ and $\mathbf{M}_{\theta f}$ represent the inertia coupling between gross body motion and small body deformation. These matrices, in addition to the inertia tensor $\mathbf{M}_{\theta\theta}$, are implicitly time dependent since they are functions of the body generalized coordinates.

In a similar fashion, the global quadratic velocity vectors can be assembled for the jth finite element of the flexible body,

$$\begin{Bmatrix} \mathbf{Q}_R^q \\ \mathbf{Q}_\theta^q \\ \mathbf{Q}_f^q \end{Bmatrix}^j = -\int_{V^j} \rho^j \begin{Bmatrix} \Pi \\ \Lambda^T \tilde{\mathbf{s}}'^T \\ N^{j^T} \end{Bmatrix} \left[\tilde{\omega}\,\tilde{\omega}\,N\,\mathbf{s}'_n + 2\,\tilde{\omega}\,N\,\dot{\mathbf{s}}'_n\right]^j dv \tag{59}$$

The inertial forcing vector $\mathbf{Q}^q$ is made up of all the terms in the equations of motion which do not contain second derivatives.

The virtual work of body forces $\mathbf{f}_v$ for the jth finite element can also be written at once,

$$\left(\delta W_6^{forces}\right)^j = \int_{V^j} \delta\mathbf{r}^T\,\mathbf{f}_v^j\,dv = \left[\delta\mathbf{R}^T \quad \delta\boldsymbol{\theta}^T \quad \delta\mathbf{s}_n'^{j^T}\right] \begin{Bmatrix} \mathbf{F}_R \\ \mathbf{F}_\theta \\ \mathbf{F}_f \end{Bmatrix}^j \tag{60}$$

Finally, the virtual work for internal constraints of the jth finite element was defined earlier,

$$\left(\delta W_5^{internal}\right)^j = \int_{V^j} \delta\epsilon^{j^T}\,\sigma^j\,dv \tag{61}$$

where ϵ^{j^T} and σ^j represent, respectively, Cauchy's deformation and strain vectors. For a viscous elastic material governed by the Kelvin-Voigt model (Christensen, 1975; Flugge, 1967), the behaviour law between stress and strain is established as,

$$\sigma^j = \mathbf{H}^j\,\epsilon^j + \mathbf{G}^j\,\dot{\epsilon}^j = \mathbf{H}^j\,\Xi^j\,\mathbf{s}_n'^j + \mathbf{G}^j\,\Xi^j\,\dot{\mathbf{s}}_n'^j \tag{62}$$

where $\mathbf{H}^j$ and $\mathbf{G}^j$ are, respectively, the elastic and viscous tensors for this behaviour law and are function of Young's modulus and poisson's coefficient. The matrix Ξ^j represents spatial interpolation deformation functions. Hence, the internal virtual work for the jth finite element can be written under the following form,

$$\left(\delta W_5^{internal}\right)^j = \delta\,\mathbf{s}_n'^{j^T}\,\mathbf{K}_{ff}^j\,\mathbf{s}_n'^j + \delta\,\mathbf{s}_n'^{j^T}\,\mathbf{C}_{ff}^j\,\dot{\mathbf{s}}_n'^j \tag{63}$$

with

$$\mathbf{K}^j_{ff} = \int_{V^j} [\Xi^T \, \mathbf{H} \; \Xi]^j \, dv \tag{64}$$

$$\mathbf{C}^j_{ff} = \int_{V^j} [\Xi^T \, \mathbf{G} \; \Xi]^j \, dv \tag{65}$$

Equations (64) and (65) are, respectively, the stiffness matrix and the viscous damping matrix of the jth element. With the body kinetic and strain energy in hand, the virtual work can be exploited to generate the system equations of motion of a single flexible body. Hence, the general form of virtual work terminal equation for each body δW_{5i}, required in the cutset equation, can be written

$$\delta \mathbf{q}^T \{\mathbf{M}\,\ddot{\mathbf{q}} + \mathbf{C}\,\dot{\mathbf{q}} + \mathbf{K}\,\mathbf{q} - \mathbf{F} - \mathbf{Q}\} = 0 \tag{66}$$

This variational equation holds for arbitrary virtual displacement $\delta \mathbf{q}$, so the terms in parentheses are the well-known equations of motion in standard form. Hence, for each flexible body in the system, the translational, rotational and viscous-elastic equations of motion can now be assembled into a partitioned matrix formulation,

$$\begin{bmatrix} \mathbf{M}_{RR} & \mathbf{M}_{R\theta} & \mathbf{M}_{Rf} \\ & \mathbf{M}_{\theta\theta} & \mathbf{M}_{\theta f} \\ Sym. & & \mathbf{M}_{ff} \end{bmatrix} \begin{Bmatrix} \ddot{\mathbf{R}} \\ \ddot{\theta} \\ \ddot{\mathbf{s}}'_n \end{Bmatrix} + \begin{bmatrix} 0 & 0 & 0 \\ 0 & 0 & 0 \\ 0 & 0 & \mathbf{C}_{ff} \end{bmatrix} \begin{Bmatrix} \dot{\mathbf{R}} \\ \dot{\theta} \\ \dot{\mathbf{s}}'_n \end{Bmatrix} + \begin{bmatrix} 0 & 0 & 0 \\ 0 & 0 & 0 \\ 0 & 0 & \mathbf{K}_{ff} \end{bmatrix} \begin{Bmatrix} \mathbf{R} \\ \theta \\ \mathbf{s}'_n \end{Bmatrix} = \begin{Bmatrix} \mathbf{FQ}^q_R \\ \mathbf{FQ}^q_\theta \\ \mathbf{FQ}^q_f \end{Bmatrix} \tag{67}$$

where $\mathbf{FQ}^q_i = \mathbf{F}_i + \mathbf{Q}^q_i$ for $(i = R, \theta, f)$. Since the total virtual work of the system of flexible bodies is the sum of the individual virtual work, the algorithm must incorporate the sum of all bodies in the formulation using a global cutset equation. Then, the variational equations of motion for flexible multibody systems may be obtained from the tree joint element which connects the whole system of bodies to the ground body through a path consisting entirely of branches. To get the contribution of all physical components to the system, the terminal virtual work equations are written for all bodies in the tree. By summing the cutset equation, similar to eq.(5), for all tree flexible bodies, the contribution of all physical components to the system virtual work equations are captured. The dynamic form of these expressions and fundamental properties of virtual work guarantee that a unique solution of the flexible set of equations of motion exists.

Depending on the topology of the mechanical system and the specified tree, the branch coordinates may not be independent quantities. If the number of coordinates is greater than the degrees of freedom, then constraint equations are required to express the dependency between coordinates. The constraint equations are obtained directly from the joints and motion drivers in the cotree, by projecting their circuit equations, similar to eq.(7), onto the joint reaction space. Then, if kinematic joint k establishes a translational connexion between points a and b located on bodies i and j, the following vectorial constraint expression must be respected,

$$\mathbf{\Pi}^{k\,T} [\mathbf{r}^i - \mathbf{r}^j] + \mathbf{r}'^k_k = 0 \tag{68}$$

where $\mathbf{r}^i$ and $\mathbf{r}^j$ are the position vectors of the fixation points of the kinematic joint k on bodies i and j while $\mathbf{r}'^k_k$ represents the length of the joint. In a similar fashion, the rotational connexion at kinematic joint k between points a and b can be written,

$$(\boldsymbol{\omega}^i + \dot{\boldsymbol{\alpha}}^i)_k + \boldsymbol{\omega}_k^k - (\boldsymbol{\omega}^j + \dot{\boldsymbol{\alpha}}^j)_k = 0 \tag{69}$$

where ω^i, ω^j and ω_k^k are angular velocities of bodies i and j and kinematic joint k, expressed in the joint reference frame. By introducing the tensor $\mathbf{E}^k$, obtained in equation (26), to eliminate all superflous constraints and substituting the relations for the derivatives of the transformation matrices, the translational and rotational geometrical constraint equations (68) and (69) can be derived twice with respect to time to obtain,

$$\mathbf{E}^k \boldsymbol{\Pi}^{k\,T} \begin{bmatrix} I & -\boldsymbol{\Pi}\,\tilde{\mathbf{s}}' & \boldsymbol{\Pi}\,\mathbf{L}_t \\ 0 & \boldsymbol{\Pi} & \boldsymbol{\Pi}\,\mathbf{L}_r \end{bmatrix} \begin{Bmatrix} \ddot{\mathbf{R}} \\ \ddot{\theta} \\ \ddot{\mathbf{s}}'_n \end{Bmatrix} = -\begin{Bmatrix} \ddot{\mathbf{r}}'^k_k \\ \dot{\omega}^k_k \end{Bmatrix} - \mathbf{E}^k \begin{Bmatrix} \ddot{\boldsymbol{\Pi}}^{k\,T}\,\mathbf{r} + 2\,\dot{\boldsymbol{\Pi}}^{k\,T}\,\dot{\mathbf{r}} + \boldsymbol{\Pi}^{k\,T}(\boldsymbol{\Omega}) \\ \dot{\boldsymbol{\Pi}}^{k\,T}\,\boldsymbol{\Pi}(\omega + \dot{\alpha}) + \boldsymbol{\Pi}^{k\,T}\,\boldsymbol{\Pi}\,\tilde{\omega}\,\dot{\alpha} \end{Bmatrix} \tag{70}$$

with $\boldsymbol{\Omega} = 2\boldsymbol{\Pi}\tilde{\omega}\,\dot{\mathbf{s}}'_n + \boldsymbol{\Pi}\,\tilde{\omega}\tilde{\omega}\mathbf{s}'$.

Together, the topological and terminal equations form a necessary and sufficient set of motion equations for FMS. The variational equations of motion for FMS may be obtained from the tree joint element which connects the whole system of bodies to the ground body through a path consisting entirely of branches. Substituting the general form of virtual work terminal equations for each element in the cutset equation for this tree body constraint or joint, one gets a complete set of equations of motion for the FMS. In general, the branch coordinates are not independent, but are related by the kinematic constraint equations. Thus, these constraint acceleration equations (70) must be appended to the set of dynamic equations (67), giving all the equations to solve for branch coordinates and finally yields the classical system differential-algebraic equations of motion for FMS.

5. Examples

By exploiting GT methods and virtual work principles, this formulation has been implemented into a computer program called **FlexNet** (for FLEXible NETwork). Given only a spanning tree with the terminal expressions for deformable bodies in the system, this program automatically generates the equations of motion. Since the selection of a proper tree only requires an elementary knowledge of graph theory, the objective consists in choosing an optimal joint tree to keep the number of branch coordinates and constraint equations to a minimum. Since the equations of motion for deformable bodies are function of a good discretization, all the constant tensors that are function of finite elements have been identified and generated by a finite element preprocessor. Hence, the preprocessor generates look-up tables that can be exploited when needed during the dynamic simulation of FMS. To enforce the constraints at the position and velocity levels, an energy algorithm proposed by (Bauchau et al., 1995) has also been implemented.

A similar symbolic software that fully exploits this graph-theoretic approach in multi-domain modelling is MapleSim, commercialized by Maplesoft. This GT formulation has been extended in the second version of the software (MapleSimII, 2011) to the analysis of mechatronic and other multidisciplinary systems such as mechanical, electrical, thermal, signal/control and hydraulic systems which can all be naturally combined in a model diagram similar the one presented in section 2. However, this software is limited to the simulation of rigid bodies and flexible beams only.

5.1 Flexible four-bar mechanism

Let us consider the example of the planar flexible four-bar mechanism described earlier in section 2. For this FMS, shown in figure 2(a), a proper tree has been highlighted in bold in figure 2(b). This example has been previously analyzed by (Khulief, 1992) and was also analyzed with the software MapleSimII. The rigid crank OA has a length of 0.3 m and is driven at a constant angular speed of $\omega = 210\, rad/s$. The flexible coupler link AB and the flexible follower BC are discretized by eight linear 3-D beam elements with bending moments of inertia equal to $3.112 \times 10^{-8}\, m^4$ and have cross-sectional areas of $1.767 \times 10^{-4}\, m^2$. Flexible links AB and BC are made of steel with modulus of elasticity of $2.0 \times 10^{11}\, N/m^2$ with mass densities of $7800\, kg/m^3$. The rigid crank is assumed horizontal at the initial state. The deflection at the mid-point of the links are mesured perpendicular to the initial links. The first two vibration modes are considered in this simulation. Shown in the figures 6(a) and 6(b) are the numerical results for the relative deflection of the mid-point of the links plotted against the crank angle θ_{31}.

Once the topology and parameters for the FMS has been defined, the translational and rotational graphs can be generated automatically. Due to the systematic nature of GT methods, the previous formulation was encoded with relative ease into a general computer program. Exploiting conventional GT methods, the cutset and circuit equations are automatically generated from the given topology. The terminal equations developped in the preceeding section are contained in a library of modelling components that can be easily updated to include new components. From the projected cutset and circuit equations, the set of motion equations governing the dynamic response of a given FMS is automatically assembled that provides insight into its structural motion. The results are in good agreement with those obtained by (Khulief, 1992) and the software (MapleSimII, 2011).

5.2 Deployment of two flexible panels

As a final example, consider the unfolding of the spatial structure, drawn in figure 7(a), composed of two flexible panels (1) and (2) attached on a rigid base. The linear graph of this flexible structure is shown in figure 7(b). Each panel of dimension $2m \times 0.003m \times 2m$ is made of steel with a Young's modulus of $2.1 \times 10^{11}\, N/m^2$, Poisson's coefficient of 0.3 and a mass density of $7800\, kg/m^3$.

The edges comprising the tree are traced in bold. The deformable plates are represented by edges e_{51} and e_{52}. The revolute joint e_{31} connects panel (1) to the ground and revolute joint e_{32} connects panel (2) to panel (1). Each panel is discretized by 32 triangular elements. The flexible panel elements are represented by edges e_{11} and e_{12}. By imposing a symmetrical meshing throughout the panels, this avoids the generation of torsion deformations outside of their respective plane. To assure good alignment of the nodes on which are fixed the revolute joints, rigid beam elements are conveniently pasted along the edges joining these nodes.

The complete deployment of the flexible panels has been achieved in $T = 14$ seconds where angles ψ_1 and ψ_2 goes from 0° to 90° and from 180° to 0°, respectively. The imposed drivers at the articulations of the structure have zero velocity and zero acceleration at the beginning

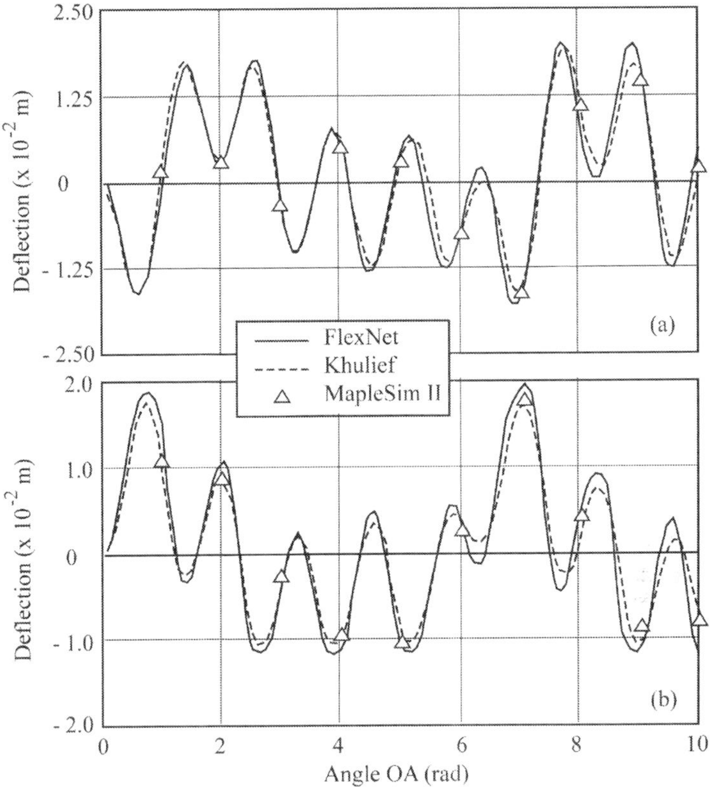

Fig. 6. Deflection of center of a) link *AB* and b) link *BC*

and end of the simulation. The angular drivers e_{61} and e_{62} are given by,

$$\psi_1(t) = \frac{\pi}{2T}\left[t - \frac{T}{2\pi}\,\sin(\frac{2\pi t}{T})\right] \tag{71}$$

$$\psi_2(t) = \pi - \frac{\pi}{T}\left[t - \frac{T}{2\pi}\,\sin(\frac{2\pi t}{T})\right] \tag{72}$$

where $\psi_1(t) = \pi/2$ and $\psi_2(t) = 0$ when $t \geq T$.

Simulations for the flexible panels were performed during $t = 20$ seconds. Results are plotted from the time of release of the panels (at $t = 0s$) through complete deployment (at $t = 14s$) and rebound effects of the panels (until $t = 20s$). Since MapleSimII is restricted to the simulation of flexible links only, figure 8 provides a comparison with the software (Adams/flex, 2011) for the deflection of the centers of the two panels considering the first four vibration modes.

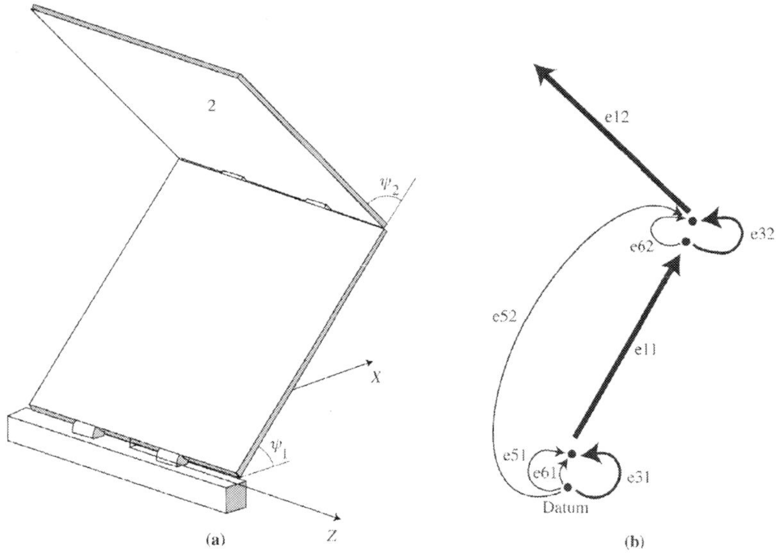

Fig. 7. a) Deployment of the panels and b) graph representation of the system

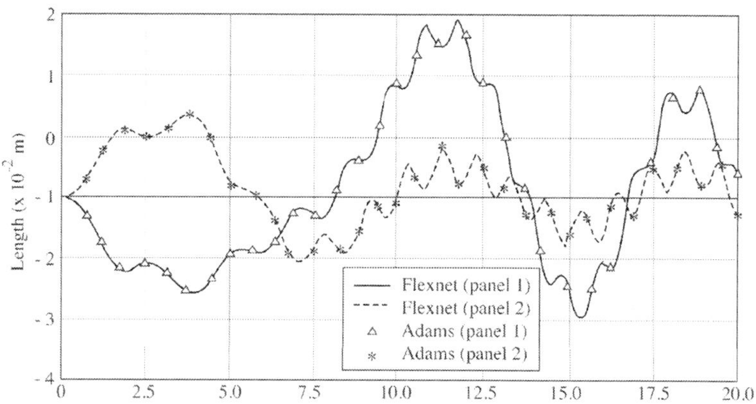

Fig. 8. Transversal deflexion of panel 1 and 2 centers

6. Conclusion

By combining the mechanical system topology with the variational virtual work constitutive equations, a new systematic graph-theoretic formulation has been introduced and used to describe the time-varying configuration of spatial FMS. This method assembles automatically the governing equations of motion in a symmetrical format where the structure and organization of the mass matrix parallels that of structural finite element mass and stiffness matrices, which are also derived using variational methods.

For open-loop systems, like the deployment of panels, a joint tree results in independent branch coordinates and a set of reduced ordinary differential equations can be generated. However, if the graph of a multibody system has closed loops, like in the case of the four-bar mechanism, a tree structure is formed by mathematically cutting the constraining elements or joints yielding the constraint circuit equations. A kinematic formulation may then be developed for the resulting spanning tree, so it neglects momentarily the effect of kinematic constraints between other bodies. While the variational equation of motion is still valid, it holds only for branch coordinate variations that are consistent with the constraint. It is, therefore, necessary to introduce the equation associated with the physical constraint.

Through graph-theoretic methods, the state-of-the-art of general multibody programs has advanced to the point where the flexibility of bodies combined to multi-domain systems can be simulated. Perhaps the most important requirement of a GT general purpose multibody computer program is the quality of the interfaces for the input and output of data. Hence, the self-formulating aspect of all programs exploiting GT methods will become very important for a productive utilization. Other features of GT methods worth mentioning for the future are the portability of the GT algorithms which should be able to adapt easily to all computer environments and the compatibility between different databases of multidisciplinary programs.

7. Acknowledgement

Financial support of this research by the Natural Sciences and Engineering Research Council of Canada is gratefully acknowledged.

8. References

Adams/flex (2011). *MSC/Software Simulating Reality, Delivering Certainty*, http://www.mscsoftware.com/Products/Modeling-Solutions/Default.aspx, last consulted July 2011.

Andrews, G. (1971). *The Vector-Network Model: A topological Approach to Mechanics*, Ph.D. Thesis, University of Waterloo, Waterloo, Ontario, Canada.

Andrews, G. (1977). *A General Re-statement of the Laws of Dynamics Based on Graph Theory*, Problem Analysis in Science and Engineering, Academic Press.

Andrews, G. & Kesavan, H. (1975). The vector-network model: A new approach to vector dynamics, *Mechanism and Machine Theory* Vol. 10: 57–80.

Arczewski, K. (1990). Application of graph theory to the mathematical modelling of a class of rigid body systems, *Journal of the Franklin Institute* Vol. 327, no. 2: 209–220.

Baciu, G., Chou, J. & Kesavan, H. (1990). Constrained multibody systems: Graph-theoretic newton-euler formulation, *IEEE Transactions on Systems, Man and Cybernetics* Vol. 20, no. 5: 1025–1039.

Bauchau, O., Damilano, G. & Theron, N. (1995). Numerical integration of nonlinear elastic multi-body systems, *International Journal of Numerical Methods in Engineering* Vol. 38: 2727–2751.

Behzad, M. & Chartrand, G. (1971). *Introduction to the theory of graphs*, Allyn and Bacon.

Bos, A. (1986). *Modelling Multibody Systems in Terms of Multibond Graphs with Application to a Motorcycle*, Dissertation Twente University.

Chou, J., Kesavan, H. & Singhal, K. (1986). Dynamics of 3-d isolated rigid-body systems: Graph-theoretic models, *Mechanism and Machine Theory* Vol. 21, no. 3: 261–281.

Christensen, R. (1975). *Theory of Viscoelasticity: An Introduction*, Academic Press, New-York.

Christofides, N. (1975). *Graph theory, An Algorithmic Approach*, Academic Press, New York.

Even, S. (1979). *Graph Algorithms*, Computer Science Press.

Flugge, W. (1967). *Viscoelasticity*, Blaisdell, New-York.

Hu, Y. (1988). Applications of bond graphs and vector bond graphs to rigid body dynamics, *Journal of China Textile University* Vol. 5, no. 4: 67–80.

Khulief, Y. (1992). On the finite element dynamic analysis of flexible mechansims, *Computer Methods in Applied Mechanics and Engineering* Vol. 97: 23–32.

Koenig, H. & Blackwell, W. (1960). Linear graph theory - a fundamental engineering discipline, *IRE Transaction on Education* Vol. 3: 42–62.

Koenig, H., Tokad, Y. & Kesavan, H. (1967). *Analysis of Discrete Physical Systems*, McGraw-Hill.

MapleSimII (2011). *High-Performance Multi-Domain Modeling and Simulation*, http://www.maplesoft.com/products/maplesim/index.aspx, last consulted July 2011.

McPhee, J. (1998). Automatic generation of motion equations for planar mechanical systems using the new set of branch coordinates, *Mechanism and Machine Theory* Vol. 33, no. 6: 805–823.

McPhee, J. & Redmond, S. (2006). Modelling multibody systems with indirect coordinates, *Computer Methods in Applied Mechanics and Engineering* Vol. 195, no. 50: 6942–6957.

Richard, M. (1985). *Dynamic Simulation of Constrained Three Dimensional Multibody Systems Using Vector Network Techniques*, Ph.D. Thesis, Queen's University, Kingston, Ontario, Canada.

Richard, M., Bouazara, M. & Therien, J. (2011). Analysis of multibody systems with flexible plates using variational graph- theoretic methods, *Multibody System Dynamics* Vol. 25: 43–63.

Richard, M., Huang, M. & Bouazara, M. (2004). Computer aided analysis and optimal design of mechanical systems using vector-network techniques, *Journal of Applied Mathematics and Computation* Vol. 157: 175–200.

Roberson, R. (1984). The path matrix of a graph, its construction and its use in evaluating certain products, *Journal of Computer Methods in Applied Mechanics and Engineering* Vol. 42: 47–57.

Shabana, A. (1986). Transient analysis of flexible multi-body systems - part1: Dynamics of flexible bodies, *Computer Methods in Applied Mechanics and Engineering* Vol. 54: 75–91.

Shi, P. & McPhee, J. (1997). On the use of virtual work in a graph-theoretic formulation for multibody dynamics, *ASME Design Engineering Technical Conference* DETC97/vib-4199.

Shi, P. & McPhee, J. (2000). Dynamics of flexible multibody systems using virtual work and linear graph theory, *Multibody System Dynamics* Vol. 4: 355–381.

Shi, P., McPhee, J. & Heppler, G. (2001). A deformation field for euler-bernoulli beams with applications to flexible multibody dynamics, *Multibody System Dynamics* Vol. 5: 79–104.

Tennich, M. (1994). *Dynamique de systèmes multi-corps flexibles, une approche générale*, Ph.D. Dissertation, Laval University, Québec, Québec.

Wasfy, T. & Noor, A. (2003). Computational strategies for flexible multibody systems, *ASME Applied Mechanics Reviews* Vol. 56, no. 6: 553–613.

Wittenburg, J. (1977). *Dynamics of Systems of Rigid bodies*, Teubner, Stuttgart.

18

Spectral Clustering and Its Application in Machine Failure Prognosis

Weihua Li[1,2], Yan Chen[2], Wen Liu[1] and Jay Lee[2]
[1]School of Mech. & Auto. Eng,
Souch China University of Technology,
[2]NSFI/UCRC Center for Intelligent Maintenance System,
University of Cincinnati,
[1]China
[2]USA

1. Introduction

Machine fault prognosis and health management has received intensive studies for several decades, and various approaches have been taken, such as statistical signal processing, time-frequency analysis, wavelet, and neural networks. Among of them, pattern recognition method provides a systematic approach to acquiring knowledge from fault samples. In fact, mechanical fault diagnosis is essentially a problem of pattern classification.

Many pattern recognition methods have been studied and applied in machine condition monitoring and fault prognosis. Campbell proposed a linear programming approach to engine failure detection (Campbell&Bennett, 2001). In Ypma's study, different learning methods, such as Independent Component Analysis, Self Organising Map, and Hidden Markov Models, were applied in fault feature extraction, novelty detection and dynamic fault recognition (Ypma, 2001). Ge et.al (2004)proposed a support vector machine based method for sheet metal stamping monitoring. Harkat et.al(2007) applied non-linear principal component analysis in sensor fault detection and isolation. Lei and Zuo (2009) implemented the Weighted *k* Nearest Neighbour algorithm to identify the gear crack level.

However, the information of machine incipient fault is always weak and contaminated by strong noises, and there is always lack of fault samples to train the learning machine. Therefore, the key issue is how to select sensitive features from the dataset for machine incipient faults prognosis, which is related to feature selection and dimension reduction, and is very useful for fault classification.

In most of medical and clinic applications, when the dimensionality of the data is high, for reducing computation complexity, some techniques might be used to project or embed the data into a lower dimensional space while retaining as much information as possible. Classical linear examples are Principal Component Analysis (PCA) (Jolliffe.2002) and Multi-Dimensional Scaling (MDS) (T. F. Cox & M. A. Cox, 2001). The coordinates of the data points in the lower dimension space might be used as features or simply a mean to visualize the data.

However, for common PHM(Prognostic and Health Management) applications, the dimensionality of the data is not as high as those in medical research, and the mapping techniques are mainly applied to reveal the correlation of features as to increase the accuracy of fault detection and identification. The selection of features also can avoid unnecessary sensors used in machine monitoring, considering the high cost maintaining. Nomikos and MacGregor(1994) firstly presented a PCA approach for monitoring batch process, the history information was linear projected onto a low-dimensional space that summarized the key characteristics of normal behaviour by both variable and their time histories. Considering that minor component discarded in PCA might contain important information on nonlinearities, a large amount of nonlinear methods were presented for the process monitoring and chemical process modelling (Dong & McAvoy,1996; Kaspar & Ray,1992; Sang et. al,2005), such as Kernal PCA (Schölkopf,1998).

Non-linear dimensionality mapping methods are more frequently recognized as non-linear manifold learning methods. The manifold learning is the process of estimating a low-dimensional underlying structure embedded in a collection of high-dimensional data(Tenenbaum et. al, 2000; Roweis & Saul, 2000). Instead of using Euclidian distance to measure samples' similarity in input space, samples' similarity in latent space is measured by their geodesic or short path distance. The deceptive close distance in the high-dimensional input space can be corrected.

Spectral clustering is a graph-theory-based manifold learning method, which can be used to dissect the graph and get the clusters for exploratory data analysis. Compared with the traditional algorithms such as k-means, spectral clustering has many fundamental advantages. It is more flexible, capturing a wider range of geometries, and it is very simple to implement and can be solved efficiently by standard linear algebra methods. It has been successfully deployed in numerous applications in areas such as computer vision, speech recognition, and robotics. Moreover, there is a substantial theoretical literature supporting spectral clustering (Kannan et.al,2004; Luxburg,2007,2008).

In most PHM applications, multi-groups of data sets from different failure modes are frequently nonlinearly distributed and mixed in a high dimensional feature space. However, an "unfolded" feature space is expected as to differentiate these degradation patterns by a designed classifier.

In this part, we first propose a spectral clustering based feature selection method used for machine fault feature extraction and evaluation, and then the samples with selected features are input into a density-adjustable spectral kernel based transductive support vector machine to train and to get the prognosis results.

2. Spectral clustering feature selection

2.1 Basics of graph theory

Given a d-dimentsional data points $\{x_1, \ldots, x_n\}$, and the similarity between all pairs of data points x_i and x_j is noted as w_{ij}. According to graph theory, the data points can be represented by an undirected data graph G=(V,E). Each node in this graph represents a data point x_i. Two nodes are connected if the similarity w_{ij} between the corresponding data x_i and x_j is positive or larger than a certain threshold, and the edge is weighted by w_{ij}. These data points can be divided into several groups such that points in the same group are similar and points in different groups are dissimilar to each other.

2.2 Laplacian embedding

BelKin(2003) indicated that Laplacian Eigenmaps used spectral techniques to perform dimensionality reduction. This technique relies on the basic assumption that the data lies in a low dimensional manifold in a high dimensional space. The Laplacian of the graph obtained from the data points may be viewed as an approximation to the Laplace-Beltrami operator defined on the manifold. The embedding maps for the data come from approximations to a natural map that is defined on the entire manifold.

The popular Laplacian Embedding algorithm includes the following steps, as shown in Fig.1.

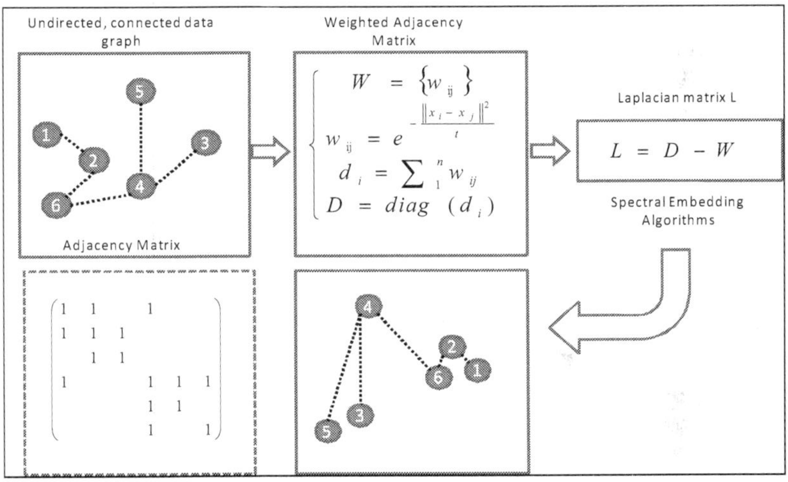

Fig. 1. The procedure of Laplacian Embedding Algorithm

Step 1: The d-dimensional dataset is viewed as an undirected data graph [10] , G = (V, E) with node set V={x_1,...,x_n}. Every node in the graph is one point in $\Re_d$. An edge is used to link node i and node j, if they are close as ε-neighborhoods which means the distance between nodes $\mathbf{X}_i$ and $\mathbf{X}_j$ satisfying $\left\|\mathbf{X}_i - \mathbf{X}_j\right\| < \varepsilon$, or if node $\mathbf{X}_i$ is among n nearest neighbors of $\mathbf{X}_j$ or $\mathbf{X}_j$ is among n nearest neighbors of $\mathbf{X}_i$.

Step 2: Each edge between two nodes $\mathbf{X}_i$ and $\mathbf{X}_j$ carries a non-negative weight $w_{ij} \geq 0$. The weighted adjacency matrix of the graph is the matrix $\mathbf{W} = \{w_{ij}\}, i, j = 1, \ldots, n$. There are different methods to configure the weight matrix. For example, the most common is

$$w_{ij} = \begin{cases} 1 & \text{if } x_i \text{ and } x_j \text{ is connected} \\ 0 & \text{otherwise} \end{cases} \quad (1)$$

Or Heat kernel

$$w_{ij} = \begin{cases} e^{-\|x_i - x_j\|^2 / t} & \text{if } x_i \text{ and } x_j \text{ is connected} \\ 0 & \text{otherwise} \end{cases} \quad (2)$$

The degree of a node $X_i \in V$ is defined as $d_i = \sum_1^n w_{ij}$. The degree matrix D is defined as the diagonal matrix with $\{d_1, d_2, \ldots, d_n\}$ on its diagonal. The un-normalized graph Laplacian matrix is defined by Luxburg(2007) as: $\mathbf{L} = \mathbf{D} - \mathbf{W}$.

Step 3: The Laplacian Eigenmap (on normalized Laplacian matrix) is computed by spectral decomposition for eigenvectors problem of $\mathbf{L}y = \lambda \mathbf{D}y$. The image of X_i under the embedding is converted into the lower dimensional space $\Re m$, given by ordered eigenvalues: $\{y_1(i), y_2(i), \ldots, y_m(i)\}$. This decomposition provides significant information about the graph and distribution of all points. It has been proven experimentally that the inner natural groups of dataset are recovered by mapping the original dataset into the space spanned by eigenvectors of the Laplacian matrix(Belkin & Niyogi,2003).

2.3 Supervised feature selection criterion by Laplacian scores

Given a graph G, the Laplacian matrix **L** of G is a linear operator on any feature vector from $\mathbf{f} = \{\mathbf{f}_1, \ldots, \mathbf{f}_m\}, \mathbf{f}_i \in R^n$

$$\mathbf{f}_k{}^T \mathbf{L} \mathbf{f}_k = \frac{1}{2} \sum_{i,j=1}^{n} w_{ij} (x_{ki} - x_{kj})^2 \quad (3)$$

The equation quantifies how much the feature vector is consistent with the structure of the G locally. For the instances closer to each other, the features that have similar value for them are contributes more on the dissimilarity matrix that is consistent with data structure. The flatter the feature value is over all instances, the smaller the value of the equation. However, instead of the feature consistency only considering instances with small distance, a complete definition of feature consistency with the data structure is clarified as the following:

Definition 1: (feature local consistency with data graph)

Given data graph G= (**V**, **E**) ($V=\{X_1, \ldots, X_n\}, E=\{W_{ij}\}$), the feature **f** is a locally consistent variant of G at level h ($0<h<1$) for a clustering C over G. If for every cluster C_k of C, there is

$$\frac{\frac{1}{n_k} \sum_{i,j \in C_k} (\mathbf{f}_i - \mathbf{f}_j)^2}{\frac{1}{n_k (n - n_k)} \sum_{i \in C_k, j \notin C_k} (\mathbf{f}_i - \mathbf{f}_j)^2} = h_k \quad (4)$$

And $h = \max(h_k)$ is defined as feature consistency index.

The definition is a ratio between inner and intra cluster variation caused by the individual feature. Perfect clustering expects less variance inter-cluster and the inverse for intra-clusters. If the feature **f** contributes to better clustering, the nominator tends to be smaller and denominator is larger. Therefore h_k is expected to be smaller. The feature consistency index h indicates the features's weakest separablility for clustering C

In terms of graph theory, similar criterion can be formulated based on Eq.(4), and configure data graph G with following similarity measurement,

$$w^{(1)}_{ij} = \begin{cases} 1/n_k & i,j \in C_k \\ 0 & \text{otherwise} \end{cases} \tag{5}$$

$$w^{(2)}_{ij} = \begin{cases} 0 & i,j \in C_k \\ -1/(n-n_k) & otherwise \end{cases} \tag{6}$$

Where $w^{(1)}_{ij}$ is the similarity measurement of samples within-class, and $w^{(2)}_{ij}$ that of samples between-class. Then the sequence of instances can be reordered to make the adjacency matrix carry closer instances along its diagonal.

$$\mathbf{W}^{(2)} = \begin{pmatrix} W_1^{(2)} & \cdots & -1/n_1(n-n_1) \\ \vdots & \ddots & \vdots \\ 1/n_p(n-n_p) & \cdots & W_{n_p}^{(2)} \end{pmatrix} \tag{7}$$

$$\mathbf{W}^{(1)} = \begin{pmatrix} W_1^{(1)} & \cdots & 0 \\ \vdots & \ddots & \vdots \\ 0 & \cdots & W_{n_p}^{(1)} \end{pmatrix} \tag{8}$$

As proved by He et.al (2006), Laplacian score of r-th feature is as the follows:

$$L_r = \frac{\tilde{f}_r^T L \tilde{f}_r}{\tilde{f}_r^T D \tilde{f}_r} \tag{9}$$

Because of $\tilde{\mathbf{f}}_r^T \mathbf{L} \tilde{\mathbf{f}}_r = \mathbf{f}_r^T \mathbf{L} \mathbf{f}_r$ (He et.al, 2006), and with the weight matrix as $\mathbf{W}^{(2)}$ and $\mathbf{W}^{(1)}$ as well as their degree diagonal matrixes,

$$\mathbf{D}^{(1)} = -\mathbf{D}^{(2)} = \begin{pmatrix} 1/n_1 & 0 & 0 \\ 0 & \ddots & \vdots \\ 0 & \cdots & 1/n_p \end{pmatrix} \tag{10}$$

The two Laplacian score $\mathbf{L}_r^{(1)}$ and $\mathbf{L}_r^{(2)}$ have same absolute value of denominators. If there exists clustering C={C_1,…, C_p } over data graph G, the nominators are as the following

$$\mathbf{f}_r^T\mathbf{L}^{(1)}\mathbf{f}_r = \frac{1}{2}\sum_{k=1}^{p}\frac{1}{n_k}\sum_{i,j\in k}(x_{ri}-x_{rj})^2 \tag{11}$$

$$\mathbf{f}_r^T\mathbf{L}^{(2)}\mathbf{f}_r = -\frac{1}{2}\sum_{k=1}^{p}\frac{1}{n_k(n-n_k)}\sum_{i\in k,j\notin k}(x_{ri}-x_{rj})^2 \tag{12}$$

Combining Eq.(4) and Eq.(11), there is

$$\mathbf{f}_\mathbf{r}^\mathbf{T}\mathbf{L}^{(1)}\mathbf{f}_r = \frac{1}{2}\sum_{k=1}^{p}\frac{h_k}{n_k(n-n_k)}\sum_{i\in k,j\notin k}(x_{ri}-x_{rj})^2 \tag{13}$$

Comparing Eq.(12) with Eq.(13), it can be obtained

$$\min(h_k) < -\frac{\mathbf{f}_\mathbf{r}^\mathbf{T}\mathbf{L}^{(1)}\mathbf{f}_\mathbf{r}}{\mathbf{f}_\mathbf{r}^\mathbf{T}\mathbf{L}^{(2)}\mathbf{f}_r} = \frac{\mathbf{L}_r^{(1)}}{\mathbf{L}_r^{(2)}} < \max(h_k) = h \tag{14}$$

Therefore, from Eq.(14), instead of the feature consistency index in Definition 1, the ratio of two Laplacian scores can also be considered as equivalent estimation of feature consistency. They are over the data graph with the configuration of $\mathbf{W}^{(2)}$ and $\mathbf{W}^{(1)}$. If the feature is consistent with these data graphs, term of $\mathbf{L}_r^{(1)}$ should be smaller and $\mathbf{L}_r^{(2)}$ be larger.

Therefore, from graph theory perspective, the supervised feature selection criterion by Laplacian score can be defined as follows

$$m = -\frac{\mathbf{f}_\mathbf{r}^\mathbf{T}\mathbf{L}^{(1)}\mathbf{f}_\mathbf{r}}{\mathbf{f}_\mathbf{r}^\mathbf{T}\mathbf{L}^{(2)}\mathbf{f}_r} = \frac{\mathbf{L}_r^{(1)}}{\mathbf{L}_r^{(2)}} \tag{15}$$

Based on the criterion, the feature can be ranked, and a simple searching engine can be defined to select appropriate number of features from the list.

3. Spectral kernel transductive support vector machine

3.1 Density-adjustable spectral clustering

Commonly, the weight of the edge in a Graph is defined by the Euclid distance between the two nodes, and it works very well with the linear data.

But for nonlinear data, such as two clusters shown in Fig.2, data points a and c belong to the same cluster, and the Euclid distance between points a and b is less than that between points a and c. Therefore, it is necessary to measure the similarity of data points in a different way, which can zoom out the path length of those passing through low density area, and zoom in those not. Then the minimum path can be obtained to replace the Euclid distance. It is very useful for machine failure prognosis, because there always exists nonlinear when machine anomaly occurring. Chapelle et.al (2005) proposed a density-sensitive distance based on a density-adjustable path length definition as follows,

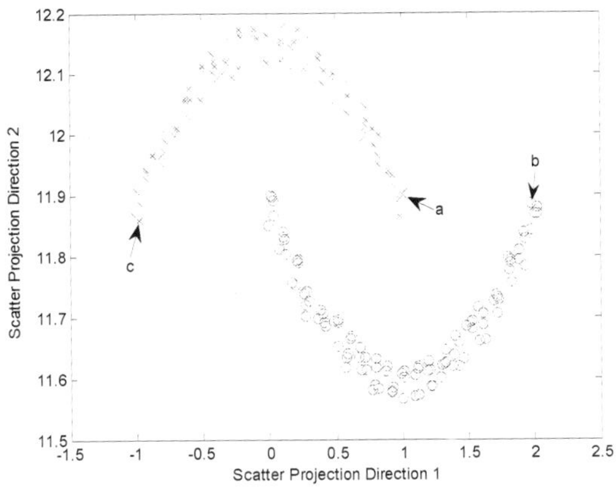

Fig. 2. Scatter Plot of two clusters based on Density-adjustable spectral clustering

$$l(x_i,x_j)=\rho^{dist(x_i,x_j)}-1 \tag{16}$$

Where $dist(x_i,x_j)$ is the Euclid distance between data x_i and data x_j, and ρ is the density adjustble factor($\rho>1$). This definition is satisfied with the cluster assumption, and can be used to describe the consistency of data structure by adjusting the factor ρ to zoom out or in the length between the two data points. Therefore, the similarity of the data point x_i and x_j can be expressed as following,

$$s_0(x_i,x_j)=\frac{1}{dsp(l(x_i,x_j))+1} \tag{17}$$

Where $dsp(l(x_i,x_j))$ is denoted as the minimum distance between data x_i and x_j, which is the shortest path based on density adjustment.

3.2 Transductive support vector machine

Support vector machine is one of supervised learning methods based on statistical learning theory (Vapnik, 1998). Instead of Empirical Risk Minimization (ERM), Structural Risk Minimization (SRM) is an inductive principle for model selection used for learning from finite training data sets, which enhances the generalization ability of the SVM. The key to SVM is the "kernel tricks", by which the nonlinear map can be realized from low dimensional space to high dimensional space. Therefore, the nonlinear classification task in low dimensional space can be converted to a linear classification, which can be solved by finding a best hyperplane in the high dimensional space.

Considering of 2-class data points, there are many hyperplanes that might classify the data. The best hyperplane is the one that represents the largest margin between the two classes, and the distance from this hyperplane to the nearest data point on each side is maximized.

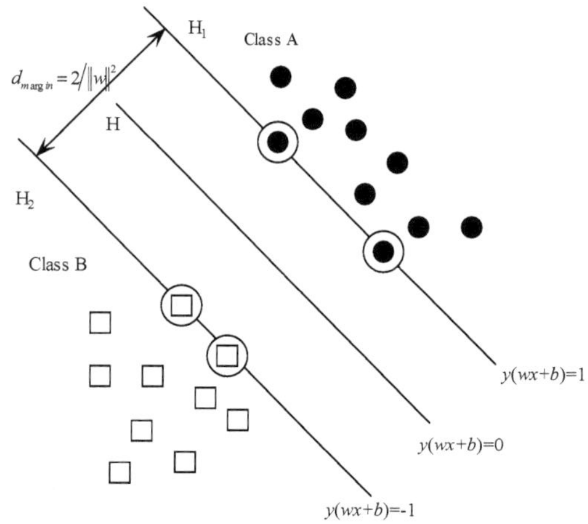

Fig. 3. The Linear Hyperplane of Support Vector Machine

As shown in Fig.3, the data points of Class A are denoted as '•', the others of Class B as '□', and the data points circled by '○' represented support vectors. These data x in the input space are separated by the best hyperplane H

$$y(\mathbf{w} \cdot x + b) = 0 \tag{18}$$

with the maximal geometric margin

$$\varphi(w)=2/\|w\|^2 \tag{19}$$

here '$\cdot$' denotes the dot product and $\mathbf{w}$ is normal vector to the hyperplane, and b is offset from the hyperplane to the margin.

The plane H1 and H2 are also the hyperplanes where the nearest data points to 'H' are located. H1 can be expressed as $y(\mathbf{w} \cdot x + b) = 1$ and H2 $y(\mathbf{w} \cdot x + b) = -1$ respectively. It reveals that finding the best hyperplane means minimizing the $\|w\|^2/2$. There are three widely used kernel function as following,

Polynomial Kernel: $K(x,y) = [\langle x,y\rangle + 1]^d$,

Gaussian Kernel: $K(x,y) = \exp(-\| x - y \|^2/\sigma^2)$,

Hyperbolic: $K(x,y) = \tanh[v(x,y) + c]$.

As for Transductive Support Vector Machine (TSVM), it is one of semi-supervised learning methods, which can combine the labelled data with amounts of unlabelled data co-training. TSVM uses an idea of maximizing separation between labelled and unlabelled data (Vapnik, 1998). It solves

$$\min:\frac{1}{2}\|w\|^2+C\sum_{i=0}^{l}\xi_i+C^*\sum_{j=0}^{k}\xi_j^* \tag{20}$$

$$s.t.:\forall_{i=1}^{l}:y_i(w\cdot x_i+b)\geq 1-\xi_i,\ \forall_{j=1}^{k}:y_j(w\cdot x_j+b)\geq 1-\xi_j^*$$

$$\forall_{i=1}^{l}:\xi_i>0,\ \forall_{j=1}^{k}:\xi_j^*>0$$

Where C and C^* are the penalty factors corresponding to labeled and unlabeled data, ξ_i and ξ_j^* are the slack factors respectively, l is the number of labeled data and k that of unlabeled. These parameters are set by user, and they allow trading off margin size against misclassifying training samples or excluding test samples.

3.3 Density-adjustable spectral kernel based TSVM

Combine the ideas of density-adjustable spectral clustering (Chapelle & Zien,2005) and TSVM, we can get the density-adjustable spectral kernel based TSVM algorithm, called DSTSVM. The data is pre-processed by density-adjustable spectral decomposition, and the processed data is input into the TSVM which is trained by gradient descent on a Gaussian kernel, then the data is classified. The implementation of the DSTSVM algorithm is as following,

Input: n-dimension data $X\{X_1,\ldots,X_m\}$ (some labelled and others unlabelled)

Parameter: density-adjustable factor ρ, penalty factor C and kernel width σ of the Gaussian kernel. (Set by user)

Output: The label of unlabelled data and the correctness of classification

Step.1 Calculate the Euclid distance matrix S of data X

Step.2 Calculate the shortest path matrix S_0 according to the Eq.16

Step.3 Construct the Graph G based on data matrix S_0. Define the similarity of between nodes as $w_{ij}=e^{-s_0(x_i,x_j)/2\sigma^2}$, and then the degree diagonal matrix can be denoted as $D(i,i)=\sum w_{ij}$.

Step.4 Calculate the Laplacian matrix $L=D^{(-1/2)}WD^{(-1/2)}$ solve the Eigen-decomposition and rearrange the eigenvalue $\{\lambda_1,\ldots,\lambda_n\}$ and corresponding eigenvector $\{U_1,\ldots,U_n\}$ in descent order.

Step.5 Select the first r nonnegative eigenvectors according to $\left(\sum_{i=1}^{r}\lambda_i\Big/\sum_{j=1}^{n}\lambda_j\right)\geq 85\%$.

Step.6 Get the new data set as $Y=U_r\Lambda_r^{1/2}\quad\{y_1,\ldots,y_m\}$

Step.7 Train the TSVM by gradient descent using the newdata and then get the classification result.

4. Case study

To demonstrate that the proposed feature selection method and DSTSVM classifier are effective in machine failure prognosis, we applied the methods in feed axis faults feature selection and classification.

4.1 Experiments

Feed axis is one of critical components in a high-precision numerical control machine tool, which always working in conditions such as high speed, heavy duty and large travel distance. This would augment the degradation of mechanical parts such as bearings, ball nuts and so on. From a preventive maintenance perspective, autonomous fault detection and feed axis health assessment could reduce the possibility of causing more severe damage and downtime to machine tool.

TechSolve Inc. collaborated with the NSF Intelligent Maintenance System Center (IMS) to investigate intelligent maintenance techniques for autonomous feed axis failure diagnosis and health assessment. For the investigation, designed experiments were conducted on a feed axis test-bed built by TechSolve. Multiple seeded failures were tested on the system such as axis front and back ball nut misalignment, bearing misalignment and so on (Siegal et.al, 2011). 13 channels (bearing and ball nut accelerometers, temperature and speed; motor power; encode position and so on) data were collected from the test-bed over a period of approximate 6 months. Since all the tests were designed to carry certain failures under different working conditions, the collected information was labeled in terms of the four condition indices including the test index, the load, ball nuts condition, and bearing condition.

Mode	Test index	Table Load	BallNut Misalignment	Bearing Misalignment	Time
1 (Health)	1	0	0	0	2010-10-20
	2	300	0	0	2010-10-22
2 (Failure1)	3	300	0	0.007	2010-11-09
	4	0	0	0.007	2010-11-22
3 (Failure2)	5	0	0.007	0	2010-11-29
	6	300	0.007	0	2010-12-01
4 (Failure1 and Failure2)	7	300	0.007	0.007	2010-12-02
	8	0	0.007	0.007	2010-12-03

Table 1. Eight working conditions of Four modes (Health, Bearing misalignment, Ballnut misalignment, and Combination)

4.2 Feature selection and fault classification

The samples were collected under 4 modes, which were Health, Failure 1(Bearing misalignment 0.007μm), Failure 2 (Ballnut misalignment 0.007μm), and Mode 4 (Failure 1 accompanied with Failure 2). Every mode had two working conditions with load at 0 and 300Kw, and 25 samples at every condition. As for each sample, there were 154 features which contain 117 vibration features (RMS, kurtosis, crest factor at different time periods, and average energy of selected frequency bands) and 37 other features (torque, temperature, position error, and power at different time periods). Therefore, there were totally 200 154-D samples used for investigation.

All the features were evaluated and ranked by Laplacian score using the proposed feature selection criterion. Among 154 features, there were 22 features selected which can reflect the data structure well with the best classification performance, which was shown in Fig.4.

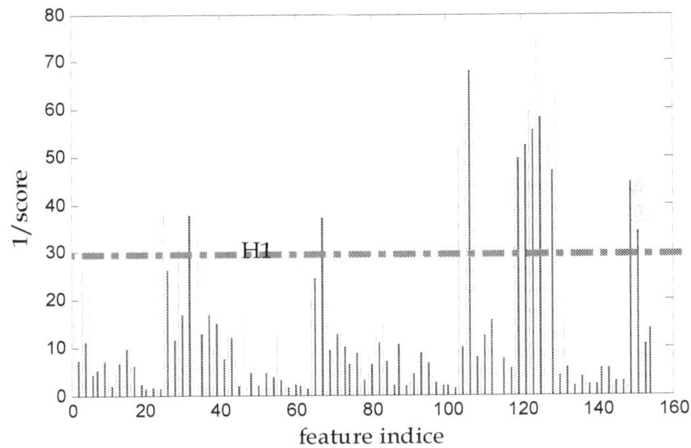

Fig. 4. Features selection based on Laplacian scores

Therefore, the input data dimension can be reduced from 154-D to 22-D. Selecting 25 labelled samples randomly from those 50 22-D samples within every class (totally 100 samples), and the remained 100 samples were regarded as unlabelled ones. Then all these labelled and unlabelled samples were input into the DSTSVM classifier for co-training. This process was repeated for 10 times, and then through 5-fold cross validation, we predicted that which class should the unlabelled samples belong to.

For testing the performance of designed DSTSVM classifier, we reduced the labelled samples to 20 and 10 respectively, and then repeated the procedure above. To verify the effectiveness and correctness, the result was compared with those using SVM (supervised) and TSVM (semi-supervised).

The 10th classification results using the data (10 labelled samples VS 40 unlabelled each class) were shown in Fig.5, Fig. 6, and Fig. 7 respectively.

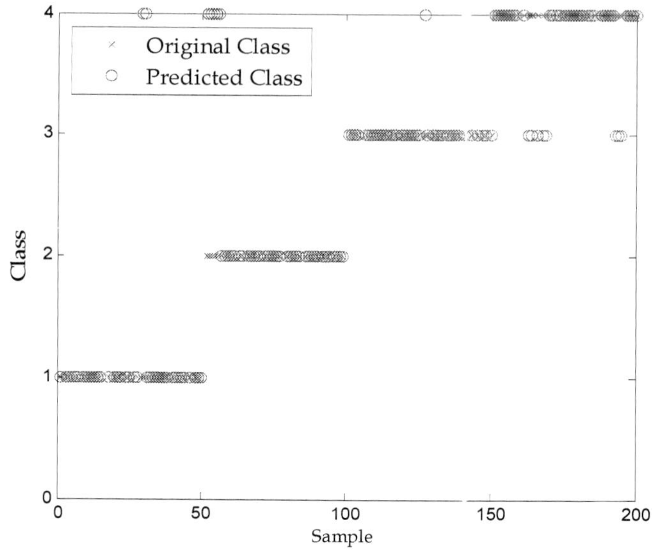

Fig. 5. The Learning result of DSTSVM

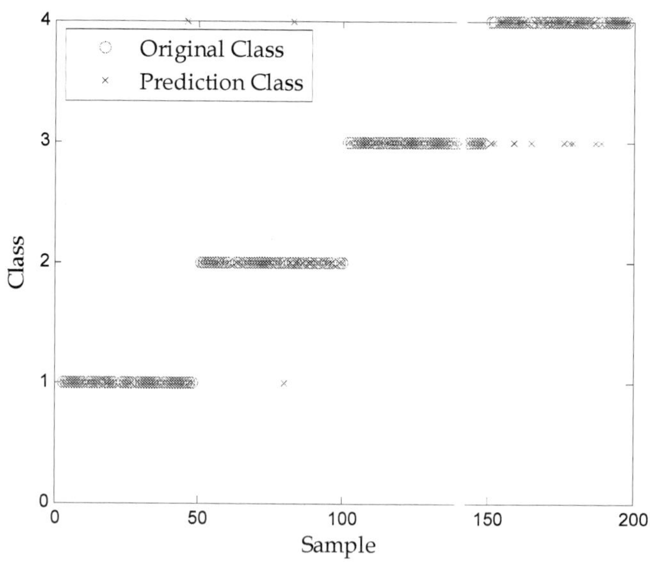

Fig. 6. The Learning result of SVM

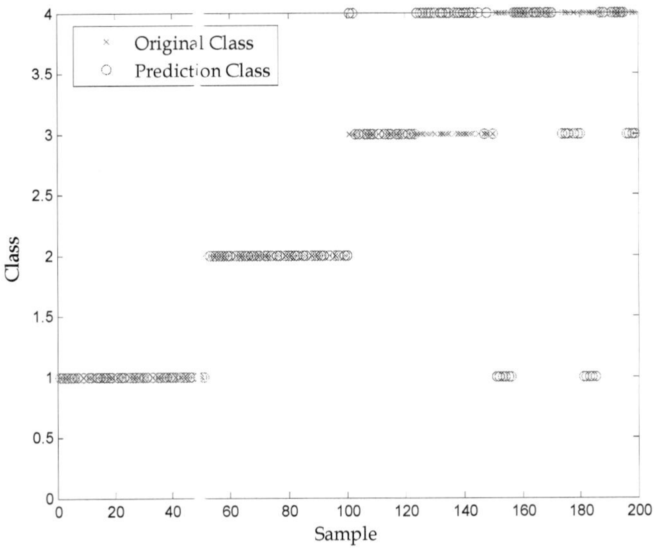

Fig. 7. The Learning result of TSVM

All of the classifiers were trained on Gaussian kernel, and the kernel width σ was set as the optimal value corresponding to the different classifiers. There are two parameters σ and ρ influencing the DSTSVM classification, and the density adjustable factor ρ reflects the data similarity measure, which also affects the Kernel function. In terms of the classification correctness, we can choose the optimal group of these two parameters (ρ, σ). The comparison results under different labelled samples were listed in Table.2.

	DSTSVM		SVM		TSVM	
Labelled vs Unlabelled	Kernel width & density factor (σ,ρ)	Ave Correctness (%)	Kernel width σ	Ave Correctness (%)	Kernel width σ	Ave Correctness (%)
(25vs25)*4	(0.75,2)	91.90	0.5	91.80	0.55	82.50
(20vs30)*4	(0.75,2)	90.92	0.5	90.42	0.55	83.33
(10vs40)*4	(0.75,2)	90.25	0.5	88.88	0.55	85.63

Table 2. The parameters and the average correctness of three classifiers

In Table.2, the average correctness means the average of 10 testing process by 5-fold CV. It can be observed that the proposed method outperforms the TSVM and equals to the supervised SVM under different labelled samples. Moreover, when the labelled data was reduced to 10 samples, it performed better than SVM, which was very meaningful to practical machine failure prognosis applications.

5. Conclusion

The proposed feature selection method can capture the structures of the input data, reduce the dimension of the data and expedite the computation process. More importantly, the classification result is also improved by this feature selection method. Compared with traditional supervised SVM learning and the TSVM semi-supervised learning method, the proposed DSTSVM performed better. Experiment results demonstrate that the proposed DSTSVM method is effective and capable of classifying incipient failures. It has great potential for machine fault prognosis in practice. Based on the current work, the proposed approach can be used to quantify and assure the sufficiency of the data for prognostics applications.

In total, the spectral clustering based method was proposed to evaluate data and to select sensitive features for prognostics, furthermore the spectral kernel based TSVM classifier was also proved to be effective in PHM applications.

6. Acknowledgment

The work described in this paper is supported in part by the National Natural Science Foundation of China (51075150), the Fundamental Research Funds for the Central Universities (2009ZM0091), and Open Research Foundation of State Key Laboratory of Digital Manufacturing Equipment and Technology (DMETKF2009010). The authors would also like to thank Intelligent Maintenance System center in University of Cincinnati and its industry collabrator TechSolve Inc. for the investigation of feed axes system.

7. References

B. Schölkopf, A. Smola, K.R.Muller.(1998). Nonlinear Component Analysis as a Kernel Eigenvalue Problem, *Neural Computation*, Vol.10, No.5,(July 1998), pp.1299–1319, ISSN 0899-7667

Campbell, C. and Bennett, K. (2001). A linear programming approach to novelty detection, *Advances in Neural Information Processing System*, Vol. 14, pp.395-401, ISBN-10 0-262-04208-8, Vancouver, British Columbia, Canada. December 3-8, 2001

Chapelle O, Zien A.(2005). Semi-supervised classification by low density separation, *Proceedings of the 10th International Workshop on Artificial Intelligence and Statistics*, pp57-64, ISBN 0-9727358-1-X, Barbados, January 6-8, 2005

D. Dong and T. J. McAvoy.(1996). Batch tracking via nonlinear principal component analysis, *AIChE Journal*, vol. 42,No.8, (August 1996). pp. 2199-2208, ISSN 1547-5905

Harkat, M-F., Djelel, S., Doghmane, N. and Benouaret, M. (2007). Sensor fault detection, isolation and reconstruction using non-linear principal component analysis, *International Journal of Automation and Computing*, Vol. 4, No. 2, (April 2007),pp.149-155, ISSN 1751-8520

I. Jolliffe.(2002)Principal component analysis, *Encyclopedia of Statistics in Behavioral Science*, ISBN 0-387-95442-2. Springer, New York

J. B. Tenenbaum, V.d.Silva and J.C. Langford.(2000). A global geometric framework for nonlinear dimensionality reduction, *Science*, Vol. 290, No. 5500, (December 2000),pp. 2319-2323, ISSN 0036-8075

T. F. Cox. and M. A. A. Cox (2001). Multidimensional scaling, Chapman and Hall(2nd Edition), ISBN 1-584-88094-3, Florida, USA

M. Belkin and P. Niyogi. (2003). Laplacian Eigenmaps for Dimensionality Reduction and Data Representation, *Neural Computation*,Vol.15,No.6 (June 2003), pp.1373-1396, ISSN 0899-7667

M. Ge, R. Du, G. Zhang, Y. Xu. (2004) Fault diagnosis using support vector machine with an application in sheet metal stamping operations. *Mechanical System and Signal Processing*, Vol.18, No.1, (January 2004), pp.143-159, ISSN 0888-3270

M. H. Kaspar and W. H. Ray.(1992). Chemometric methods for process monitoring and high performance controller design, *AIChE Journal*, Vol. 38, No.10, (October 1992), pp. 1593-1608,ISSN 1547-5905

M. Li, J. Xu, J. Yang, D. Yang and D. Wang. (2009). Multiple manifolds analysis and its application to fault diagnosis, *Mechanical systems and signal processing*, Vol.23, No.9, (November 2009) ,pp. 2500-2509, ISSN 0888-3270

P. Nomikos and J. F. MacGregor.(1994). Monitoring batch processes using multiway principal component analysis, *AIChE Journal*, Vol.40, No.8,(August 1994), pp. 1361-1375, ISSN 1547-5905

Q. Jiang, M.Jia, J. Hu and F. Xu. (2009). Machinery fault diagnosis using supervised manifold learning," *Mechanical systems and signal processing*, Vol.23, No.7, (October 2009), pp. 2301-2311, ISSN 0888-3270

R. Kannan, S. Vempala, and A. Vetta.(2004). On clusterings: Good, bad and spectral. Journal of the ACM, Vol.51, No.3, (May 2004), pp.497–515, ISSN 0004-5411

Skirtich, T., Siegel, D. and Lee, J. (2011). A Systematic Health Monitoring and Fault Identification Methodology for Machine Tool Feed Axis. *MFPT Applied Systems Health Management Conference*, pp.487-506, May 10-12, 2011, Virginia Beach, VA, USA

S. T. Roweis and L. K. Saul.(2000). Nonlinear dimensionality reduction by locally linear embedding, *Science*, Vol. 290, No.5500, (December 2000),pp. 2323-2326, ISSN 0036-8075

U. Von Luxburg. (2007). A tutorial on spectral clustering, *Statistics and Computing*, Vol.17, No.4, (December 2007), pp. 395-416, ISSN 0960-3174

U. von Luxburg, M. Belkin, and O. Bousquet.(2008) Consistency of spectral clustering. *Annals of Statistics*, Vol.36, No.2, (April 2008),pp.555–586, ISSN 0090-5364

Vapnik, V. (1998). Statistical Learning Theory. Wiley, ISBN 0-471-03003-1, New York, USA

W.C Sang, C Lee, J Lee, H Jin, I Lee. (2005). Fault detection and identification of nonlinear processes based on kernel PCA, *Chemometrics and intelligent laboratory systems*, Vol.75, No.1, (Januray 2005), pp.55-67, ISSN 0169-7439

W. Yan and K. F. Goebel. (2005). Feature selection for partial discharge diagnosis, *Proceedings of the 12th SPIE: Health Monitoring and Smart Nondestructive Evaluation of Structural and Biological Systems IV*, Vol.5768, pp. 166-175, ISBN 0-8194-5749-3, March 19 - 22, 2007, San Diego , California,USA

X. He, D. Cai, P. Niyogi.(2006). Laplacian score for feature selection, *Advances in neural information processing systems*, Vol.18, p507-515, ISBN 0-262-19568-2, December 4-7,2006, Vancouver, British Columbia, Canada

Y Lei, M Zuo.(2009). Gear crack level identification based on weighted K nearest neighbor classification algorithm, *Mechanical Systems and Signal Processing,* Vol.23,No.5, (July 2009),pp.1535-1547, ISSN 0888-3270

Ypma, A. (2001). Learning methods for machine vibration analysis and health monitoring, *PhD Dissertation,* ISBN 90-9015310-1, Delft University of Technology, Delft, Netherlands.

Z. Zhao and H. Liu, (2007). Spectral feature selection for supervised and unsupervised learning, Proceedings of the 24th International Conference on Machine Learning , pp.1151-1157. ISBN 978-1-59593-793-3, June20-24 ,2007, Corvallis, OR, USA

19

Combining Hierarchical Structures on Graphs and Normalized Cut for Image Segmentation

Marco Antonio Garcia Carvalho and André Luis Costa
School of Technology, University of Campinas
Brazil

1. Introduction

The image segmentation task is to divide an image into regions of interest that are suitable for machine or human operations. The machine ability of recognizing and distinguishing objects, or its parts in a scene, is the main goal of computer vision domain. This is a critical issue because the judgement of good or bad segmentation is usually subject to humans.

Extensive studies have been accomplished for image segmentation. The segmentation algorithms are commonly categorized according to the image characteristics borders and regions (Gonzales & Woods, 2000). In the first one, the image is divided based on its discontinuities, *i.e.*, the places where abrupt intensity changes occur. Regarding to the region segmentation, this happen when there are similarities of color or texture, for example, between neighboring pixels. In spite of these categories, the problem is to find a good partitioning of an image among several possible to be achieved.

Several algorithms in image segmentation can be formulated from the partitioning of graphs. This means using graphs as image models or representations and then apply a criterion or methodology in order to split it into subgraphs. The existing literature on graph partitioning is wide, but we are interested on a particular approach, the called Normalized Cut introduced by Shi & Malik (1997).

A graph cut consists of removing edges consistently in order to generate two subgraphs. The Normalized Cut approach is a graph-cut technique based on Spectral Graph Theory responsible for generating balanced subgraphs through the removal of the smallest possible number of edges. The Normalized Cut approach uses concepts by Fiedler (1975) in the manipulation of the second smallest eigenvector of the graph representative matrix as a guide for graph partitioning. The inherent bias of this technique is that balanced partitions for image segmentation cannot be appropriate for some images when small number of partitions is desired (*e.g.*, images with an easily detectible object and an uniform background). A survey of application of Spectral Graph Theory is given by Spielman (2007).

There are several ways of generating the graph model representing the input images. The graph commonly used as input to the Normalized Cut implementation is that one based on the pixel grid similarity. We propose two alternative representations of graphs known as Quadtree and Component Tree similarity graphs. These graphs decompose the image into partitions and thus carry hierarchical information that can be useful on segmentation task.

Another goal is to reduce the computational cost, due to the reduction of the graph size, compared to using the pixel similarity graph.

Finally, we show experiments using Normalized Cut and Quadtree and Component Tree similarity graphs. In addition to the Component Tree, we propose the use of the Reverse Component Tree in order to profit the relevant information in decomposition process of an image. The results are classified using a benchmark provide by The Berkeley Image Database (Martin et al., 2001).

This chapter is organized as follows. Section 2 introduces graph concepts, including our Quadtree and Component Tree based similarity graph. Section 3 presents graph cuts and Normalized Cut theory. Some related works also are described in this section. An overview of the proposed approach is given in Section 4. Experiments in sampled images are done in Section 5 and further comments of the experiments, conclusions, as well as suggestions of future work are done in Section 6.

2. Graph representation

In digital image processing, a graph is commonly used to model digital images (Wilson & Watkins, 1990). In the Normalized Cut segmentation technique the input graph is called *Similarity Graph* (Shi & Malik, 2000), that we explain in details in Section 3.3. In a similarity graph the edge weights should reflect the similarity between the nodes connected by them, and are given by a *Similarity Function*. Here we present the methods for building a similarity graph that we have used in the experiments described in Section 5.

There are several approaches to represent an image as a similarity graph. In the next subsections we present some fundamental concepts on graphs, and four image-graph representation approaches: based on the *Pixel Grid* (Shi & Malik, 2000) , *Multiscale Pixel Grid* (Cour et al., 2005), based on the *Component Tree* (Carvalho, Costa, Ferreira & Cesar-Jr., 2010), and based on the *Quadtree* (Carvalho, Costa & Ferreira, 2010). Approaches based on the *Component Tree*, *Quadtree*, and *Multiscale Pixel Grid* rely on hierarchical structures to model an image as a graph, and provide different segmentation results when compared to the classical non-hierarchical pixel grid approach.

2.1 Basic concepts on graphs

A *graph* is a mathematical structure employed to model or to describe objects and their relationships, *e. g.*, a composition relationship can describe objects and their constituent parts. Let $G = (V, E, W)$ be a non-directed weighted graph; V is a set of *nodes*, E is a set of *edges* $e(i, j)$, $i, j \in V$, and W is a set of *weights* $w(i, j)$, $i, j \in V$. For each edge $e(i, j) \in E$ exists an associated weight $w(i, j) \in W$, that can be represented by a single value or a set of values. Two nodes i and j are *adjacent*, represented by $i \sim j$, if there is an edge connecting i and j. Given a node $i \in V$, its *degree* d_i corresponds to its number of neighbours, and its *strength* s_i (Wilson & Watkins, 1990) to the sum of its edge's weights. A *subgraph* of a graph $G = (V, E, W)$ is a graph $G' = (V', E', W')$ where $V' \subseteq V$, $E' \subseteq E$, and $W' \subseteq W$.

A *path* $\pi = (i_1, i_2, \ldots, i_n)$, $i_n \in V$, is a sequence without repeated nodes where $i_k \sim i_{k+1}$, $k = 1, 2, \ldots, n-1$. Two nodes are *connected* if there exists at least one path between i and j. In a *connected graph* G all pair of nodes are connected. A *cycle* is a path where $i_1 = i_n$. A *tree* is a connected graph with no cycles.

2.1.1 Graphs and matrices

A graph and its features can be represented using matrices (Wilson & Watkins, 1990). The adjacency between graph nodes can be described by an *Adjacency Matrix* A with size $n \times n$, where n is the number of nodes, $|V|$, of graph $G = (V, E, W)$. The matrix elements $a(i, j)$ are 1 if $i \sim j$, $i, j \in V$, or 0, otherwise. Similarly, the *Weight Matrix* W, also with size $n \times n$, $n = |V|$, can store the graph weights $w(i, j)$, $i \sim j$, $i, j \in V$. The *Degree Matrix* D is diagonal with $d(i, i) = d_i$, where d_i is the degree os node $i \in V$. Finally, the *Laplacian Matrix* L is defined as $L = D - A$ for unweighted graphs, or $L = D - W$ for weighted graphs. The Laplacian matrix is commonly used on Spectral Graph Theory (Spielman, 2007).

2.2 Graph based on the Pixel Grid

In this *Pixel Grid-based* image-graph representation each pixel is taken as a graph node, and two pixels within a r distance are connected by an edge. Shi & Malik (2000) have used this approach as the first one for their Normalized Cut technique. This approach have been introduced in the experiments as a landmark for compare results with other approaches.

2.2.1 Multiscale Pixel Grid

The *Multiscale Pixel Grid* graph decomposition algorithm introduced by Cour et al. (2005) works on multiple scales of the image grid to capture coarse and fine detail levels. The construction of the similarity graph is done according to their spatial separation, as in the following Equation

$$W = W_1 + W_2 + \ldots + W_s, \tag{1}$$

where W is a weight matrix that represents a graph composed by independent subgraphs W_s, s corresponds to a scaled pixel grid.

In the Multiscale approach there exists one different radius for each image scale s. Thus, two pixels i and $j \in W_s$ are connected only if the distance between them is lower than a radius R_s. The radii values are a tradeoff between the computation cost and the segmentation result. The Multiscale approach can alleviate this situation by using recursive sub-sampling of the image pixel grid.

2.3 Graph based on the Component Tree

The *Component Tree* (CT) (Carvalho, Costa, Ferreira & Cesar-Jr., 2010) is a hierarchical representation of a digital image after thresholding operations between its minimum and maximum gray values (Mosorov & Kowalski, 2002). There exists a relation of inclusion between components at sequential gray levels in the image, explained below by the partition definition (Carvalho, 2004).

Definition 1. *A partition P of an image I is a set of disjoint regions R_i, $i \in \mathcal{N}$, where $\bigcup_i^n R_i = I$ and $R_i \cap R_j = \varnothing$, $i \neq j$.*

A cross-section I_k of an image I is a binary image defined as (Mosorov & Kowalski, 2002; Najman & Couprie, 2006):

$$I_k = \{x \in I / I(x) \geq k\}. \tag{2}$$

In the CT, the *Connected Components* (CC) of all cross-sections are organized in a tree structure. There exists an edge between two connected components CC^i_{k+1} and CC^j_k when $CC^i_{k+1} \subseteq CC^j_k$ (inclusion relation); k is a cross-section identifier, i is a CC in cross-section $k+1$, and j is a CC in cross-section k. The connected component of the first cross-section corresponds to the whole image domain and it is called root. The leaves are the elements of the CT that have no children. A fast algorithm to build the CT is given by Najman & Couprie (2006). Fig. 1 shows a gray scale image I and its five cross-sections I_k. The Component Tree for image I is depicted in Fig. 2(a).

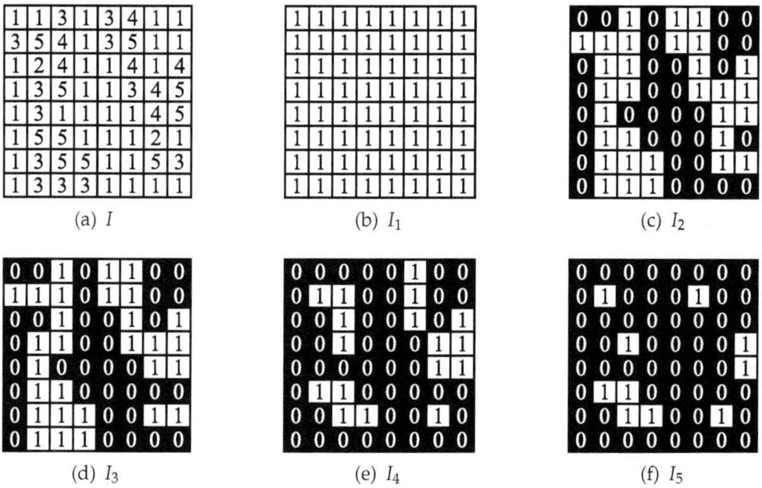

(a) I (b) I_1 (c) I_2

(d) I_3 (e) I_4 (f) I_5

Fig. 1. Thresholding image graylevels to build cross-sections. (a) a grayscale image I and (b)-(f) its five cross-sections.

When observing the traditional CT model, one realizes that the tree will be composed by only *white* components, *i. e.*, components with value 1. There still information in the cross-sections related to the *black* components. In fact, these components can provide more relevant information in particular cases. Therefore, we have defined the Reverse Component Tree (RCT) (Carvalho, Costa, Ferreira & Cesar-Jr., 2010) where two connected components CC^i_k and CC^j_{k+1} are linked when $CC^j_k \subseteq CC^i_{k+1}$; k is a cross-section identifier, i is a CC in cross-section $k+1$, and j is a CC in cross-section k. Unlike described for the CT case, the roots of the RCT's are formed by the connected components of the last cross-section. Fig. 2(b) shows the Reverse Component Tree for image I, presented in Fig. 1(a).

In order to build a connected similarity graph, we combine Component and Reverse Component Trees. This similarity graph will be used in the graph cut process. First, a connected subgraph $G_k = (V_k, E_k, W_k)$ is created for each cross-section I_k, where the nodes

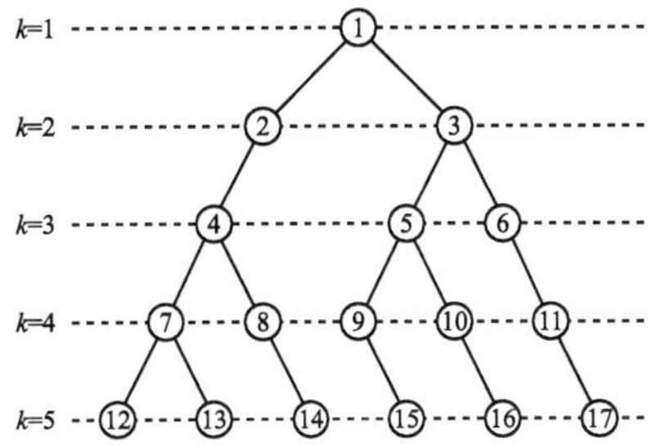

(a) Component Tree

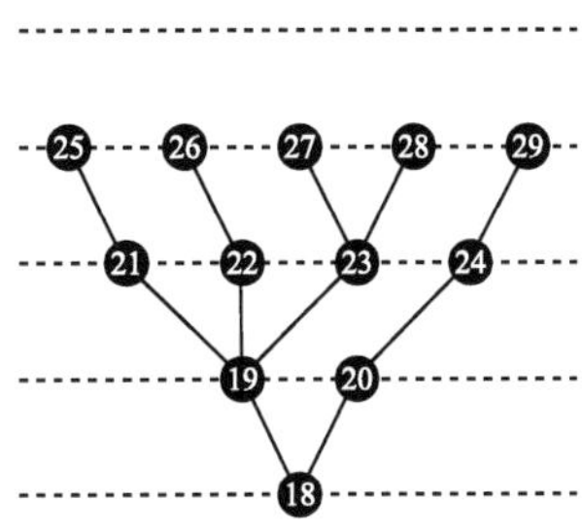

(b) Reverse Component Tree

Fig. 2. Component Tree and Reverse Component Tree from grayscale image presented in Fig. 1(a).

$v_{k,n}$ correspond to the connected components CC_k^n; $k \in \mathcal{N}$ is a cross-section identifier, and $n \in \mathcal{N}$ is a connected component identifier. Given two nodes $v_{k,i}$ and $v_{k,j}$, $v_{k,i} \sim v_{k,j}$ if $\text{distance}(v_{k,i}, v_{k,j}) \leq r$, where $r \in \mathcal{R}$ is the connection radius. After built, the k subgraphs are connected by adding the edges from the CT and RCT. The weight of each edge should reflect the likelihood of different connected components. Some of them are difference between areas, density, average gray levels and standard deviation, and Euclidean distance.

One strong characteristic of CT method is the generation of multiple image partitions at once. Because a cross-section I_k corresponds to the whole image, there is one image partition for each cross-section.

Finally, it is important to note that some images can produce a high quantity of connected components, especially in the presence of noise. Therefore, it is useful to apply some pre-processing on the image before starting the CT computation such as, gaussian filter, normalization of the gray values into a smaller range, and merging of identical subsequent cross-sections.

2.4 Graph based on the Quadtree

A Quadtree is a data structure formed from the recursive decomposition of a space (Samet, 1984). In the image processing domain, a quadtree usually maps an image and its regions into a directed acyclic graph (Consularo & Cesar-Jr., 2005).

The decomposition process is simple: The initial region corresponds to the whole image and is associated to the root node; each region in the image should be recursively decomposed into exact four new disjoint regions until they satisfy a defined criterion of homogeneity. Fig. 3 shows a Quadtree decomposition example. The decomposition criterion choice in this case was to exist regions with only one value.

In practice, the regularity of the Quadtree decomposition limits the application of this method to square images with edge sizes 2^n, $n \in \mathcal{N}$. One solution is to relax the regular decomposition, allowing a more suitable number of regions. But the greatest

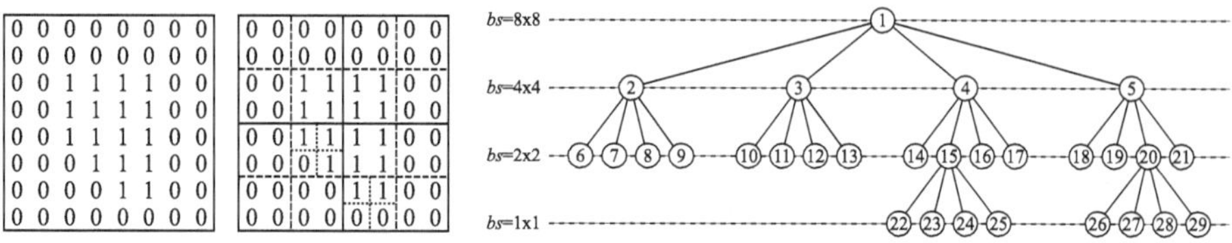

(a) I (b) Regions (c) Quadtree

Fig. 3. Quadtree decomposition. (a) original image. (b) decomposed regions. (c) corresponding Quadtree.

difficulty in creating the quadtree is the choice of the decomposition criterion. There are different criteria proposed, such as the standard deviation or entropy of image gray levels (Consularo & Cesar-Jr., 2005).

In our quadtree approach (Carvalho, Costa & Ferreira, 2010) for image segmentation, we proposed applying the Canny (Canny, 1986) (1986) filter in the image before the decomposition. This filter has low sensitivity to noise in images. By removing pixels with low gradient and thresholding the resultant ones, this process results in a binary image with border pixels highlighted. This procedure was chosen because:

1. after the filtering, the image results in a binary matrix. Then, facilitating the decomposition criterion definition, that a region should be decomposed when it is not formed entirely by ones or zeros (Samet, 1984);
2. the edge detection operation drastically reduce the size of data to be processed, while at the same time preserves the structural information about object boundaries (Canny, 1986).

In our work (Carvalho, Costa & Ferreira, 2010), the main reason for using a Quadtree image representation was to reduce the similarity graph size. Thus, in this technique the graph is generated using only the regions associated to the Quadtree leaves. Each region is associated to a node and for each region a centroid pixel is defined as the representative pixel. The nodes of the similarity graph are linked together if their representative pixel distances are less than a given radius r, similar to the pixel grid approach. However, it is useful to consider the nodes region sizes to calculate the radius r.

The number of nodes on the similarity graph can be influenced by the choice of the edge detector parameters. The number of regions obtained by the proposed technique will vary according to the image features. Also, the parameters of the edge detection filter can be manually specified, in order to change its sensibility.

3. Graph Cut and Normalized Cut

A graph cut partitions the set of nodes V of a graph $G = (V, E, W)$ into two disjoint subsets A and B, and can be expressed by the following equation (Shi & Malik, 1997):

$$\text{Cut}(A, B) = \sum_{u \in A, v \in B} w(u, v), \tag{3}$$

where $w(u,v)$ are the edges removed from G.

This formula indicates the degree of dissimilarity between G_A and G_B, the corresponding subgraphs to the node subsets A and B, respectively. There are a lot of ways to solve the problem of graph cuts. One of them, proposed by Wu & Leahy (1993), solve this problem removing the smallest possible number of edges. However, in some cases this approach can produce isolated nodes. A study about types of graph cut is given by Soundararajan & Sarkar (2001).

A graph cut can be accomplished by means of *Spectral Graph Theory*. In this approach, the matrix eigenvectors that represent graphs are analyzed and used as parameter in order to partition a graph.

3.1 Spectral Graph Theory

The *Spectral Graph Theory* (SGT) studies the eigenvalues of the graph matrices, also called graph spectrum. Algebraic methods used to analyze matrices of graphs are especially effective in treating regular and symmetric graphs (Chung, 1997). The matrices commonly used are adjacency matrices and the SGT establishes a relation between the graph spectrum and the graph features.

The use of graph spectrum information for graph cuts has a great contribution from Donath & Hoffman (1972); Fiedler (1975); Pothen et al. (1990). Fiedler proposed that the second smallest eigenvector v_2 of the Laplacian matrix, also called the Fiedler vector, has in a given row $v_2[i]$ a numerical information about node i, also called the characteristic value of the node. The graph nodes can be partitionated by grouping them according to their value in the Fiedler vector. The commonly way used to group nodes is the characteristic values signals.

3.2 The Normalized Cut

The *Normalized Cut* (NCut) technique (Shi & Malik, 1997) is a theoretic method for graph partitioning. Its goal is to find a balanced cut in a graph, in order to generate two or more subgraphs. This technique solves the problem stated by Wu & Leahy (1993) in their minimum cut criteria for graph cutting. Applying this method for image segmentation is possible with a proper image-graph representation, where the subgraphs obtained from graph partitioning represents the image regions. The NCut in a graph G is calculated by the following equation:

$$\mathrm{NCut}(A,B) = \frac{\mathrm{Cut}(A,B)}{\mathrm{SumCon}(A,V)} + \frac{\mathrm{Cut}(A,B)}{\mathrm{SumCon}(B,V)}, \tag{4}$$

where A and B are the node subsets of subgraphs G_A and G_B, subject to $A \cup B = V$ and $A \cap B = \varnothing$; $\mathrm{Cut}(A,B)$ is defined in Equation (3); $\mathrm{SumCon}(A,V)$ is the total weight of the edges connecting nodes from a subgraph G_A to all nodes in the original graph G; and $\mathrm{SumCon}(B,V)$ is similarly defined to a subgraph G_B.

The optimal NCut is the one that minimizes Equation 4. The problem in minimizing Equation 4 is that it is only trivial for small graphs. For bigger graphs, it has a NP-Complete complexity. Shi & Malik (2000) extended this equation and found a well-known equation in linear algebra called the Rayleigh Quotient. It can be minimized using spectral graph properties of the graph's Laplacian Matrix described by Fiedler (1975), *i.e.*, its minimum value is λ_2, the second smallest eigenvalue (Golub & Loan, 1989).

The graph partitioning is guided by the eigenvector v_2, where each value $v_2[i]$ will represent a graph node i. To split a graph, a threshold value is used and the graph nodes are partitioned in two subsets. The most common threshold values are zero, the median value in v_2 or the one that minimizes the NCut value.

3.3 Similarity Graph

In a *Similarity Graph* the edge weights represent the degree of similarity between the linked nodes. For graphs that represent images, the similarity can be determined by a function of intensity, position and other image pixels features. A measure of similarity regarding the intensity and the position of image pixels is given by (Shi & Malik, 2000):

$$W_{\mathrm{IP}}(i,j) = \begin{cases} e^{-\left(\frac{\alpha^2}{d_p}\right)-\left(\frac{\beta^2}{d_i}\right)}, \text{ if } \alpha_2 < r \\ 0, \text{ Otherwise} \end{cases}, \tag{5}$$

where $\alpha = ||P_i - P_j||$ and $\beta = ||I_i - I_j||$ are respectively the distance and the difference of intensity between pixels i and j; r is a given distance (also called graph connection radius); and d_p and d_i are set as the variance of the image pixels positions and intensity. This grouping cue used separately often gives bad segmentations because some natural images are affected by the texture clutter.

The intervening contours is another measure to evaluate the affinity between two nodes by measuring the image edges between their correspondent pixels. The intervening contour similarity function is given by (Cour et al., 2005):

$$W_{\mathrm{C}}(i,j) = \begin{cases} e^{-\left(\frac{\max_{(x \in \mathrm{line}(i,j))} \varepsilon^2}{d_C}\right)}, \text{ if } \alpha < r \\ 0, \text{ Otherwise} \end{cases}, \tag{6}$$

where $\mathrm{line}(i,j)$ is a straight line joining pixels i and j and $\varepsilon = ||\,\mathrm{Edge}(x)||$ is the image edge strength at location x.

These two grouping cues can be combined as (Cour et al., 2005):

$$W_{\mathrm{IPC}}(i,j) = \sqrt{W_{\mathrm{IP}}(i,j)\, W_{\mathrm{C}}(i,j)} + W_{\mathrm{C}}(i,j). \tag{7}$$

3.4 Related work

There is a wide range of recent work in image segmentation using the Normalized Cut technique. The contributions are focused on improving the algorithm performance, others on proposing different image-graph modelling and others on the application of this technique for real-world applications.

In several works, the image model used is the similarity graph built by taking each image pixel as a node. In this case, the node pairs within a given radius r are connected by an edge. This graph will be explained in the next section.

Monteiro & Campilho (2008) proposed the Watershed Normalized Cut, which uses the regions from the Watershed image segmentation as nodes for the similarity graph. The Watershed region similarity graph is either used by Carvalho et al. (2009) for comparison with the primitive pixel affinity graph in yeast cells images segmentation. Ma & Wan (2008) used Watershed based similarity graphs to segment texture images.

The primitive normalized cut enhancement was also studied and applied by many researchers. Cour et al. (2005) proposes a Normalized Cut adaptive that focus on the computational problem created by long range graphs. The authors suggested the use of multiscale segmentations, decomposing a long range graph into independent subgraphs. The main contribution of this technique is that larger images can be better segmented with a linear complexity. Sun & He (2009) proposed the use of the multiscale graph decomposition, partitioning the image graph representation at the finest scale level and weighting the graph nodes using the texture features.

Tolliver & Miller (2006) suggested an improvement of the normalized cut technique. They proposed the use of the *k* first eigenvectors for graph partitioning as the *k*-way Normalized cut. The difference is that these eigenvectors modify the edges weight in the graph, resulting in new graph matrices, and the *k* first eigenvectors are calculated again in the new Laplacian Matrix. The authors proved that this procedure changes the *k* first eigenvalues to zero. Spectral graph theory concepts about the Laplacian matrix informs that the number of eigenvalues equal to zero shows the number of connected components in a graph. Their algorithm returns these connected components. Cour et al. (2005) suggested another improvement by dividing the graph in scales and processing them in paralell. This approach can segment large images graphs with high conections with linear complexity.

Tao et al. (2008) proposed a new image thresholding technique using the normalized cut. The graph similarity matrix proposed is now based on pixel gray levels, reducing the matrix size and the computational cost. So, a new matrix M is created, where $M(i,j) = \text{Cut}(V_i, V_j)$ with i and j being two given gray levels. Using this matrix, the normalized cut is then calculated to each threshold value, If the normalized cut related to a given threshold value t is below a prespecified value, this threshold value is adequate to separate the objects from the background in this image.

Grote et al. (2007) suggested the normalized cut for extracting roads from aerial images. In their graph, pixels are the graph nodes and the similarity matrix uses contours, hue and color in the image pixels. this approach uses the *k*-way normalized cut, with *k* being large to avoid road and non-road pixels mixture. Senthilnath & Omkar (2009) compared this technique with other state-of-art road extraction approach, proving that the normalized cut based technique works better. Other normalized cut aplications in the literature are the noise reduction in images by Zhang & Zhang (2009) and the colour image segmentation by Tao et al. (2008).

4. Normalized Cut segmentation workflow

Given an image I, we build a similarity graph $G = (V, E, W)$, from Quadtree and/or Component Tree representations. The image segmentation process based on Normalized Cut technique can be applied by two distinct methods: recursive Two-way and K-Way. The block diagram presented in Fig. 4 illustrates the complete image segmentation process.

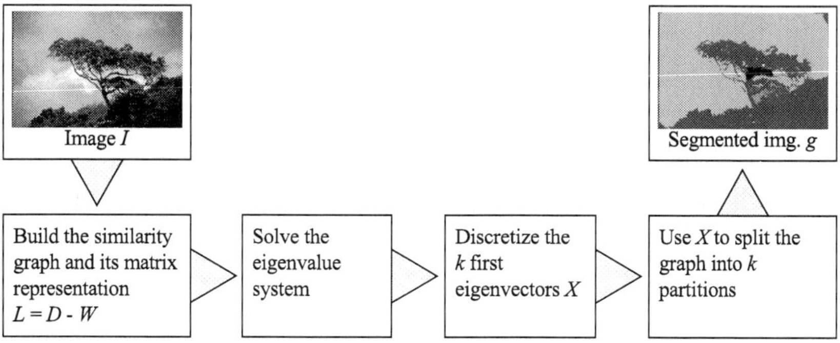

Fig. 4. Workflow of the image segmentation technique based on Normalized Cut.

The similarity graph obtained from Quadtree and Component/Reverse Tree representations is done according to the details explained previously and its parameters are described in Section 5. They have hierarchical information that is exploited in the graph cut process. The eigenvectors of the Laplacian matrix are obtained from the solution of the following equation:

$$(D - W)v = \lambda D v. \tag{8}$$

At this moment, it is possible to use only the second eigenvector v_2 in order to provide two partitions of the graph G and reapply the process to obtain recursively a large number of partitions. A partition should be divided by analysing a specified cut value. This technique is known as Recursive Two-Way NCut. In the other hand, it is possible to discretize the k first eigenvector X, were $X = [v1, v2, \ldots, vk]$ and use them directly to implement the graph partitioning into k desired partitions. This partitioning process is called K-Way Cut and corresponds to the block sequence presented in Fig. 4.

5. Experimental results and discussion

We have performed k-way Normalized Cut segmentation in 100 grayscale test images from *Berkeley Segmentation Benchmark*[1] (Martin et al., 2001). The goal of these experiments is to compare the techniques for building the similarity graph based on *Pixel Grid* (Shi & Malik, 2000), *Multiscale Pixel Grid* (Cour et al., 2005), *Quadtree* (Carvalho, Costa & Ferreira, 2010), and *Component Tree* (Carvalho, Costa, Ferreira & Cesar-Jr., 2010). Fig. 5 show a collection of 9 selected images.

The Berkeley's benchmark rely on human image segmentations to state the segmentation algorithms assertiveness, according to Precision (P) and Recall (R) metrics (Davis & Goadrich,

[1] Available at http://www.eecs.berkeley.edu/Research/Projects/CS/vision/bsds/ (last accessed September, 2011).

Fig. 5. Selected images from Berkeley's benchmark. (a) 3096. (b) 21077. (c) 42049. (d) 85048. (e) 97033. (f) 119082; (g) 147091. (h) 167062. (i) 241004.

2006; Martin et al., 2001). Precision is the probability that a pixel marked as a border is in fact a border pixel, and is given by

$$P = \frac{TP}{TP + FP}, \tag{9}$$

where TP is the number of true positives, and FP the number of false positives. The precision P decrease as increases the number of false positives. Recall, also called *hit rate*, is the probability that the border pixels marked by the machine are the same as the border pixels marked by humans, and is defined as

$$R = \frac{TP}{TP + FN}, \tag{10}$$

where FN is the number of false negatives.

These two metrics are summarized in the F-measure (Davis & Goadrich, 2006)

$$F = 2 \cdot \frac{P \cdot R}{P + R}, \tag{11}$$

that is used as the score metric by Berkeley's benchmark to ranking the algorithms effectiveness.

5.1 Experiment setup

The experiments were perfomed according to the workflow presented in Section 4 with k-way method. The connection radius for the *Pixel Grid* graph was $r = 10$ and the edges weights were given by Equation (6). For the *Multiscale Pixel Grid* approach were used one radius for each scale, which were $r_1 = 2, r_2 = 3$ and $r_3 = 7$ and the edge weights were given by Equation (6). The *Quadtree* weights were also given by Equation (6), and their radii given as

$$r_{i,j} = \frac{1}{2}\max(v_i^{\phi x} + v_j^{\phi x}, v_i^{\phi y} + v_j^{\phi y}) + k, \tag{12}$$

where $v_i^{\phi x}$ and $v_i^{\phi y}$ are repetively the horizontal and the vertical diameter of region correspondent to node $v_i \in V$; $v_j^{\phi x}$ and $v_j^{\phi y}$ are similarly defined for node $v_j \in V$; and $k = 10$.

The Component Tree was generated with radius $r = 25$ for the subgraphs. The attributes used to build our CT similarity graph were difference of area, distance, standard deviation of the gray levels and density. For the edges that links the subgraphs, the weights were multiplied by a factor given by the following equation:

$$f = \frac{NC_{Fi} + NC_{Fj}}{2 + |\,\mathrm{d}(i) - \mathrm{d}(j)|}, \tag{13}$$

where NC_{Fi} and NC_{Fj} are the number of CCs of the cross-sections that has the nodes i and j respectively; and $\mathrm{d}(i)$ and $\mathrm{d}(j)$ are the degrees of nodes i and j respectively, related to the CT. After the CT segmentation procedure the various partitions generated for each image were converted to a single one by two distinct approaches: manually by selecting the partition that seemed to be the better image segmentation by a criterion of resemblance to the original image; automatically by merging pairs of partitions with highest mutual information iteratively. These approaches sets our experiments on image segmentation based on CT as semi-automatic or automatic procedures.

5.2 Results, discussion, and future works

The Berkeley's benchmark combine the individual scores from all segmentations of each algorithm in a single final score that determine the algorithm overall ranking. In our experiments the first place in the ranking was for the *Multiscale Pixel Grid* approach and the last place was for the automatic *Component Tree*. Fig. 6 show the overall scores obtained for each similarity graph method.

The segmentation scores for some individual images, however, are quite different from the algorithm's overall score. Fig. 7 show the individual scores for each image with each algorithm. We can observe that even the automatic CT approach, which is the worst ranked algorithm, has the highest score to about ten images. A similar result was obtained by the Semi-automatic CT approach. Put together, they account for 20% of the better scores for individual images. Not surprisingly, they also have the highest overall *Recall*, 0.65 and 0.64

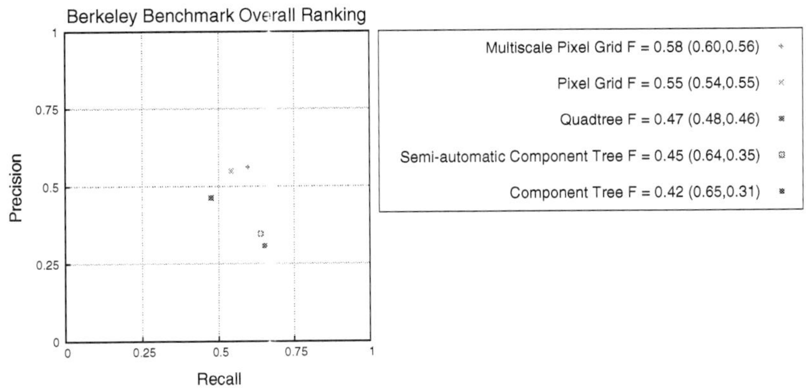

Fig. 6. Algorithms overall ranking. The two values between parenthesis at the right box represent (R,P).

for automatic and semi- automatic methods, respectively, against 0.60 for the best ranked algorithm.

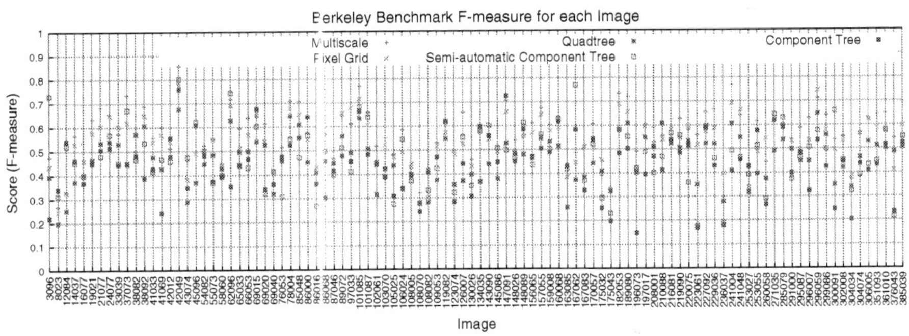

Fig. 7. Berkeley benchmark score (F-measure) for each image.

In the chart shown at Fig. 7 one can yet observe a clear trend for the Multiscale and the Quadtree approaches to follow the scores obtained by the classical Pixel Grid method: Multiscale with a little better, and Quadtree with a little worse scores. We can associate this trend to the fact that these algorithms are using the same similarity function.

Despite these quantitative analisys, it is also important to make a qualitative analisys of the segmentation results. Thus, are shown in Fig 8 one machine segmentation for each image shown in Fig. 5, and its human segmentations.

The computational performance is also an important requirement for the Normalized Cut technique. When Cour et al. (2005) proposed the Multiscale approach to generate the similarity graph, one main objective was to reduce the NCut computational cost. It is also the objective of the Quadtree approach. Fig. 9 show a chart with the time each algorithm took to process the segmentation. There is a strong correlation between the Component Tree

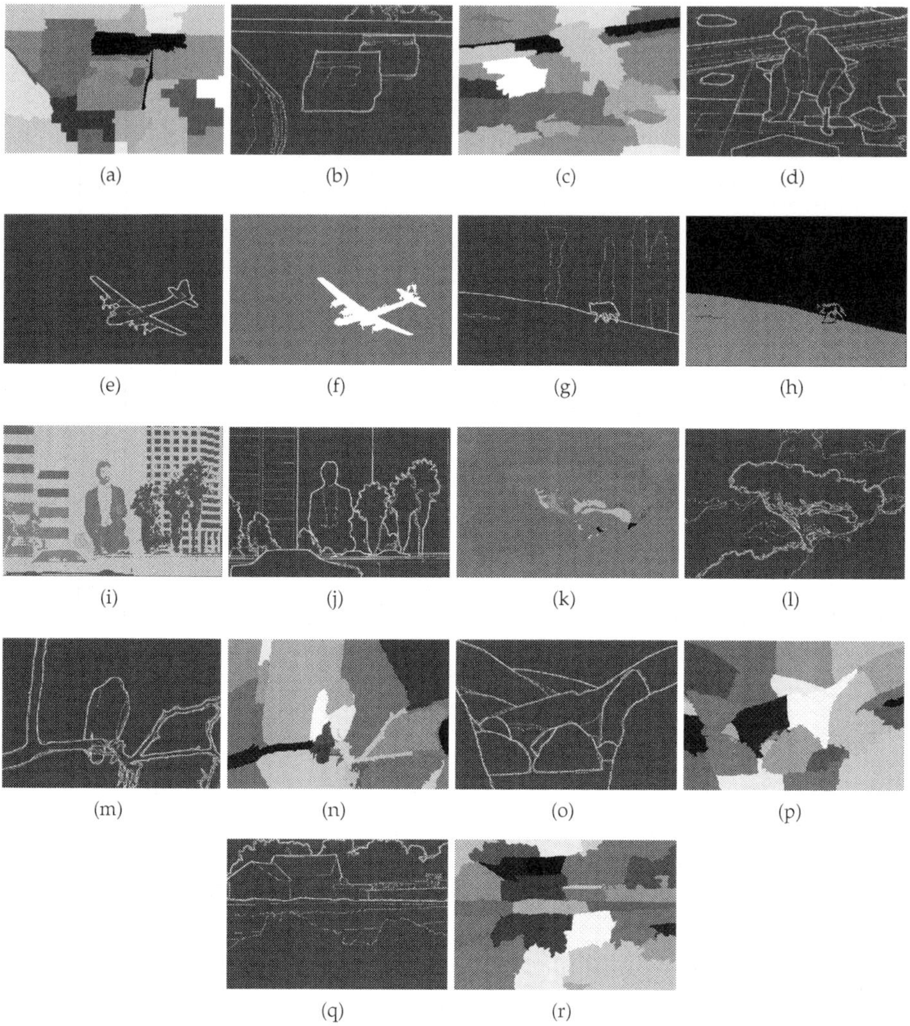

(a) (b) (c) (d) (e) (f) (g) (h) (i) (j) (k) (l) (m) (n) (o) (p) (q) (r)

Fig. 8. Selected segmentations. (a) 21077 and (c) 85048 segmentations by Quadtree method. (f) 3096 and (h) 167062 segmentations by Semi-automatic Component Tree method. (i) 119082 and (k) 147091 segmentations by Component Tree method. (n) 42049 and (p) 241004 segmentations by Multiscale Pixel Grid method. (r) 97033 segmentation by Pixel Grid method. (b) 21077, (d) 85048, (e) 3096, (g) 167062, (j) 119082, (l) 147091, (m) 42049, (o) 241004, and (q) 97033, human segmentations from Berkeley benchmark.

and the Quadtree methods. That indicates that they are similarly sensitive to the image's data, but their overall performance are, respectively, the lower and the higher ones. The overall performance of the Multiscale algorithm is higher than the overall performance of the Pixel Grid algorithm, but is lower than the performance of the Quadtree method. Despite the lower performance, only the Component Tree can generate multiple image partitions at once. This problem can be alleviated by implementing the Najman's (Najman & Couprie, 2006) fast algorithm to build the Component Tree.

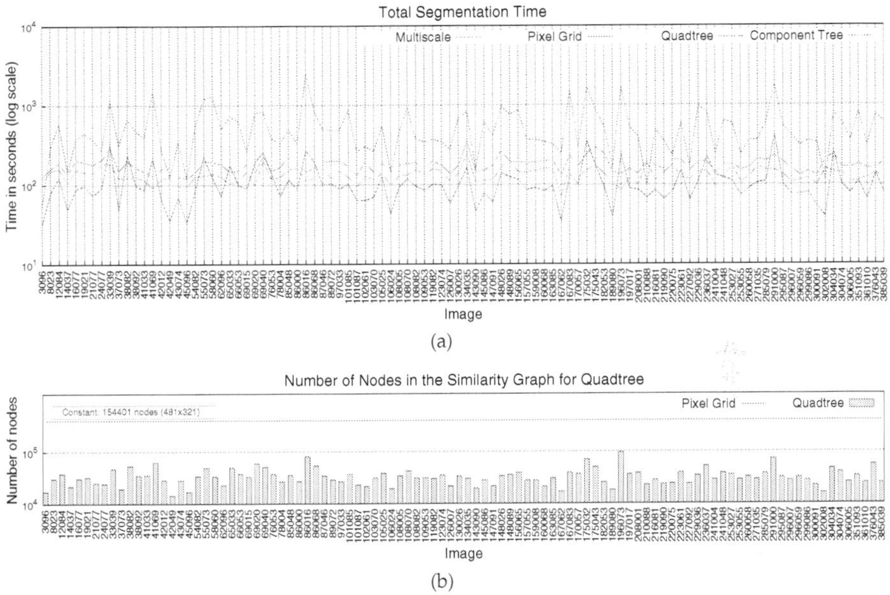

Fig. 9. Algorithms performance. (a) execution time for each image. (b) number of nodes in the similarity graph for Quadtree representation.

The chart in Fig. 9(b) show the number of nodes in the similarity graph generated by the Quadtree approach. Notice that the number of regions in the graph has direct impact to the algorithm's performance.

For future works we see that the Component Tree is the most promising method, despite its worst effectiveness and efficiency. Its implementation can be improved to reduce the computational cost. A more detailed study about the similarity criteria has the potencial of reducing the false positive rate.

There are future works for the Quadtree approach as well. Once the nodes represent regions instead of pixels, the study of texture and other region-based similarity criteria would improve the method effectiveness. It is also reasonable to explore further the hierarchical information of the Quadtree, that would lead the design of a new multiscale approach.

6. Conclusion

In this Chapter we proposed an approach to implement image segmentation based on graph modelling and Normalized Cut technique. Performing graph partitioning by means of Normalized Cut has been widely used in the specific literature. The possibility of generate balanced partitions has shown that this approach is efficient. The proposed similarity graphs, build from the Quadtree and Component Tree structures, proved promising compared to the traditional modelling based on pixel similarity graph. We performed comparisons using two-well established metrics, the Precision and Recall values. An additional aspect to be considered in the proposed graph models is exploring the hierarchical structures of both, Quadtree and Component Tree. Besides, we exploit a little more the Component Tree and proposed the Reverse Component Tree as a way to better represent the information contained in the image cross-sections.

The experimental results accomplished on images from the Berkeley Database show that use regions, or primitive regions to be specific, instead pixels seems to be a better strategy to segment images by Normalized Cut approach. In addition, the new image representation had the advantage of reducing the number of graph nodes and, therefore, improved the algorithm performance.

7. Acknowledgment

This work is supported by FAPESP (São Paulo Research Foundation) – Proc. 2010/14759-0.

8. References

Canny, J. (1986). A computational approach to edge-detection, *IEEE Transactions on Pattern Analysis and Machine Intelligence*, pp. 679–700.

Carvalho, M. A. G. (2004). *Análise hierárquica de imagens através da árvore dos lagos críticos*, PhD thesis, Faculdade de Engenharia Elétrica e Computação- FEEC.

Carvalho, M. A. G., Costa, A. L. & Ferreira, A. C. B. (2010). Image segmentation using quadtree-based similarity graph and normalized cuts, Lecture Notes in Computer Science, v. 6419, pp. 329-337.

Carvalho, M. A. G., Costa, A. L., Ferreira, A. C. B. & Cesar-Jr., R. M. (2010). Image segmentation using component tree and normalized cuts, *Proceedings of the XXIII Brazilian Symposium on Computer Graphics and Image Processing (SIBGRAPI2010)*, Gramado - Brazil, pp. 317-320.

Carvalho, M. A. G., Ferreira, A. C. B., Pinto, T. W. & Cesar-Jr., R. M. (2009). Image segmentation using watershed and normalized cuts, *Proc. of 22th Conference on Graphics, Patterns and Images (SIBGRAPI)*, Rio de Janeiro - Brazil.

Chung, F. (1997). *Spectral Graph Theory*, American Mathematical Society.

Consularo, L. A. & Cesar-Jr., R. M. (2005). Quadtree-based inexact graph matching for image analysis, *Proceedings of the XVIII Brazilian Symposium on Computer Graphics and Image Processing (SIBGRAPI2005)*, Natal - Brazil, pp. 205–212.

Cour, T., Bénézit, F. & Shi, J. (2005). Spectral segmentation with multiscale graph decomposition, *Proc. of IEEE Computer Society Conference on Computer Vision and Pattern Recognition - CVPR'05*, Vol. 2, pp. 1124–1131

Davis, J. & Goadrich, M. (2006). The relationship between precision-recall and roc curves, *ICML '06: Proceedings of the 23rd international conference on Machine learning*, ACM, pp. 233–240.

Donath, W. & Hoffman, A. (1972). Algorithms for partitioning graphs and computer logic based on eigenvectors of connection matrices, *Technical report*, IBM.

Fiedler, M. (1975). A property of eigenvectors of nonnegative symmetric matrices and its applications to graph theory, *Czech. Math. Journal* 25(100): 619–633.

Golub, G. H. & Loan, C. F. V. (1989). *Matrix Computations*, John Hopkins Press.

Gonzales, R. & Woods, R. (2000). *Digital Image Processing*, Addison-Wesley.

Grote, A. et al. (2007). Segmentation based on normalized cuts for the detection of suburban roads in aerial imagery, *IEEE Proceedings of Urban Remote Sensing Joint Event* pp. 1–5.

Ma, X. & Wan, W. (2008). Texture image segmentation on improved watershed and multiway spectral clustering, *Proceedings of International Conference on Audio, Language and Image Processing - ICALIP*, pp. 1693–1697.

Martin, D., Fowlkes, C., Tal, D. & Malik, J. (2001). A database of human segmented natural images and its application to evaluating segmentation algorithms and measuring ecological statistics, *Proc. 8th Int'l Conf. Computer Vision*, Vol. 2, pp. 416–423.

Monteiro, F. C. & Campilho, A. (2008). Watershed framework to region-based image segmentation, *Proc. of IEEE 19th International Conference on Pattern Recognition - ICPR*, pp. 1–4.

Mosorov, V. & Kowalski, T. M. (2002). The development of component tree for grayscale image segmentation, *Proc. of International Conference on Moderns Problems of Radio Engineering, Telecommunications and Computer Science – TECSET*, Slavsko – Ukraine, pp. 252–253.

Najman, L. & Couprie, M. (2006). Building the component tree in quasi-linear time, *IEEE Transactions on Image Processing* 15(11): 3531–3539.

Pothen, A., Simon, H. D. & Liou, K.-P. (1990). Partitioning sparse matrices with eigenvectors of graphs, *SIAM J. Matrix Anal. Appl.* 11: 430–452.
URL: *http://portal.acm.org/citation.cfm?id=84514.84521*

Samet, H. (1984). The quadtree and related hierarchical structures, *ACM Computing Surveys* 16(2): 187–261.

Senthilnath, M. R. & Omkar, S. N. (2009). Automatic road extraction using high resolution satellite image based on texture progressive analysis and normalized cut method, *Journal of the Indian Society of Remote Sensing* 37(3): 351–361.

Shi, J. & Malik, J. (1997). Normalized cuts and image segmentation, *Proceedings of the IEEE Computer Society Conference on Computer Vision and Pattern Recognition*, pp. 731–737.

Shi, J. & Malik, J. (2000). Normalized cuts and image segmentation, *IEEE Transactions on Pattern Analysis and Machine Intelligence (PAMI)* 22(8) pp. 888-905.

Soundararajan, P. & Sarkar, S. (2001). Analysis of mincut, average cut and normalized cut measures, *Workshop on Perceptual Organization in Computer Vision*.

Spielman, D. (2007). Spectral graph theory and its applications, *Proc. of 48th Annual IEEE Symposium on Foundations of Computer Science*, pp. 29–38.

Sun, F. & He, J. P. (2009). A normalized cuts based image segmentation method, *Proc. of II International Conference on Information and Computer Science*, pp. 333–336.

Tao, W., Jin, H., Zhang, Y., Liu, L. & Wang, D. (2008). Image thresholding using graph cuts, *IEEE Transactions on Systems Man and Cybernetics Part A-Systems and Humans* 38(5): 1181–1195.

Tolliver, D. & Miller, G. (2006). Visual grouping and object recognition, *Graph partitioning by spectral rounding: Applications in image segmentation and clustering*, pp. 1053–1060.

Wilson, R. & Watkins, J. (1990). *Graphs: An Introductory Approach*, John Wiley and Sons.

Wu, Z. & Leahy, R. (1993). An optimal graph theoretic approach to data clustering: theory and its application to image segmentation, *IEEE Trans. Pattern Analysis and Machine Intelligence*, Vol. 15, pp. 1,101–1,113.

Zhang, L. & Zhang, J.-Z. (2009). Image denoising based on statistical jump regression analysis and local segmentation using normalized cuts, *Acoustics, Speech, and Signal Processing, IEEE International Conference on* pp. 661–664.

20

Camera Motion Estimation Based on Edge Structure Analysis

Andrey Vavilin and Kang-Hyun Jo
University of Ulsan,
Korea

1. Introduction

The estimation of camera motion is important for several video analysis tasks such as indexing and retrieval purposes, motion compensation and for scientific film analysis. From an aesthetical point of view, camera motion is often used as an expressive element in film production. Motion content can be used as a powerful cue for structuring video data, similarity-based video retrieval, and video abstraction

Motion estimation and motion pattern classification problem have been extensively investigated by the scientific community for semantic characterization and discrimination of video streams. Moving object trajectories have been used for video retrieval [1-3]. Camera motion pattern characterization has been efficiently applied to video indexing and retrieval [4-7]. However, the main limitation of the latter methods is that they deal only with the characterization of the detected camera motion patterns, without explicit measurement of the camera motion parameters. As a result, the acquired information is of limited interest, since it can be used primarily for video indexing and retrieval.

There are different types of camera motion: rotation around one of the three axes and translation along the x and y-axis. Furthermore, zoom in and out can be considered as equivalent to translation along the z-axis. Existing methods can be classified as optical flow methods and feature correspondences based approaches. Let us also mention recursive techniques based on extended Kalman filters [8] which track camera motion and estimate the structure of the scene. In the case of an uncalibrated camera, interesting approaches are described in [9, 10]. The use of optical flow avoids the choice of "good features". In [11] differential approaches of the epipolar constraint are described. In [12], the optical flow computed between two adjacent images in a video sequence is linearly decomposed on a database of optical flow models. The authors of [13] propose a comparison of algorithms which only use optical flow for estimating camera.

In this work we present an approach for recovering graph-based structures from images. This structure is then used for estimating 3D camera motion. Our approach is based on detecting straight line segments. After several prefiltering operations such as bilateral filtering and Hough transform, preceding by the edge detection is applied. Then a result of transformation analyses in order to detect local maximums. Reverse transform of these maximums gives us a several straight lines presented in the image. We use an intersection of these analytical lines with detected edges in order to find straight line segments. On this step we also detect intersections between line segments. For each intersection point we compute rank based on number of connected points. After transforming image into graph we search for similar structural elements in the graph of previous frame. This process is based on searching subgraphs consists of vertices with similar ranks. After finding correspondence points camera motion is estimated as a combination of translation and rotation.

2. Camera motion model

In this work we considered eight-parameter perspective model defined as follows:

$$x_i^2 = \frac{a_0 + a_2 x_i^1 + a_3 y_i^1}{a_6 x_i^1 + a_7 y_i^1 + 1}$$
$$y_i^2 = \frac{a_1 + a_4 x_i^1 + a_5 y_i^1}{a_6 x_i^1 + a_7 y_i^1 + 1} \quad (1)$$

where (x_1^1, y_1^1) and (x_i^2, y_i^2) are the coordinates of the same point in the consequent frames at t_1 and t_2 respectively and $(a_0, \ldots, a_7)$ are the motion parameters. Various motion models can be derived from this mode. For example, in case of $a_6 = a_7 = 0$ it is reduced to affine model, and setting $a_2 = a_5$, $a_3 = -a_4$ and $a_6 = a_7 = 0$ will give us a translation-zoom-rotation model.

In [14] any vector field is approximated by a linear combination of a divergent field, a rotation field and two hyperbolic fields. The relationship between motion model parameters and symbol-level interpretation is established as:

$$\begin{aligned} Pan &= a_0 \\ Tilt &= a_1 \\ Zoom &= \frac{1}{2}(a_2 + a_5) \\ Rotation &= \frac{1}{2}(a_3 - a_4) \end{aligned} \quad (4)$$

Error in esti mation parameters is defined as:

$$\varepsilon(a) = \sum_{i=1}^{N} \left\| p_i^2 - f(p_i^1, a) \right\| \quad (2)$$

where N is the number of corresponding points, $p_i^1 = (x_i^1, y_i^1)$ and $p_i^2 = (x_i^2, y_i^2)$ are the corresponding points in first and second frames, $a = (a_0, \ldots, a_7)$ is a transformation parameters vector and *f()* is a transformation function defined by (1).

Using this model definition, problem of camera motion estimation could be formalized as the error minimization problem:

$$M = \arg\min_{a} \varepsilon(a) \tag{3}$$

Where M defines estimated camera motion parameters.

It is well known that, by taking some particular point p as the origin of the coordinate system with coordinates z, any infinitely differentiable function f(x) could be approximated using Taylor series:

$$f(z) = f(p) + \sum_i \frac{\partial f}{\partial z_i} z_i + \frac{1}{2} + \sum_i \frac{\partial^2 f}{\partial z_i \partial z_j} z_i z_j + \ldots \approx c - b \cdot z + \frac{1}{2} z \cdot A \cdot z \tag{4}$$

where

$$c \equiv f(p) \qquad b \equiv -\nabla f \,|\, p \quad [A]_{ij} = \frac{\partial^2 f}{\partial z_i \partial z_j} \,|\, p \tag{5}$$

The matrix A which consists of a second partial derivatives of the function is also called Hessian matrix of the function at p [15]

In approximation of (4) the gradient of f is easily calculated as

$$\nabla f(z) = Az - b \tag{6}$$

In Newton's method gradient is set to 0 to determine the next iteration point.

The gradient of error function ε with respect to parameters a has components

$$\frac{\partial \varepsilon}{\partial a_k} = -2 \sum_{i=1}^{N} \frac{\left[p_i^2 - f\left(p_i^1, a\right)\right] \partial f\left(p_i^1, a\right)}{\partial a_k}, \qquad k = 0, 1, \ldots, 7 \tag{7}$$

Taking second order partial derivatives gives

$$\frac{\partial^2 \varepsilon^2}{\partial a_k \partial a_j} = 2 \sum_{i=1}^{N} \left[\frac{\partial f\left(p_i^1, a\right)}{\partial a_k} \frac{\partial f\left(p_i^1, a\right)}{\partial a_j} - \left[p_i^2 - f\left(p_i^1, a\right)\right] \frac{\partial^2 f\left(p_i^1, a\right)}{\partial a_k \partial a_j} \right] \tag{8}$$

It is conventional to remove the factors of 2 by defining

$$\alpha_{kj} = \frac{1}{2} \frac{\partial^2 \varepsilon^2}{\partial a_k \partial a_j} \tag{9}$$

$$\beta_k = \frac{1}{2} \frac{\partial \varepsilon}{\partial a_k} \tag{10}$$

Making [a]=1/2A in equation (6), in terms of which that equation can be rewritten as the set of linear equations

$$\sum_{i=1}^{N} \alpha_{ki} \partial a_i = \beta_k \tag{11}$$

SVD is used to compute transformation parameters form overdetermined set of linear equations (11).

In the proposed work initial translation was estimated prior to pan-tilt-zoom estimation based on center of gravity of corresponding feature points in consistent frames. To remove outliers voting idea was used. After finding correspondences between frames each pair of matching points "votes" for its offset. Then points with small number of offset votes are discarded.

3. Image to graph conversion

However, the most challenging part in camera motion estimation is finding correspondences between two frames. In proposed work this process is based on searching similar edge structures in the frames. Input image is represented as a graph based on edges and their intersections. Intersection points are ranked according to the number of connections. Algorithm for transforming image into graph is presented in Fig.1.

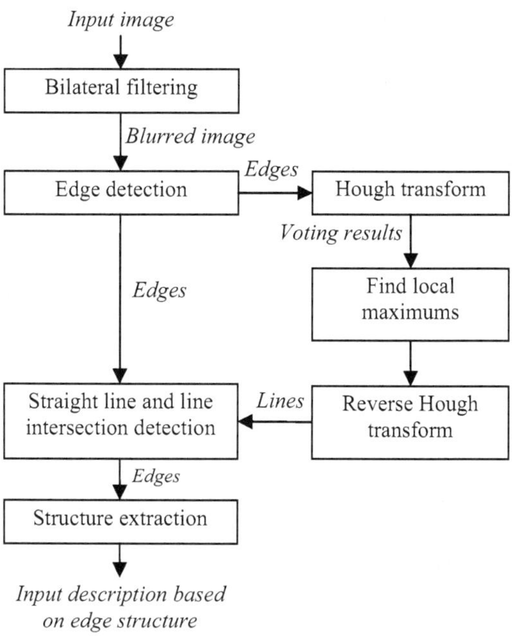

Fig. 1. Transforming image into graph

The proposed method is based on matching edge structures inside the images. Robustness of the algorithm depends on the quality of detected edges. Thus, we try to discard small edges and edges with small magnitude before recovering structures. One of the most effective way to remove such edges is a bilateral filtering [18]. We used bilateral filtering to blur image while preserving strong edges (Fig.2(b)). This allows us to reduce number of small edges. With a Gaussian function $g(x,\sigma)=\exp\left(-x^2/\sigma^2\right)$, bilateral filter of input image I at pixel p is defined as

$$bf(I)_p = \frac{1}{k}\sum_{q\in I}\left[G\left(\|p-q\|,\sigma_s\right)\cdot G\left(|I(p)-I(q),\sigma_I|\right)\cdot I(q)\right] \tag{5}$$

where σ_s controls the influence of spatial neighbourhood, σ_I the influence of the intensity difference and k is a normalizing coefficient defined as

$$bf(I)_p = \frac{1}{k}\sum_{q\in I}\left[G\left(\|p-q\|,\sigma_s\right)\cdot G\left(|I(p)-I(q),\sigma_I|\right)\right] \tag{6}$$

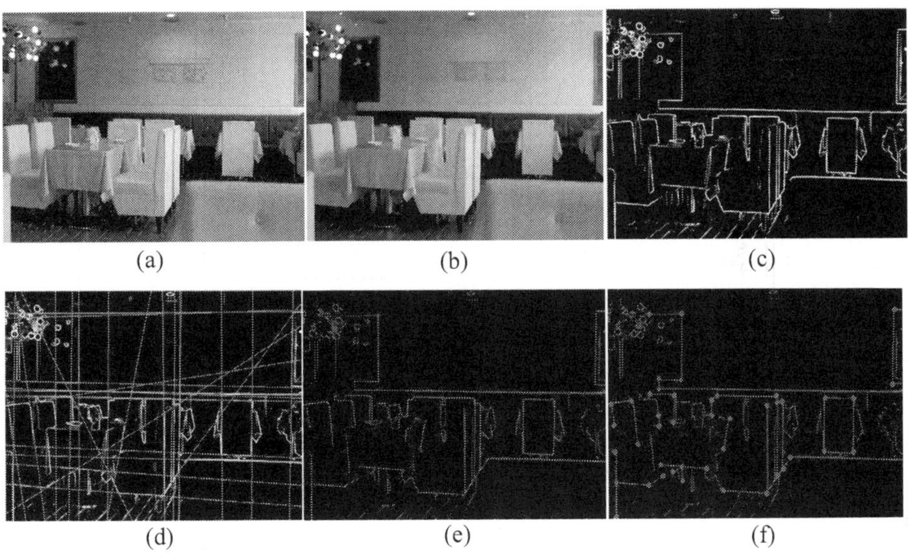

Fig. 2. Example of image to graph transformation. Refer text for details.

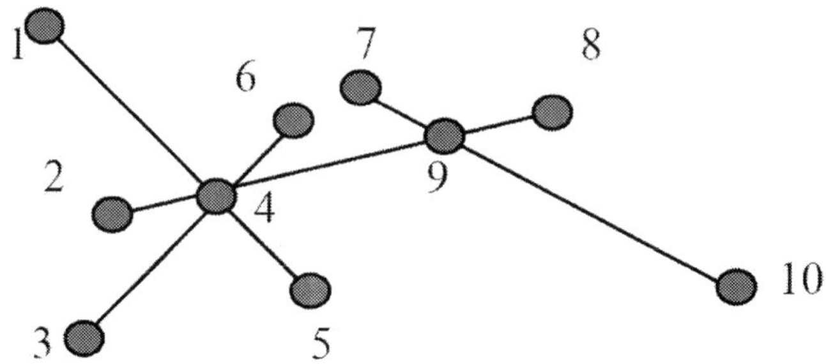

Fig. 3. Example of graph structure.

Next step is edge detection (Fig.2(c)). In this work Sobel edge detector was used. Edges with magnitude less than 50 were filtered out during this step. Remained edges were mapped into ρ, φ space using Hough transform. As a result 2-dimensional voting array was generated. Local maximums of this array correspond to strongest edges in the image. Using reverse Hough transform for these maximums we obtain set of lines (Fig.2(d)). Intersection of these lines gives us straight line segments (Fig.2(e)) and their intersections (Fig.2(f)). The purpose of these steps is to obtained graph-like structure. In further processing we use information about edge intersections (vertices) and their connections (edges). The computational time of the proposed algorithm might be reduced by removing Hough transform. It is not very important to detect exactly straight lines between vertices. The important information is their connectivity. However, using straight lines instead of edges allows more robust detection of edge intersection.

Information about edges could be represented in the form of a graph $<E,V>$ where $v = \{v_1, ..., v_m\}$ is a set of vertices obtained from intersections and $E = \{e_1, ..., e_n\}$ is a set of edges. Each vertex is described by its coordinates and rank which shows how many connections this vertex has. Edges of graph show connections between vertices. To compute rank of the vertex we used the following idea. Let's consider the structure presented in the Fig.3 as a graph, obtained after edge detection. It has nine edges $e_1 \ldots e_9$, ten vertices $v_1 \ldots v_{10}$ and could be described by the following connectivity matrix :

$$C = \begin{bmatrix} 0&0&0&1&0&0&0&0&0&0 \\ 0&0&0&1&0&0&0&0&0&0 \\ 0&0&0&1&0&0&0&0&0&0 \\ 1&1&1&0&1&1&0&0&1&0 \\ 0&0&0&1&0&0&0&0&0&0 \\ 0&0&0&1&0&0&0&0&0&0 \\ 0&0&0&0&0&0&0&0&1&0 \\ 0&0&0&0&0&0&0&0&1&0 \\ 0&0&0&1&0&0&1&1&0&1 \\ 0&0&0&0&0&0&0&0&1&0 \end{bmatrix}$$

Let's define j-th order rank of the i-th vertex as a number of vertices which could be reached from i-th vertex by j steps. First order rank of the i-th vertex shows how many vertices are directly connected to it. Thus, the v_1 will have first order rank $r_1^1 = 1$ and the v_4 will have $r_4^1 = 6$. Second order rank shows how many vertices could be reached from the i-th vertex in two steps. Thus, $r_1^2 = 6$ and $r_4^2 = 9$. Finally, n-th order rank shows how many vertices could be reached from i-th vertex in n steps. This ranking could be used to evaluate complexity and size of the substructures. Rank table for the graph presented in Fig.3 is shown in Table 1. Let's define the highest order of the rank $rMax$ as the minimal order which satisfies the following condition:

$$rMax = j \mid r_i^j = n \forall i \geq rMax \tag{7}$$

where n is the number of edges in graph.

The highest order for this graph is 3. Using higher order rank is useless for that graph as long as it would have same values. However, in common case, using higher order ranks allows to make matching process more effective by detecting more complex structures inside the image.

	Vertices									
	v_1	v_2	v_3	v_4	v_5	v_6	v_7	v_8	v_9	v_{10}
r_i^1	1	1	1	6	1	1	1	1	4	1
r_i^2	6	6	6	9	6	6	4	4	9	4
r_i^3	9	9	9	9	9	9	9	9	9	9

Table 1. Vertex ranks

These ranks have the following properties:

- Maximum rank could not be higher than number of edges.
- Maximum rank is equal to the number of edges if and only if the graph does not contain loops.
- Highest order of the rank shows diameter of the graph: maximum number of steps required to reach any vertex from any other.

After transforming two frames into graphs problem of finding correspondences between them could be reformulated as a problem of finding sub-graphs with similar structure. We start our search with finding correspondences for vertices with high rank. During this process spatial information could also be considered. Thus we try to find corresponding vertex which would have the same rank and will be located close to the reference vertex. In the future work we this step may be improved by searching correspondences for groups of vertices instead of matching them one by one. As the result of this step we obtain two set of points P and Q which are used to estimate camera motion as it was described.

Matching idea is based on searching similar substructures in the image graphs. Typically, images contain many simple substructures. These substructures have a small maximum rank order *rMax*. Furthermore, most of the vertices have small rank of first and second order, while very few of them are ranked higher than 6. Thus we start searching of correspondences from the structures with highest ranks. In the graph presented on Fig.3 such vertices are v_4 and v_9. They have ranks 6 and 4 respectively. As long as they are connected we will try to search for two connected vertices with ranks 4 and 6 in the next frame.

To simplify matching process we try to find substructures with more complex structure. This problem is solved by computing rank of vertices of higher orders.

Some edges could be lost in image sequence due to noise, camera movement and movement of objects in scene. It may cause differences in the structure of image graphs. To solve this problem the following ideas were used:

1. We tried to match structures located closer to the center of frame first in order to avoid loosing edges due to camera motion.
2. We consider that vertex i in one frame may correspond to vertex j in other frame even if their ranks are not exactly same. Thus, for each vertex in first frame we select several candidates which ranks are differs less than 30%. After candidates are selected for all vertices we try to choose best corresponding pairs using spatial information.

To decrease number of incorrect matches and to increase the preciseness of matching algorithm matched points were additionally compared using Cross-Hexagon Search (CHS) algorithm [19]. Coordinates of matched graph vertices were used a block centers and offset between matched points in consistent frames was used as initial offset. As long as CHS is used for verification of matched feature points, it can be changed to any block-based feature matching algorithm such as Diamond Search [20] or Three-Step Search [21].

4. Experimental results

All experiments were done on Intel Core 2 Duo with 2Gb memory under Borland Builder environment. Program was not optimized for the maximum performance, thus, computational time, shown in Table 2, could be decreased.

Stage	Average time (sec)
Bilateral filtering	0,31
Edge detection and Hough transform	0,2
Representing image as a graph	0,03
Ranking	Less than 0,01
Graph matching	0,17
Total	0,72

Table 2. Average computational time for 200 vertices.

To evaluate matching quality several types of experiments were done. First group of tests considered planar camera motion (translation and rotation around camera optical axis). Image sequences with camera smoothly by shifted by 20 cm in different directions and rotated by 20 degrees around its optical axis were made (see Fig.4 for example). To evaluate quality of camera motion estimation average and maximum absolute errors were computed. Results for all groups of tests are shown in Table 3.

(a)

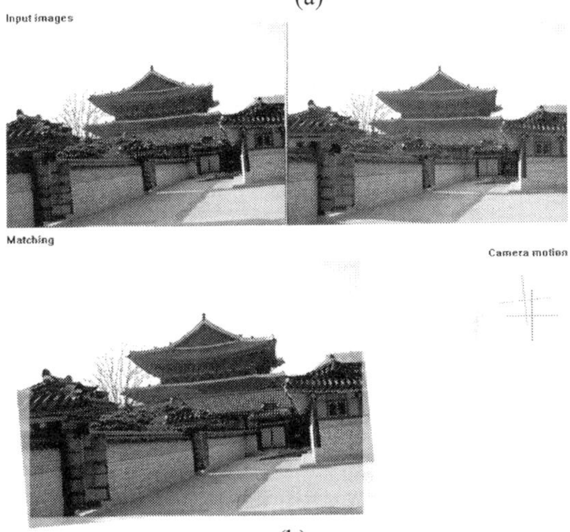

(b)

Fig. 4. Planar camera motion estimation for translation (a) and translation with rotation (b).

Second group of tests was used to evaluate algorithm performance for full 3D camera motion with known real camera trajectory. Three kinds of scenes were used: static scenes, scenes with moving objects and scenes with high amount of natural objects (trees, grass etc). Example of camera trajectory estimation is shown at Fig.5~6.

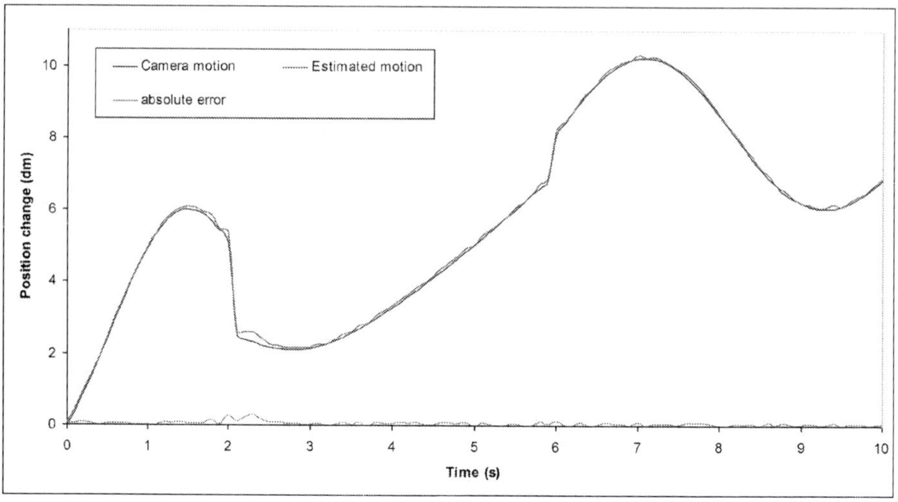

Fig. 5. Estimated trajectory for translation and zoom.

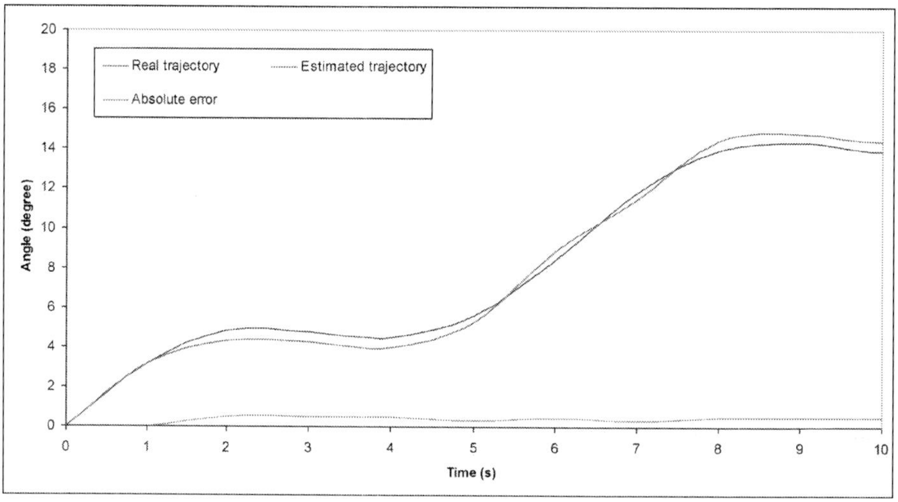

Fig. 6. Estimated trajectory for rotation.

Additionally, these tests were used to evaluate performance of algorithm with and without CHS correction. (Fig.7,8). It is easy to see, that using additional verification step for correspondent points could decrease estimation error, with relatively small increasing of computational time (about 0,07 sec).

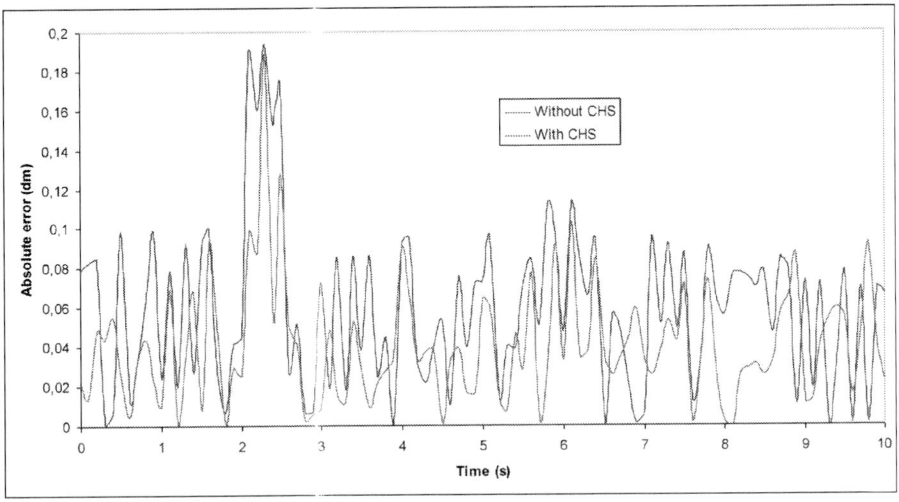

Fig. 7. Absolute error for translation and zoom.

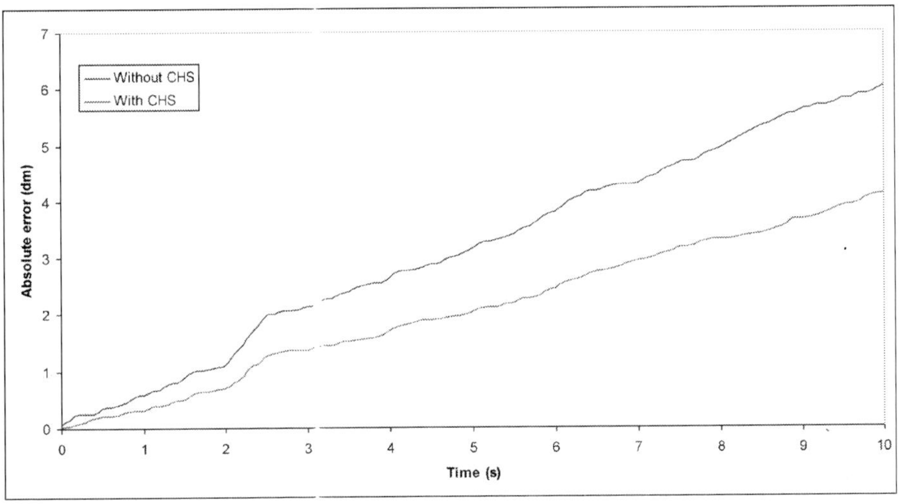

Fig. 8. Accumulated absolute error for translation and zoom.

In last group of tests image sequence with predefined camera motion trajectory was used to evaluate error depending on number of graph vertices used for matching result is shown in Fig.9.

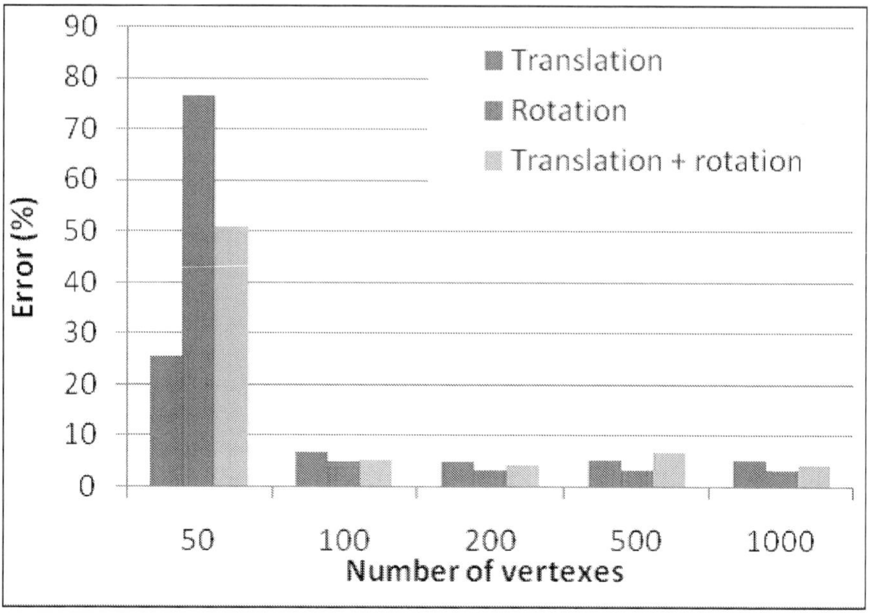

Fig. 9. Computational error depending on number of vertices.

	Planar motion	3D motion			3D motion with CHS		
		Static scene	Moving objects	Natural scene	Static scene	Moving objects	Natural scene
Average absolute error	0,59	0,44	0,59	4,61	0,33	0,37	4,3
Maximum absolute error	0,6	3,7	3,93	9,02	2,21	2,47	8.98

Table 3. Computational error (cm)

Table 3 shows that the proposed method can effectively estimate camera motion for scene with moving objects. However, its weak point is natural scenes with small number of geometrical objects.

5. Conclusion

In this paper we introduce an algorithm for converting images into graphs based on edges structure and graph matching algorithm based on vertex ranking. Proposed method could be used in different applications such as camera motion estimation, stereo matching, motion compensation, background model generation and many others. The proposed method provides efficient image-to-graph mapping for urban scenes. In case of natural scenes additional prefiltering may be required for removing unimportant information from edge image. In this paper we also presented simple algorithm for camera motion estimation based on parametric motion model. In future works we would like to improve the performance of the proposed algorithm to work in a real-time applications. Furthermore, algorithm could be improved for natural scenes by using different type of features.

6. Acknowledgments

This research was supported by the MKE(The Ministry of Knowledge Economy), Korea, under the Human Resources Development Program for Convergence Robot Specialists support program supervised by the NIPA(National IT Industry Promotion Agency) (NIPA-2010-C7000-1001-0007) and post-BK21 at University of Ulsan.

7. References

[1] W. Lie and W. Hsiao, "Content-based video retrieval based on object motion trajectory," in Proc. IEEEWorkshop on Multimedia Signal Processing, Dec. 2002, pp. 237–240.

[2] W. Hu, D. Xie, Z. Fu, W. Zeng, and S. Maybank, "Semantic-based surveillance video retrieval," IEEE Trans. Image Process., vol. 16, no. 4, pp. 1168–1181, Apr. 2007.

[3] Y. Jianfeng and L. Zhanhuai, "Modeling of moving objects and querying videos by trajectories," in Proc. 10th Int. Multimedia Modelling Conf., Washington, DC, 2004, pp. 373-380.

[4] Y.-P. Tan, D. D. Saur, S. R. Kulkarni, and P. J. Ramadge, "Rapid estimation of camera motion from compressed video with application to video annotation," IEEE Trans. Circuits Syst. Video Technol., vol. 10, no. 1, pp. 133–145, Jan. 2000.

[5] L.-Y. Duan, J. S. Jin, Q. Tian, and C.-S. Xu, "Nonparametric motion characterization for robust classification of camera motion patterns," IEEE Trans. Multimedia, vol. 8, no. 2, pp. 323–340, Apr. 2006.

[6] X. Zhu, A. K. Elmagarmid, X. Xue, L. Wu, and A. C. Catlin, "InsightVideo: Toward hierarchical video content organization for efficient browsing, summarization and retrieval," IEEE Trans. Multimedia, vol. 7, no. 4, pp. 648–666, Aug. 2005.

[7] T. Lertrusdachakul, T. Aoki, and H. Yasuda, "Camera motion characterization through image feature analysis," in Proc. ICCIMA'05, Aug. 16–18, 2005, pp. 186–190.

[8] A. Yao and A. Calway, "Robust estimation of 3-d camera motion for uncalibrated augmented reality", Technical Report CSTR-02-001, Dept of Computer Science, University of Bristol, 2002.

[9] O. Faugeras, Q.T. Luong, and T. Papadopoulo. "The Geometry of Multiple Images". MIT Press, 2000.

[10] M. Pollefeys, M Vergauwen, K Cornelis, J. Tops, F. Verbiest, and L. Van Gool "Structure and motion from image sequences" Proceedings of Conference on Optical 3-D Measurement Techniques V, pp. 251-258, 2001.

[11] Y. Ma, J. Koseck_a, and S. Sastry. "Linear differential algorithm for motion recovery: A geometric approach", IJCV, vol.36(1), pp.71-89, 2000.

[12] S.C. Park, H.S. Lee, and S.W. Lee, "Qualitative estimation of camera motion parameters from the linear composition of optical flow", PR(37), vol. 4, pp.767-779, 2004.

[13] Y. Tian, C. Tomasi, and D.J. Heeger, "Comparison of approaches to egomotion computation" IEEE Computer Society, Conference on Computer Vision and Pattern Recognition, pp.315-320, 1996.

[14] E. Francois and P.Bouthemy, "Derivation of qualitative information in motion analysis," Image Vi-sion Computing, vol.8, no.4, pp. 279-287, Nov.1990.

[15] W.H. Press, B.P. Flannery, S. A. Teukolsky, and W.T. Vetterling, Numerical Recipes in C: The Art of Scientific Computing. Cambridge, U.K.: Cambridge Univ. Press, 1988, pp.59-70, pp.656-706.

[16] R. Grompone von Gioi, J. Jakubowicz, J-M.Morel and G.Randall, "On Straight Line Segment Detection", Journal of Mathematical Imaging and Vision, vol.32(3), pp.313-347, November 2008.

[17] C. Beumier, "Straight-Line Detection Using Moment of Inertia", IEEE International Conference on Industrial Technology, pp.1753-1756, 15-17 Dec. 2006.

[18] C. Tomasi and R. Manduchi, "Bilateral Filtering for Gray and Color Images", Proceedings of the 1998 IEEE International Conference on Computer Vision, Bombay, India, 1998.

[19] S S. Zhu, J. Tian, X. Shen, K. Belloulata,"A new cross-diamond search algorithm for fast block motion estimation", the IEEE Int. Conf. Image Processing, *ICIP2009*, Cairo, Egypt, 07-11 Nov. 2009, Vol. I, pp. 1581-1584.

[20] Belloulata, K., Shiping Zhu, Jun Tian, Xiaodong Shen, "A novel cross-hexagon search algorithm for fast block motion estimation", Systems, Signal Processing and their Applications (WOSSPA), 2011 7th International Workshop on, On page(s): 1 - 4, Volume: Issue: , 9-11 May 2011

[21] Li Ren-xiang, Zeng Bing, Liou M. L, "A new three-step search algorithm for block motion estimation," IEEE Transactions on Circuits and Systems for Video Technology, vol. 4, pp. 438-442, April 1994.

21

Graph Theory for Survivability Design in Communication Networks

Daryoush Habibi and Quoc Viet Phung
Edith Cowan University
Australia

1. Introduction

Design of survivable communication networks has been a complex task. Without establishing network survivability, there can be severe consequences when a physical link fails. Network failures which may be caused by dig-ups, vehicle crashes, human errors, system malfunctions, fire, rodents, sabotage, natural disasters (e.g. floods, earthquakes, lightning storms), and some other factors, have occurred quite frequently and sometimes with unpredictable consequences. To tackle these, survivability measures in a communication network can be implemented at the service layer, the logical layer, the system layer, and the physical layer.

The physical layer is the base resource infrastructure of the network, and to be able to protect it, we need to ensure that the physical topology of the network has sufficient link and node diversity. Without this, protection at higher layers will not be feasible. With the implementation of Dense Wavelength Division Multiplexing (DWDM) in the optical backbone of metropolitan and long-haul networks, greater flexibility is achieved in providing alternate routes for light-path connections. However, the survivability problem at the physical layer remains the same. In fact, it becomes even more critical, because each link of a backbone network carries huge amounts of traffic and the failure of an optical component, such as a fiber cut or a node failure, may cause a very serious problem in terms of loss of data and profit.

The physical topology of a network is considered to be survivable if it can cope with failure scenarios occurring at network components. In other words, the physical topology must remain connected under the failure scenario. For example, to cope with single link failures in the network, the physical topology must be at least 2-connected, meaning that there is at least 2 link-disjoint paths between any two nodes in the network. Generally, to protect against the failure of any set of k links in a network, the physical topology of that network must be $(k+1)$-connected. Menger's theorem (Menger, 1927) gives the necessary and sufficient condition for survivability of networks at the physical layer, using the connectivity between network's cut-sets. However, the computational complexity of this model grows exponentially with the size of the network, since a network with $|V|$ nodes would yield $2^{|V|} - 2$ cut-sets. Therefore, the cut-set technique cannot efficiently deal with even moderate size networks of say 40 nodes, and larger networks are out of computational reach of this technique. Testing for survivability of large networks can be done using a technique called bi-connected components of a graph introduced by W. D. Grover (Grover, 2004). This technique can determine vulnerable links and nodes of the network. However, verifying network survivability is just the first step in network planning, after which we need to apply appropriate protection routing schemes using such techniques as Shared Backup Path Protection (SBPP), Pre-configured Protection Cycles (p-cycle), or ring protection. It is therefore very helpful if the algorithm used for determining the physical survivability of the network can also provide additional information which is of benefit to protection design.

2. Chapter outline

It is generally understood that research in transport networks has a close connection to graph theory. A graph can be used to present key aspects of a network, such as its topology and/or the associated capacity. Indeed, a network consists of many more elements such as the physical equipment (e.g. OADMs, OXCs, etc.), fibre cables, and so on. The objective of this chapter is to provide an overview of network connectivity in relation to network protection design. In addition, this chapter also aims to introduce and analyse the advantages and disadvantages of methods and algorithms for searching network connectivity as well as sets of disjoint and distinct paths for protection design.

Given these objectives, the chapter is organized as follows. Section 3 discusses the connectivity property of graph in relation to network protection design. Section 4 discusses two approaches to establishing the survivability of physical topology. In Section 5, we present the problem of diverse routing and graph algorithms. Finally, we close this chapter in Section 6 by summarising the key aspects of network connectivity in network protection design.

3. Graph connectivity in relation to network protection design

Practically, different traffic requirements over a network would require different connectivity between nodes. Some traffic demands may require no protection, or may only need to be carried when possible. In contrast, other traffic demands may ask for a full protection against either single-link failure, dual-link failures or other types of failure. Hence, the required connectivity between nodes would be different for these varied protection requirements. This section first presents the general requirement for network connectivity in which the network can at least be protected against any single failure scenario, e.g. the failure of any single link or node of the network. In this case, the physical topology of the network must be 2-connected.

Fig. 1. Two connected graph versus biconnected graph

The protection mechanism is designed to maintain the continuity of services under network failures. The failure can be minor such as a channel failure, or be more significant such as failure of groups of links or nodes. As far as the connectivity of the physical topology is concerned, the failure may be in a single link, a single node, a group of links, a group of nodes. Protection design cannot cover all failure scenarios. Instead, it will consider the set of specific (or predetermined) failures. For example, protection design against single link failures needs to determine the recovery routes for services so that they can maintain their services under the failure of any single link in the network. To do that, the network connectivity must provide at least 2 *disjoint* paths between any source and destination nodes. The term "disjoint" here is with respect to the failure scenario, meaning that the "disjoint" paths must not suffer from the same failure. For example, for single link failures, the 2 paths must be link-disjoint. Similarly, for single node failures, the 2 paths must be node-disjoint.

Fig. 1 shows an example of a pair of link-disjoint paths (Fig. 1(a)) and node-disjoint paths (Fig. 1(b)). It can be easily seen that link-disjoint paths may share nodes along their paths, e.g. node 3 on paths p_1 and p_2 in Fig. 1(a). Hence, link-disjoint paths may not be node-disjoint. On the other hand, node-disjoint paths are always link-disjoint.

A graph which provides at least 2 link-disjoint paths between any two nodes is 2-*connected*. With stronger connectivity, a *biconnected* graph is able to provide at least 2 node-disjoint paths between any two nodes.

Generally, a network must provide at least K link-disjoint paths between any node-pairs to be able to protect against simultaneous failure of $K - 1$ links. The graph of such networks is said to be *K-connected*. The rest of this chapter will mainly discuss network connectivity which supports single link and single node failures, known as 2-connected and biconnected.

4. Establishing physical survivability

This section presents the procedures for establishing network survivability against single-link failures which is one of the most common failure scenarios occurring in practical networks. As discussed, the physical topology of a network can only be survivable under single-link failures if and only if it is 2-connected. Manual verification for survivability is only suitable with small networks where designers can perform the verification in just few seconds or few minutes. However, manual verification may take hours or even days for large scale networks. Furthermore, it is prone to human errors. Therefore, automatic survivability verification is important in both theory and practice. The concept of survivable networks is more complex than the concept of connectivity in graph theory. In addition, efficient automation algorithms based on graph theory can help designers to reduce the computational time and avoid human errors. This section presents techniques for evaluating the physical survivability of networks. Firstly, we outline and analyse the strengths and weaknesses of a popular method, namely the cut-set method. Then, we introduce two comparable techniques that can deal with network sizes of many thousand nodes (Habibi et al., 2005). One technique is based on Depth-First Search (DFS) and the other uses properties of 2-connected graphs.

4.1 Survivability via cut-sets

A network is survivable if the size of every cut-set of the network is equal to or larger than 2. At a glance, this definition leads to a view that the network has nodal-degree of two, meaning that every node in the network is connected to at least two other nodes. Since every node is connected to at least two other nodes in the network, on the surface this property seems to be able to offer two disjoint paths between any two nodes in the network. In fact, this is a misconception. If a network is 2-connected then the nodal degree of all nodes in the network is equal to or larger than 2. The reverse does not hold, however, in that a network in which the nodal degree of all its nodes equal to or larger than 2 is not always 2-connected. The topology in Fig. 2 illustrates this concept. In that Figure we can see that path $(3-5-6)$ is a bridge that connects two subsets of network nodes $X = \{1,2,3,4\}$ and $Y = \{6,7,8,9\}$. As a result, all paths between nodes $x \in X$ and $y \in Y$ must share the same path $(3-5-6)$. Hence, although all nodes in this network have a nodal degree equal to or larger than 2, it is not a 2-connected network.

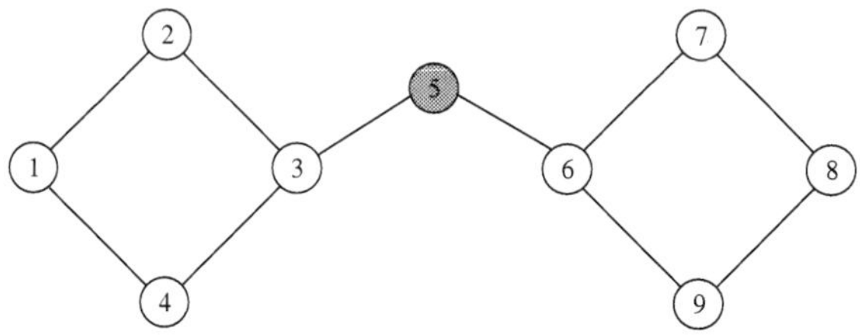

Fig. 2. An illustration of the failure of the nodal degree technique

Therefore, all algorithms for verification of network survivability based on node-degree of two may yield undesirable and inaccurate results and hence are not reliable. The cut-set assumption described below has been preferred for the accuracy of network survivability verification.

Let $G = (V, E)$ be a network topology. A cut in G is a partition of V into parts S and $\bar{S} = V \setminus S$. Each cut defines a set of edges consisting of those edges in E with one end-point in S and the other in $\bar{S}$. This edge set is referred as the cut-set $CS(S, V \setminus S)$ associated with the cut $\langle S, V \setminus S \rangle$. Let $|CS(S, V \setminus S)|$ be the size of the cut-set, being the number of links between S and $V \setminus S$. Thus, according to the cut-set assumption, **a network is 2-connected if** $|CS(S, V \setminus S)| \geq 2, \forall S \subset V$. If S is a subset of only a single node in the network, then the cut-set assumption is essentially the same as the node-degree assumption.

Since the cut-set assumption is related the number of links connected between two subsets of a cut, it can assure the network to offer **link-disjoint paths**, but **not node-disjoint paths**. In other words, a configuration of the network that satisfies the condition of the cut-set assumption can provide at least one link-disjoint path-pair between any distinct pair of source node and destination node.

The implementation of the cut-set assumption is not complex but its computational time for large scale networks is its biggest disadvantage. The number of cut-sets increases exponentially with the number of network nodes and is calculated as (Grover, 2004):

$$N_{cutset} = 2^{|V|} - 2$$

where N_{cutset} is the number of cut-sets in the network, and $|V|$ is the number of network nodes.

Table 1 shows the example of the number of the possible cut-sets, N_{cutset}, versus the number of network nodes $|V|$. The number of cut-sets doubles with an increase of one node in the network. For instance, N_{cutset} in a network of 20 nodes is over 1 million; and it is over 32 million with $|V| = 25$; which is $32 (= 2^5)$ times larger than $|V| = 20$; and the number of cut-sets in the networks of $|V| = 30$ nodes is up to 1 billion cut-sets. So, the cut-set technique becomes intractable even with moderate scale networks ($20 \leq |V| \leq 30$).

$\|V\|$	20	25	30
N_{cutset}	1,048,574	33,554,430	1,073,741,822

Table 1. The number of cut-sets versus the number of network nodes

In summary, the node-degree assumption is simple but not reliable for the verification of network survivability. Meanwhile, the cut-set assumption is only applicable for link-survivable networks, and it is intractable with large scale networks. The verification ability of these two assumptions for different connectivities of the physical topology are summarised in Table 2. The node-degree assumption cannot verify any type of physical topology that has potential to support network survivability (namely 2-connected and biconnected networks) whereas the cut-set assumption can verify the survivability of a network that is 2-connected but cannot identify exactly a 2-connected topology or verify a biconnected topology. Next, we propose an approach that can classify network topologies, and determine if they are unconnected, (1−)connected, 2-connected or biconnected.

	Network connectivity			
	Disconnected	(1-)Connected	2-connected	Biconnected
Node-degree assumption	Yes	Yes	No	No
Cut-set Assumption	Yes	Yes	Yes	No

Table 2. Performance of two common assumptions in terms of network connectivity

4.2 An approach to verifying physical topology for designing network survivability

Let $G(V,E)$ be the graph presenting the physical topology of a network. If the degree of any node in G is zero, the graph is disconnected. If the degree of any node in G is 1, the graph cannot be 2-connected or biconnected. For the sake of network survivability design, from here after, we assume that the degree of every node in the graph is at least 2. This condition allows every node to belong to a biconnected component or a bridge. Let G' and G'' be two biconnected components of the graph G. The relationship between G' and G'' determines the connectivity of the graph:

- If G' and G'' have at least 2 common nodes, then G is a 2-connected graph with no cut-node (i.e. node bridge) or cut-link (i.e. link bridge). In other words, G is a biconnected graph.
- If G' and G'' only have one common node, then G is a 2-connected graph with an *articulation node* which is the common node.
- If G' and G'' are separated by a cut-link (or a cut-path), then G is not a 2-connected graph, and the cut-link (or cut-path) cannot be protected.
- If G' and G'' have no common links or nodes, then G is a disconnected graph.

The key point for determining the connectivity of a graph is to find all biconnected components in the graph and check the relationship between these components. Biconnected components can be found using either Depth-First Search (DFS) or the properties of the 2-connected graph.

4.2.1 Finding biconnected components using Depth-First Search (DFS)

Algorithm 1 outlines the pseudo-code for verifying a 2-edge-connected graph. The principle is to find a bridge (edge) via articulation nodes - a cut at one of these nodes would disconnect the graph. A bridge is an edge or a path segment that connects two biconnected component neighbourhood. A graph is 2-edge-connected if it contains no bridge. The DFS algorithm for finding biconnected components was proposed by Robert Tarjan (Tarjan, 1971), and subsequently, revised for a particular study in survivable mesh networks in (Grover, 2004). Algorithm 1 is a modified version of the original DFS algorithm in (Grover, 2004; Tarjan, 1971) that allows for the verification of the 2-edge connectivity of a physical topology.

The underlying concept behind this search is to firstly "depth" explore unvisited nodes, called "depth search", via a walk through incident edges from the current node (v). At any depth search, the current visited node is pushed to a stack. The depth search continues until there are no unvisited nodes reachable from the current node. The search is "backtracking" by examining visited nodes in the stack and continuing depth search at these nodes. The algorithm is terminated when there are no nodes in the stack.

Algorithm 1 Depth-First Search for 2-connected graph

Require: A graph $G(\mathbf{V}, \mathbf{S})$ presented the physical topology of a given network.
Ensure: Return **true** if G is two connected, otherwise **false**

```
count ← 1;
Set current node v ← v0; //start at node v0
Set dfs[v] = btk[v] ← count++;
repeat
    if (there is an unvisited incident edge e of v) then
        if (∃w ← v is unvisited) then
            dfs[v] = btk[v] ← count++;
            Push stack ← v;
            Current node v ← w;
        else
            btk[w] = min(btk[w], btk[v])
        end if
    else
        Pop w ← stack; //parent of node
        if (btk[v] ≥ dfs[w]) then
            Record w is an articulation node
        else
            btk[w] = min btk[w], btk[v];
        end if
    end if
    Current node v ← w;
until (there is no node in the stack)
if (there is no edge bridge between any two articulation nodes) then
    return true;
else
    return false;
end if
```

Two parameters are assigned to each visited node v, the $dfs[v]$ and the $btk[v]$, to discover articulation nodes. The $dfs[v]$ identifies the "depth first search" order of the node v when it is visited for the first time. The $btk[v]$ is determined using "back tracking" as follows:

- Initially, $btk[v]$ is assigned a value equivalent to the value of $dfs[v]$ when the node is first visited.
- $btk[v]$ is then updated as $btk[v] = \min(btk[v], dfs[w])$ when it has a neighbour w through an unvisited edge, and w is an ancestor of v.
- The value of $btk[w]$, where w is the parent of v, is also updated during the backtracking step as $btk[w] = \min(btk[w], btk[v])$.

The calculation of the value btk helps determine if a node v is a cut node (or articulation node) when $btk[v]$ is larger than or equal to $dfs[w]$, where w is the parent of v.

4.2.2 Finding biconnected components using property of 2-connected graphs

Alternatively, based on the properties of 2-connected graphs, biconnected components can be built from a simple and small cycle by adding the so-called H-paths to the cycle. Let H be a biconnected component on the graph G. A H-path is a non-trivial path on G that meets H exactly at its end nodes. The following proposition and proof are adopted from (Diestel, 2000).

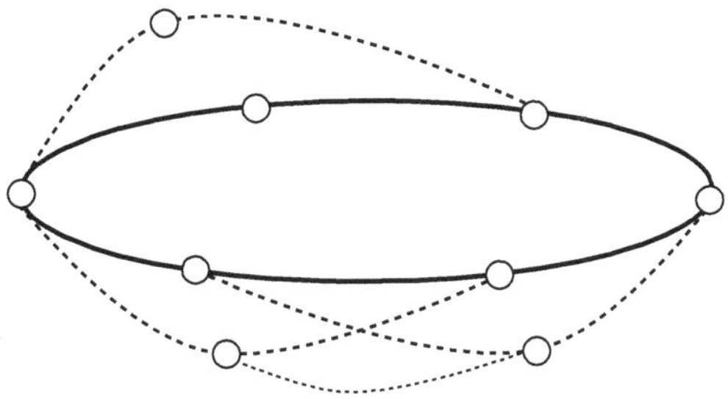

Fig. 3. The construction of 2-connected graphs

Proposition 4.1. *A graph is 2-connected if and only if it can be constructed from a cycle by successively adding H-paths to graph H already constructed.*

Proof. Clearly, every graph constructed as proposed is 2-connected. Conversely, let G be a 2-connected graph, then G contains a cycle, and hence a maximal subgraph H is constructable, as evident in Fig. 3. Any edge $x, y \in E(G) \setminus E(H)$ with $(x, y) \in H$ defines a H-path. Then, H is an induced sub-graph of G. If $H \neq G$, then by the connectedness of G, there is an edge vw with $v \in G - H$ and $w \in H$. As G is 2-connected, $G - w$ has a $v - H$ path P. Then wvP is a H-path in G, and $H \cup wvP$ is a constructable sub-graph of G. □

Based on this proposition, we can use the relationship between network's cycles or 2-connected graphs to verify the survivability of its physical topology.

An undirected graph is thus seen as the combination of all fundamental cycles. Using Algorithm 2, these fundamental cycles can be found from a spanning tree $T(V, E')$, $E' \subset E$ of a graph $G(V, E)$ (eg. the spanning tree highlighted by thick lines in Fig. 4).

Algorithm 2 Finding cycles

Require: A tree T and and edge e whose end-nodes is in T.
Ensure: A cycle P formed by T and e.

$(s, d) \leftarrow$ end-nodes of e;
$queue \leftarrow [node.s, node.P]; check \leftarrow 0;$
while $(check = 0 \& queue \neq \emptyset)$ **do**
  $[v] \leftarrow head(queue);$
  $queue \leftarrow queue - head(queue);$
  if $(v.s = d)$ **then**
    $check = 1; P \leftarrow v.P;$
  else
    for (all v_k is neighbour of v_s) **do**
      $node.s \leftarrow v_k; node.P \leftarrow P \cup v_k;$
      push *node* into *queue*;
    end for
  end if
end while

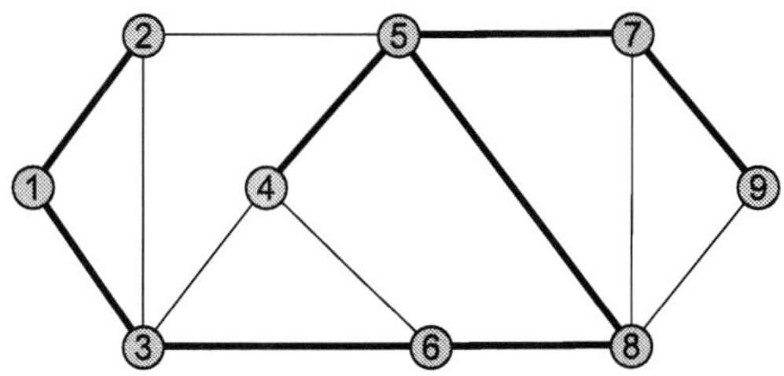

Fig. 4. Spanning tree on an arbitrary graph

However, it is not easy to find all of the fundamental cycles in the graph. For instance, in Fig. 4, the edges represented with thin lines are not part of the spanning tree (shown by thick lines). If any of these edges are added to the tree, it will form a unique cycle, but such cycle is not necessarily a fundamental cycle (eg. consider adding edge $2-5$). Any set of cycles found from the spanning tree can be used to verify the survivability of the topology from which it is generated. An algorithm for finding a set of cycles through spanning tree of a graph is represented in Algorithm 2. An efficient method for finding fundamental cycles of a graph, referred to as *Paton's* algorithm, is outlined in (Paton, 1969). Further discussion of this topic is outside the scope of this chapter.

The connectivity of the graph then can be determined using Algorithm 3. Note that the **set of remaining links** contains links in the graph but not in the tree.

5. Graph algorithms for diverse routing in protection design

Previously in this chapter, we have discussed the connectivity of the physical topology to support the problem of designing multiple quality of protections. However, the assurance of connectivity at the physical layer is only the first step to ensure traffic demands can be conveyed from the source to the destination. Once a physical layer is given, the main goal of the Logical Topology Design (LTD) is to determine routes for traffic flow in the most efficient

Algorithm 3 Construct biconnected components

Require: A spanning tree T of the graph G and the set of remain links.
Ensure: Set of biconnected components.

1: Firstly, a biconnected subgraph $G_i, i = 1$ is found by picking up a link e in the set of remain links and joining it with a unique path in the tree between end nodes of e.
2: a new biconnected subgraph $G_j, j = i + 1$ is constructed from a remain link and a unique path between end nodes of that link. If G_j have more than one node in common with a component $G_k, k = 1 \ldots i$, join $G_k \leftarrow G_k \cup G_j$. Otherwise, a new biconnected subgraph G_j is recorded, $i \leftarrow i + 1$.
3: Repeat step 2 until there is no remain links left.
4: The set of constructed biconnected components $G_1, G_2, \ldots, G_i$ is return.

way, that is to minimise the amount of physical resources utilised, particularly the amount of capacity utilisation. One approach is to enumerate the set of best candidates for each demand. In network protection design, these candidates can be distinct paths or disjoint paths. The disjoint paths are to ensure the success of the recovery process from network failures. On the other hand, the distinct paths provide the flexibility in selecting the most efficient working and backup routes. This section presents graph algorithms to support the diverse routing problem including finding K shortest (least cost) paths, finding two disjoint paths and finding K shortest disjoint path-pairs between any two nodes in a network.

5.1 Algorithm for finding K shortest paths between two nodes in the network

A set of all paths between two nodes can be used to select the best paths on which traffic flows between these nodes may be carried. All paths between two nodes in the graph can be found using either the Breath-First Search or the Depth-First Search. However, the number of all paths increases exponentially with the size of the network. Hence, finding all paths for routing is not a practical approach for real-time provisioning. In addition, the number of best selected paths is very small compared to all possible paths. Therefore, finding a small set of best eligible paths would be more practical and computationally efficient.

This section discusses and analyses the complexity of algorithms presented in the literature. We outline an efficient graph algorithm for finding K shortest paths between any two nodes in the network. This algorithm is an adaptation from (Martins et al., 1998) for directed graph to undirected graph.

Model selection used in survivable network design employs a set of potential candidates as inputs and selects optimal candidates as outputs. Input candidates differ depending on the protection techniques used. This can be either a set of paths for routing working flows, backup routes (in non-joint optimisation approaches), a set of disjoint path-pairs or a set of cycles in p-cycle design. This section introduces a basic algorithm used as a subroutine for finding input candidates for routing working flows and backup routes in non-joint optimisation approaches; the K shortest (minimum) paths algorithm.

K shortest paths is a classical graph problem that has been widely studied (Eppstein, 1998; Martins et al., 1998; Martins & Santos, 2000). Eppstein *et al.* (Eppstein, 1998) proposed a k shortest path algorithm between any two nodes in a digraph in time complexity of $O(|E| + |V| \log |E| + K)$, where $|V|$ is number of nodes, $|E|$ is the number of edges and K is number of paths required. Martins *et al.* (Martins et al., 1998) present two algorithms for

Algorithm 4 K shortest paths algorithm

Require: An undirected graph $G(V, E)$, a pair of source and destination nodes and the number of shortest paths required.

Ensure: A set of K - shortest paths over graph G from s to d.

1: To assure the possible repetition of the algorithm in a path between a pair of source-destination nodes (s, d), the given network is enlarged with a super source node S and super destination D, with zero cost edges $(s*, s)$ and $(d, d*)$. Following this, the shortest tree from source node s to other nodes in the network is obtained, and the first shortest path is marked as $p_1 = \{s_0(= s), s_1, \ldots, s_{r-1}, s_r(= d)\}$ from s to d.

2: Determine the first node s_h in p_1 such that s_h has more than a single incoming edges. If a node s'_h , of which the incoming edges are the incoming edges of s_h except those coming from s_{h-1}, does not exist, then generate the node s'_h, else determine the next node s_i in p_1 that has not alternate yet. The cost $d(s, s'_h)$ of shortest path from s to s'_h is calculated as:

$$d(s, s'_h) = \min_x \left(d(s, x) + d(x, s'_h)\right)$$

where (x, s'_h) are incoming edges of s'_h.

3: For each $s_j = \{s_i, \ldots, s_{r-1}\}$, generate s'_j following the same rules as s'_h, but with one more incoming edge of (s'_{j-1}, s'_j). Clearly, the shortest path from s to s'_j is the second shortest path from s to s_j. Therefore $p_2 = \{s_0, \ldots, s_i, \ldots, s'_{r-1}, s_r(= d)\}$ is the second shortest path. Repeat step 2 to determine next shortest path $p_k (k = 2, 3, \ldots)$ until $k = K$.

the K shortest paths problem, one based on a label setting algorithm and another based on a label correcting algorithm. The results show that these algorithms perform better than the algorithm in (Eppstein, 1998). The K-shortest path algorithm employed in this study is adapted from (Martins & Santos, 2000), which is proposed over a directed graph approach. Building on this idea, this study has developed an algorithm (Algorithm 4) which is relevant for an undirected approach as well. This algorithm runs with the time complexity of $O(K \times |E|)$, where K is the number of shortest paths required and $|E|$ is the number of undirected edges in the graph.

5.2 Algorithm for finding two disjoint paths (disjoint path-pair) between nodes in the network

Finding a disjoint path-pair between two nodes in the network is a basic solution for protection design in which the primary and secondary paths must not suffer from the same failure. Basically, finding a pair of disjoint paths can be done in two steps. In the first step, the first path is determined from the original graph. Then, all edges contained in the first path are removed from of the graph. The second disjoint path is determined from the residual graph. Both paths are usually determined using any shortest path algorithm such as Dijkstra's algorithm (Dijkstra, 1959) or Bellman-Ford algorithm (Bellman, 1958). The two step approach is simple in both concept and implementation. There is, however, no guarantee that the total cost of the found disjoint path-pair is minimum. In addition, this approach may fail to find a solution in some cases even when a disjoint path-pair exists between the two nodes. An example of a trap topology is shown in Fig. 5. It is easy to see in Fig. 5(a) that there are two disjoint paths between nodes 1 and 4. However, by using the two-step approach, the first shortest path may be path p_1 $(1 \rightarrow 2 \rightarrow 3 \rightarrow 4)$ as shown in Fig. 5(b). The second path is determined after all spans contained in the first path (edges $\{(1-2),(2-3),(3-4)\}$) are removed. It can easily be seen that the second path can not be found since the graph is disconnected between nodes 1 and 4.

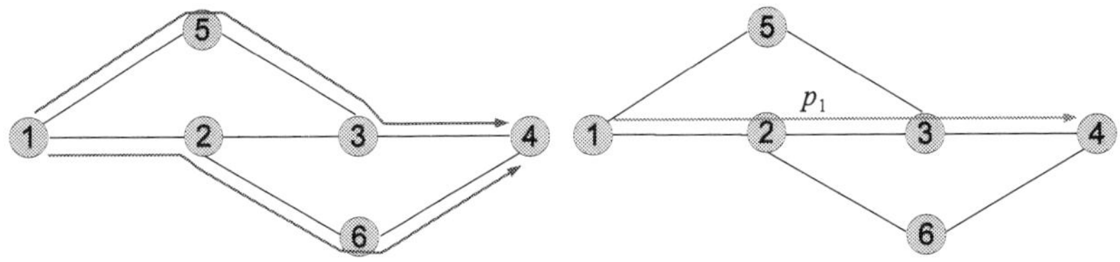

(a) A pair of edge-disjoint paths is created (b) Find the first shortest path p_1

Fig. 5. An example of trap topology

To resolve these two drawbacks, a graph algorithm, known as the one step approach, for determining a shortest disjoint path-pair was first proposed by Surballe (Surballe, 1974) and modified by Bhandari (Bhandari, 1994; 1999) to adapt to the negative weight of edges. The algorithm, as its name implies, determines the first and the second disjoint path simultaneously.

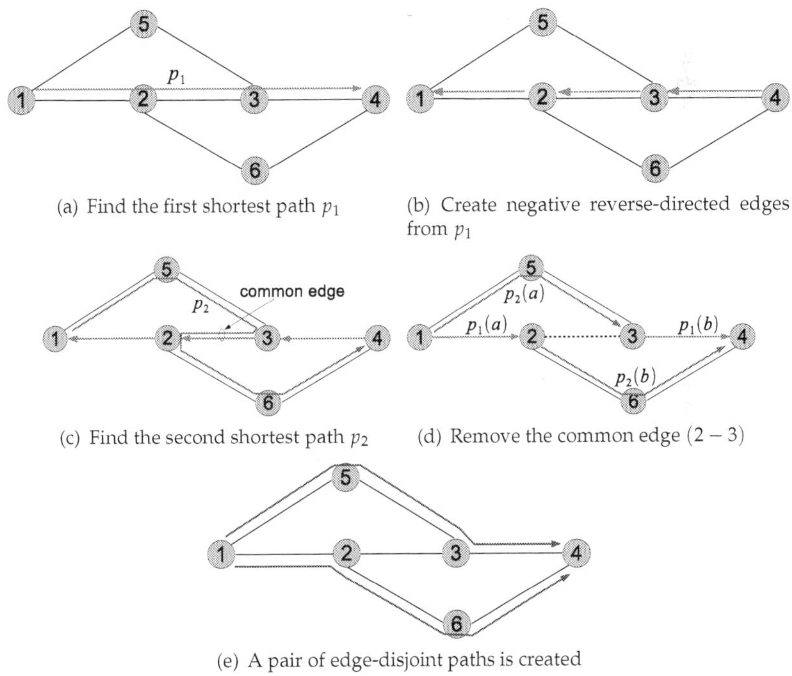

(a) Find the first shortest path p_1

(b) Create negative reverse-directed edges from p_1

(c) Find the second shortest path p_2

(d) Remove the common edge $(2-3)$

(e) A pair of edge-disjoint paths is created

Fig. 6. An illustration of the one-step approach to resolve trap topology

Let us assume that a shortest disjoint path-pair needs to be determined between the source node s and the destination node d. The one step algorithm is outlined as follows:

- Find a shortest (least cost) path between the source node s and the destination nodes d, and denote it as p_1 (Fig. 6(a)).
- Mark the direction of each edge traversed in p_1 from s toward d as positive.
- Remove all directed edges on the shortest path p_1 and replace them with reverse direction edges by multiplying -1 to the original edge cost (Fig. 6(b)).
- Find the least cost path from s to d in the modified graph using the modified Dijkstra's algorithm, and denote it as path p_2 (Fig. 6(c)).
- Remove any edge in the original graph traversed by both p_1 and p_2 (Fig. 6(d)). These are called interlacing edges.
- Identify all path segments remaining after the process of the edge removal (Fig. 6(e)) which forms a pair of disjoint paths from the source node s to the destination node d.

5.3 Algorithm for finding K shortest disjoint path-pairs between nodes in the network

In path protection techniques such as path restoration, or shared backup path protection, there are two sets of candidates needed for provisioning of the working flows and the backup routes. Finding and employing these two sets independently may compromise the protection conditions as the backup and working paths must be disjoint. There is no guarantee that each working route has a disjoint path in the corresponding set of backup routes. In addition, using two different sets of candidates also increases the number of decision variables used in model selection which increases the complexity of both space requirement and computational time. Another approach is to determine one set of candidates in which each candidate is a disjoint path-pair serving as a primary and a backup route. This set would always satisfy the disjointness requirements for protection and reduce the complexity in both time and space of model selections such as Integer Linear Programming (ILP) and Mixed ILP (MILP). By combining algorithms in Sections 5.1 and 5.2, this section introduces an algorithm for finding K shortest (least cost) disjoint path-pairs between two nodes in the networks.

Algorithm 5 K disjoint-paths pairs (KDPPs)

Require: An undirected graph $G(V, S)$ source node s, destination node d, and K, the number of shortest disjoint-paths pairs required.
Ensure: A set of K shortest disjoint-paths pairs.
1: Find a shortest path between s and d, denoted by p.
2: Define the direction of each edge traversed in p from s to d as positive 1.
3: Remove all directed edges on the shortest path p and replace them with reverse direction edges by multiplying the original edge cost with -1.
4: Find K shortest path (least cost) paths from s to d in the modified graph using the K shortest path algorithm (Algorithm 4). Denote them as the set of paths $P = \{p_1, p_2, \ldots, p_K\}$.
5: For each pair of paths $(p, p_i), i = 1 \ldots K$, remove any edge of the original graph traversed by both p and p_i. These are called interlacing edges. Identify all path segments from the rest of edges. These from disjoint-paths pairs, denote as $\{(w_1, r_1), (w_2, r_2), \ldots, (w_K, r_K)\}$.

The two-step and one-step approaches can be used to find the set of disjoint path-pairs. They are simple and computationally efficient. However, since these approaches provision traffic streams sequentially without back-tracking, sometimes no solution may be found even when a feasible solution does exist. In fact, the graph theory approach is more applicable in online provisioning than in offline provisioning. These approaches have been extensively studied in the literature (Patre et al., 2002; Sen et al., 2001; Xin et al., 2002; Zhang et al., 2003). Authors in (Xin et al., 2002) investigated survivable routing based on both the two-step and the one-step approaches, namely Separate Path Selection (SPS) and Joint Path Selection (JPS) respectively. These approaches aim to optimise the network resource utilisation of each traffic connection by minimising the total cost of the primary and backup paths. The performance of these approaches is evaluated for different protection path cost functions. The results have shown that JPS performs substantially better than SPS and also scales very well in terms of the network resource abundance. In addition, JPS can utilise network resources better than SPS. In (Zang et al., 2003), the two-step and one-step approaches are also investigated, but with a different objective function based on the blocking probability. The simulation results have shown that the one-step approach significantly outperforms the two-step approach in this case. The improvement in blocking probability is significant, around 10%-20%, especially when fixed routing is used.

In this section, the one-step approach is used as a sub-function in an algorithm for finding K shortest disjoint path-pairs between any two nodes in the graph. The pseudo code of this algorithm is shown in Algorithm 5. This algorithm is then proved to yield K distinct disjoint-path pairs. Since a path pair found from one step algorithm was proved to be disjoint in (Bhandari, 1999) , it is only necessary to prove that the K found path pairs do not coincide with each other.

Proof. Let $P = \{P_k | k = [1 \ldots K]\}$ be the set of K pairs of disjoint paths yielded from Algorithm 5, where $P_k = \{w_k, r_k\}$ is the kth pair.

Let $P_i = \{w_i, r_i\}$ and $P_j = \{w_j, r_j\}$ be any two disjoint-path pairs yielded from the first shortest path p and paths p_i and p_j $(i, j \in [1 \ldots K])$ respectively. This study proves that P_i and P_j do not coincide.

Since p_i and p_j do not coincide, there exists at least one edge e_k contained in p_i but not contained in p_j. Following this, it is proved that e_k can only belong to either P_i or P_j. If e_k is contained in p then e_k is obviously not contained in P_i. However, since e_k is not contained in p_j, e_k is not an interlacing edge of (p, p_j) and hence e_k is in P_j. Conversely, if e_k is not contained in p, then e_k is in P_i. In addition, since e_k is not contained in both p and p_j, e_k is not contained in P_j. Therefore, P_i and P_j do not coincide and the K found disjoint-path pairs are distinct from each other. □

6. Conclusion

In this chapter we have investigated and discussed the connectivity of graphs in relation to the requirements of protection of traffic demands in practical networks. We have discussed and analysed the complexity of several methods for verifying the connectivity of the physical topology of a network. Diverse routing was then addressed as an important problem in designing network protection, followed by the introduction of three algorithms for finding distinct and disjoint paths. These algorithms address the challenges for network protection design using graph theory.

7. References

Bellman, R. (1958). On a routing problem, *in Quarterly of Applied Mathematics* 16(1): 87–90.

Bhandari, R. (1994). Optimal diverse routing in telecommunication fiber networks, *Proceedings of the 13th IEEE Networking for Global Communications.*, Vol. 3, Toronto, Ont. , Canada, pp. 1498 –1508.

Bhandari, R. (1999). *Survivable Networks: Algorithms for Diverse Routing*, Kluwer Academic Publishers.

Dijkstra, E. (1959). A note on two problems in connection with graphs, *Numerische Mathe-matik* 1: 269–271.

Diestel, R. (2000). *Graph Theory*, Springer-Verlag.

Eppstein, D. (1998). Finding the *k* shortest paths, *SIAM Journal on Computing* 28(2): 652–673.

Grover, W. D. (2004). *Mesh-based Survivable Networks: Options and Strategies for Optical, MPLS, SONET/SDH, and ATM networking*, Prentice Hall PTR.

Habibi, D., Nguyen, H., Phung, Q. & Lo, K. (2005). Establishing physical survivability of large networks using properties of two-connected graphs, *TENCON 2005 2005 IEEE Region 10*, IEEE, pp. 1–5.

Martins, E. D. Q. V., Pascoal, M. M. B. & Santos, J. L. E. D. (1998). The *k* shortest paths problem, *Technical report*, CISUC.

Martins, E. D. Q. V. & Santos, J. L. E. D. (2000). A new shortest paths ranking algorithm, *Investigação Operacional* 20(1): 47–62.

Menger, K. (1927). Zur allgemeinen kurventheorie, *Fund. Math* 10(95-115): 5.

Paton, K. (1969). An algorithm for finding a fundamental set of cycles of a graph, *Communications of the ACM* 12(9): 514–518.

Patre, S. D., Maier, G. & Martinelli, M. (2002). Design of static WDM mesh networks with dedicated path protection, *Infocom*.

Sen, A., Shen, B., Bandyopadhyay, S. & Capone, J. (2001). Survivability of lightwave networks - path lengths in WDM protection scheme, *Journal of High Speed Networks* 10(4): 303–315.

Surballe, J. (1974). Disjoint paths in a network, *Networks* 4: 125–145.

Tarjan, R. (1971). Depth-first search and linear graph algorithms, *Proc. th Annual Symposium on Switching and Automata Theory*, pp. 114–121.

Xin, C., Ye, Y., Dixit, S. S. & Qiao, C. (2002). A joint lightpath routing approach in surviavble optical networks, *Optical Networks Magazine* 3(3): 13–20.

Zang, H., Ou, C. & Mukherjee, B. (2003). Path-protection routing and wavelength assignment (RWA) in WDM mesh networks under duct-layer constraints., *IEEE/ACM Transactions on Networking* 11(2): 248–258.

Zhang, J., Zhu, K., Sahasrabuddhe, L. & Yoo, S. B. (2003). On the study of routing and wavlength assignment approaches for survivable wavelength-routed WDM mesh networks, *Optical Networks Magazine* 4(6): 16–28.

22

Applied Graph Theory to Improve Topology Control in Wireless Sensor Networks

Paulo Sérgio Sausen, Airam Sausen and Mauricio de Campos
Master's Program in Mathematical Modeling, Regional University of Northwestern Rio Grande do Sul State (UNIJUI)
Brazil

1. Introduction

This chapter presents solutions for computing bounded-distance multi-coverage backbones in wireless networks. The solutions are based on the (k,r)-CDS problem from graph theory for computing backbones in which any regular node is covered by at least k backbone members within distance r, offering a variable degree of redundancy and reliability.

Advances in lower power-consumption processors, sensor devices, embedded systems and wireless communication have made possible the development and deployment of Wireless Sensor Networks (WSN).Such networks have been used, for instance, in safety and military applications for the purpose of monitoring and tracking geographic boundaries. In industrial applications, WSN may be used for automating manufacturing processes, for monitoring building structures, and in environmental systems for monitoring forests, oceans and precision farming Akyildiz, Su, Sankarasubramaniam & Cayirci (2002).

A WSN is usually composed by a large number of small nodes, called *sensor nodes*, each one having a processing unit, a radio transceiver and an antenna for wireless communication, one or more sensor units (e.g., temperature, movement), and a power unit usually equipped with a low capacity battery. Due to its limited power resources, and because batteries cannot be easily replaced, nodes are built out from power saving components.

To save energy,both approaches apply the partial or total turn-off of some node units. The rule of thumb is to keep active only those units (or components) necessary for performing the sensor network tasks. However, it is not an easy task to decide which nodes should sleep and which should be active at any given time, because these decisions strongly depend on the application running on top of the network. It is also undesirable to keep nodes inactive for too long, because it can impact the network *Quality-of-Service* (QoS).

Topology control through the construction of backbones can offer better support for broadcasting and routing of data packets. The total or partial turn off of nodes not comprising the Backbone constitutes the main motivation for employing such structures in WSNs. Reduced power consumption, and longer network lifetime, are potential benefits when applying Backbones to a network of sensors, because only a subset of nodes need to be active at any time to support basic network services.

In contention based medium access protocols using a single channel, the number of collisions of packets increases as we increase the number of competing nodes. By reducing the total number of active nodes, backbones can potentially reduce the end-to-end delay among sensors and sinks, and possibly extend the network lifetime due to the reduced energy consumption. In addition to that, it might be possible to provide better Quality of Service (QoS) for WSNs.

The basic criteria of QoS in WSN (i.e., *area coverage*) can still be guaranteed by not totally turning off the sensor nodes. Given that the radio is the most expensive element in terms of energy consumption Margi et al. (2006), by just turning it off and leaving the other components active we can still manage to save on energy.

In Ad Hoc networks Alzoubi et al. (2002); Bao & Garcia-Luna-Aceves (2003a), and more recently in WSNs Dai & Wu (2005); Paruchuri et al. (2005), the computation of Backbones has been considered through the computation of some variant of Connected Dominating Set (CDS). A set of nodes in the network is considered a Dominating Set (DS) if all nodes in the network belong to this set or, otherwise, are adjacent (i.e., neighbors) to at least one DS node. A DS is said to form a CDS when the graph induced by the DS is connected (i.e., the DS induces a Backbone for the network).

The problem of computing a CDS of minimum cardinality for any arbitrary network topology, a Minimum CDS (MCDS), constitutes an NP-complete problem Garey & Johnson (1978a), and requires knowledge of the entire network topology. Distributed solutions for computing approximations to the MCDS problem have been proposed in the literature Chen & Liestman (2002); Das & Bharghavan (1997). Even though such solutions aim at reducing the total number of dominating nodes, it has been shown that in wireless networks there is a tradeoff between redundancy and reliability Basu & Redi (2004). Too much redundancy is not desirable, but too little may compromise the network connectivity. This is of special concern to WSNs, because nodes are more vulnerable to failures due to the environments in which they operate.

Dai e Wu Dai & Wu (2005) proposed a distributed solution for computing a k-connected k-dominating Backbone for wireless networks. Their approach combines multiple domination and the k-vertex connected property, which guarantees that a CDS remains vertex connected even when removing up to $k-1$ nodes from the backbone. The shortcomings of this approach have to do with the required high degree of redundancy in the network topology.

In this chapter we propose the first centralized and distributed solutions for computing *bounded-distance multi-coverage backbones* in WSNs. This means that any sensor node is covered by multiple backbone members within a bounded-distance. To guarantee these properties, the (k,r)-CDS mechanism is employed for computing the Backbone. The multiple domination parameter, k, defines the minimum number of backbone nodes covering any regular sensor node. The bounded-distance parameter, r, defines the maximum distance to k backbone nodes for any other sensor in the network. The centralized solution provides an approximation to the optimum solution, and it is used as a lower bound when evaluating the performance of the distributed solution. The distributed solution is source-based in the sense that usually the base-station (or sink) is the focus of attention in a WSN.

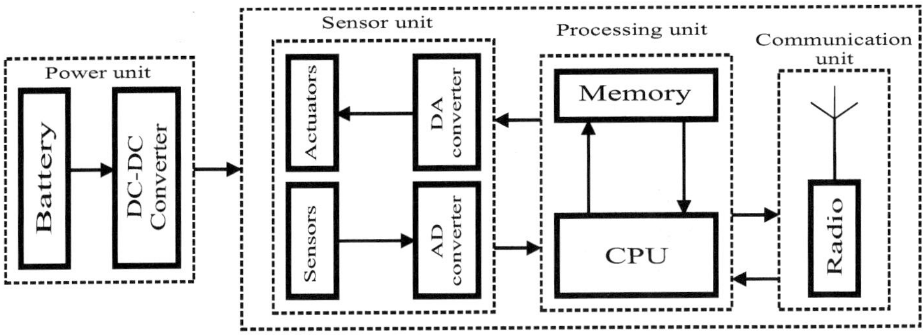

Fig. 1. Sensor node: basic structure

2. Wireless Sensor Networks

A Wireless Sensor Network may well contain hundreds or thousands of small autonomous elements called sensor nodes, and each sensor can feature a large variety of sensors (e.g., temperature, speed, acoustic, seismic). In many cases, nodes are randomly spread over remote areas, making it difficult to perform any maintenance to the nodes. Hence, a node remains live while it has enough battery capacity for its normal operation, and the network lifetime strongly depends on the remaining capacity of the nodes in the network.A sensor node has a few basic components (see Figure 1) Akyildiz, Su, Sankarasubramaniam & Cayirci (2002); Raghunathan et al. (2002) as follows:

- *Power Unit*, usually a battery, which acts as the power source for all node's components;
- *Sensor Unit* that contains a group of sensors and actuators;
- *Processing Unit* which includes a microprocessor or a micro-controller;
- *Communication Unit* which consists of a short range radio for wireless communication.

3. Domination in graph theory

An undirected graph $G = (V, E)$ consists of a set of vertices $V = \{n_1, \ldots n_k\}$, and a set of edges E (an edge is a set $\{n_i, n_j\}$, where $n_i, n_j \in V$ and $n_i \neq n_j$). A set $D \subseteq V$ of vertices in a graph G is called a *dominating set* (DS) if every vertex $n_i \in V$ is either an element of D or is adjacent to an element of D Haynes et al. (1998). If the graph induced by the nodes in D is connected, we have a *connected dominating set* (CDS). The problem of computing the minimum cardinality DS or CDS of any arbitrary graph is known to be NP-complete Garey & Johnson (1978b).

A variety of conditions may be imposed on the dominating set D in a graph $G = (V, E)$. Among them, there are *multiple domination*, and *distance domination* Haynes et al. (1998). *Multiple domination* requires that each vertex in $V - D$ be dominated by at least k vertices in D for a fixed positive integer k. The minimum cardinality of the dominating set D is called the *k-domination number* and is denoted by $\gamma_k(G)$. *Distance domination* requires that each vertex in $V - D$ be within distance r of at least one vertex in D for a fixed positive integer r. In this case, the minimum cardinality of the dominating set D is called the *distance-r domination number*, and is denoted by $\gamma_{\leq r}(G)$.

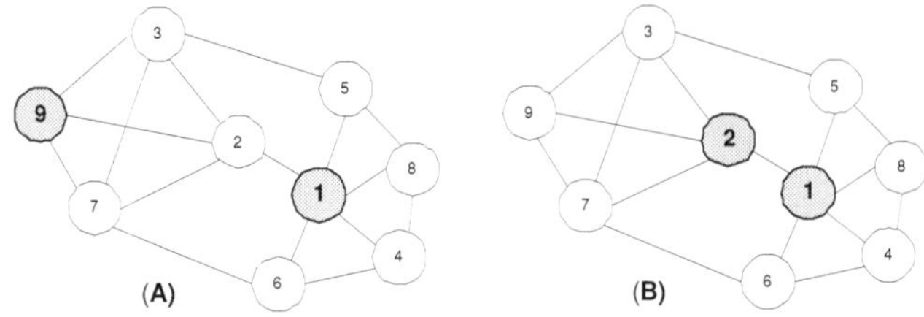

Fig. 2. *Dominating set* examples (gray nodes are *dominating*): (A) Dominating Set (DS); (B) Connected Dominating Set (CDS).

Henning et al. Henning et al. (1996) have presented some bounds on the *distance-r domination number* $\gamma_{\leq r}(G)$. They show that, for an integer $r \geq 1$, if graph G is a connected graph of order $n \geq r+1$, then $\gamma_{\leq r}(G) \leq \frac{n}{r+1}$. An algorithm that computes a *distance-r dominating set* within the established bounds is also presented.

The (k,r)-DS problem is defined Joshi et al. (1993) as the problem of selecting a minimum cardinality vertex set D of a graph $G = (V,E)$, such that every vertex u not in D is at a distance smaller than or equal to r from at least k vertices in D. The problem of computing a (k,r)-DS of minimum cardinality for arbitrary graphs is also NP-complete Joshi et al. (1993). Figure 2 (A) show example the Dominating Set and Figure 2 (B) show the Connect Dominating Set example.

Joshi et al. Joshi et al. (1993) have provided centralized solutions for solving the (k,r)-DS problem in *interval graphs* (IG). A graph G is said to be an interval graph if there is a one-to-one correspondence between a finite set of closed intervals of the real line and the vertex set V, and two vertices u and v are said to be connected if and only if their corresponding intervals have a nonempty intersection. Even though the solutions presented by Joshi et al. Joshi et al. (1993) are optimal, IGs are limited to very simple network topologies.

4. *Clustering* and topology control

In wireless sensor networks (WSN), nodes must coordinate among themselves because they cannot assume any fixed infrastructure (e.g., access points). Broadcasting of signaling messages is the underlying mechanism for coordination, and the broadcast can target a portion of the network (e.g., gathering neighborhood information), or the entire network (e.g., discovering routes on demand).

Coordination in WSN includes operations such as neighborhood discovery, organization of nodes (i.e., topology control and clustering), and routing. Examples of organization of nodes include the location of services, computing an efficient backbone for the broadcasting of signals, and routing of data packets.

Organization of nodes can be proactive or on demand. While operations to build such structures require broadcasting of signaling messages, these structures make broadcast operations scale to much larger portions of the network. That is, the hierarchical structure functions as a backbone, on top of which broadcasting can be performed more efficiently.

A virtual hierarchy is also possible. In this case, nodes are organized not depending on their physical location, but based on some other criteria. For example, the virtual topology could be comprised only by nodes speaking a given protocol. In this case, a virtual link exists between any pair of nodes whenever they are talking to each other using the specified protocol.

In some cases, the predefined hierarchical address of each node reflects its position within the hierarchy Tsuchiya (1988). In heterogeneous networks (i.e., networks composed of nodes with different capabilities in terms of energy, bandwidth, processing power, and transmission power), not only the physical location but also the resources of each node can be used as a criteria for deciding the role of each node within its sub-structure.

There are two broad categories of hierarchical architectures in ad hoc networks: *clustering* Chen et al. (2004), and *topology control based on hierarchies* Bao & Garcia-Luna-Aceves (2003b); Li (2003). These architectures can be employed to extend the network lifetime Bandyopadhyay & Coyle (2003); Chen et al. (2001); Younis & Fahmy (2004), achieve load balancing Bao & Garcia-Luna-Aceves (2003b), and to augment network scalability Heinzelman (2000); Li (2003).

With *clustering* Chen et al. (2004), the substructures that are condensed in higher levels are called *clusters*. For each cluster there is at least one node representing the cluster, and this node is usually called a *cluster-head*. Cluster-heads act as leaders in their clusters, providing some service to their members. As an example, a cluster-head could be an access point to the outside network, or it could be a *sink* for collecting information from a group of sensors (cluster members) in a wireless sensor network Akyildiz, Weilian, Sankarasubramaniam & Cayirci (2002).

Topology control and clustering are closely related problems. While the former defines a physically connected *backbone* of the network (i.e., the backbone nodes are connected, and they cover all nodes in the network), the latter constructs a *virtual backbone* (i.e., the set of cluster-heads do not necessarily compose a connected component of the network, even though they cover all nodes in the network).

Hierarchical structures are used for broadcasting, transmission of control messages, and routing data packets. The selection of nodes for the backbone will have a direct impact in the overall performance of the protocol. In most cases, dominating nodes are selected using some distributed dominating set algorithm, and if a backbone is desired, auxiliary nodes are selected to connect the dominating nodes.

5. Centralized (k, r)-CDS mechanism

In this section we shows the centralized soluction for computes a (k,r)-CDS for any connected networks. The network can be abstracted as a graph $G = (V, E)$ where the set V includes all nodes (i.e., vertices), and the set E includes all links (i.e., edges). The centralized solution for the (k, r)-CDS problem requires that the entire network topology be known. The centralized solution applies a *greedy* heuristic usually employed to optimization problems when there is the need for defining a group of candidates by optimizing the value of a given metric. The centralized mechanism guarantees that all nodes in the network, with the exception of those that comprise the Backbone, are covered by k members of the Backbone within distance r. It is assumed that all nodes have an unique identifier (i.e. ***id***) and they know the whole network topology.

While carrying out the algorithm, colors are ascribed to nodes to reflect their states during the selection process. To begin with, all nodes are colored **White**. A node is colored **Gray** when it becomes a candidate to the Backbone. Once a node joins the Backbone, the node is colored **Black**.The heuristic chosen for selecting nodes for the (k, r)-CDS is described as follows:

1. Initially, all nodes in the network are colored white.
2. The node with the largest r-hop neighborhood (i.e. $u \in V$ with maximum value for $|N_r^u|$) is colored black. Ties are broken lexicographically by considering the highest ***id***.
3. Next, all nodes adjacent (i.e. neighboring nodes) to the black node are colored gray.
4. The gray node with most white neighbors is then selected and colored black. Ties are broken by choosing the highest ***id***. This procedure continues until the conditions in item 6 are satisfied.
5. In the absence of any white nodes, the node with the most gray neighbors is considered as the next member of the Backbone.
6. The process comes to an end when all regular nodes have been covered by at least k members of the Backbone (black nodes) within distance r; i.e., when all nodes in the network, except those that are members of the Backbone, have met the (k,r)-CDS specification.

5.1 Example

Figure 3 shows the computation of a (2,2)-CDS for a particular network topology. Black nodes are members of the Backbone. For this configuration, nodes that do not belong to the Backbone are covered by at least two nodes of the Backbone at most two hops distant. Initially, all nodes are colored white, and have their degrees calculated (Figure 3(A)). For example, the node with id 3 displays the marking $(7, -, 0)$, which indicates that it has seven neighbors within two hops (i.e., $r = 2$), and it is not covered by any black nodes yet (indicated by the third parameter set to zero).

The node with the largest 2-hop neighborhood (i.e., $u \in V$ with maximum value of $|N_2^u|$) is colored Black (Figure 3(B)). At this point, there is a tie among nodes $0, 2$ and 5. In this case, the node with the largest ID (i.e., node 5) wins. Following that, the neighboring nodes to node 5 are colored gray, while its r-hop neighborhood is accounted for this new Backbone node (i.e., all nodes within distance 2 from node 5 are covered by this node).

Node 0 is the Gray node covering the most White neighbors (nodes 4 and 6), hence it is chosen for the Backbone and colored Black. Therefore, all its neighbors are colored Gray (Figure 3(C)). The remaining gray nodes hold only one White neighbor. Once node 0 has been selected, all its r-hop neighbors (i.e., nodes $2, 3, 4, 6, 7, 8, 9$) have their parameters updated to reflect coverage by node 0 (Black nodes do not need to be covered, for they are part of the Backbone).

The process goes on by selecting the Gray node that has the most White neighbors (Figure 3(D)), and in this case node 9 is selected for untying purpose. After this last selection, the Backbone is complete, and all network nodes are covered by at least two Black nodes within distance 2. The Backbone is then formed by nodes 0, 5, and 9.

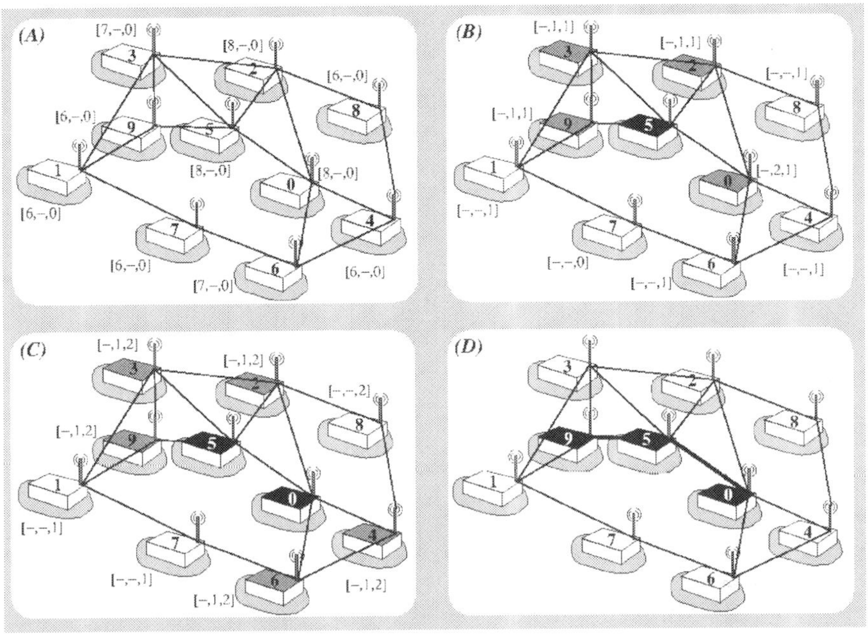

Fig. 3. Exemple (2,2)-CDS applying the centralized solution

5.2 Formal analysis

A WSN is modeled as a graph $G = (V, E)$, where V is the set of sensor nodes, and E is the set of wireless links. Each node in V is associated to its Euclidean coordinates. A link between any pair of nodes u and v exists (i.e., $(u, v) \in E$) if and only if the Euclidean distance between the pair of nodes is smaller than or equal to their transmission range (assumed to be the same for all nodes in V).

A set $V' \subseteq V$ forms a CDS for network G if all nodes in $V - V'$ are adjacent to least one node in V', and the sub-graph $G[V']$ induced by V' is connected.

Lemma 1. *Connectivity is preserved by augmenting a connected component with any node adjacent to the connected component.*

Proof. This can be proved by induction on the cardinality of the connected component. The base case is when the connected component is composed by just one node. Now consider a connected component with cardinality $n - 1$. A node adjacent to any node in the connected component augments its cardinality to n, and keeps the component connected because of the adjacency property. □

Theorem 1. *The centralized mechanism correctly computes a (k, r)-CDS Backbone for any arbitrary connected graph $G = (V, N)$.*

Proof. To account for node's coverage, k sets are used, $D_0, D_1, D_2, ..., D_k$, where D_i represents the nodes covered by at least i nodes from the Backbone within distance of r hops. Initially, all nodes of G are in D_0. The inclusion of a new member to the Backbone can promote one or more nodes from D_i to D_{i+1} for all $i < k$. The nodes elected for the Backbone are immediately inserted into D_k. The first Backbone node, b_0, is the node with the largest r-hop neighborhood in the graph. Whenever a tie occurs, the node with the largest identifier (i.e., **id**) is selected. In each iteration, a new backbone node, u, is selected among the neighboring nodes to the Backbone (i.e., N_B) such that the selected node has the largest number of uncovered neighbors (i.e., $\forall\ n \in N_B$ we have that u maximizes $\sum_{i=0}^{k-1} |D_i \cap N_1^n|$). The connectivity property is guaranteed by Lemma 1. The process ends when all nodes are covered, or all nodes belong to the Backbone (i.e., $D_k = V$). Assuming networks with a finite number of nodes, n (i.e., $n = |V|$), the number of iterations is at most n; therefore, the computation ends within a finite period of time. □

6. Distributed (k, r)-CDS mechanism

Unlike the centralized solution, the distributed (k,r)-CDS solution does not require the information about the whole network topology. All nodes are required to know only their r-hop neighborhood. The (k,r)-CDS extends the (k,r)-DS mechanism Spohn & Garcia-Luna-Aceves (2006) proposed for ad hoc networks. The (k,r)-DS mechanism is used for the construction of bounded distance multi-clusterhead clusters (i.e., each regular cluster member is covered by several clusterheads within a bounded distance), but it does not connect the clusterheads among themselves (i.e., that is why it is a DS).

As for the centralized solution, the distributed mechanism computes a (k,r)-CDS of the network. However, the computation of the Backbone is accomplished distributively. In addition to that, to adhere to the characteristics of sensor networks, the construction of the Backbone stems from a particular node which could be the Base Station (BS) in the network.

We assume that any node in the network could be the BS. Moreover, there could be more than one BS. However, in this work we consider a single BS per network, which is randomly chosen among all nodes in the network. It is also assumed that each node has an unique identifier, and they have knowledge about their r-hop neighborhood. The mechanism is carried out in two phases as described as follows.

In phase 1 the BS initiates the process by sending an Information Message (IM) to their neighbors reporting the Distance to the Base Station, dBS, initially set to zero by the BS itself. On receiving this message, a node updates its distance to the BS and announces its dBS to its neighbors through a new IM message. If a node gets more than one notification message, any message announcing a shorter distance to the BS triggers a new IM message so that any neighbor can eventually learn about a shorter path to the BS. Considering that all transmissions are reliable, after a finite period of time, and possibly after many retransmissions, all nodes in the network learn their shortest distance to the BS.

The second objective of this phase consists of obtaining the r-hop neighborhood topology, which requires r rounds of messages exchange. In each round, the nodes broadcast information about their known neighbors, and their respective distances. After r rounds, all nodes come to know their neighbors within distance r. By piggybacking the information about each node's distance to the BS (i.e., their dBS), at the end of this phase nodes also learn the distance from each r-hop neighbor to the BS.

Phase 2 starts immediately after the completion of phase 1. It is during this phase that nodes elect k nodes from their r-hop neighborhood to become part of the Backbone. After that, the node announces its elected nodes throughout its r-hop neighborhood. The election is based on the information gathered during phase 1.

The BS node actually starts the election process by electing the k nodes closest to itself (i.e. those with the smaller dBS in the neighborhood). Any ties are broken choosing the node with the largest degree, and persisting the tie the node with the largest ID wins. The BS creates and transmits to all its neighbors a message called Election Message (EM) carrying a list called Backbone Members (BM) with the k elected nodes.

Upon receiving an EM message, a node performs - just once - the selection of its Backbone Members. The criteria are similar to those used by the BS with the restriction that only nodes belonging to the Backbone, or those adjacent to it (i.e. neighbors to Backbone members), can be elected. This restriction guarantees the Backbone connectivity property(i.e. the creation of a CDS), and it reduces the total number of Backbone members because nodes already in the Backbone are likely to cover multiple nodes in the neighborhood.

After a node elects its Backbone members, the BM list in the EM message is updated to reflect any changes to the list, and the message is then transmitted to its neighbors. In addition to that, a Notification Message (NM) is sent to all (if any) new elected nodes (i.e., nodes that were not listed in the original BM list). The election process continues until all nodes in the network have elected their Backbone members. At any stage, a node that has already carried out its election and receives another EM message will just discard it. [1]

6.1 Example

Figure 4 shows the computation of a (2,2)-CDS for a particular WSN. As previously, Black nodes represent Backbone members. Initially, node 0 is selected as the BS, and it is colored Black (Figure 4(A)). Given that $r = 2$, all nodes are familiar with their neighborhood up to 2 hops. The first field in the marking process (shown close to each node in the Figure) identifies the dBS value. The second field indicates whether a node belongs to the Backbone or it neighbors a Backbone member (value 1), otherwise it is set to value 0. The third field indicates the **Degree** of a node.

Using the information obtained during phase 1, the BS selects its two members for the Backbone (Figure 4(B)). Notice that the BS selects itself (because it is a Backbone member by default) and another node from its r-hop neighborhood. The list of elected nodes is transmitted to the BS neighbors through an EM message.

The first elected node embodies the BS itself since $dBS = 0$ and because it starts the whole process. Node 5 is the second elected node for it exhibits the largest id while node 2 ties in Degree and distance (i.e., dBS) with node 5. The election of nodes 0 and 5 reflects on the marking of nodes $2, 3, 4, 6$ and 9, demonstrating that they are either members or neighbors of

[1] To handle periodical elections, one could use an election identifier in the EM message to allow nodes to know when they should re-elect their Backbone members.

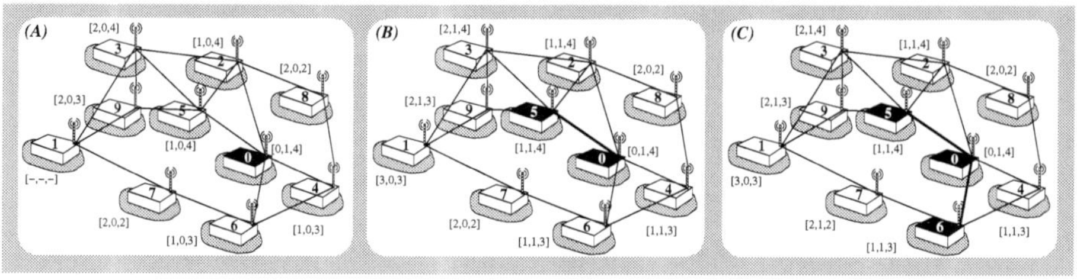

Fig. 4. Exemple (2,2)-CDS applying the distributed solution

a Backbone member. On the sequence, all BS neighbors perform their elections. All nodes with $dBS = 1$ (i.e. the nodes $2, 4, 5$ and 6) elect nodes 0 and 5 as members of the Backbone, triggering a new EM message to be sent to their neighbors.

For nodes two hop distant from the BS (i.e., $dBS = 2$), we have that nodes $3, 8$ and 9 elect nodes 0 and 5, and node 7 elects nodes 0 and 6 (Figure 4(C)). The marking of node 7 is updated demonstrating that this node is a neighbor of a Backbone member. Node 1 which has $dBS = 3$ receives the EM message and elects nodes 5 and 6 as members of the Backbone. This ends the election since all neighbors of node 1 (which is the node farther away from the BS) have already completed their election. The Backbone is then composed by nodes $0, 5$ and 6.

6.2 Formal analysis

To prove the correctness of the distributed (k,r)-CDS mechanism, we have to show that it is *safe* (i.e., the algorithm computes a (k,r)-CDS of the network), and that it is *live* (i.e., it completes within a finite period of time).

Lemma 2. *Phase one of the distributed solution has message complexity of $O(n \cdot r)$, where n is the number of nodes in the network and r is the distance parameter.*

Proof. During each round, nodes send messages to all their one-hop neighbors. Phase one takes r rounds. Assuming a network of n nodes, phase one requires $n \times r$ messages to complete. Therefore, the message complexity of phase one is of order $O(n \cdot r)$. □

Lemma 3. *After r rounds of successful transmission of message m, the message is propagated up to r hops away from the originating node.*

Proof. This can be proved by induction on the distance d from the node starting the process, n_0. The base case is when $d = 0$, meaning that the starting node itself knows the message it created to be propagated throughout the network. Now consider a node u at distance $r - 1$ from n_0. Once node u retransmits message m to all its one-hop neighbors, the message eventually reach any neighbor r hops from n_0. □

Theorem 2. *The distributed solution correctly computes a (k, r)-CDS Backbone for any connected graph $G = (V, E)$ during phase two.*

Proof. We assume that any node $i \in V$ knows its r-hop neighbors (i.e., N_r^i), as well as their distances to the base station i_0 (Lemma 3). The base station, i_0, is selected as the first backbone node. On its turn, node i_0 selects for the backbone the $k-1$ nodes closest to itself (i.e., first it tries to select among its neighbors within distance one, then, if necessary, within distance two, and so on until $k-1$ nodes are selected). The selected nodes repeat the process, taking as candidates to backbone members those nodes from their r-hop neighborhood which are closer to the base station, i_0, and also requiring that any candidate must be adjacent to or already a member of the backbone. The latter requirement, guarantees the connectivity of the Backbone (Lemma 1). After node i_0 has selected its $k-1$ backbone members, the base station announces the list of elected nodes to its neighbors, which in turn repeat the process by performing their own election. The election is carried out just once by all nodes in the network (duplicate announcements are just discarded). Considering that messages take a finite period of time to propagate throughout the network, the whole election takes a finite period of time to complete. Given that any node must elect k members among its r-hop neighborhood, and that any elected node must be adjacent to nodes already in the Backbone or members themselves, the connectivity and coverage properties are guaranteed. □

7. Performance analysis

The centralized and distributed (k,r)-CDS mechanisms are compared through extensive simulations using a customized simulator. Network topologies are created based on the ***unit disk graph*** model Clark et al. (1990). According to this model, any pair of nodes, A and B, are said to be connected if the Euclidean Distance between their coordinates is smaller or equal to R, the transmission range of any node. We assume $R = 15m$ for all nodes (i.e., a homogeneous networks). Nodes are randomly placed over the terrain, and only connected topologies are taken into account. For each configuration, we gather results for 30 trials.

Nodes	Diameter	Degree
200	11,7±0.7	11,8±0.6
400	10,9±0.4	24,2±0.7
600	10,6±0.5	36,6±0.8
800	10,3±0.5	49,0±0.9
1000	10,1±0.3	61,4±0.9

Table 1. Parameters for Scenarios 1

For the simulations we assume an ideal MAC protocol with no collisions, ensuring that all transmissions are successful. The same assumption is made in related work Spohn & Garcia-Luna-Aceves (2006); Wu & Dai (2003). All topologies evaluated in the simulations are assumed to be static (i.e., no mobility). Because there is no known optimum solution for the (k,r)-CDS problem, the proposed centralized solution is used as a lower bound when evaluating the performance of the distributed solution. The simulations encompass a series of experiments changing the distance parameters (i.e., r) and the coverage parameters (i.e., k). All experiments are repeated for 30 trials corresponding to different network topologies.

To gather representative statistical samples, two scenarios are considered. Table 1 presents the average standard values for the **Diameter** (i.e., the largest shortest distance between any pair

Nodes	Diameter	Degree
200	11,9±0.7	12,2±0.6
425	18,0±0.5	11,7±0.5
750	23,2±0.6	12,0±0.0
1185	29,4±0.7	12,0±0.0
1720	35,4±1.0	12,3±0.5

Table 2. Parameters for Scenarios 2

of nodes) and the **Degree** (i.e., average number of one-hop neighbors) over 100 samples for first scenario.

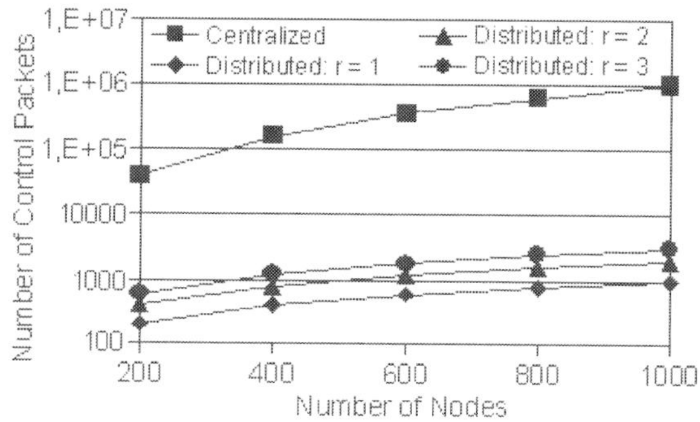

Fig. 5. Control message overhead

In the first scenario, the network diameter stays almost unchanged as the average degree increases with denser networks. As for the second scenario (see Table 2), the network density is kept the same by increasing the terrain size for larger networks. As a consequence, the average degree remains almost the same but the network diameter increases (i.e., the networks are sparser compared to the ones from the first scenario).

To compare the two proposed heuristics, two performance metrics are evaluated: ***control message overhead***, the total number of control messages exchanged for gathering topology information (centralized mechanism), or for the execution of the two phases in the distributed mechanism; ***total number of Backbone nodes***, the total number of nodes that each mechanism selects to form de Backbone.

Figure 5 shows the results for the message overhead regarding the first scenario. Results for the second scenario are omitted because they are similar to those from the first scenario. Considering a network composed of n nodes, the centralized mechanism incurs $O(n^2)$ messages exchange due to the topology dissemination process. In the distributed mechanism, the control overhead depends on the distance parameter r, because the nodes need to obtain information regarding the r-hop neighborhood. Given that all nodes participate in this process, it incurs a $O(n \cdot r)$ message complexity.

As expected, the centralized mechanism presents the best results for the first scenario (Figure 6). As the distance parameter r increases, the performance of the distributed

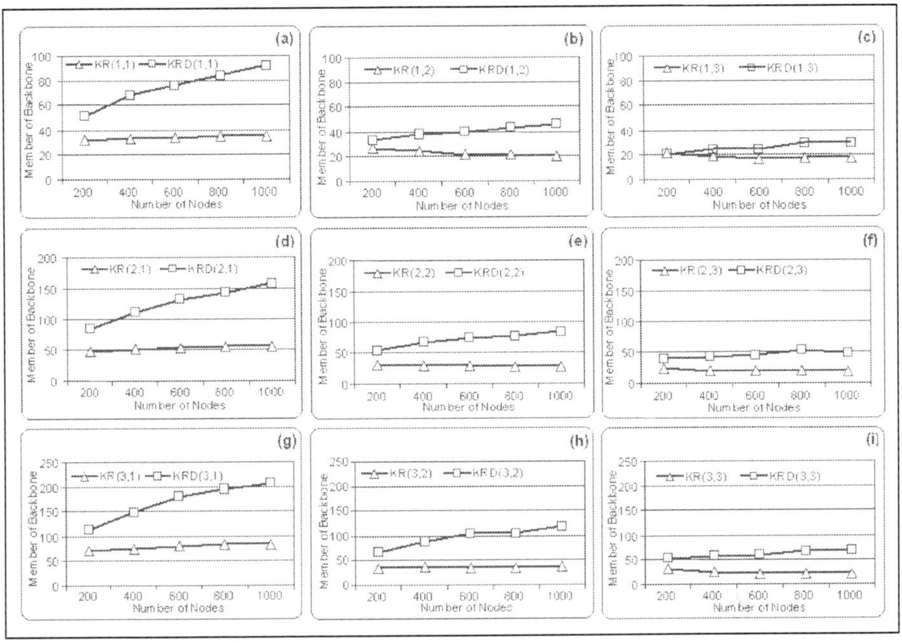

Fig. 6. (k,r)-CDS results for scenario 1

mechanism gets closer to the performance of the centralized mechanism (Figures 6(c), (f), and (i)). The best results are achieved for networks with 200 nodes (Figure 6(c)), when the centralized mechanism elects 20.8 nodes in average, whereas the distributed mechanism elects 21.4 nodes in average. The difference between the two approaches becomes more prominent for larger networks (e.g., networks with 1000 sensor nodes). As the network gets denser, the distributed mechanism elects more nodes. Because nodes elect k nodes among their r-hop neighborhood it is likely that more candidates satisfy the election requirement (i.e., nodes already in the backbone or adjacent to any backbone node), incurring on more redundancy when compared to sparser networks. For the future work we intend to apply some pruning mechanism to reduce redundant backbone members.

For the second scenario, we have chosen to keep node density steady while varying the network diameter. The simulation results (Figure 7) show an increase in the total number of Backbone nodes for both mechanisms. This is due to a better distribution of sensor nodes (i.e., sparser networks). As expected, the centralized mechanism presents better results for most experiments. However, the two heuristics compare to each other in the $(1,2)$-CDS and $(1,3)$-CDS configurations (Figure 7 (b) and (c)). As noticed in the first scenario, as the distance parameter r increases, the two approaches present similar results. On the other hand, the difference between the performance for both solutions reduces compared to the first scenario.

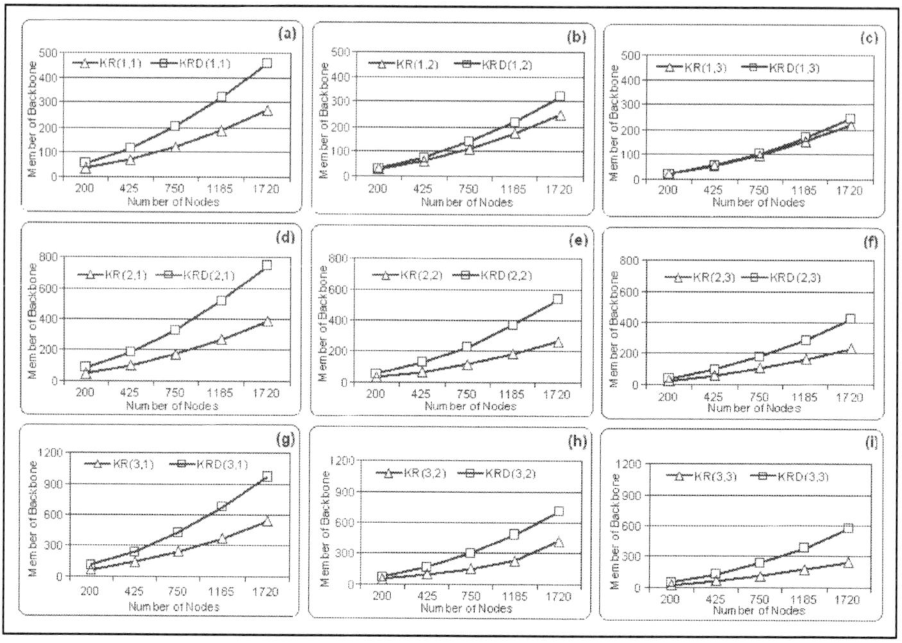

Fig. 7. (k,r)-CDS results for scenario 2

8. Conclusion

We presented the first centralized and distributed solutions for computing *Bounded-Distance Multi-Coverage Backbones* in Wireless Sensor Networks (WSNs). Backbones have the (k,r)-CDS properties, which include the minimum number, k, of nodes in the backbone covering any regular node, as well as a bounded-distance, r, to the covering nodes.

Given the characteristics of WSNs, redundancy is desirable. Therefore, any mechanism requiring redundancy (e.g., data gathering, routing) could take advantage of topologies with the (k,r)-CDS properties. By limiting the distance to the backbone, it could well translate to bounded-delays when accessing the backbone. In any situation, the solutions presented in this paper provide new basis for designing protocols for WSNs.

We compared the centralized and distributed mechanisms through extensive simulations using a customized simulator. Given that the centralized solution is unsuitable for WSNs, because of the incurred control overhead, it is used as a lower bound when evaluating the performance of the distributed solution. It is shown that even though the distributed solution builds larger backbones, it does not incur on much control overhead.

As future work, we are planning applying a pruning mechanism to the distributed solution during the election process. In face of that, one can expect Backbones of smaller cardinality compared to the original solution. We also plan to include other coverage metrics (e.g., area coverage) within the selection process, and load balancing for members of the backbone (i.e., nodes should alternate roles as backbone members in order to prolong the network lifetime).

9. References

Akyildiz, I. F., Weilian, S., Sankarasubramaniam, Y. & Cayirci, E. (2002). A survey on sensor networks, *IEEE Communications Magazine* 40(8): 102–114.

Akyildiz, I., Su, W., Sankarasubramaniam, Y. & Cayirci, E. (2002). A survey on sensor networks, *IEEE Communications Magazine* 40(8): 102–114.

Alzoubi, K. M., Wan, P.-J. & Frieder, O. (2002). Distributed heuristics for connected dominating sets in wireless ad hoc networks, *Journal of Communications and Networks* 4(1): 22–29.

Bandyopadhyay, S. & Coyle, E. (2003). An energy efficient hierarchical clustering algorithm for wireless sensor networks, *IEEE INFOCOM*, pp. 1713–1723.

Bao, L. & Garcia-Luna-Aceves, J. J. (2003a). Topology management in ad hoc networks, *MobiHoc*, ACM Press, New York, NY, USA, pp. 129–140.

Bao, L. & Garcia-Luna-Aceves, J. J. (2003b). Topology management in ad hoc networks, *MobiHoc '03: Proceedings of the 4th ACM international symposium on mobile ad hoc networking & computing*, ACM Press, pp. 129–140.

Basu, P. & Redi, J. (2004). Movement Control Algorithms for Realization of fault Tolerant Ad Hoc Robot Networks, *In IEEE Network* 18: 36–44.

Chen, B., Jamieson, K., Balakrishnan, H. & Morris, R. (2001). Span: An energy-efficient coordination algorithm for topology maintenance in ad hoc wireless networks, *MobiCom '01: Proceedings of the 7th annual international conference on mobile computing and networking*, ACM Press, pp. 85–96.

Chen, Y. P. & Liestman, A. L. (2002). Approximating minimum size weakly-connected dominating sets for clustering mobile ad hoc networks, *MobiHoc*, ACM Press, New York, NY, USA, pp. 165–172.

Chen, Y. P., Liestman, A. L. & Liu, J. (2004). *Ad Hoc and Sensor Networks*, Nova Science Publisher, chapter Clustering algorithms for ad hoc wireless networks.

Clark, B., Colbourn, C. & Johnson, D. (1990). Unit disk graphs, *Discrete Math* 86: 165–177.

Dai, F. & Wu, J. (2005). On constructing k-connected k-dominating set in wireless networks., *IPDPS*, IEEE Computer Society, Denver, CA, USA.

Das, B. & Bharghavan, V. (1997). Routing in Ad-Hoc Networks Using Minimum Connected Dominating Sets, *ICC* pp. 376–380.

Garey, M. & Johnson, D. (1978a). *Computers and Intractability: A Guide to NP-Completeness*, Freeman, San Francisco, California.

Garey, M. R. & Johnson, D. S. (1978b). *Computers and Intractability*, Freeman, San Francisco.

Haynes, T. W., Hedetniemi, S. T. & Slater, P. J. (eds) (1998). *Fundamentals of Domination in Graphs*, Marcel Dekker, Inc.

Heinzelman, W. (2000). *Application-Specific Protocol Architectures for Wireless Networks*, PhD thesis, Massachusetts Institute of Technology.

Henning, M. A., Oellermann, O. R. & Swart, H. C. (1996). The diversity of domination, *Discrete Mathematics* 161(1-3): 161–173.

Joshi, D., Radhakrishnan, S. & Narayanan, C. (1993). A fast algorithm for generalized network location problems, *Proceedings of the ACM/SIGAPP symposium on applied computing*, pp. 701–8.

Li, X.-Y. (2003). *Ad Hoc Networking*, IEEE Press, chapter Topology Control in Wireless Ad Hoc Networks.

Margi, C. B., Petkov, V., Obraczka, K. & Manduchi, R. (2006). Characterizing energy consumption in a visual sensor network testbed, *in Proceedings of the 2nd IEEE TridentCom* .

Paruchuri, V., Durresi, A., Durresi, M. & Barolli, L. (2005). Routing through backbone structures in sensor networks., *ICPADS*, Vol. 2, Fuduoka, Japani, pp. 397–401.

Raghunathan, V., Schurgers, C., Park, S. & Srivastava, M. B. (2002). Energy-aware wireless microsensor networks, *IEEE Signal Processing Magazine*, 19(2): 40–50.

Spohn, M. A. & Garcia-Luna-Aceves, J. J. (2006). Bounded-distance multi-clusterhead formation in wireless ad hoc networks, *Ad Hoc Networks (Elsevier)* . http://dx.doi.org/10.1016/j.adhoc.2006.01.005.

Tsuchiya, P. F. (1988). The landmark hierarchy: a new hierarchy for routing in very large networks, *SIGCOMM '88: Symposium proceedings on communications architectures and protocols*, ACM Press, pp. 35–42.

Wu, J. & Dai, F. (2003). Broadcasting in ad hoc networks based on self-pruning, *IEEE INFOCOM* pp. 2240–2250.

Younis, O. & Fahmy, S. (2004). Heed: A hybrid, energy-efficient, distributed clustering approach for ad hoc sensor networks, *Transactions on Mobile Computing* 3(4): 366–379.

23

A Dynamic Risk Management in Chemical Substances Warehouses by an Interaction Network Approach

Omar Gaci[1] and Hervé Mathieu[2]
[1]*ISEL, Le Havre University*
[2]*LITIS - ISEL, Le Havre University*
France

1. Introduction

Supply chain is a set of activities involving a group of commercial actors to create a product or a service to satisfy a customer demand. The actors are the ones who form the supply chain, they are suppliers, transporters, manufacturers, distributors, retailers, customers. The objective of every supply chain is to maximize total supply chain profitability.

The Supply Chain puts in interaction a set of entities to provide to the final client the right product (or service) at the right time. Raw material suppliers, manufacturers of parts and components, assemblers, original equipment manufacturers, distributors, retailers, and customers are the main interacting entities of supply chain (SC) systems (Forrester, 1961).

In this chapter, we model Supply Chain as Complex Adaptive System (CAS) (Holland, 1996). CAS postulates that the activities of the constituting entities contribute to a specific emergence which corresponds to a global behaviour. Thus, the system is composed by active and adaptive intelligent agents. Their behaviours, interactions and adaptations lead to the emergence of the system behaviour.

We propose to study activities of storages in a warehouse of chemical substances. Then, this warehouse is subject to restriction in business processes executed every day: operators must respect a segregation strategy which consists in avoiding any mixing of incompatible chemicals. To reproduce the actions of forklift operators, we propose a Multi-Agent System which is the support of CAS modelling. Then, during agent movements for handling pallets from their reception into their storage locations, we define a dynamic graph where the vertices represent agents in activities and edges measure the distance between agents. The study of this dynamic graph shows that the average mean distance remains weak meaning that agent are often close each other. From this observation, we deduce a strategy for a dynamic risk management that gives the priority to agents whose betweenness is superior to the other agents that handle pallets of incompatible chemicals.

This chapter is organised as follows. In section 2, we present the main features of a Complex Adaptive Supply Chain and notably the existing support to simulate such a Supply Chain through Multi-Agent System. In section 3, we describe the existing solutions to reproduce

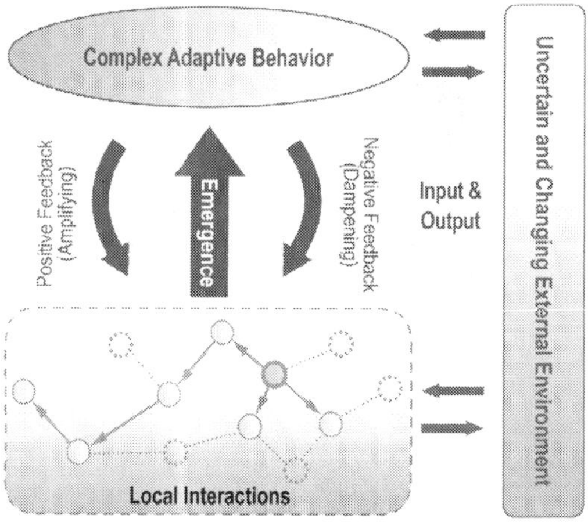

Fig. 1. Emergence from local interactions in Complex Adaptive Systems.

the activities of storages in a warehouse of chemical substances. In particular, we highlight the JADE framework for Multi-Agent simulations. In section 4, dangerous goods in logistics are studied and also the current regulation that warehouse must comply with. In section 5, we present our solution to reproduce the activities of storages in the studied warehouse by implementing a Multi-Agent system. In section 6, we study the dynamic graph resulting from agents handling actions and we deduce a dynamic risk management strategy.

This work is funded by German BMBF and French ANR as part of ReSCUeIT project.

2. Complex Adaptive Supply Chain

The theory of Complex Adaptive Systems (CASs) is presented by Holland (Holland, 1996) as a new paradigm to study the organizations and the dynamics of multi-scale systems whose evolution and adaptability leads to a global behaviour. A CAS can be considered as a multi-agent system with seven basic elements. According to Holland, the first four concepts are aggregation, nonlinearity, flow and diversity. They represent the characters of agents and influence the adaptability and the system evolution. The last three concepts, tagging, internal models and building blocks, are specific mechanics for agents to communicate with each other and also with the environment. The environment is itself subject to evolution notably because of the agent interactions which compete or cooperate from a same resource or for achieving a specific goal. As well, since the environment changes, the agents' behaviour evolve as consequence.

The main remarkable property which characterizes a CAS is the emergence of highly structured collective behaviour over time from the interactions of simple entities (Holland, 1996). The emergence of a complex adaptive behaviour from the local interactions of the agents is illustrated in Fig. 1. Then, the CAS and its environment evolve in the same time in order to maintain themselves in a state of quasi-equilibrium.

Considering a CAS consists in studying non-linear phenomena, non-exhaustive knowledge, a large state numbers and dynamic changes in environment. The main challenges when we reproduce a CAS are to produce a global behaviour by emergence under unpredictable conditions.

2.1 Complex Adaptive Systems as Multi-Agent Systems

In a Complex Adaptive System, CAS, a global behaviour emerges over time into a coherent form, adapting and organizing themselves without any singular entity controlling or managing the global structure or node interactions (Holland, 1996).

Complex Adaptive Systems are commonly implemented and simulated by Multi-Agent System, MAS, (Julka et al., 2002; Kwon et al., 2006; Swaminathan et al., 1997) which represents a general and flexible framework to describe and model autonomous systems including their interactions. An agent is basically a self-directed entity with its own goals and has a means to interact or to communicate with other agent.

2.1.1 Multi-Agent Systems

A MAS is formed by a network of computational agents that interact and typically communicate with each other.

The approach described by MAS consists in representing explicitly the individuals or the entities which compose the studied population. The system can then be ecological, social economic, etc. The goal is to produce a model for the entities, for the environment and for the mutual interactions. When the entities and their interactions are modelled, it remains to study the evolution of the relation through the simulation of their collective behaviour.

The understanding of the global MAS dynamic is viewed according to two levels, the microscopic (the study of the individual dynamics) and the macroscopic (the observation of the collective behaviour resulting of the entities interactions).

In (Conte, 1999), the authors propose two conceptual approaches deduced from the modelling of social phenomena:

- The top-down approach, which enables to deduce the microscopic phenomena, the goals or the individuals' motivations starting from the macroscopic observations;
- The bottom-up approach in which the hypothesis are established on the individual behaviours, their motivation or their way of interacting. The observation of their collective behavior is then compared to the macroscopic phenomena observed in the modelled system to eventually discuss the hypothesis formulated at a microscopic level (Epstein & Axtell, 1996). The bottom-up approach is specific to the most individual based models which propose such models to explain or characterize observed collective behaviours.

2.1.2 The agent properties

The agents considered in MAS are used in a broad variety of applications and are defined by the following way (Ferber, 1999):

The term 'agent' denotes a hardware or (more usually) software-based computer system, that has the following characteristics (Casterfranchi, 1995):

- *Autonomy*: an agent acts without any intervention from its environment and possesses rules to control its action and internal states;
- *Social ability*: an agent interacts and communicates with other agents using a specific agent-communication language;
- *Reactivity*: an agent perceives its environment and is able to answer to any solicitations;
- *Pro-activeness*: an agent is not only reactive to a stimulus from its environment, it is also able to exhibit goal-directed behaviour by taking the initiative.

2.1.3 The type of agents

Agents are defined by their capacities and according to these properties, different levels of complexity characterize agents. Such complexity depends on the task that agents have to carry out and on the environment surrounding them. In (Ferber, 1999), agents are classified according to their architectures:

- *Simple reflex agents*: These agents are basic because their actions depend on stimulus. Their act are then subject to specific conditions. The past is not considered and none memory influence the present reactions.
- *Model-based reflex agents*: These agents cannot perceive their whole environment but keep track of their environment they cannot currently observe. Then, they possesses an internal representation of their environment called 'model of the world' to evaluate the environment evolution and the impact of the agent's actions on this environment. These agents select their action according to condition-action rules. The conditions only depends on the model of the world, and not on the current perception of the environment.
- *Model-based, goal-based agents*: These agents have goals describing desirable situations to choose an action because the current state of the model of the world is not always enough to select an action efficiently. The model of the world represents a state from which the agents evaluate how the world would be after an action. The action is chosen in order to the agent goals are satisfied and the model of the world state is a parameter taken into account.

2.1.4 Applications of Multi-Agent Systems

MAS are commonly exploited to model and simulate one of the three followings types of applications:

- *MAS for studying complexity*. These studies regroup social models such as the segregation model of Schelling (Schelling, 1971) artificial life simulation with the Sugarscape (Epstein & Axtell, 1996) and Reynold's Boids models (Reynolds, 1971) and also logistics models (for example traffic simulations (Burmeister et al., 1997)). These models are built with simple reactive agents and a set of rules without any need of resource planning or coordination. The simulations are monitored relying on qualitative measures (emergent communities, emergent flocking, emergent behaviour) and/or quantitative (average generation, average agent movements, average awaiting time). These models are then studied as well from a top-down approach than with a bottom-up approach.
- *MAS for studying Distributed Intelligence*. These studies are relative to planning (Pollack & Ringuette, 1990) and particularly cognitive social interactions Doran (n.d.); Gilbert (2005); Sun (2001). The main goal is to reproduce human cognition through

cognitive agents (Sloman & Logan, 1999). These developed models use complex, situated and communicating agents to study the behaviour of cognitive formalism (Taatgen et al., n.d.; Wray & Jones, n.d.).

- *Application development with MAS*. Existing toolkits provide technical tools to develop software agents described in (Jennings et al., 1998). Software agents are then Semantic Web agents, Beliefs-Desires-Intention (BDI) agents in expert systems, or agents for network metamanagement. These toolkits include a development environment to implement MAS, it can be considered equivalent to a simulation engine.

Further, in this chapter, software agents are used and the JADE platform is used as framework for the development.

3. Multi-Agent System to study warehouse activities

The activities of modelling and simulating offer applications in scientific and industrial fields. These works improve the understanding and the reliability of design of various systems.

In the context of supply chain, the study of warehouse activities is motivated by the following goals:

- test by a software a virtual version of a warehouse before implementing and using the real system;
- collect information to support discussion with the customer;
- simulate the warehouse activities to improve business or security procedures;
- generate reproducible error situations.

In this chapter, we are interested in simulating storage activities in a warehouse of dangerous goods to evaluate the segregation policies efficiency and to propose a reliable risk management to maintain these segregation strategies.

3.1 Existing softwares in warehouse simulations

Over the years, different tools have been developed to help designers and users to model and simulate warehouse activities. Existing tools can be divided in three groups: GUI-based simulation softwares, framework libraries and specialized programming languages (Colla & Nastasi, 2010).

There is few simulation tools designed for the application of supply chain activities. Among them, we can cite the commercial tools eM-Plant. It can be used for visualization, planning and optimization of production and logistics. FlexSim (*Flexsim Simulation Software*, n.d.) is another commercial software which enables fast and easy modeling, clear visualization as well as reuseability of models.

The agent-based approach appears to be a powerful tool for the development of complex systems and is exploited in industrial applications (Weiming et al., 2000). This approach is used in many fields such as manufacturing, process control, telecommunication, air traffic control, transportation systems, information management, electronic commerce, etc.

Among the existing agent-based applications for the simulation of supply chain activities, we can cite Repast, SeSAm, NetLogo, SDML or AnyLogic.

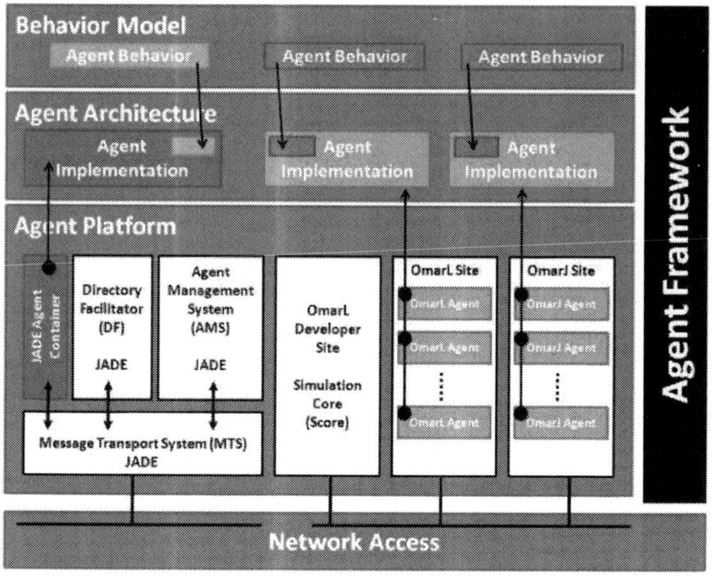

Fig. 2. Description of Agent Framework.

3.2 Existing frameworks for Multi-Agent warehouse simulations

It exists many different types of frameworks dedicated to the agent development. They are built from different theories and principles and allows then their classification. The definition of an agent framework is the following: an agent framework is a dedicated structure or platform to the development of software agents and based on a specific technical architecture.

An agent framework covers a set of missions relative to agents development, platform development, agent architecture and agent behaviour models as shown by Fig. 2. Then, an agent development platform is a structure which encompasses and support the entire life cycle of agents and provide in the same time a communication interface for agent interaction. This agent development platform commonly provides an API that defines the manner an agent communicate within the platform (Bellifemine, Caire, Trucco & Rimassa, 2007). As well, the agent architecture constitutes itself a framework for creating behaviour models. A behaviour model represents the architecture content and usually represents different forms of knowledge. The behaviour can be viewed as the result of the architecture and its content (Lehman et al., 2006).

The Java Agent Development Environment (JADE) is an agent platform used further in this chapter to implement a Multi-Agent System. JADE is a platform for the creation of MAS and contains a message transport system (MTS). This MTS, constitutes a network interface for developing distributed agent networks. As well, an Agent Management System (AMS) is available and allows the supervising of agent access control to the MTS and a directory facilitator (DF) for creating distributed services. In JADE, an agent is an instant that runs in the agent platform, then the agent has a determined life cycle by the AMS. Each agent is able to communicate with the other and possesses a queue for sending and receiving messages. An agent instance represents a container for the agent internal structure. The JADE agent platform is a middle-ware that complies with the specifications of the Foundation for Intelligent Physical Agents (FIPA) (Bellifemine, Caire, Trucco & Rimassa, 2007).

3.3 JADE platform for warehouse activities simulations

JADE is a software development framework fully implemented in JAVA language aiming at the development of multi-agent systems and applications that comply with FIPA standards for intelligent agents (Bellifemine, Caire & Greenwood, 2007). JADE is an agent framework and provides then a set of technical features to the development of MAS such as:

- *A distributed agent platform*. The platform can be easily shared and hosted in different machines when each machine possesses its own Java Virtual Machine;
- *FIPA-Compliant agent platform*. This means that the platform provides a set of functionalities such as Agent Management System, a Directory Facilitator and an Agent Communication Channel;
- *Communication with ACL messages*. The standard ACL ensures efficiently in the message transport between agents.

Communication of agents consists in sending and receiving messages, the FIPA ACL language is used to represent the messages. Each agent possesses an incoming message box and messages can be blocking or nonblocking during a determined blocking time. As well, JADE offers the possibility of filtering messages: it is possible to utilize advanced filters relative to different fields of the incoming message such as sender or ontology.

To build agent conversations, FIPA defines a set of standard interaction protocols such as FIPA-request and FIPA-query that can be exploited as standard for agent communication. When a conversation starts between two agents, JADE distinguishes two roles: the initiator who is the agent that starts the conversation and the responder who communicates with the previous one. This protocol architecture implies that the initiator sends a message and the responder can potentially reply by refusing the message indicating the incapability to continue with the conversation. The responder can also answer with a agreed message indicating that the communication between the two agents is established and can continue. After receiving a message, the responder performs potentially an action and must send back a message to describe such an action. In case that the action has failed, a failure message indicates that the action was not successful. JADE provides behaviour for initiator and responder roles according to FIPA interaction protocols. Then, the classes *AchieveREInitiator* and *Responder* provides homogeneous implementation of interaction protocols with methods for handling the different communication phases.

In JADE, agents actions or missions are implemented by the implementation of *behaviours*. These behaviours are defined as threads that can be composed or not, and allows agents to achieve their intentions. Such behaviours can be initialized, suspended and spawned at any given time. Then, the agents possess an action list that is executed through their behaviours. The JADE platform uses one thread per agent and not one thread per behaviour due to resource concerns (the number of running threads is limited). As well, a scheduler (unreachable for developers) organizes via a round-robin strategy the behaviours already created and instantiated in the queue. The coding of a behaviour offers the possibility of releasing the execution control when blocking mechanisms are used. The behaviours are executed in the method action().

The behaviour of agents is defined by a *Behaviour* class that can be specialized to defines a set of other behaviours. A behaviour is composed by several methods so that it is possible to describe the different state transitions. From this root behaviour, children behaviours can be deduced and notably the *SimpleBehaviour* and *CompositeBehaviour*. Behaviours that specialize or descend from *SimpleBehaviour* represent atomic simple tasks that can be executed several times according to the developer coding. As well, behaviours from *CompositeBehaviour*, are able to use multiple behaviours according to the children behaviours. Then, the agent tasks are executed not directly through the current behaviour but inside its children behaviours. For that purpose, the *FSMBehaviour* class executes the children behaviours. The *FSMBehaviour* class is able to maintain the transitions between states and to select the state coming after the current one. It is possible to register some of the children of an *FSMBehaviour* as final states. This type of behaviours terminates once one of its children has finished its execution.

4. Dangerous goods in logistics

A good is considered as dangerous when it may present a danger on the population, the environment or on the infrastructures according to its physicochemical properties or because of the reactions it can imply. A dangerous good can be flammable, toxic, explosive, corrosive or radioactive. According to the new CLP regulation, dangerous goods are considered as chemical substances in the European Union.

4.1 Dangerous goods identification

Considering the important number of substances, there is a clear need for dangerous goods classification. Amongst the existing classification of dangerous goods, the following distinctions exist:

- chemical family (acid, alcohol, amide, etc.);
- chemical reaction (oxidation, reduction, combustion).

We remark that the vocabulary becomes quickly specialized. To avoid this technical aspect, the dangerous goods are described in function of their reactions. Thus, the danger that represents the manipulation of dangerous goods depends on the properties of each product. Some goods represent only one risk whereas others regroup several.

The CLP (Classification, Labelling, Packaging) regulation is relative to the chemical substances imported or commercialized in the European Union. This regulation entered into force in January 2009 and will be totally applied in 2015.

4.1.1 Obligations under CLP

CLP provides a global obligation for all suppliers in the supply chain to cooperate. This cooperation is necessary to make the different suppliers meet the requirements for classification, labelling and packaging.

4.1.2 Terminology

A new terminology is used, terms of existing regulation are kept whereas news are adopted. The term substance is used to designed hazardous material and the transformation of these substances into a new one is called mixture.

As well, the properties of substances are described according to three properties: physicocochemical, toxicological and ecotoxicological. According to these three criterion, the definition of hazard classes helps to classify a substance. Then, a hazard class defines the nature of a hazard, it can be physical, on health or on the environment.

4.1.3 Classification of substances

CLP possesses specific criteria of classifications that are rules that allow associating a substance to a class of hazard or a category in this class. In particular, the classification process is based on the substance concentrations to establish the effects of those substances on the health and the environment.

CLP defines three hazard classes and 28 categories, such as:

- 16 categories for physical hazards;
- 10 categories for health hazards;
- 2 categories for environmental hazards.

For example, the physical hazards regroup explosives, flammable gases, solids, aerosols, liquids. The health hazards are relative to acute toxicity, skin corrosion, irritation and sensitization. The environmental hazards address hazardous to the aquatic environment and hazardous to the ozone layer.

4.1.4 Labelling

A substance contained in packaging should be labelled according to the CLP rules with the following information (called labelling elements):

- the name, address and telephone number of the supplier of the substance;
- the quantity of the substance in the packages;
- hazard pictograms;
- signal word;
- hazard statements;
- appropriate precautionary statements;
- supplemental information.

A substance contained in packaging is labelled according to the CLP rules and contains a set of information such as name of the supplier of the substance, quantity of the substance in the packages or hazard pictograms, see Fig. 3.

The CLP regulation helps then the identification of chemical substances through the supply chain since it provides a standard framework for the classification, the labelling and the packaging of substances.

Fig. 3. Pictograms used in CLP regulation.

4.2 Dangerous goods storage

Among dangerous goods, products can react violently when they are in contact. For these reasons, they must be stored in separate places. The strategy of storage consists in avoiding incompatible products to be neighbours. To avoid any storage of incompatible goods and risks of chemical reactions in case of wrong manipulation, segregation policies are established. Fig. 4, summarizes the incompatibilities between chemical substances.

Segregation policies in dangerous good warehouses consist in storing products according to their physicochemical properties. This strategy is static and doesn't take into account the possible movements of incompatible goods (by forklifts for example) that can be present in the same place at the same time.

The segregation can be achieved by the use of an impervious barrier or by a separation distance sufficient to prevent mixing. The segregation policies are also subject to constraint storages. According to the nature of goods, specific storage conditions must be respected. Among storage constraints, we can cite the most obvious such as storage conditions (humidity, heat and light). The respect of these constraints is ensured by safety equipments: sprinkler, smoke detector, particles detector or temperature probe.

Consequently, to make a warehouse of dangerous goods secured, different types of safety equipments are needed and a reliable segregation is used. In this chapter, we propose to simulate such a warehouse and to study the emergent collective behaviour of the MAS constituted by the warehouse actors.

Danger Code	F	F+	T	Xi	O	Xn	N	C
F	+	+	-	+	-	+	-	-
F+	+	+	-	+	-	+	-	-
T	-	-	+	+	-	+	-	-
Xi	+	+	+	+	-	+	+	-
O	-	-	-	-	+	-	-	-
Xn	+	+	+	+	-	+	-	-
N	-	-	-	+	-	-	+	-
C	-	-	-	-	-	-	-	+

Fig. 4. Identification of compatibilities between dangerous goods. The letter F means inflammable, F+ means very inflammable, T means toxic, Xi means very irritant, means O oxidizing, Xn means noxious, N means polluting and C means corrosive.

5. Simulation of warehouse activities by a Multi-Agent System implemented with JADE

Agent considered represent forklift drivers and the warehouse structure is then the agent environment. Fig. 5 shows the warehouse architecture which is composed of a forklift base, corridors, docks where pallets are temporally stored and five racks.

5.1 Forklift agent

Forklift agents are simple reactive agents that are positioned in their base and wait for a message from the central warehouse scheduler. This scheduler is actually a random generator which creates truck arrivals and sends messages to forklift driver agents so that they go to docks to unload the truck. Once the truck is completely unloaded, forklift driver agents continue their actions and store pallets in their rack position.

As shown by Fig. 6, agents react and communicate through messages. Firstly, agents are in their base and when they receive a message *GoToDock* they receive also the dock number and they consecutively move according to the *moveToDock(dockNum)* method. The agent motion follows warehouse corridors and this method provides to agents the set of corridors to use in order to reach the dock number *dockNum*. When the agents is in position, he confirms his position to the centralized scheduler and replies a message *atDock-DockNum*. This means that he is operational and the scheduler communicates with him to ask him to begin the unloading with an *Unload* message. If the scheduler has sent another message type, the agent would move back to the base. To unload the truck, the agent executes the *unloadTruck* method and confirms the end of handling operations with a message *EmptyT-dockNum*. Once more, the scheduler can choose to call back the agent to the base or to send him a message *Storage* so that the agent uses the method *storePalletsFrom(dockNum)*. This last method indicates to the

Fig. 5. Representation of the studied warehouse. Agents are located in their base and follow corridors to go to docks or racks.

agents the corridors to follow until the storage place in rack. When, the agent finishes the storage of pallets, he sends a message *StoredP-DockNum* and move back to his base.

The forklift driver agents evolve in a warehouse which represents their environment. They interact with a set of objects enumerated in the class diagram presented in Fig. 7. As shown, a forklift agent is a software agent defined according to an *ID* which is typically a number. His position is monitored in two dimensions and the current *Corridor* where he is evolving is given. As well, the *status* variable provides a means to know if the agent is in activity or if he is waiting in the base. In the class *Pallets*, the *hazardType* attribute gives the type of dangerous goods present on the pallet and it is the same for *Racks* that stores only restricted types of dangerous goods.

6. An interaction network approach for a dynamic risk management

The interaction network approach proposed in this section consists in monitoring in real-time the forklift agent movements and to detect a risk of incompatible chemicals mixing. To achieve such a goal, the warehouse is viewed as a dynamic graph where forklift agents who are active in the warehouse represent vertices that can be removed when they move back to their base. Edges link the vertices which represent agents and are weighted by the euclidean distance between agents in the warehouse. By this way, it is possible to consider a dynamic graph that puts in interaction forklift agents whose edges represent distance between them. The goal is then to detect the risk of incompatible chemicals mixing when the distance between agents is insufficient.

```
addBehaviour(new CyclicBehaviour(this) {
private static final long serialVersionUID = 1L;

public void action() {
int dockNum;
String msgType1, msgType2, msgType3;
ACLMessage msg1, msg2, msg3;
ACLMessage rep1, rep2, rep3;

// Waiting message from scheduler
msg1 = receive(MessageTemplate.MatchPerformative(ACLMessage.INFORM));
if (msg1 != null){
  msgType1 = msg1.getContent().substring(0,8);
  if (msgType1.equals("GoToDock")){

    dockNum = Integer.parseInt(""+msg1.getContent().substring(8,9));

    moveToDock(dockNum);     //move to dock
    rep1 = msg1.createReply();
    rep1.setContent("atDock"+dockNum);
    send(rep1);              // moved at dock

    msg2 = receive(MessageTemplate.MatchPerformative(ACLMessage.INFORM));
    if (msg2 != null){
      msgType2 = msg2.getContent().substring(0,8);
      if (msgType2.equals("Unload__")){

        unloadTruck(dockNum);    //unload pallets from a truck
        rep2 = msg2.createReply();
        rep2.setContent("EmptyT"+dockNum);
        send(rep2);              // pallets unloaded from the truck
        }

        msg3 = receive(MessageTemplate.MatchPerformative(ACLMessage.INFORM));
        if (msg3 != null){
          msgType3 = msg3.getContent().substring(0,8);
          if (msgType3.equals("Storage_")){

            storePalletsFrom(dockNum);// store pallets from a dock
            rep3 = msg3.createReply();
            rep3.setContent("StoredP_"+dockNum);
            send(rep3);              // pallets stored from the dock
          }
        }
      }
    }
goToBase();
}
```

Fig. 6. Behaviour of forklift agents. They react after receiving messages and confirm their action by replying.

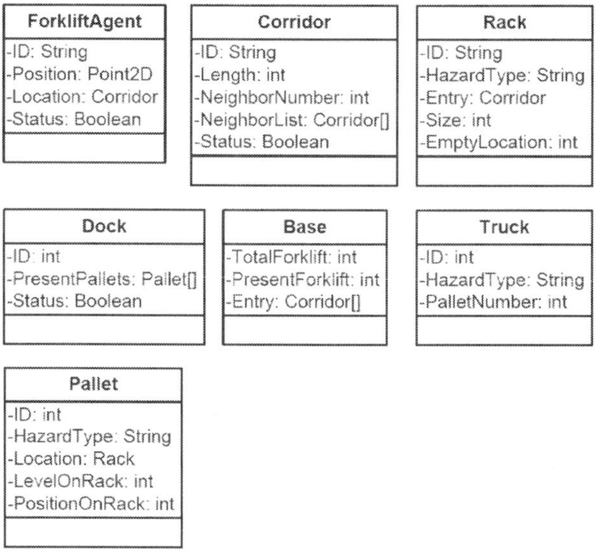

Fig. 7. Classes used to reproduce the activities of storage in a warehouse of chemical substances.

6.1 Dynamic graphs

Many systems, both natural and artificial, can be represented by networks, that is by sites or vertices bound by links. The study of these networks is interdisciplinary because they appear in scientific fields like physics, biology, computer science or information technology. The purpose of these studies is to explain how elements interact inside the network and what are the general laws which govern the observed network properties.

From physics and computer science to biology and the social sciences, researchers have found that a broad variety of systems can be represented as networks, and that there is much to be learned by studying these networks (Broder et al., 2000). Indeed, the study of the Web (Albert et al., 1999), of social networks (Wasserman & Faust, 1994) or of metabolic networks (Jeong et al., 2000) are contribute to put in light common non-trivial properties to these networks which have *a priori* nothing in common. The ambition is to understand how the large networks are structured, how they evolve and what are the phenomenon acting on their constitution and formation (Watts & Strogatz, 1998).

Nevertheless, to study the dynamic of a phenomenon through a graph, we need tools able to describe the graph topology evolution over time. The works relative to random graphs (Erdos & Rényi, 1959) provide a generic dynamic model which describe graphs whose edges are added according to a specific probability.

More recently, the interest for dynamic graphs has increased notably because of their potential application in communication, urban traffic or social sciences. The dynamic graphs allow studying the graph topology evolutions relying on dynamical metrics able to describe the graph properties when it evolves over time.

Now, we give some graph theory definitions to propose a definition of dynamic graphs.

A graph G is formally defined by $G = (V; E)$ where V is the finite set of vertices and E is the finite set of edges each being an unordered pair of distinct vertices.

Let f be a function defined on the vertex set as $f : V \rightarrow N$, then the triple $G = (V; E; f)$ is a node weighted graph. As well, let g be the function defined on the edge set as $f : E \rightarrow N$, the triple $G = (V; E; g)$ is an edge weighted graph.

In (Harary & Gupta, 1997), the authors classify the dynamic graphs as a function of the graph evolution:

- Node dynamic graphs, the vertex set V changes over time
- Edge dynamic graphs, the edge set E is modified over time
- Node weighted dynamic graphs, the f function evolves over time
- Edge weighted dynamic graphs, the g function varies over time

6.2 Graph metrics

Different graph measures allow characterizing graphs. Here, the proposed metrics provide measures for global description and also for individual vertices so that it is possible to identify the influence of a vertex in the modelled warehouse.

6.2.1 Distance and diameter

The distance in a graph $G = (V, E)$ between two vertices $u, v \in V$, denoted by $d(u, v)$, is the length of the shortest path connecting u and v.

A graph diameter, D, is the longest shortest path between any two vertices of a graph:

$$D = \max\{d(u,v) : u, v \in V\}$$

The mean distance is defined as the average distance between each couple of vertices:

$$L = \frac{2}{n(n-1)} \sum_{u,v \in V} d(u,v)$$

6.2.2 Mean degree

A degree of a vertex u, k_u, is the number of edges incident to u. The mean degree, z, of a graph G is defined as follows:

$$z = \frac{1}{n} \sum_{u \in V} k_u = \frac{2m}{n}$$

6.2.3 Node betweenness

The betweenness of a node is defined as the total number of shortest paths between pairs of nodes that pass through this node. It measures the influence of a node in a network. The betweenness of a node t, denoted $B(t)$ is defined as follows:

$$B(t) = \sum_{u \neq v, u \neq t, v \neq t} \frac{\sigma_{uv}(t)}{\sigma_{uv}}$$

where σ_{uv} is the number of shortest paths between the nodes u and v, and $\sigma_{uv}(t)$ is the number of shortest paths between u to v that pass through t.

6.3 Simulation and results

We assume that the warehouse is well dimensioned and at last one agent is available to perform a truck unloading or a pallet storage. Once a single or several agents react, they perform handling operations according to their behaviours. Then, agents are located in their forklift base and wait for a truck arrival. When a truck is in position, agents react and move into a dock. Another reaction is needed in order to agents unload the truck. The movements of agents follow the warehouse corridors. The time spent by agents to unload a truck or to store pallets is the average time observed in the real warehouse. The objective is to simulate a behaviour close to the reality.

In this case study, we consider that the warehouse stores three types of chemical substances denoted A, B and C. Each product must be stored only in its rack location and the segregation consists in avoiding that a product is stored in another rack. We consider 6 forklift agents and 10 trucks with a cargo of 33 pallets by truck. We launch a simulation and we study the dynamic graph resulting for agents activities.

Fig. 8 shows the evolution of the mean distance denoted l and the diameter, D. It appears that the means distance evolves between 30 and 150 which is the consequence of the warehouse dimensions. As well, the diameter being an upper bound of distances in interaction networks, we expect that the mean distance l will be lower than D. The mean degree is studied in Fig. 9 and shows that it evolves between 1 and 6. This means that at least two agents are in activities in the warehouse and when they are all outside their base, the mean degree will be 6.

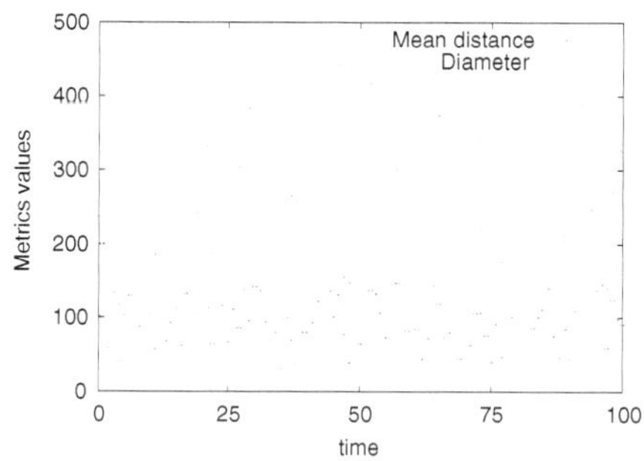

Fig. 8. Mean distance and diameter of the resulting graph from agent activities.

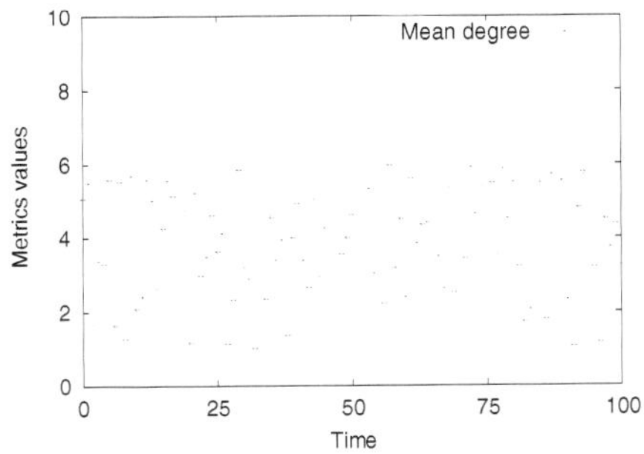

Fig. 9. Mean degree of the resulting graph from agent activities.

This first study about the dynamic graph resulting from agents handling operations put in evidence that they are not all present in same time in the warehouse. The average distance between agents is still weak in front of the upper bond expressed by the diameter.

Our goal is to develop a dynamic risk management strategy to maintain a segregation during the agent movements. In front of results presented above, we deduce a strategy presented in Algorithm 1. Then, when two agents are present in the same corridor, the type of handled goods determines if these forklift agents can share this corridor. In case that incompatible products are transported by agents, a topological measure is exploited, typically the node betweenness, to determine the priority between these agents. We consider that the agent

Algorithm 1: Algorithm to maintain a dynamic segregation between agents

Input:
F_a: set of forklift agents
Data:
$f_a, f_a^{'}$: forklift agent
$B(f_a)$: betweenness of the current agent
$HazType(f_a)$: hazard type of chemicals handled by the current agent
$Corr(f_a)$: corridor length of the current agent
$reorienteAgent(f_a)$: current agent is reoriented into another corridor

```
begin
    foreach f_a ∈ F_a do
        foreach f'_a ∈ F_a do
            if dist(f_a, f'_a) < Corr(f_a) then
                if HazType(f_a)andHazType(f'_a) are incompatible then
                    if B(f_a) > B(f'_a) then
                        reorienteAgent(f'_a)
                    else
                        reorienteAgent(f_a)
```

whose betweenness is superior, has the priority and the other agent is reoriented into another corridor. If the next corridor is in the same configuration, the agent will change again until be in presence of incompatible chemicals. Therefore, the dynamic risk management strategy is defined as a prevention of incompatible chemicals crossing in corridors. Any risks of crossing or mixing is mitigated by the routing of agents into another corridor when this agent possesses a weaker betweenness that the other one.

7. Conclusion

In the global context of logistics and supply chain management, we are interested in the manner to model the SC. A Complex Adaptive Model, CAS, approach is then well studied for modelling supply chain systems considering the structural and behavioural dynamics. In a CAS, the interactions of the agent population and the environment evolution contribute to the emergence of a global behaviour.

This chapter presents an approach to study warehouse of chemical substances involving human actors. We have modelled the activities and the actors to implement a Multi-Agent System, MAS from which we want to reproduce segregation violation during the goods movements. Then, the warehouse becomes a CAS where agents accomplish their goals (typically handling operations) and whose mutual interactions are susceptible to violate segregations.

We propose a dynamic graph to describe the agents movements in the warehouse. Then, vertices represent agents when they are in activities and removed once they move back t their base. Edges are defined between vertices and are weighted by the distance between agents. The study of this graph by topological measures such as the average distance, the diameter and the mean degree show that agents are effectively close each other during their handling operations. We deduce a dynamic risk management to maintain segregation even when chemical substances are handled by agents. Thus, when the distance between incompatible goods is insufficient, a study of the two involved agents node betweenness determine what agent is redirected into another corridor. By this way the crossing and the mixing of incompatible goods is mitigated.

8. References

Albert, S., Jeong, H. & Barabasi, A.-L. (1999). The diameter of the world-wide web, *Nature* Vol. 401(No. 4): 130–131.

Bellifemine, F., Caire, G., Trucco, T. & Rimassa, G. (2007). Jade programmer's guide.

Bellifemine, F. L., Caire, G. & Greenwood, D. (2007). *Developing Multi-Agent Systems with JADE*, Wiley, MA, USA.

Broder, A., Kumar, R., Maghoul, F., Raghavan, P., Rajagopalan, S., Stata, R., Tomkins, A. & Wiener, J. (2000). Graph structure in the web, *Computer Networks* Vol. 33(No. 1): 309–320.

Burmeister, B., Haddadi, A. & Matylis, G. (1997). Application of multi-agent systems in traffic and transportation, *IEE Proceedings of Software Engineering*, IEEE Computer Society, London, pp. 51–60.

Casterfranchi, C. (1995). Guarantees for autonomy in cognitive agent architecture, *in* M. Wooldridge & N. R. Jennings (eds), *Lecture Notes in Computer Science: Intelligent Agents*, Springer-Verlag, Heidelberg, Germany, pp. 56–70.

Colla, V. & Nastasi, G. (2010). Modelling and simulation of an automated warehouse for the comparison of storage strategies, *in* G. Romero Rey & L. Martinez Muneta (eds), *Modelling Simulation and Optimization*, InTech, Rijeka, Croatia, pp. 471–486.

Conte, R. (1999). Social intelligence among autonomous agents, *Computational & Mathematical Organization Theory* Vol. 5(No. 3): 203–228.

Doran, J. (n.d.). Can agent-based modelling really be useful?, *in* N. J. Saam & B. Schmidt (eds), *Cooperative Agents: Applications in the Social Sciences*, Springer, pp. 57–81.

Epstein, J. & Axtell, R. (1996). *Growing Artificial Societies, Social Science from the bottom up*, Cambridge MA MIT press, MA, USA.

Erdos, P. & Rényi, A. (1959). On random graphs I, *Publicationes Mathematicae* Vol. 6(No. 1): 290–297.

Ferber, J. (1999). *Multi-Agent System: An Introduction to Distributed Artificial Intelligence*, Harlow: Addison Wesley Longman, MA, USA.

Flexsim Simulation Software (n.d.).
URL: *http://http://www.flexsim.com/*

Forrester, J. W. (1961). *Industrial Dynamics*, Cambridge MA MIT press, MA, USA.

Gilbert, N. (2005). When does social simulation need cognitive models, *in* R. Sun (ed.), *Cognition and multi-agent interaction: From cognitive modeling to social simulation*, Cambridge University Press, Cambridge, UK, pp. 428–432.

Harary, F. & Gupta, G. (1997). Dynamic graph models, *Mathematical and Computer Modelling* Vol. 25(No. 7): 79–87.

Holland, J. H. (1996). *Hidden order: how adaptation builds complexity*, Reading, MA, Addison Wesley, MA, USA.

Jennings, N. R., Sycara, K. & Wooldridge, M. (1998). A roadmap of agent research and development, *Autonomous Agents and Multi-Agent Systems* Vol. 1(No. 1): 7–38.

Jeong, H., Tombor, B., Albert, R., Oltvai, Z. N. & Barabasi, A.-L. (2000). The large-scale organization of metabolic networks, *Nature* Vol. 6804(No. 407): 651–654.

Julka, N., Karimi, I. & Srinivasan, R. (2002). Agent-based refinery supply chain management, *Computer Aided Chemical Engineering* Vol. 26(No. 12): 1771–1781.

Kwon, O., Im, G. P. & Lee, K. C. (2006). Mace-scm: A multi-agent and case-based reasoning collaboration mechanism for supply chain management under supply and demand uncertainties, *Expert Systems with Applications* Vol. 33(No. 3): 690–705.

Lehman, J. F., Laird, J. & Rosenbloom, P. (2006). A gentel introduction to soar, an architecture for human cognition.

Pollack, M. E. & Ringuette, M. (1990). Introducing the tileworld: Experimentally evaluating agent architectures, *Proceedings the Eighth National Conference on Artificial Intelligence*, AAAI Press, Boston, MA, USA, pp. 183–189.

Reynolds, C. W. (1971). Flocks, herds and schools: A distributed behavioural model, *Computer Graphics* Vol. 21(No. 4): 25–34.

Schelling, T. (1971). Dynamic models of segregation, *Journal of Mathematical Sociology* Vol. 1(No. 2): 143–186.

Sloman, A. & Logan, B. (1999). Building cognitively rich agents using the sim agent toolkit, *Communications of the Association of Computing Machinery* Vol. 42(No. 3): 71–77.

Sun, R. (2001). Cognitive science meets multi-agent systems: A prolegomenon, *Philosophical Psychology* Vol. 14(No. 1): 5–28.

Swaminathan, J. M., Smith, S. F. & Sadeh, N. M. (1997). Modeling supply chain dynamics: A multi-agent approach, *Decision Sciences* Vol. 29(No. 3): 607–632.

Taatgen, N., Lebiere, C. & Anderson, J. (n.d.). Modeling paradigms in act-r, *in* R. Sun (ed.), *Cognition and Multi-Agent Interaction: From Cognitive Modelling to Social Simulation*, Cambridge University Press, pp. 29–52.

Wasserman, S. & Faust, K. (1994). *Social network analysis: methods and applications*, Cambridge University Press, Cambridge, UK.

Watts, D. J. & Strogatz, S. H. (1998). Collective dynamics of 'small-world' networks, *Nature* Vol. 393(No. 6684): 440–442.

Weiming, S., Qi, H., Hyun, J. Y. & Douglas, H. N. (2000). Applications of agent-based systems in intelligent manufacturing: An updated review, *Advanced Engineering Informatics* Vol. 20(No. 4): 415–431.

Wray, R. E. & Jones, R. M. (n.d.). An introduction to soar as an agent architecture, *in* R. Sun (ed.), *Cognition and Multi-Agent Interaction: From Cognitive Modelling to Social Simulation*, Cambridge University Press, pp. 53–78.

24

Study of Changes in the Production Process Based in Graph Theory

Ewa Grandys
Academy of Management in Łódź
Poland

1. Introduction

New areas of knowledge can only be created based on earlier scientific output. To identify possible cognitive gaps, the existing knowledge of management was analysed, which allowed dividing the knowledge hierarchically into three levels of organizational management, enterprise management and production management. The lowest position of the last level in the hierarchy does not make it is less important, especially in the present economic situation of the world that struggles with the impacts of the global crisis.

Graph theory is a field of knowledge offering a broad range of applications. A novel approach was using the theory to build a production management model based on the concept of an inverted tree (with many entries and one exit), as this type of a model reflects the real-life determinants affecting the production of short life cycle goods. The conducted investigation involved clothing companies that produce such goods. Clothing manufacturers deciding to start production invariably expose themselves to considerable risk. This risk can be reduced by obtaining more information on customers' expectations, fashion trends, the conditions of acquiring materials necessary for making the designed models, as well as manufacturer's technical and technological capacity for actually producing the garment. One assumption as made during the investigation was that the analysed product would not be a single design, but a series of garments comprising a fashion collection [6]. It was also necessary to assume a process-based approach to production management that in the opinion of many authors boosts enterprise effectiveness [5, 7]. With these assumptions in mind, the production process was broken down into four main subprocesses (product creation, setting up product manufacturing, manufacturing and sale) and their subdivisions. The presented production management model is based on this breakdown.

According to the research, apparel as a category of the short life-cycle goods is made in a production process (consisting of product creation, the setting up of the manufacturing processes, procurement of intermediate materials and sale) that spans 18 months [6]. In this relatively long time, the actual production circumstances and those predicted at the planning stage are very likely to show significant differences. Why the changes appear will not be explored in the article to keep it concise, but their occurrence will be assumed *a priori* as a fact. This study was designed to investigate the negative effects of the changes delaying the completion of a production process.

It must be remembered that the production cycle for the short life-cycle goods has a pre-determined date when the sale should start. The fact that the delays observed during the research usually resulted from management errors committed for a lack of an appropriate tool aiding production management helped identify a cognitive gap, following which a method for analysing process changes was developed. The method was called a Production Process Control Tree (PPCT).

2. The production cycle model for short life cycle models

2.1 Short life cycle products

The investigation concentrated on production management that in the theory of management deals with providing scientific solutions to production problems. Concentrating on processes „and not on jobs, people, structures and functions makes it possible to watch the main purpose of the process and not its components" [11]. The process-based approach was adopted to create a production cycle model for short life cycle products (SLCP). The term "life cycle" has been „derived from natural sciences, after an analogy between living organisms and products was found. They are too destined to be born, mature, age and die" [1]. The popularity of the term increased with the European Commission's project of 2005 *„The European Platform on Life Cycle Assessment (LCA)"* [25], which extended the notion of life cycle over business and politics. These circumstances increasingly justify the search for regular patterns (cycles, loops, or equilibrium points) that systems tend to [16]. The role of product life cycle was also commented on by P.F. Drucker [3], who stated that it could be used as a tool for evaluating firm's position. Further, R. Kleine-Doepke [12] mentioned life cycle together with the experience curve concept and the results of research conducted under the PIMS (*Profit Impact of Market Strategy*) program, as the third of the factors that contributed to the development of the portfolio planning methods. All these circumstances provided an inspiration for focusing the study on the management of production of the short life cycle products. Such products have one of the below characteristics:

- the length of the selling period depends on product design, and fashion shows cyclical changes,
- the end of the production period is determined by objective constraints on sales (e.g. alternating seasons in the case of clothing),
- the length of production cycle is incommensurate with the selling period.

Typical products whose life cycle is decided by their design are clothing and footwear. Their selling time is correlated with the passing of seasons that together with the seasonal character of fashion trends subject production management to strict discipline. Products manufactured for too long become unsaleable. The manufacturers of durable goods use the positive aspect of fashion to stimulate demand (motor vehicles, interior design articles, etc.).

2.2 Formulation of the research hypothesis

According to M. Marchesnay [19], a theory is constructed via a process consisting of the following stages: formulation of a hypothesis, construction of a hypothesis confirmation procedure, confirmation by means of an empirical test or mathematical-logical evidence, assessment of the confirmation success rate, formulation of conclusions (theoretical/practical). This sequence is criticised by persons advocating the phenomenological approach who believe that understanding the examined phenomena is more important than measuring them. This approach is justified in the case of a heuristic research and scientific procedure. However, M. Marchesnay's procedures are appropriate when the researcher's reasoning is linear. With these reservations in mind, the following hypothesis was formulated:

The management of production of the short life cycle products is a process of determined duration, consisting of four cyclical subprocesses. The cycles are staggered with respect to each other by fixed time intervals.

For the hypothesis to be confirmed an appropriate investigation had to be conducted and its results analysed. The management science proposes in this case a three-stage model of analysis comprising decomposition (into the building blocks), description and integration [23]. The presented algorithm was used at the further stages of the investigation.

2.3 Process decomposition and a description of its components

The process applied to produce garments was divided into four main sub-processes: product development, preparation of production, production and sales. As far as the short life cycle products are concerned, separating product development from all other actions related to the production preparation process is justified. An example of the SLCP is fashion articles whose production is determined by seasonality of sales. Two fashion collections are usually created, i.e. for the spring-summer and autumn-winter seasons.

2.3.1 The garment development subprocess

This subprocess is carried out between 1 February (of the year preceding product release) and 1 August for the spring-summer collection and between 1 August and 1 February of the next year for the autumn-winter collection.

New product designs are created based on the external and internal sources of information. The latter usually account for more than 55% [15]. This rate, however, does not apply to fashion articles. Their originality is assessed by means of criteria laid out in the copyrights. For a season's collection to be created, information has to be collected from several sources:

- design guidelines formulated by fashion creators,
- data provided by a survey of a market segment targeted by the enterprise,
- information about the relevant garment constructions and manufacturing technologies that will be used subject to the availability of appropriate equipment.

A talented designer and the person's ability to assimilate the design guidelines, whose new informative contents alter the knowledge of the trends in fashion development, are a prerequisite for starting the work on a collection. The relevant guidelines can be sought in Paris, Milan, etc., at international fashion shows. As observed, some fashion elements are recurrent; yet, they are never copied, but introduced after some modifications. This justifies the statement that all models of a season's collection are new. Products that are attractive for the buyers (because of their design, quality and price) involve interaction with the customers. Data offered by market surveys are an important source of information, allowing the manufacturer to look at a product from a broader perspective [18]. However, a design that is attractive but priced against the expectations of the targeted market segment will render sales unsuccessful. The responsibility for setting prices rests on an authorised group of persons who take account of the design manufacturing data (material and labour costs, etc.). Design attractiveness is the main criterion affecting the level of prices. A market failure is certain when the season's collection is released too late. This fact demonstrates the importance of the time factor for the production cycle of seasonal products.

2.3.2 The production preparation subprocess

This subprocess is carried out between 1 June and 1 December for the spring-summer collection and between 1 December and 1 June of the next year for the autumn-winter collection.

The production preparation subprocess consists of:

- preparation of the technical and technological documentation,
- procurement of the necessary materials,
- planning and organizing the product manufacturing subprocess.

From the standpoint of the operations to be carried out within the production preparation subprocess, it is not important whether the team of workers responsible for the subprocess will be based in their parent company or at the service provider's site [9]. The technology to be used must correspond to the selected materials and the available machines (either owned or belonging to other party). Modern enterprises prepare the necessary documentation using Computer Aided Manufacturing systems (CAD) that are common in the Polish medium and large-sized manufacturing companies today. The author pioneered the implementation of the first of such systems in Poland in 1987. Other activities related to the preparation of documentation include:

- sequencing the technological operations,
- selecting the machines and pieces of equipment necessary to perform the operations,
- calculating the times necessary to complete each operation.

These documents allow setting up the product manufacturing subprocess, estimating the wages to be paid to the piece-rate workers, the direct production costs, etc.

Material procurement, which is a separate activity, is equally important. The domestic clothing industry buys its materials from suppliers based in the EU (the high end of the apparel market) and in Asian countries (the other segments). The geography of the suppliers usually has a bearing on fabric quality, wearability and price, the latter being a key factor shaping the final price of a product. Fabric patterns are picked by the designers who take into account the designs to be produced, while the procurement personnel is responsible for analysing the submitted offers and making choices that are optimal for the firm. All procurement, although the contract signing process is exposed to the pressure of time, must be carried out prudently. The type of payment (advance payment, pay on delivery, deferred payment) is an important aspect of negotiations concerning the terms of supply. Optimization of the procurement process is vital for enterprise functioning.

The organizational setup of the product manufacturing process must integrate the following areas:

- human (the necessary number of workers with the required skills and available at the right time and place),
- technical (the availability of the machines and equipment),
- material (the optimal quantity of materials stored in the working areas and available when needed).

The above areas decide about the type of the manufacturing system that will be used: an assembly line, an assembly line with sections, sections with synchronised working teams, a flow system or an arrhythmic system [27]. Other factors that influence the production preparation process include the size of an order, the possibility of making several models simultaneously, etc. The organizational efforts must optimize manufacturing times and costs, as well as providing a product of expected quality (in relation to manufacturers' expenses and target buyers' preferences).

2.3.3 The product manufacturing subprocess

This subprocess is carried out between 1 August and 1 February of the next year for the spring-summer collection and between 1 February and 1 August for the autumn-winter collection.

A characteristic feature of garment production is the input of manual labour. In the developed countries, small series of garments containing particular large inputs of manual labour are produced for the high-end market segments. Regardless of the target buyer, garment production consists of two main stages: cutting out garment elements and their assembly. The operations performed at the two stages depend on the organizational plan and technological documentation prepared beforehand.

The first of the two stages comprises the following operations:

- fabric layers are spread along the cutting table to form a stack (in a manual or automated process),
- the layout of the templates to be cut out is transferred on the stack of fabric,
- garment elements are cut out from the fabric with dies, portable oscillating knives, stationary cutting machines, or automated cutting systems,
- adhesive inserts are bonded with the cut-out elements or sections thereof that need stiffening / strengthening,
- the cut-out elements are numbered/marked,
- the cut-out elements are checked for quality,
- the cut-out elements are bundled up (e.g. 50-piece bundles) and stored.

The cutting room setup aims at keeping the cutting machine busy at all times, as the machine is a central piece of equipment that decides about the output of the semi-finished products. The continuous operation of the cutting machine can be ensured via one of two modes. The first of them requires the keeping of spare stacks of laid-out fabric, which increases the amount of work in progress. The second method allows accomplishing a steady workflow by feeding into the machine sections of stacked fabric that are prepared simultaneously on two or several tables. Therefore, the cutting room operations are mainly determined by the available equipment.

The cut-out elements are then transported to the sewing room so that a finished product can be assembled. The garment assembly process is preceded by the following procedures:

- reorganization of the working team as required by the technical and technological documentation, allowing for the installation of the necessary machines and equipment and the verification of their reliability,
- cooperation with the Production Preparation Department in making a model ready for production.

All technological operations in the sewing room can be divided into three groups:

- sewing,
- adhesive bonding,
- thermal processing of a product.

Thread joints are the basic technology employed in garment manufacturing. The sewing machines are divided into universal, semi-automated and automated machines. The automated sewing machines are the state-of-the art technology, but garment complexity makes them more appropriate for performing specific jobs or making simple products. Stitching quality is assessed against the in-house standards, as it ultimately affects the quality of a finished product.

Adhesive bonding makes use of a diffusion process that takes place between adhesive particles and the substrate. Adhesive joints are divided into bonded, heated and welded. A popular adhesive bonding method is contact heating. In most cases, two layers of fabric are bonded together with an adhesive. The elements to be bonded are heated on one side and then mechanically pressed together. The bonding process can be applied to a surface (e.g. inserts reinforcing the chest elements of a jacket), linearly (adhesive stitching) or in a dot-like manner. The criterion for the division is the area exposed to bonding. Adhesive bonding is now an important part of the garment manufacturing process, greatly reducing its time.

In terms of technology, the thermal processing of garments can be divided into:

- forming, i.e. the shaping of garment elements by applying force, temperature and by moistening, is a major process in the production of heavy garments (overcoats), as the shape of their elements depends also on factors other than the construction of particular elements alone;
- product upgrading by pleating, applying permanent press, as well as surface or local dyeing of finished products in which process the design is transferred from a paper template onto the product by pressing them together;
- steaming that involves the use of steaming dummies in order to remove minor workmanship defects or to freshen up a product after it has been stored for a long time or cleaned;
- the interim pressing operations performed at different stages of the assembly process; they have a strong effect on the quality of final pressing and are carried out immediately after the cut-out elements have been joined together, as after attaching the lining such joints become inaccessible;
- final pressing that determines the ultimate product quality; the operation can be performed with a whole range of specialist machines and pieces of equipment.

Smart clothes are different from the other types of clothing not because of their construction (that can be copied) but due to fabric quality, the quality of the assembly process and thermal processing.

2.3.4 The sales subprocess

This subprocess is carried out between 1 February and 1 August (one year after the product development process was started) for the spring-summer collection and between 1 August and 1 February for the autumn-winter collection.

The Kotler model [14] as applied to the sales subprocess is well known, so it will not be discussed here to make the article concise. Because the scientific output in this field is considerable, it was decided that repeating it would be pointless.

3. Product life cycle and production cycle

The earlier quoted authors suggested that it was possible to present research results as a Kotler curve [14] extended to include the earlier subprocesses. The curve describes a product life cycle as sales in time (fig. 1).

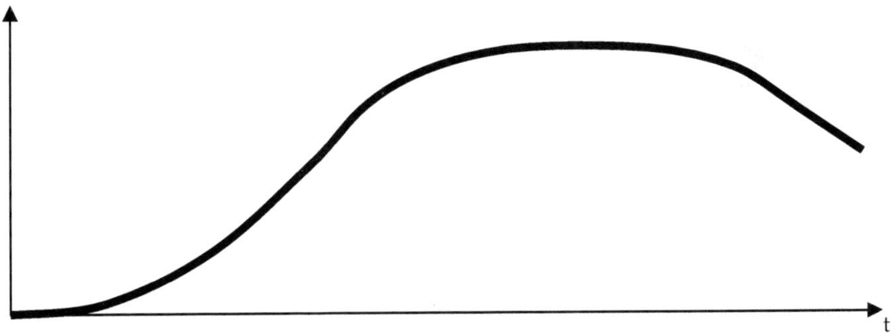

Fig. 1. Product life cycle - Kotler curve
Source: developed after Ph. Kotler, *Marketing Management, 11th ed.*, Prentice Hall 2003, p. 328

According to Kotler [14], the sales curves vary depending on the product (fig. 2):

A. stylish products (architecture, furniture, etc.),
B. fashion articles (clothing, footwear etc.),
C. products with temporary popularity (Rubik's cube, yo-yo, etc.).

The B curve reveals some special character of the fashion articles. The graph is fully adequate when a fashion article is meant as one model of a product. However, the investigation has confirmed that the classical product life cycle approach can be applied to clothing too (fig. 1), if we assume that such products do not represent a single design but a set of designs comprising a seasonal offer, which is in fact the final product of an enterprise. This knowledge encouraged the author to present the investigation's findings graphically as a Kotler curve extended to include the earlier production management subprocesses. Consequently, an original production cycle model for the SLCP was created, approximating the temporal work intensity distribution in the particular components of the production process. According to Waszczyk and Szczerbicki [26], such approximation is rarely treated as model falsification. It is rather assumed that some developments taking place in the economic reality were omitted from the model. The Leśkiewicz [17] accuse the approach of being internally inconsistent, i.e. combining unrealistic assumptions and a strongly accentuated previdistic function of the economy. Nevertheless, Waszczyk and Szczerbicki [26] view things differently: a solid description provided at the stage of constructing an explanatory model lends credence to its prognostic value. The long-time research conducted by the author of this article allows her to confirm this opinion.

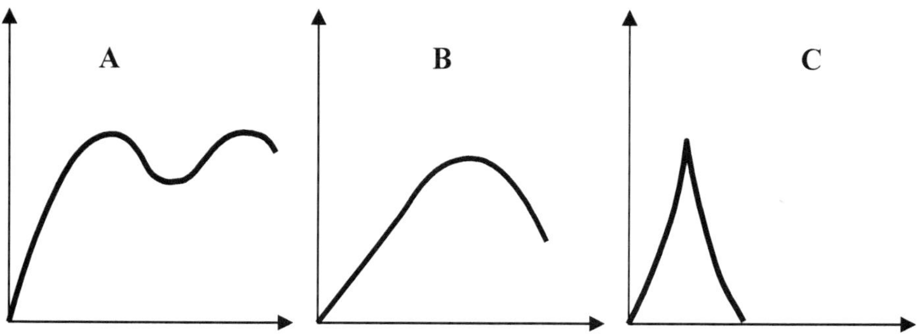

Fig. 2. Life cycles: A - stylish products, B - fashion articles, C - temporarily popular products.
Source: developed after Ph. Kotler, *Marketing...*, op. cit., p. 330

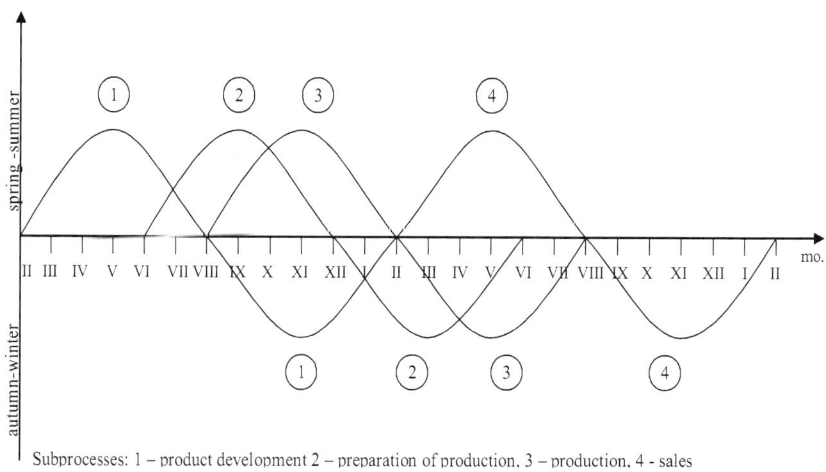

Fig. 3. The SLCP production cycle model.
Source: developed by the author.

The constructed production cycle model (fig. 3) is underpinned by the author's empirical study, the findings of which were verified in the course of her 18 years' long business practice. Although the changing circumstances impeded the correct time measurements, the cyclical character of the production process enabled their verification. For the model to be created „the reality had to be appropriately smoothed out" [12]. It is justified to state now that the presented model sufficiently reflects the actual situation. Author's good knowledge of the research subject is confirmed by the attached description of the production process. All these circumstances together allow concluding that the evaluation [26] of the constructed model' prognostic properties is fully relevant.

In the presented production cycle model, sales are only one of the subprocesses (curve 4). The x-axis separates operations necessary to prepare two clothing collections in a year; these related to the spring-summer season run above the axis, while operations concerning the autumn-winter collection are below it. The curves illustrate the rising and falling intensity of work in the particular subprocesses during the execution of a seasonal collection, as well as determining their acceptable completion times. The curves are shifted with respect to each other by a time interval indicated by the research findings. Although it is possible for the interval to show minor variations, the regular occurrence of a constant time interval is a fact. The interval is:

- four months between curves 1 and 2,
- only two months between curves 2 and 3,
- as many as six months between curves 3 and 4.

Because each of the four subprocesses goes on for as long as 6 months, the production process could be spread over 24 months. The possibility of reducing the time by four months (between curves 1 and 2) and two months (between curves 2 and 3) as demonstrated by the research findings shortens the production process to 18 months. It is also worth noting that the start dates for the spring-summer collection (curve 1 above axis x) and the autumn-winter collection (curve 1 below axis x) are shifted against each other by 6 months. The knowledge of this fact allows optimizing the management of production of seasonal products having a determined manufacturing completion time.

4. A production management model for short life-cycle goods

Production management must always arise from a plan. Every „plan involves a performance imperative. An organization striving to comply with the imperative becomes less flexible and less perceptive of what is going on around it. On the other hand, the increasingly turbulent environment requires organizations to show flexibility, so that unexpected events [...] representing opportunities can be used, while those posing threats avoided [...] "[16]. The changes in the functioning of domestic enterprises are well illustrated by the events that took place at the turn of the 20th c., which demonstrated how the transition of 1989 contributed to the formation of a new economic reality in Poland [7]. After the domestic market was opened, the inflow of imports increased. As a result, stronger competition in the market reduced the range of selling opportunities. These circumstances substantiate an investigation into the ways of improving the effectiveness of production management that provides companies with more favourable market positions.

A production management model for the short life-cycle goods was built following the stages below:

Stage I. Empirical aggregation of actions making up the production process.
Stage II. Using the Altshuller method for verifying causal relationships between particular actions.
Stage III. Making a schedule of the actions and determining their times.
Stage IV. Building the model based on graph theory.

The fact that the author had researched the area for many years helped verify the process constituents and the causal relationships between them were found using the Altshuller method. For the sake of illustration, let us show the applied method with respect to the subprocess representing the creation of a fashion collection.

The evaluation of the attractiveness of clothing designs (5) is the critical action in the string of events presented in diagram 1. The acceptance of the designs means that the next steps can be taken, i.e. the sample room team can prepare a sample of the designed model.

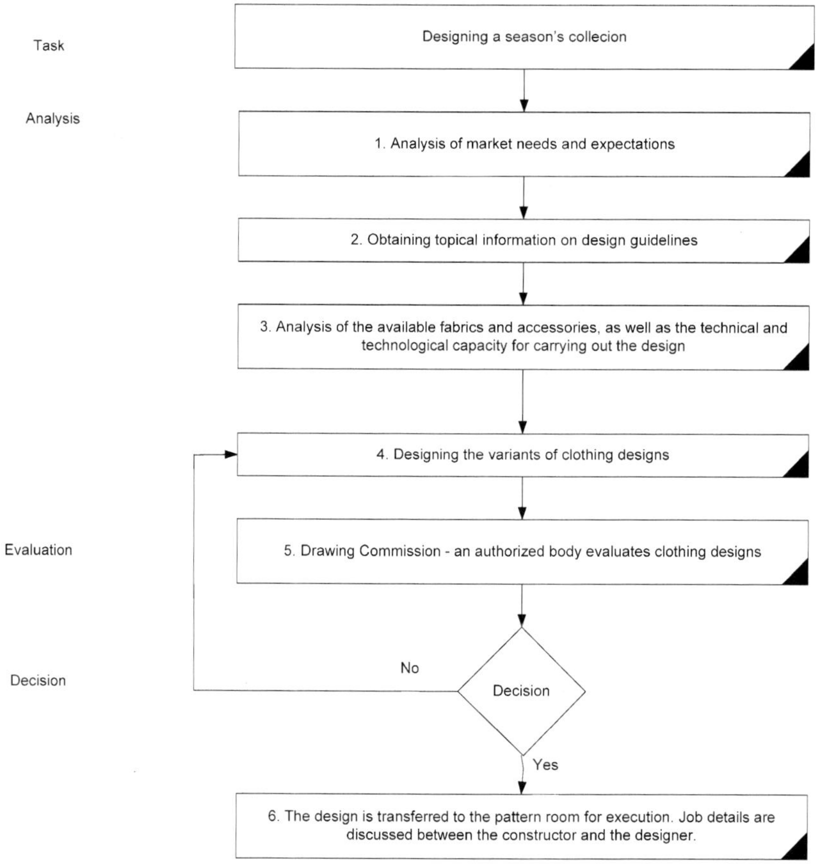

Diagram 1. An algorithm illustrating a fashion collection design process.
Source: developed by the author

Otherwise, the proposed models have to be redesigned. This procedure is repeated until the group of specialists appointed by the enterprise board decides that the outcomes are satisfactory (the number of designs meets the manufacturer's needs).

The Altshuller method applied to evaluate the results of all strings of events allowed scheduling the process correctly. The duration times of the strings were determined empirically and then verified using special catalogues being in possession of every clothing manufacturer. The actual duration times of identical actions may vary between particular manufacturers, as they operate in different technical and technological environments. Therefore, a production management model should follow from an investigation conducted in the concrete enterprise. Because process scheduling is widely discussed topic in the literature [2, 4], for the sake of keeping this article succinct we only wish to note that the schedule produced in the course of this investigation provided a basis for constructing a production management model.

The number of points for starting the model construction corresponded to the number of entry points to the process. The points are the leaves from which each branch consisting of many events (vertices) and of actions (edges) denoting their execution originates. The edges do not provide any information on their duration times, indicating only the sequence of events. At the next stage of tree development, particular branches converge to ultimately form the root, i.e. the final event. With these rules in mind, two assumptions were formulated to build the model:

- the start time of each string of actions depends on the process external and internal determinants,
- the duration of an action is a deterministic value expressed in terms of specific units.

Let us consider whether the second assumption is not a simplification possibly leading to the creation of an unrealistic model. We need to bear in mind that in the case of the short life-cycle goods the time for performing each elementary action can be allowed to deviate from the schedule only to a limited degree, because product selling must start at a predetermined point in time. Therefore, the deterministic time assumption actually relates to some expected time, the length of which is estimated based on long-time experience and many measurements. A starting point for future research could be the adaptation of the model to a situation where the elementary actions have non-deterministic (i.e. described by a random variable) execution times.

The production management model was built along the following lines:

1. Each process action is represented by an edge with a label indicating its duration.
2. There is one vertex for one intermediate state of the process. A vertex is a place where all edges symbolizing actions immediately preceding the state described by the vertex end and where an edge representing an action leading to the next state has its beginning.
3. The tree leaves are equivalent to the initial states of the strings of actions.
4. The root of the tree denotes that the process is complete and the product is ready.
5. Chronologically later process stages are closer to the root than the earlier stages, because the tree is oriented to the root.

6. Each vertex u can be assigned pairs of numbers $p(u)$ and $q(u)$ denoting the earliest and latest acceptable times of starting actions originating in the vertex.

Let us explain now the exact meanings of the notions and terms used in this article.

The earliest acceptable action start time $p(u)$ is the time when the state u appears, assuming that the preceding actions were performed on schedule.

The latest acceptable action start time $q(u)$ represented by an edge originating in the vertex u allows completing the entire process on schedule, provided that all the following actions are performed on time.

For each vertex u of the production management model, the following inequality exists:

$$p(u) \leq q(u) \tag{1}$$

If the strong inequality $p(u) < q(u)$ is met, then some extra time is available to the state u, which can be used to make up for any earlier delay in the string of actions. The acceptable length of this delay is given by $q(u) - p(u)$ and it is not likely to affect the process completion time, unless the times of the next actions grow longer. However, if the equality $q(u) = p(u)$ takes place, any delay in the string of actions preceding the state u may defer the process completion time. Therefore, the extra time $r(u)$ available to the state u (i.e. the difference between the latest and earliest acceptable start times for an action) can be defined as:

$$r(u) = q(u) - p(u) \tag{2}$$

Based on the above, other assumptions can be formulated:

- if $r(u) = 0$, the state u will be called sensitive,
- if $r(u) > 0$, the state u will be called resistant.

To simplify the formulas, a state in the process represented by a vertex (e.g. u) will be treated as identical with that vertex, so the term state u will be used. Analogously, an action originating from the state u and having the state v as its end will be equated with the u-v edge and called the u-v action for the sake of clarity. The time of its execution will be denoted as $t(u\text{-}v)$. These assumptions allow forming a production management model as a tree. Let us present its portion corresponding to the product creation subprocess (diagram 2).

The designer does his job (4), which is central to the design making subprocess, based on the leaves (actions 1, 2, 3 in diagram 1). The accepted drawings (5) are transferred to the sample room (6). At the same time, visually attractive fabrics are being sought, selected and purchased for the sample room (7−11). The fabrics and the prepared markers (12) are used for making the cutouts (13) that are then assembled with the accessories (14) to make a sample of the model (15). Parallel to that, the abridged model documentation is being prepared, so that the manufacturing costs can be calculated (16−20). The finished models are evaluated for their appearance and functionality (21). The accepted ones are priced and added to the fashion collection (22). If the production process were designed as part of B2B services involving the delivery of corporate clothing (employees meeting with customers shape their employer's image), then body measurements (23-26 in diagram 3) would precede the making of the markers.

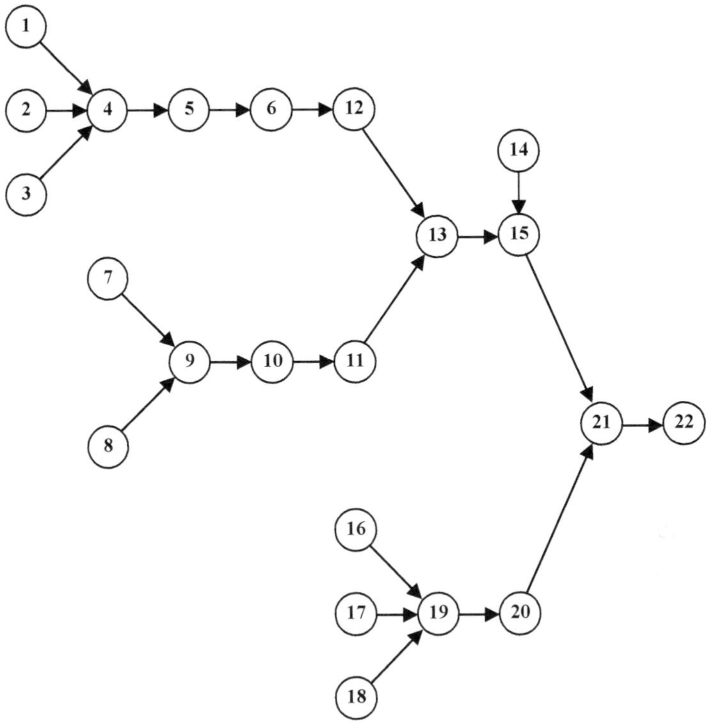

Diagram 2. A production management model - the product creation subprocess.
Source: developed by the author

The decisions giving the green light to the production of particular models (subsequent to consumer focus group, shows at fairs, etc.) initiate the following processes:

- market grading (27–31),
- delivery of the necessary materials (32–37),
- pattern making (38–41),
- preparation of the technical and technological documentation for the sewing room (42–46),
- operational planning (47–51),
- product manufacturing (52–60).

The discussed production management model is illustrated graphically in diagram 3, but without repeating the string of actions that has already been shown in diagram 2 (the product creation subprocess). Let us concentrate our discussion on the product manufacturing subprocess, which is determined by only several vertices. Therefore, the vertex 52 stands for assembling the „job order" (i.e. the putting together of all materials, accessories, the earlier made sample, and the technical and technological documentation for

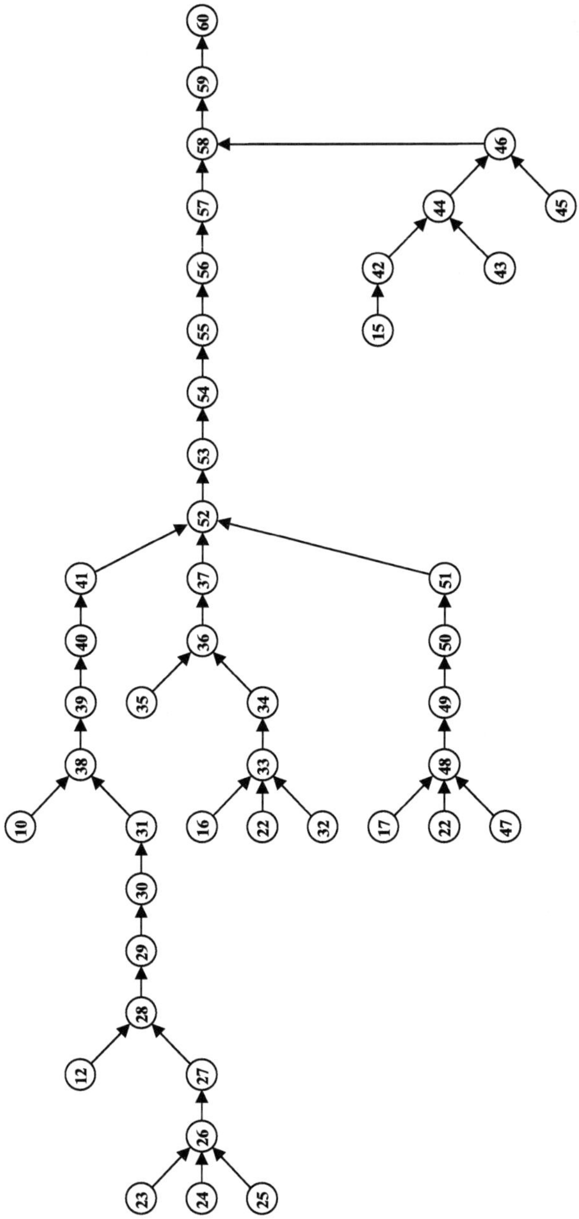

Diagram 3. The production management model.
Source: developed by the author

the manufacturing process), checking the order's completeness and then delivering the complete set to the manufacturing team. The vertices 53–57 represent the cutting room operations (spreading the fabric into stacks, dividing the stacked fabric into sections, making the patterns either automatically or manually, applying the stiffening inserts (if necessary), checking the cut-outs for quality and bundling them together into units of input delivered to the sewing room).

The cutouts and the technological documentation for their assembly meet at the vertex 58 being the string of operations performed in the sewing-room (the operations may vary depending on the model of clothing and the sewing room equipment). For instance, it takes several tens of operations to assemble the cutouts of an overcoat. Given that the construction of the product manufacturing subprocess has already been discussed in another original study by the author [13], it does not seem necessary to repeat it. The vertex 59 is the inspection of the finished product quality and the vertex 60 represents its delivery to the warehouse. Taking into account that the main goal of the investigation was to build a model of production management process, the aggregation of the elementary jobs into sub-processes seems rational.

5. A study of changes in the production process for short-life cycle goods

5.1 A critical path and an Indicator of Process Resistance in the production management model

The critical path of the tree determines the duration of the production process, in the same way as a network's critical path does. By identifying the critical path of the production management model and by calculating the Indicator of Process Resistance (IPR) to change the manager can estimate the degree to which the process completion date is at risk.

Let us present a procedure for finding a critical path or paths of the production management model that do not offer time reserves. Their number provides an indication of the process resistance to changes. The tree has at least one critical path, but every path running between an initial state and a final state can theoretically be a critical one. Then the production process is likely to end later than scheduled, because of changes increasing the duration of any of its constituent tasks. Production processes based on management models with a large number of critical paths are not resistant. The most resistant are processes having only one critical path. This shows that a production management model should be analysed while still being planned, as the range of the model verification options is the greatest then.

Let us present a procedure that was developed to identify the critical path of a production management model shaped as a rooted tree. Let the vertex w correspond to the tree's root (a final event of the production process). Among the states directly preceding the state w there is a state u having a time reserve $r(u) = 0$. If all states coming before the state w had time reserves, then the state w would have a time reserve too. This contradicts the assumption on which model [6] was founded, i.e.:

$$p(w) = q(w), \text{ i.e. } r(w) = 0 \quad (3)$$

Applying the same reasoning to the state u and its preceding states, we infer that there is some state v preceding the state u, for which $r(v) = 0$. This procedure should be repeated until we discover that a state without a time reserve is one of the initial states (let us call it the vertex a). The path starting at a and ending at w will be called a **critical path**. Accordingly, each state on the critical path is a critical state, particularly the initial state a.

While trying to identify the critical path we may discover that the analysed critical state u is preceded by more than one critical state. Then more than one critical path goes through the state u. This means that **the production management model (for the short life-cycle products)** has as many critical paths as critical initial states. Let us suppose that the model has n initial states containing k critical states. According to the earlier observations, the value of k is within the range:

$$1 \le k \le n \tag{4}$$

Consequently, the **Indicator of Process Resistance** to unexpected changes can be calculated as follows:

$$\text{IPR} = \frac{n-k}{n} = 1 - \frac{k}{n} \tag{5}$$

where: IPR – Indicator of Process Resistance to unexpected changes,
n– the number of the initial states (tree leaves),
k– the number of the critical states among the initial states.

IPR's extreme values are obtained for $k = n$ and $k = 1$. They define the range of values for the created indicator, i.e.:

$$< 0; 1 - \frac{1}{n} > \tag{6}$$

When every path in the production management model is critical, then $k = n$ and the IPR = 0. In the model with a single critical path $k = 1$ and the IPR is close to one, because it is calculated as:

$$\text{IPR} = 1 - \frac{1}{n} \approx 1 \tag{7}$$

It can be assumed that such defined **IPR's value measures the process resistance to changes that delay its completion.** The indicator can be used for assessing the production management model's design, as well as its actual performance (each time it has been modified). When the IPR is 0, then the timely completion of the production process is very much at risk, should any change extending the duration of any of its tasks occur. This means that the IPR is a synthetic measure of process resistance to changes, regardless of the stage they affect.

5.2 The PPCT as a method of investigating changes in the production process

A production management model (an inverted tree) provides information on the tasks, their duration and relationships. This aggregate knowledge allowed developing a method that:

- controls the duration of the process-related tasks,
- monitors changes affecting task duration,
- allows adjusting the model, when the changes delay the production process end date.

Let us present the **Production Process Control Tree** (PPCT) method, which was specifically developed for the short-life cycle goods. Let us note that the occurrence of some state u can be delayed with respect to the time $p(u)$, because of one of two reasons:

- one of the states directly or indirectly preceding the state u, e.g. a, occurs later than $p(a)$,
- one of the tasks preceding the state u, e.g. a-u, stretches over a longer period than the scheduled time $t(a\text{-}u)$.

where: $p(u)$ – the earliest moment of commencing the task originating in the vertex u,
$p(a)$ – the earliest moment of commencing the task originating in the vertex a,
$t(a\text{-}u)$ – the time for performing the task between the vertices a and u.

The delayed occurrence of the state u may make shift the production end to a later date. This is certain to happen, when u is a critical state. In a general case, **a delay will only take place when the delayed occurrence of the state u affects the commencement of the nearest critical state situated on the path linking the state u and the tree root**. However, the delay of the state u may also be "absorbed" by the time reserves of the states following u.

For the production management model to monitor changes, we need to find the times $p(u)$ and $q(u)$, representing the earliest moment of commencing each task and the latest moment of ending each task, respectively. According to the literature, the following rules can be applied to find the duration of the tasks:

- a deterministic rule for tasks carried out according to the company's own rules that explicitly prescribe task's deadline or duration,
- a probabilistic rule for tasks of duration determined empirically by an experienced expert.

The knowledge of the rules for determining the duration of tasks and time reserves played an important role in developing the PPCT method. Each time reserve indicates the length of time by which a task can extend without the production management model having to undergo adjustment. Considering that a production process is shaped by many variables, the constructed model has to be dynamic, enabling even some modifications to the schedule in case the end date of the production process becomes uncertain.

Let us suppose that we have a production management model shaped as an inverted tree. The duration of particular tasks and the moments when the initial states of tasks should start are also known. The duration of the task transforming the state a into b is denoted as $t(a\text{–}b)$ and the earliest moment when the state u can commence is denoted as $p(u)$. Let us create an algorithm for this production management model to find $p(a_i)$, $q(w)$ and $q(a)$. The values will be used when the production management model will have to account for the impacts of variables affecting the production process. So:

- $p(a_i)$ is the earliest allowed moment when the task originating in the vertex a_i should commence; it will be calculated according to formula (8) below,
- $q(w)$ is the latest allowed moment of ending the final process activity w; it will be calculated according to formula (11) below,
- $q(a)$ is the latest allowed time when the task originating in the vertex a should end; it will be calculated according to formula (13) below.

Let us use this method for calculating the time $p(u)$ for the vertex u, which is not a tree leaf (i.e. an initial state). In the considered tree, the offspring of the vertex u are the vertices that come immediately before it. Then:

$$p(u) = \max \{p(a_i) + t(a_i–u)\} \quad \text{for } i = 1, \ldots, k \tag{8}$$

where: $p(u)$ – the earliest moment when the task originating in the vertex u should commence; $p(a_i)$ – the earliest moment when the task originating in the vertex a_i should commence, $t(a_i-u)$ – the duration of the task between the vertices a_i and u.

The above **rule helps to find the moments p(u), first for the states directly following the initial states and then recurrently for all vertices of the tree representing a production management model.**

Let w be a state equivalent to the tree root and $p(w)$ the actual end date of the production process. If T is the scheduled end date, then the process will end as planned when:

$$p(w) \leq T \tag{9}$$

If otherwise, the product will not be ready on time. This problem can be handled by adjusting the process, which entails some restructuring of the production management model. Continuing the earlier procedure, we determine the moment $q(u)$, i.e. the latest allowed time when the state u should commence. Naturally, the relationship:

$$q(w) = T \tag{10}$$

still holds.

Building on the earlier assumption about the management of production of short life-cycle goods, we can write that:

$$\mathbf{p(w) = q(w) = T} \tag{11}$$

where: $p(w)$ – the earliest allowed moment when the task originating in the vertex w (the tree root) should commence,
$q(w)$ – the latest allowed when the task w, being the final task of the production process, should end,
T – the scheduled process end.

If the equality $p(w) = q(w) = T$ does not take place, then the condition (11) can be met by introducing a dummy state w and assuming that:

$$p(w') = T \text{ and } (w–w') = T - p(w) \tag{12}$$

The time $t(w–w')$ shows the shift in the product completion date, thus providing information on the observed change's effect on the production process. According to assumption (11), **the vertex w ending the production process (i.e. the tree root) is a critical state**. So, the moment $q(u)$ of the state u is determined and the state a precedes the state u towards the root. Then $q(a)$ can be defined using the following equation:

$$\mathbf{q(a) = q(u) - t(a–u)} \tag{13}$$

where: $q(a)$ – the latest allowed moment when the task originating in the vertex a preceding the vertex u should end,
$q(u)$ –the latest allowed moment when the task originating in the vertex u should end,
$t(a–u)$ – the duration of the task between the vertices a and u.

The value on the right hand-side of equation (13) is determined precisely, as there is only one edge that starts at a and ends at u. Consequently, the formula needs neither a minimum operator nor a maximum operator. The formula (13) allows recurrent determination of the time $q(u)$ for each vertex of the tree, which property is utilised in the PPCT method to monitor changes.

Changing production circumstances may extend the amount of time that is needed to end the process. This threat must result in an immediate correction of the model data. In other words, changing circumstances should generate warnings about a possibly delayed product completion date.

The PPPCT method we propose for investigating production changes compares the duration of each task with its scheduled time. Let us assume that a task $a-x$ was performed in time $t'(a-x)$, which extended beyond its scheduled time $t(a-x)$ by n units. Then we have:

$$t'(a-x) = t(a-x) + n \tag{14}$$

Let us also assume that the path linking the state x and the tree root successively goes through the states $y_1, y_2, \ldots, y_k$, so the path is given as $x - y_1 - \ldots - y_k - w$. We additionally assume that all tasks preceding the state a were performed on time, meaning that the activity $a-x$ started at the moment $p(a)$. Then, one of the three possibilities takes place:

$$1^\circ \quad p(a) + t(a-x) + n \leq p(x), \text{ or} \tag{15}$$

$$2^\circ \quad p(x) < p(a) + t(a-x) + n \leq q(x), \text{ or} \tag{16}$$

$$3^\circ \quad q(x) < p(a) + t(a-x) + n. \tag{17}$$

where: $p(x)$ - the earliest moment when the task originating in the vertex x should commence,
$q(x)$ - the latest moment the task originating in the vertex x should end,
$p(a)$ - the earliest moment when the task originating in the vertex a preceding the state x should commence
$t(a-x)$ - the duration of the task between the vertices a and x,
n - the number of units by which the duration of the task $a-x$ has been extended.

Let us explore now the meaning of the three situations and find the algorithms to deal with them.

Should the first case occur, the production process end date runs no risk of being delayed, because the earliest moment when the task y_1 (initiation of the activity x) should start takes place after the length of time allocated to activity $a-x$ elapses. So the model of the process does not need any modifications, but replacing the time $t(a-x)$ by $t'(a-x) = t(a-x) + n$. In this case, the production manager does not have to be informed about an event if occurred, as its influence was neutral.

In the second case, the production process is not exposed to any direct threat to its timely completion, because the state x has the time reserve $r(x) = q(x) - p(x)$. The task $a-x$ will end not later than $q(x)$, being the latest allowed moment for the task $x{-}{-}y_1$ to commence. In this situation, the tree requires the following modifications:

i. the time $(a-x)$ has to be replaced with $t'(a-x) = t(a-x) + n$,

ii. each state on the path $x - y_1 - \ldots - y_k - w$ has to be assigned a new commencement time using the formula (8) and some obvious changes have to be made to the formula symbols (u has to be replaced with the right vertex name and a_i with its preceding vertices).

The production manager has to be notified of the changes, but no action is required to prevent the production process from running late.

Two things need to be raised at this point: 1) the moments $p(x)$, $p(y_1)$, $p(y_2)$, ..., $p(y_k)$ have to be recalculated, because the changes may have transformed the resistant states into critical ones, thus affecting the process structure; 2) the moments $q(x)$, $q(y_1)$, $q(y_2)$, ..., $q(y_k)$ do not change, because the scheduled process end date $T = p(w) = q(w)$ that depends on them remains the same.

In the third case, the production process end date will be exceeded, because the state x needs more time to end than its time reserve $r(x)$ allows. Hence, the model has to be modified as follows:

i. the time $t(a-x)$ has to be replaced with $t'(a-x) = t(a-x) + n$,
ii. each state on the path $x - y_1 - \ldots - y_k - w$ has to be assigned a new commencement time using the formula (8) and some obvious changes have to be made to the formula symbols (u has to be replaced with the right vertex name and a_i with its preceding vertices),
iii. the process end date T has to be replaced with $T' = p(w)$, assuming at the same time that $q(w) = p(w)$, where the time $p(w)$ represents a new process end date calculated at step (ii),
iv. now the latest allowed moments of starting tasks that have not been carried out yet have to be determined, their duration of the tasks remaining the same.

The steps (i) ÷ (iv) **readjust the model of the process**. The production manager has to be notified of the situation to decide about the next steps after analysing the new model. The manager may choose to shorten the sequence of activities $x - y_1 - \ldots - y_k - w$ by introducing organizational, technical or technological improvements. If the intervention is effective and, for instance, the time $t(y_i - y_{i+1})$ becomes shorter by m units, then the steps (i) ÷ (iv) should be repeated, with the time $t(y_i - y_{i+1})$ at step (i) being replaced by $t(y_i - y_{i+1}) - m$.

Because decisions on taking actions causing dynamic adjustment of the model usually increase product manufacturing costs, the company board has to grant the production manager an appropriate scope of authority. Otherwise, the PPCT method enabling interactive management of production processes will not be as effective as it can be. If the duration of the longest path of the tree ensures following the intervention that the production process will end as scheduled, then the process is continued. If otherwise, the production manager has to notify the Board (or another relevant body) of the situation, which may choose to discontinue the production process (after estimating the losses) or to carry on.

6. Conclusion

The presented operational algorithm allows concluding that the empirical verification of the production model for the short life cycle products confirms the hypothesis of the determined duration of the production process. The process consists of four subprocesses that run cyclically and are staggered with respect to each other by constant time intervals. Because the main building material of the management science is the inductive methods that enable drawing general conclusions from empirical research [22], the presented modelling results can be assumed to have a scientific value. The generated model of the product manufacturing cycle is central to company management. Its importance goes beyond the possibility of synchronising the subprocesses alone. The prolonged production of the SLCP shortens the available selling period, and in the extreme case it can completely ruin the sales. This situation is caused by the seasonal character of sales, the time of the year when a clothing article can be worn, etc.

A production management model based on an inverted tree concept (graph theory) allows an innovative, graphical representation of a management process applied to the production of short life-cycle goods. Although an inverted rooted tree has not been used in management theory so far, there are good reasons for constructing it, because it can help:

- identify the sensitive graph routes, i.e. those determining process duration,
- develop a unique measure of process resistance to change (PRI) enabling an immediate evaluation of the production management model for the designed production process or after each process modification caused by changes arising during its execution,
- develop a method for analysing changes in the management of production of short life-cycle goods that allows its user to have active control over the process.

The amount of material discussing the above issues is quite extensive, so it will be presented in other articles that will be published in this periodical.

All computations (necessary to design the original tree, to determine its longest path and to readjust the production management model) can be performed in real time, once an appropriate computer software has been developed. The need for the management process to integrate technology, organizational issues and IT, regardless of the supervisory, stimulating role of the process manager, was accentuated by B. Nogalski [20]. The software should be built around the aforementioned algorithm that enables study of changes in the production of the short life-cycle goods. The software helps implement the method we propose in business practice. Making decisions under the pressure of time is a key problem that companies manufacturing short life-cycle products have to resolve. Modern production management methods, including the PPCT, combined with IT tools are the only ones that make it possible to:

- analyse a production process and its changing circumstances on an on-going basis,
- make decisions in real time to offset the negative impacts of changing process circumstances,
- minimize the losses a company may incur should it decide to discontinue the production process, because every step forwards generates unnecessary costs (augmenting the losses).

The proposed method for analysing changes in the production process can improve the effectiveness of companies making short life-cycle goods that function in turbulent environments. According to the *Global Trends 2025* report prepared by the National Intelligence Council, such environments are becoming the norm today [21]. The report reveals not only problems, but also opportunities that arise from unexpected changes creating new economic realities.

7. References

[1] Ayres R.U., Ayres L., Rade I., *The Life Cycle of Cooper, Its Co-Products and By-products*, Kulwer Academic Publishers, Dordrecht 2003

[2] Burchard-Korol D., Furman J., *Zarządzanie produkcją i usługami*, Wydawnictwo Politechniki Śląskiej, Gliwice 2007
[3] Drucker P.F., *Natchnienie i fart, czyli innowacja i przedsiębiorczość*, Wydawnictwo Studio Emka, Warsaw 2004
[4] Durlik I., *Inżynieria zarządzania. Strategia i projektowanie systemów produkcyjnych*, Agencja Wydawnicza Placet, Warszawa 2007
[5] Grajewski P., Nogalski B., *Potencjalne źródła niesprawności w organizacji procesowej*, [in:] M. Romanowska, M. Trocki (ed.), *Podejście procesowe do zarządzania*, Wydawnictwo SGH, Warszawa 2004
[6] Grandys E., *Production Cycle Model for Short Life-Cycle Models*, "Fibres & Textiles in Eastern Europe" 2010, No. 1
[7] Grandys E., *Impact of External Determinants on the Functioning of Polish Clothing Manufactures*, "Fibres & Textiles in Eastern Europe" 2010, No. 3
[8] Grandys E., *Productions Management Model for Short Life-Cycle Goods*, "Fibres & Textiles in Eastern Europe" 2010, No. 4
[9] Grandys E., Grandys A., *Outsourcing – an Innowation Tool in Clothing Companies*, "Fibres & Textiles in Eastern Europe" 2008, No. 5
[10] Gutenberg Th., *A Review of Improvement Methods in Manufacturing Operations*, "Work Study" 2003, Vol. 52, No. 2
[11] Hammer M., Champy J., *Reeingineering the Corporation – Manifesto for Business Revolution*, Nicholas Brealey Publishing, London 1994
[12] Kleine-Doepke R., *Podstawy zarządzania*, Wydawnictwo C.H. Beck, Warsaw 1995
[13] Kołacińska E., *Zastosowanie teorii grafów w kierowaniu zespołami szyjącymi*, „Odzież" 1977, nr 9
[14] Kotler Ph., *Marketing Management. 11th ed.*, Prentice Hall 2003
[15] Kotler Ph., Amstrong G., *Principles of marketing*, 4th ed., Prentice Hall, London 1989
[16] Krupski R., *Innowacje w planowaniu strategicznym*, [in:] H. Bieniok, T. Kraśnicka (ed.), *Innowacje zarządcze w biznesie i sektorze publicznym*, Wydawnictwo Akademii Ekonomicznej w Katowicach, Katowice 2008
[17] Leśkiewicz I., Leśkiewicz Z., *Zarys metodologii ekonomii (część II i III)*, WNUS, Szczecin 1999
[18] de Luca L.M., Atuaehbe-Gima K., *Market Knowledge Dimensions and Cross-Functional Collaboration: Examining the Different Routes to Product Innovation Performance*, "Journal of Marketing" Vol. 71, January 2007
[19] Marchesnay L., *L`economie et la gestion sont – elles des sciences? Essaie d`epistemologie*, „Cahier de l`EFRI" Universite Montpelier 2004, Vol. 11, No. 1
[20] Nogalski B., *Restrukturyzacja procesowa w zarządzaniu małymi i średnimi przedsiębiorstwami*, Oficyna Wydawnicza Ośrodka Postępu Organizacyjnego Spółka z o.o., Bydgoszcz 1999
[21] National Intelligence Council, *Global Trends 2025: A Transformed World*, Washington, U.S. Government Printing Office, November 2008, www.dni.gov
[22] Sudoł S., *Nauki o zarządzaniu. Węzłowe problemy i kontrowersje*, Wydawnictwo TNOiK, Toruń 2007
[23] Szczerbicki E., *Management of Comlexity and Information Flow In Agile Manufacturing*, [in:] A. Gunasekaran (ed.): *The 21st Century Competitive Strategy*, Amsterdam 2001
[24] Szczerbicki E., Jinadasa P., *Modelling for Performance Evaluation In Complex Systems*, „Systems Analysis, Modelling, Simulation" 2000, Vol. 38
[25] *The European Platform on Life Cycle Assessment*, http://lca.jrc.ec.europa.eu
[26] Waszczyk M., Szczerbicki E., *Metodologiczne aspekty opisowego modelowania w naukach ekonomicznych*, Zeszyty Naukowe Politechniki Gdańskiej, Gdańsk 2003
[27] Więźlak W., Elmrych-Bocheńska J., Zieliński J., *Odzież. Budowa, własności i produkcja*, Wydawnictwo Instytutu Technologii Eksploatacji – PIB, Radom 2009

25

Graphs for Ontology, Law and Policy

Pierre Mazzega[1,2*], Romain Boulet[3] and Thérèse Libourel[3]
[1]*UMR GET, IRD, CNRS, Université de Toulouse III*
[2]*International Joint Laboratory OCE, IRD – Universidade de Brasilia*
[3]*UMR ESPACE-DEV, IRD, Université de Montpellier II*
[1,3]*France*
[2]*Brazil*

1. Introduction

Since the post-war decades, Public Policies are required increasingly as a preferred tool to promote collective action. Today these public policies are developed through sophisticated participatory schemes involving a variety of actors, public or private. Indeed in the current context of globalization though the State and its administration are key actors (Henry, 2004), their influence fades gradually into a more diffuse institutional environment (Oström, 2005) involving a multitude of other actors (Hassenteufel, 2008). For example at the two ends of the spectrum of governance, we find on one hand the increasing involvement of supranational entities, on the other hand the involvement of nongovernmental organizations.

Therefore, the stated aims of their implementation and the means to achieve them are the result of negotiations and of - at least partial - consensus with stakeholders. In representative governments especially, the trend is growing imposing accountability as regard to the implementation and effects of these policy devices. Following the same trend it becomes mandatory to lean projects of public policy on impact analyses (André et al., 2004; Bourcier et al., 2012) themselves regulated by legal provisions (e.g. European Commission, 2004). These changes induce or reinforce specific phenomena of interest here: a) the systemic nature of law and public policy (and "public action", an expression that might have a more explicit connotation from a dynamic point of view); b) the gradual - yet limited - disappearance of a singular authority (as could be the State) having the monopolistic power necessary for the shift in or the centralized decision-making; c) the emerging nature of the direct or indirect (desirable or undesirable, internalized or externalized, etc.) effects induced by the policy and law.

These introductory remarks that are part of an intellectual position rather than of a due demonstration, lead us to propose a dialogue between the analysis of public policy and the analysis of complex systems. We take the risk of turning to the analysis of law and public policy as complex systems whose implementation mobilizes law, economics, sociology, policy and administrative sciences, and which *understanding* relies on these disciplines but

*Corresponding Author

also, in its foundations, on ontology or mathematics (though we are aware that the scale of this ambition is balanced by the modesty of the results presented here).

The modeling of law and public policy is an emerging field of research aiming in particular at understanding their "functioning", at simulating *ex ante* their potential impacts, at finding ways of achieving a desirable goal (back casting), at producing tools for decision support, at allowing the participative drafting of legal texts or policy, especially by using ICT (Information and Communication Technology) or approaches developed for the analysis and structuring of social networks. Two objectives are achieved in this chapter: a) cover part of the literature of recent years in this field; b) illustrate our point with original results drawn mainly from the analysis of law and policy in the wide field of environment and sustainable development.

In Section 2 we present some basic notions in graph theory and network analysis routinely used in this article (and in other cited articles). Our choice is to limit ourselves to a very small number of tools and concepts from graph theory while providing more opportunities for application in law or political science. In Section 3, an ontology-inspired approach is used to represent the law and public policy (and the associated knowledge) in the form of graphs whose analyses are powerful to discover and interpret cognitive and operational structures in these systems. We hope that the dividend of the example will double as our analysis focuses on the representation of current research conducted on the application of ICT in e-governance and modeling of public policies. In Section 4, we present various types of graphs induced by the law and whose analysis leads to propose a quantitative approach to some aspects of legal complexity. In particular the analysis of environmental treaties of international law adds a new graph structure to those previously identified in the analysis of networks of references between laws.

We proceed similarly in Section 5 for public policies considered in terms of organized action. It is in this case a policy of management of water resources implemented in France at the scale of a hydrological basin (large water cycle) where many uses are competing in particular in period of low water. Some perspective for expanding the areas of graph theory that will have a great interest in the modeling of Law and policy are briefly mentioned in Section 6 with concluding remarks.

2. Graphs for the analysis of complex systems

From a general perspective graph theory is today a cornerstone of the study of complex systems. In this chapter we use a few fundamental concepts, measures and estimation methods developed in graph theory and network analysis, that provide us with privileged ways to conceptualize, formalize, model and visualize structural properties of legal and policy systems and to identify their non trivial properties. Both the use and development of these concepts and methods have proven to be fruitful in the study of large interaction networks in sociology or in biological sciences, where emerging structures like small-worlds or scale-free structures are recurrently exhibited. In return, we hypothesize that the contemporary legal and policy “fabrics” pose original problems that may trigger new developments in graph theory and network analysis. In order to show their relevance for the study of legal and policy systems in the next sections, we restrict our "toolbox" to the following limited set of concepts and estimators (the analysis methods and algorithms will be indicated through the cited references only).

2.1 Concepts

A graph is a mathematical object consisting of two sets: a set of vertices (or nodes) and a set of edges (or links), an edge linking two vertices. This mathematical structure of graph and its related analysis tools are used to model real phenomena of interaction between objects that are networks (see e.g. Brandes and Erlebach, 2005). We now introduce basic vocabulary of graph theory that will be used in this chapter. An induced *sub-graph* H of a graph G is a graph whose set of vertices is included in the set of vertices of G and there is an edge between two vertices of H if and only if there is an edge between these two vertices in G.

An undirected graph is *connected* if there is a path between any two vertices. A *connected component* of a graph is a sub-graph of maximum size (in particular a connected graph has one and only one connected component: itself). A directed graph is *weakly connected* if the underlying undirected graph is connected. It is *strongly connected* if there is a directed path (in each direction) from each vertex to any other vertex. A *strongly connected component* is a maximal strongly connected sub-graph.

A vertex v is a *neighbor* of a vertex u if there is an edge between u and v. The *neighborhood* of a vertex u is the sub-graph induced by the set of its neighbors and the *degree* of u is the number of its neighbors. A *complete graph* is a graph where each pair of vertices is linked by an edge. A *clique* in a graph is a complete sub-graph. Several matrices can be associated to a graph such as the adjacency matrix A whose (i,j)-element is 1 if vertex i is linked to vertex j and is 0 otherwise.

2.2 Measures

Understanding the architecture of a network first passes through a structural analysis. Networks are of many different kinds - simple, directed, weighted, labeled, etc. - which requires the development of specific indices to measure their properties. Some indices measure basic characteristics of the network such as the number of vertices or nodes n, the number of edges or links m, the density d of the network (defined by the ratio between the actual number of links and the total possible number of links) and the mean degree.

The indices measuring the global connectivity of the network are built on the notion of shortest paths in the network. A *shortest path* between two vertices is a path (a sequence of consecutive edges) of minimal length. Global connectivity is then evaluated by the *mean of the shortest paths lengths* l, the *characteristic path length* L (median of the means of shortest paths; Watts, 2003) or the *diameter* D (the length of the longest shortest path in the graph). Two indices, called clustering coefficients, measure the local connectivity. The *first clustering coefficient* $C1$ is defined by the average density of the neighborhood of a vertex. *The second clustering coefficient* $C2$ is the ratio between the number of triangles in the network and the number of connected triples in this network which can also be seen as the probability to have a link between two vertices linked to a common vertex.

In order to evaluate the position of a vertex in a graph, three notions of centrality have been defined (Freeman, 1979). The degree centrality C_D measured by the degree of a vertex, the betweenness centrality C_B related to the number of shortest paths going through a vertex and the closeness centrality C_C of a vertex based on the mean distance to the other vertices. Then the centralization of a network is the normalized sum of the differences between the vertex with the highest centrality and the centralities of the other vertices in the graph. A zero (resp. unit) value of the network centralization corresponds to a non centralized (resp. most centralized) network. The *degree distribution* is the probability distribution of the vertex degrees; for each integer *k* it gives the probability to have a vertex of degree *k*. Other indices may be introduced dealing more particularly with the impact on the network structure of weights or the presence of different kinds of links (Boulet, 2011; Boulet et al., 2011b).

2.3 Finding communities

An essential step in network analysis is the research of communities. In a social network, some people can be gathered into communities. Following this example of community we can extend this notion to networks of different nature (networks of legal texts, lexical networks, etc.) analogously defined as groups of vertices more densely connected to each other than the rest of the graph. Detecting communities in networks is a very active field of research in network analysis and we shall consider only a few of the existing algorithms.

Several algorithms have been developed relying on various methods. The walktrap algorithm (Pons and Latapy, 2005) is based on random walks on graphs with the underlying idea that a random walk would be trapped into a community. The fast greedy algorithm (Clauset et al., 2004) aims at greedily maximize the modularity (a criterion assessing the quality of a partitioning) of the resulting partitioning. Finally spectral methods (von Luxburg, 2007) are based on eigenvalue decomposition of matrices associated to a graph which embeds the graph in an Euclidean space on which we can use statistical clustering.

A special community is worth mentioning here, the *rich-club* (Zhou and Mondragon, 2004). A rich-club is formed when the vertices with highest degree (the rich vertices) are highly interconnected and form a very dense group (a club). They therefore constitute a central and influent community in the network.

2.4 Types of graphs

An *Erdös-Rényi random graph* (Erdös and Rényi, 1959) is a graph where an edge is put between two vertices with a uniform probability p. It is known (Watts, 2003) that such a graph have a tight global connectivity (the randomness of edges creates shortcuts) and low clustering coefficients (the local density looks like the overall density). Then the indices presented earlier allow distinguishing several classes of graphs. A *small world* network (Watts, 2003) is a network with a tight global connectivity (nearer than that of a random graph) and a high local connectivity (much larger than that of a random graph). A *concentrated world* (Boulet et al., 2011a) is a dense graph with some highly interconnected vertices having the highest centrality measures. A *scale-free network* is a graph with a power-law degree distribution. Therefore it has a lot of vertices with a low degree and few vertices with a high degree (sometimes called hubs). It contrasts with Erdös-Rényi random graphs, the degree distribution of which is centered to a mean value and follows a Poisson distribution. A directed graph is a graph with directed edges. A special kind of directed graph is a tournament in which there exists an edge between any two vertices (it can be seen as a complete directed graph).

3. Ontology as a network

The title of this section calls for comments. First, even if we exclude *a priori* from the scope of our discussion the field of philosophy, the term "ontology" has no unambiguous acceptance. By the 1980s, the field of computer engineering and knowledge representation takes the term to define a computational model for performing automated reasoning. In 1995, T. Gruber says that "an ontology is a formal, explicit specification of a shared conceptualization" (Grüber, 1995). In 2009, he refines his remarks by stating that "an ontology defines (specifies) the concepts, relationships, and other distinctions that are relevant for modeling a domain. The specification takes the form of the definitions of representational vocabulary (classes, relations, and so forth), which provide meanings for the vocabulary and formal constraints on its coherent use" (Grüber, 2009). Finally, the pragmatic issues converge in the statement that "an ontology is a tool and product of engineering and thereby defined by use ». The key issues opened by these proposals relate to how to make the best choice of language, and how to set objectives of use of these ontologies.

3.1 Languages and objectives for ontology

In terms of languages, it is interesting to quickly scan the history. Originally, we find the semantic networks (Quillian, 1968) which are doubly labeled directed graphs, the vertices being labeled by concepts, the arcs being labeled according to relators between concepts. Then follow, the most significant proposals emanating from Minsky, Sowa, Brachman and Levesque. Minsky (1975) proposes an approach based on the notion of a grain of knowledge or frame and specifies that « here is the essence of the theory: when one encounters a new situation (or makes a substantial change in one's view of the present problem) one selects from memory a structure called a frame. A frame is a data-structure for representing a stereotyped situation. Attached to each frame are several kinds of information. We can think of a frame as a network of nodes and relations. The "top levels" of a frame are fixed, and represent things that are always true about the supposed situation. The lower levels have many terminals-"slots" that must be filled by specific instances or data».

Sowa (1984) proposes the conceptual graph formalism. Those are bipartite graphs with two types of nodes: concept-nodes and relation-nodes. Knowledge representation can be defined in a specific area, this being reflected in what is referred to as a support and includes two lattices: the concepts and relationships pertaining to the chosen field. The reasoning is based on semantics in first order logic, but a more original view suggests compensating the mechanisms of logical inference by graph operations in particular the homomorphism of graphs (called projection; Chein and Mugnier, 2009). Brachman (1979), Brachman and Levesque (1985, 2004) propose extensions to the language of frames and semantic networks from semantic-based description logics. They introduce the notions of concept, role and individual and rely on an inference mechanism based in particular on subsumption.

These theoretical propositions are the heart of various studies conducted to date. They are accompanied by proposals for operational developments, the most iconic of them being probably KIF (Knowledge Interchange Format) on the initiative of the consortium DARPA Knowledge Sharing Effort (Genesereth, 1992), the Ontolingua project (Gruber, 1992) until the arrival of the Semantic Web following the original article by Berners-Lee et al. (2001), which paves the way for many of the proposals in terms of protocols, languages, standards (XML Extensible Markup Language, Resource Description Framework RDF, RDF Schema, OWL Web Ontology Language) and tools. In the field of legal studies these researches are now flourishing (Casanovas et al., 2007; Sartor et al., 2011).

Let us return to the question of the use and purpose of ontology design in the context of knowledge of public policies. It is now commonly accepted (Guarino, 1998; Gangemi et al., 2001) that ontologies can be stratified by level of generality or abstraction (Figure 1): a) top-level ontologies describe very general concepts like space, time, material, objects, events, actions, etc., which are independent of one problem or particular application domain. They specify very general abstract knowledge whose content depends on the degree of formalization; b) domain ontologies and problem-solving ontologies or task ontologies that describe, respectively, the knowledge related to a generic domain (like medicine or aviation) or generic activities (as water management) by a specialization of the concepts presented in the top-level ontologies; c) application ontologies describe concepts depending both on a field and on a particular task. They are specializations of the two previous types of ontologies.

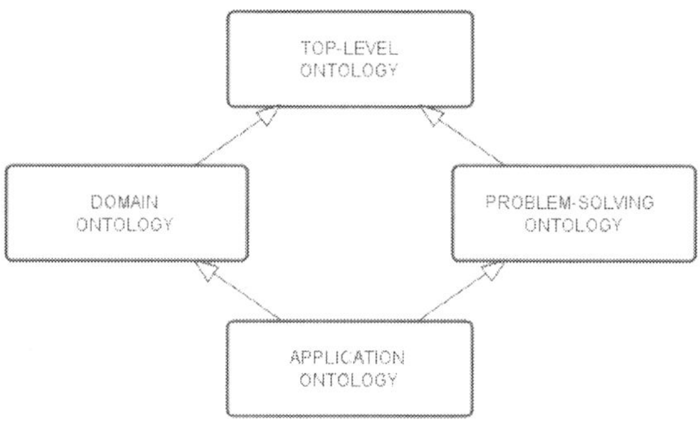

Fig. 1. Scheme of the stratification of ontologies by levels of generality and abstraction.

Overall, it appears that the graphs are essential in the development of knowledge representations and ontologies, and that the synergy between different approaches is important (Farquhar et al., 1995). The example we now develop tackles with the representation of a field of knowledge. The approach taken may not be consistent with the *doxa* but illustrates the types of exploration that allows the use of graphs in the field.

3.2 Classification and phenomenological graphs

Let us return to some fundaments. We here call "classification graph" a graph built on the relationship of subsumption ("is a" relationship) that binds an instance to its class membership. According to an Aristotelian-type classificatory approach, a concept (e.g. an agent of the administration) may be both a special case - one instance - to a larger class (the agents) and a (sub-) class for other more specific instances (e.g. the prefect). The support structure of these univocal classifications is of course the tree-graph that we propose to call "class graph". According to its purpose, this structure is effective and unambiguous.

But by destroying any flexibility of interpretation, this normativeness may be undesirable. Let us consider an example which is specific to Law. The judge is asked to reinterpret terms or concepts in a manner more consistent with the acceptance that tends to prevail in a constantly evolving social context. Thus the "family" of the Civil Code of 1804 is no more precisely that *family* of a society that tends to recognize the single-parent family, same-sex parents or surrogate mothers. Sometimes it follows a reassessment of existing case law, the judge taking a unique position that other judges will adopt later. For schematic that can be our example (indeed, the departure from precedent is less about the interpretation of terms than about the reinterpretation of a point of law which, presumably, involves an entire ontological environment), a sociologically-oriented ontology should be able to allow, in the organization of its classes and of their instances, the occurrence of multiple relations of subsumption (one instance being subsumed to several classes), in a way more conform to uses than in line with normativeness of any *a priori* model (should it be dominant).

Incidentally, we move from the trees (and forests) to the wider world of all graphs. These graphs then capture the structure of a conceptualization of a system that relies on a variety of types of objects and typed relations, a "model" or “ontology”. In this chapter we propose to call these structures “phenomenological graphs” - or “*pheno-graph*” for short - because they capture the observable structure (whatever the means of observation) of relationships between entities whose existences are attested.

There are various ways to build such a model, based on pragmatic approaches in the fields of law or public policy. One of them is of particular interest in this section. It is based on the terminological analysis of large corpus of texts (legal texts, texts describing public policies, regulations, etc.). The analysis of terminology and text mining can also be based on a representation of the knowledge domain in the form of ontology, the text analysis revealing more or less reinforced relationships between terms or concepts (or even invalidating the relevance of some ontological relations in this context or by inducing new links).

Formally, this type of analysis consists of two levels say a tree-like classification for supervision and the texts revealing a more general network of entities linked by heterogeneous relationships (such double structure is described in Mazzega et al., 2011). Let us now work an example of a double structure - ontological and phenomenological - in the field of research mapping.

3.3 Illustration: Research in e-governance & policy modeling

The CROSSROAD European project produced a public report on the state of the art on the field of ICT research in electronic governance and policy modeling (CROSSROAD, 2010) from which we here extract and analyze the data structure. This research field is divided in five domains divided in areas and sub-areas as follows: 1) Open government information and intelligence for transparency (4 areas; 18 sub-areas; *associated color*: orange); 2) Social Computing, citizen engagement and inclusion (4 areas; 14 sub-areas; green); 3) Policy modeling (4 areas; 18 sub-areas; yellow); 4) Identity management and trust in governance (4 areas; 18 sub-areas; blue); 5) Future internet for collaborative governance (5 areas; 25 sub-areas; purple). In this list we attribute a color to each research domain and to its afferent areas and sub-areas for the purpose of graph visualization.

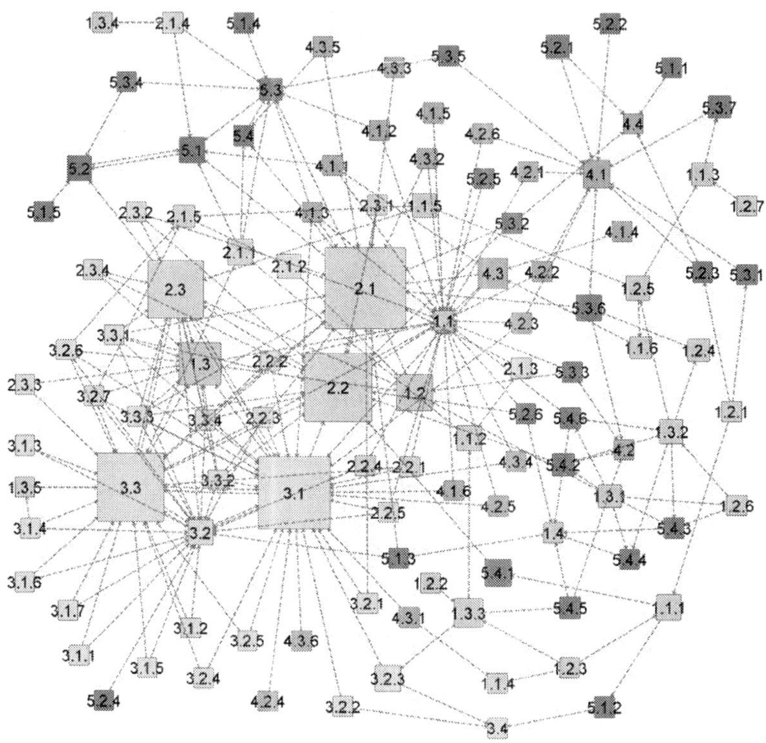

Fig. 2. A representation of the *pheno-ICT graph* with the size of each vertex being linearly related to its betweenness degree (see text). Vertices of the same color belong to the same research domain.

The full mapping of this field of research shows the type of double structure mentioned above, say: a) a tree structure - that we call *onto-ICT graph* (not represented here) - induced by the organization of this field of research in the above mentioned 5 domains (see below), 21 areas and 93 sub-areas (grouped under the term "research topics") that are the 119 vertices of the graph, with 114 edges; b) a network structure – which principal connected component we call *pheno-ICT graph* (111 vertices, 245 edges) - in which topics (research domains, areas or sub-areas) are linked by pairs when the specific researches they cover are explicitly related in a noticeable amount of scientific publications or when these publications refer to specific terminologies preferentially associated with these topics.

In Figure 2 we give a representation of the *pheno-ICT graph* that enhances the relative magnitudes of betweenness centrality associated to the vertices. The correspondence between the labels of the vertex ("x" type label for domain,"x.x" for area, "x.x.x" for sub-area) and research field they cover can be found in CROSSROAD (2010). Let us now imagine some simple scenario (about research policy for policy research). Should we organize some meeting in ICT research in electronic governance and policy modeling, what should be the title of the sessions? A convenient choice might be to choose those topics with the highest degrees in the *pheno-ICT graph*. If now some (financial or human) resources are available to strengthen research where should it be primarily allocated? Such a choice of course depend on the criteria for decision making but a strategy could be to support those topics that present a high betweenness centrality, because they will reinforce the synergy between various research communities and strengthen the whole research system.

Label	Name of the research topic	Betweenness Centrality Index (rank)	Normalized Degree (rank)
2.1	Social Computing	1.00 (01)	0.64 (05)
3.1	Policy Analysis (in policy modeling)	0.86 (02)	1.00 (01)
3.3	Visualization (in policy modeling)	0.80 (03)	0.75 (03)
2.2	Citizen Engagement	0.78 (04)	0.46 (06)
2.3	Public Opinion Mining & Sentiment Analysis	0.60 (05)	0.39 (07)
1.3	Visual Analytics (in open government information)	0.36 (06)	0.39 (07)
1.2	Linked Data (in open government information)	0.26 (07)	0.14 (13)
4.3	Trust (in governance)	0.16 (08)	0.11 (17)
1.3.3	Analytical Reasoning (in visual analytics)	0.14 (09)	0.07 (22)
4.1	Identity Management	0.12 (10)	0.36 (09)
5.4.1	Web Accessibility (in human / computer interactions)	0.11 (11)	0.07 (22)
5.3.6	Public Service Aggregation, Mash-ups & Orchestration	0.10 (12)	(>25)

Table 1. Ranking the first twelve research domains, areas or sub-areas of ICT research in electronic governance and policy modeling by decreasing (normalized) betweenness centrality index (as extracted from the pheno-ICT graph) considering only entering links. The normalized degree (and rank) of the research topics are also given for comparison.

In Table 1 we give the first twelve research topics ranked by decreasing (normalized) betweenness centrality index. The normalized degree (and corresponding rank) of the research topics are also given for comparison. It appears that though they do not have a high rank of connectivity, several topics have a high rank in terms of betweenness centrality. This is the case for the first topic "social computing" (betweenness centrality rank=1; connectivity rank=5) that is about the application of web social software in public-sector activities and the support to social interaction and collaboration (and with the associates terminology: social networking, content syndication in government portals, blogging and micro-blogging, collaborative writing tools, feedback, rating and reputation systems - CORSSROAD, 2010). It is interesting to notice also that several topics among the most connected with the other topics are not in the short list of high betweenness centralities: area 1.1 "open & transparent information management" with degree 0.89 (2d rank), area 3.2 "(policy) modeling and simulation " (degree 0.75 - 3rd rank), area 5.3 "multi-channel access and delivery of next generation of public services " (degree 0.32 - 10th rank), areas 1.4 "findings (in open government information and intelligence for transparency)" and 5.1 "cloud computers (for collaborative governance)"(degree 0.21, 11th rank).

	Index	Non-oriented *pheno-ICT* Graph	Average Indices of *Erdös-Rényi Graphs*
General Characteristics	n	111	109.56
	m	239	239.08
	d	0.039	0.040
	k	4.31	4.36
Global Connectivity	l	3.25	3.34
	L	3.15	3.24
	D	8	6.92
Local Connectivity	C1	0.34	0.092
	C2	0.12	0.038
Network Centralization	C_D	0.24	0.055
	C_B	0.11	0.037
	C_C	0.27	0.15

Table 2. Small world indices calculated on the non-oriented *pheno-ICT* graph and for comparison on a set of 1000 *Erdös-Rényi* random graphs with the same size and order. n is the number of vertices, m the number of edges, d the density, k the average degree, l the length of the average shortest path, L the characteristic length, D the diameter, C1 the first clustering coefficient, C2 the second clustering coefficient, C_D the degree centrality, C_B the betweenness centrality and C_B the closeness centrality (see Sec.2).

On one hand these simple findings can be useful for designing a research policy in this field, as briefly suggested by our quite trivial scenarios or by many others related to real life situations. On the other hand it is interesting to see if the pheno-ICT network belongs to a known class of graphs. We consider the undirected graph (some geodesics do not exist on the directed graph) for which we assess the general indices as well as the global and local connectivity (Table 2). The random model used for comparison is the G(n,p) model of *Erdös-Rényi* (See Sec.2) where there is an edge between two vertices with a probability p equal to the density of the graph. The examination of these connectivity indices leads us to conclude that this network is a *small world*. Indeed, it fills the following two conditions: a) tighter global connectivity similar to that of random graphs; b) strong local connectivity, much higher than that of a random graph. So we are dealing with a type of graph which shows the structure of many social networks the study of which is enriched with other concepts opened to interpretation, but that we will not discuss in this chapter.

We also observe that the (non-oriented) *pheno-ICT* network exhibits high values of the betweenness centrality (but not of the closeness centrality) when compared to random graphs. We interpret this indicator as showing that the work developed in many topics (domains, areas or sub-areas) are routinely called upon to involve or interest not only directly related topics but also other neighboring topics albeit slightly more distant (on the network). In a sense, this feature reflects the strong identity and overall coherence of research in the field of ICT research in electronic governance and policy modeling.

4. Law-induced networks

According to the classic positivist theory of law (knowing that we do not consider here the Common Law), legal norms must obey a hierarchical organization implying that the norms of lower degrees should not be in conflict with the norms of higher degree (Kelsen, 1960). At the top of the pyramid of norms is the Constitution, more or less expanded with a "block of constitutionality", followed by the organic and other laws, decrees, etc. With the rise of Community, European and International law, also with the proliferation of sources of law, this hierarchical organization is deeply upside. The doctrine echoes these on-going transformations (eg. Ost & van de Kerchove, 2002; Delmas-Marty, 2007) that are also subject of much debate in the democratic representative bodies.

For example in France, the positions of the Court of Cassation and of the Council of State have been for nearly 15 years in opposition as to the primacy of European law over national law, until the adoption of a common position recognizing it during a reversal of precedent of the State Council (see Bécane et al., 2010). Of course this rule is accompanied by measures not to amputate the representative bodies of their ability to legislate or to exercise control over norms produced outside their assemblies, the national legislature thus acquiring a role in the European legislative process (Article 88-4 of the Maastricht Treaty).

So we perceive that under the combined effects of globalization and the empowerment of communities and organizations (e.g. NGOs) network structures appear in all domains of Law and policy. Different kinds of networks: institutional networks (the link being instantiated by roles, powers, information flows, etc.), networks associated to the process of decision-making (e.g. EU), networks and flows in law-making, etc. But outside of these role and power games the analysis of which is subtle, another phenomenon reflecting the overlapping of legal systems can be easily observed and studied. Although its range is relatively minor (it is of interest for some operational services of law broadcasting like LEGIFRANCE www.legifrance.gouv.fr/, EURLEX eur-lex.europa.eu/en/index.htm, etc. and also for codification), its analysis allows starting the development of measures of certain manifestations of "legal complexity": this phenomenon is the emergence of networks of citations between legal texts (Bourcier and Mazzega, 2007a; Bommarito and Katz, 2010). The citations between legal texts results from a self-organizing process, no top authority being in charge to manage the constant flow of legislative regeneration, neither at the national nor regional or global level.

Based on previous work, we will support the next two assumptions that do not deny the concerns of the science involved in the analysis of complex systems, namely: a) that the types of structures found in the network of citations depend on both the size of the object in question and the scale of resolution for their analysis; b) that the "canonical" representation of a field of knowledge - in this case the legal knowledge - deserves to be coupled with a representation based on the analysis of emerging phenomenological graphs. We will then give further arguments in favor of these two hypotheses, based on an empirical analysis of the bipartite network of environmental treaties of international law.

4.1 Scale matters in law

Let us start with small scales. The article is classically considered as the smallest entity that deployed in a broader frame - law, code - should have a legal content making sense of its own. Yet we have found up to 4 levels of subdivision in a significant number of articles in the environmental code, and we have estimated their frequency distribution and length of text statistics (Bourcier and Mazzega, 2007b). The association of a graph of citations to a corpus relies on the choice of the resolution for analysis: should we keep all the subdivisions or stop at the granularity of articles (with 1266 of them in the environmental code, legislative part)? This choice is in fact dictated by the objectives of the thematic analysis. However we understand intuitively that the absorption of certain entities (e.g., subdivisions of articles) in the entity of which they are parties (e.g. article) increases the density of the network by aggregating the parts in the local whole and assigning all edges to it.

On the other side of the spectrum of sizes, the choice of a definition of the analyzed object is just as important. The environmental code has in a sense a unity conquered by the legislature (especially with regard to the rural code) but partly arbitrary since it cites (or is quoted by) 35 other codes, several EU Directives, international treaties etc. Considering at a given time all of the existing law in the world and its ramifications (to which corresponds a global legal-graph), being interested only in the French environmental code, or in all of the codified French law (which associated graph we call hyper-code), is equivalent to extract an induced sub-graph and analyze it separately. This sub-graph can be seen as associated to an ontology-derived community which does not have the emerging character of the phenomenology-derived communities we will consider below. Indeed the ontology-derived communities are deliberately constructed by the legislature, or in this case, coder (two "actors" that deserve being considered themselves as communities of actors).

The use of approaches presented in Section 3 also allows identifying vertices with remarkable properties: for example, articles (resp. Codes) of high degree centrality or high betweenness centrality in the environmental code (resp. hyper-code graph; Mazzega et al., 2009; Boulet et al., 2011a). Thus, as in many complex systems the choice of the analysis resolution and of the size of the object changes the characteristics and properties of the associated graphs, but also the graph type and hence the paradigm of interpretation.

4.2 Alternative representation of legal knowledge

The matter of a code - as the Environmental Code - is usually organized into divisions - books, titles, chapters, sections, articles - that form a tree structure (table of content). However, another organization is behind it, which brings together the divisions with a high density of inter-citations (the main connected graph component associated with the legislative part of the Environmental Code has 980 vertices and 2186 edges). The use of multiple algorithms for partitioning the graph associated to a corpus, allows identifying stable (say found by all algorithms based on different criteria for partitioning - cf. Sec. 2.2) "hidden" communities of its divisions - including articles - which are semantic units pertinent for the interpretation of the law.

Two points are worth noting: a) the existence of these phenomenological communities is known neither to the legislature nor to the lawyer, b) some of these emerging communities do not coincide with the ontological divisions, necessary in the planned organization of the code (Boulet et al., 2010). Conversely some ontological divisions are not in any stable community, such as for example the provisions relative to New Caledonia or Antarctic (a result that we keep to interpret). In other words, the codified substance could be distributed in a different cognitive representation and determined according to objective criteria (reproducible between codes - possibly from different countries).

Similar results are obtained when analyzing the hyper-code graph of citations among all codes of the French legal system produced using the same codification methodology and whose vertices are the codes (52 to date). Thus we have mainly highlighted (Boulet et al., 2011a,b): a) a rich-club (see Sec. 2.3; Colizza et al., 2006) including the 10 most central and influential codes of the French legal system; b) a stable community of 12 codes governing the legal areas linked to social activities, their regulation and security; c) a second stable community of 11 codes governing the legal areas related to land management, the territories and their resources. Only the analysis of hyper-code code could lead to identify those communities whose existence should challenge the doctrine, their existence being previously unknown.

4.3 Illustration: A tournament of international treaties

We now consider the state (as of 2010) of ratification of the 42 environmental international treaties by the 196 countries (or entities of equal status, such as the European Community) members of the United Nations (see the Chapter XXVII of the database of international treaties of the United Nations http://treaties.un.org/Pages/ParticipationStatus.aspx). Initially we built a graph with a link between countries A and B if both have ratified at least one common treaty. The links are then weighted by the number of common treaties ratified by the two countries. The partitioning of this graph showed two groups (Boulet et al., 2012): one group of 38 countries with only Canada being not part of continental Europe, and a group bringing together 158 countries.

In a second step, we seek a graph showing a higher discriminatory power of any developed strategies for ratification by member countries. For this we used the following rule: a link is established from country B to country A if B is the first country to ratify a particular treaty after ratification of that treaty by A. A second rule must be established with respect to N countries simultaneously ratifying the same treaty: a) link the N countries, which induces a clique in the graph or b) not link the N countries, which induces a stable graph. In the following analysis we use option (a) as our second rule. The graph (196 vertices, 2832 links) we obtain is shown in Figure 3. The hypothesis that motivates the analysis of this graph is that the sequence of dates of ratification reveals (whether collaborative or competitive) collective political strategies of countries (Louka, 2006).

The five countries most ready to sign the environmental treaties are (ranked by decreasing order of the degree centrality) Norway, Finland, Hungary and at the same level, France and Luxembourg. The countries with the highest betweenness centrality, and thus being somewhat in the stream of the temporal succession of ratifications are (ranked by decreasing order of betweenness centrality) Hungary, France, Belgium, Romania and Norway. These simple results show unambiguously the active role of Hungary, Norway and France about the environment on the international stage.

We find four stable communities with 41, 39, 22 and 10 countries respectively. Most European countries (in a geographical sense) are the second community, alongside the United States, Canada, Japan, New Zealand and Burkina Faso. The contrasting positions of these countries with regard to Europe, in particular on issues related to the climate change and energy policy suggests that this grouping into a single community rather reflects an antagonist-type of interaction. Note that this community also has the largest clique of the graph composed of 18 countries (Germany, Austria, Belgium, European Community, Denmark, Spain, Finland, France, Greece, Ireland, Italy, Japan, Luxembourg, Netherlands, Portugal, United Kingdom of Great Britain and Northern Ireland, Slovakia, Sweden).

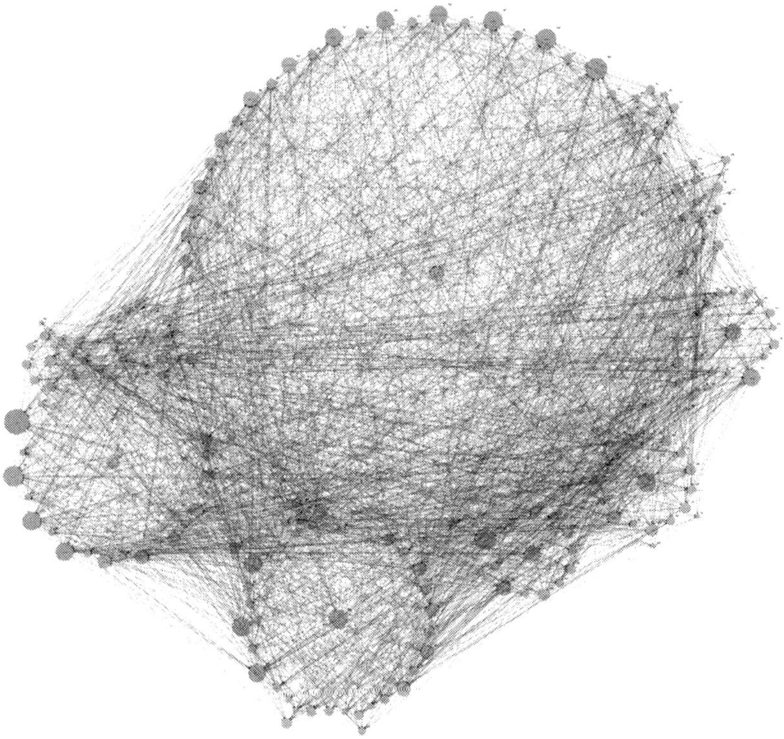

Fig. 3. A representation of the oriented graph associated with the ratifications of the environmental treaties and conventions of International Law. The vertices are 196 countries (or analog legal entities like the European Community) of the world. A link is drawn from B to A if B is the first country having ratified a given treaty just after country A. The larger orange (resp. smaller green) vertices represent countries with the highest (resp. lowest) betweenness centrality (see text).

Among the emerging countries, Brazil, China and India are in the third community (22 countries), but not South Africa (in the 4th community). The Russian Federation does not appear in any stable community (as defined here in Sec. 2.3), as also 83 other countries.

Countries suffering from acute chronic internal conflicts, backed to failing States, are among the countries that have ratified the least environmental treaties, a fact that reveals a simple inspection of their degree centrality. The logic behind the arrangement of the first community, made up of many countries from different geographical, geopolitical or economic regions, is not easy to identify. This probably results from the existence of several smaller sub-communities but whose ratifications are interspersed.

So if these early results are promising (as we think about the other 28 chapters that bring together hundreds of treaties), a more detailed analysis of these data, taking into account the particular dates of ratification themselves and a diachronic knowledge of the major world events, should identify more subtle patterns of international relation strategies as expressed by the evolution of international law (Schneider & Urpelainen, 2012).

5. Graphs for policy analysis

The analysis of citation networks between legal texts foreshadows network analysis for components and links of heterogeneous networks that may be associated with public policy. We have already mentioned that throughout the life cycle of policy (agenda-setting, formulation, decision making, implementation, evaluation; Howlett and Ramesh, 2003) are mobilized a variety of actors (individual or group, institution, etc.) and of resources.

One objective of these models is to provide tools for the *ex-ante* assessment of the potential impacts of these policies. This ambition is very high and we believe should be seen as a horizon to strive for rather than an achievable goal in the near future. Indeed at the individual scale, actors' behavior is unpredictable, their resilience and creativity never limited even if in a highly regulated or binding frame. However, at the collective level, patterns of behavior are observed and can be analyzed using proven methodologies. The analysis of graphs associated with the representation of certain aspects of public policy adds to the available (or developing) tools promoting a better understanding of these instruments of the "public" collective action. Rather than remain at this level of generality we prefer in this section to develop an example who keeps illustrative in general. This is the development of a simulation platform of the impact of new norms for managing water resources at the scale of a hydrological basin.

5.1 A framework for water policy

The water management in France is governed by various legal provisions, including the Law on Water and Aquatic Environments 2006 (LEMA, 2006) which adopts tools to achieve by 2015 the goal of "good" water state as set by the European Water Framework Directive (WFD, 2000). Basically the water management is organized at the scale of large hydrological basins. Southwest of the French metropolitan territory, the Adour-Garonne basin (AGB) covers about 120 000 km^2, with a rate of precipitation of 600 mm to 2000 mm/year, a potential for runoff of 90 km^3/year and large stocks of water in the aquifers. About 7 million people are distributed over 6900 municipalities and 35 cities with more than twenty thousand inhabitants (most such data are provided by the website of the Adour-Garonne Water Agency www.eau-adour-garonne.fr/).

Average annual withdrawals are 2.5 km^3, being roughly equally distributed between the three main uses, namely drinking water, industrial uses and agriculture. However, the water availability and uses are very uneven over the year: during the low water period (summer and early autumn) agricultural levies represent 80% of the withdrawals for about 645 000 irrigated hectares. During the heat wave of 2003 the withdrawal for irrigation has nearly doubled compared to average years. On the other hand, the climate change scenarios predict that 2003 will be in terms of rainfall better than the average year of the 2050's (Pagé & Terray, 2011). Consequently, the management of low water is the first priority of the Adour-Garonne Water Agency. The water uses must also be balanced with the preservation of aquatic ecosystems and environmental services, two issues that the EU directive and the LEMA (2006) explicitly raised as priorities.

On the scale of the Adour-Garonne basin, the water policy and its implementation was prepared with the participation of governmental administrations, territorial and other communities, associations, the civil society, etc., over several years, as described in the master water planning and management report (SDAGE AG, 2010) and in the associated implementation program (PDM AG, 2010), documents whose provisions may be legally opposed to other sectoral policies (territorial development, economic development, etc.). More locally, across the river basin management units (sub-basins), the low-water management plans specify the measures to regulate water uses within the environmental, social, economic and ecological constraints associated to periods of low flow.

In the MAELIA project (Multi-Agents for EnvironmentaL norms Impact Assessment) we develop a hybrid model combining a multi-agent system, model equations and GIS to estimate the societal, economic and environmental impacts of new "norms" implementation in the basin. We focus specifically on the new device that will limit water withdrawals for irrigation in many watersheds. To evaluate *ex ante* the potential impacts of this new frame, we represent in the model both the behavior of key actors involved in the water uses or management, but also the environmental (including hydrology) and climate dynamics as well as the main activities (especially agriculture) developed by the actors that may have a direct or indirect effect on the resource. To achieve this goal it is first necessary to identify the key actors, the activities they lead, the resources (material and cognitive) they use or generate, and the social and environmental processes the entire system depends on (Sibertin-Blanc et al., 2011; Thérond et al., 2011). This step was carried out by an interdisciplinary participatory method that results in the production of a conceptual model presenting only the essential elements of the management of low water in the basin.

5.2 Illustration: Basin-scale low water management

The conceptual model is built up on the basis of various UML diagrams (OMG, 2005). Figure 4 shows the main one, namely the actor- resource diagram (see Sibertin-Blanc et al., 2011 for some other diagrams). The vertices are instantiations of the following classes: actors, material resources, cognitive resources (including the norms: legal texts, programs, directives, etc.). The links are of different types (with cardinalities that we discard here): actors' activities, social processes, environmental processes or conceptual relationships between the linked entities. We are interested in the structure of the graph associated to this conceptual model of the low water management in the Adour-Garonne basin.

The graph has a single component of 66 vertices and 87 edges. It is weakly connected, with only one strongly connected group of vertices formed of two material resources (equipment for drinkable water catchment; equipment for raw water catchment and flow like canals, pipes, etc.), two "actors" (remembering that the term « actor » can refer to a group of actors: raw water distributors; clean water distributors) and one cognitive resource (structure of water prices and charges). Functions or operations associated with the vertices with the highest degree of connectivity must be modeled accurately because they directly affect the states of many others. These are in particular (by decreasing degree) the farmers, the (public or private) equipments, socio-professional categories (regarded as consumers of drinking water in municipalities), all types of water tanks, the land sub-parcels.

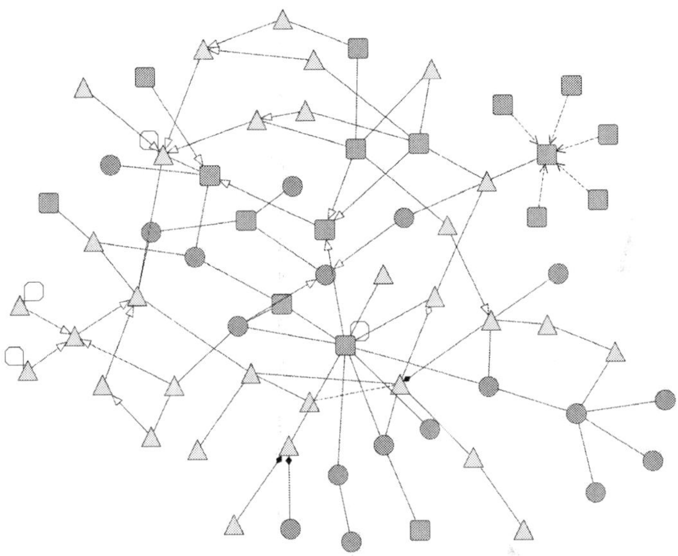

Fig. 4. The graph associated to the conceptual model of the law water management in the Adour-Garonne basin (France). The colors of the vertices indicate their type: actors (orange round rectangles); cognitive resources and norms (green circles); material resources (yellow triangles). The labels, attributes and functions associated to each vertex in the UML model have been removed to clarify the graph (some of them being given in the text).

On the distribution drawn on Figure 5 we see that around ten vertices present a significant betweenness centrality index. These vertices are the following ones: (label=49) Raw water distributors; (09) Manager *of* engineering structure (dams, etc.); (61) Manager of water catchment; (47) Clean water distributors; (57) Water tanks; (07) (Public or private) Equipments; (14) Equipment for water catchment; (17) Equipment for drinkable water catchment; (00) Geo-referenced territorial unit; (01) Plots. From a perspective of how the dynamical model works, the behavior of these entities (including changes in their respective states and comparing them with empirical data) should be given special attention. Indeed their intermediate position a priori designate them as being likely to exhibit abnormal behavior in the case all processes and activities modeled are not adequately represented or adjusted against each other.

A look at the global and local connectivity indices estimated for this graph does not allow us to characterize it as a small-world network. Although the overall connectivity is tightened (L= 4.14, D = 8) and close to that of random graph (L = 4.58, D = 11.32), the local connectivity is low (C1 = 0.41 C2 = 0027): the first clustering coefficient is artificially high due to the large number of vertices of degree 1, the second clustering coefficient is low. Moreover, the graph contains only two triangles.

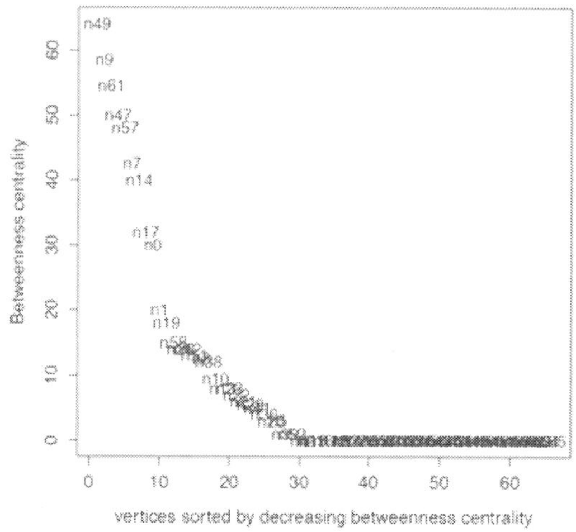

Fig. 5. Distribution of vertices of the low water management graph (Fig.3) in descending order of their degree of betweenness centrality.

All these results concern the static structure of the conceptual model of low water management. From the conceptual model is then derived a dynamic model where all the social and environmental processes (represented by computer codes) change over time the state variables (or attribute values) of the actors and resources. The analysis of the dynamic properties of this type of model must use a range of other tools (Mesbahi and Egerstedt, 2010), including statistics we will not address here, but whose scope covers any multi-agent system, being dedicated to the modeling of public policies and of their potential impacts or to any other complex system dynamics.

6. Conclusion

As was briefly shown in this chapter network analysis is useful for many purposes in Law and Policy: to identify emerging cognitive sets or patterns (groups of concepts); to make a functional mapping of the components of a complex system and of their interaction; to carry out all stages of modeling (from the definition of a referential representation to the setting up of a conceptual model and its implementation in a simulation platform for impact assessment) ; to analyze social dynamics (like strategies, coalition dynamics, etc.).

Many other concepts can be requested from graph theory (Jungnickel, 1999) to highlight the hidden properties of legal corpuses or public policies. For example we mentioned in Sec.4 the impact of the aggregation of nodes (corresponding to different choices of resolution) in a root vertex on the density and other measures associated to a network. A similar transformation occurs when passing from a given graph to the graph of its stable communities. Graph theory can provide fundamental knowledge on the incidence of these operations on the main measures associated with the studied networks, which would constitute a major theoretical and methodological contribution to the analysis of complex legal and policy systems.

As soon as graphs are involved in formal representations, their comparison provides a methodology for comparing the complex legal and policy systems they capture. Such issues appear especially in ontology alignment, in the identification and analysis of functional similarity of actors' positions in governance schemes, in the comparison of policies or legal systems between different sectors or countries, etc. Techniques of graph mining (Cox and Holder, 2007) would be particular useful in conjunction to text mining, a huge amount of data being accessible today via institutional public web sites and data base systems (as illustrated in this chapter with LEGIFRANCE, EURLEX or the UNO data basis on the multilateral treaties).

Another exciting area of research is to provide a graph-related equivalent to concepts developed and tested in the social sciences, especially law and political sciences. Different schools of thought have developed conceptualizations of central concepts such as power or role (among many others), which could be translated in terms of graphs and their properties and thus be enriched by the theoretical contributions of mathematical research.

Finally, the legal and policy "factories" are in constant work. The objects they produce continuously change, reform themselves, aggregate or distinguish each others. The approach to these phenomena by graphs that are either the support for dynamics (Egestedt and Mesbahi, 2010), flows or events, or even whose topology changes is therefore essential.

We can even imagine that these formal approaches based on graph theory will soon be integrated in the design of inter-sectoral integrative policies, thus responding to a growing need for multi-level societies, as evidenced by the everyday news.

7. Acknowledgment

R. Boulet benefits from a post doctoral grant of the CARTAM-SAT project (FEDER 2007-2013 operational program in French Guyana). This study is partly funded (see Sec. 5) by the RTRA *Science and Technology for Aeronautics and Space* (http://www.fondationstae.net/) in Toulouse (France) under the MAELIA project (http://maelia1.wordpress.com/). The yEd Graph editor has been used for producing the figures. Statistical properties of networks have been computed with R and the library igraph (http://www.rproject.org/).

8. References

André, P.; Delisle, C. E. & Revéret, J. P. (2004). *Environmental Assessment for Sustainable Development - Processes, Actors and Practice*, Presses Intern. Polytechnique, École Polytechnique de Montréal, ISBN 2-553-01138-5, Québec, Canada

Bécane, J.-C.; Couderc, M. & Hérin, J.-L. (2010). *La Loi*, Dalloz, ISBN : 978-2-247-08761-7, Paris, France

Berners-Lee, T.; Hendler, J. & Lassila, O. (2001). The semantic web. Scientific American, 284(5), pp. 34-43

Bommarito, M. J. & Katz, D. M. (2010). A Mathematical Approach to the Study of the United States Code (March 25, 2010). Physica A, Vol. 389,19, pp. 4195-4200

Boulet, R. (2011). Introduction d'indices structuraux pour l'analyse de réseaux multiplexes. *Actes 2de Conf. Modèles et Analyse des Réseaux: Approches Mathématiques et Informatique*, October 19-21, Grenoble, France, *in press*

Boulet, R.; Mazzega, P. & Bourcier, D. (2010). Network analysis of the French environmental code, In *AICOL Workshops 2009:* Beijing, China / Rotterdam, The Netherlands, Casanovas, P., Pagallo, U., Sartor, G. & Gianmaria A. (Eds.), LNAI 6237, Springer, Heidelberg, Germany, ISBN 978-3-642-16523-8, pp. 39-53

Boulet, R.; Mazzega, P. & Bourcier, D. (2011a). A network approach to the French system of legal codes - Part I: analysis of a dense Network. Artificial Intelligence & Law, vol.19 (4), 333-355

Boulet, R.; Mazzega, P. & Bourcier, D. (2011b). A network approach to the French system of legal codes - Part II: the role of the weights in a network, *submitted*

Boulet, R.; Mazzega, P. & Bourcier, D. (2012). Réseaux normatifs relatifs à l'environnement : structures et changements d'échelles. In *Politiques Publiques Systèmes Complexes*, Bourcier, D., Boulet R. & Mazzega P. (Eds.), Hermann, Paris, France, *in press*

Bourcier, D. & Mazzega, P. (2007a). Toward measures of legal complexity, *Proc. 11th Intern. Conf. Artificial Intelligence & Law*, Stanford Law School, ACM Press, ISBN 978-1-59593-680-6, New York, USA, pp. 211-215

Bourcier, D. & Mazzega, P. (2007b). Codification, law article and graphs, In *Legal Knowledge and Information Systems*, JURIX, Lodder, A.R. & Mommers L. (Eds.), IOS Press, ISBN:1586038109, pp. 29-38

Bourcier, D.; Boulet, R. & Mazzega, P. (eds.) (2012). *Politiques Publiques Systèmes Complexes*, Hermann, Paris, France, *in press*

Brachman, R. J. & Levesque, H. J. (Eds.) (1985). *Readings in Knowledge Representation*, Morgan Kaufmann, San Mateo, USA (CA)

Brachman, R. J. (1979). On the epistemological satus of semantic networks. Findler, pp. 3-50

Brachmann, R. J. & Levesque, H. J. (2004). *Knowledge Representation and Reasoning*, Morgan Kaufmann Publishers, Elsevier, ISBN: 1-55860-932-6, San Francisco, USA

Brandes, U. & Erlebach, T. (2005). *Network Analysis - Methodological Foundations*, Springer, ISBN: 3-540-24979-6, Berlin, Germany

Casanovas, P.; Noriega, P., Bourcier, D. & Galindo, F. (2007). *Trends in Legal Knowledge - The Semantic Web and the Regulation of Electronic Social Systems*, European Press Acad. Publ., ISBN: 8883980492, Florence, Italy

Chein, M. & Mugnier, M.-L. (2009). *Graph-based Knowledge Representation: Computational Foundations of Conceptual Graphs*, Springer Verlag London, ISBN: 978-1-84800-286-9, London, UK

Clauset, A.; Newman, M. E. J. & Moore, C. (2004). Finding community structure in very large networks, *Physical Review E* 70:066, 111, doi:10.1103/PhysRevE.70.066111

Colizza, V.; Flammini, A., Serrano, M. A. & Vespignani, A. (2006). Detecting rich-club ordering in complex networks, *Nature Physics*, 2, pp. 110–11

Cox, D. J. & Holder, L. B. (2007). *Mining Graph Data*, Wiley & Sons, ISBN: 13 978-0-471-73190-0, New Jersey, USA

CROSSROAD, (2010). A participative roadmap for ICT research in electronic governance and policy modeling - State of the art analysis. D1.2, FP7-ICT-2009-4 SA Project

Delmas-Marty, M. (2007). *Les Forces Imaginantes du Droit III - La Refondation des Pouvoirs*, Le Seuil, ISBN2020912503, Paris, France

Erdös, P. & Rényi, A. (1959). On random graphs, *Publicationes Mathematicae*, 6, pp. 290–297

European Commission, (2004). Commission Report on Impact Assessment: Next steps - In *Support of Competitiveness and Sustainable Development* SEC(2004)1377 of 21 October 2004

Farquhar, A.; Fikes, R., Pratt, W. & Rice, J. (1995). *Collaborative Ontology Construction for Information Integration*, Knowledge Systems, AI Laboratory Department of Computer Science, KSL-95-63

Freeman, L. C. (1979). Centrality in social networks: conceptual clarification, *Social Networks*, 1(3), pp. 215–239

Gangemi, A.; Guarino, N., Masolo, C. & Oltramari, A. (2001). Understanding top-level ontological distinctions, *Proc. of IJCAI 2001 Workshop on Ontologies and Information Sharing*, Gómez Pérez, A., Gruninger, M., Stuckenschmidt, H. & Uschold, U. (Eds.), Seatle, USA

Genesereth, M. R. & Fikes, R. E. (1992). *Knowledge Interchange Format*, Version 3.0 Reference Manual. Technical Report Logic-92-1, Computer Science Department, Stanford University, USA

Grüber, T. R. (1992). *Ontolingua: A Mechanism to Support Portable Ontologies*. Technical Report KSL 91-66, Knowledge Systems Laboratory, Stanford University, USA

Grüber, T. R. (1995). Toward principles for the design of ontologies used for knowledge sharing, *Intern. J. Human-Computer Studies*, 43 (5-6), pp. 907–928

Grüber, T. R. (2009). Ontology, In the *Encyclopedia of Database Systems*, Liu, Ling; Özsu, M. Tamer (Eds.), Springer-Verlag, *ISBN* 978-0-387-35544-3, Berlin, Germany

Guarino, N. (1998). Formal Ontology in Information Systems. In *Formal Ontology in Information Systems*, Guarino N. (Ed.) *Proceedings of FOIS'98*, Trento, Italy, June 6-8, 1998. IOS Press, ISBN: 9051993994, Amsterdam, The Netherlands, pp. 3-15

Hassenteufel, P. (2008). *Sociologie Politique : l'Action Publique*, Armand Colin, coll. U Sociologie , *ISBN*-10: 2200019858, Paris, France

Henry, N. (2004). *Public Administration and Public Affairs* (9th Ed.), Prentice-Hall Inc., ISBN10: 0-13-222297-3, Upper Saddle River, NJ USA

Howlett, M. & Ramesh, M. (2003). *Studying Public Policy - Policy Cycles and Policy Sub-Systems*, Oxford Univ. Press, *ISBN*-10: 0195417941, Oxford, UK

Jungnickel, D. (1999). *Graphs, Networks and Algorithms*, Algorithms and Computation in Math. Vol.5, Springer, ISBN 3-540-63760-5, Berlin, Germany

Kelsen, H. (1960). *Pure Theory of Law* (2d. Ed.), M. Knight, trans. (1967), University of California Press, Berkeley, USA

LEMA, (2006). *Loi n°2006-1772 du 30 décembre 2006 sur l'eau et les milieux aquatiques*, JORF n°303 (31/12/2006), texte n°3, p.20285 sq. http://www.legifrance.gouv.fr/

Louka, E. (2006). *International Environmental Law*. Cambridge Univ. Press, ISBN-13: 978-0-521-86812-9, Cambridge, UK

Mazzega, P.; Bourcier, D. & Boulet, R. (2009). The network of French legal codes. *Proc. 12th Intern. Conf. Artificial Intelligence and Law*, ACM 2009, ISBN 978-1-60558-597-0, Barcelona - Spain, June 8-12, pp. 236-237

Mazzega, P.; Bourcier, D., Bourgine, P., Nadah, N. & Boulet, R. (2011). A complex-system approach: legal knowledge, ontology, information and networks. In *Approaches to*

Legal Ontologies: Theories, Domains, Methodologies, Sartor, G., Casanovas, P., Biasiotti, M. A. & Fernández-Barreira, M. (Eds.), Springer, ISBN 978-94-007-0119-9, Berlin, Germany, pp. 117-132

Mesbahi, M. & Egestedt, M. (2010). *Graph Theoretic Methods in Multi-Agent Networks*, Princeton Series in Applied Math., Princeton Univ. Press, ISBN: 9780691140612, Princeton, USA

Minsky, M. (1975). A Framework for Representing Knowledge, In *The Psychology of Computer Vision*, Winston, P. H. (Ed.), McGraw-Hill, USA

Ost, F. & van de Kerchove, M. (2002). *De la Pyramide au Réseau? Pour une Théorie Dialectique du Droit*, Publ. Facultés Univ. Saint-Louis, ISBN2802801538, Bruxelles, Belgium

Oström, E. (2005). *Understanding Institutional Diversity*, Princeton Univ. Press, ISBN: 9780691122380, Princeton, USA

Pagé, C. & Terray, L. (2011). New fine-scale climate projections on France for the 21st century: scenarios SCRATCH2010. Climate Modelling and Global Change Technical Report TR/CMGC/10/58 (in french). Centre Européen de Recherche et de Formation Avancée en Calcul Scientifique (CERFACS), Toulouse, France

PDM AG, (2010). *Programme de Mesures du Bassin Adour-Garonne 2010-2015*, Comité de Bassin AG / Ministère de l'écologie, de l'énergie, du développement durable et de la mer, adopté le 16 nov. 2009, http://www.eau-adour-garonne.fr/

Pons, P. & Latapy, M. (2005). Computing communities in large networks using random walks. *Journal of Graph Algorithms and Applications*, 10(2), pp. 191–218

Quillian, M. R. (1968). Semantic memory, In *Semantic Information Processing*, Minsky M. (Ed.), M.I.T. press, Cambridge, USA (MA), pp. 216-270

Sartor, G.; Casanovas, P., Biasiotti, M. A. & Fernández-Barreira, M. (Eds.) (2011). *Approaches to Legal Ontologies: Theories, Domains, Methodologies*, Springer, ISBN 978-94-007-0119-9, Berlin, Germany

Schneider, Ch. J. & Urpelainen, J. (2012). Distributional conflict between powerful states and international treaty ratification. International Studies Quarterly, *forthcoming.*

SDAGE AG, (2010). Schéma Directeur d'Aménagement et de Gestion des Eaux du Bassin Adour-Garonne 2010-2015, Comité de Bassin AG / Ministère de l'écologie, de l'énergie, du développement durable et de la mer, adopté le 16 nov. 2009, http://www.eau-adour-garonne.fr/

Sowa, J. F. (1984). *Conceptual Structures, Information Processing in Mind and Machine*, Addisson-Wesley, ISBN: 0201144727, USA

von Luxburg, U. (2007). A tutorial on spectral clustering, *Statistics and Computing* 17(4):395416, URL http://arxiv.org/abs/0711.0189, 0711.0189.

Watts, D. J. (2003). *Small Worlds: The Dynamics of Networks between Order and Randomness*, Princeton University Press, ISBN: 9780691117041, Princeton, USA

WFD, (2000). *Directive 2000/60/EC of the European Parliament and of the Council of 23 October 2000 establishing a framework for Community action in the field of water policy*, Available from: http://eur-lex.europa.eu/en/

Zhou, S. & Mondragon, R. J. (2004). The rich-club phenomenon in the internet topology, *IEEE Communications Letters*, 8(3), pp. 180–182